FIRE
THIS TIME

**The Watts Uprising
and the 1960s**

FIRE
THIS TIME

The Watts Uprising
and the 1960s

Gerald Horne

DA CAPO PRESS
New York

Library of Congress Cataloging-in-Publication Data

Horne, Gerald.
Fire this time: the Watts uprising and the 1960s / Gerald Horne.—
1st Da Capo Press ed.
    p.   cm.
Originally published: Charlottesville, Va.: University Press of Virginia,
1995.
Includes bibliographical references and index.
ISBN 0-306-80792-0 (alk. paper)
    1. Watts Riot, Los Angeles, Calif., 1965. 2. Los Angeles (Calif.)—
Race relations. 3. Afro-Americans—Civil rights—California—Los Ange-
les. I. Title.
F869.L89N344   1997
979.4′94053—dc21   97-5211
                                                                CIP

First Da Capo Press edition 1997

This Da Capo Press paperback edition of *Fire This Time* is an
unabridged republication of the edition published in Charlottesville,
Virginia in 1995, with minor emendations. It is reprinted by
arrangement with the University Press of Virginia.

Published by Da Capo Press, Inc.
A Subsidiary of Plenum Publishing Corporation
233 Spring Street, New York, N.Y. 10013

Manufactured in the United States of America

CONTENTS

ILLUSTRATIONS

Figures 1–5, 16 courtesy of the Southern California Library for Social Studies and Research

Figures 6–14 courtesy of the Bancroft Library, University of California–Berkeley

Figure 15 courtesy of the Library of Congress

Maps

ABBREVIATIONS

ACLA   Archives of the City and County of Los Angeles
ACLU   American Civil Liberties Union
AFDC   Aid to Families with Dependent Children
AFL-CIO   American Federation of Labor–Congress of Industrial Organizations
ANC   African National Congress of South Africa
BPP   Black Panther party
CAP   Community Alert Patrol
CHP   California Highway Patrol
COINTELPRO
            Counter-Intelligence Program of Federal Bureau of Investigation
CORE   Congress of Racial Equality
CP   Communist party
CRC   Civil Rights Congress
CSU   Conference of Studio Unions
CURE   Catholics United for Racial Equality
FBI   Federal Bureau of Investigation
FFA   Ford Foundation Archives
FHA   Federal Housing Administration
FPRA   Fire and Police Research Association
FTAW   Food, Tobacco, and Allied Workers Union
GOP   "Grand Old Party," i.e., the Republican party
HUAC   House Un-American Activities Committee
ILWU   International Longshoremen's and Warehousemen's Union
LA   Los Angeles
LACHRC   Los Angeles County Human Relations Commission
LAPD   Los Angeles Police Department
LBJ   Lyndon Baines Johnson
MAPA   Mexican-American Political Association
MLK   Martin Luther King, Jr.
M-Ls   Los Angeles Provisional Organizing Committee for a Marxist-Leninist
            Communist party
NAACP   National Association for the Advancement of Colored People

ABBREVIATIONS

NLG	National Lawyers Guild
NOI	Nation of Islam
NUL	National Urban League
N-VAC	Non-Violent Action Committee
OEO	Office of Economic Opportunity
OIC	Opportunities Industrialization Center
PP	Progressive party
SCLC	Southern Christian Leadership Conference
SLANT	Self-Leadership for All Nationalities
SNCC	Student Non-Violent Coordinating Committee
SOW	Sons of Watts
TALO	Temporary Alliance of Local Organizations
UAW	United Auto Workers
UC	University of California
UCLA	University of California–Los Angeles
UCRC	United Civil Rights Committee
UPRI	Urban Policy Research Institute
US	United Slaves
USC	University of Southern California
USCCR	U.S. Commission on Civil Rights
USSC	United States Strike Command
WLCAC	Watts Labor Community Action Committee
WNA	Westminster Neighborhood Association

ONE

Context

INTRODUCTION

A T LEAST 34 PEOPLE DIED IN LOS ANGELES
during the Watts Uprising of August 1965; 1,000 more were injured, and
4,000 arrested. Property damage was estimated at $200 million in the
46.5-square-mile zone (larger than Manhattan or San Francisco) where approximately 35,000 adults "active as rioters" and 72,000 "close spectators" swarmed. On hand to oppose them were 16,000 National Guard, Los Angeles Police Department, highway patrol, and other law enforcement officers; fewer personnel were used by the United States that same year to subdue Santo Domingo.[1]

Within the larger area of conflict, the twenty-square-mile district of Watts-Willowbrook was devastated. In its eastern portion lived one-sixth of Los Angeles County's black population of little more than one-half million (the county included the city and other territory); two-thirds of the adult residents had less than a high school education and one in eight was illiterate. Income levels were lower than any other section of the county except for the skid row district of downtown LA.[2] Though most of those killed were black, most of the property damage was suffered by a ruling elite and middle class who were predominantly white.

In the area bordered by Washington Boulevard to the north, Rosecrans Avenue to the south, Alameda Street to the east, and Crenshaw Boulevard to the west, 261 buildings were damaged or destroyed by fire, along with almost all of the latter's contents. The epicenter of destruction was on 103d Street. In one three-block area 41 buildings occupied primarily by food, liquor, furniture, and clothing stores were demolished. Few homes, churches, or libraries were damaged, a fact that supports the contention that the Watts Uprising was no mindless riot but rather a conscious, though inchoate, insurrection.[3]

■

In the period before the Red Scare, Los Angeles possessed one of the stronger left and progressive movements in the nation; this left was based predominantly in the working class—trade unions—and the black community, work-

3

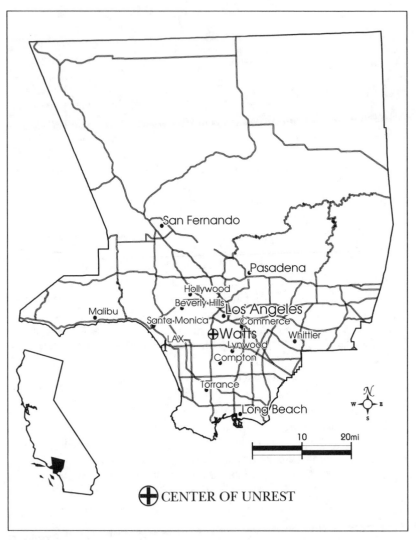

Los Angeles

ing class and middle class alike; the middle class did not exercise the hegemony in black political life that it came to later. The repression of the left created an ideological vacuum that would later be filled by black nationalism, and this nationalism exploded in Watts in August 1965. This nationalism eventually had at least three strands: the Nation of Islam, "cultural nationalists," and the Black Panther party; the first two assumed primacy during the 1960s, while the latter—which had ties to the reviled left—disappeared. To comprehend the background for these epochal changes, it is instructive to survey briefly the history of the left in Los Angeles.

As late as 1947 journalist Eugene Lyons claimed that the Communist party had a more secure foothold in the entertainment industry in LA than in any other industry in the nation. David Caute has claimed that from the 1930s through the 1950s, there were approximately three hundred Reds in Hollywood.[4] The influence of LA Communists extended further than did that of their comrades in other parts of the nation because they had within their ranks lavishly paid screenwriters like John Howard Lawson and Dalton Trumbo (for a time the highest-paid writer in Hollywood); they could pay higher dues, which meant production of more literature (including a weekly regional newspaper), hiring of more functionaries, and many other activities. That Lawson and his colleagues were materially successful only served to attract more adherents to their banner; California's own singular version of the "American Dream"—a fantasy of affluence, sunshine, and good times—exerted a powerful and pervasive influence on the citizenry. Lawson and Trumbo demonstrated that one could be a leftist and enjoy that dream too.

Testifying before the House Un-American Activities Committee in 1952, former Communist leader Max Silver maintained that at the party's zenith in the 1940s there were 4,000 Communists in the city, with an extensive number of branches among professionals (especially doctors and teachers), oil workers, auto workers—and Negroes.[5] Despite the city's well-deserved reputation as an antiunion redoubt, Los Angeles had one of the highest concentrations of Communists in the nation. This political movement had a significant representation in a key union, the International Longshoremen's and Warehousemen's Union.

Before the Red Scare dawned, Pettis Perry was the leading black Communist in Southern California. He was from a poor, working-class background and, like so many others, joined the party as a result of the Communist role in the ultimately successful struggle to free the Scottsboro Nine, a group of

African-American males imprisoned and slated for death because of allegations that they had raped white women.

In a brief memoir Perry recalled the severe repression exerted on party members and the broader left, suggesting that because of the notorious "Red Squad" of the Los Angeles Police Department, the party was outlawed until the early 1930s; leftists were "beaten, jailed, some maimed for life," he maintained. In 1937 Perry spearheaded a struggle in LA that forced a number of retail stores to hire black women as clerks. By 1938 he was chairman of the party in LA County. That same year he received more than 65,000 votes when he became the first Negro to run for the State Board of Equalization; he received a like number of votes when running for Congress in 1940. In 1942, as the first Negro to run for secretary of state, he received over 40,000 votes.[6] By 1965 the Communist party in California only rarely was running candidates for offices; if it had been putting more on the ballot, it is highly unlikely that they would have fared that well.

Perry's contentions about repression of the party apparently are no exaggeration. The left journal *New Masses* noted that elites "all have the jitters" because of the 1934 General Strike in San Francisco, spearheaded by ILWU leader Harry Bridges, a presumed Red. Bridges, unlike Perry, was "well-born," having left Melbourne traveling east to the San Francisco Bay area. He seemed worse to some than the ultimate alleged class traitor, Franklin Delano Roosevelt. "Let anyone who doubts American fascist potential come to Los Angeles and see them realized" was one writer's conclusion. It was difficult in the 1930s to circulate propaganda, appear on a picket line, or hold a radical play without being battered by the Los Angeles Police Department.[7]

Just as civil rights activity in the Deep South in the 1960s was to energize Los Angeles, changes in the national political landscape in the 1940s were similarly influential. The impact of the victory of Ben Davis, a black Communist from Harlem, elected to the New York City Council in 1943, was felt in Southern California.[8] The World War II alliance between Moscow and Washington made it more difficult automatically to categorize Communists and leftists as traitors, thus marking an advance of the left across the country. The acceleration of factory production during the war was accompanied by an increase in black migration from the south to LA, and an increase in union organizing efforts. Ties between blacks and Reds were strengthened and would remain strong for some time after the war.

In 1946 Charlotta Bass, the publisher of the *California Eagle,* the city's leading black newspaper, asked John Howard Lawson, by this time the leader of the party in Hollywood, to join her board of directors.[9] Bass would go on to play a leading role in former vice president Henry Wallace's Progressive party. Her overtures to Lawson and her ties to this left-wing party were not then deemed unusual. Her political odyssey exemplifies the decline of the organized left in Black LA and the rise of narrow nationalism.

In the early fall of 1949, Bass's friend Emil Freed, a Jewish trade unionist, had been imprisoned for his tireless labor on behalf of the striking workers of the Conference of Studio Unions. He was told that Bass's paper the *Eagle* "is being given a rough time. . . . the Southside is being flooded with free copies of other Negro papers to kill its circulation and advertisers have been approached."[10] This campaign proved successful; the *Eagle* had been driven out of business by 1965; in its wake arose the *Los Angeles Herald-Dispatch,* a militant right-wing nationalist organ that engaged in baiting of the Jewish community, especially the black Jewish celebrity Sammy Davis, Jr., and provided an initial forum for the Nation of Islam.

This turn of events was a blow to the black community of LA. Bass had collaborated with Loren Miller, a black lawyer who led the successful struggle in the 1940s against enforcement of racially restrictive covenants in deeds. The long-range repercussions of this struggle would be felt when Proposition 14, designed to overturn fair-housing legislation, became a major issue in the elections of 1964. The collaboration of Bass and Miller against restrictive covenants exemplified the potential for important contributions by the black middle class to progressive struggles on race and reform.

Bass was also close to the writer Arna Bontemps, who as a young boy would frequently visit her office. Over the years, as Bontemps developed a reputation as a writer, he had cooperated informally with the left. However, when in 1961 Bass asked her younger friend if he would consider coming to Los Angeles for a speaking engagement for the benefit of the *People's World,* the Communist weekly, he demurred. Times had changed.[11]

The Civil Rights Congress, an alleged Communist front, was formed in 1946; its chapter in Los Angeles included a broad sprinkling of left-influenced unions with substantial black membership. On the chapter's board at various times were representatives of the ILWU; the Food, Tobacco and Allied Workers Union; and the United Furniture Workers Union. The chapter's sponsors in 1946 ranged from Lena Horne to Frank Sinatra.[12] The CRC provided a visible channel through which people could join together across racial lines to combat bigotry in a militant fashion; moreover, it was a living and graphic reminder that there were numerous nonblacks of goodwill who were willing to fight racism generally and police brutality against blacks specifically. The cases it targeted, such as that of the black prisoner Robert Wesley Wells, received statewide, national, and international recognition.

The CRC boasted a score of branches citywide with hundreds of dues-paying members and thousands of supporters. In addition to expressly political activities, the CRC sponsored films on racial prejudice, regularly observed Negro History Week, and organized classes on the history of civil rights struggles, along with folk-singing, plays, and other cultural activities. In 1952 the Hollywood branch of the CRC held an extraordinary conference to "examine and study the problem of white chauvinism, to exchange ideas and experiences."[13] By 1965 the very idea of holding such a conference in LA would seem far-fetched.

The CRC also worked closely with the left-influenced National Lawyers Guild, establishing in 1949 a lawyers' panel that eventually comprised fifty-three attorneys. Most of these lawyers were white, but most of their cases concerned police brutality against blacks.[14] The CRC collaborated with other forces on the left, such as the Hollywood Writers' Mobilization; they worked effectively against racially restrictive convenants in deeds, carrying on the work of Loren Miller and Charlotta Bass. In an unprecedented move, pressure from the left led to the Screen Actors Guild adopting a resolution "pledging to use all its power to oppose discrimination against Negroes in the motion picture industry."[15] Later, Dalton Trumbo was pivotal in organizing a conference at the Hollywood Masonic Temple that lambasted "treatment of minorities in film."[16] When the liberal—though anti-Communist—Helen Gahagan Douglas, a prominent figure in Hollywood, entered the race for a congressional seat in 1946, the Republicans selected Fred Roberts, who was black, to run against her. But black voters chose to cast most of their votes for Douglas—a future victim of the Red Scare—and she triumphed.[17]

Though the CRC had chapters from coast to coast, the LA contingent was one of its strongest. As branch after branch fell victim to the Red Scare, the unit in LA remained viable virtually until the CRC's demise in 1956. In 1955 it was discovered to no one's surprise that the LA branch had been infiltrated by the FBI; the local executive secretary of the CRC was an informant for the FBI, paid to disrupt activities. This was a prelude to COINTELPRO, the Counter-Intelligence Program of the Federal Bureau of Investigation, launched in 1956, which was designed to obliterate organizations like the CRC. COINTELPRO and related initiatives were successful; by 1965 the CRC had disappeared and with it the kind of multiracial activism for which it was noted. Despite the disintegration of this primary "Communist front," the federal government maintained a keen interest throughout the 1960s in the LA Communist party, holding numerous investigative hearings designed to intimidate real and potential leftists, particularly those who advocated a more aggressive variety of trade unionism.[18]

Nevertheless it was impossible to liquidate the LA left altogether in part because there remained a modicum of support for its singular brand of militant antiracism and trade unionism, particularly among blacks and, to an extent, among the Jewish population. When the Communist Bernadette Doyle ran for state superintendent of public instruction in 1950, she received 500,000 votes in a bipartisan primary; her party affiliation was not listed on the ballot, but her credentials were well known, and like Pettis Perry, she received a hefty number of votes from blacks.[19]

Still, the Red Scare took its toll. It was well recognized that disaffected blacks were a prime recruiting target for Communists, and this realization led directly to anti–Jim Crow concessions; but the price paid for these concessions was the weakening of the left and strengthening of the ultraright, especially within the Los Angeles Police Department, which proceeded to run rampant without fear of challenge. In South LA, the behavior of the LAPD was more closely akin to that of marines than of social workers.

There was a particular fear that blacks, given the atrocious racism they faced, would turn Red, and this led directly to pressure to disavow any taint of radicalism. Hence, in 1952, prominent black actresses Hattie McDaniel and Louise Beavers felt obligated to "disavow and repudiate the conference on equal rights for Negroes" planned by left-wing forces in Hollywood.[20] Yet a study released that same year showed there was "not one Negro secretary, cutter, art director, cameraman, grip, reader, prop man, accountant . . . in the motion picture industry." According to the Hollywood Arts, Sciences, and Professions Council, which sponsored both the conference and the study, "a blacklist [against the left] could not exist today [in the film industry] if it were not based on a 300 year old blacklist against the Negro people."[21] The import was that the illiberalism sustained by Jim Crow facilitated the conservative attack on the left in Hollywood.

With the defeat of the left-influenced Conference of Studio Unions, gone was the possibility to move the recalcitrant studios to hire more blacks or to portray them accurately. Los Angeles was a major battleground during the domestic Cold War, and the consequences of this conflict were to be felt in 1965; the strength the left had managed to amass had the potential to affect dramatically the plight of African-Americans in cinema in all respects. Despite an alleged "civil rights revolution," this promised transformation had not occurred by August 1965.

Blacks had been barred effectively from one of the most vital industries in Los Angeles; worse, that same industry often libeled blacks on those few occasions when it represented them. Yet blacks were forced to stand apart from the one force—the left—that was seeking to reach across racial lines to combat this exclusion and defamation in a militant fashion.

By 1963 the *New York Times* was reporting that "many" of the studios "have no Negroes." By 1969 the Equal Employment Opportunity Commission had asked the Justice Department to bring suit against both the studios and the unions on the basis of their failure to hire or include blacks.[22] Though they had distanced themselves from the left in Hollywood, blacks had not been rewarded with jobs; worse, an ideological and organizational vacuum created by the erosion of left influence was being filled by an often narrow black nationalism.

■

The creation and subsequent filling of this vacuum defines the meaning of the Watts Revolt of 1965 and, indeed, the meaning of the 1960s. By the time the 1960s arrived, it was clear that Jim Crow not only had to go but was going. However, the civil rights movement had its most dramatic and substantive impact in the Deep South, not Los Angeles. For many black Angelenos it was disorienting to hear talk of a revolution in race relations but to see little evidence of it in their lives. Moreover, by 1965 militant and multiracial confrontation of police brutality and other ills was disappearing; in such an environment it became easier to imagine that a monolithic Euro-American populace stood opposed to the faintest hint of black progress.

Unions, hampered by Red Scare restrictions, such as the Taft-Hartley bill, found it difficult to organize or embrace the black migrants flooding into Southern California. Thus excluded, these migrants turned in growing numbers to the Nation of Islam, attracted by its doctrine of self-sufficiency and "do for self." Blacks were faced with a paradox: at the same time they were undergoing a proletarianization process in their move from the fields of Texas and Louisiana to the factories of Los Angeles, unions and working-class ideology were declining while the fundamentally middle-class ideology of the NOI was ascending. This "Nation of Shopkeepers" ideology not only created illusions about the economic destiny of blacks, it also served to reinforce the passive acceptance of the decline of unions. Gangs, with their dream of emulating other racial and ethnic groups by constructing illicit commercial empires, played a similar ideological role. Significantly, both gangs and the NOI recruited heavily in prisons, where the Civil Rights Congress previously had chalked up some of its more important victories; with the decline of unions and working-class organizations there was a concomitant growth in the ranks of the "lumpen proletariat" and its own distinct ideology.[23]

Part of the appeal of the NOI was its relentless pursuit of a middle-class ideal in the oppositional garb of Islam; its promise to "clean up" the perceived rough edges of the incoming black migrants paralleled what the National Urban League was attempting. Though the community that both purported to represent was predominantly working class, both organizations stressed the donning of the middle-class uniform of suit and tie as a route to respectability. The National Association for the Advancement of Colored People was firmly in the grips of a more traditional middle-class leadership, exemplified by the light-skinned banker H. Claude Hudson. As working-class organizations declined, gangs flourished by stressing racial, religious, and family ties.

Eventually the rise of gangs influenced the nascent Black Panther party and the NOI, as well as music, dress, language, cinema, and other areas of peculiar relevance to Los Angeles. This influence was transmitted via the BPP to the predominantly white Students for a Democratic Society, the Weathermen or "Weatherpeople," and others.

The rise in influence of gangs brought with it a brand of black nationalism that hurt black women. Nationalism generally can have negative consequences for women, and the black nationalism developing in LA was no exception.[24] Part of the "liberation" proclaimed by many male black nationalists in LA was the "right" to emulate the patriarchy of the Euro-American community. Moreover, the influence of gangs and the lumpen proletariat with their penchant for settling disputes through violence and their devaluing of women through prostitution complicated male-female relations in the black community. The subjugation of black women served to negate many of the positive aspects of black nationalism, such as pride in being black. Still, these gangs filled a socioeconomic vacuum left by the decline of unions and a love and caring vacuum left by the weakening of family structure.

The black nationalism that ultimately detonated in Watts was not just a reaction against white racism; it was also a reaction against the historic and stereotypical notion that blacks were the "female" of the races: subordinated, subordinate, dominated, timid. Through black nationalism a slice of race cum gender privilege could be reclaimed by means of a sometimes brutal masculinity that, after all, was normative among other races and ethnicities in the sprawling city of Los Angeles.

That black nationalism was ignited in Los Angeles should not have been surprising given the atmosphere of what might be called "compounded racism." Not only was the city torn by the simple biracial polarity that existed in most of the country, it was also home to other groups—principally Mexican-Americans and Asian-Americans—who often carried negative ideas about the darker skinned. Moreover, many black Angelenos had roots in Louisiana, where conflicts between lighter- and darker-skinned blacks had a lengthy history. In an environment where class consciousness had been suppressed, color consciousness was enhanced, providing fertile soil for the growth of black nationalism.[25]

Black nationalism, in part, represented an attempt to create a bond between darker- and lighter-skinned blacks and to curb tensions that had developed because, among other reasons, employers of whatever hue often favored the latter over the former. Similarly, societal norms infected by white supremacy dictated to darker women and men that through skin lighteners and hair straighteners they should mimic their lighter counterparts. To be sure, black nationalism did not simply arise in Southern California in 1965; it was a phenomenon that had waxed and waned in the United States since at least the nineteenth century, just as Islam was no stranger to Africans in the Americas.[26] What was relatively new about this black nationalism was its potent antiwhite character and, to a lesser extent, its muscular nature. The Nation of Islam was born in the early 1930s, but at that time there was a left movement to provide a multiracial and militant alternative; thus, the NOI's ranks were thin. As the left weakened, however, the NOI began to grow: by 1965 the NOI probably had as many members and influenced as many as the Civil Rights Congress at its zenith. The rise of the NOI in LA made for a contradictory and confused black nationalism. The theology of this sect maintained that blacks were Asiatic at a time when black nationalism to many meant an identification with Africa along with pride in nappy hair and dark skin. The NOI's identification with Asia was at times the cause of some ambivalence among its adherents.

Nationalism was not monolithic. Aside from the NOI, there were "cultural nationalists," often artists and intellectuals influenced by the transatlantic currents of Negritude, as well as anti-imperialists who identified with armed struggle in Africa, Asia, and Latin America but did not want to fight for their government in Vietnam or Santo Domingo—or Watts.

The Black Panther party, which bloomed in the ashes of Watts, had ties to the diminished left. Its internationalism was an enhanced reflection of what its members had experienced in a California that diverged sharply from the national pattern of simple biracial polarity. However, the socioeconomic decline of South LA and related factors created conditions favorable for the flourishing of gangs and a culture that left a deep and damaging imprint on everything it touched, including the BPP. Concomitantly, COINTELPRO targeted the BPP, and this hastened its demise.

There is a link that joins the apparently conflicting agendas of the middle-class ideology of the NOI, "cultural nationalists," the NAACP leadership—and the gangs. The NOI, the cultural nationalists, and some of the gangs clamored for blacks to control businesses in black communities. This was a touchy issue since to some it implied a form of "ethnic cleansing" in South LA; it was made more sensitive by the left's lengthy campaign for Negro self-determination with its inference of black control of institutions in the black community. When the goal of black control moved toward realization, those who were positioned to benefit were many black entrepreneurs close to the NAACP leadership and the Sons of Watts, an organization viewed by many as a glorified gang.

Working-class blacks did benefit in the aftermath of the revolt. Many received government jobs and joined public-sector unions. However, they rarely asserted themselves with the kind of working-class ideology that was expressed in South Africa, for example, by the mostly black Congress of South African Trade Unions. The right wing's constant emphasis on reducing the size of government ensured that these black workers would face constant insecurity.

The NAACP was affected profoundly by the Red Scare. It was forced to oust from organizational influence black and nonblack leftists alike. Those whites who fought racism militantly were branded as Red or Pink and purged.

Frank Barnes, the militant president of the Santa Monica branch, was suspended from his post office job on loyalty charges after organizing a picket line for jobs at a local Sears Roebuck store. In the charges, filed pursuant to Executive Order 9835, it was alleged that he had been and was at that time "affiliated or sympathetic with an organization, association, movement, group, or combination of persons designated by the Attorney General as subversive." Barnes was also a fervent advocate of internal democracy in the centralized NAACP, and shortly thereafter he was ousted from the presidency; removing him from influence set the stage for the NAACP in LA to be dominated by middle-class professionals often distant from the concerns of working-class black Angelenos.[27] By 1965 the NAACP would hesitate to collaborate with Communist union leaders like John Howard Lawson or Emil Freed or even a union leader who simply ran afoul of the Red Scare, such as Frank Barnes.

The triumph of the middle class in the NAACP ultimately was harmful for South LA. As black migrants flowed into Southern California after World War II, they were associated with the dislocation their arrival was said to bring. More blacks meant more opportunities for antiblack racism and more competition for scarce housing and employment. Many of the new arrivals in Watts particularly were scorned for their alleged untidiness, viewed as a relic of their rural backgrounds. Unlike many in the middle class, they did not wear suits and ties daily because their employment did not require it or allow it. Unlike those bourgeois leaders at the apex of the NAACP leadership, they did not have deep roots in Southern California. Year-of-arrival consciousness became a substitute for class consciousness.

By the time of the Watts conflagration of 1965, the NAACP was scorned and deemed out of touch with the black masses. That this leadership tended to be lighter skinned than the majority of the community they purported to represent became an issue of no small significance in August 1965. Similarly, the black Christian church had failed to attend to the temporal needs of many of its parishioners. Taken together, the perceived failures of these two venerable institutions created an opening for the Nation of Islam with its militant rhetoric about presumed oppressors.

The triumph of the middle class in the NAACP underscored the vitality of the California Dream. Those with attractive homes, well-tailored suits, large cars, and hefty bank accounts were thought to be better people and happier; this description did not apply to many in South LA. The events of 11–18 August 1965 assumed the form of a "food riot," an eruption of commodity fetishism, and a potlach of destruction among those denied the dream. The organizational channels through which the marginalized traditionally had expressed their anger had been eroded.

In the resulting void along with nationalism, year-of-arrival consciousness, and the like arose generational conflict. Justifiably, the youth of 1965 asked what the older generation had done to combat Jim Crow; many of the youth did not recall or were made to forget the militance of W. E. B. Du Bois and Ben Davis, not to mention Pettis Perry. Thus, the answers they received were incomplete, unsatisfying, unimpressive. The younger generation concluded that there had been an excess of middle-class prudence and the time had come for militance. Unfortunately, this laudable response was colored by the ascending influence of gangs, whose often violent bravado could have benefited from a dash of prudence.

Although the case of *Brown v. Board of Education* in 1954 and the Montgomery bus boycott of 1955 precipitated a new conversation on race, South LA was not disposed to participate in it. The sacrifices of black youth, from Emmett Till to the Student Non-Violent Coordinating Committee, earned them a distinct place at the table, along with the NOI, cultural nationalists, gangs, the BPP, and the NAACP; to many of the youth, all appeared attractive except the last. Simultaneously, the attack on Aid to Families with Dependent Children—i.e., welfare—was not just an attack on women, it was an attack on youth.

Hence, the meaning of the 1960s cannot be divorced from what had happened in the 1950s, most notably, the Red Scare. Those forces arising in the 1960s were marked indelibly by what happened in the previous decade. Ironically, this meant that those activists who arose in the 1960s not only were obligated by the prevailing consensus to keep apart from figures like Ben Davis, John Howard Lawson, Pettis Perry, and Frank Barnes, they often were unaware of their existence.

The decline of the left also set the stage for the rise of ultraright forces bent on eviscerating the public sector; it was the government—city, state, and federal—that sought to hamstring racial discrimination via legislation and regulation, and the weakening of this sector had a negative impact on blacks. Government was the chief employer in LA; in it blacks—City Councilman Tom Bradley for one—were placed at the highest levels, as they were not generally in the private sector. The attack on government was, in effect, an attack on blacks.

The Watts Uprising was a milestone marking the previous era from what was to come. For blacks it marked the rise of black nationalism, as blacks revolted against police brutality. But what began as a black revolt against the police quickly became a police revolt against blacks. This latter revolt was a milestone too, one marking the onset of a "white backlash" that would propel Ronald Reagan into the governor's mansion in Sacramento and then the White House. White backlash proved to be more potent than what had given it impetus, black nationalism. This too was the meaning of the 1960s.

■

To discuss the Watts rebellion without examining its roots in the global political economy would be to offer an incomplete and faulty analysis. As evidence, one has only to consider the rich and exciting school of scholarship that seeks to explain the abolition of slavery in the British Empire, and ultimately in all of the Americas, by examining broader questions of political economy. Even those who do not accept every aspect of this thesis have been forced to engage it.[28]

Thus far, those who have examined a question of similar epochal significance—the dismantling of legalized racial segregation—have avoided, for the most part, incorporating in their analysis broader questions of political economy and the global correlation of forces, despite the fact that this dismantling took place as the Cold War began and as policy makers admitted freely that their actions were motivated by global developments.

I have argued that just as the conflict between capitalism and slavery led to the abolition of bonded labor, the conflict between capitalism and the possibilities of socialism led to the abolition of formal Jim Crow. I am certain that at some point in the twenty-first century, historians will be obligated to tackle this important question—the dismantling of legalized segregation—by reference to the Cold War. Similarly, I am convinced that these future historians will be captivated by the apparent paradox that as Jim Crow subsided, black nationalism grew; and, concomitantly, that as the presumed liberalizing influence of anti–Jim Crow measures were exerted, conservatism began to grow. My thesis is that the solution to these seeming conundrums can be found by examining the declining fortunes of the left. Besides seeking to comprehend the uniqueness of the black experience in the West, examining the dynamics of insurrection, and reflecting on class, race, ethnicity, gender, and age, this book seeks to chart the impact of the world on Afro-America and vice versa.

Its domestic context aside, the Watts Revolt in its scale and intensity brought to the forefront the question of national security. In some respects it offered a paradigm of what might happen if a nuclear warfare emergency arose: there were hints of martial law, military rule, and a coup d'état. The revolt even sparked fears in some quarters that the Soviet Union had manipulated the situation or could take advantage of it. These fears were not unprecedented. Historically, there had been concern that disaffected blacks would be sympathetic to the blandishments of foreign powers, thus jeopardizing existing sovereignty.

In February 1942 Japan launched the last direct frontal attack on the U.S. mainland, a stone's throw from where I once resided in California; during World War II blacks, via the NOI, had manifested some sympathy for Tokyo's claim to be "protecter of the colored races."[29] California was not distant from Vietnam and was not only part of the Atlantic world; it was also part of the Pacific. Military spending in this region boosted the University of California by way of research dollars lavished on science departments and contractors like Douglas Aircraft and TRW. Thus, the call in August 1965 by a number in Watts to support the National Liberation Front and the Communist party

1. In this pre-1948 photo, a black man observes housing from which he is excluded because of race.

in Vietnam angered and frightened many; this call was echoed shortly there-after by some BPP activists.[30] The BPP had political relations with Cuba, China, North Korea, and other forces deemed hostile to Washington. This global context was a decisive factor facilitating domestic civil rights conces-sions.[31]

The impact of the Mexican heritage of California must be considered also. Blacks could receive civil rights concessions for national security reasons; in California there was the added incentive of a competing, compounded racism. By the time Los Angeles experienced another burst of civil unrest in 1992, the city's Latino, or Spanish-speaking, population was growing more rapidly than monolingual blacks. This created an opportunity for blacks in the city and state to assume the position of "middle man minority" and conse-quently to gain top posts in City Hall and Sacramento much more rapidly than their Latino counterparts.

In 1965 a major concern among white elites was whether concessions

2. In the fall of 1946, Ronald Reagan (*center at microphone*) appeared in an antiracist radio play sponsored by a "Communist front," called "Mobilization for Democracy."

to blacks after August 1965 would send the message to Chicanos that more militance would be rewarded. In a state where race relations meant more than biracial polarity, where by 1992 not only the Spanish-speaking but Asian-Americans as well outnumbered blacks, it was difficult for blacks in the city and state not to be internationalist in outlook. But this could mean contact with many deemed potentially antagonistic to Washington—those with roots in Ho Chi Minh City, for example—or at least could open the door for neighbors like Mexico to take advantage of regional problems.[32] Demographers suggest that the population trends of today in California, where blacks are just ahead of Native Americans in numbers, like many other trends eventually will sweep eastward from here. Thus, blacks and nonblacks alike across the nation can benefit from understanding this state's peculiar experience.

Renewed affinity with the continent of Africa was supposedly at the heart of black nationalism. Yet, the February 1965 murder of Malcolm X in New York City by his former NOI comrades weakened the relations he had developed with Nasser's Egypt and Nkrumah's Ghana. The NAACP was loath to associate with its logical counterpart, the African National Congress of South

3. Civil Rights Congress leader William Patterson (*left*) and local leader Anne Shore appear at a 1949 LA rally.

Africa, because of the ANC's alliance with South African Communists.[33] "Cultural nationalists" expressed ideas remarkably similar to those of Leopold Senghor of Senegal and his doctrine of "Negritude." Janet Vaillant has maintained that colonial repression in this West African state undergirded this philosophy. "Cut off from the give-and-take of local politics, to which they had become accustomed," she noted, "young educated Senegalese were thrown back on ideas and theories. Unable to act for the time being, they considered cultural questions with added fervor."[34]

By 1965 many blacks were "cut off" from anti-imperialist and trade union politics; "cultural questions" filled the vacuum. Writing poems was deemed to be more important than who controlled the means of production. And just as Senghor's praxis was marked by the bacchanalian influence of Baudelaire and Rimbaud, the cultural nationalists in LA were marked by a certain liber-

4. Dalton Trumbo bids farewell to fellow left luminaries from the film industry and friends as he goes off to prison. *Left to right:* Helen C. Nelson Bessie; Alvah Bessie; the Reverend W. M. Small of New Light Baptist Church; Trumbo; Herbert Biberman; Mrs. Carl Crain; Rev. Crain, pastor of Long Beach Christian Church; Margaret Larkin Cole; Albert Maltz; Lester Cole.

tine abandon that took full advantage of the unfolding "sexual revolution," a revolution that was marred by the rise of gangsters and their particular approach to heterosexual and homosexual relations. Thus sexual abandon, along with year-of-arrival consciousness and nationalism, evolved to fill the vacuum created by the erosion of class consciousness.

The transatlantic influence exemplified by Negritude may not have been accidental. In 1956, the year the CRC dissolved and the left went on the defensive in the midst of revelations about Stalinist rule, Senghor addressed a host of black intellectuals, including Richard Wright and Mercer Cook—but not Du Bois, who was barred because the government would not grant him a passport—at a forum in Paris apparently backed by Paris and Washington.[35] Anti-Communists maintained that Moscow influenced virtually every nation in the world through the manipulation of local Communists. But global influence was far from being a Communist monopoly. The Women's Christian Temperance Union had shown that women could organize across national

5. Charlotta Bass (*center*), publisher of the *California Eagle*, campaigns for Congress in October 1950.

boundaries, influencing social policies in many nations.[36] Martin Luther King, Jr., was influenced profoundly by India.[37] Certain forms of black nationalism could also be produced and reproduced and were influenced by global trends, be they from Tokyo or Dakar.[38] Cultural nationalists in LA might agree rhetorically with Amilcar Cabral that there should be a "return to the source," to Africa, for inspiration; but the anti-Communist environment in which they existed made it more likely that their source would more closely resemble Leopold Senghor than Nelson Mandela.

In the 1990s nationalism of various brands is spreading in the aftermath of the left's decline; this trend has taken hold in neighborhoods from LA to Kabul.[39] This is a global development. In sum, just as Toni Morrison has complained that race is a looming absence in the discourse on U.S. literature, we must acknowledge that considering the African-American experience while ignoring the looming presence of the rest of the world does a disservice to all sides, including the U.S. experience as a whole.[40] In the pages that follow I sketch the impact of race, region, class, gender, age, and the like on postwar Los Angeles; but all of these factors must be considered in the light of developments in Vietnam, the Soviet Union, China, Africa, the world.

1

Toward Understanding

ISTORIANS OF THE BLACK URBAN EXPERIENCE HAVE
concentrated on New York and Chicago, tending to ignore the nation's
second largest city, Los Angeles.[1] Yet events in 1965 and 1992, the evolution of rap music, the proliferation of gangs, sensational trials, and the growth of various forms of nationalism suggest that LA is a city worthy of deeper investigation.

A closer examination of the nation's largest state would deflect the inaccurate assumption that the history of distinct regions east of the Mississippi River is applicable to California, which entered the Union by way of conquest from Mexico, a factor that continues to impact every aspect of this region. Just as enslavement of African-Americans and genocide against Native Americans must be the starting point for the explication of much of U.S. history, in California the added factor of conquest from Mexico must be noted. To understand the roots of the 1965 insurrection involves a consideration of factors beyond the usual black-white bipolarity and broader factors beyond the immediate issues of police brutality and unemployment.

Some have felt that Southern California has been a racial Eden for African-Americans, while others have argued the opposite. It seems that both views have a kernel of truth. The presence of sizable Latino, Native American, and Asian-American groups of color served as a lightning rod at once diffusing the bigotry absorbed almost exclusively by African-Americans in the East and South and compounding and heightening the impact of racism in a manner detrimental to blacks. Watts 1965 in part was an expression of this trend.

This is not intended to slight the "Black Question" when considering California, for persons of African descent have been there at least since the beginning of the Columbian era. One writer has observed that "as early as 1510, California . . . was reputed to be an island inhabited by black, passionate Amazons." The first person of African descent is said to have set foot in California in 1535.[2]

Black presence has also been a historical factor in Los Angeles itself. Of the 94 settlers who founded this Southern California town in 1781, 26 are said to have had some African ancestry. Still, it would be mistaken to equate the history of New York City—where African-Americans by the mid-eighteenth century already had tried to burn down the city twice—with Los Angeles, where according to the 1880 census there were a mere 100 blacks.[3]

Likewise, it would be mistaken to assume no major difference between the black experience in the West and that of the East and South. Certainly antiblack racism existed; the question is to what extent the presence of sizable Latino, Asian, and Native American populations—and the relative dearth of African-Americans—mediated or enhanced antiblack racism. Suggestive is the comment of Joseph Franklin that from 1889 to 1939 in the Mountain and Pacific regions, 166 people were lynched, of whom only 12 were black.[4] Roger Daniels and Harry Kitano have argued that the size of a national minority in relation to other groups determines the effect of social proscription. Hence, when the African-American population is exceeded by the Asian-American population—as often was the case in the West—the bulk of prejudice was directed against the latter.[5]

In nineteenth-century Los Angeles and California, most violence was aimed at the Mexican, Indian, and Asian populations, because the black population was negligible. Indeed, the violence in this frontier town was substantial and pervasive and cannot be separated from the insurrection of 1965. One commentator suggested that between 1850 and 1870 the City of Angels was "the wildest, toughest, hell-for-leather town west of the Rockies." LA was a town full of "drifters, thieves and con men, who, in addition to everything else, were for the most part racist and given to cruel outbursts of violence," most of it aimed at Mexicans, Indians, and Chinese. Both LA and San Francisco had vigilantes, but in the former "'fighting crime' was" more often "racially motivated."[6]

A significant percentage of LA blacks migrated from Oklahoma, Texas, and Louisiana, and a significant percentage of those killed in August 1965 hailed from these states. Texas slaves were known for utilizing the tactic of fire against their enemies; the "Texas Troubles" of mid-1860 occurred when the "weather was extremely hot," and the "ruinous fires" set "spread fear across the entire South."[7] As in 1965, a number of blacks were killed as a direct result. Louisiana was the site in 1811 of the nation's largest slave insurrection, along with later substantial slave resistance. "Pelican State blacks were subjected to a greater degree of violence than Negroes in other parts of the South during the late nineteenth century."[8] Oklahoma had its own form of "compounded racism" as a number of the Native American peoples owned black slaves; moreover, this state was the home of the "Okies," who had their own distinct expressions of racism. The violent roots of LA combined with the insurrectionary and violent memories of many of its black residents suggest a combustible pairing.

California's racial composition and its late entrance into the United States of America are unique and dominating factors.[9] "Early Los Angeles was thoroughly integrated since house lots were distributed to the settlers without reference to racial characteristics."[10] This pattern was largely absent in the East and South. California was under Mexican rule until the mid-nineteenth century, and Mexico City's hostility to slavery was more pronounced than Washington's. This did not mean Los Angeles escaped racism—in fact, it was a hotbed of Confederate sympathy during the Civil War—it only meant that it had much more of a "rainbow racism" than other U.S. cities did: racism was not solely or predominantly of the typical black-white dichotomy that obtained elsewhere. It was what I call "compounded racism."

Moreover, one can speak of a "compounded racism" in that African-Americans were not only subjected to bias by whites but also had to confront Mexican, Japanese, and other cultures that were either biased against darker peoples or unable to surmount an overall U.S. prejudice against darker peoples. Likewise, African-Americans were not immune from active or tacit participation in bigoted acts against other minorities, such as the internment of Japanese-Americans during World War II.

■

The fluidity of a rapidly developing situation and the bigotry absorbed by other minorities at times allowed black women the opportunity for economic advancement. Biddy Mason was born in 1818 as a slave; her masters migrated to California in 1851. She was part Cherokee and Choctaw, like many others defined as black. Ultimately she was freed and became a major property owner in the city of LA.[11]

What may be the oldest Southern California black community was begun in 1905. James Furlong helped to transform a truck farm into a thriving housing tract that took his name. Furlong Tract was bounded by Alameda Street, Long Beach Boulevard, 50th Street, and 55th Street. In 1941 the LA Housing Authority purchased the area for low-income housing and built what are known today as the Pueblo Rio Housing units.[12]

Val Verde, the "black Palm Springs," was founded in northern Los Angeles County in 1924 during an era when discrimination kept African-Americans from enjoying the basic amenities of California life: sunny beaches, picturesque parks, resorts, and hotels. Bruce's Beach, a popular black-owned resort in Manhattan Beach, was forced to close years before.[13]

As the African-American population of LA began to increase at the beginning of the twentieth century, "Negrophobia" increased concomitantly. As late as 1910 it was possible to say that African-Americans were less segregated than Asian-Americans. The construction and opening of the Panama Canal and the growing U.S. role in the Pacific ignited black migration to California. A hotel was erected on Central Avenue in LA that catered to black guests, and other blacks began to flock to this area. This migration engendered a backlash by some white property owners and realtors who sought to ensure that blacks moved to this area of the city and no other through such mechanisms as the imposition of racially restrictive covenants in property deeds.[14]

In the 1920s the Ku Klux Klan was resurrected in Southern California, as it was elsewhere. Its members' attention was diverted by the comparatively large Asian-American and Latino populations, though they did not ignore blacks.[15] The Klan's rise fed the the development of nationalist sentiments among blacks, along with a thriving chapter of Marcus Garvey's Universal Negro Improvement Association.[16]

The same decade also witnessed the acceleration of LA's suburbanization, and race was no negligible factor in this process. More affluent Euro-Americans were not only fleeing their rural brethren but African-Americans as well.[17] Simultaneously, blacks were moving from the Central Avenue area and migrating farther south to an area called Watts, named after C. H. Watts, a Pasadena real estate and insurance man who also operated a livery. It developed as a black island in an otherwise white sea of southeastern LA County. This growth did not escape the attention of the KKK. Paying homage to Carl Van Vechten, some Angelenos had begun referring to Watts as "Nigger

Heaven."[18] There was fear that a black town with black elected political leadership could be utilized to advance black interests in the region.

Watts was hemmed in on the east by a string of nearly lily-white cities and towns—notably South Gate, Lynwood, and Bell—and on the south by Compton. Until the 1950s Lynwood described itself as "the friendly Caucasian city"; Compton had one Negro resident in 1930. The area to the north was covered by a network of racially restrictive convenants that extended from Slauson Avenue to 92d Street. From 1937 to 1948 there were over a hundred lawsuits enforcing these convenants in LA Superior Court, and mortgages, in any case, were difficult for African-Americans to obtain. Blacks were contained in Watts; they were denied self-determination after the city of LA succeeded in annexing Watts in 1926.[19]

The social and spatial isolation induced by the hypersegregation of Black LA was not without consequence.[20] Arna Bontemps argued that "here removed from the influence of white folks, [blacks] did not acquire the inhibitions of their city brothers. [It] was like a tiny section of the deep south literally transplanted." As the 1930s began Watts, according to Sonora McKeller, "was all but barren land." Houses were few and far between, with the emptiness interrupted by Japanese produce gardens. "Where today we see storm drains and cemented gullies, in those days the people of Watts fished for crawfish and catfish in mud and slime." There were "Chinese lottery dens," "honky-tonks," and "speak-easies" and "bootleg whiskey, gin and home brew. In each spot a lone piano played by a local boy provided the entertainment." From this milieu, similar to what had happened in the sister city of New Orleans, a number of top-flight jazz musicians came to maturity.[21]

Watts was incorporated into LA in part to broaden the tax base in order to pay for precious water brought by the Owens Valley Aqueduct. But the narrowness of its lots limited the size and quality of the homes to be built, guaranteeing that only a persecuted minority like blacks would be attracted there. This persecution also made it likely that residents of Watts would not be indifferent to the appeal of the left, as the Socialists and then the Communists found support there.[22]

■

In 1966 *Time* proclaimed that LA was "probably the fastest growing city in the history of the world." This was hyperbole but did suggest the flux that had been gripping Southern California for at least the previous forty years.

From 1925 to 1940, 284,549 whites came to LA and only 14,758 "non-whites," but most of this latter group were blacks, who grew to two-thirds of the community of color.

LA was an antiunion town as a direct result of the furor surrounding the bombing of the *LA Times* building in 1910, and this helped to ensure an ample supply of cheap white labor. The subsequent trial of labor and left advocates and the resultant growth of the right wing in Southern California was a dominant factor in shaping racism there; cheap white labor feared cheaper black labor, and captains of industry manipulated one against the other. Almost no blacks were employed in the city's booming tire and auto plants during the early 1930s. They were excluded from most unions, except the left-influenced Packing House Workers. The exclusion from the private sector led blacks to turn to the public sector for jobs, but obstacles were there also; teaching jobs were generally not available. In Pasadena blacks were barred from public swimming pools, but in a uniquely LA twist, so were Japanese, Chinese, Filipinos, and Mexicans.[23]

LA had a population of 6,000 in 1870, 50,000 in 1890, and 320,000 in 1910. From 1920 to 1930 the population grew from 577,000 to 1.24 million. The automobile accelerated this growth. In 1919 the city had the "highest ratio of automobiles per capita of any major city" in the United States. Four years later a mass-transit network, the Pacific Electric Railway, was developed and covered over 1,164 miles with its streetcars. Watts was the site of the Pacific Electric shops, and a major junction for southbound trains was in this black community. The destruction of the electric transit system is an oft-told tale, most recently in the Hollywood film *Who Framed Roger Rabbit?* The social isolation of Watts began when the "red rail cars" were removed in 1940s.[24]

The triumph of automobile use meant growth of the oil industry. There were major oil fields no more than twenty miles from the center of the city. Oil fuels industrial expansion. LA became the center of the oil equipment and service industry; the second largest tire-manufacturing center; the headquarters of the western furniture, glass, and steel industries; and the regional center for the aircraft, automotive, chemical, and trucking industries. Instead of developing an industrial core surrounded by residential suburbs, the city developed an administrative-residential center surrounded by an industrial suburban network. As a result, most of the working-class residents lived in suburbs, not in the city. The scattering of the working class in fragmented suburbs forestalled the development of their political strength and, perhaps, their class consciousness. The working class worked in the industrial suburbs but did not necessarily live or vote there, which furthered the hegemony of business owners and their effort to maintain LA as an open shop. This aided the development of a hidebound conservatism, often accompanied by racism and fear of competition from black and other minority workers.[25]

Langston Hughes captured the complexity of LA and race at this time. The city, he said, "seemed more a miracle than a city, a place where oranges sold for one cent a dozen, ordinary black folks lived in huge houses with 'miles of yards,' and prosperity seemed to reign in spite of the Depression." Yet he felt that Hollywood "might just as well be controlled by Hitler."[26] The social scientist Charles Johnson also noticed this racial complexity. "In certain plants where Mexicans were regarded as white, Negroes were not allowed to mix with them; where Mexicans were classed as colored, Negroes not only worked with them but were given positions over them. In certain plants Mexicans and whites worked together; in some others, white workers accepted Negroes and objected to Mexicans; still in others white workers accepted Mexicans and objected to Japanese."[27] When employers hired African-Americans, they preferred the light-skinned variety. According to James Gregory nothing bothered Okies more "than California's system of racial and ethnic relations." They were shocked by signs reading "no white laborers need apply." The conflict between their past and present realities helps to explain why a raw racism became a "source of group identity" for many of these migrants from a state known as "Little Dixie."[28]

Los Angeles historically has been hospitable to the unconventional, not only in its racial complexity. "Vedanta, Theosophy, Rosicrucianism, spiritualism, New Thought, and the Self Realization Fellowship. . . . Krishnamurti, Paramahansa Yogananda, Ernest Holmes and Aimee Semple MacPherson. Nudism, body building, ethical vegetarianism, Theocracy and homeopathy. . . . circus tent revivalism, militant atheism, the Nation of Islam and the Church of Wicca" all flourished in LA.[29] Apparently there was something about this region that spawned uniqueness; many writers have pointed to the tendency in the United States for migrants to flee west in order to reinvent themselves on the edge of the continent, the last frontier. This spawned innovation and difference.

It is striking that the movement led by the African-American Father Divine in the 1930s was predominantly black in New York, while in Los Angeles he attracted "middle and upper middle class" whites; moreover, his movement in LA "displayed a broader and more intense politicalization" than elsewhere in the nation.[30] Los Angeles, along with its pattern of race relations, was peculiar, and the patterns of Chicago and New York do not altogether encompass this city. The fact that an insurrection with the depth of that of 1965 arose there first and not elsewhere seems understandable given this context.

■

The deft chronicler of Southern California Carey McWilliams saw this region as a great laboratory of experimentation, a forging ground, a place where ideas, practices, and customs move, prove their worth, or are discarded.[31] In LA in the 1960s many blacks came to feel that this great laboratory had produced a Frankenstein monster of bias that deserved to be discarded. LA had been subjected to enormous strain as a result of massive migration; this combined with unique racial tensions and related subjective factors produced an explosion.

The fiction of LA should also be considered. One critic has remarked about the preeminent novelist of LA, Raymond Chandler, that in his work "law enforcement is untrustworthy; business has become a sanctuary for deceivers; the professions are riddled with chicanery. . . . the city becomes a graphic symbol of THE BIG LIE—the cardinal deception of American civilization . . . a depraved regional society [with] . . . fraudulence at the heart of the culture."[32] The black migrants, like others flocking to this region, were in search of something more. When they were confronted with the grim reality, they were as disillusioned as others, except their disillusionment was leavened with an anger about racism and a history of militance.

Black fiction has not ignored these tendencies. Paul Carter Harrison's play *The Great MacDaddy* represents Los Angeles as a netherworld where, in the words of one critic, "Africans in America lose their ancestral minds. . . . [where] black folk engage in all manner of social, moral and political corruption."[33] For others—such as Nona Hendryx in her affecting song "Can I Speak to You Before You Go to Hollywood?"—LA was the site for blacks to discard the bonds of community and revel in egotism. Chester Himes framed the issue most portentously. At one point one of his characters in *Lonely Crusade* proclaims, "You might say the fate of the working class of the world depended on us here. . . . As the West Coast goes, the nation goes. As the nation goes, the world goes."[34] In his exaggeration Himes underscored the essential point that LA is both unique and an incubator of trends for future export.

■

The thousands of blacks migrating to LA in the 1930s and 1940s were faced with a contradictory reality. There were sizable communities of color that often deflected bigotry that traditionally was directed toward blacks exclusively. Yet some of these same communities were influenced by bias against darker peoples. Still, despite the restrictive convenants, the job segregation, blacks kept coming.[35]

In 1910 there were an estimated 7,599 blacks in LA; by 1940 this figure had risen to 55,114, and by 1944, to 118,888. Watts doubled in size from 1940 to 1946. During the 1940s California received the largest decennial population increase of any state in the nation's history. Such significant population growth inevitably induces a crisis of rapid change and disorientation; neighborhoods appear overrun, local institutions seem besieged. [This was especially the case in 1940s LA when some of the growth was among the traditional bête noire of U.S. society, while the white population was growing similarly via a heavy influx of Okie migrants.] The venues where the races crossed paths were a flashpoint. In March 1943 a black passenger charged that a white conductor pushed him off a streetcar and beat him with a wrench. White drivers and conductors complained of attacks from blacks on the Central Avenue line. Through strikes and threats to walk out, the Association of Street, Electric Railway, and Motor Coach Operators forced the confinement of Negroes to menial jobs such as janitors and coach cleaners.[36]

World War II transformed the West from a raw-materials colony for the East to a metropole in its own right, and government spending was crucial in this process. Black labor was needed in defense plants, which spurred migration. But formidable barriers existed, particularly in the realm of housing and transportation. Following the lead of the Federal Housing Administration, savings and loans associations refused loans to blacks in white neighborhoods; in 1940 the FHA underwriting manual contained requirements that discriminated against blacks and made the adoption of racially restrictive convenants a condition for FHA insurance of new construction. Blacks were unable to reside close to the aircraft and shipbuilding plants, and very few of the mass transit red cars were useful in transporting them to these sites; there were no runs at night, and bus, taxi, and jitney drivers were reluctant to drive in to or out of South LA at night. Blacks were mostly excluded from the booming film industry of Culver City, Burbank, and other distant areas.

Despite the labor shortage during the war, it took a spirited protest led by black women in 1942 to force war-related industries to open their doors a crack to black workers; even then Deputy Mayor Orville Caldwell recommended that black migration to LA be halted. Herded into ghettos from which there was no escape, hounded on the job, surrounded by other communities of color who were not immune to color biases, LA blacks were forced to be tightly knit; they left work at the same time, fearing white violence. It was inevitable that embryonic gangs would eventually emerge.[37]

Still, it would be mistaken to view African-Americans as the sole target of bigotry, for it was during this time that Japanese-Americans were rounded up and herded into concentration camps. No better example of the compounded and contradictory nature of LA racism is the fact that blacks, in a sense, were a beneficiary of this process as "Little Tokyo" was emptied and became "Bronzeville." Anti-Nippon sentiment was particularly virulent in LA. According to John Modell, "One out of three people in Southern California wished to see the Nisei placed in concentration camps, as compared with only one out of seven elsewhere on the Coast."[38]

The black minority did not distinguish itself in protest, though the bigotry of this process inevitably was harmful to its long-term interests. Maya Angelou, a witness to this process in San Francisco, recalled "indifference to the Japanese removal. . . . since they didn't have to be feared, neither did they have to be considered. . . . No member of my family and none of the family friends ever mentioned the absent Japanese."[39]

Black protest was dulled because some did benefit. Edwin Louis Petty came to LA from Memphis in 1932 and worked for a Japanese-American produce broker in the city market at Ninth and San Pedro streets. After the internment he became a state licensed broker, buying from farmers and selling to local stores and markets. In 1944 he opened his own commission house. Some of his accounts were among the most prominent chain stores in LA; that year he was generating sales of $750,000. He had replaced his Asian-American boss.[40] The need for black labor during the war, along with the appeals made by Tokyo, then Moscow, to African-Americans, paved the way for an expansion of the black middle class, a process that was to accelerate in the wake of *Brown v. Board of Education* in 1954.

There was also intraracial conflict. Louisiana, from which many LA blacks migrated, had a highly color-conscious African-American community, in part because of the elevated antebellum status of mulattoes. Color conflict was exacerbated in LA when lighter blacks were favored for certain jobs.[41] One of the ironies of the 1965 insurrection is the fact that not only whites but lighter blacks were attacked because of the color of their skin and what that was thought to represent.

Not all Black Angelenos were pleased with the massive influx of black migrants during the war. These newcomers often hailed from rural areas and were not attuned to urban folkways, and some were darker than those who were objecting to their presence. These migrants also had to face hostility from Mexican, Chinese, European, and others who feared labor competition.

Walter Mosley's fictional hero Easy Rawlins noted that in his neighborhood in LA "almost everybody . . . had come from the country around southern Texas and Louisiana." He lamented the presence of "snobs. They thought that their people and their block were too good for most of the rest of the Watts community. They frowned on a certain class of people buying houses on their streets and they had a tendency to exclude other people from their barbecues and what not. They even encouraged their children to shun other kids they might have met at school or at the playgrounds because it was the Bell Street opinion that most of the black kids around there were too coarse and unsophisticated."[42]

The three-tiered racial hierarchy of much of Louisiana, the evolution of a "colored" population perched midway between those defined as "Negro" and "white," was felt in Los Angeles. Dorothy Dandridge, the light-skinned black actress, symbolized how race, gender, color—and its handmaiden class—could conflate tragically in LA in the 1950s. These swirling pressures pushed her to the point of suicide.[43]

A color and class conflict among blacks has been noted by social scientists as well. Alonzo Smith has observed that "prior to World War II, Los Angeles had more of a middle-class black community than the southern and northeastern cities." Then thousands of poorer black migrants arrived. Harlan Dale Unrau has limned the "tendency toward intra-racial friction between upper and middle class blacks and lower-class blacks"; this led to "year consciousness," or status determined by what year one arrived. There was a perception that lighter skin correlated with early arrival in LA. This year consciousness may have influenced the strategies of civil rights organizations, which focused more on restrictive covenants—a particular concern of the middle class—

than on public housing, a particular concern of the strapped sector of the working class.[44]

Gerald Nash has said that "both blacks and whites also charged that the influx of southern blacks bred problems since some behave boisterously"; in Venice "two mass meetings of black residents protested against the construction of a new housing project for blacks (in a black neighborhood)." Such a fissure distanced middle-class civil rights organizations from their less affluent compatriots, leaving the latter defenseless and making inchoate outbursts like that of 1965 the major vehicle of protest.[45]

The contradictory nature of race relations in pre–Cold War LA is reflected in the memories of musician Buddy Collette, who recalled an easygoing relationship among racial groups.[46] Woody Strode, the UCLA gridiron hero who became an actor, has spoken similarly. He grew up in South Central LA, 51st and Holmes, in the 1920s; it was a "predominantly black neighborhood," though he recalled relatively smooth interaction among the Mexicans, Italians, and Germans in the vicinity. He ascribed the easy interaction to the relative absence of blacks and felt that as their population grew, tensions increased. This African-American stated that through the 1940s a "black man couldn't walk through Inglewood after dark. They had a sign posted: 'NO JEW AND NO COLOREDS ARE WELCOME IN THIS TOWN!'"

Yet that LA was a place apart was signaled by the experience of his fellow black football star Kenny Washington, who lived among Italians: "I swear he was nothing but a nice Italian kid. He couldn't speak good English; he had an accent that was half-Italian." Strode did not see it as accidental that the "three responsible for integrating pro sports in America"—himself, Washington, and fellow UCLA star Jackie Robinson—all hailed from LA and therefore had a special approach to race relations. This LA idyll was interrupted rudely when he joined the military. "What a slap in the face that was. For twenty seven years I thought I was equal." Misty-eyed memory aside, Strode was probably correct when he stated, "To the best of my knowledge, UCLA was the first major university to have four black kids playing key roles" on the football team.[47]

Strode was also correct when he suggested that racial tensions rose as the black population increased. This—along with the fact that newcomers would work for less—may help to explain why older black residents were resentful of the newcomers. Quintard Taylor has detected a similar resentment in the Pacific Northwest. Moreover, the fact that the newcomers in turn felt that older residents were too timid and that a more aggressive posture was needed can be detected in LA.[48] An expropriated Japanese-American community—who saw blacks taking their place—and a Mexican-American population that had suffered through the so-called Zoot Suit attacks of 1943 added their own irritation to this seething racial cauldron.

Chester Himes caught some of these tensions. His protagonist announced bitterly that "Los Angeles is the most overrated, lousiest, countriest, phoniest city I've ever been in." A prominent black physician "went into a restaurant where he's been eating for years and they didn't want to serve him." Was racism responsible? No, "Southern Negroes are coming in here and making it hard for us."[49] Solidarity had withered, atomizing had increased.

Suburbanization and the removal of jobs from areas immediately accessible to blacks accelerated after the war; exclusionary zoning and FHA policies hastened this process. The overall quality of black life fell precipitously during this period.[50] Building public housing in South LA was a source of contention. The Jordan Downs project of 512 units was completed months before the war ended, just after the 142 units of Imperial Courts. Hacienda Village, 184 units, was finished a few years before. Yet this housing was deemed to be "semi-permanent" or "temporary," which has led some to conclude that this was also the view of the black population that moved in.[51]

Vehement protests erupted when blacks sought to move to nearby Willowbrook.[52] In 1945 lawsuits challenging racially restrictive covenants were filed in LA at a rate significantly higher than that of most of the nation.[53] A researcher for the American Council on Race Relations expressed concern about the perilous course of integration in Watts itself, which by now was 80 percent black: "Threats of violence [are] common and have been made equally by Mexicans and whites against the expanding Negro population." Powerful real estate interests apparently had "selected" Watts as "an area of Negro segregation"; this in turn heightened "tension between the incoming Negroes and the Mexicans. . . . returning Mexican veterans, resentful over the striking changes which have occurred during their absence, have in some cases threatened to band together to expel the Negro invaders." In 1947 there was "for the Negro and Mexican, inequality in income, employment opportunity, educational opportunity and housing, for the white, ignorance, prejudice, insecurity and a thousand and one personal frustrations. Add to these an irresponsible press, the policies of real estate agencies and mortgage companies and a prejudiced police force." The same situation existed eighteen years later.[54]

The Los Angeles Police Department was a major problem. In July 1946 after a highway patrolman shot in the back and killed a fleeing black suspect, "a near riot situation occurred at the corner of Adams and Central." The *LA Times* during this period was specifying race in want ads. Perhaps as a direct result, in 1948 "there were no black workers at the new GM plant in Van Nuys. . . . black [taxi] drivers said they were never sent to Beverly Hills or Hollywood, or the Wilshire District." "Why," Alonzo Smith has asked plaintively, "during the late 1940s when fair employment practices legislation was being passed in other parts of the country, did it fail in California?" The compounded racism—the complex interaction between and among several racial groups—of the largest population center, LA, is a partial explanation.[55]

Meanwhile, Watts was becoming blacker and more decrepit. Patricia Rae Adler has asserted: "The never adequate sewers stank in the summer, there was not enough water to flush the toilets, not enough pressure to fight fires. Health facilities were inadequate." Public housing was sited in this area that already had more than its share of the poverty-stricken. She concluded, "The social fabric of the community could not withstand the strain." The Red Scare decimated whatever resistance had emerged, and this "absence of organizational activity perpetuated the voicelessness of the Negro electorate."[56]

Still, black migrants continued flooding in. More blacks migrated to California in the 1950s than any other state. The black population of New York City increased nearly two and a half times, in Detroit it tripled, and in LA it increased eightfold. The blacks were greeted by a compounded racism and caught in a crisis of rapid change. They were coming to the city while jobs, which historically had been disproportionately in the suburbs, continued to flow into outlying regions.[57]

■

There were many causes and reasons for the tumultuous events of August 1965 in LA; it should have come as a strange surprise only to those who were not paying attention. Strikingly, a consensus quickly emerged that this was no riot, a term that could just as easily be applied to spring antics in Fort Lauderdale or Palm Springs. No, said the editorial broadcast on the CBS radio affiliate in LA as fires were being damped, "This was not a riot. It was an insurrection against all authority." To drive the point home, the words were repeated with emphasis, "This was *not a riot*. If it had gone much further, it would have become civil war." Citing an atypical source, the Peking radio, it called those recent events "a veritable revolutionary movement."[58]

The "CBS Reports" TV broadcast in December 1965 agreed, except it spoke of the "revolt." KMPC radio in LA called it a "virtual civil insurrection probably unmatched since" the Civil War. The left-wing National Lawyers Guild was not isolated when it underscored that "in the profoundest legal and moral sense, those men, women and children were revolting against injustice." The scholars David O. Sears and John B. McConahay substantiated this view when they noted that the "legally constituted authority . . . was overthrown" in the black community.[59]

So it was an insurrection, but the question remained: Why did it happen? There was immediate focus on issues like police brutality, unemployment, poverty, and the like. As the situation was returning to "normal," the *LA Times* addressed this question. It blamed the "social structure," not "whitey" or "the whole Negro race," though it added in what came to be a popular refrain, "the civil rights movement, middle class oriented here, failed the poverty stricken." It also pointed to Proposition 14, a measure passed by the state's voters in 1964 and widely viewed as bolstering residential segregation. The Reverend H. H. Brookins, a well-known black pastor, remarked that "other cities are old and have lived with this problem longer. . . . Where the most hope is built up, the awakening to reality hurts the most."[60]

In a backhanded way a number of analysts agreed with Rev. Brookins. Curt Moody, former director of the Community Relations Conference of Southern California, intoned that "a person coming out of the south with a vision of the Promised Land . . . finds that Los Angeles is not the Promised Land he had expected." The prominent journalist Theodore White was curious as to why such a conflagration would hit the "green lawns, palm trees, flower beds, white frame houses . . . open spaces, airy school houses with huge playgrounds, large parks with swimming pools" of LA. Why LA? For here "Negroes have lived better than in any other large American city." This was a repetitive theme of eastern journalists discovering South LA for the first time. How could such horror occur in a land of sunshine and palm trees?[61] Others looked at LA and concluded that its freeways that could transport commuters could also move insurrectionists easily and that its walls and fences encouraged an alienating isolation.[62]

The British journal the *Economist* sought to contextualize the insurrection, relating it to similar uprisings in Malaysia and Sudan and the "double grievance" of class and race: "Outbreaks like this are part of the price we are going to pay for a society in which more and more people live in cities and do deadly dull work and waste their leisure." [63] An analyst for the AFL-CIO did not disagree and added that this economic malaise was "intensified by two basic economic factors . . . the technological revolution in agriculture and . . . the decline of manufacturing production and maintenance jobs." [64]

Others groped for another kind of context. The sociologist Robert Blauner saw the "so-called riots" as "a preliminary if primitive form of mass rebellion against a colonial status." [65] The idea of African-Americans as a nation within a nation was revived during this period. Thus, the Trotskyite Socialist Workers party cited the South African militant I. B. Tabata, who asserted that the insurrection "reminded me of my own country." [66] The pastor Dr. Edwin T. Dahlberg likened what happened in LA to "guerilla warfare" in Vietnam. The conservative columnists Rowland Evans and Robert Novak felt obligated to discuss the idea that "guerilla warfare in our cities" would be inevitable unless "preferential treatment" was accorded blacks. [67] Beverly Hills psychoanalyst Dr. Frederick Hacker, who interviewed a number of participants in the insurrection, confirmed this approach when he concluded that they were not despairing but saw themselves as "freedom fighters liberating themselves with blood and fire." The rebellion, he insisted, had a positive impact on blacks in that before it occurred "Negro children saw their fathers as helpless and frightened objects of the arbitrariness of white men in uniform," but their outlook changed afterwards. [68]

Was it anomalous that Watts would explode as the civil rights movement was dramatically transforming the plight of African-Americans? One comprehensive analysis concluded that "civil rights policies" did decrease "the gap between black and white incomes, but that this effect is confined to the South." [69] The recognition of this fact drove Martin Luther King, Jr., to move his crusade north to Chicago. It was also dawning on elite circles that a stigmatized black labor force consigned to low wages might be ultimately counterproductive, though profitable in the short term. A report in the *Harvard Business Review* related this abuse of black labor to the fact that a "severe shortage in skilled manpower" reigned and added that "the purchasing power of the Negro community is way below what it would be were Negroes receiving the same remuneration and opportunity as whites of equal ability." *Newsweek* agreed and affirmed that when blacks spend more on housing, they have less to spend on "refrigerators, stoves and furniture." An analysis for the commission that investigated the insurrection supposed that if more of an effort had been made to curb economic discrimination against blacks "such that today Negro-white salary and employment figures were comparable, the white race would itself have made extremely significant economic gains from this."[70] These opinions help to explain the tentative effort during the 1960s to improve the lot of African-Americans.

One upshot of the insurrection was the number of studies and investigations by social scientists of the beleaguered community of South LA. Indeed, researchers may have been the ultimate beneficiary of those fires of summer. The countercultural *LA Free Press* commented in wonder, "The special investigations and reports, surveys, articles, books, lectures, conferences and programs virtually defy enumeration; at UCLA alone, a recent inventory of projects focusing on the south central area counted a minimum of 35."[71]

A major insurrection in a major U.S. city was sufficient to spur elites to try to understand why. Some explanations were bizarre; one sought to blame a book by James Baldwin.[72] This may be why the reclusive and recondite novelist Thomas Pynchon was coaxed from seclusion briefly to examine the insurrection for the *New York Times Magazine*.[73] Others wondered if there was something about blacks that caused them to rebel while Chicanos did not.[74] Watts "has probably been more carefully examined than any riot that has ever occurred."[75]

Studies by social scientists of what they called the "riot" were a minor cottage industry.[76] However, the soundness of some perspectives could be questioned. Vernon Mark, who utilized sources from apartheid South Africa, entitled his contribution "Does Brain Disease Play a Role in Riots and Urban Violence?"[77] The idea that African-Americans might be crazy was not an unusual theme, and this inevitably led to suggestions as to how their brains should be fixed. Such an approach reached the daily press as columnist George Todt indicated that the revolt was "caused by weak character traits in uncivilized human beings who yielded to their savage emotions in a barbaric display of ill will and hate."[78] Overall, August 1965 marked the onset of a highly beneficial era for those employed as social scientists. *LA Times* writer Art Seidenbaum mused, "I have a mental image of a USC sociologist interviewing a man on the street who turns out to be a psychologist from UCLA."[79]

The McCone Commission, appointed by Governor Edmund ("Pat") Brown to investigate the revolt, interviewed community activist Archie Hardwick, who put the point bluntly: "This was a male revolt directed at the white power structure. There is a different type of Negro emerging from the 18 to 25 year old bracket. . . . they identify with Malcolm X's philosophy. . . . During the riot the women were out on the streets cheering the men on."[80] Watts did mark a leap forward for various nationalist discourses with masculinist overtones.

Charles Silberman warned the readers of *Fortune* that Watts meant that black anger would no longer be turned inward but directed outward. Paul Bullock felt that the revolt bolstered the self-esteem of the residents and gave the area "an identity and a touch of glamor. . . . The foreign visitor to Los Angeles is now more likely to tour Watts than MGM or Forest Lawn."[81] The rebellion had a powerful psychological impact and marked a watershed in the evolution of black militance.

It seemed that August 1965 marked the point when LA blacks decided no longer to tolerate misery. Or so suggested the novelist Chester Himes, who stated that "Los Angeles hurt me racially as much as any city I have ever known. . . . The only thing that surprised me about the race riots in Watts in 1965 was that they waited so long to happen." Bill Lane, writing in the black-owned *LA Sentinel*, was of like mind: "A Negro gets mad when he daily sees social patterns that tell him he is living in a white world. . . . The Negro is quiet, but mad, when he sees no Negro secretaries in big firms where Negroes spend much money, place their mortgage escrows and the like." The expression of this anger could no longer be ignored. Former Harvard president James Conant called this anger among the youth "social dynamite" and warned of a veritable holocaust unless this problem was addressed.[82]

In Selma, Alabama, whose difficulties earlier in the year helped light the fuse in LA, Watts hit home. "All through the South whites began locking their doors more carefully and laying in extra supplies of ammunition for their hunting rifles. Watts might be more than two thousand miles away, but some of the Black Belt whites' most terrifying nightmares . . . [were] being played out in color on their own living room television screens. The blacks also had tv sets and the whites knew they were watching too. Watching and thinking—what?"[83]

The revolt led to a wrenching and agonizing reappraisal of race relations. A recurrent theme was that black leadership had lost touch with the black masses. Social scientists like H. Edward Ransford began to conclude that the civil rights movement itself spoke more to the interests of a "middle class . . . with 'rising expectations' for full equality," while the revolt revealed a "very different population—one whose members are intensely dissatisfied, feel powerless to change their position, and have minimum commitment to the larger society. . . . for them, violence is a means of communicating with white society."[84]

The socioeconomic fault lines of California were apparent in August 1965. Tom Wicker of the *New York Times* suggested that "not since the bank holiday in 1933 has the established order in America been more drastically challenged." More ominously, he added, it appeared that "now as then much of that order has to be changed if we [are] to preserve the rest." Concurring from the left, Mike Davis has stated that Watts was "the worst shock to ruling class nerves since the near victory of the Socialist Party in the 1912 mayoral election."[85] A Gallup poll showed that Watts led to civil rights replacing Vietnam as the greatest concern of those polled.[86] The Reverend Don Boyd of the First Methodist Church in LA reflected the worries of many parishioners when he found in the August events parallels with the prophesies of Isaiah.[87] From all quarters and all sectors it was evident that the Watts Insurrection was a blazing turning point.

For a brief moment the fires of LA illuminated stark realities about the region and the nation. E. J. Hobsbawm has commented with clarity about how such a conflagration can distill an essence. Searing conflict dramatizes crucial aspects of the social structure that are strained to the breaking point. He continued, "Moreover, certain problems cannot be studied at all except in and through such moments of eruption, which do not merely bring into the open so much that is normally latent, but also concentrate and magnify phenomena for the benefit of the student, while—not the least of their advantages—normally multiplying our documentation about them."[88]

What are called riots are rarely spontaneous in the ultimate sense, even the riot by the LAPD against Black LA in August 1965. They occur in the context of an elaborate train of social, economic, and political events.[89] Moreover, riots have been a fundamental aspect of the political culture of the United States.[90] The Atlanta riot of 1906, which amounted to an antiblack pogrom, had an electrifying effect on the political and intellectual life of African-Americans. It became more difficult to countenance the perceived timidity of Booker T. Washington's philosophy. The Swing Rebellion in nineteenth-century England had a dramatic impact on Whig and Tory alike, not unlike the way the Watts Rebellion affected Democrats and Republicans alike.[91]

Uprisings like those in Watts in 1965 are akin to a toothache in that they alert the body politic that something is dangerously awry. Their dramatic nature grabs and holds attention and can motivate sweeping social reform and/or repression. Uprisings also can be inspirational. The character and tactics of the Jamaican slave rebels of 1831 were strikingly similar to those of the

Swing Uprising just months earlier.[92] The character and tactics of Watts 1965 were imitated in Newark, Detroit, and a host of other cities.

In addition, there are striking similarities between what happened in Los Angeles in 1965—and 1992—and what took place in Bombay between December 1992 and March 1993. There the death toll from "riots" and bombings was in the .thousands. As one careful study explains what happened in the world's sixth largest city, deindustrialization, the crushing of a militant labor movement, and a decline in class consciousness combined to exacerbate religious and ethnic tensions. Nationalism and sectarianism flourished along with gangs. In rough outline, this is what happened in LA. The study adds the cautionary note that four centuries ago, Goa was a thriving city, larger than London. "What killed it? Not the plague. No, it was the Inquisition. Hounding people for their religious beliefs destroyed the economy. Hindus, Jews, Muslims went to other places. . . . Plagues do not destroy cities. Neither do floods nor earthquakes. What can destroy cities is bigotry and intolerance."[93]

The weight of this admonition about bigotry was rarely far from the minds of many who endured the Watts Revolt. Elite institutions like the *Los Angeles Times* and the University of California were pushed to more progressive approaches as a result of August 1965, just as the Republican party of Southern California was pushed in an opposing direction. Some African-Americans were drawn to new forms of nationalism as epitomized by the Black Panther party, the Nation of Islam, and the forces surrounding Maulana Ron Karenga, just as other blacks chose the related goals of economic nationalism and middle-class aspirations. Mexican-Americans, inspired by the example of Watts 1965, initiated the Brown Berets and the Chicano/a movement, which too had its strain of nationalism. This legacy was multiplied during the "riot" that swept LA again in 1992.

Nationalism was magnified after the onset of the Red Scare as militant organizations, which could have attracted and channeled the energy of blacks, were marginalized or destroyed. And just as blacks in LA mostly came from Texas and Louisiana where fierce rebellion was not uncommon, they also came from a continent where mass uprising against colonial rule was equally commonplace.[94] A people with a tradition of rebellion in a nation with a similar history guarantees convulsion.

TWO

Uprising

2

Rising Up

THE TURBULENCE OF AUGUST 1965 THAT SWEPT across Black Los Angeles—conveniently but inaccurately denoted as the Watts "Riot" or Uprising, it stretched far beyond this one area—was a surprise to some but not to others. The progressive black attorney Loren Miller apparently predicted in May 1964 something akin to what happened fourteen months later. At least that is what Stanley Mosk, California attorney general and later state supreme court judge, was told. Miller was said to have foreseen "violence in Los Angeles" as "inevitable"; he also envisioned "the appointment of a commission who will damn the civil rights leaders and the [police] chief alike." He was prescient.[1]

∎

E. R. Haines, executive assistant at the LA County Department of Parks and Recreation, was in a position to sense the tensions gathering in 1965. A bit more than a year earlier at Bethune Park, there was "an incident at a swimming meet where a white boy had won a contest [and] was beaten up by Negroes after the competition. At Athens Parks there was a riot last winter at a football game between teams from Bethune Park (Negro) and Alondra Park (white) resulting in one white boy being hospitalized. A carnival that was held at Will Rogers Park in July had to be closed down ahead of time due to fighting, drinking, etc. by large numbers of youth between the ages of 16 and 21 years."[2] These incidents often were exacerbated by an abusive police presence. On Memorial Day in 1961, these tensions led to an "alleged riot between citizens and police" that could have been as explosive as the 1965 conflagration.[3] In LA, where there was often a tendency to flee the immense number of small homes for open spaces, parks had become battlegrounds.

The turmoil of the civil rights movement in the Deep South also had reverberations in LA. As in the South, pastors like the Reverend H. H. Brookins played a crucial role; he was chair of the United Civil Rights Committee, which cooperated with the California Democratic Council. In June 1963 at the Statler Hilton Hotel, Brookins helped to organize a large meeting with many city leaders in order to raise pressing issues of "housing, education, employment and law enforcement." A few months later his friend Tom Bradley was elected to the city council, one of the rare times that a black had been elected to office from a predominantly white constituency in any state west of the Mississippi; Watts was considerably south of his district.[4]

Yet the scholar Harry M. Scobie concluded, after scrutinizing "250 incidents of Negro protest demonstrations . . . since approximately May 1963" until 1965, that these "protests accomplished very, very little."[5] This opinion may be overly harsh, although it is easy to understand. In April 1964 tensions involving young blacks and police erupted at Jefferson High School.[6] During the summer of 1964, a report was filed with Democratic governor Pat Brown detailing the deteriorating conditions and attitudes in South LA.[7] No vigorous action was taken. Worse, the initiative on the fall ballot, Proposition 14, was viewed widely among African-Americans as a crude attempt to maintain housing segregation and keep blacks penned in South LA; this measure would overturn moderate fair-housing legislation. This could mean a return to the bad old days of de facto racially restrictive covenants in deeds; this could mean black renters and homeowners being forced to compete for scarce stock in an inflationary market.[8] It was feared that this November ballot measure would also reinforce school segregation, ensuring the continuation of inferior education for blacks.[9] The Negro Political Association of California was created in partial response but to no avail.[10]

Selma erupted in 1965. Deprivation of voting rights there and the racist response of the Alabama authorities to protests built tension in Los Angeles; a number of demonstrations were held in sympathy and solidarity, while others focused on similar local grievances. Rabbi Alfred Wolf, chair of the county Commission on Human Relations, suggested in January 1965 that this body had "been successful in keeping down tensions in many areas." Van de Kamp's, a chain of restaurants, had been targeted by local activists because of its reluctance to hire "Negro waitresses" on the grounds that they would not comport with its "Dutch motif." Other targets of protest were Sears Roebuck, Safeway, Thriftimart, and other companies accused of discriminatory hiring practices. Strikingly, such commercial enterprises were targeted in a different manner eight months later. Rabbi Wolf lamented the "higher unemployment rate" among blacks and worried that "with the rising influx of people to California, [this] could complicate the situation." [11] The LA historian Mike Davis, in words that dovetail with Rabbi Wolf's, said that "the Watts Rebellion was, among other things, a protest against the racist 'Cotton Curtain' that excluded blacks from the higher-wage jobs in the industrial belt east of Alameda Street." [12] Commerce, Vernon, and other areas were in a universe separate from Black LA, though only miles away.

The Human Relations Commission did seek to monitor the situation, but the fear of black labor had been operating unchecked for too long. The HRC's words carried little weight with City Hall. In mid-March 1965 it met amid an "apparent deterioration of police-community relations." Blacks on the HRC's staff recommended having a "meeting with the leadership of the Muslims." The influence of the recently slain Malcolm X was prevalent in LA; those influenced by the NOI were stressing strongly in 1965 the issue of police brutality against blacks.

The LA authorities were concerned about the recent protests in sympathy with Selma. The HRC felt that the "demonstrations at the Federal building seemed to have no organization, leadership, control or defined objective. . . . twenty-seven persons had thrown themselves in front of mail trucks and had been arrested for felony charges." Rabbi Wolf "commented that there seems to be a tremendous groundswell of indignation and frustrations because of Selma." Though Alabama was distant, feeling had emerged that there was one people—black people, not Negroes—involved in these struggles.

Rabbi Wolf's ear may have been closer to the ground than others; he then moved to the next item, "concern of some of the Jewish agencies that Negro anti-Semitism might be growing." This was rooted in the economic relationship of merchant and customer. John Buggs suggested a "series of vignettes" on a local radio station in an effort to ease tensions. [13]

In March 1965 there were five continuous days of demonstrations at the Federal Building. The *LA Times* expressed concern that these "mass civil rights" protests were "turbulent" and "obstructed federal business." Simultaneously, 3,000 faculty members at LA City College held a rally focused on

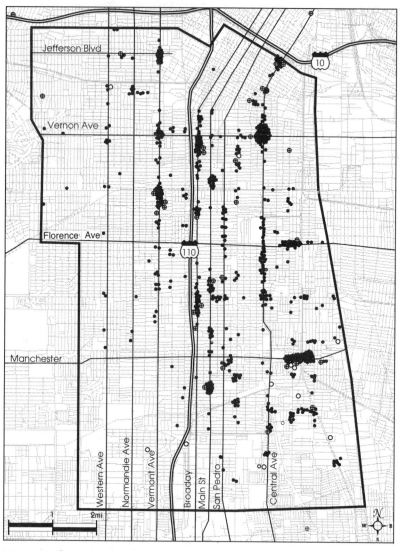

Major areas of unrest in August 1965

Selma and passed a resolution backing the Voting Rights Act being debated in Washington.[14]

By June the Congress of Racial Equality chapter upped the ante by launching a demonstration in the foyer of the mayor's office focusing on the issue of Yorty's blocking the dissemination of antipoverty funds from Washington. In the weeks preceding the August conflagration, CORE was involving hundreds in militant demonstrations throughout the city.[15]

Naturally a special concern of LA activists was their brethren in Louisiana, where many Southern California blacks had roots. A particular issue was the major corporation Crown Zellerbach and its practices in Bogalusa where the armed Deacons for Defense—a precursor of the Black Panther party—were based. The clamor about Bogulusa and the Deacons was sufficiently intense that just before the uprising the South LA assemblyman Mervyn Dymally went to Louisiana to investigate; he returned with the reassurance that the Deacons were "non-violent," though, not contradictorily, he noted that they "guarded him" and "that many Negroes are armed in Louisiana."[16]

But it was not just politics that was roiling the waters. H. M. Bruce of Van Nuys worriedly warned City Hall about the incendiary plays by the black playwright LeRoi Jones, *The Toilet* and *The Dutchman*.[17] Jones, soon to become Amiri Baraka, was an influential black nationalist during the 1960s before becoming attracted to Maoism.

Any who merely followed the public record of what was going on would not have been surprised by the fires of August. The Los Angeles elite, including the Yorty regime and Police Chief William Parker, were not sufficiently alert to have anticipated an impending uprising.[18]

■

The 144 hours of disturbances in August 1965 did not occur exclusively in Watts; the epicenter was, however, South LA, which included Watts. There continues to be amazement that such turmoil could burst forth among the sunshine, palm trees, and horizontal environs of that area. When President George Bush toured the area after the "riot" of 1992 he was struck by the "'wide streets, relatively neat frontyards and obvious pride in the little houses along there' because he associated urban troubles with 'high buildings and tenements and hopelessness.'" Bush remarked, "This is open and rather pretty."[19]

In a sense Bush can be seen as the latest victim of a "New York–centric" approach to urban affairs, associating urban problems with high-rise housing projects and apartment buildings in a cold-weather clime; this tendency was not absent in 1965 either. To be fair, this approach does have a grounding in reality. Staff member William Colby reminded the McCone Commission about the widespread opinion that "Los Angeles was number 1 as the place where Negroes are better off." Perhaps because of the affluent stratum of black sports figures and entertainers, cinema and television representations, the appealing climate, or all of the above, the city was favored by many black migrants, not only from the traditional southern areas but also increasingly deteriorating midwestern cities like St. Louis.[20]

Despite the claims of Colby, a number of blacks viewed the City of Angels as "spiritually below the Mason-Dixon line, without the nastiness of park benches labeled 'for colored,'" and "40 years behind the rest of the country."[21] The neighboring community of Compton had been the home of the young George Bush some years earlier, but it was developing a complexion that he would have had difficulty in recognizing. Integration was proceeding fitfully there, in part because of a local newspaper that by any measure could be considered as incredibly racist.[22]

Watts was becoming a bastion of blacks in the southern part of LA County. By 1965 it had a population of 34,800.[23] Even then Eldridge Cleaver, who was in Folsom prison, recalled bitterly how the very term *Watts* had become an epithet, "the same way as city boys used 'country' as a term of derision. To deride one as a 'lame' who did not know what was happening (a rustic bumpkin), the 'in-crowd' of the time from L.A. would bring a cat down by saying that he had just left Watts."[24]

On top of the regional insult suffered by all blacks, those of Watts had an added burden to bear that gave added intensity to their anger; they not only faced interracial pain but the intraracial variety as well. Stanley Sanders, another son of Watts and its first Rhodes scholar, has added his own interpretation. He blamed the building of Jordan Downs, Nickerson Gardens, Imperial Court, and other housing projects that came to hold a significant percentage of the black poor as being partly responsible for Watts's image. Out of this vortex emerged gangs like the Black Swans and the Farmers. Each project spawned different gangs, and conflict was not unknown. Speaking in 1990, Sanders recalled that "most middle class blacks" were "afraid to come to Watts." With a remaining scintilla of bitterness, he recalled rejection at a dance because he came from Watts. He and his friends were deemed "outcasts." They were "looked down on" by other blacks. They were the "bottom of [the] barrel," he continued. He remembered not only a "color line" but an "economic" line. There was economic conflict that had both interracial and intraracial consequences. The same could be said of color conflict. There was not only the usual white chauvinism; there were "very few fair skinned blacks in Watts," and these were perceived as discriminating against their darker brothers and sisters, referring to folks in Watts as "those black niggers in Watts" as if they were "a whole different race." This combination of resentments—a compounded racism in sum—helps to explain why LA exploded first and with a fervor dwarfing contemporaneous outbursts.[25]

Herb Atkinson, who in 1965 was vice president of the South LA Transportation Company and the Atkinson Transportation Company, took a different tack toward Watts. After the disappearance of the Pacific Electric Railway, passengers on his buses increased; his company had gotten involved in this business when Huntington interests controlled the rail lines and would not extend their reach to Watts. The citywide Rapid Transit District refused to accept his transfers. This post–World War II development, he told the McCone Commission at a hearing held in South LA in November 1965, was a turning point for Watts; until then there was a "community spirit here, a cohesiveness. They had a Coordinating Council. We had a Chamber of Commerce. . . . Many of our good people, leaders here began moving to the westside. And they left a sort of a vacuum here. . . . we seemed to have more of the type of people who were just struggling so hard to keep body and soul together that they had no time for community activities. . . . we began to notice that the children were more difficult to deal with. . . . there was more a chip-on-their-shoulder attitude. . . . Even in junior high and high school, they were asserting their rights, and so forth." Interestingly, hardly any of his buses were damaged during the August eruption.[26]

As Atkinson's words indicate, the business-government elite bears major responsibility for fomenting the conditions that led to the Watts Uprising of 1965. The examples abound. The Red-baiting that routinely and repetitively painted public housing as a Communist plot thereby limited residential options, lubricated the path for the preferred option—a massive land giveaway of Chavez Ravine to LA Dodgers owner Walter O'Malley—increased urban crowding, dispersed Chicanos into competition with blacks for low- to moderate-income housing, and ignited tensions.[27]

Mayor Sam Yorty, emulating Alabama's Governor George Wallace, figuratively stood in the door of City Hall blocking the distribution of federal antipoverty funds from Sargent Shriver's Office of Economic Opportunity to Watts and other poverty-stricken neighborhoods. For the combative Yorty it was a question of right-wing philosophy and real concern about where money would flow, who would supervise the flow, and what strengthened constituencies could result. Yorty also may have sensed that this kind of reform eventually could undermine him.[28]

Even an amenity as mundane as street lighting—a major factor in crime prevention—was inferior in Watts. "The lighting on Wilshire Boulevard in the Miracle Mile sector is quite brighter than the lighting [of] 103rd Street through the business sector of Watts. Likewise, the lighting on Hollywood Boulevard is about five times as bright as the lighting on 103rd Street."[29]

South LA was a circumscribed realm of diminishing opportunity. A UCLA research team under contract from the U.S. Department of Commerce submitted a massive study in December 1964, "Hard Core Unemployment and Poverty in Los Angeles," that lamented the "fantastic incidence of tuberculosis" and the inevitable "interrelatedness of environment, income and disease." The study argued that "heavy immigration from the South means in effect that the Los Angeles area is importing many of the problems resulting from continuing Southern failure to provide adequate and nondiscriminatory" education. It detailed the "tendency for non-whites to have had [to make] a relatively higher down payment than whites" for housing. Possibly worst of all was that "most respondents fail to perceive any concrete employment benefit from the increased civil rights action of recent years."[30]

Thomas Sheridan of the McCone Commission staff later attributed the fires of August to a number of factors. LA was "so sprawling . . . that a riot here is much harder to control." But most of all, he blamed "agitators." He saw a clear sequence of events over a two-year period that led to unrest in South LA. The 28 August 1963 March on Washington, the 22 May 1964 civil rights sit-in at the Bank of America in San Francisco, the July-August disturbances in seven eastern cities, the passage of the War on Poverty program and major civil rights legislation on 20 August 1964, the fall 1964 protests at Berkeley followed by the arrest of 814 people in December, the March 1965 protests at the Federal Building in LA, the sit-ins at Van de Kamp's, the protests in Selma, and the anti–Vietnam War protests in northern California in March 1965 were storm signals. The "agitation" helped to create both a climate of protest and a dramatization of searing problems.[31]

Sheridan's initial point should not be downplayed either. LA was "sprawling," yet it had inadequate mass transit in a region known for jobs sited in far-flung suburbs. The city had the country's greatest number of automobiles per 1,000 inhabitants and for a long time had "one of the lowest percentages of street areas of any of the major cities" in the country. In a city of freeways, too many blacks often were left stranded.[32]

But Sheridan's analysis was outweighed by negative characterizations of other kinds of "agitators" who were said to be to blame for the civil unrest. Dick Carter, an owner of Hilo Engineering and Manufacturing, told the chief counsel of the McCone Commission that Saul Alinsky, the well-known social reformer, made an "extremely provocative" speech in LA on 1 July 1965 that "excited the Watts riot." Carter was irate, calling Alinksy "no good . . . a disrupter . . . [who] teaches people how to disrupt society by street action." The problems revealed by the fires of August would have been easier to solve if Carter had been right. But he was not.[33]

■

It was uncommonly warm on Wednesday, 11 August 1965, in Los Angeles. This was the continuation of a heat wave; the high temperature on 12 August of 92° was the lowest maximum of the previous five days. It was even hotter on 13 August. Heat has been pointed to as a factor in murder rates going up in various regions during August of any year.[34] A number of psychologists and other analysts were quick to point to the weather as a catalyst in sparking the uprising, while others pointed to the combination of heat and smog.[35]

As the embers were still cooling, Professor Richard Hankey, who taught courses in police administration, charged flatly that the weather was a significant factor in heightening unrest. He argued forcefully that "hot weather increases the crimes of violence" and added the related factor that "blighted and poor residential districts" had "few air-conditioners and fewer swimming pools"; moreover, there was "little privacy" in the small homes in densely populated neighborhoods that many of the poor were forced to occupy.[36]

The argument positing heat as a factor in igniting the uprising was susceptible to racist interpretation, paralleling as it did old bromides about heat making the "natives restless." Yet the argument was so prevalent in 1965 that William Colby of the McCone Commission staff wrote a useful memorandum speculating on the connection between heat and "race riots" during the

1917–64 period, concluding that all except one took place during the summer.[37]

Other analysts have observed that there was a full moon on 12 August and have speculated on the impact of the tides on the oceanside city of Los Angeles. A *Los Angeles Times* report of 13 August 1965 has fueled this kind of conjecture: "More strange lights, similar to the 'ball of fire' spotted in the sky Tuesday night, were seen Wednesday night. . . . One unofficial explanation is that they were meteorites."[38]

■

The stopping of Marquette Frye by the California Highway Patrol was the spark that ignited this insurrection. He was born Marquette Price on 3 July 1944, the third of four children of Rena Davis and C. L. Price, in Lima, Oklahoma. When he was six months old, he and his mother moved to Hanna, Wyoming, and in 1957 they came to LA; at that point his mother was remarried, to Wallace J. Frye, whose name her son took. Marquette was small, 5 feet 7 inches and 130 pounds, not big enough to confront police authorities successfully. At this juncture he was living at 11620 Towne in South LA and was unemployed. He was a high school dropout with a juvenile record. His brother Ronald, who accompanied him on the evening of 11 August 1965, was a year younger and three inches taller. Their mother, who intervened in the arrest of her sons, was forty-nine years old in 1965 and also had been born in Oklahoma; though she was seven inches shorter than Marquette Frye, she was not small, weighing in at a hefty 147 pounds.[39]

Marquette Frye's version of what happened that evening differs markedly from that recounted by the police authorities. Despite the heat wave the temperature had fallen to a mild 75° on the evening of 11 August with humidity of 67 percent. As he recalled it all, his brother had just been discharged from the U.S. Air Force, and to mark the occasion they decided to drive in their 1955 Buick to the home of two young women where they talked and imbibed vodka and orange juice. At 6 P.M. on this Wednesday, they were stopped by the California Highway Patrol. The CHP was about to let him go when another patrol car pulled up containing officers with a nastier attitude. Impolite words were exchanged. His mother, who lived nearby, arrived. By that time a crowd had gathered; they were "friendly and joking and ribbing the officers a bit." His mother, however, took issue with the authorities, "and the first officer then twisted her arm behind her back and seemed to lift her off the ground and put handcuffs on her, causing her to cry and scream, due to the pain. The crowd then got boisterous." An officer hit Frye "extremely hard on the front of my head . . . and then I noticed an officer standing next to me with a shotgun pressing against my temple."[40] A patrol door was slammed on his legs, and he was kicked by an officer after he was tossed roughly in the car. He was struck on the head again while being driven away. There were contusions on his head to bolster his allegations.[41]

With Rashomon-like implications, California highway patrolman Lee Minikus did not accept Frye's version of events. That evening this eight-year CHP veteran was alone on patrol in county territory just outside of the city limits when a motorist told him that a drunken driver was weaving north-bound on Avalon Boulevard. He spotted Frye's Buick at 122d Street and pulled him over at 116th Street in city territory. Technically this was not Watts. Frye, he said, failed a sobriety test as a crowd gathered. Frye's brother "stood by quietly." Then his mother "came from nearby home and began berating her son." Marquette Frye, he implied, responded to this challenge to what some might call his manliness by turning on Minikus. Minikus drew his gun when Frye would not enter the squad car. Frye yelled at one point, according to the officer, "Go ahead, kill me." At this juncture Rena Frye jumped on Minikus's back. Someone in the agitated crowd of 200 hit another officer on his head. California Highway Patrol officer Larry Bennett pulled out a shotgun and ordered the growing crowd to disperse. The officers retreated in automobiles with the three Fryes in tow.[42]

According to Rena Frye, the officers "slapped me on the face and hit me on the knee with a blackjack" as she was being driven off. She says that she was not physically abused at 116th Street, but the rumor that she had been caused hell to break loose.[43] The belief that Joyce Gaines was attacked also enraged the crowd; she was a 5 foot 7 inch, 132-pound unemployed twenty-one-year-old black woman wearing a barber's smock that made her look pregnant. The idea that a woman in that condition had been assaulted by authorities not unknown for doing such things incited the crowd. The district attorney, for his part, said that she had spat on an officer, provoking his re-sponse.[44] The patriarchal, though comprehensible, complaint emerging from slavery that black men could not protect their families and "their" black women apparently enkindled a major twentieth-century insurrection. The masculinist origins of the black nationalism that emerged from Watts 1965 can be marked at this point.

Ralph Reese, of 724 East 118th Street, told an interviewer a story focused on CHP motorcyclists who sought to get the crowd to disperse by riding on sidewalks; this inflamed the crowd, he recalled, since it was seen as jeopardizing the safety of children. In addition, "police officers called them 'black' and they had never been called that before." This was one of the things "that the young people had never really encountered on any prior occasion and they were startled by it. [Reese] said it became a real battle with the community defending themselves against an armed attack. He said that people just had to defend themselves because they considered the police representative of the white class holding them down."[45]

A *LA Times* journalist wrote: "Rocks began flying, then wine and whisky bottles, chunks of concrete, pieces of wood—anything that could be thrown. The targets were anyone or anything strange to the neighborhood—mostly vehicles. . . . The police department dispatched 80 helmeted men into the area. . . . Police tried pulling back and closing off the area where the rioting was worst on the theory that their absence might calm things down. But the experiment didn't work." A station wagon belonging to a TV station was burned.[46]

Thomas Sheridan, chief counsel of the McCone Commission, examined various accounts and interviews of scores of officers and civilians; he scrutinized "numerous photographs and documentary corroboration." His account basically tracks that of CHP officer Minikus, albeit with more detail. At 7 P.M. Minikus stopped the Fryes, at 7:05 he radioed for assistance, at 7:12 two fellow officers arrived (along with Rena Frye), and the crowd swelled from 200 to 500. After Mrs. Frye admonished her son for drinking, he became more belligerent, according to Sheridan. By 7:23 the Los Angeles Police Department had arrived, and the crowd had grown to about 1,500; at 7:26 the officers departed with those who had been arrested, and Frye's Buick was towed away by a truck. By 7:30 the patrol cars arrived at the county sheriff's Firestone station. There Mrs. Frye hit an officer in the groin, and she was punched in the nose. At 10:45 the Fryes were transported to the central jail. Sheridan discounted the stories of the Fryes and Joyce Gaines.[47]

Mayor Yorty charged subsequently that CHP officers inflamed the situation by keeping the Fryes at the scene too long in the face of alleged entreaties by the LAPD to evacuate the scene.[48] This was not the only criticism of the authorities' actions. A most serious charge was the failure of law enforcement to protect property when the crowd erupted. Frank Beeson, Jr., was in command at the strategically located 77th police precinct on the evening of

11 August. He was thirty-five years old, a Navy veteran who lived in suburban Whittier with his wife and two children. In these respects he was a typical LAPD officer. Beeson "personally made the decision not to shoot looters. . . . He had tried repeatedly to get a decision on this matter at a higher level but ran into constant delay and bickering over many hours." The command-control-communications system of police authorities was a tangled mess. There was a "complete breakdown at the administrative level."

Yet Beeson's recollections could possibly be impeached on the grounds of bias; not only was he a principal, but he held racist views, believing that "Negroes have nothing to be proud of and that they have no history or outstanding members of their race . . . score lower on IQ tests," and so on. He supported Proposition 14 and was convinced that Communists were behind the civil rights movement. His jaundiced view of blacks was shaped by his work, which involved frequent interactions with the 247 bookmakers, 200 prostitutes, 166 gambling houses, 5 private gambling houses, and 3 bordellos that he claimed were located in his district. His frequent encounters with the lumpen proletariat gave him the impression that all blacks were of this class.[49]

Daryl Gates would go on to serve as police chief during the civil unrest of 1992 in Los Angeles, but in 1965 he was a substitute inspector of Patrol Area 2 and field commander. He has confirmed that the command-communication-control system was inadequate. Three police agencies were involved on 11 August—the CHP, the LAPD, and the county police headed by the sheriff—and their "radios were not" all "set to the right frequency to communicate." This confusion contributed to the decision to withdraw. Gates has contended that because the authorities were seen as the cause of the crowd's anger, they decided to withdraw. Looking back, he has called this "faulty wisdom" and an "unwise decision." Their tactics were based on what they had much experience in crushing: confrontations with amassed union strikers. They were not prepared for the inchoate "guerilla" conflict of August 1965. Yes, the general usually does fight the last war, for good reason, implied Gates: "I kept searching for a great big crowd that I could confront with all the tactics I had learned." He "tried to make a perimeter," but the boisterous crowd behaved as if a "crazed carnival atmosphere had broken out."[50] Ironically, the feared symbol of the Red Scare—striking workers—haunted the authorities as they entered a new era of black militance. They thought they were fighting the Conference of Studio Unions class war of 1945–46, but this was a new day.

Other accounts vary from official and unofficial recollections. The Emergency Control Center Journal reported a crowd of 2,000 at 116th and Avalon as early as 7:45 P.M., though with "no organized leaders; isolated groups only."[51] Another official noted that by 8:18 complaints had been registered that autos in transit through that area—especially at Imperial and Avalon—were under siege, "attacked by missile throwing mobs. By 11:45 pm the situation had deteriorated and the attacking of newsmen and the burning of vehicles had begun."[52] The 12 August *LA Times* reported a "five hour melee" in "an eight block area" that was "near chaos. . . . Avalon Blvd., which is lined mostly with apartments and homes in the area, was littered with debris. But few buildings were damaged." A page-one headline blared, "1000 Riot in LA."[53]

The progressive black journalist Almena Lomax writing in the *Berkeley Post* charged that the Frye incident was trumpeted hysterically by television reporters eager to cover a "riot" similar to "last summer's Harlem." The authorities initially looked the other way as the situation in South LA spun out of control but acted speedily when fires were set near downtown police headquarters, she claimed.[54]

Benjamin Perry, a retired government employee, lived at 627 East 107th Street, just off Avalon. He was there when the Fryes were arrested. A community leader, he had served as president of the Will Rogers Park Council and proudly called himself "a grass roots person." That night he heard what sounded "like a thousand sirens. They were coming down every side street and down Avalon Boulevard. . . . and I remarked to my wife that 'The King of Siam' just arrived. I think I will go out and see him." He counted twenty-five officers, heard name-calling, and saw spitting. He too heard that Joyce Gaines was pregnant and was beaten. After that, hostilities increased, and cars were stoned on Avalon. Perry began to act as a traffic cop, directing motorists down side streets so they would not be assaulted. At about 9:30 P.M. "followers of Malcolm X" arrived, shouting "Let's burn . . . baby, burn." He recalled, "When a car came down the street, if you stuck three fingers out that way and yelled 'blood brother,' you weren't attacked."[55]

On 11 August 1965 Leon Smith, a black attorney employed by the Human Relations Commission, was at home in upscale Baldwin Hills, about to go to a party. He idly turned on the television and was stunned by what he saw taking place in South LA. His coworker John Buggs called to urge that he go immediately to Watts. He arrived at Imperial and Avalon at 11:15 P.M. and saw cops swinging their clubs and wading into crowds, and cars, driven by whites, being stoned. Shortly thereafter another black HRC worker, Herbert Carter, received a call from John Buggs asking him to go to Imperial and Avalon as well. This graduate of California State University had been working two and a half years with the HRC focusing on "tension control," especially in integrated housing. He lived near Crenshaw Boulevard and therefore arrived speedily on the scene. He saved a reporter from attack but that did not save him from harassment by the police; when he told an officer that he was with the HRC and wanted to cross police lines, he was threatened with a beating.[56]

At 12:05 the HRC staff suggested to the LAPD that it close Imperial Highway and that "uniformed white officers be taken out of the immediate area inasmuch as they were mainly the object of attack. That Negro officers be sent into the area." Buggs, Smith, and Carter were all black. Their nationalist-inspired suggestion later was criticized heavily, though the authorities adopted a tactic that was criticized even more, withdrawing from the fray. At 12:20 Buggs arrived; half of the crowd, he said later, were spectators, a fourth were "out of sympathy" or hostile to the "rioters," "while another fourth were actively angry and involved." His coda? "Well, it was bound to happen."[57]

The angry crowd was energetic and did not begin to diminish until 4 A.M. on 12 August. Mayor Yorty was stunned: "It was a strange riot; it was stop and go because they'd all get real tired about two or three o'clock in the morning and they'd go home and sleep till two o'clock in the afternoon and then they'd come out and start rioting."[58] Yorty was unfamiliar with the weekend schedules of many blacks, who went to parties until the early hours of the morning and then slept a few hours before awakening for another round of activity.

The first supermarket to be looted was at 116th and Avalon.[59] By 8 A.M. on this hot 12 August 1965, matters had heated up again. There was a heavy antiwhite emphasis and references to Vietnam. One comment heard at Imperial and Avalon that morning was "If I've got to die, I ain't dying in Vietnam, I'm going to die here."[60] Things slowed down as the day wore on, then sped up again at 6:45 P.M. as darkness loomed. People were driving and walking to Imperial and Avalon, while others decided to duplicate Imperial and Avalon in their own neighborhoods.[61]

Leon Smith went home and went to bed but by 10 A.M. on Thursday, 12 August, was up and at 116th and Avalon watching youths tossing rocks at passing cars. *Times* reporter Philip Fradkin and photographer Joe Kennedy were attacked "either because of our white faces or the mobile radio antenna, which perhaps made the station wagon look like a police car." Fradkin noted that "the car in front of us, driven by a Negro, was not hit."[62] The turmoil was being characterized as a race riot, but unlike the nineteenth-century variety, here blacks were much more on the offensive on a racial basis. The Emergency Control Center reflected the disarray when it noted in its journal that false calls were being placed to distract the authorities and then reported that 900 white male youth were "heading for affected area" from Orange County, San Bernadino, and other sections of LA. "They're mad over it."[63]

■

The Reverend Casper Glenn, pastor of Bel-vue Community United Presbyterian Church at 675 East 118th Street in the heart of the commotion, had "special clinical training in psychiatry" and had experience in developing interracial churches; he had done so successfully at his last assignment in Tucson. He had moved to LA in November 1964.

At 8:30 A.M. he went to the barbershop and found the window broken. Then a television cameraman arrived. He recalled, "They had one of the boys put his head through the window and the other boys leer in the background. The picture has become quite famous." Television, he said, exacerbated smouldering tensions: "Across the street I saw t.v. cameramen have a man take his shirt out and with his bare chest showing, wave his hands and talk vehemently."[64]

The situation was out of control. The HRC staff, which contained a critical mass of blacks, decided to meet; the HRC had been established by the county precisely to defuse tensions, but the organizers had never imagined something of this magnitude. The staff was prompted to hold a community meeting in Athens Park, not far from the turbulence. John Buggs was blunt about the purpose; they wanted to start a "counter rumor . . . 'It's all over; it's all off. Everybody stays in tonight.'" The HRC sought to organize teams to spread this rumor. Buggs conceded that he advocated "illegal activity: If they walked up on a group of kids, or an individual, who seemed to be inciting a riot, to unobtrusively as possible escort him away, put him in a car and put him in jail and get him out of the community before night fell."[65] Due process was not mentioned; black human relations operatives were willing to dispense with constitutional niceties because it was clear that the situation was deteriorating rapidly.

The HRC staff gathered 100–150 adults and about 100 youth at Athens Park; the presence of some of these youth was unexpected. The light-skinned black congressman from the area, Augustus Hawkins, attended along with the white men who represented the area on the city council and county board of supervisors respectively, John Gibson and Kenneth Hahn. The affluent NAACP leader H. Claude Hudson (who could easily have passed for white) and his colleague from the association, Norman Houston, arrived, as did the Reverend Mr. Brookins.[66] The presence of these melanin-deficient men at a meeting designed to becalm young blacks seemed to have agitated them instead.

By noon of 12 August it was 87° with humidity of 49 percent; an intensely bright sunshine penetrated the smog. By 1:50 the gathering at Athens Park had begun. But Buggs and the HRC staff were not able to control the agenda or the flow of the meeting. They had spread a rumor that the turbulence had ended, then called a meeting to ratify this assertion. However, those with a differing agenda decided to show up and argue otherwise. Uninvited television cameras captured a moment that was broadcast widely and apparently inflamed white racial fears: a black youth vowed to take the tumult out of the ghetto into posher areas. The idea of black youth marching into Beverly Hills with guns sent more than a frisson of apprehension coursing from Pacific Palisades to Simi Valley. Buggs was fuming. In a stage whisper he said, "Get another kid up here to refute this." But it was too late. Buggs blamed television for unnecessarily inflaming the situation: "Now the tragedy of that situation was that he was the only person that was shown on the television screen." Conveniently edited out were the noes that greeted the youth's brash declaration.[67] Television's hunger for inflamed human drama stoked white fears about blacks and helped to bring on racial conflict.

The edited broadcast of the Athens Park meeting excited many, though it omitted striking and articulate suggestions by other black youth. Rev. Glenn recalled that the "boys spoke succinctly and sanely of police problems." They urged that Avalon should be "blocked off from Imperial to 120th and all east-west streets leading into it [from] Stanford on the East and Towne on the West. They didn't think anybody should come in who didn't live there . . . both Negro and white. The boys further suggested there be a dance at Avalon and 116th so that tempers could cool off and the young people could feel that they had gained something of a victory." Only black police would patrol the area, and the dance would end at 11 P.M. The soothing sounds of Martha and the Vandellas blasting in the streets and an empowering victory for black youth seemed a small price to pay, but the authorities were not buying.[68]

Kenneth Hahn, the powerful white caudillo of Black LA, called the youth "hoodlums."[69] He claimed that he "ordered" Buggs to have this meeting, thus discrediting Buggs and his proposals in the eyes of many.[70] Buggs, Brookins, Hudson, and others tried to salvage the situation by meeting with gang leaders, but their demand that white police be ousted from the neighborhood could not be met, and an impasse ensued.

The HRC had failed to extinguish the fires and, through no immediate fault of its own, had helped to accomplish the opposite. Many of the interested parties showing up at Athens Park had been arrested the previous evening. The sight of their "bloody heads" was a red flag to the bull that was the crowd. Later Buggs conceded that the "residents in Watts had a feeling that they had given the police a licking and that they were not going to let the police forget it." But Buggs was most upset about television's "incalculable damage." Buggs felt that he had a 50 percent chance of "stopping the whole thing by 4 o'clock that afternoon"; he then discovered that "one cannot plan in an atmosphere of television cameras, tapes, flashbulbs." The "integrationism" of the NAACP-oriented leadership confronted "nationalism" at the meeting, as many of the youth were demanding that all whites must leave.[71]

The ubiquitous Ralph Reese, along with Buggs' colleague Jim Burks, had proposed the meeting afterwards with the gangs. Reese, who earlier had been spotted arranging interviews with reporters, planted the idea that gangs were "getting ammunition ready, guns ready, etc. There were five of these groups and after the meeting, Reese and his companions contacted all five." Or at least they agreed to do so.[72]

Claude Hudson, the affluent banker and dentist who held an important NAACP post, was not pleased with the Athens Park meeting either. After the meeting he went to Avalon Boulevard but was told by LAPD officers that it was too dangerous for him to be in the area because of "his light complexion." Shaken, he then went over to Rev. Glenn's church, but there "a number of men in the parking lot told him the same thing." Presumably the white elite was not the only force inattentive to its environment, for Hudson conceded, "I thought that was sensible, although I had never thought of it before."[73]

The angry young man who had threatened mayhem against whites earlier at Athens Park allegedly cried afterwards. "He did not know what to say and was told to say what he had."[74] By whom? This was not clear. Yet his words had frightened many whites, and they also could contribute to the fear of lighter blacks like Dr. Hudson. But the larger question to be answered was, what was the import of the angriest and darkest forces allegedly seeking revenge against others?

By 8 P.M. Herbert Carter had returned to Imperial and Avalon. The crowd was "older," and there was an "atmosphere of grim belligerence; the carnival mood had evaporated."[75] The irresistible force was meeting the immovable object: the police were becoming "much firmer" also. Clarence Moore, twenty-four, then of 11715 Success Avenue, worked for the city's housing authority; he was married and had three children. On 12 August at 9 P.M. he was at Imperial and Success and "heard voices apparently coming from a loudspeaker saying 'Niggers! You niggers, come on outside!'" He saw three squad cars with Euro-American officers driving slowly east on Imperial Avenue. "All hell [broke] loose."[76]

Everette Hodge was also out and about on the evening of 12 August. A divorced forty-one-year-old black man, he had migrated from Chicago four years earlier. He was born in Haskell, Oklahoma, and now worked as a janitor in Van Nuys at the California Department of Employment and owned a service station on Broadway in the heart of the black community. At 110th and Avalon he informed police that he had just witnessed looting at 108th and Avalon. One officer tersely told him: "I've got a wife and two children. I'm not going to make any effort to stop anyone from stealing. They can steal the whole town if they want to."[77]

Similar activity in Beverly Hills would have met a different response. This passive attitude toward South LA was an expression of alienation by the protectors of property from the property they were sworn to protect. Yet whatever alienation existed soon was to be blown away with a fusillade of buckshot.

3

Death in the Afternoon, Evening, and Morning

T WAS NOW 13 AUGUST, AND THE AUTHORITIES HAD lost control of South LA. It was an especially bloody and unlucky Friday the Thirteenth, as a veritable record was set in the killing of African-Americans. To some this appeared to be the only way to keep the flames from spreading—and to stop the spread of the idea that oppressed blacks did not have to obey the authorities.

■

This kind of insurrectionary activity was inchoate and diffuse, but it was not totally disorganized. During the heat of the battle, Police Chief William Parker announced: "This situation is very much like fighting the Viet Cong. . . . We haven't the slightest idea when this can be brought under control." Deputy Chief Roger Murdock felt that the way to handle this guerrilla warfare was "to put as many people as we can in jail. . . . That's certainly no secret."

Later, after the fires had cooled, journalist Theodore White agreed with Parker: "Modern Negro violence is not simply rioting but an urban form of guerilla warfare" that needed to be confronted with new "weapons and tactics." Strikingly, White conceded the black nationalists' argument, even using androcentric terms: "It is, at this time, perhaps necessary to find out how to create some form of Negro self-government coupled with Negro responsibility in the big cities which will give Negroes that sense of control over their own destinies that all men so dearly require." [1]

Devising tactics to confront the police was not new to Black LA. Days after the rage had subsided, the black journalist Bill Lane recalled that "Los Angeles was the first city I ever saw where citizens quickly rise up, overpower police officers, chase them, take their guns and wreck their cars. I saw one case in Los Angeles where four Negro women snatched a white cop off his motorcycle, beat him up, took his gun and choked him with a bicycle chain. Only two weeks before the riot a whole neighborhood of Mexican-Americans stormed two white cops who tried to arrest a Mexican housewife on a traffic charge. . . . Such scenes have been numerous in the last four years in Los Angeles." [2]

The beleaguered John Buggs later remembered different tactics at Imperial and Avalon during the height of the uprising.

> About every three minutes a foray of automobiles rushed into the center [of the intersection] with sirens screaming and with red lights flashing . . . and officers jumped out of their cars in groups of ten and twenty and rushed at the youths that were throwing rocks from the corners. . . . The kids had a plan of action. They had rocks cached in the alley to the south on Imperial Boulevard and when rushed by the police they ran into the alleys, from the depths of which they pelted the pursuing officers who promptly ran out faster [than] they had run in. The only two arrests made in these forays were two Negro girls between the ages of nine and twelve.

That was not the only form of tactical sophistication. "In the larger stores, department stores and clothing stores the first target was the credit records. These were destroyed before the place was burned." The civil rights movement, Buggs would say later, "never involved nor did it really include the Negro of lower socio-economic status. . . . [In LA] it is a middle class movement for middle-class people . . . with middle class goals." [3] Guerrilla tactics inspired by Vietnam were the inevitable response and distorted mirror image of petit bourgeois leadership.

The National Advisory Commission on Civil Disorders, known as the Kerner Commission, appointed by President Lyndon Johnson to investigate the causes and consequences of these urban rebellions, confirmed Buggs's view that the bulk of "window smashing, looting and arson" did not begin until quite late in the evening of 12 August and the early morning of 13 August. [4] Guerrilla tactics were also a response to and a cause of the increased police militance that appeared on that unlucky Friday.

True guerrilla tactics were used after this escalation took place. On 13 August at 3:30 P.M. the Emergency Control Center Journal recorded "6 male Negroes firing rifles at helicopter from vehicle, 109th & Avalon." This time the ECC was not engaging in puffery. Looking back, the Euro-American left-ist Michael Meyerson noted, "I distinctly remember during the Watts riots, young men firing on LAPD helicopters in emulation of the South Vietnamese liberation army."[5] Governor Brown did not view such tactics so romantically, since he subsequently had to curtail an aerial tour of South LA because of "sniper fire."[6] Delta Airlines flight 805 carrying 127 passengers had to change course because "rioters were shooting at planes." A major flight path into LAX, the main area airport, led directly over the heart of the area of unrest. Numerous flights had to be rerouted because of sniper fire and billowing smoke.[7] It has been suggested that the authorities fabricated the reports of sniper fire in order to justify the carnage they unleashed; however, County Supervisor Warren Dorn, testifying under oath at a hearing, recalled being "grateful" when his flight into LA from Santa Barbara was on a "slow plane and a high-flying plane [since] there were shots as we went over the troubled area." At that point he went off the record.[8]

There was a method to what was called looting. Often a number of per-sons would ride by a store in a car, get out, break windows, return to the car, and drive to another area. In their wake other cars would come by and begin to seize and load the merchandise. The McCone Commission added, "The burning did not start until the looting was completed in most instances."[9]

Police radio channels were interrupted by clandestine radio messages, which the city council viewed as further evidence of organization.[10] The McCone Commission concluded that the youth "had some type of com-munication system because occasionally teenagers and young adults could be spotted using telephone booths. After making these calls, the youngsters would again get into their cars, headed for new locations. . . . the destruction appeared to be organized by reason of the types of businesses attacked and the expertness of the burning."[11] Some youth who had broken into stores donned clerks' aprons in order to fool the police.[12] Those who entered Boys Market near 105th and Imperial had transmitter radios in order to intercept police calls.[13]

Robert Richardson, a light-skinned black who worked at the *Times* in sales, was recruited by management to cover the tumult; his added melanin finally was deemed to be a plus. In reporting from this quasi-war zone, he noted another form of organization: "One finger meant he was a Watts man, two meant a Compton man and three fingers meant a man from a Willowbrook area."[14] The LA Public Library was reported to have received a huge number of calls for books dealing with explosives when it opened on 13 August, and "this continued until the library withdrew such books from circulation at approximately 11:30am on August 14."[15]

Lieutenant General Roderic L. Hill of the National Guard noticed that the events "had an organized aspect . . . I feel certain that there were roving groups of a few people each employing 'hit and run' tactics" and "mobile communications."[16] Others suggested that some black youth wore a quasi-military uniform of "black pants and dark turtle-neck sweaters," which the Black Panther party later adopted.[17]

Almena Lomax thought that this new spirit of unity and militance in devising tactics meant that though "Negroes lost the battle," they had "won the war." Despite the destruction it was hard "not to feel a certain sense of triumph. . . . All over the city, Negroes feel this . . . there is a strange, hushed, secretive elation in the faces of the 'bloods.'" Yet she too was taken by the organization of events: "Everybody was listening in on their broadcasts and knew as soon as they did where the latest outbreak was." The sense of unity and seriousness was signaled by the fact that "there had been but one report that anyone [who] talked to me called a 'family dispute' . . . and usually, especially on weekends there are scores . . . you know that white people will never take Negroes for granted again."[18] This last point was premature though understandable euphoria; the main point was, however, that out of the uprising had developed forms of organization, bonds of unity, and deftness of tactics that were to be manifested in the Panthers and related groups.

■

Unity came at a high price given in blood. Many in South LA may have felt they could seize merchandise with impunity in light of the initial reluctance of the police to arrest them; this impression proved to be false, but it did embolden some to the point of death.[19]

Ulysses Prince of the HRC staff was told by one black man at Avalon and Imperial late in the evening of 12 August, "I've got my 'stuff' ready, I'm not going to die in Vietnam, whitey has been kicking ass too long." In the face of such sentiments, the HRC requested that nonblack officers be withdrawn. When Deputy Chief Roger Murdock reportedly replied that the only advantage would be that black cops could not be seen as easily at night, the credibility of HRC and the authorities was damaged even further in the eyes of South LA.[20] Guns were rife, and this too unsettled the police. Two men who were arriving for work late in the evening of 12 August were killed "with a volley of bullets fired from a mystery car into the parking lot where they stood" at 2015 East Olympic Boulevard. Neither was included in the official toll of thirty-four deaths, said the *Los Angeles Herald Examiner.* With the dawning of 13 August, the land of oranges was to be drenched in blood.[21]

Most of this blood was spilled as a result of weapons fired by the LAPD, county police, National Guard, and CHP. Of all these law enforcement authorities, the LAPD and the sheriff's force were feared most by the South LA community. In a study of coroner's inquests in the county from 1 January 1962 to 31 July 1965, attorney Hugh Manes found there were sixty-five inquests involving homicide by officers during that time, and only one ended with a verdict other than justifiable homicide, a case "in which two officers 'playing cops and robbers' in a Long Beach Police Station shot a newspaperman." Of these sixty-five victims, twenty-seven were shot in the back, twenty-five were unarmed, twenty-three were suspected of theft or other nonviolent crimes, and four had committed no crime at the time of the shooting. The "overwhelming majority" of the cases involved the notorious LAPD.[22]

A volatile situation had developed. A black community with deeply held grievances was revolting. A police department with a history of violence at first had retreated, had been humiliated by stone throwers, then mystified by the carnival atmosphere, and it was eager to retaliate. A larger community was becoming increasingly hysterical, fearing that the firebell that had rung in the night was not only heralding the spreading of flames but the invasion of angry Negroes.

The press had painted a picture of an *intifada.* The *Los Angeles Times* of 13 August reported that

> 7000 persons rioted . . . as stores were looted and set afire, automobiles were destroyed and 75 persons were injured, including 13 policemen and two firemen. . . . Rioters were reportedly firing guns at policemen and civilians. . . . Rifles and machetes were reported stolen. . . . Gas-filled bottles made into Molotov cocktails reportedly were being hurled into cars and crowds and a number of motorists said they were dragged from their cars and beaten by groups of

Negroes. . . . Numerous automobiles were reported burning throughout the eight block area and motorists who were beaten by the mobs
sought sanctuary in nearby homes. Fire trucks and ambulances were
unable to enter the area to fight the fires and pick up the injured
because of the danger from flying rocks, bricks and fire bombs. The
Fire Department and hospitals reported receipt of many false reports
designed to lure vehicles into the riot area.

The reality on the ground was, if anything, more chaotic than what the
Times reporter observed or was told. On 13 August at seventeen minutes after
midnight a store at 109th and Avalon was looted for "weapons." Minutes
later there were reports of "breaking into war surplus stores" on Avalon
between 104th and 108th.[23]

■

The governor of the state, Pat Brown, was in Greece on 11 August. County
sheriff Peter Pitchess was also out of town. It was clear that local police could
not handle the situation, and the demand arose that the National Guard be
called in. Yet moving thousands of troops to LA proved to be no simple task,
particularly when key leaders were indisposed.

LAPD chief William Parker later recalled that he sensed that further help
would be needed after he heard that a market was "looted" at 116th and
Avalon on 12 August early in the morning.[24] By 5 P.M. he was in touch with
the adjutant general suggesting that his forces might need support.[25] Twenty-
four hours later seventy-six stores had been burned or looted and eighteen
vehicles burned.

In the early afternoon of 12 August, Lieutenant Governor Glenn Anderson, who was ninety miles north of LA in Santa Barbara, "was informed about
the trouble in Watts." He did not leave until 7 P.M., arriving in LA at 9:05.
On the morning of 13 August, he was "assured that the situation was contained," so he "left for Berkeley" for a meeting of the Regents of the University
of California. He was misinformed. By 12:45 P.M. he had traveled to McClellan Air Force base to meet with National Guard leaders, and three hours later
he made the fateful order to commit these troops.[26]

Richard Kline of the governor's staff told Parker on Thursday evening
that Anderson was coming to LA for urgent consultations. But, Kline later
admitted, "the Chief, in effect, cries wolf too often. . . . I have a hunch if the

police of Oceanside had called up . . . Sacramento and said, 'I need the National Guard.' We would have sent it out. But Chief Parker called up and going though our mind is the question, 'Well, is it serious?'"[27]

It was serious. Friday afternoon H. Claude Hudson wandered to 103d Street, a major shopping area. This businessman was dumbfounded by what he saw. "Even if an officer would take his revolver from his holster, some member of the mob would yell to him 'Put it back' and in every instance as I observed they did put their revolvers back into holsters." This longtime civil rights leader felt that "nothing short of martial law" would suffice to halt this unfolding process. Self-interest did not motivate him to leap to this chilling conclusion, for his bank, Broadway Federal Savings, only suffered broken windows though "buildings were burned and looted north of me and south of me."[28]

Official reports noted that on 103d Street on Friday morning there was a "group of about 3000 persons ranging from very young children to elderly adults . . . in a three block area . . . engaged in general looting."[29] Not far away at Broadway and Manchester, it was reported that 500 to 1,000 people were "looting stores . . . more units needed."[30]

That evening the first official death by gunshot wound was recorded. Leon Posey was a slightly built twenty-one-year-old African-American. This native of Texas had a distinctive goatee in the fashion of his neighborhood; he lived at 126 West 93d Street. He died not far away, at the hands of the LAPD, at 6:30 P.M. at 89th and Broadway in a death ruled "accidental" by the coroner. According to Emerson Lashley, Jr., a witness to the shooting, Posey was "standing outside the barber shop." They had gone there together, and serendipity dictated that Lashley was in a chair and not standing where his friend met his death. "People had started gathering, you know, further down, north of Broadway. So, he would go outside, to see, you know, just what was going on. . . . the next thing I knew, then I heard some shots. Then, I just saw him fall." Police were apparently firing wildly, and "people were running."

At the hearing investigating the circumstances of the death or, as it was appropriately titled, the coroner's inquisition, Lashley was asked, "Didn't you tell [LAPD] that you saw a large group of Negroes throwing rocks and bottles at the police officers?" Lashley denied this, but he was not allowed to complete his impassioned rebuttal. Another witness, Leroy Simon, through his attorney asserted the Fifth Amendment and was excused. By the time this hearing occurred—13 October, two months after the slaying—the idea had spread that despite the global publicity, these deaths would be treated like countless others executed by the LAPD. Said Simon's attorney, "Well, my client does not desire to be a party to a whitewash."

Edwin Lewandowski of the LAPD recalled people "hurling rocks and jeering and shouting, yelling. . . . Somebody heaved a rock, which went through my window. . . . As more officers arrived at this location, other officers were under fire. . . . We formed a skirmish line. . . . Most of the officers there had guns and some officers were shooting over the heads of these people into the air, and there was firing going on at the officers from different directions." Philip Cox of the LAPD saw not only rocks being thrown but "bottles and chunks of cement" as well. His testimony underscored the notion that the previously passive response of the LAPD had lulled the crowd into a state of false security. "I heard several people yelling: 'They can't shoot. Mayor Yorty told them not to shoot. They have orders not to shoot. They have got blanks in their guns.'"

As the crowd's brio was surging, so was the officers'. "The crowd kept pushing down on us, and we appeared to be at a point of losing control." Shortly after that moment of apprehension, he noticed Posey dead on the sidewalk. Donald Joachimstaler of the LAPD added, "People were in groups of 10 and 15; male Negroes would charge into us, throwing things at us." A fellow officer "had been struck with a bullet on the top of his head . . . it was about an inch above the hairline, which might possibly indicate that the bullet came from a high angle into his head. . . . remains of a .38 caliber bullet [were recovered] which, of course, is used by the Police Department."[31]

It remains unclear if snipers had been shooting at the LAPD at that moment. At 6:30 P.M. on 13 August, rumors were circulating that the National Guard would be called because the LAPD could not control the situation; some saw this as damaging to the police's organizational ego. Simultaneously a black community weighted down with years of oppression and with encoded memories of resistance was striking back and accumulating the merit badges and necessities of consumer society—couches, food, fans. Leon Posey, the young black Texan, was the first victim of this historic departure.

It did not take long for word to circulate among the crowd that Posey had been shot. Ulysses Prince of the HRC was at Imperial and Avalon at 8:30 P.M. on 13 August, and it did not appear to him that the killing of Posey had intimidated the crowd: "Things were going crazy." He recalled police cars "driving in an elliptical circle" and an atmosphere of unalloyed chaos. However, he was a light-skinned black and thus was nervous about having been dispatched by his bosses to that area "because it was getting dark" and word was already out that the crowd's vengeance was including persons of his hue. He decided to leave.[32]

Thus, Prince was not nearby when Ronald E. Ludlow, a twenty-seven-year-old, 6 foot 2½ inch, 191-pound white male, met his death by gunfire at 8:55 P.M. at Imperial and Wilmington. Deputy Sheriff Ludlow was shot in the lower abdomen while struggling to hold three suspects in custody. It was thought to be an accident, though a young black, Phillip Brooks, was prosecuted. The shooting of Ludlow was a turning point. It was at this juncture that a community revolt against the police was transformed into a police revolt against the community.[33]

Fifty minutes later Homer Ellis, a forty-four-year-old black man, was killed at a liquor store at 2800 South Central. He was suspected of looting a store, but he did not have a weapon. He was blasted in the chest; his heart was perforated, and his right lung suffered a massive hemorrhage. The officers wounded three others, though these suspects were not armed either.[34]

George Adams, Jr., a beefy 6 foot 1 inch, 205-pound, forty-five-year-old native of Louisiana, was at 82d Place and Main Street when he too suffered a gunshot wound to the chest at the hands of a LAPD officer. He too suffered a massive hemorrhage. It was 9:48 P.M., three minute after Ellis's death. Adams was married and resided at 11662 Blue Street. His twenty-year-old friend Robert Louis Crowder of 212 West 106th Street was present during the slaying. He recalled officers instructing them to move; right after that he heard shots, "one, at first . . . [then] 10, 15 shots." Apparently someone in the crowd "said he was going to take the gun away from the cops." One shot hit Adams, who was then placed in a car and driven to the hospital. But he was dead by the time they reached Broadway and Manchester.

Joseph F. Scanlon of the LAPD testified that he had just left a "looted . . . liquor store" at 82d Street and San Pedro and had "three prisoners from this store in the rear seat of the police vehicle with me. . . . As we approached the intersection of 82nd Place and Main Street, we could see all these people. As we rounded the corner, they were shouting, and threw some missiles at us, some rocks and bottles. All of a sudden, my partner Davis yelled: 'Look out, they are shooting.' . . . there was a man on the corner with a Panama hat on, and he was pointing a gun at our car and fired. . . . my attention was drawn to the left . . . and there was a man on that side of the street in a pink t-shirt. He also was pointing a gun at our vehicle." Scanlon felt his life was at stake: "[He] fired twice at him" and drove away. John Heene of the LAPD was with Scanlon and also heard shots fired by "a male Negro, approximately 35, six feet in height." He too did not feel there was time to reflect. "I immediately returned six rounds of fire." Richard Rankin of the LAPD was in a separate car. Adams, he said, not only fired but also "crouched down and ran along the wall of the business." He claimed that Adams's shots hit a pickup truck. Rankin "fired three rounds" at Adams for good measure.

With Rankin was Gary Bebee. He was the fourth officer to fire a weapon at George Adams. "I dropped to one knee and fired one shot from the shotgun." Like the others, he did not stop to see what their handiwork had wrought "due to a hostile-growing crowd at the intersection and fearing for the welfare of our own lifes and for the welfare of the officers that had been shot at."

It was apparently Bebee's shot that killed Adams; his shotgun blast discharged twelve pellets. The man in the "Panama hat," who was said to be firing a weapon too, apparently hit no one. The Adams family hired a lawyer to attend the hearing that investigated the death, and he objected strenuously to the attempt by LAPD investigator Pierce Brooks to justify the promiscuous firing by officers by suggesting that Adams had been committing a felony. Like the other deaths caused by the authorities, this deprivation of life was ruled accidental, despite fatal wounds in the chest and entrance wounds in the back.[35]

Two minutes after the Adams slaying, Calvin Jones, a bearded, thirty-one-year-old, dark-complexioned black native of Oklahoma, was hit at 110th and South Main with a shotgun pellet in the back that perforated his heart, aorta, and right lung and caused massive hemorrage. Carl Charles Blackman of 121 East 111th Place, who was with him at the time "on the sidewalk, about 30 feet" away, said, "I was directly 'astride' the police officers that were doing the shooting" though he was "fleeing the scene." There were eight shots. Jones "appeared to have been shot in the right leg and stumbled, and came down; and then, there were four or five more shots; and he didn't move anymore." Alfred McGee of 142 East 126th Street was there too. The officers "pulled in, hit the curb right next to me, and when the officer stepped out, he shot in the air." Jones "came out of the store behind me, and ran down the street, and one officer hollered: 'Halt, or I'll shoot;' and another officer was shooting in the air at the time. . . . The deceased kept running and he fired again in the air. One officer hollered: 'Halt,' and he shot again, and went down." William Jackson of Compton and Frank Brown of 1425 E. 123d Street both refused to testify.

Nelson Crow of the LAPD recalled "12 to 15 people inside a shoe store" as he and his partner proceeded south on Main Street. "As we exited the car, approximately four or five of these persons inside the store came out of the window." He had detained them all when he heard the word "Halt"; he then decided to fire. His colleague Alvin Miller of the LAPD said, "All the suspects had hands and arms full of articles." He chased Jones and yelled, "Halt." "At this point, the deceased threw down the articles he was carrying and spun at us from the waist." The fatal shots hit Jones in the back and buttocks. Frank Alexander of the LAPD fired his shotgun as Jones "spun around from the waist up . . . his right hand was out of sight in the vicinity of his waist . . . only the upper part of his torso turned." As the chase of Jones proceeded, a crowd of about four hundred gathered, shouting, he recalled, "Kill them. Let's kill the whites." [36]

There were questions about Jones's death, like those of the others. Why didn't they shoot this unarmed man in the leg? How was he shot in the back, if he was running away and then spun his torso toward the officers who fired? Why shoot to kill for a box of shoes? But logic and answers were going up in flames, along with the City of Angels.

Charles Shortridge, a tall and sturdy eighteen-year-old African-American, had grown to 6 feet 4 inches and 185 pounds and lived at 619½ East 87th Street in the heart of the black community. Forty minutes after Calvin Jones was slain, he was hit by shotgun pellets in the left side of his scalp and face and neck; he was said to be sacking a store at 8201 South San Pedro. Jones was shot for shoes, Shortridge for liquor; but no one was indicted or tried for either death as "justifiable homicide" was the coroner's conclusion in both cases.

John Henry Nichols, the clerk at the Do-Rite Market, like many had decided to remain at the store to protect it. Shortridge, he said, entered the store when "all the windows were practically knocked out . . . the liquor section had been just torn up, cigar cases and everything." His coworker, James Lawrence, fired the fatal shot. Another colleague in the store that night, Richard Jackson, saw Shortridge "enter the store, walking in a slow kind of tipping manner. . . . he walked past the cash register, going towards the beer box and that is the time the shot was fired." Neither Jackson, Lawrence, nor Nichols knew if Shortridge was armed. The black teenager was hit with the full force of a 12-gauge shotgun, though he was unarmed and no one called out a warning. Despite the fact that there were distinct wounds in the back of Shortridge's head and that it is unclear whether Shortridge ever picked up the beer, the coroner's inquiry was typically perfunctory. Lawrence did not even receive a mild rebuke for taking the life of Charles Shortridge.[37]

■

The horrified *LA Times* told its predominantly Euro-American audience that "blocks of businesses owned by 'whitey' were burned. . . . As the firemen began to control the blazes the crowd became more brazen. 'White devils, what are [you] doing in here?' they chanted to newsmen." The press descended en masse upon neighborhoods accustomed to being ignored and found that residents who had been forcibly denuded of the subversive language of class had no alternative but to use the language of race. "One teen-age girl shouted: 'White men, you started all this the day you brought the first slave to this country.'"

"Another called out: 'You created this monster and it's going to consume you. White man, you got a tiger by the tail. You can't hold it. You can't let it go. The next time you see us we'll be carrying guns. It's too late, white man. You had your chance. Now it's our turn.'" The *Times* went on to tell of Frank T. Rose, presumably white, a sixty-five-year-old resident at 618 107th Street; he was beaten by some from the crowd, though others from the crowd saved him. The mood in that neighborhood, the paper said, was "ugly, almost hopeless, sickening."[38]

It had, indeed, been an ugly Friday the Thirteenth. Many whites in LA had conjured up a monster image of blacks in the streets with guns seeking retribution for racial crimes. This was a perception. The reality was that the LAPD was busily moving in the streets of South LA with monsterlike ferocity, guns blazing. The police were joined by shopkeepers and their friends willing to kill over a bottle of barley, hops, and water. Meanwhile, flames were leaping forth not just from guns. Flames were engulfing Los Angeles, which the novelist Edward Stewart called "a city with a forest inside it."[39]

■

The authorities had unsheathed their weapons and decided to fire this time. In turn, some residents of South LA resorted to the antebellum tactic of fire this time. California was described by one analyst as "the most flammable place on earth."[40] Stewart has observed that "the Los Angeles region has the fastest burning ground cover in this part of the hemisphere."[41] The city was in the position of a hemophiliac beset by vampires. It was being subjected to arson by merchants and angry residents alike, yet this original desert and drought-prone area was having its precious water steadily drained away. Los Angeles was an "overtapped oasis," where the dearth of water was as relevant to the culture as in any other hydraulic society.[42]

The fire department was as Negrophobic as any other major city institution. As a direct consequence, firefighters were harassed and even fired on by South LA residents. In 1952 there were 8 blacks in the department of 2,500; from that time on there had "been a concerted effort to exclude Negroes." Blacks were barred by doctors manipulating arbitrary criteria in a discriminatory manner and by equally arbitrary training and apprentice procedures. In 1965 there were approximately 59 black firefighters, though 1,000 more "men have been added to the force since 1952."[43]

Racially segregated fire stations exited in LA until 1955. Yvonne Brathwaite, then working for the McCone Commission and later a member of the U.S. Congress, found that the fire department had not even bothered to hire "Negro clerical workers"; if they made the civil service list, they were barred after oral interviews.[44] Those hired faced "ethnic slurs, daily taunts and acts of cruelty." Paul Orduna, who by 1991 was assistant chief and the department's highest-ranking black, remembered that he "worked in silence, ate alone and slept in a bed that was separated from the rest of the men." Yet when Watts erupted in 1965, the bias that was said to be too massive to attack frontally cracked suddenly. "They wanted me to sit up front to make sure everyone knew they had a black firefighter . . . so they wouldn't get attacked." African-Americans were now "premiums." After the smoke cleared, some affirmative action did ensue; insurrection had proved useful in melting patterns thought to be glacial.[45]

The department later complained that "intelligence" during the fires of August was inadequate. However, the department was aware that black publications—such as the *Crusader* of Robert Williams, published in Cuba—carried lengthy articles on how to construct the feared Molotov cocktails.[46] By one account thirty-two persons were arrested for arson during the uprising, a small number not commensurate with the sizable fear and panic ignited by arsonists.[47]

Father Samuels of the Westminster Neighborhood Association, who also had been involved with CORE, argued that the fires were the result of broken electrical connections and a decaying infrastructure. The authorities begged to differ. The Watts experience was studied for lessons in fighting insurrectionary fires, since according to Colonel Rex Applegate, Molotov cocktails were "first used in quantity" there.[48]

Department captain J. Slade Delaney recalled that "our main concern was that the flames would get out of control. In which case, they could have swept westward all the way to the ocean. Who knows how many might have lost their lives if this had happened? And it could have." Flames can create a wild velocity of their own; once out of control a firestorm can move with the force of a tornado, destroying every structure and living organism in its way. If this had happened, said Delaney, "we would have had to dynamite a path to keep the flames from crossing the city. That barrier conceivably would have been a mile or more strip along Crenshaw Boulevard." A black community would have been sacrificed to save the rest of the city, though Delaney did not note if those residents or their representatives would have been consulted by his virtually lily-white department. This grim scenario did not unfold, though Delaney went on to add that because of the breadth and intensity of the flames, the death toll from the fires of August 1965 was actually much higher than reported since, he said, bodies were turned to ashes or what remained of them was buried in massive rubble.[49]

The Ford Foundation was struck by the fact that 75 percent of the firefighting equipment of the county was committed to the vicinity of Watts at precisely the time when the dry season was closing in with its ominous threat of ruinous brushfires. Such a prospect inspired the foundation to donate more funds to the beleaguered city.[50]

A study for the System Development Corporation in Santa Monica concluded that the "conditions encountered during the Watts Riot were somewhat similar to expected nuclear attack conditions." Under siege, the fire department adopted the guerrilla tactic of "hit and run" to fight fires. This new approach would be useful during nuclear war, the study concluded, since "more fires would be expected than there would be manpower equipment and facilities to cope with them."[51]

The *LA Times* added that 85 percent of the city's force was engaged by the revolt, leaving "the harbor, West Los Angeles and San Fernando Valley" bereft of protection. *Fire Engineering,* a professional journal, reported later that "rarely in the history of the nation's fire service has any fire department faced the situation that confronted" LA, one like "that faced by European cities during the incendiary raids of World War II." It was like war. "If a building was ablaze and would obviously be a total loss, the firemen were left unhampered. If it was only partially involved, they could expect a heavy barrage of paving blocks and bottles which would force them away from the area until the fire could completely involve the building and those nearby." [52]

The LAPD was often tied down protecting firefighters, allowing stores to be deprived of goods with impunity. Chief Parker recalled later, after viewing a film of a fire on Newton Street, that "they are fighting three fires. . . . and then without any apparent involvement suddenly two buildings across the street just seem to erupt." It was surmised that magnesium might have been used to produce such an effect, which led them to further surmise that there had been organization in the midst of the chaos. "A very small group of people could have done every bit of this major burning, every bit of it." [53]

Residents of South LA interviewed subsequently did recall seeing Molotov cocktails thrown. [54] Vernon Brooks conceded that he learned to make them in combat in Korea. Thurman Moore observed that some stores were burned because they happened to be "Jewish owned and operated"; he was accused of setting fire to the Vons grocery store at 5029 South Vermont. [55]

The decision by some residents to employ fire this time upset the LA elite more than the decision by the authorities to fire this time on some residents. The potent combination of guns and fire showed no signs of weakening as a bloody Friday the Thirteenth receded, and a new day, 14 August 1965, dawned.

4

Fire/Guns

IT WAS NOW 14 AUGUST 1965. SINCE THE EVENING of 11 August, Southern California had been facing the twin threats of blazing fires and blazing guns. The shedding of the blood of the inhabitants of South LA was having an impact. The commitment of thousands of National Guard troops would soon act as a blanket to suppress the flames of insurrection.

■

The authorities were concerned about armed Negroes, and the Negroes were concerned about armed whites, in and out of uniform. Southern California was a haven for various and sundry ultraright fanatics, including the John Birch Society and the Minutemen, both of which had interlocking links with the LAPD. This region was also part of the West where arms proliferation was a part of life. This, combined with the hysterical fear that armed blacks would be marching on white LA in a bid to settle historical accounts forcibly, led to a run on gun shops.

At the Brass Rail gun shop at 711 North La Brea, an armed clerk in a replay of the Old West searched entering customers in order to forestall holdups. One store owner said that some of these novice customers "don't even know which shoulder to put a gun to, but they want a gun to protect themselves." These greenhorns were not subjected to the practice meted out to others: "Checkpoints were set up and hundreds of guns were taken away from Negroes." The *Los Angeles Times* added that "many" were taken from "children." There was an apparently false report that "an armed truckload of Negroes wearing red armbands was invading the downtown area."[1]

Governor Brown warned that the mass buying of arms by whites was dangerous. His measured remarks were contradicted by Chief Parker's contrary admonitions. Gun shops reported heavy business in white areas in the sale of all types of firearms and ammunition; a number were said to have exhausted their stocks. Usually weekend sales of firearms amounted to 862, but this time a state record of 2,038 was set; according to figures supplied by the *Times,* only sixty-eight buyers were black.[2]

But those were only official records; illegal sales were not recorded. The authorities made the confiscation of arms, together with fighting fires, a top priority, and thousands of weapons were seized, particularly from blacks. Along with food stores and liquor stores, the merchandise in gun shops was a special target for roving bands. It was feared that "Negro hoodlums and juvenile gangs may be storing them underground for use in future times of violence." *Life* magazine said that guns were being cached in "outlying areas" for "safekeeping."[3] One result of the uprising was the placing of weapons in the hands of future Black Panthers, gang members, ultrarightists, and lumpen elements of all colors. Gun sales in the state "jumped 500% in the week following the Los Angeles riots," and "less than 2% of the purchasers were Negroes," said Attorney General Thomas C. Lynch.[4] KABC-TV believed that this pattern of gun purchasing reflected the lack of "confidence in constitutional authority." Many of these newly minted gun enthusiasts may have been part of a developing trend, the formation of rifle clubs. *Closer Up,* a right-wing newsletter, hailed this trend, which it claimed was inspired—ironically—by the advice to blacks given by Robert F. Williams on how to make Molotov cocktails.[5] Charles Shortridge was killed by an armed civilian as he walked toward a bottle of beer; his death was a sign of this domestic arms race.

In the weeks after the uprising, federal agents arrested a Cuacomonga egg rancher—William Huntington Garner, fifty-seven, of 10024 Turner Avenue—and confiscated rockets, smoke bombs, ammunition, bulletproof vests, and more. He was affiliated with the Christian Defense League, which "opposed Negroes, Jews and Communists."[6] Years later, leaders of the neo-Nazi Aryan Brotherhood mused about attempting to "drop a tub of cyanide into the aqueduct" of LA, blowing up power and telephone lines, launching armed struggle, and capitalizing "on the strife to recruit frightened whites" in a conscious replay of 1960s LA.[7]

∎

Those in uniform were more effective in killing blacks than ultraright civilians, and this was particularly the case on Saturday, 14 August. This was a day when there was an acceleration of the killing of South LA residents by the authorities in an attempt to end the tumult once and for all. For most of the day a pall of black-gray smoke hovered over the typically smoggy city. Commercial airlines continued to alter their flight patterns to avoid smoky areas, police and news helicopters, and snipers.[8]

Angelenos awakened to a city still on fire. "Eight Men Slain; Guard Moves In" was the *LA Times* headline that greeted them that morning. Related outbursts were reported to have spread from Venice to Pasadena, and the turmoil reached the edge of City Hall. Fires blazed most consistently from 41st Street to 108th Street. The temperature on Friday had leaped to 94°; Saturday it would rise to 97°.[9]

Firefighters were having difficulty in suppressing the blazes; scores of fires raged out of control. Those firefighters able to reach the flames were assaulted with rocks, debris, and curses from angry residents. The *Times* reporter watched "looters, including women and small children . . . grabbing everything in sight." The number in the streets seemingly amounted to an estimated "7000."

"Hostility toward authority and toward whites was evident everywhere. Mobs torched businesses believed owned by Caucasians." Though the LAPD was busily firing on residents in certain areas, it "left some areas unpatrolled because they were too dangerous to enter." Police radios crackled with reports of emergencies: "Manchester and Broadway, a mob of 1000. . . . 51st and Avalon, a mob of 1000." A crowd penned down the LAPD by ringing the notorious 77th Street police station; police and news helicopters hovering overhead were fired on. The Watts post office on 103d Street was invaded and ransacked. Chief Parker reported that his forces were "nearing exhaustion." Little wonder. One detachment of "700 helmeted and shotgun carrying officers fought a virtual guerilla war during the night with mobs of frenzied Negroes."[10]

Panic had descended on the armed and civilian authorities. John W. Billett, an assistant to the governor, was at the corner of Avalon and Santa Barbara with other leading officials in the early hours of the morning of 14 August. Suddenly, at 12:50 A.M. he noticed a gray car with doused headlights barreling toward them at "60 miles an hour." A National Guardsman was struck by the speeding car in a scene captured in *Life* magazine. The black person who was driving "was thrown to the ground, and he was literally beaten against the pavement" by the guard, while his passenger was shot in the abdomen.[11]

Lieutenant General Roderic L. Hill, adjutant general of the California Guard, was present, and this led to a change in his force's tactics, which to that point had ceded the shooting role to the LAPD. "I was the one who personally gave the order to load the weapons at approximately 1:00 am Saturday." But even here the influence of the LAPD was not absent, as the man leading the troops that night under Hill's command, a "brigade commander," was a LAPD officer. The guns were loaded, then used, and the guard was credited with killing eight of the official total of thirty-four slain.[12]

There were 5,760 guardsmen in the streets at 12:30 P.M., and less than three hours later there were 9,958.[13] Ultimately, 60 percent of the state's entire force had to be called out.[14] These numbers were leveraged by the imposition of a curfew over a huge 46.5 square miles, two-thirds of that in the city and the other third in the county.[15] Over twenty-five years later, the *Times* conceded that the curfew was racially coded, in that it was "not confined to the blocks on fire. It applied to any area in South Los Angeles where African-Americans lived: 20 square miles, as far north as what was to become the Santa Monica Freeway. Any place blacks would be was officially deemed dangerous."[16] Blacks were not oblivious to the way they were subjected to collective punishment regardless of their individual character or actions. In the absence of class consciousness, such sweeping punishments in turn generated a collective indictment and dislike of whites.

The LAPD was deluged with calls, some designed to jam its phone lines and communications. Some officers were lured into buildings and ambushed by crowds. The fire department reached a peak of activity at 1 A.M. on 14 August, and it began to slacken off at this point, suggesting that the peak of the insurrection itself had been reached. Yet that evening Division Chief George Brunton requested more flak suits and police protection in the face of "increased sniper activity."[17]

By the end of the day, the death toll had exceeded the toll of U.S. deaths recorded during the same period in Vietnam and surpassed all the losses recorded in similar urban disturbances in the United States in 1964. The scene resembled Vietnam, as guardsmen behind jeep-mounted machine guns blazed away "over the tops of cars and anything else that moved in the curfew area." It was becoming difficult to limit violence to Southeast Asia and not have it wash up on these shores. The Wild West had arrived in force in the twentieth century. Already Watts was being called "the worst American race riot since the 1943 uprising in Detroit."[18]

■

Montague Whitmore, also known as Carroll Andrew Shaw, of 740 East 50th was a thirty-seven-year-old native of Texas; he was a heavyweight, 6 feet tall and 195 pounds. On 14 August at 12:20 A.M., he was subjected to a gunshot and shotgun barrage in the back that perforated his aorta and both lungs, with massive hemorrhaging, along with various pellet wounds in the back of his head. He was killed. The LAPD did the shooting in this incident at 59th and Vermont. Since he was accused of committing a felony when he was shot, the coroner's jury adjudged this to be justifiable homicide. Lee Logan reported that "I observed two vehicles parked in front of Pep Boys and Hudson Shoe Store" at 59th and Vermont. "The trunks of both of these vehicles were open. . . . I observed a suspect come from the broken front window of Pep Boys. In his arms were various non-descript articles." Then he saw him "enter the front window of Hudson Shoe Store." There were four suspects, Whitmore among them. The LAPD chased them. "I heard another shotgun, which sounded like a shotgun firing, and the suspect fell."

Ronald L. Borst of the LAPD recalled that "Officer Bradfield had the shotgun pointed out at the suspect and told him to stop. I walked up behind him, with my back to Hudson Shoes and began searching the suspect with my left hand; I had my revolver in my right hand." He heard a "noise." A suspect behind him "rushed at me and knocked me to the ground. . . . I was in a dazed condition." Larry Bradfield, who fired the shots that killed Whitmore, chased him forty yards toward the junior high school on Vermont. "I then fired a third shot at the suspect, and he fell behind the ledge."[19]

Charles Shortridge was shot because he seemed about to take a bottle of beer. Now Montague Whitmore was killed because he appeared to be taking "non-descript articles." The authorities conducting the inquiry into how these men met their fates evidently were not concerned about the propriety— legal and otherwise—of a shoot-to-kill procedure directed at unarmed suspects in the midst of committing what were arguably misdemeanors. Nor did they pursue apparent ellipses in the testimony of witnesses. The devising of nonlethal methods to detain suspects was not considered. The authorities and the press did not consider it of note that Whitmore was shot in the back and the head, rather than his legs.

Warren Earl Tilson, a fireman, was killed ten minutes after the slaying of Whitmore when a wall collapsed as the fire department fought a blaze at a market at 120th and Central. Tilson was a thirty-one-year-old white man who lived in suburban Torrance at 1161 Levinson; like so many of the others slain, he hailed from Texas; he was a lithe 6 feet 1 inches and 174 pounds. Captain J. Slade Delaney recalled that "there were quite a few spectators" and there "had been looting . . . from the start, up until the wall fell, we had bottles thrown and various bricks . . . we had quite a major fire going at the front, and we were rather unprotected from the rear." There was "no police protection" though the "worst problem was the car traffic. We had cars with three to six people coming down quite fast, driving over our hose lines, going between our apparatus and the store." Then the wall of the store fell, and "the whole area collapsed, which covers approximately 25 or 30 feet." Tilson was crushed by the wall. Antone P. Jasich of the fire department concluded that the fire was "incendiary in origin, or set by human hand."[20] It was chaotic. Scores of residents milled around or seized merchandise as firefighters fought a blaze in the store. Snipers apparently were present, though the LAPD was absent. A sheriff's deputy had been killed; now a firefighter. Twenty minutes later the guard loaded its weapons, and the carnage increased.

An hour after the fateful order to load weapons, Albert Flores, Jr., forty years old, divorced, born in California, and living at 8181½ Dearborn Avenue in South Gate, was shot in the head, suffering severe cerebral lacerations. He was killed as he sought to run a roadblock at 102d and Compton, or so it was said. It was deemed to be justifiable homicide. Robert Peter Nelson, the commanding officer of Company A, 1st Batallion, 160th Infantry of the National Guard, was there. He had supervised the construction of a roadblock that consisted only of "a sign . . . a table . . . a trash can." Only one man was posted at the barricade; the rest of his men were stationed on the sides of the streets. It was well lit, he said, and there was a combined force of eleven or twelve of his men and LAPD. At 1:45 A.M. he spotted Flores in his car. "This Mercury pulled up behind the first car. . . . It stopped behind the first car for just an instant, and then it pulled out around that car, gunned the motor, and started going through the road block." "Halt" was yelled, and then immediately the car was fired on by four or five guardsmen and LAPD officers. Flores's car "got about halfway down the block; then, it appeared to go out of control and swerved into a pole, where it stopped."

Michael Gorman of the guard said that Flores "stopped for, maybe a second or two seconds, and then 'floored' the car, pulled around to the left of the car that was stopped there, and proceeded through the barricade." All present fired. Fifteen minutes later Michael John Patzakis, a captain and battalion surgeon of the 160th Infantry, arrived and found that Flores still had the "smell of alcohol." The autopsy found "acute alcohol intoxication" and several gunshot wounds, one "penetrating right cheek," another "penetrating left eye and orbit," and one in the back. This Latino was listed as a "Caucasian male."[21]

Would it have been possible to stop Flores without killing him? Was it necessary to shoot him in the face? A car going that fast with a severely wounded driver could have been a threat to bystanders or property. Why was the barricade so flimsy? Were the guardsmen trying to lure unsuspecting drivers into running past the solitary man at the roadblock so that they could unload a barrage? Was there a better way to halt the uprising?

Thomas Ezra Owens was as single, twenty-two-year-old black native of California who resided at 1911 West 43d Street. He was said to be running from a store with a box in his hand when the LAPD yelled, "Halt," to no avail. Ronald D. Rouse of the LAPD Wilshire Division saw Owens at 1 A.M. "traveling east bound on Vernon, when I observed three male Negroes walking west on Vernon from McKinley. Two of the Negro fellows were carrying boxes. . . . The third Negro fellow was pushing this shopping cart, which was loaded with groceries." He drove by the market with a shotgun, not issued by the LAPD, at the ready. "I saw a suspect run from the market, northeast across McKinley, towards an awaiting vehicle, which was a 1958 T-bird, white." Rouse leaped from his car and chased the suspect who "was carrying a box of what appeared to be canned pop."

"I saw a suspect run from the doorway, carrying objects in his hands." He uttered the obligatory "Halt," but the suspect kept sprinting, so he fired his shotgun, as did his partner, Patrick McDonald. Owens "fell at the curb." The 6 foot 2 inch, 188-pound man collapsed with a staggering "50 entrance wounds," many in his back and others in his chest and trunk. In his car the officers said they found "liquor, tv dinners, soda pop, beer, about 78 or 79 bottles of wine and beer and liquor."[22]

Minutes after Thomas Owens's death, one of the youngest victims met his death. Carlton Elliot, also known as Carlton Reynolds, was seventeen, black, and a native of Arkansas; he was small, 5 feet 8½ inches and 137 pounds. He lived in Compton at 13329 Penrose. He died of gunshots to the chest, "penetrating" his "heart with massive hemorrhage." Vincent Alexander of 674 East 36th Street lived near Griffith and Jefferson, the site of Elliot's death. "About this time, I was next door, outside with the people next door. We kept seeing a lot of young kids about five or six years old going into this liquor store" that had been broken into. "So I decided to go down and see what was going on, you know. On the corner is a service station, and the man that owns the service station was standing outside, talking to someone."

Alexander spoke briefly to them. "As soon as I crossed the street to go back home, the police car drove up." At this juncture, "this young fellow ran out of the liquor store. . . . He was carrying a box, and a police officer said, 'Halt.' When they said 'Halt,' I jumped behind a tree. Then, they said 'Halt' again, and he threw the box and he kept running." As Alexander hid behind the tree, "the police officer fired one shot, and I thought it had missed him, because it passed right by me. The boy stumbled, and he went under a car. . . . Then three officers came around and looked under this car, and I think they asked the boy, was he all right . . . and they left him laying there, and they left. The man that owned the car, he came, and he drove his car off. He didn't know anybody was under there. . . . So I went back, and he was laying down there. The other people that they had stopped that were in the liquor store, they let them go." The officers were in motion in their car when one decided to shoot, Alexander said.

Walter Dudley of 2726 West 54th Street was on his way home. He was told what had happened, and he and a friend took Elliot to the hospital. The black youth "never said a word" and probably was already dead. Claude Chaisson of 850 East Jefferson was across the street, "in the service station garage that I own." He had owned this business since 1952 and was considered a pillar of the community. Like other merchants he "had been staying at my place of business at nights, to keep people from hauling stuff from my place." He saw the liquor store being ransacked, saw Elliot removing objects from the store, and saw an officer firing. "It was a police officer; four of them was together. . . . there wasn't no firemen there at that time. . . . I seen the officers pulled out on the corner of Jefferson and Griffith real fast and got out of the car. I heard one policeman holler 'Halt'; he hollered 'halt' twice, and I heard the shots."

Michael Bergman of the LAPD saw the black youth leaving the liquor store with a "box in his hand." He screamed, "Halt." But "the suspect threw the box to the ground and started running." Elliot reached 36th and Griffith, and Bergman yelled, "Halt," again to no avail. So "I fired one shot at the suspect while I was still in the police vehicle." He claimed that he was one hundred feet from Elliot. "He continued to run; he didn't falter or stumble," and he got away. Then there was "yelling; bottles smashed against the building beside me." He decided to depart. C. A. Higbie of the LAPD added, "Sometime after the shooting, the entire building that encompasses the liquor store, a meat market and a two story unoccupied apartment house was completely destroyed by fire." Two firefighters were wounded in the vicinity earlier, he said.

As Thomas Hooker of the LAPD approached the intersection of Griffith and Jefferson in his car, he heard "the ringing of a 459 burglar alarm. . . . As I exited from the right front of the vehicle, I yelled to the large group of people . . . 'Halt.'" He too claimed to have seen Elliot leaving the liquor store with a box.

> The suspect then veered to the right and started running southbound down the sidewalk. I began to pursue him on foot. I had only taken one or two steps when, out of the corner of my eye, I noticed another adult male suspect, standing near the building, reach into his front pocket. . . . I stopped and directed my attention to this suspect and covered him with my service revolver, fearing he had a weapon in his pocket. . . . [then] I heard one of my partner-officers yell "Halt" and heard one shot fired. . . . suspect that I had originally started to pursue was at the opposite end of the building. . . . He gave no visible evidence that he had been struck by a shot. . . . He disappeared . . . running.

The officers then arrested a group at the liquor store. "As we rounded the corner onto 36th Street, we observed two male adults in a parked vehicle at the curbing. . . . It was obvious that both men were eating some sort of barbecued food." The officers questioned them; then came the "smashing of glass to my right and rear" and "obscene . . . muttered threats." This distracted them from Elliot, who apparently escaped, he claimed. He was concerned about his safety since "we had been cautioned by people . . . to use extreme care as two firemen had been shot in the vicinity of Jefferson and Griffith while fighting a fire."[23]

Possibly because of Elliot's youth, more witnesses decided to participate in the coroner's hearing, which was typically boycotted because seen as biased in favor of the authorities. Yet, the verdict—justifiable homicide—was the same. The authorities and the press did not ask why a youth was shot for allegedly taking liquor. Was it necessary for the officers to fire from their car and keep going? Was it necessary to fire at all, and if so, was it necessary to shoot him in the heart?

Less than an hour later Andrew Houston, Jr., a forty-one-year-old native of Louisiana, was shot in the head at 1505 East 103d Street; his skull was fractured, his brain was lacerated, and he died. A National Guardsman fired the shot. David Labowitz of the guard recalled that "a Cadillac had gone down the street and fired several shots" at them. Douglas Warren Mercer of the guard was posted at the Watts substation, on the same side of the street and just across the alley from the 103d Street hotel where the killing took place. He heard shots come from there. "I saw a man standing in the doorway leading out to the balcony on the second story." Mercer "fired a warning shot into the building beside him. . . . he immediately moved out of my sight and into the hallway, and then he reappeared." Was Houston now frightened and pondering how he could leave this building which was now being fired on? That thought did not occur to Mercer. "I believe he was going to be shooting at the police officers in the street . . . [so] I shot him." He fired once, and, he said, there was no more sniping after that. He could not say that Houston had a gun when he shot him in the head just above the eye.

This point was relevant because William C. Johnston, Jr., of the guard arrived at the hotel after the shooting and found a "fully-loaded .22 rifle, with a sawed-off stock and a .22 automatic revolver, fully loaded." Early Cludy, the investigator for the district attorney, testified that the guns' "ownership was never ascertained."[24] The coroner's jury actually posed a few perfunctory questions. But the conclusion—justifiable homicide—was the same. No juror asked if the guard should adopt another procedure concerning the shooting of unarmed suspects in urban settings; and if the guard was forced to shoot the unarmed, could it avoid aiming for their heads? Could the guard have considered asking suspects to exit the hotel with their hands up before shooting? With rumors spreading about crazed motorists running roadblocks, firefighters and officers being shot or shot at, and other authorities being pelted with blocks of pavement, a guard and police corps unskilled in handling such urban insurrections was striking out wildly in a blunt attempt to bring back order.

■

At 5:30 A.M. Leon Cauley was shot and killed at 6120 South Vermont (then a retail store, now a library) by the LAPD as he was said to be in the act of looting.[25] At 6:45 A.M. Miller Judson, also known as Miller Burroughs, a thirty-year-old black male of smallish stature, 123 pounds and 5 feet 9½ inches, was hit with a shotgun wound in the back, perforating his aorta and intestines with a massive hemorrhage. He was said to be suffering from acute ethanol intoxication.[26]

Fifteen minutes before the slaying of Leon Cauley, Fentroy Morrison George, a twenty-one-year-old black man from Texas who lived at 6210½ South Broadway, was "shot by police while looting" at 62d and Broadway. The gunshots penetrated the left anterior and posterior of the chest walls of this "well-developed and nourished Negro male," as the coroner described the 6 foot 2 inch and 183-pound victim. In this case, George's family hired an attorney, Stanley Malone, to monitor and intervene in the coroner's hearing. Malone made a valiant effort to protect the interests of his clients. He asked that witnesses be segregated so they could not hear what preceding witnesses were saying and adjust their testimony accordingly. The coroner denied this request and concluded that justifiable homicide was involved.

George was said to be removing clothes from his home, which was above a commercial enterprise that was on fire, to the 1961 Corvair owned by his friend Harold Battle. Battle said that they "heard gunshots . . . so we started running." Bystander George Chandler remembered a confused scene with officers firing wildly; "one police officer emptied his gun in the air." The LAPD's Michael Wilson saw a building on fire and two blacks placing clothes in a car. He assumed they were committing a felony, thereby making deadly force appropriate to stop them. A NBC cameraman, Houston Hall, also assumed that George was looting and began to film him. A tow-truck driver arrived and made the same assumption; his truck rammed the Corvair to disable it, and another tow truck pulled behind the car to bar escape at the suggestion of the NBC cameraman. The owner of the clothes store below George's apartment identified the clothes taken from the Corvair as belonging to the store. Still, the question remained: Was it necessary to shoot George in the chest to keep him from taking clothes, whoever they belonged to?[27]

A few hours later at 4881 Compton Avenue, William Vernon King, also known as William Vernon Caston, a thirty-seven-year-old, 128-pound, 5 foot 8 inch native of Louisiana, was shot by the LAPD "while looting a liquor store." There were shotgun wounds in his chest perforating his heart and both lungs with massive hemorrhage. The body showed signs of "acute ethanol intoxication."[28]

It had been a bloody morning. Negroes had been shot in the heart and head for allegedly taking such items as clothes and liquor. Rumors about snipers and organized Negro gangs were proliferating. This was making the normally itchy trigger finger of the LAPD tingle; the National Guard was inexperienced in handling such onerous tasks as civil unrest, and its men were "weekend warriors," many of whom had joined the guard to avoid the Vietnam-style conflict they were now engaged in. Though fires had begun to slacken off at 1 A.M., this fact did not become clear until much, much later. Firefighters were traumatized, demoralized, and horrified at the prospect of fighting fires under fire. White male journalists, who were interpreting and filtering reality for a larger audience far distant from the curfew zone, were inexorably presenting a view that reflected the shock and horror at being attacked on racial and status grounds. One could view what was happening as blacks versus the establishment, or black against white, or black male residents of South LA versus white male authorities mostly from the suburbs or the valley. These different ways of seeing suggest why the conflict was so searing and underscore why the tumult impacted race relations so severely.

The patterns established in the early morning of 14 August continued as dusk approached, after a hiatus during daylight. The idea that "the night belongs to us" was becoming current in South LA. Simultaneously, the Euro-American community, though in many instances distant from the events, could see the smoke, fire, and guns on television, even if they were not experiencing it directly.

■

Nathaniel West suggested that Southern California bred more hate groups than the rest of the country combined. He attributed it to the bitterness of people who came to live in the sunshine and glamour and found instead boredom and disappointment.[29] No doubt there was something to this. The image transmitted by mass media of Southern California could easily leave the impression that everyone in this distant place was a tanned movie star having fun, but this stereotype failed to capture the entire Euro-American experience.

The ascendancy of Barry Goldwater in the GOP in 1964 and the racially charged battle in California over housing integration and Proposition 14 seemed to give a boost to neo-Nazi activity in LA. The offices of the Glendale Citizens against Proposition 14 were threatened with bombings and invaded. It was said that African-Americans there "were not allowed to walk the streets after dark. It was rumored that Negroes were not served in restaurants."[30]

The authorities displayed a meticulous interest in black participation in the events of August 1965, but they were not so keen in their investigation of the role of the white community despite the substantial organized ultra-right white presence in the region. One report stated that 14 August was the day that rumors began to reach police of impending organized black raids on white neighborhoods and the downtown business district.[31] The northern-most point of the curfew area was only four miles from Beverly Hills. Apprehensive, the veteran screenwriter Henry Greenberg, who lived in this affluent area, asked his children to stay home and not go to the beach that weekend.[32] Daniel Horowitz of Beverly Hills recalled the strange experience of watching the tumult on television while his black maid in uniform served them at a wedding.[33]

Fear and apprehension were only one side of the picture. One black man saw a "1964 or '65 Dodge with a Caucasian, it got stopped on Wilmington right at 105th. . . . and they opened the trunk of that man's car. He had rifles for an army . . . he had machine guns; they opened up the back of his seat; he had so many bullets that he could start anything he wanted. . . . He was over there selling that stuff to them colored peoples."[34] Trains containing guns and other goods routinely traversed South LA and were waylaid at times.

Other Euro-Americans had different purposes. Early on in the uprising, a yellow 1965 Buick Riviera—a rather large car—was driven into the mostly black Jordan Downs housing project by two white men who fired at residents. Rather than calling the police—whom they did not trust—some residents decided to break into a pawnshop, get guns, and respond more forcefully to the white men if they returned. This same source reported that it was white men in a blue Mustang who broke into the Watts post office and took "things from certain mail bags inside," not blacks as officially reported.[35]

As the flames were still raging, the *Times* noted the presence in the curfew zones of a "small band of Minutemen" who rescued besieged white women from "Negroes. . . . The men were wearing green berets and boots into which their pants were tucked like paratroopers." The interlocking directorate between the ultraright organizations and the authorities facilitated alliances, the validity of the *Times* tale aside. John Rousselot of the John Birch Society claimed in 1965 that 3 DA investigators, 25 LAPD officers, 15 sheriff's deputies, and other law enforcement personnel were members of his organization; he denied, however, the charge that 2,000 officers were members, though he freely acknowledged that a number of retired judges, along with retired and active FBI agents, belonged.[36]

Whatever the size of the Birch faction, its ideas and those of the Minutemen seemed to be spreading among whites. An informant dispatched by President Johnson to the scene reported back that Sam K. Cook, a "Director of California Moderate Democrats," advised that he would furnish weapons to his group. Though his group was small, the fact that he was allied to the armed and dangerous Minutemen meant he had to be taken seriously.[37]

LAPD officers, deputies, and guardsmen were returning to their mostly lily-white neighborhoods with horrific tales about burning and sacking, "white-baiting," sniping, and more. They were also talking on television and radio. This was a factor in helping to spread white fear, which in turn was infecting the men in uniform. This miasma of fear—and at times loathing—assured that the evening of Saturday, 14 August, would be eventful.

■

Willie Curtis Hawkins, a thirty-one-year-old black native of Texas, 6 feet 1 inch, 165 pounds, and mustachioed, was shot and killed by the LAPD at 7:14 P.M. that evening. James A. Benton of the LAPD claimed that he saw Hawkins "running from the vehicle which we were pursuing on 87th Place." He had spied Hawkins in the car and then saw him leap out and flee after helping to take items from a clothing store at 8750 South Broadway. He pulled out his 12-gauge shotgun after yelling the mandatory "Halt."

Kenneth Neal Henderson of the LAPD, Benton's partner, observed "one defendant placing an armful of clothing in the trunk of the vehicle. . . . another suspect was coming from the rear of the store with an armful of clothing. . . . The back door was open of the store . . . [I] ordered the suspects to halt." He was armed with both a .38 caliber weapon and a 12-gauge shotgun but decided to fire the latter. Hawkins's niece, Daisy Pittman of 1364 East 142d Street in Compton, testified at the inquest, but the intimidating atmosphere of an official hearing forced her to say little. Hawkins had been hit in the chest, causing hemothorax and laceration of the lung; there were also wounds in his face and his left upper arm. He too had acute ethanol intoxication.[38]

Curtis Lee Gaines, Jr., was a stocky—5 feet 9½ inches, 198 pounds—twenty-four-year-old mustachioed black man, a churchgoing Protestant, living at 935 West Palmer in Compton. This native of Arkansas was shot in the back by an LAPD officer with a shotgun; the pellets perforated his left kidney and intestines, inducing a massive hemorrhage, and penetrated his right buttock. He died. His death was ruled justifiable homicide. Eddie Harris, his first cousin, was circumspect at the coroner's hearing about what happened. Pearl Williams of 1026½ East 14th, who was at the scene of the killing, a store at 1211 East Washington, gave a terse mixed message: "Yes, I will testify. I don't know anything about it anyway."

Glen A. Bachman of the LAPD narcotics division said that at about 5:45 P.M., "I was in a partial uniform. I was in plainclothes, wearing my badge on the front of my shirt and wearing a riot helmet . . . accompanied by my brother officer, Sgt. James A. Salagi. . . . We were southbound on Central Avenue at Washington, when I intercepted a radio call 'officer needs help, Washington and Essex.' . . . I noticed that extensive looting was taking place. . . . There were fires; in fact, as I recall, the Thrifty Drug Store directly across the street was burning. The plate-glass windows on Golds Department Store, which face on Central Avenue, were completely demolished." He "took several people into custody for burglary [and] looting."

He then entered the department store, which was in "total darkness." Sergeant Len A. Leeds was there; both were unsure if anyone else was present. Suddenly, a "person appeared to jump from the larger shelf . . . it appeared that this person was attempting to disarm Sgt. Leeds. . . . I could see this person holding onto the gun barrel of Sgt. Leeds' shotgun . . . and appeared to be going through the door. . . . At this time, I reached around Sgt. Leeds with my own pistol and fired [a] shot. At the same time I fired my pistol, Sgt. Leeds fired his shotgun."

Sergeant Leeds corroborated this story. "I had on a hard helmet; I had on khakis; I had my badge on my shirt front and I had on the Sam Brown, or the leather goods of a uniformed officer." As he approached the store, he saw about thirty-five "people going from the loading door to the vehicles with their arms loaded with clothing and other items. . . . As I approached, they all appeared simultaneously to throw everything into the air and start running back into the store . . . to the storeroom portion." It was "darkened." Then "one person jumped from my right, from behind the doorway, and jumped onto my right side. I shook this person loose and continued into the room. . . . a second person . . . ran into my right side . . . at this time I discharged one round from the shotgun at waist level." He could have shot a fellow officer accidentally.

Undeterred, the intrepid Sgt. Leeds proceeded. "I could hear other persons in the room breathing and moving. I could not see anyone or anything." He called for surrender of whoever these apparitions were. A voice responded, "Hold it. I am coming out with my hands up." He was "startled" when this person materialized "a foot away from me, facing me. . . . My first reaction was to get this person away from me. . . . I shoved out with my shotgun, striking him in the upper portion of his body." Stunned, the suspect fled. At that point, the officer said, Bachman arrived, and a suspect (it was unclear if this was the previous one or ones) chose an inopportune moment to jump "from the shelf towards me"; he "grabbed the shotgun which I was holding. We turned in a half-circle, probably all the way around. We pushed back and forth for some time, struggling for the shotgun . . . the stock of the shotgun was captured." The suspect, who turned out to be Curtis Gaines, pulled away and ran. "I fired with my shotgun," and Gaines, a black man with no previous record, died.[39]

Others unlucky enough to encounter the LAPD escaped scathed but alive. At 8:15 P.M. on 14 August, Mercedes Madrid was a passenger in her car which was being driven by Robert Lee Tyler, who lived at 5919¼ South Figueroa. They made a right turn at the intersection of Beach near 102d; she was shot in the leg as Tyler turned the wheel. Then they were ordered out of the car after this forced stop. As she stepped from the car with her hands in the air, a LAPD officer choked her, until a guardsman made him stop. She was taken into custody, then later released; she remained unclear about what she had done to merit such treatment.[40]

As it happened, the area that Madrid and Tyler had turned into was one of the fiery cruxes of the uprising. There was a barricade there posted by the guard. Forty-five minutes after the confrontation with Madrid, Charles Patrick Smalley, a black man in his twenties, was shot in the head by a guardsman after refusing to stop at the barricade, or so said the guard. He was thin, 5 feet 11 inches and 138 pounds, and mustachioed with brown eyes; this single native of Louisiana resided not far from the scene at 200 West 103d Street. The fatal shot penetrated his brain, inflicting multiple contusions, lacerations, and skull fractures. He was not intoxicated.

Sergeant John Sutherland of the guard said, "At 9:00 pm, we had a trailer in the middle of the intersection, several trash cans, broken glass and a car that we had previously stopped." That auto belonged to Madrid. He saw Smalley at 8:45 P.M. "We were still under heavy sniper fire" as another car proceeded toward them. "I yelled 'halt' several times in a loud tone of voice. . . . I was just screaming 'halt' as loud as I could. The vehicle accelerated at a higher rate of speed than it was when it first started out . . . I fired two warning shots" as the car reached an estimated forty-five miles per hour. He fired again, this time at the car. After Smalley was hit, "the vehicle went completely out of control; hit a building."

As Sutherland recounted his story at the coroner's hearing, the deceased's representative, Albert Jones, demanded "the right to cross-examine the witness." The coroner brusquely denied this request. Jones insisted that "the code" did not compel the denial and denounced the "farce" and "kangaroo court." The only official effort to find out what happened to Smalley ended like most of the other inquiries, with a verdict of justifiable homicide.[41]

The law enforcement authorities had decided to make a stand at 103d Street, called Charcoal Alley because this business district was in flames and the area was abuzz with residents helping themselves to merchandise. At 103d and Grape streets, Ramon L. Hermosillo, a nineteen-year-old Latino listed as "Caucasian," was shot at a blockade. This brawny 5 foot 8 inch, 168-pound resident of 9517 Street and native of Texas was killed when the gunshot hit his chest, penetrating his left lung and heart and causing a massive hemorrhage. His uncle, who was with him, survived. Yes, he said, they saw the roadblock, those "cone shaped things in the street," as they were going west on 103d at thirty-five to forty miles per hour. He insisted that the time was 7 P.M., but the authorities insisted just as vigorously that it was 8:15.

Randall Woods, the captain in the California National Guard commanding Company C, 1st Battalion, 160th Infantry, 40th Division, was patrolling the roadblock when he noticed Hermosillo's 1957 Chevy Bel-Air heading toward him. "I heard some one yell, 'Here comes another one' and I looked up and I saw this car travelling at what I estimated to be between 40 and 50 miles an hour. I heard another guardsman yell 'halt' and then several guardsmen yelled 'halt,' and then there was a shot. . . . the vehicle . . . swerved to the left and came to rest in front of a poultry market. . . . we started receiving fire from a brick wall near the apartment house on 103rd and Hickory." There were several snipers "wearing red armbands."

This description was corroborated by John Jackson of the guard. Guardsman Victor David Subian recalled the Chevy accelerating at the roadblock; while firing, "we received sporadic sniper fire from an apartment house . . . and this I observed personally. . . . We had been given instructions, approximately 9am that day, to keep an eye out for a red-orange 1957 Chevrolet, which had been reported firing at police." He was the only witness making this assertion. He was also the "first one in the area" to report the presence of "approximately 10 people wearing red armbands on their left arms, and one who had the appearance of being a leader of some sort, wearing a red rosette over his lapel." [42]

At 9:30 P.M. at a drugstore at Miramonte and Florence, Joe Nelson Horn, also known as Joe Nelson Bridgett, was shot and killed. This twenty-two-year-old black native of Louisiana was 6 feet 1 inch and 165 pounds and resided at 5961 South Avalon. It was reported that he "fired at the [LAPD] officers wounding two . . . the officers returned the fire." Horn suffered a perforation of the heart after eight gunshot wounds to the chest. [43]

The authorities were reclaiming South LA block by block, shot by shot. The National Guard was becoming as trigger happy as the LAPD. Bullets were whizzing through the hot night air; there probably were snipers, though it is not certain if one killed four-year-old Bruce Moore, who was shot while playing in his yard at 11:15 P.M. at 8800 Mary Avenue. He was the youngest victim of all, shot in the chest with resultant cardiac lacerations and massive hemothorax. His family was stunned by it all, and his mother was unconsolable. The mainstream press and the authorities expressed no outrage. [44]

Not only blacks were under fire in the rainbow that was Los Angeles. Juan Puente's death was reported at 11:50 P.M. at 10411 South San Pedro. This 5 foot 11 inch, 181-pound native of Texas was shot by the LAPD in the abdomen with damage to his liver and lung and massive hemorrhage. Richard Young of the Foothill Division of the LAPD was traveling northbound on "San Pedro, approaching 104th, at which time my partners and I observed two men come out of a broken window of a hardware store at that location. We proceeded to the hardware store and stopped at the corner. . . . the deceased stepped out of the window [of the hardware store] and began walking southbound. . . . as he reached the edge of the building, where the driveway is, between the house and the hardware store, he turned westbound in the driveway and began running." He chased Puente fifty feet, then stopped. "I heard the bushes rustling in this area. . . . at this time, my partner, Officer Wagner, ran around my right and in front of me to the other corner of the building. As he was coming behind me, I ordered the deceased twice to come out with his hands up, at which time all motion stopped in the corner."

Officer Ronald D. Wagner said:

> As the deceased came out of the window, he had his hands clasped in front of him, as if he were carrying something. His body was casting a shadow on the front of his person, so I couldn't tell exactly what he had in his hand. . . . I stepped into the shadows and, after a few seconds, my eyes became accustomed to the dark light, and I could see the deceased standing in the bushes. . . . I ordered the deceased approximately two or three times to come out. On the last command, the bushes started moving, but I could see the deceased's feet and they were not moving. At this time, I became afraid for my life and the life of my partner, because I thought the object which the deceased was carrying might have been a weapon and he was going to use it.

At this point, Wagner stated, "I fired one shot" from eight feet away. Perhaps Wagner was so nervous because his regular assignment was the valley and now he was in alien territory.

No one pressed Wagner on his testimony about "light coming from the front of the store, which also shone down the driveway" and why he was not able to see Puente clearly. Instead, the officers were asked leading questions: "And you felt that this man had just committed that burglary; is that right?" Evidence that most likely would have been inadmissible at a trial was introduced, such as Puente's prior arrest and conviction record, along with other damning facts.[45]

■

It had been a day of spilled gore. Fire this time had been concentrated in the southerly reaches of the city of Los Angeles. Businesses were in flames or ransacked or both, and their owners had been complaining steadily about what others already had perceived as a pusillanimous approach by the authorities in addressing this problem. As Sunday morning approached and Watts readied to don its finery for the weekly church ritual, jeeps filled with armed soldiers continued to rumble through the streets. Their presence and their actions, along with those of the increasingly agitated LAPD, served to put down an unfolding civil insurrection.

5

"The Hearing Children
of Deaf Parents"

ATURDAY, 14 AUGUST, WAS A TURNING POINT IN squashing the uprising. The decision by the authorities to enforce the curfew—most notably on 103d Street—simply by shooting those who appeared to be violating their edict sparked rising anger. In an atmosphere in LA where the Red Scare had stifled the process of Euro-Americans flocking militantly to the civil rights banner, black militance increasingly took on antiwhite characteristics. This was facilitated by the fact that most of those pulling the triggers, giving the orders, fighting the fires, commenting on the airwaves, and shrinking in fear were Euro-American. The black leaders like Pettis Perry and Charlotta Bass who ascribed antiblack behavior to class and ideology had been squelched, so some African-Americans had little option beyond ascribing such behavior to race. Antiwhite expressions were not the sole mode of dissent; but it did appear that these words and actions captured attention, particularly when class realities and expressions were denied. Concessions through working-class organization had been blocked. One of the few alternatives remaining was concession through lumpen organization: gangs and insurrection. Though the bloodshed of 14 August chased many blacks back into their homes, it would take a few more days to short-circuit what already was being called the Watts Uprising.

■

The National Guard and the LAPD could argue that their response was so strong because of the fiery militance they faced. Molotov cocktails were being tossed, snipers were sighting targets, and there was some evidence that all this was organized.[1] Adrian Dove, a consultant to the state Department of Industrial Relations, joined James Burks, Fred Scott, and Carl Martin of the city probation department's Group Guidance Unit—its "street corner gang workers"—in surveying the scene. "We wore old clothes and drove an old car." The fires were still burning as they conducted interviews, thirty in the curfew zone, including "some businessmen" and "50 gang teenagers." They also snapped photographs.

What struck them was the selective nature of the burning. In one block the Urban League's Watts project was "the only unburned building left in its block. A Negro owned restaurant was left standing and unlooted while a furniture store next door was burned to the ground. Some white businesses were still operating and had not been bothered." They found, contrary to most reports, that "poor people of both races" were plundering stores and "for the first time in many years, all of the Negro gangs in the LA ghetto have called for an end to the fighting between each other." In some areas water and electricity had been turned off, and police cars were cruising carrying five men with four shotguns extended from the windows.[2]

The momentum of the revolt was propelled forward by what Dr. Paul O'Rourke, Governor Brown's special assistant for antipoverty planning, called "hard core youth, gang leadership, between the ages of sixteen and twenty." This intelligence was gleaned from gang liaisons like Burks, HRC personnel, and other blacks with ties to the authorities.

> The spread-pattern of the riot coincided with the territories—the "turf" or "sets"—of the major, hard-core gangs. . . . The method of operation used in the entering and firing of buildings was identical with the highly effective guerilla tactics in use for many years by these same gangs when they fight among themselves. The safe conduct signs and signals, which allowed Negroes to pass unharmed through active riot areas, were of gang origin. [These] included the familiar two finger, victory sign for the Slausons, three raised fingers representing the Watts Gang V and [the] familiar [circle] of the thumb and forefinger forming a zero—the sign of the Gladiators.

O'Rourke warned that if the gangs were not confronted, there would be a "recurrence—or worse—of the bloody riots," but this time featuring sharp clashes with white gangs. These black gangs had not received sustained attention as long as it seemed that their activity was concentrated on each other and other blacks, but when businesses, the police, the guard, and others were attacked, suddenly the gangs became public enemy no. 1.[3]

Sizable numbers of "non-gang" blacks were surging through the streets too. "Sweet" Alice Harris, now a leading community activist in South LA, has recalled, "We looted but didn't burn." Residents not in gangs took advantage of the situation to seize groceries or destroy credit records.[4]

Lelia Hodge, a black shopkeeper in South LA, noted that early on in the uprising she saw two black men running south of Jefferson Boulevard. The taller one was shouting, "The whitey has to go," and she was advised to put "Blood brothers–Negro owned" on her window. When she asked why they burned, they told her, "We haven't got anything, our parents didn't have anything, we are not looking to get anything, and we just don't give a damn." She asked who they were, and they said, "We are the Brothers. . . . We are not like CORE. We are violent and we mean business." They assailed the philosophy of nonviolence, increasingly associated with Dr. Martin Luther King, Jr. "As long as the Ku Klux Klan is riding and burning, we, the Black Brothers, are going to also ride and burn." They wore armbands and carried walkie-talkies.[5]

Even when those affiliated with gangs or belonging to or identifying with the Nation of Islam were not in the streets in organized detachments, these two forces possessed the only organized, militant ethos left in the community in the wake of the ideological devastation of the Red Scare. Thus, even when these militants were not present in fact, their ethos or presumed ethos was being adopted en masse by black youth, many of whom were repelled by the sight of blacks in the South being beaten by racists—and not striking back—and many of whom had been abandoned by mainstream civil rights organizations.[6]

The vernacular associated with the NOI was now in wide use. A Pacifica Radio reporter recorded a black youth shouting during the time of the revolt that the "whole atmosphere has changed . . . everything is 'brother, brother.'" This language was being linked with disgust over the war against Vietnam: "If this is a white man's world, let him fight the war." These statements from the streets not only reflect NOI influence; the militant tone and words that could easily be characterized as antiwhite could also be deemed anti-imperialist, and it was this aspect, as much as anything else, that captured attention in an increasingly anti-Communist United States.

Pacifica captured the bitter attacks on black clergy—"hypocrites," "cuss 'em and spit on 'em"—and black leadership generally: "Negro leadership has been an incestuous middle class affair." But overriding all else was the anger toward the police, those who cry law and order but "kick down doors," make "illegal arrests," and resort to beatings, while expecting blacks to be law-abiding.[7]

The signs were all about that this turn in the black movement was nigh. The historian Clay Carson, then toiling as a reporter, interviewed Woody Coleman of the Non-Violent Action Committee shortly before the revolt, who uttered words at odds with the philosophy of his organization. "I'm looking for a bloodbath this summer. We're going to get tired of being peaceful and non-violent without getting anything. We're still getting crumbs; we're going to get a big slice of that cake." Carson observed, "His ideal is to have a 'mean and nasty organization, where people have everything to gain and nothing to lose.'" Coleman called Dr. King "a 'misguided or misinformed individual'" and expressed admiration for the NOI.[8]

Even if the authorities had not been paying attention to the *LA Free Press,* there was ample evidence that race relations in LA had taken a dangerous detour. Before the uprising there had been random assaults on cars bearing whites.[9] After the uprising one analyst tried to explain to a worried, predominantly white audience what this all meant. Today's "Negro," he said, had "neither the psychological defenses nor the social supports that permit passive adaptations to" racism. "In a sense," he concluded, "they are the hearing children of deaf parents."[10]

Coleman's words seemed to become reality during the uprising. Vengeance was taken, especially on the LAPD. At one point a black man was reconnoitering the command post at 49th and Avalon. He then walked to South Park, and shortly thereafter a crowd came out of South Park and attacked the command post, forcing it to move to 55th and Avalon. "He was recognized as Muslim," the LAPD noted.[11]

Whether this man was with the NOI or not, the fact is that a new approach toward Euro-Americans and the police was developing in Black LA. Rhett Jones has observed that historically black hatred of whites was muted and subtle in the United States, especially compared to other parts of the Western Hemisphere. Some scholars were so struck by this restrained attitude in the face of Negrophobia that blacks were termed dismissively the "female of the races."[12]

The nonviolence message of Dr. King combined with the publicized beatings of his followers, along with the new popularity of Malcolm X and the NOI and the decline of competing left groups, led to an erosion of this restraint. The increased racial identification by blacks that came with this erosion was substituted for a rising mobility, the lack of which then fed back on dislike of whites.[13] The antiwhiteness was so vigorous and unrestrained precisely because these angry sentiments had been curbed for hundreds of years.

Paradoxically, black nationalism was a common platform and one way to reconcile tensions among darker and not so dark blacks; just as "white identity" was consummated at an altar of antiblackness, "black identity" was sanctified as antiwhiteness. Some lighter-skinned blacks—men and women alike—could demonstrate their fealty to this latest stage of black nationalism by fiery nationalist advocacy, thus deflecting attention away from their own hue, which might have made their allegiances suspect.

LA faced not only the national bipolar racial dilemma but tensions between African-Americans and Chicanos, which Yvonne Gerioux, the executive director of Family Service of LA, claimed were "steadily increasing since World War II." There were also tensions between blacks and many Jewish merchants, between darker- and lighter-skinned blacks, between recently arrived and already settled blacks. Gerioux complained that "there are also invisible barriers between living areas. The Vernon Area Negroes don't go to the Crenshaw Area. The Negroes west of Crenshaw don't go back to Watts." She had encountered "the type of situation where one Negro has risen socially above his past and finds it too painful to associate with this past in his mind, and so refuses to tolerate socially those from his past social level." As a result of this encrusted race- and class-driven anger, "the riot was a release of tension."[14] There was an apparent correlation between darker skin and lower income; studies showed that the darker skinned seemed to bear deeper antiwhite feelings and seemed more willing to use violence to address their plight.[15] When the authorities sought to bar not only whites but light-skinned blacks from "Viet Watts," such studies were bolstered.[16]

The piercing hatred for whites was stunning. Michele LeGrace of Gardenia, twenty-one years old, said that the windows of her car were smashed and a jeering crowd yelled color-coded comments at her. Richard Sexton, twenty-four, of 1245½ East 80th Street, was beaten on the head, kicked in the ribs, and dragged from his car, which was then burned. An acerbic eighteen-year-old black woman did not flinch in describing the kind of antiwhite action experienced by LeGrace and Sexton. "I threw bricks and rocks and anything I could get my hands on . . . to hurt them. We were throwing at anything white. Why not do it to you guys. You're doing it to us."[17]

Robert Richardson, the newly recruited black reporter for the *Times,* was flabbergasted by it all.

> I went along with the mobs, just watching, listening. It's a wonder anyone with white skin got out of there alive. I saw people with guns. The cry went up several times—"Let's go to Lynwood!" whenever there weren't enough whites around. Every time a car with whites in it entered the area the word spread like lightning down the street: "Here comes whitey—get him!" The older people would stand in the background egging on the teen-agers and the people in their early 20s. Then the young men and women would rush in and pull white people from their cars and beat them and try to set fire to their cars.[18]

Another commentator remarked that some blacks would have marched on the all-white municipality of Lynwood or other areas in the early hours of 13 August, "but it was getting late and many of them had to go work Friday morning."[19]

Richard Mojica, a forty-year-old salesman who could be regarded as La-tino, described an attack by twenty blacks. "It was that look on their faces—a look of pure hate. They just kept coming toward our car and the Negro woman that led them kept screaming, 'Kill them, kill them, kill them.' You've never seen such hatred. . . . Something has made those people awfully mad to show that much hatred." Mojica was left to ponder this anger with "his car in ruins, his fiancee seriously wounded and his memory seared."[20]

An award-winning Pacifica Radio broadcast captured many of the angry voices in the streets. To the lilting soundtrack of "White Man's Heaven Is Black Man's Hell," by the increasingly popular NOI calypsonian Louis Far-rakhan, taunting blacks affirmed that "the white man is low and dirty." There were numerous references to "Mr. Charlie" and bitter accusations: "White man will say 'good morning' to [the] Spanish before [the] Negro. . . . Negro will talk back, Spanish will obey." Violence was not abjured. "If the white man has the white Ku Klux Klan, we must form [the] black Ku Klux Klan." The mildest comment was, "I don't believe all of them are devils, just most of them."[21]

This real wrath seemed to engender a fevered reaction from the authorities and the Euro-American community at large. On the evening of 15 August, the police were told officially:

> "The Blood" (enforcement arm of Black Muslims) plan their Grand Finale sometime tonight in the ravaged riot areas. Their manpower will come from Hollywood, Beverly Hills and Encino. . . . Caller identified self as Willie Owens, 948 E. 49th St. Receiver of message believes call was attempting to draw attention away from Pasadena, Encino, Hollywood and Beverly Hills area. The Watts debacle was formulated last Christmas [1964] by a 300 member syndicate and scheduled for Friday, August 13, 1965. [They] changed their mind. This caused a new party to be formed within this party called "The Blood." This new party gained numbers and forced the Muslims to go along with the original plan which erupted prematurely by younger impatient members before heavy duty weapons could be obtained.[22]

This report was largely inaccurate, but it reinforced the lurking idea that African-Americans would one day seek retribution for centuries of racist sins, and that day was now. Undoubtedly, this pervasive feeling fueled the bloody reaction by the guard and the LAPD. Along the same line, the repeated black comments about forming a black KKK were an indication that something had gone terribly wrong.[23]

Nevertheless, it would be a mistake to assume that antiwhite expressions were evinced by all residents of South LA or all those who took to the streets. When Adrian Dove entered Jordan Downs during the height of the revolt, "we were repeatedly asked to express their idea that this was not a war against all whites. We were told that this was and will be a continued war against the LAPD and Chief Parker. . . . They pointed to the large number of white kids from CORE and N-VAC who are roaming about unmolested." White-owned businesses were attacked for being "non-residents" as much as for ethnicity.[24]

Nicholas Beck, the thirty-two-year-old UPI reporter who was saved from a beating by one group of blacks because of the intervention of a "Negro civil rights worker," could dispute the notion of unanimity of antiwhite feeling among blacks.[25] Still, the popular journalist Charles Silberman concluded that "the riot dramatized a fundamental change in Negro-white relations. . . . What is new is that Negroes have begun to reveal and to express—indeed, to act out—the anger and hatred they have always felt, but had always been obliged to hide and suppress behind a mask of sweet docility." The hatred of "everything white," he said, was "much more overt and explicit in Watts this year than Harlem last year." He added ominously, "The young Negro radicals are also moving toward black nationalism," and, in response, Dr. King was being forced to turn his attention away from the Deep South.[26]

Some light-skinned blacks also felt in jeopardy during the heat of the revolt. H. Claude Hudson of the NAACP said in a matter-of-fact tone that "my complexion is so fair, that when I'm stopped by a police officer he probably doesn't even know I'm connected with the Negro race until he has seen my identification or the neighborhood in which I live."[27] He decided to spend a good deal of time at home during 11–17 August 1965. The light-skinned Ulysses Prince of the HRC was detailed to the streets; he decided to wear a sign reading "I am a brother" so there could be no mistaken reaction to him.[28] John Buggs recalled that Prince "didn't go the first night" to the curfew zone. "I didn't want him to go, because he is very light and I was afraid for him to go down there by himself."[29]

Twenty-five years later Frieta Shaw Johnson recalled that her then husband was fair-skinned with blue eyes; another black mistook him for a white man and shot up his bus.[30] The light-skinned congressman from South LA, Gus Hawkins, decided he "had to be careful going through" his district because "there was a strong hostility to whites in the neighborhoods at that time. It hurt me not to be able to get around the area," but he was afraid someone "might take a shot" at him thinking he was "a white passing through." He recalled being in Will Rogers Park in the curfew zone "walking from the clubhouse out to my automobile and some fellow ran down to attack me on the basis of 'here's whitey in our neighborhood.'" Hawkins said friends who knew he is black rescued him. He did not report the incident, he said, but it taught him a lesson."[31] One lesson learned by some was that black nationalism could bind blacks of varying hues and, perhaps, forestall the recurrence of such tensions.

Many blacks saw the revolt as an opportunity to settle scores with those of a different color who were perceived somehow as the enemy.[32] This was not altogether rational, as evidenced by the fact that the light-skinned Louis Farrakhan—the poet laureate of the streets—might have been attacked on the basis of color in Watts by darker brethren who did not recognize him. Still, it is hard to dispute the perception that Watts marked the point when masses of blacks were manifestly demonstrating that Dr. King's ideas were not accepted universally. Ironically, many of the protesters saw themselves as realizing the ideas of Malcolm X when they attacked those of a different hue, though he had clearly taken steps away from such a philosophy in the wake of his Mecca visit in 1964, if not before. But what was buoying the protesters was not necessarily the doctrines of Malcolm X—correctly perceived or not—but a lingering hostility to establishments deemed to be dominated by whites and perceived as bastions of bias.

■

Few residences were burned down, or schools, or churches, and only one library was damaged. These were not targeted, but it seemed that firefighters were. While they were fighting fires, often "they would see right down in the same block a car drive up with four men in it, and right behind them a truck. They would break into a building, load the truck, beep-beep, beep-beep on the horn. Everybody would come out of the building, one man would go back in with a bucket of gasoline, throw it into the building, ignite it, and away they would go. . . . our men were shot at, had bricks and large chunks of concrete and asphalt thrown at them, and they were literally driven away" from fires. The top command of the department was forced to give orders that in such cases the firefighters should "let the buildings burn."

Raymond Hill of the department said black gangs, who had "trucks and signals with horns and everything," organized the attack. In the melees the department's "heavy pieces of equipment" were damaged, 25 percent of the 400 total, "and over 40 of them had all their windshields broken out" and "a couple of tires shot out"; thirty-two of his men were injured, four were shot, one was killed, and many others were hit by "flying missiles." On 12 August one of his men "was driving a fire apparatus from Manchester and Hoover and he went across Manchester to Avalon and from Avalon to Imperial Highway, that's 28 blocks, and he said during that entire 28 blocks they were literally bombarded with missiles all the way, both windshields were broken out . . . one chunk of concrete came through the windshield and one hit the man on the neck." His colleague Antone Peter Jasich added that protesters used "flammable liquids" and Molotov cocktails. He inadvertently discovered "on Pasadena Avenue in the northeast section of town . . . a factory . . . putting the molotov cocktails together." [33]

The fire department's methods of detecting the location of fires were inadequate. Bands of protesters running from site to site were starting fires, while the department "received no formal authenticated information" but had to

rely on the mass media and the "grapevine." The department tuned into television to ascertain the site of major fires; its telephones were overwhelmed
not only with calls of assistance but with calls designed to tie up its lines. Its
radio frequencies were not up to the task. These handicaps are even more
surprising when it is considered that the pace of events in the Deep South
had caused the department to hold high-level meetings to plan its response
in the event of a "racial incident, riot or civil disobedience." Days before the
uprising it had met about such an eventuality.

There had been a breakdown in communications between the city and
county fire departments and related agencies. K. E. Klinger, an engineer, had
made pointed suggestions about how to respond in the future, recommending better intelligence and technology. A helicopter for the department—the
Bell 204B was "the very type machine and operation presently being used so
successfully by our armed forces in Vietnam"—was deemed a top priority.
"Viet Watts" was becoming more than a slogan. In a precursor of the "high-
tech" approach to urban unrest, Klinger also suggested that the department
purchase other aircraft that could detect and map fires, using airborne infra-
red scanners and "associated electronic readout systems."[34]

Though the department was uncanny in making plans for the future, it
was not so adept in interpreting the past. One of the reasons it had been
meeting in anticipation of trouble in South LA was because "over a two-year
period" there had been sharp "verbal exchanges, abusive language . . . rock-
throwing" and the like by residents there. The department for many years
had conducted fireworks displays in South LA on July 4, "but our firemen
were abused to such a point verbally and physically that we stopped putting
on these shows." And these attacks happened only at the hands of black
people, according to Hill and Jasich.[35] The August assault demoralized the
fire department and ignited hostility toward protesters; yet firemen stopped
fighting one fire "in order to rescue looters who were trapped on the upper
floor of a large retail establishment," and another crew delivered a baby in the
heart of the curfew zone. The U.S. Army, which later studied in detail the
star-crossed relationship between firefighters and protesters, also was surprised that "the utility companies would not go into the disturbance area to
disconnect services. On numerous occasions, fire personnel with inadequate
training and equipment had to handle high voltage electric lines." This
"posed a serious threat."

The fire department was running out of patience and, worse, water. Ambulances were refusing to enter the curfew zone, which was only increasing the ire of residents. By 14 August 200 fires were burning, including 40 deemed major fires of "a second alarm nature." That day there were 20 large structural fires; as for an additional 20 minor fires in autos, sheds, and the like, the department elected not to respond. Department brass was concerned that there were not enough companies to cover the remaining "93 percent of the city"; this department with the third largest amount of fire equipment in the nation had seven engine companies in reserve but "no personnel to man the 7 engines." A whopping "90 percent of all street alarms reported" in LA were false "under normal conditions"; on 14–15 August this figure went even higher, so the department decided to ignore all street alarms. It could have been worse. There were no fires during this period "in any manufacturing plant or huge structure." [36]

■

Though no major plant was destroyed, business—notably big business—did suffer grievously during the fires of August. The harm it endured was a central reason why these events were investigated so assiduously. With the atmosphere unsuitable for shopping or doing business, many businesses—particularly retail stores—closed down for this period. Employee absenteeism was high. [37]

Pacific Telephone and Telegraph, Richfield Oil, and Union Oil all had outposts in the curfew zone that were damaged. Thousands of phones were out of order, and severe damage was inflicted on lines, cables, and poles. Power distribution lines belonging to the LA Department of Water and Power were damaged, leading to a cessation of water; a power outage at the 99th Street pumping station was caused by the burning of cables. [38]

The major grocery chains were targeted, along with liquor stores. White Front, a leading retail store at 7600 Central, was set fire three times. [39] On the other hand, commercial glass shops did landslide business, working day and night to meet the flood of orders; new police car windshields were in great demand. [40]

The San Fernando Valley was miles away from the heart of the curfew zone, but it was close enough so that major department stores there recorded a 50 percent decline in retail sales. Business along Sunset Boulevard and La Cienega also dropped by half. Tourism, a major industry, was wounded. Migration to the state was affected. James Stowell, chief of the state Agricultural

Department inspection station in Yuma, Arizona, estimated that two hundred fewer cars crossed the border during this period.[41]

Despite the ferocious anger, it would be foolhardy to ascribe all the damage in South LA to the residents. Looking back twenty years after the fires, Marnesba Tackett, one of the residents, declared that many of the merchants "set the torch to their own stores. I was in the real estate business at the time, and one of our clients said to a salesman of mine that it's too bad that the riots didn't come this far and take my store. Interestingly enough, that store did catch fire some months later."

Tackett also noted the correlation between the growing anger and growing militance among African-Americans. Not only did this lead to the proliferation of "buying and ownership of handguns"—many of which were turned by blacks on each other—it also led to the growth of "a group that felt we should adopt scare tactics." This group tended to advocate separatism and narrow nationalism and fed the youth's need for militance to confront an often hostile society. As for Tackett, she was sufficiently cowed to the point where she reluctantly "became quiet in terms of [advocating] integrated education and there were others who felt the same thing and reacted in that way."[42]

No class discourse was available to explain to the black masses what was happening. For example, grievances against grossly exploitative practices of some merchants were at times ascribed more to their Jewishness than to their class background. One analyst hypothesized that "about 80% of the businessmen in the riot area were Jews" and they were the "hardest hit victims during the riot."[43] Jesse Robinson, a fifty-three-year-old pillar of the black community (this UCLA alumnus worked as a postal worker, owned a management company, taught junior college, and served as president of the Board of Trustees of Compton Union High School), saw an anti-Jewish pattern in the events. Days after the conflagration he went to Watts and talked to his old friends. He was told that there was much "burning" by "individuals outside of the Watts area." He referred to "a group of rioters with rifles, trucks with gas on them burning in a selected fashion . . . Jewish stores."[44]

The Central Avenue blocks, known as Charcoal Alley II, and the original Charcoal Alley, 103d Street—two of the primary shopping districts in South LA—were both devastated. Weeks after the damage Richard Marshal of South LA was still seething with anger about how "we, the older people, felt exploited. We wouldn't buy anything. There were just a bunch of Jews selling us second class merchandise for first class prices. One time I went into Mr. Sobbs to get a pair of swimming trunks. He sold them to me and the rubber was rotten because they had been on the shelf so long." He was not totally insensitive to the class dimension, noting that "the riot was a chance to get even with the power structure."[45]

This latter comment makes it clear that caution is required in assessing the extent of anti-Jewish fervor in South LA. Consider the experience of Hyman Hanes, executive director of the Sixth Region of the Jewish War Veterans, who operated a thrift shop at 47th and Broadway that was left unscathed. He had an "excellent reputation for fairness in the community" and, crucially, had a black manager who remained on the premises during the entire period. Nonetheless, the decline of a class discourse and the rise of strains of Islam that were not congenial to Judaism in the midst of a nation where anti-Semitism never was far from surfacing combined to make life difficult for many Jewish merchants in South LA. The ripple effect included lessening Jewish support for black causes.[46] Many blacks did not distinguish between Jewish merchants and those that were called "white" or "Caucasian." Much of their anger existed because these people were merchants, not because they were Jewish. Otherwise, Hyman Hanes would have suffered the fate of other Jewish merchants in South LA.

Peter Sarnoff owned Paramount Cleaners and Laundry at 401 West Compton Boulevard and a number of other shops in the area. The cleaners, he discovered, was torched during the revolt by Charles Muldrow, a disgruntled former employee. The tall, thin Muldrow, twenty-three, lived at 208 West 97th Street. On 2 November 1965 he ran into Sarnoff and instructed him to close his other businesses or sell and move out; he said he was acting on behalf of "a Mr. Kinambu" described by Muldrow as "a rich Japanese."[47] Whether Muldrow was dissembling or not, any merchant in South LA in 1965 would have had difficulty, as Korean-American merchants discovered in 1992, amid black nationalists of various class backgrounds who viewed non-black stores in their neighborhood as an indignity.

Many small businesses were ruined during this time. Richard Walker, white, lived at 3204 Euclid Avenue in Lynwood but with his parents owned Willowbrook Feed and Hardware at 12907-11 Willowbrook. He remained in the store the evening of 13 August, guns at the ready, and he stayed until 4:30 P.M. the next day. By the time he returned at 9 P.M. on 15 August, his store had been burned down completely. He suspected a "young white man," a local activist, was the culprit. Walker was gratified that some of his customers—who were mostly black—brought food and drink to him as he stayed in the store, though to avoid incurring the ire of others, they "did it at the back door so that the rioters would not see." Yet he was horrified by what he saw in the streets. "They saw all the Negro community go wild. The people looked glassy-eyed as though they were under the influence of narcotics."[48]

It wasn't just white merchants that were touched. Cornelio Jacobs was a Filipino from Torrance who owned a barbershop in Willowbrook. At the suggestion of a police officer, he left his shop on 13 August, returned the next day at 7:30 P.M., and stayed until 9:30 A.M. on the fifteenth. At 12:30 that afternoon he turned on his television and saw his shop burning. The $7,000 loss was too much to overcome; he went to work for another barber.[49]

Black merchants tried to ride the nationalist wave by placing signs on the windows of their stores reading "Negro owners" or, more fashionably, "Blood Brother," "Soul Brother," "Negro Blood," or "Black Blood Bros." Many of these stores were left untouched even when areas around them were reduced to ashes.[50] This was visual evidence of the parallel aims shared by blacks who were burning and those who (probably) were not. Nevertheless, a number of black merchants were burned out despite their race, which underscores a class aspect of the events. Their fate did not prevent one shopkeeper from putting a sign on his store reading, "Me Chinese, but me Blood Brothers too."[51]

There were countless reasons why blacks might be upset about business practices in their neighborhoods. The 4300 block of Central, which was destroyed, was an area where "no Negroes [were] allowed to rent business fronts."[52] The notorious savings and loans associations in South LA charged higher interest rates than their branches elsewhere did, redlined relentlessly, and treated their customers with scorn.[53] Almost half of the "high credit businesses" were totally wiped out, while only three out of forty "low credit businesses suffered damage to the same extent."[54] Much of what became looting was sparked initially by harried efforts to snatch credit files from businesses.[55]

To understand fully the breadth and depth of the revolt, it is necessary to understand the role of business. Some businesses overcharged customers or disrespected patrons; others were the repository of the commodities that were either necessities or the symbols of self-esteem. Thus, Bruce Michael Tyler has characterized what happened in South LA as a "consumer riot with racial, political and class overtones." There is something to this thesis. However, if it is intended to detract from the overall importance of the revolt, it is misguided. For these turbulent events had enormous impact, not least on the all-important bond market and the state's ability to raise funds in the capital markets.[56]

■

Perhaps because of the perceived threat of the uprising—a burning city, worried capital markets, slumping retail businesses, harassed firefighters, nervous Euro-Americans, and angry African-Americans—the authorities sought mightily to smash it. And this often involved bloodshed, which flowed inexorably from the evening of 14 August to the morning of 15 August.

Frederick M. Hendricks, a nineteen-year-old black student, was living at 1406 Via Los Santos; on 15 August just after midnight this slender 5 foot 9 inch 133-pounder died after he was shot in the neck; lacerations "innominated [his] artery," causing a massive hemorrhage. He was shot while seeking to leave a store with liquor. James Cullins, manager of a nearby hotel, saw Hendricks walking to a liquor store on Utah; there were three "boys" altogether. "They pulled out a trash barrel . . . and started pounding on the window" of the store. Suddenly police appeared, in "plain clothes with white crash helmets on." Hendricks fled. An officer cried, "Halt," then shot him "three times" when Hendricks did not obey.[57]

Minutes later Eugene Shimatsu, an eighteen-year-old Japanese-American residing at 3460 Second Avenue, was shot in the chest by an LAPD officer at a liquor store at 5440 West Washington.[58] At that exact moment, 12:55 A.M., in another part of town, Joseph Wallace, a twenty-nine-year-old black man living at 1459 East 90th Street, was shot by a guardsman while trying to drive past a barricade at 59th and Avalon, or so they said. A gunshot wound lacerated his lung and induced hemorrhaging. Troy Bryan Hill of the 85th Armored Division recalled how it happened. He was proceeding down Slauson Avenue as a passenger in a quarter-ton jeep, with a three-quarter-ton truck following behind. They noticed coming down the road toward them "at, it seemed like, a high rate of speed," perhaps fifty miles per hour, a light-colored car. It was after midnight, and curfew was 8 P.M.

"I immediately took it upon myself to assist in stopping this car. It appeared to me that he was trying to get away, so I had my driver pull perpendicular to the road and had the three quarter ton block the rest of the road." Wallace didn't "seem to slow down at all." Undaunted, Hill "motioned my men out of their vehicles . . . and I had them get behind the vehicles and load their weapons, chamber rounds. . . . I was armed with the .45 automatic pistol as it was, oh, I would say about half a block from me, I could see it apparently wasn't going to stop or slow down, so I fired a couple of shots over the car, in an attempt to stop him some way."

Wallace did not stop;

> he continued on . . . his speed carried right on into the intersection, and there were only a few feet between his car and my vehicles. I figured my men were behind it, so I fired at that time; I fired into the car . . . I fired all my rounds, six or eight rounds. . . . the last round . . . he turned, he skidded . . . and slid down in the other direction . . . and up on the curb. . . . I motioned my men and they all fired, too, at that time. . . . he hit a power pole and came to rest in the middle of the block . . . I felt at that time that maybe he either had hit on the accelerator or he was trying to get away again. So, I instructed my men to open fire.

Although the information was offered at the coroner's hearing that Wallace was an ex-convict, that fact was unknown when he was shot, fired on time and time again. His death was ruled justifiable homicide.[59]

At 4:25 A.M. Lonnie Cook was killed by the guard while allegedly running a roadblock at 62d Place and Vermont Avenue.[60] By 7:50 A.M. the sun had risen on a new day, but old patterns persisted, as Paul Harbin, a fifty-three-year-old black man, ruefully discovered. He was huge, 280 pounds and 5 feet 8 inches, and lived at 1325 Walnut. Those with Harbin at the time were reluctant to speak about what happened, which left it to the LAPD to shape the event. John Moreland of 1942 South Central said bluntly, "I don't know anything."

Thomas W. Hooker of the LAPD was not so reticent. He had gone to the Shop-Rite supermarket at 2004 South Central. "The windows had been broken out; part of the market, the north half of the market had been burned. . . . I heard noises coming from the market . . . I ran across the parking lot towards the market." It was "quite dark, and my vision was cut down, due to the display racks." It was 5:15 A.M., he recalled. "I heard my partner yell: 'Hold it, police. . . .' I heard running . . . and observed two persons in front of me . . . I heard my partner yell . . . 'Hold it, police.'" He spotted Harbin. "I heard several shots." He then apprehended Moreland, who was with Harbin. He saw an "object" in Harbin's hand. Nathan Johnson of the LAPD said that Harbin then began to run. Harbin was twelve feet away and terribly overweight, but Johnson decided that only lethal force could stop him. He fired three shots at Harbin, who as it turned out had nothing in his hands. Apparently the hefty Harbin was taking meat to eat, though by the time he confronted the LAPD, he had dropped it. His death was deemed justifiable homicide too.[61]

By the evening of the fifteenth, things were simmering down but not totally under control. Blacks had been losing blood by the bucket, but they were not alone. Richard Lefebvre, a twenty-three-year-old white man, was hit with a shotgun blast to the chest, perforating his heart and right lung with a massive hemorrhage. That evening the police received a call about the throwing of rocks and other things at cars by a crowd of about three hundred at 15th near California. As the LAPD arrived at the scene, Lefebvre and a few others began to run away, with the police in hot pursuit. The LAPD contended that the suspects turned and began firing, and the officers simply returned fire.

George Medak of the LAPD added, "As we stopped our vehicles, we saw debris flying in our direction—bricks, bottles." Another officer, Richard Lee Zylstra, provided a different wrinkle. "My partner and I attempted to effect an arrest on a female Negro. As we tried to assist her to the patrol car, a large group of male Negroes came up on us, yelling at us, throwing missiles, bottles, bricks. Three female prisoners and a male Negro attempted to take the prisoner away from me . . . finally, had to let her go, in fear of her own safety." Other officers responding to a distress call hurried to the scene, shotguns cocked. According to Officer Stewart Gordon, three men tried to take his shotgun. "I held it in the air; I put my finger on the trigger; it was loose, as though it had been fired." Apparently Lefebvre was shot when he tried to wrest the shotgun away from Gordon.[62] Here was a white man killed, shot through the heart with a shotgun blast, with officers' stories varying as to how it happened; some said he was fleeing, and others said he was wrestling. Justifiable homicide was the decision, nonetheless.

The same result obtained when Neita Love, a sixty-seven-year-old black woman, was shot at 51st and Avalon while allegedly driving through a roadblock. She lived at 1523 East 23d Street. She was shot in the neck with the bullet severing her spinal cord. This native of Louisiana had been at a friend's house on 87th Street for dinner, and she was on her way home. She was traveling at a rate of thirty miles per hour, had not been drinking, and was accompanied by her husband. There was light traffic as she approached the fatal intersection at 9 P.M. Apparently she knew of the curfew and had stopped her car when the shooting began. Lieutenant Robert John Geary of the guard begged to differ. So did Sergeant Gerald Garcia, who argued that he yelled, "Halt," but the car kept going and then accelerated as the headlights were doused. Private Yasue Kita agreed; he was the one who opened fire. The lawyer, Leo Branton, who spoke for this gray-haired old lady, was irate. He insisted vociferously that the car had stopped when the shooting took place, contrary to the recollections of the guardsmen. He charged further that the district attorney had done an inadequate investigation, an accusation that bedeviled each coroner's hearing.[63]

The list of victims was widening from Latinos to Asian-Americans, Euro-Americans, and senior citizens. The authorities were determined to enforce the curfew at any cost. Black LA had gone to church to pray on Sunday, 15 August, in a ritual that stretched back decades. They prayed amid fire and rubble and jeeps with armed soldiers. A new work week was beginning on Monday, 16 August, for a city that had been out of control since 11 August. More blood would be shed before the authorities could resume control; and when they did, they discovered they were now dealing with a different community.

THREE

Conflict

6

Black Scare

IT WAS NOW 16 AUGUST. THERE WERE STILL POCKETS of resistance. Conflagrations had spread beyond the boundaries of LA. As white Angelenos watched their televisions in horror, the fear began to spread—notably after the Athens Park meeting where it was promised—that the fires would be brought directly to their doorstep. One Angeleno warned his compatriots that they should "load the weapons and prepare for the worst," rather than being "defenseless people cowering in their homes, hoping that the marauders will strike their neighbors rather than themselves."[1] In Beachwood, a mostly white section of the county, there was concern that brushfires would be set intentionally that would engulf the entire neighborhood.[2]

Early on in neighboring Compton, Rosecrans Plaza, a "wealthy shopping center" built in 1963 and with twenty-two businesses, was rumored to be a target. On Saturday afternoon bands of black youth arrived there, but Leroy Conley, a black man who headed the Business Men's Association there, organized a rival band armed with weapons, including shotguns. To Conley it was a class, not a race, confrontation: "We were all working together. There wasn't any black or white."[3]

Maxcy D. Filer, another black leader in Compton, encountered black youth stoning a white motorist. "I was trying to steer the white man away. He wouldn't turn. He pulled up and stopped . . . Go on, please, I told him. Instead he stepped out of his car. 'I am a minister' he said. He turned to the crowd. 'Let us pray,' he told them." These youth were in no mood to get on their knees. "He was knocked to his knees" instead. "I could see blood. 'Please,' I told him. 'Don't go down. Get up, get in your car and get out of here.' I helped him back in and he got away."[4]

These were scattered incidents. Compton was not a major battleground during the uprising; many denied later that any disturbance had taken place there at all.[5] Nevertheless, after the uprising more whites there and elsewhere in the county moved farther south to Orange County. During the turbulent days of August, there had been only a few reports of disturbances in that conservative redoubt, and these focused on "Negroes cruising in cars" and "bothering students at Orange Coast College in Costa Mesa." Some black families who lived in Orange County in August 1965 feared that the racist right wing headquartered in this fount of reaction would exact revenge on African-Americans.

In Buena Park a Molotov cocktail landed in the backyard of a black family, "striking apprehension that some whites might be assuming the role of avengers." An officer in Long Beach was killed, there was a related outburst in San Diego, and store windows were smashed in Pasadena. Reports of violence were received in San Bernadino to the east. In Bakersfield to the northeast, a dusty town of Okies, Molotov cocktails were tossed, there was an attempt to ransack a gun store, and white avengers sought to invade black areas with deadly weapons.[6]

There was concern that incidents would spread farther north to the San Francisco Bay area; there was nervous reassurance that "workers in this field don't think there is quite the degree of repressed hate against whites among Negroes here that was evident in Watts." Things may have been chilled up north, but in Des Moines the governor called out the National Guard to protect the Iowa State Fair. In faraway Washington, D.C., there was tangible fear that the predominantly black city would explode; some Euro-Americans there were reported to have "slept fitfully."[7] Watts was a factor in subsequent major conflagrations in Detroit, Newark, Miami, and other urban battlefields. Though police in Detroit "carefully studied" Watts, that did not help appreciably when the city went up in flames in 1967. Tactics deployed in the streets of South LA by protesters were emulated by their counterparts across the nation.[8]

Nor did the specter of Watts stop at the U.S. border. There was fear that the example of Watts would be imitated in Britain. Headlines about "Race Wars" showed up in Sunday papers in Europe, and editorials in the United

Kingdom backed the Labour government's pending plan to curb immigration from the West Indies and Asia.[9] Television stations in Germany and newspapers and magazines from Milan to Sweden, from Australia to Vancouver, provided coverage.[10] Writing from Athens, *New York Times* columnist C. L. Sulzberger warned that although preventing future uprisings would "cost not only immense sums but also immense effort," it was not just a "matter of internal U.S. policy. It is also a matter of vital foreign policy."[11]

■

On 16 August at 1:53 A.M., Aubrey Griffin, a thirty-eight-year-old native of Oklahoma, was Monday's first victim. This thin, 5-foot-11-inch, 156-pound black man worked at the Berkshire Furniture Store. He received eleven shotgun wounds in his chest at his home at 314 West 93d Street. The LAPD officers had gone there because he had reputedly shot at a guardsman minutes earlier. When he refused their demand to come outside with his hands raised, they shot through the closed door and killed him.

His wife, Rowena Griffin, disputed this version of events. "We were in bed, and we heard a noise, something scaring us; we got up. . . . We started to the hall and my husband told me to stay in the bedroom. . . . I heard the front door close. I heard all the shots come in my house." "No time" elapsed between the door closing and the shots being fired, she said. Aubrey Gene Griffin, Jr., home from his post in the U.S. Air Force, was watching television as his father stepped outside; fifteen seconds passed, then he came back inside, "closed the door, took a step, and then a volley of bullets came through the front door."

John L. Freitas of the guard alleged that he had been fired on at 93d and Broadway. He spotted Griffin. "Well, there was a warning to 'Raise your hands,' etc.; and this person ran inside the house." Freitas was twenty yards away and shouted for Griffin to "come out." A combined force of twenty-five LAPD and guardsmen surrounded the house. "The lighting was very good; visible." Frona Garcia of the guard heard the original shot at Freitas and saw Griffin two minutes later. When the LAPD arrived and went to the house, the officers demanded that Griffin raise his hands, but he ran inside. The "lighting was real good. . . . It was a clear night."

The LAPD's Glen Roy Mozingo was told that a man "shot at them [the guard] from the house with the light on the porch." He saw Griffin running into the house and demanded that he come out. The response, he said, was a blunt "Fuck you. Come in and get me." Two shots rang out, and the door slammed, whereupon they opened fire. No gun was found on the body. Gary Walter Boyd of the LAPD, one of fifteen police officers there, agreed with his partner, Mozingo. "I had a 12-gauge shotgun I borrowed from a friend. . . . I saw Mr. Griffin run into the house . . . I shot twice with my shotgun towards the front door." He entered the rear of the house, and "there was still some shooting going on. . . . So, I had to crawl on the floor, and I started crawling down the hall." He was not certain, but "it appeared to me, sir, that [shots] did come from the front porch." Pierce Brooks of the LAPD testified that a search after the shooting led to recovery of a .32-caliber weapon; "however, the investigators that looked at this gun, one of them an expert, told me that, in his opinion, this gun had not been recently fired."[12]

It seems that a mistake was made, and Aubrey Griffin, a working man, a husband, a father—a living contradiction of traditional ideas about the black family—paid with his life. Though the zenith of the uprising had long since passed, the LAPD did not hesitate to shoot first and ask questions later.

The streets of South LA were emptying, and the curfew was being observed, but there was another problem. The massive publicity had brought sightseers to the streets. By the morning of 17 August, thoroughfares were "jammed bumper to bumper." Others seeking to see the now famous Watts from the freeway had to be protected from residents dropping objects from the overpass by posted guardsmen. Ringling Brothers and Barnum and Bailey canceled their shows in the curfew zone, incurring a $250,000 loss. Angelenos had found another sight to galvanize their attention: the aftermath of an uprising. But they were premature. There was more violence to come. The LAPD had decided to go the presumed source of the problem by attacking the temple of the Nation of Islam.[13]

■

The Nation of Islam, the religious sect headed by Elijah Muhammad, whose antiwhite theology was combined with black nationalism, had established a major base in Los Angeles. Many factors help to explain this; the color consciousness of Black LA provided fertile ground for the NOI's denunciations of the "white devils." The shallow historical roots of Black LA combined with the Negrophobia they were forced to endure made African-Americans there highly susceptible to the call of the NOI. The Red Scare and the concomitant abandonment of class struggle (and blacks) by many unions led, according to Donald Craig Parson, to "dissensious" politics or the "autonomous movement, unmediated by the party or state." This too helped to propel the NOI.[14]

As the 1960s dawned the NOI stood as one of the few symbols of militance in Black LA. The NAACP chapter had long since been identified as striving for middle-class goals with middle-class leadership, which automatically excluded the majority of African-Americans, who happened to be working class. The thrust of the NOI program was middle class—opening businesses—and it recruited heavily in prisons and among the lumpen proletariat, yet the abandonment of the black working class by unions and civil rights organizations made this sector susceptible to NOI blandishments also.

The reputation of the NOI was burnished—ironically—because the LAPD tended to perceive it as a threat; hence, there was a "rapid growth of that city's Black Muslim temple." A quirky local black newspaper, the *Herald-Dispatch*, "had forged an editorial and financial alliance with the Nation of Islam and had begun publishing a weekly column by Malcolm [X] entitled 'God's Angry Men.'" A biographer of Malcolm X, Bruce Perry, has stated the NOI got the idea of starting its newspaper, *Muhammad Speaks*—probably its principal device for extending its influence—from its LA experience.[15]

In 1962 a violent shoot-out between the LAPD and the NOI had left a number of Muslims and one officer wounded. The NOI alleged this battle was precipitated when "more than 100 savage policemen crashed their way into Mosque NO. 27 without warning or provocation, shooting and killing and leaving in their wake, one dead, Ronald Stokes, two permanently crippled and several others wounded." William 12X Rogers was one of those left "paralyzed from the waist down for life, his spine shattered by a police bullet."[16] Endearing the NOI to Black LA was the fact that Elijah Muhammad provided Rogers with an electric car so that he could get around. This gesture and the overriding fact that the NOI seemed to be the only organized force interested in confronting the hated LAPD brought more adherents to their door.

An all-white coroner's jury ruled that Stokes's death was justifiable homicide. What also led to admiration of the NOI was the rumor—apparently not totally inaccurate—that "Black Muslims" from coast to coast converged on LA as a result for the purposes of revenge. According to Bruce Perry, "Eventually a number of brothers secretly decided to act on their own. They began hanging out at night on skid row. Vengefully, they fell upon their inebriated, solitary victims, some of whom did not survive." This continued until Malcolm X called a halt to the bloodletting.[17]

Los Angeles proved essential in the evolution of Malcolm X and his split with the Nation of Islam. After this confrontation with the LAPD, Malcolm longed to concentrate further on the secular concern of police brutality; however, he was reined in by Elijah Muhammad, who feared such a confrontation with the authorities and steadfastly maintained that he was leading a religious sect, not a political organization. Still, rumors about NOI retaliation—true or not—inevitably reached the ears of the LAPD. It seems that the LAPD began to target the easily identifiable well-dressed NOI members with their bowties, closed-cropped haircuts, and *Muhammad Speaks* in hand.[18] The resultant tensions confirmed some of Elijah Muhammad's worst fears.

By 1965 the LAPD-NOI relationship had frayed. Weeks before the uprising the Board of Police Commissioners was meeting to discuss the issue of NOI members hawking their papers at 8th and Wall streets, near the Traffic Court Building. The board requested an opinion from the city attorney, seeking to ascertain if this activity could be barred. Beginning in May 1965 "a total of five man hours was extended in surreptitiously photographing these persons with moving pictures at distances of from 30 to 100 feet." This eight-minute film showed that the NOI modus operandi was "to take one of their papers from under their left arm, place it in their right hand, and walk along for several paces at the side of a potential customer with the newspaper near the front portion of the customer's body." This approach allowed the NOI to proselytize, even if a paper was not sold, a further worry for nervous police.[19]

When South LA erupted, a ready-made villain was already in place—the NOI. Though some, in the fashion of the day, pointed to "Communist" agitators as the villain, this was a hard proposition to sell in the wake of a thorough Red Scare and routing of the left. Attorney General Thomas Lynch pointed to NOI leader John Shabazz as the man who lit the fuse. As early as April, Lynch had fingered the NOI as a "potential, present and future danger" to the nation. Chief Parker concurred. A representative of Mayor Yorty cited their "hate" literature.[20]

Monna Utter of Albuquerque worriedly wrote the McCone Commission and confided that an "old gentleman in Puente" passed on the information that a train had gone through town carrying "train loads of Negros." She wondered, "Is it possible that Black Muslim type haters could have been sent to the ghetto population centers to provoke violence?" Gary Allen of the Birch Society fused the Red and Black scares by claiming that the revolt was "planned, engineered and instigated" by "some forty to fifty Negroes sent by the Communists into" LA by an "intellectual elite" called "The Organization." This, he claimed, was the result of a Communist-NOI alliance.[21]

An "anonymous letter" from Philadelphia not only blamed the NOI for the revolt but alleged a NOI tie with the "Black Dragon Society" and that Elijah Muhammad was the "son of a Japanese Intelligence Officer." That this claim was communicated via a high-level government official lent it a certain credibility. A related analysis sought to blame Charlie Sims of the Deacons for Defense and Justice, who had been on the radio before the revolt, but it too referred to the "Black Dragons . . . founded in 1930 in Detroit by Major Satakata Takahashi (alias Naka Nakane) . . . of the Japanese Imperial Intelligence Service." Elijah Muhammad, the analysis continued, "is of Japanese-Negro parentage, Takahashi is his father." It was noted that when Malcolm X was shot, the first person to reach his side was a woman of Japanese descent.[22] Just as the Red Scare involved the specter of Moscow, the Black Scare invoked Tokyo.

These allegations about the NOI were being ventilated at the highest levels. Attorney General Ramsey Clark was dispatched by the White House to monitor events in South LA. During the afternoon of 16 August, he was informed by a "confidential source of unknown reliability" that the NOI "held a meeting yesterday of 200 members. At this meeting the Muslims allegedly took credit for the Los Angeles riots and made plans to burn Jewish owned businesses in the troubled area. The Muslims also allegedly threatened to kill [Dr. King] if he comes to [LA]."[23]

Part of the problem was that a fine distinction was not being drawn between instigation by the NOI and the influence of the NOI. For example, when asked how he knew that the NOI and not someone else was involved in a specific anti-LAPD activity, John Buggs did not point to the members' distinctive dress but their language: "Generally Black Muslims refer to other Negroes as Brother. This is not a euphemism that is always used by Negroes to each other."[24] But Buggs should have known that things were changing; soon many blacks were addressing each other as "brother" and "sister," and certainly, all were not part of the NOI. However, his statement was suggestive of the ideological hegemony being established by the NOI.

Curiously, much of Black LA was identifying with Malcolm X, who had been estranged from the NOI at the time of his death in early 1965 in part because he wanted to move the NOI in a more political direction; his opponents preferred more emphasis on theology. Yet, it was these same opponents who, ironically, benefited from Malcolm's murder and reaped the benefits in Black LA of the political direction they had rejected.

Archie Hardwick of South LA's Westminster Neighborhood Association was pointed about this in an interview. "This was a male revolt directed at the white power structure. . . . they identify with Malcolm X's philosophy." This androcentric attitude reflected the real problem that the matrifocal black society had in adjusting to the patriarchal United States and, in addition, to the developing male chauvinist black nationalism. Hardwick also touched on a real issue of separatism that was to bedevil the mainstream civil rights movement. Following Malcolm X and the so-called Five Percenters, he said, black youth "found meaningful" the "belief that since the Negro won't be accepted by the white society he must live and create his own society." [25]

■

The final act in the Watts Uprising took place on 18 August—exactly one week after the commotion had begun—when the LAPD assaulted the Muslim Temple. Minister John Shabazz of the NOI had charged two days before that the LAPD and the National Guard were seeking to provoke an incident. They had made, he said, "filthy remarks and have taunted us by flashing lights in the window."

The guard and LAPD were frustrated, for they had wanted to confront a detachment face to face, but like the Redcoats in 1776 and the U.S. military in Vietnam, they had been forced to deal with diffuse guerrilla bands instead. The Muslim Temple at 5606 South Broadway was the kind of stationary target they had been pining for. They bombarded it with between 500 and 1,000 rounds of ammunition; fifty-nine Muslims were arrested, and eight others were cut by flying glass.[26]

Though the authorities denied it vehemently, LAPD informant Louis Tackwood claimed subsequently that he—at the instigation of the Special Investigations Section of the LAPD—"made the controversial anonymous phone call August 18, 1965 informing Newton Division police that guns were stashed at the Black Muslim Mosque." The LAPD's story was different, though not necessarily in contradiction with Tackwood's, claiming it had adequate provocation for its actions. The point that could not be avoided, however, was that no arms were confiscated from the temple.[27]

The previous hours in the city had been typically turbulent. The Rams-Cowboys game proceeded, though the crowd of 31,579 at the 90,000-seat Coliseum—in the heart of the curfew zone—was noticeably on edge. In Maywood a sniper fired at police from a second-floor surplus department store. Shotgun-carrying officers captured him minutes later. They had expected to nab an African-American, but twenty-six-year-old Nikolai Pakhomoff described himself as Persian.

This uproar was mild compared to what happened on South Broadway. The official report was that an anonymous call was made at 1:43 A.M. to the LAPD. By this time 12,400 guardsmen—the entire 40th Armored Division—were in the process of withdrawing from LA. The caller said there were arms and other illicit materiel at the temple. Said Sergeant William Biddell, "When we pulled up, pellets" started "pounding the car and we were immediately in a train of heavy fire." A sheriff's car reportedly was hit twice on the roof, and there were other reports of shots fired in the surrounding vicinity. The officers crouched behind cars, firing into the building. The two-story stucco building was besieged; soon it was riddled with bullets, and every window was broken. Officers entered the building. Files were removed, along with membership lists. Muslims were fleeing in all directions, including—it was said—into the sewers. Other Muslims were led away with shotguns aimed at their heads.[28]

The *LA Times* was pleased with the comeuppance doled out to the uppity Muslims. "The fanatical Black Muslims never have permitted a white man to enter their mosque." But, the newspaper announced, that "taboo was broken Wednesday." There was seditious literature about. "The floor was littered with hundreds of leaflets which exhorted, 'Stop Police Brutality.'" The newspaper was shocked by other touches. "On a chair, strangely for the Muslims are non-Christians, was a painting of Jesus Christ." The *Times,* the paper of record for the state, apparently was unaware that the NOI often employed Christian symbolism to attract African-Americans to Islam; it was a reason for the group's popularity in Black LA.[29]

The *Times* did not bother to investigate the flimsy LAPD story, as it had neglected to ask questions about the preceding spate of killings by the LAPD. However, Assemblyman Mervyn Dymally and City Councilman Billy Mills were not as restrained. Mills, in particular, did yeoman service, as his investigation involved a reading of the transcripts of the police, fire, and civil defense committees of the council that inquired into the assault, together with reports from the police department, fire department, and the hospital that treated the victims. He also personally inspected the premises. His conclusion was simple: the attack was an "unwarranted, unjustified and irresponsible use of police power." He was suspicious of why an anonymous telephone call would lead to the dispatching of forces from the guard, LAPD, sheriff's office, and highway patrol.[30]

Dymally wondered why the authorities shot into the temple before issuing a warning and why those taken into custody were "quietly released." He was not alone in his skepticism. Frank Miller, president and manager of the United Veterans Club, located at 5874 South Broadway near the temple, said that at the time the temple was being assaulted, the LAPD smashed windows of cars on the street and attacked other buildings unlucky enough to be close to the NOI headquarters. He said that as many as "25 shots" were fired into an apartment over a garage at 5868 South Broadway; "twenty-four shots hit the sign above the roof of the club. In all, approximately 300 shots hit the front of the club and the barber shop next door." Bullets pierced the walls of the club and "the barber shop next door." What had begun on 11 August as a black uprising primarily against the police had concluded with a police uprising against blacks.[31]

Councilman Mills was incensed and sought to use this incident as a lever to reform the LAPD. The problem was obtaining cooperation. Witnesses were afraid to testify. News organizations were reluctant to give him footage of the raid. The normally somnolent Board of Police Commissioners that was duty-bound to ride herd over the LAPD made, in his opinion, a "concerted effort to sweep the incident under the carpet to protect the image of the department." Yet he kept digging, revealing later that the LAPD may have set fire to the temple.[32]

The McCone Commission also raised questions about the police version of events. It relied heavily on the eyewitness account of Robert L. Brock, a forty-one-year-old black veteran originally from Shreveport, who lived nearby at 600 West 54th Street. At 1:30 A.M. he saw the LAPD "without provocation" fire on the temple. If his story was correct, commission investigator William Gilkey concluded, "this would refute allegations of testifying police officers as to the exact time of the gunfire in the area surrounding the Muslim Temple."[33]

The NOI painted the scenario in apocalyptic terms. Elijah Muhammad answered his own question as to why the LAPD would do such a deed. "For what? Just because they are devils and that is their nature. Allah revealed them as a race of devils. They were created to hate, deceive, murder and kill the black man." He told his followers that "they desire an excuse to shoot and kill the Muslims" but "'vengeance is mine', saith the Lord and 'I will repay.'" *Muhammad Speaks* predicted that the raid was the "prelude to America's doom!"[34] The NOI rhetoric would have seemed out of place in LA twenty years earlier; in 1965 it fell on receptive ears in Black LA.

One might think that the invasion and destruction of a house of worship by the state would have galvanized those who viewed the First Amendment at holy writ. But the local press yawned when it did not cheer. It was left to the *LA Sentinel,* the black paper, to warn, "If we deny full protection of the law to the Black Muslims, then we will soon begin bending our laws and protective powers to exclude Negro Catholics, red-haired Baptists, green-eyed Presbyterians, dark-haired American Legionaires and grey-eyed Shriners." Outside the black community, these words were falling on deaf ears.[35]

Inside the black community the raid helped to propel the NOI to folk hero status. The Watts Uprising was decentralized; it was a mass uprising and not organized in inception and conception. However, it was mostly hailed by a South LA community reeling from police brutality, unemployment, and other ills. It was scorned by many others, who sought to blame the NOI for the disruption. In response the NOI's stock soared among younger blacks particularly, because the Muslims were one of the few organized forces who seemed to be confronting the authorities with militance.

The apotheosis of this process came when Marquette Frye, the man whose arrest triggered the uprising, joined the NOI. It was ironic that one of the reasons for the falling out between Malcolm X and the NOI was the secular path he preferred, focusing on police brutality and related urban ills. Yet the NOI, at least in LA, was following the path of this heretic. On 15 August, Frye spoke at the temple. The handbills advertising his appearance bore the slogan, "Stop Police Brutality."[36]

Frey's recruitment was a coup for the NOI and a sign of its heightened profile among blacks. Even Harlem congressman Adam Clayton Powell, always alert to the direction of the prevailing winds, seemed to be edging closer to the NOI's banner. The hearings of his House Education and Labor subcommittee held in Watts in the midst of the rubble were trumpeted in *Muhammad Speaks.*[37]

The NOI continued moving steadily down the secular path; in its paper, next to the photo of the ultimate radical, Che Guevara, was an article lambasting the "KKK-type police brutality" of the LAPD.[38] Minister John Shabazz of the NOI in LA was exhibiting the signs of celebrity, cited increasingly in the press and facing more threats and harassment from opponents.[39]

The only coherent explanation that seemed to make sense to Black LA—tales of mad scientists creating evil white devils and the absence of competing narratives aside—was that of the NOI. Its concept of the white man as devil may not have been accepted in full, but certainly the tendency to engage in group stereotyping—the essence of Negrophobia—was being reversed and turned on Euro-Americans. Moreover, the behavior of the LAPD—before, during, and after the revolt—seemed satanic to many.

This left LA elites in a quandary. Asa Call of the McCone Commission wanted to avoid "witnesses who have extremist or prejudiced positions. . . . By this I mean racists, Muslims, etc." Yet, he wanted the commission to examine "the influence and leadership of Muslims in the Watts community" as a priority. How it could perform the latter task without talking to the NOI was left unexplained.[40]

Similarly, the commission felt compelled to pay obeisance to the new nationalism that the NOI symbolized. Other commissioners wanted Minister Shabazz to testify in Watts in order "to gain the confidence of the people"; moreover, they were advised to "be sure to have colored lawyers present—that an all-white Commission and staff would hinder the investigations." The presence of the NOI had become the touchstone of credibility in Watts. The new nationalism also had led to affirmative-action decisions that at least benefited some black lawyers.[41]

The NOI faced its own quandary. After all, it was for separatism, which was part of its attraction in Watts; yet, it was increasingly being drawn into nitty-gritty domestic concerns, such as police brutality, a path that had led directly to the estrangement of Malcolm X. When a team from the commission met with Minister Shabazz, his lawyer, Edward Jacko, tried to place responsibility for the negative image of the NOI on misstatements by Malcolm X and added that, in any event, the NOI did not want to be involved in solving poverty and other domestic problems since separatism was the answer.[42]

Though thousands may not have been joining the NOI, thousands were supporting it ideologically. Mervyn Dymally, the South LA assemblyman of Trinidadian and East Indian extraction, took note of the statement in the *Sacramento Bee* that "the quickest way for a Negro to gain self-respect seems to be to stand up to the white man or to taunt 'Uncle Tom' at any Negro leader who does not voice hatred of 'Whitey.'"[43]

After the uprising Ron Karenga and other newly minted nationalists organized "the first in what is planned to be an annual memorial service for Malcolm X" at 5326 South Central Avenue; his widow, Betty Shabazz, was scheduled to speak.[44] Shortly after that, plans were bruited for the incorporation of Watts as "Freedom City," an idea seen as consistent with the newly developed "Black Power" thesis of the Student Non-Violent Coordinating Committee and viewed as an aspect of the rapidly developing separatism. Symptomatic of the times was that the moderate Yvonne Brathwaite, who had just been working for the McCone Commission, did not frown at the idea.[45]

The NOI's growing popularity in South LA was signified when *Jet*, the popular black weekly, warned about the "challenge" presented by "LA Muslims" to "Negro leadership in [the] Ghetto." Even Dr. King, it said, had to "invoke the name of Elijah Muhammad to get a hearing in the riot-scarred community."[46] Maurice Dawkins, black and a future Republican then serving as associate director of VISTA, an antipoverty agency, warned bluntly that the choice was stark: "We shall convert Muslims rather than let Muslims convert us." He counseled a massive effort to convert NOI members to Christianity.[47]

Such dire predictions and remedies were symptomatic of the fact that a turning point had been reached in Black LA. The revolt had propelled the NOI forward, and along with it a new militant, antiwhite style. After comparing Watts-LA and Woodstock-Capetown, James O'Toole agreed that August 1965 marked a departure in that it inspired Black LA not to internalize anger but to express it outwardly. Analysts were discovering that in the aftermath of the revolt, there had developed a correlation between positive views of the NOI and black militance. Tom Tomlinson added, "In the eyes of most black and white citizens the Black Muslims were the only exponents of black radicalism."[48]

A confidential planning document prepared by law enforcement authorities to counter a future revolt focused not only on "the Negro" but also "the Black Muslims." The document stressed that now they must treat blacks with "extreme courtesy" in order to defuse their anger, "irregardless of poverty." Fortunately, they reassured themselves, this was a localized phenomenon: "The above conditions are peculiar to the Watts and Willowbrook area. We have other Negro communities where the above is not true." It was unclear if the "childish minds" it ascribed to blacks were found only in Watts-Willowbrook or also in these tamer areas.[49]

Blacks were changing in the aftermath of the uprising; much of their language had begun to reflect the new nationalism epitomized by the NOI.[50] White elites were paying attention. Richard Simon, a high-level official of the LAPD, though he compared the NOI to Nazis, stated flatly that except for the NOI, blacks had insufficient pride.[51] What was evolving was a grudging acceptance of the NOI and the new nationalism. This was understandable, for unlike the Red Scare—which raised a threat to what was dearer than life itself, private property—the so-called Black Scare as evidenced by the NOI stood for separatism and was ambivalent about dipping into public coffers to fight poverty. Here was a scare that could possibly be accommodated, particularly if police brutality could be contained.

The ultraright American Eugenics party went further in endorsing the new nationalism, in particular its separatist overtones, in language that could have been lifted from the nationalists themselves: "Only negro police should patrol the negro area. . . . The negro community should have only negro employers and employees. . . . Negro nationalist groups should be encouraged so that a measure of 'pride' in their race can be held up as a symbol." Of course, there was also language that the new nationalist might have taken umbrage to: "Negroes on welfare, especially those not married, should be prohibited from having children." The party also advised that as many blacks as possible should be repatriated to Africa; many nationalists would have agreed about this too.[52] Some conservatives felt that nationalists' emphasis on identity was a welcome respite from the left's emphasis on income redistribution and working-class unity across racial lines.

∎

The Watts Uprising helped to set in motion a nationalism that filled an ideological void in Black LA. The Black Scare was unpredictable; it could and did present a threat to the person of some elite whites. The stories and pictures of whites being pulled from their cars and attacked were frightening to some with melanin deficiency. But, akin to the old Jack Benny joke, where the comedian is torn when the robber demands, "Your money or your life," LA elites recognized that the nationalists could be accommodated in a way that their militant predecessors of the left could not. As long as separatism was decoupled from reparations, the NOI-influenced nationalism not only did not present a threat to private property, it could even be helpful—along with racism—in keeping apart those who might want to unite jointly against the LAPD and the elites it was sworn to protect. The problem for blacks was that the blows from LAPD batons raining steadily down on their heads— overwhelmingly by white officers commanded by white elites—made any notion of "black and white unite and fight" seem like a delirious dream not even worthy of Hollywood.

7

Iron Fist

THE LOS ANGELES POLICE DEPARTMENT HAS BEEN pointed to as the principal malefactor, the signal offender in angering blacks to the point of insurrection. Yet the LAPD was not a thing in itself; it did not operate autonomously but at the behest of the political and economic elites who administered the city. It is true that the LAPD had a certain amount of leeway because of the structure of the city's charter, but as the crisis in LA of 1991–92 over the beating of Rodney King and the firing of Daryl Gates demonstrated, this autonomy could melt when elites decided that it was engendering a counterproductive police brutality. Still, it cannot be denied that under the leadership of Chief William Parker, the LAPD seemed to take to the task of hammering African-Americans with a macabre relish. This was particularly so during the week of 11–18 August 1965.

The brutality of the LAPD was so obvious that it had not escaped the attention of usually circumspect journalists. In 1961 Theodore White called the force "the most cruel in the nation." Thirty years later Lou Cannon of the *Washington Post* was prompted to call LA a "police state" because of the depredations of the LAPD.[1] Even before the 1960s the LAPD's reputation for lawlessness had been well established. In the late 1930s the LAPD organized a "bum blockade" near California's desert borders—far from its jurisdiction— "to discourage dissidents from entering" the state. The department was notorious for its "widespread abuse" of Mexican-Americans "on the border as well as within the city." As for African-Americans, the LAPD was typically contradictory. It was one of the first departments to have black officers in uniform, "though it remained profoundly racist in its policies, allowing black

134

officers to work in only two areas, both of them in black communities . . . police patrols were also segregated . . . black officers were not allowed to patrol a white beat." The LAPD was venal; it had a reputation for being one of the more corrupt departments, notably in the 1930s and 1940s when it countenanced the involvement of mobsters in gambling and other illicit activities.[2]

Like Tom Bradley, Earl Broady of the McCone Commission—then serving locally as a judge—had been one of LA's early black officers. In 1965 he reflected on a time when "all Negro traffic officers worked on Alameda Street, and you got that exhaust and smoke all day long. All of us had to work on Alameda Street. There was a great stink about this thing. . . . Also, all Negro officers always work in the Newton Division. . . . Now they say they ought to be congregated where they can take care of Negroes, and they don't want to do this."[3]

Recalling those days, Joe Walker, a black officer, remarked: "I was just out of the academy when they teamed me up with this guy. . . . His policy was to stop and hopefully arrest any black man he observed in a more expensive automobile than he owned." His partner "amassed more felony arrests than anyone else in the division and in a relatively short period of time rose through the ranks to captain." Highlighting the force's continuing corruption, Walker also recalled that when the eruption finally came in 1965, among those seizing merchandise from stores were not only residents but LAPD officers as well.[4]

Mike Rothmiller, a white former officer, has drawn an ugly portrait of Negrophobia in the LAPD over the past few decades. "Racism was expected, part of the group persona. Shrink from it and you were an odd duck, perhaps a pink one. . . . race hatred was nonetheless a dominating force." Officers lied in arrest reports on routine felony cases. "Some loonies did manage to bluff their way through the department's psychological screenings. . . . These were crazies whose ultimate goal was to waste someone, lunatics who liked nothing better than to inflict pain." Some officers randomly and arbitrarily beat and tortured black men, even those who were not suspected of anything. "Bending fingers back, twisting ears, tightening handcuffs into medieval torture devices, slamming the victim's head into the door while placing him in a vehicle" were some of their milder techniques. "Sometimes they dangled suspects by their ankles from the edge of buildings." Overwhelmingly, their illegalities were perpetrated against black men, who were perceived to be least able to protest effectively.[5]

During the Christmas season of 1959, in a typical maneuver, the LAPD gave out official bulletins to merchants describing how African-American and Chicano shoplifters operated; nothing was said about white shoplifters. This was just a continuation of a department policy that explicitly set a quota on arrests of blacks. Raids and arbitrary arrests of suspects in Black LA led to inflated statistics, which led to more raids and arrests, which led fearful white constituents and politicians to approve Chief Parker's ravenous demands for more resources and influence. The resultant police records handicapped those blacks when they applied for jobs.[6]

Police units were integrated in 1961; and despite the small number of black officers, this may have abated the brutal practices. But immediately preceding the insurrection, there were a series of serious clashes between blacks and officers. Things seemed to reach a peak during the crucial election year of 1964. Despite this horrendous record, the *LA Times* consistently opposed the idea of a civilian review board to rein in the department.[7]

Black women were not immune from assault by the authorities. Sonora McKeller recalled later the many stories "over the years," told "too often to discount." "A woman is walking home alone after dark. The patrolmen pull their car up to the curb, get out and flash a light in the woman's face. She is asked to walk a certain distance and told that she is under the influence of either narcotics or alcohol and that she is to get into the car to be taken to jail. She is next driven to a secluded spot, assaulted and beaten."[8]

Why was the LAPD so brutal? There were many targets for its hatred—not just African-Americans but Latinos, Asian-Americans, and Native Americans too—and this might have compounded racism geometrically and exponentially. After the beating of black motorist Rodney King in March 1991, veteran LA litigator Stephen Yagman said that brutality may be worse in LA because officers were compensating for the fact that LA was so large and sprawling yet had a comparatively low ratio of police to citizens.[9] This brutality was a form of draconian deterrence, intended to make potential lawbreakers think twice before risking arrest by the LAPD.

The notorious 77th Street Division—in the heart of the August 1965 curfew zone—was a veritable heart of darkness for Black LA. One angry black complained that "you'll find more people in jail in the 77th Precinct than anywhere in the city of Los Angeles, on suspicion, suspicion . . . don't wear tennis shoes, because if you wear tennis shoes, you might go to jail, you might go to jail for suspicion. . . . They search you in all ways. You spread your legs."[10] Tennis shoes were not viewed by the LAPD as comfortable footgear but as "felony flyers" that could be used to escape quickly from the scene of a crime.

With little internal check on the LAPD, the department was left to investigate itself. The Board of Police Commissioners, which some thought should be the departmental watchdog, was a toothless terrier. In 1964 there were more excessive force complaints from whites than blacks—sixty-three versus forty-two (as well as thirteen from Latinos and three from "others")—though this may have been a function of black reluctance to step forward. In 1964, 12 officers resigned in lieu of disciplinary action, 11 were removed after hearings, and 9 were suspended; 470 officers altogether received disciplinary action during this year.[11]

At the apex of the LAPD and symbol of their iron-fist policy toward blacks was Chief William Parker, a native of South Dakota who arrived in Southern California in 1927 with his parents. He passed the bar in 1930 and earned his military spurs during World War II. This military experience epitomized a central problem with the LAPD: it approached the policing of Black LA as if it were an alien community during wartime. Chief Parker boasted about his experience in helping to "plan the invasion of France" and as "one of 1500 men in the theater that were privileged to read all of the invasion plans." This, he suggested, had been helpful experience in subduing South LA.[12] He helped to train the police in Germany after the war, and this experience may have been a factor recommending him when he was appointed chief in 1950.

Quickly he distinguished himself for his propensity to make one insulting statement after another about African-Americans and Chicanos. "You cannot ignore the genes in the behavior pattern of people" was Parker's comment on the significant number from these two minorities that wound up in prison. During the uprising he compared blacks to "monkeys in a zoo." He once noted that "of all types of professional people, workers and citizens, women school-teachers have the least respect for police officers." As flames consumed the city, he conjectured—inaccurately—that LA would be 45 percent black by 1970 and wondered, "Now how are you going to live with that without law enforcement."[13]

Despite its bluster and reputation for toughness, the LAPD was unprepared to confront the guerrilla tactics deployed in Watts during the insurrection. Yet at the hearing before the McCone Commission, weeks after the raid on the NOI Temple, Parker was typically cantankerous and unapologetic. He blamed the California Highway Patrol and its initial handling of the arrest of the Fryes for the conflagration. He castigated tacticians of civil disobedience such as Dr. King and the communications media for their presumed role in generating conflict. CORE and the NOI came in for special condemnation. Yet he could not avoid admitting being bewildered about the turn of events. "I had never read about a riot that ran this way, where the people rested the first night and then the next night. . . . Our men were, I think, as perplexed by this spectacle as anyone else, and if you look at the film . . . you will see their hesitation to move." [14]

This bewilderment did not prevent his legions of supporters, especially in the San Fernando Valley and among whites, from praising his savage crushing of the uprising. He was inundated with commendations. However, there was no "white united front" backing the chief. Republicans in the state assembly failed in a bid to praise him officially over the stalwart objections of Democrats. [15]

Winslow Christian, a former superior court judge then serving as executive secretary to the governor, was caustic in his evaluation of Parker, taking pointed exception to the chief's notion that "they are underneath and we are on top at this point" in reference to South LA–police relations. [16] Even the Federal Bureau of Investigation expressed concern about his stewardship; relations were so icy that officers were not allowed to go to the FBI's training academy, though Parker maintained the reason was because he resisted the effort to establish a national clearinghouse on organized crime, as occurred under Attorney General Robert Kennedy. [17]

There was an organized presence of ultrarightists within the department. Michael Hannon, who worked there for seven years, pointed out in 1965 that at the Newton police station—in a district where relations with blacks were less than ideal—the lunchroom "resembled nothing so much as a Birch Society 'Americanism Center.' Rightist propaganda such as Life Lines, Human Events, Dan Smoot Report, and American Opinion abounded." The department allowed Fred Schwarz and his rabidly racist Christian Anti-Communist Crusade to hold meetings at stations and encouraged officers to attend. Yet Hannon was subjected to disciplinary action because he worked with the Socialist party. When Major General Edwin Walker, the rebellious and racist officer who had stirred up much strife in the Deep South, appeared at the Shrine Auditorium in July 1965 to support Proposition 14 and other racist policies, a number of police officers attended. [18]

The John Birch Society had a foothold in the department. By some estimates there were 2,000 members in various area law enforcement agencies.[19] By other estimates there were 2,000 members in the department alone, or roughly one-third of the membership.[20] High-level political leaders who knew about this infiltration apparently did not consider it important enough to question publicly. Though a "law and order" mentality dominated the department, LA during the 1960s led the nation in bombings—conducted mostly by neo-Nazis and the ultraright—and few of the perpetrators were brought to justice.[21]

The Community Relations branch of the department made sporadic efforts to rein in the ultrarightists. Memorandums were issued demanding that officers desist from "thoughtlessly wearing campaign slogans and insignia on visible portions of their clothing while on duty." Many white officers supported Proposition 14 in 1964, interpreted widely as a racist initiative. Directives were issued mandating that "objectionable material" concerning this measure and related sensitive topics be kept off bulletin boards at stations, but this too was widely ignored.[22] At the same time Hannon and the left were hampered severely by official and unofficial means from circulating their views in a like manner.

Days after the rebellion City Councilman Tom Bradley complained about "scurrilous" fake NAACP membership forms found on station bulletin boards reading: "Marital status: Check one: Shacked up___Making out___Worn out___Still trying___" and "I believe in equality: that Niggers is better than white folks is" and "Make of auto: Check: Lincoln___ Imperial___Cadillac___."[23]

Right-wing officers and firefighters combined to form the Fire and Police Research Association, which published the *Fi-Po News*. According to William Becker, an assistant to the governor, FPRA was "the organizational base of the radical right and possibly the organization front of Birchers and people more extreme than that." Its agenda was the usual hodgepodge, ranging from blaming the revolt on the Reds to blasting Bob Dylan. Its influence on the department—membership aside—was palpable. Captain Thomas King of the LAPD thought blacks to be inferior, considered the civil rights movement to be Communist dominated, and praised the Birch Society. His views were far from being atypical.[24]

Such views often were translated into action in the streets. Patterns of brutality tended to escalate in 1965. Congressman Augustus Hawkins of

South LA found the LAPD to be "abusive and arrogant" and accused them of trying "to control things by force." [25] This abuse cut across class lines in the black community; white officers often bore a fiery resentment toward black middle-class men driving expensive cars. These officers evidently could not tolerate this violation of the credo that blacks should remain "hewers of wood and drawers of water." Simultaneously, their monolithic handling of blacks heightened nationalism among the black middle class and made it more difficult for them to conceive of themselves as distinct from their less affluent brethren. James Williams, executive director of the LA World Trade Center Authority, said in 1965 that he had been stopped while driving twelve times by the LAPD in the past six years and was treated roughly each time. [26]

Willie F. Brown, an unemployed migrant from Mississippi, married with two children and a resident of 12609 South Willowbrook, recalled seeing handcuffed black men beaten with batons by officers. [27] Bill Lane of the *LA Sentinel* was flabbergasted when he saw officers "both white . . . making a Negro woman 'walk the line.' She had been driving her car, had banged into the back of a white couple's car at a stop light. Her speech was thick. Her eyes were somewhat glassy. . . . The crowd which had gathered was obviously put out over the scene, which was on Central Avenue near Vernon. . . . To me, the whole thing was something that should not have been conducted on the street." [28]

Even with the indignities, the August detonation could have been avoided if prophylactic measures such as a vigilant police commission had been in place. However, the United Civil Rights Committee, a mainstream grouping, had filed numerous complaints with the Board of Police Commissioners that were met with pro forma—and hostile—investigations designed to clear officers of culpability. [29] A report by the local American Civil Liberties Union affiliate concluded that "police malpractice is a very real thing, a routine of false arrests, illegal searches, rousts, beatings, intimidations, verbal abuse and official sanction by inaction, and no Negro is immune." The "roust," or illegal arrests to get people off the streets, was frequently used in South LA. This was accompanied by disparate treatment. Along Central Avenue when officers pulled a traffic violator to the curb, they approached the car with drawn guns; but the guns were holstered in similar circumstances in the valley or West LA or Hollywood. Traffic violators were frisked as a matter of course in Watts; not so in predominantly white areas. Yet police illegality was not directed against African-Americans solely. The ACLU concluded that illegal searches and seizures and illegal arrests were rampant in LA, and blacks were not the only victims.[30]

Thus, what began as a black "riot" aimed principally at the police became quickly a police riot aimed principally at blacks. As the flames were still leaping, a *Sentinel* editorial complained that too often "white policemen come into minority neighborhoods reflecting a chip on both shoulders by their attitudes." The tactics scored by the ACLU were used with promiscuity, along with invading homes to make arrests without benefit of warrants. In short, by August 1965 South LA was under paramilitary siege.[31]

It worsened with the Frye arrest. Richard Brice, thirty, a shopowner at 11701 South Avalon, agreed with those who recalled seeing an officer "jamming" a club into Marquette Frye's stomach. "When that happened, all the people standing around got mad." So did he. Bobby Daniels, twenty-three, a maintenance man living at 852½ West 61st Street, had just returned from fishing. "We got out of the car and these 15 officers ran up to us. They jabbed us in the back with clubs and told us to get off the street. They jumped . . . on us, laughing about it."[32] The consensus in the neighborhood was that the blatant behavior of the LAPD triggered the revolt.

Things got worse on 14 August and after. Bobby Daniels provided a sworn statement that the shotgun wounds in his chest and arms came at the hands of the LAPD on 12 August at 9:30 P.M. at Imperial and Avalon; the next day he saw thirty officers at 88th and Broadway fire into a crowd of fifty, standing seventy-five feet away. "I saw one boy fall and learned later he had been shot in the back of the head. At about the same time, I saw a woman dragged from her house with blood covering her back. . . . The police fired indiscriminately into the house." Two hours after Daniels was shot, Leslie Lackey was beaten mercilessly by four officers at 118th and Avalon.

Sarah Mae Barker of 1030½ East 46th Street was arrested on 13 August and taken into custody at the Sybil Brand Institute for Women until 29 August. When she returned home, she found that her home had been burglarized and all her furniture and clothes had been taken. She suspected police officers as the culprits. Her neighbor Emma Nieves corroborated this suspicion. On the afternoon of 17 August, the LAPD came to her home claiming they were searching for stolen goods; then other officers went to Barker's home, took her belongings, placed them in a guard truck, and drove away.

That same day Jesse Staten was at his apartment at 762 West Colden when two officers knocked on his door and said they wanted to look around.

He let them in. They inquired about the provenance of his television and asked for the receipt. He did not have it. So he was dragged off to the 77th Street station. Then he was released but had to walk home. "On Manchester and Broadway I saw a shirt on the sidewalk and I picked it up." He was stopped and arrested again and taken back to the 77th, then downtown "to the 'glass house.'" He spent seven nights at the Lincoln Heights jail before he was released.

Delois Wilson, a thirty-one-year-old, 5-foot-4-inch, 130-pound black woman residing at 3039 Shrine Place, was arrested on 14 August at 12:30 A.M. for looting. On her way to the store that evening, four police cars and a wagon approached. The officers "knocked me to the ground. One choked my neck between his legs and two or three . . . started beating me with their night sticks on my legs, chest, back and hip. I lost my wig, shoes and purse."

Later that day Leo Sanders was driving by Florence and Broadway but was stopped by "heavy traffic." Three officers approached. One "hit me with the butt of his gun, a shotgun, and another cop hit me with the butt of his shotgun on my left side. The other officer hit me on the right side. I fell in the street behind my car . . . I lay there in the street approximately 30 to 45 minutes before I was able to drive to a doctor. . . . I have never been arrested nor have I had any previous encounters with police officers."[33]

Other sources substantiate the broad point that a random, racist, arbitrary violence was unleashed against the residents of South LA during a hectic week in August 1965. Roadblocks were the site of a number of killings, and one photograph shows officers at one of these venues with an ominous sign reading, "Turn left or get shot." Suppose a driver was illiterate or could not read English well? Another photograph showed five black men lined up against a wall as six officers and two guardsmen with bayonets held them at bay.[34]

A *Times* reporter on 14 August spoke to a forty-year-old black woman who had lived in the city for seventeen years and who considered herself a "responsible" person. She stated: "I have never heard policemen talk like they did last night. . . . My husband and I saw 10 cops beating one man. My husband told the officers, 'You've got him handcuffed.' One of the officers answered, 'Get out of here nigger. Get out of here, all you niggers.'"[35]

Archie Lee Howard was stopped by the LAPD and the guard on 14 August in the evening at 68th and Hoover. "As I opened the door and stepped out with my hands up, a police officer began hitting me across the top of the head with his billy club." He was beaten three different times that evening by the LAPD. Black women were not exempted by the LAPD. Carrie Lee Smith was driving with her baby on 16 August but got stuck in traffic. She got out of her car to look around but was arrested and taken to the 77th. A "police officer named Anthony Joyce made a remark saying 'it must be jelly cause jam don't shake that way'" in a salacious reference to her buttocks. At the station "the people there [said] there were women there that was beaten, stomped, killed, shot. One woman had her teeth knocked out, another was shot in the side, another shot in the foot, one had her eye almost knocked almost out."[36]

DeKovan Richard Bowie recalled that "riding down the street the police didn't care who they shot at—they would just start shooting. Lots of people that I have come in contact with haven't even gone to a doctor. They are scared. They are doctoring on themselves." He heard officers refer to a resident as "black son of a bitch . . . need to be back in Africa."[37] Another black man, Larry Allen Overby, was on his way home on 18 August when a squad car with four officers pulled him aside. They questioned him, and "then one officer turned and hit me in the mouth causing the loss of 4 teeth and 8 broken."

With the quelling of resistance, it seemed that the LAPD—ironically—escalated its cruelty. In a sworn statement Benjamin Doakes averred that on 18 August at 3:30 A.M. he was sitting on a chair in a shoeshine parlor at 57th and Central when two police cars—with three officers in each—arrived and commanded all to leave. After a brief exchange of words, "one officer clubbed me with the butt end of his shotgun and knocked me out completely . . . my nose was broken, my cheek bone was cracked and four of my ribs were broken. I almost lost my right eye . . . advised I would be shot if I didn't run." He was hospitalized for three days.[38]

This police riot had unintended consequences. It served to reinforce the NOI contention that "whites are devils," for there were no other competing militant explanations.[39] It brought more protesters to the streets, with more anger. One of these protesters, who only gave the name Joe, got involved when he heard an officer yell, "Nigger." The LAPD, he said,

> never took time to stand and talk. They were hitting everyone. Girls and little kids. The cops drove up to clusters of people and got out of their cars and started swinging at everyone with their billy clubs. . . . That's what got the people mad. . . . The average person out there in

the streets knew what it was and he considered it a war. . . . At first
it was against the white police. Then—not just the police, but all
whites. . . . After the rioting started, more and more other whites just
seemed to keep coming into Watts. . . . They came to see us put on
a show. . . . They say it wasn't organized—but it was. Not in the regular sense. But the people met in the park and talked about what had
happened and what they planned to do that night.[40]

After the uprising ended officially, the truculence of the LAPD continued.
Roger Wilkins, nephew of NAACP leader Roy Wilkins and a Justice Department official, was stopped by the police on 23 August at 11 P.M. and subjected
to a harrowing interrogation.[41] On 26 August, Lionel Lewis—twenty, single,
Los Angeles City College student, and not so high on the social totem pole
as Wilkins—was working as usual for Cassidy Distributing Company hand-
ing out free samples. He had stopped to use the toilet at a bowling alley, when
an officer approached and began beating him and shouting, "You niggers have
messed up Watts, but you better stay out of Eagle Rock."[42]

The normally staid *LA Sentinel* became worried. They were stunned
about the "flood of telephone calls and office visitations from persons making
charges of police brutality." But it continued. The West Side Social Club at
4607 South Western was a haven for black city employees. It had about seven
hundred members, who were the sort of hardworking, taxpaying blacks that
many of the right-wingers in the LAPD said they did not object to; yet weeks
after the uprising the LAPD raided this establishment in response to accusations of gambling and wrecked the club. The viciousness of the assault seemed
to reflect a kind of compounded class and race resentment, akin to the
lynching of prosperous black shopkeepers in the late nineteenth-century
Deep South.[43]

Such attacks directed across class lines at blacks were like a recruiting
broadside for the NOI. Interviewed during the height of the rebellion, Minister John Shabazz railed at Dr. King and his philosophy, denounced the "white
man," and added, "This is war." He linked it all to the conflict in Vietnam
and contributed the idea of the "black man being an Asiatic, fighting an
Asiatic war."[44]

Though new recruits may not have been knocking on the door of the
NOI Temple to gain admittance, there was little doubt that the ideas of Minister Shabazz were becoming hegemonic in South LA and the brutality of the

LAPD was a major reason. On this same radio broadcast featuring Minister Shabazz, Bob Freeman and Cleveland Wallace of CORE recounted numerous instances of police illegality in Watts before 1965 and complained that very little of this was covered by the press. They sought to explain—without reference to demonizing—why police officers were stoned by crowds and why whites generally were assaulted. Freeman used the phrase "power structure," not "white man" or "white devil," to describe the foe. Such language was emblematic of the nascent new-left Panthers, which soon were to meet their Waterloo.

■

Councilman Tom Bradley on 30 September 1965 mourned the fact that so many blacks were still "fearful of reprisal" at the hands of the LAPD. He criticized the labors of the McCone investigation, which he said had not been active enough to ferret out this information and other issues. Referring to the revolt he noted that some of his former comrades in the LAPD confided that "there were a number of cases where in their judgment there was no sound basis for shooting, and, in a word they said it was murder. . . . they were just taking advantage of a situation. . . . I talked with this woman who said that she was in a building and observed the officers actually shooting at people without any justification." Bradley said bitterly that "we have never had a Negro captain" in the LAPD and lamented that "there is no Negro lieutenant today." He denounced departmental segregation and the continuing difficulty in ensuring that "Negro and white officer[s] could work together in a radio car." [45]

Social scientist Gary Marx has explained that "the behavior of some social control agents," such as the LAPD, "seemed as much to create a disorder as to control it." Given the racial tensions in LA in 1965, "using ethnically alien police to stop an ethnically inspired riot may be equivalent to attempting to put out a fire with gasoline." The LAPD had lost critical legitimacy among many blacks, and its officers were viewed "not as neutral representatives of the state upholding a legal system but as armed representatives of their ethnic communities." [46]

In its defense the LAPD could argue—as it often did—that "no municipal police department in this country has ever been called upon to cope with a situation of such magnitude" as that of August 1965. This was true; extreme situations often bring forth extreme reactions. Nor had the LAPD escaped unharmed; ninety officers had been injured, and at least 2 police cars were destroyed and 178 of them damaged. To H. C. Sullivan, a high-level LAPD official, the relatively sparse ranks of the LAPD plus the injuries created a "manpower shortage that was intensified by the necessity of repressing the riot and still affording the necessary police protection to the citizens in the remainder of the city."[47]

The force of the uprising gathered strength in part because of the LAPD's lack of preparedness. It did not have enough vehicles of various categories, according to Sullivan, and when more and more of those it did have were disabled, the department was weakened further. It had "no mobile jail capacity," which impeded taking away people the officers apprehended; this may have led to shooting or otherwise disabling large numbers of suspects on the spot as officer frustration grew. Similarly there was an "inability to make mass bookings in the field." Sullivan was also upset about the communications problems; various frequencies on the radio spectrum used by the LAPD, National Guard, CHP, and sheriff's office were limited. "Having only one command and surveillance frequency curtailed airtime to a point that endangered many officers . . . walkie-talkies were in severely short supply." There was a dearth of shotguns, and so some had to be "donated by local merchants" or "borrowed."

The LAPD may have been the leader of the police riot by design. The overall strategy was to turn over "the positive, repressive actions against the rioters" to the LAPD and let the guard "hold areas over which control had been established." After all, the LAPD knew the terrain and should have known some of the people in the neighborhoods.[48] Given the designation of the LAPD as the attacking force, it is easier to comprehend the brute force of its approach. This approach juxtaposes neatly with the department's initial timidity; protesters were stunned and confused when timidity was supplanted by ferocity. One of those milling about in the streets on the afternoon of 13 August, Leon Smith, felt that the lethargic approach of the LAPD in those early hours convinced some that there was a de facto license granted to take merchandise.[49]

One reason why the LAPD was ill prepared to deal with race conflict was because it was embroiled in a class conflict, the "policing of a labor dispute" at the Harvey Aluminum Company at 190th and Normandie. Deputy Chief Roger Murdock said this detracted from the department's ability to confront South LA; on the other hand, the high level of mobilization and tension that the strike brought may have ultimately harmed South LA.

Murdock arrived on the scene after the Fryes had been taken away, on 11 August at 10:15 P.M. He felt the situation was becalmed because by 11:30 or earlier most residents had drifted away. But by 8:30 P.M. on 12 August he was called back to South LA, because the protesters had just taken a good night's sleep before returning to the fray. Then he had to deal with the frantic ministrations of John Buggs and his entourage, who were beseeching the brass to replace white officers with certain youth recruited by the HRC, called "muscle," and with the few black officers. According to Murdock it was they—and not he, as widely reported to his chagrin—who said, "We think the colored officers would make less of a target." Murdock firmly opposed this proposal to use black officers exclusively because, he said, they "have a problem dealing with their own people. And they have a problem because in lots of jurisdictions colored officers aren't allowed to arrest white people." Black officers were enforcing law that was applied unequally, and this alienated broad sectors of South LA.

Murdock was to the right of Buggs in that the latter's nationalist-tinged affirmative-action proposal might have been more successful in smashing the insurrection. And that was the point and part of the reason why black nationalism had such an appeal and why affirmative action could have surprising origins; having blacks repress other blacks was a kind of nationalism that many could embrace. Murdock was not lagging on this question altogether. He was quick to point out that "we had colored officers in there in plainclothes for intelligence purposes." It was obvious that the revolt could proliferate or be extended unless more black officers could be deployed.[50]

Deputy Chief Thomas Reddin also was baffled by the starting and stopping of the uprising on 11–12 August, which had not occurred "back east" in 1964. The 77th Division was at the point of the counterattack partly because of the "criminality of 77th Division residents," he argued. He tried to exculpate his force in psychological terms, citing his men's "personality traits" of being "tolerant" and "resistant to fear" with "control over [their] emotional expressions." Others would argue that these latter two factors, if anything, helped to explain the viciousness of the department's response. To be wound up tightly was not necessarily the best psyche needed for the LAPD to handle the complex class and race tensions in South LA.

The attack on the Muslim Temple is a case in point, and Reddin went to great pains to show why the LAPD's actions there were eminently reasonable. He stated that when the officers arrived, "the front door was opened for them and they were let into the temple"; he did not say who was courteous enough to do this in the midst of insurrection with rumors swirling about LAPD retaliation against the NOI. Then suddenly shots were fired from the temple at the officers' parked cars, he remembered. With that provocation the LAPD fired round after round at the temple. At that juncture other officers entered an open rear door, he recounted, and let in even more officers. "There was a grand melee resulting in all sorts of fights and foot races and wrestling matches" and then "a fire broke out." This fire seems to have ignited spontaneously; the McCone Commission did not bother to ask how. It was all a strangely appropriate conclusion to a week beginning with blacks rebelling primarily against police and ending with police primarily rioting against a rapidly growing symbol of black militance.[51]

Murdock and Reddin were not alone in seeking to explain or explain away the department's behavior. Richard Simon, yet another white male deputy chief in a city replete with minorities (he administered the Community Relations branch of the LAPD), attempted to explicate why the LAPD's reaction was so Negrophobic. "The Caucasian officers," he remarked, using the common term of the period to denote whites or Euro-Americans, "found it difficult to distinguish the Negro who is a professional man, strictly a law observer and the Negro who was a lawbreaker," who presumably was not of that elevated status. He did not explain, nor was he asked, how or if he could make similar distinctions within other racial groups. That the official with supervision over community relations would look at the issue this way illuminated, if it did not explain, why blacks of all classes could be subjected to police attack.

This statement was a bit much for Simon's questioner, the usually restrained Judge Earl Broady. "You say police brutality is a phony charge." "That's right," answered the unflappable Simon. Well, intoned the judge, "then in the next breath you say policemen have gone to prison for every charge set out in the Penal Code." "Oh yes," responded Simon brightly. "We have the problems, we always have had."[52]

Murdock, Reddin, and Simon all were defensive and supportive of the department's actions in August 1965. Daryl Gates sharply criticized the LAPD response from a safe historical distance in his 1992 memoir, but in 1967 when he had the opportunity to comment on his experience as "Captain, Commander of Intelligence Division" and "field commander" two years earlier, he was reticent.[53] Not so, Lieutenant Frank Beeson, Jr., who was on the scene early on 11 August and who took credit for making the decision not to shoot "looters." He lambasted Parker and lamented how he "had tried repeatedly to get a decision on this matter at a higher level but ran into constant delay and bickering over many hours." Sure, there were deputy chiefs on the scene, like Murdock. "However, no one relieved [Beeson] of command though department rules state that suggestions are not to be made by superior officers in the field unless they assume command. In fact similar situations prevailed throughout the five days of rioting." Some had the authority, others took the responsibility, and this uncoordinated approach may have fed the inchoate departmental response.[54]

The lawless tactics of the LAPD that contributed to the uprising were not unknown to local elites before August 1965. In a confidential communication Judge J. B. Lawrence of the municipal court in San Bernadino told Warren Christopher, the influential attorney working with the McCone Commission, that he would do well to investigate to see if a

> disproportionate number of cases in which there has been proof of illegal searches or seizures or of confessions extracted by force or fraud have arisen in Los Angeles. I have twice heard from reliable sources (that is, law enforcement officers) that the [LAPD] maintains a robbery squad or commercial burglary detail which, when a tip-off enables them to stake out the scene of a crime in advance, habitually prefers to kill the offender than to arrest him. . . . When I review a person's criminal record for any purpose, I give no weight whatsoever to a Los Angeles felony arrest unless it is followed by a conviction, since in my opinion, it frequently means merely that the defendant was in the wrong place at the wrong time. This is said to be particularly applicable to Negroes.

He sharply questioned reports about snipers and instructed Christopher bluntly, "I am suggesting that there are reasonable grounds for the hostility which is felt by the lowest economic class" toward the LAPD. The eminent judge provided Christopher with a road map so that he could discover the shady side of the LAPD, but there was no adequate follow-up; the problem was left to fester until the 1990s.[55]

On Saturday, 14 August, the LAPD headquarters itself was under siege and had to be patrolled, which tied down more officers. "Inside, for the first time in the memory of Carroll (Spud) Corliss of the *Times,* dean of the police press corps, policewomen took their guns from their handbags and strapped them on. Officers reported for duty carrying their own shotguns and hunting rifles, at their superior's suggestion. . . . A request for the short-barreled riot guns went out over the statewide police teletype. Response came from far away as" San Francisco.[56]

Officers were being shot, two in Long Beach on 15 August alone. Stations throughout the region were being deluged with threatening phone calls promising fires and bombings "in an apparently organized 'campaign of terror,'" proclaimed the *Times*. Other callers were claiming that the freeways were being assaulted by snipers; this rumor terrorized travelers and hampered the transport of officers to scenes of conflict. The number of officers injured jumped dramatically from 13 August to 15 August, mostly because of the tossing of brick and rocks; the majority of these injuries took place up and down Avalon from 103d to 113th. The department insisted that this situation had to be considered before accusing it of rioting.[57]

Black officers and personnel of the LAPD were in an anomalous position. They lived in communities under fire; their neighbors, their friends, their families were the ones being frightened by—or participating in—the spectacle of an insurrection in their backyard. But the black authorities were obligated to follow the orders and edicts of superiors in the force who often held openly Negrophobic attitudes.

Sergeant Vivian Strange, a black woman, an NAACP board member, and a member of the force since 1942, was shocked at how Chief Parker's office became discombobulated when it heard that forty-three NOI members had landed at the main LA airport in the midst of the uprising. Panicked, the officers called the airport and inquired about descriptions of Negroes arriving at the airport. It turned out the black males observed were from a post office workers union.

Sergeant Strange, a dignified black woman, was often treated by her fellow officers like "a prostitute or a drunk." Officers often were forced to roust such alleged "deviants" as a regular part of their workweek and rarely encountered darker peoples in their segregated neighborhoods; this made them susceptible to perpetrating such stereotypes against Sergeant Strange. Strange complained to the "Division Commander, who regarded it as nothing." She too complained about police training, indicating that too much time was spent on "how to shoot weapons" but little on "human nature." The paramilitary LAPD was not composed of amateur psychologists and held no yearning for such an orientation. Its job was to subjugate neighborhoods, not win them over.

The Parker mentality mixed uneasily with that of Strange and other black professionals. She admitted candidly to being stirred by the civil rights movement as it crested in Selma, and she said that the "emergence of independent Negro nations in Africa has had the same effect."[58] The changing political situation helped to influence some black officers to resist the trend of ruthlessness toward their "blood"; this was a positive aspect of the developing nationalism. As a result, black cops were harassed severely by fellow officers, guardsmen, and other authorities.[59] In turn, to prove their reliability, some black cops felt obliged to heighten brutality against Black LA.

Parker's office was an organizational mess at a time such a situation was needed least. LA elites knew this. An eyewitness told Warren Christopher that on 13 August at 4:15 P.M. he was in the chief's office and it was wracked by "bedlam."[60] But the nature of Parker's appearance before the McCone Commission helps to explain why local and national elites were in no hurry to castigate and isolate the LAPD chief and/or his practices, an omission that can be counted as one of the major failures of LA's leaders. John McCone, former CIA director, reminded Parker about the recent "Panama riots . . . and the recent revolution in the Dominican Republic," where African-derived peoples had played central roles and where "police brutality was an issue." The events of August 1965 had been an insurrection; there were high stakes, and stern measures were necessary. The right-wing notion that Black LA was there to be subjugated because it was potentially revolutionary fodder was the guiding principle, and this ethos only backed up Parker's incompetence and brutality.

McCone went on to mourn the police officers killed in Santo Domingo, "600" of them, he said, a statement in obvious sympathy with Parker's burden. The chief added that he found it "startling" that referring "to a Negro male as boy, regardless of age, is considered brutal. To refer to a Negro woman by her first name is absolute taboo." The diligent chief had asked the vice president of a large university if it was acceptable to call a black woman a "Negress" and was told that it was; but, he fumed, he could not do so under LAPD rules. He was dumbfounded about the evolution of the etiquette of language.

He was more sensitive about language directed at his officers, or at least the men. "This is an oppressive assignment to give these young men who have been taught to be courteous and [are] addressed as an individual who has sexual intercourse with his mother." "Motherfucker," an increasingly popular term in the nation and Black LA and symbolic of the increasing encroachment of lumpen culture, was not scrutinized by the LAPD in order to divine deeper meanings that would help the officers accomplish their mission; it was just condemned. Parker expressed no similar concern about epithets tossed by fellow officers at the 4 percent of the force that was black; however, he was solicitous enough to them to contend that "the Negro police are treated worse than the Caucasian police" in the larger community. But what was the "most downtrodden, oppressed, dislocated minority" in this country? Blacks? Black cops? Chicanos? No, "the police of this country," said Parker. Though the chief was not predisposed to psychology, sociology was another question. The problem with African-Americans, he maintained in an argument foreshadowing future discourses, was that "the people who have progressed moved out of" Watts, while the "flotsam and jetsam" have remained.

Yet, sociology aside, Parker's job involved, among other things, being prepared to handle the kinds of emergencies that beset LA in August 1965. And the fact was that the department was not prepared to do so. To cite one example, Parker stated that his main purpose during those days was to arrest as many people "validly" as he could: "I don't want illegal arrests because those will cause us trouble." However, this depopulation strategy was foiled by the lack of vehicles to transport those arrested away, inadequate systems for booking suspects in the field, and the like. This issue—which minimally might have aided in suppressing later uprisings—was not pursued aggressively by the McCone Commission. Instead, Parker was on the receiving end of soft queries, such as when Asa Call of the commission inquired gently about "harassment or brutality." Toward blacks? No, "toward the police." [61]

Though the McCone Commission failed to go after the chief or his practices when he testified or afterward, others were not so timid. He was now the whipping boy of the black community. Pickets at police headquarters were now more regular. [62] Police brutality was now an issue that would spark the formation of the Black Panther party. Publicly it seemed the chief was feeling the stress, for his misstatements seemed to increase as time proceeded. Six months after the uprising he was claiming that it had started spontaneously but had been exacerbated by persons with bullhorns. In fact, as the *Times* carefully pointed out, the bullhorn "was actually a police bullhorn borrowed by a person trying to help the police." [63]

The Republican party and the ultraright, now in the political ascendancy in Southern California, were behind Parker. [64] A number of residents of South LA also were not displeased with the department's rough handling of the insurrectionists. Mrs. Ozie Gonzaque had lived in Watts twenty-two years; her husband had worked for the North American Aircraft Company for fifteen years. She was conservative and supportive of the department's tactics.[65]

Others in Watts disagreed, and they were joined in their concern by Herbert Carter of the HRC staff. He had sought to provide training in human relations for law enforcement personnel, but it boomeranged; "for some of the officers it had merely crystallized their antagonistic attitudes and their identification of human relations concerns as 'radical.'" These officers "were active in far right organizations," unsympathetic to the Negro, and held deep biases against the NOI; worse, they maintained an "'on guard' approach to all unfamiliar Negroes."[66]

■

City Councilman John Gibson was not alone in his opinion that the officers supervised by LA County sheriff Peter Pitchess were hated less by blacks.[67] Certainly, they were more sophisticated. Pitchess had coordinated the production in January 1963 of a detailed "Disaster Law Enforcement Instructional Guide [for] Crowd and Riot Control" that covered a huge swath of territory from San Luis Obispo County, 200 miles to the north, to Orange County, LA County's southern neighbor. Unlike the LAPD practice, this document did not disdain psychology and, in fact, made interesting points about the psychology of mobs, in a manner not dissimilar from that of academicians. It isolated such factors as novelty, anonymity, contagion, and panic as helping to spread mob activity. "The mob leader is of great importance in inciting a crowd to mob action," it explained, and should be dealt with forthwith.

The guide gave a flexible definition of what constituted a riot—it simply involved "two or more persons acting together" lawlessly—which served to facilitate heightened mobilization by the department early on. History was even consulted, for the document included an instructive and detailed exposition of the Whiskey Rebellion of 1791–94. What the sheriff learned from history and law was that there were "[three] basic principles in riot control": have a plan, "rapidly execute" it, and "be firm." The LAPD failed, in the estimation of some, on all counts. Like the reviled Chinese government, Pitchess suggested that there was a symmetrical triad of tactics as well: dispersing forces rapidly, preventing assemblies, and arresting leaders. Pitchess mirrored Lenin, who argued for firmness in executing insurrection, by arguing for firmness in pulverizing insurrection. "Never use blanks." Organize forces thusly: "⅓ force attack, ⅓ reserve, ⅓ support."

"Crowd and riot control formations" were highlighted, including the "wedge, diagonal & line," with refinements like the "squad wedge," "squad diagonal," and "squad line." From the point of view of military tactics, Pitchess and his cohorts did not sufficiently explore the question of adapting such formations to guerrilla maneuvers. But there was a lengthy section on the creative use of the baton and the "Japanese strangle." Employment of this measure eventually was to cost the city thousands in damage claims: "When the baton is on the right side of the opponent's neck and against the cartoid artery on the left side, the supply of oxygen-giving blood to the brain will be shut off, causing temporary unconsciousness." The "American strangle" was also explained.

Pitchess displayed his cool realism by even making reference to the Cold War to explain why insurrections occur: "We live in a 'cold war climate' but one that engenders 'hot' emotions." Such an analysis placed him miles ahead of most historians and other analysts at the time. When this document was updated in April 1963, as the Cold War waxed, it included listings countywide of radio frequencies of various law enforcement agencies, along with numbers of rifles, shotguns, sedans, and wagons. The June 1963 version had a lengthy discussion of alternatives to pursue in case of nuclear attacks, chemical and biological warfare, and the like.[68]

But with all this planning, when Watts blew up, Pitchess was on vacation, and the bumbling LAPD took the lead. The sheriff's force was able to respond en masse to a request from the city on 12 August at 10:07 P.M. for reinforcements, but like the LAPD it had 200 men tied up at the Harvey Aluminum strike.[69] There were 3,800–3,900 officers in the department, with 5.8 percent black, and 1,500 nonofficers, of whom 27.2 percent were black.[70] Their Community Relations detail, a de facto intelligence unit, seems to have been more effective than their LAPD counterpart.

Though the sheriff's force seemed to be more in tune with the times than the LAPD, its record was not without blemish. Willie F. Brown, a black man who came to California from Mississippi in 1940, was stinging in his rebuke of county officers' frequent harassment of African-Americans. Tellingly, the novelist Chester Himes focused on the brutality of the sheriff's men, and not the LAPD, in his angry *Lonely Crusade*.[71]

Pitchess was honest enough to note that "within the past year or two" there had been police and community conflicts that could have reached the level of Watts but had not for various reasons. But Pitchess's central point afterward was that LA had gotten off easy in August 1965; he recognized that the fact that the National Guard was in mobilization for summer camp had allowed the authorities to mount a more forceful response than they could have ordinarily.[72]

Chief Parker was not impressed with the sheriff, however. When asked why the latter's office was not held as culpable for the Watts outburst, the chief replied bluntly, "Because he sits there and keeps his mouth shut and doesn't get in trouble with anybody." Worse, the sheriff "made his deal" with the U.S. Civil Rights Commission and other unreliable liberals.[73] LA's leaders chose to back Parker, when they easily could have compared his record negatively to that of Pitchess, undermined the chief, and gotten rid of him.

■

The LAPD's reach theoretically did not extend beyond the borders of the city. In those parts of LA County, the sheriff and/or local forces reigned. Compton was one of those areas. Its chief, William K. Ingram, was a self-described "white, protestant, native Kansas, born 1909." He was like Parker in many ways, having served in the military, the U.S. Navy, where his "primary responsibility was security"; he performed so admirably that he moved up to work during the early stages of the Red Scare with "the new President's Loyalty Program background investigation of employees." In 1953 he came to Compton as chief. Though many may have forgotten the inroads the left had made among blacks before the Red Scare, this was well within Chief Ingram's memory. Blacks as "revolutionary fodder" was not an alien concept for him.

By 1965 his town had split in two, with the west side being mostly black and the east side mostly white. Of the 76,600 population, he estimated that 40 percent were black, and this portion was growing rapidly as, not accidentally, white population declined. However, less than 10 percent of his force was black. He did ensure that his force's training included "at least six hours in" public relations, "at least two hours in race relations," combined with "four hours in riot control."

Compton was not untouched by the adjoining fires, though most of its businesses survived intact. The "looting" was "minor," according to the chief; he credited the response of his force, which went on twelve hours on–twelve hours off duty with no time off on weekends from 14 August to 26 August.[74]

This lack of reported damage can be ascribed to overly legalistic approaches. Benjamin Friar of 1314 West 138th Street in Compton recalled that on 12 August he was "hit with stones and sharp arrow like objects propelled by 12 Caucasian males at the corner of Central Avenue and Rosecrans Boulevard." He called the Compton police but was informed that he was hit "in the county and that, therefore, the City of Compton had no jurisdiction."[75] The LAPD took a similar approach. However, Ingram's tactics were not so questionable as that of his Long Beach counterpart, Chief William J. Mooney, who was praised by the *Sentinel* because he was able to "quell the riot" by having his "600 man force" adopt the legally flawed approach of entering the "troubled Negro section chasing people off the streets and back into their houses."[76]

■

It was the California Highway Patrol that stopped the Fryes, and this led directly to the revolt. Inevitably, the way the patrolmen handled this matter was criticized, often by self-serving LAPD brass seeking to shift the spotlight from their own activity. Chief Parker blamed the CHP on the nationally televised program "Meet the Press," at state senate hearings, and anywhere else there was an open microphone.[77]

The CHP had a lot to explain, Parker's criticisms aside. Its reputation among blacks was not sterling; perhaps 3 of 3,000 officers were black. Its leader, Bradford Crittenden, conceded that the CHP was freely "labeled as a white organization," and his background as a labor attorney apparently had not prepared him to alter this. Crittenden gamely sought to defend his record and rebuke Parker as being "neither factually nor actually correct," and the rhyme of his reason gave resonance to the fact that the CHP may have been a tad more innocent than the LAPD. However, the CHP with its predilection for arbitrarily stopping blacks who happened to be driving in expensive cars was not totally blameless for South LA's lack of confidence in the fairness of law enforcement.[78]

The National Guard proved to be the decisive factor in subduing South LA. This kind of activity was not its forte, and it committed numerous blunders as a result. Many of the recruits were raw, poorly trained, and racially insensitive. Their often chaotic reaction to the events of August 1965 cannot be ascribed to lack of planning. Beginning in August 1963, right after the massive March on Washington addressed by Dr. King, the guard's leader,

Lieutenant General Roderic Hill, initiated a series of meetings about how to respond to civil disorder and threats to maintaining rule. These meetings included the deputy chief of the LAPD, Roger Murdock.[79]

An emergency plan was developed and updated. On 13 October 1964 it was changed to allow the deployed forces to carry hand grenades. It was an elaborate plan of approximately a hundred pages that seemed to be aimed as much at Moscow as South LA. The use of "passwords and countersigns" was outlined, and the key areas of arms, food, transport, medicine, payroll censorship, communications, and burials were covered. A section recommended paying civilians for ongoing supplies with invoices. The enemy within was not neglected: "Known subversive or disaffected personnel within the state military forces will be disposed of by appropriate administrative or punitive action." Thus, the possibility of a coup would be negated.[80]

Through the fall of 1964, as ultrarightists gained strength in the GOP and as the battle over Proposition 14 created hard feelings, the National Guard and the LAPD held a series of meetings, with the state's attorney general kept apprised. The LAPD was viewed with Birmingham in mind. "The City has no police dogs; it does not condone their use nor the use of fire hoses. . . . It does contemplate the use of tear gas." The understanding they reached bolstered Murdock's contention that "the city police force would be assigned to crowd control duties without reference to race." The rules of engagement said, "Bayonets would be fixed but weapons would be loaded only upon specific orders to do so."[81]

Despite this meticulous planning, the guard did not—perhaps could not—envision the breadth and depth of what confronted it in August 1965. But just as Chief Parker deflected attention away from his department's performance by pointing to the inadequacies of the CHP, he was similarly generous with blame when it came to the guard. He was joined by others who accused Lieutenant Governor Glenn Anderson—in charge initially because the governor was in Greece—of being derelict in responding to the city's call for the guard.[82] This charge was at the heart of the conventional wisdom about the Watts Uprising. It was investigated thoroughly by many and almost derailed Anderson's budding political career. He was derided as the man who fiddled while Watts burned.

More than once, Anderson was forced to recount the chronology of his actions. Early in the afternoon of 12 August while he was in Santa Barbara, he was informed about the troubles in Watts; he left for LA by 7 P.M. and arrived at 9:05 P.M. He met there with Lieutenant General Hill and others. He too was fooled by the protesters' decision to get a good night's sleep, because he left for Berkeley the next morning at 7:25 A.M. for a University of California regents meeting. By 12:45 P.M. he went to McClellan Air Force base to meet again with General Hill, and by 3:50 he had ordered troops committed.

The next morning he flew over the curfew zone in a helicopter. He was "low enough so that I could almost recognize people that were looting and going in and out of stores." Anderson was the top man in charge, in a sense, and this fifty-two-year-old Euro-American man born in Hawthorne was taken aback by what he had seen. According to John McCone, he was not up to the task. The McCone Commission subjected him to a grueling and minute examination of his actions and his presumed lethargy in calling out the guard.

In a sense this was unfair to Anderson. Not only did he have to worry about the wildness of a Birch-infested LAPD, even black leaders—like Rev. Brookins—were said to be demanding that he declare martial law throughout the county. He had to deny committing the ultimate sin of meeting with the highly influential Minister Shabazz. McCone was not persuaded that such pressures were exculpatory. He chided Anderson for being critical of Chief Parker and consulting insufficiently with him. Anderson countered that he was concerned about the chain of command and the fact that the guard, once deployed, remained under Hill's control and not Parker's or Pitchess's.[83]

Anderson mistrusted Parker, and so did most of those surrounding Pat Brown. One McCone Commission staffer was told "off the record" that "members of the Governor's staff, with which Anderson was in close touch, were intensively considering the political implications of actions, including calling or not calling out the National Guard. Particularly vis-[à]-vis Yorty's political plans." They were concerned that the peripatetic right-wing mayor would be bolstered by a display of the iron fist. On the other hand, they were concerned that if they did not send in the guard and Watts continued to burn, they would be accused of being weak-kneed liberals.[84]

Anderson drew analogies between his actions and other emergencies, such as the General Strike in San Francisco in 1934 and the Zoot Suit Riots during the war. He tried to explain that the number of guardsmen called out in 1934 was a fraction of the 13,000 dispatched in 1965, thus making comparisons of approaches inappropriate. Moreover, strikers were more likely to proceed in organized formations, which made them easier to contain than fragmented guerrilla bands. He painstakingly explained that calling out the guard would denude Northern California where there was "equal concern then, [for] that was the morning that the troop train for VietNam was going in through Berkeley." He refreshed recollections about protesters who reclined on train tracks and the way this activity might veer beyond the control of local police. But all his interrogators wanted to know was why it took him so long to call out the guard.[85]

Anderson sought to ward off his assailants. He insisted that within two hours of Parker's request of 1,000 guardsmen, he put in a call for three battalions. This deployment was done at a "quicker speed . . . than any similar assembling of troops to put down civil unrest in the entire history of our nation." Within twenty-four hours 13,000 troops were dispatched, and the inevitable happened; the state had to call the White House for "federal troops . . . because the rest of the state was being drained of National Guard forces."[86]

Richard Kline, an assistant in charge of the governor's LA office, backed Anderson and refuted Parker. When he called the chief in the midst of the turmoil, he too detected bedlam. Worse, "when I mentioned the Negro community, he became very agitated and, in effect, exploded and said he didn't want to have a meeting with any Negro leaders or with anybody." Parker, he said, not only objected to Anderson, he was angry at Pitchess too. It was simplistic just to blame Anderson, Kline said. "We found ourselves floundering a little bit in not being able to determine, really, whether we should take more of an initiative than we did or whether we should make the Police Department make the decisions." The chief, he continued, was the culprit, not Anderson. He scared whites and blacks when he went on television and told people in the curfew zone, "this vast area, to please stay in your homes." The problem was not Anderson failing to call out the guard quickly enough but Parker not redeploying officers quickly enough from other beats in the area of disturbance. Kline accused the chief of worsening the situation on 12 August by pulling back some forces. The problem, according to this former reporter, was that Sacramento had a hard time taking Parker and his opéra bouffe seriously.[87]

But Warren Dorn, a powerful LA County supervisor, echoed the prevailing elite line that it was not Parker but Anderson who was responsible because he "did not want to take the responsibility or suffer the political consequences of calling out the guard."[88] The Parker versus Anderson debate was a typical elite diversion, avoiding the central fact that deteriorating socioeconomic conditions, more than the actions or inaction of any person, caused the Watts Uprising. Trying to portray Anderson as a scapegoat was misleading analytically and factually.

■

The *San Francisco Chronicle* claimed that 1,750 guardsmen were called out the last time on 6 July 1934 for the General Strike.[89] By 1965 the guard was rusty and unprepared for the magnitude of its job. Emergency plans aside, it had been preparing for something else altogether, something akin to what the U.S. Strike Command organized in 1964. The USSC had deployed a hundred thousand army and air force men to stage the "largest peacetime war games in American history, as two mythical countries, Calonia and Neezona, fought for weeks to control the Colorado River south of Needles. Uncounted thousands of living things got destroyed, along with thirty-six young soldiers."[90] Anticipating an assignment overseas, the guard was less prepared for its central task of holding down neighborhoods in LA while the LAPD was dispersing and confronting protesters. At its peak on 2 P.M. on 14 August, there were 13,393 guardsmen on duty in the curfew zone.[91] This group included a closely knit structure of senior guard officers, many of whom had served together as a team in Korea, supervising rawboned recruits.[92]

Michael Harris, who is black and lived in Watts during this period, recalled twenty-five years later that the "vast majority of guardsmen were from such places as Redwood City and Eureka and had little or no exposure to or understanding of African-Americans and our problems."[93] This was partially true. Lieutenant Colonel Thomas Haykin commanded the First Battalion, 160th Infantry, composed of men from Glendale, Burbank, Pasadena, and North Hollywood, which "was the first to go into riot-torn Watts Friday." Some were eighteen, and the average age was twenty-one or twenty-two; most were white, some were African-American or Chicano. Haykin viewed this experience in the context of past maneuvers. "It was like taking a village. . . . It was tough and it was isolated. . . . But tactics and training are not war and Watts was war." However, none of his war experiences or the maneuvers he had participated in prepared him for what he faced in Watts. "When our relief (the 49th) came up Sunday night we absolutely could not pull out. We were in a running fire fight, and we had to stay in there and battle it out until midnight. In warfare . . . this just doesn't happen."

The feelings of his inexperienced troops ranged from "incredulity to pity for the innocent people involved."[94] Many in South LA could not believe the rampaging of the guard, either. One analyst concluded that Central between 22d and Slauson was not so bad but in Watts proper the guard "seemed as if they were under a different set of orders. They rode down 103rd Street with their guns pointed directly at the people." The "worst roadblock of all" was at 103d and Wilmington.[95]

Jimmy Walker, a resident of the area, said that he had seen guardsmen "drive down 103rd Street shooting out street lights and later shoot into a fast moving '57 Chevy."[96] Two and a half decades later Michael Harris was still "haunted by the searing image of two of my neighbors lying dead in the street, their bodies riddled with bullet wounds as young guardsmen stood over them, magazines emptied, bayonets affixed, looking up at me quizzically, seemingly searching for answers."[97]

Howard Morehead, a black cameraman working for CBS, said he had no problem in dealing with the crowd during those days. "The most trouble I received was from the police and National Guard. Early on Saturday it was quite possible that the young guardsmen were frightened and did not know what they were doing. Some did not even know how to challenge me or ask me for identification." Despite all of the emergency and contingency planning, the guard was not prepared. But what could prepare these troops for the experience of guarding trapeze artists in a circus at the Sports Arena from angry area residents storming on the periphery?[98]

Nevertheless, Julian Hartt, whose beat for the *Times* was military affairs, assessed the guard's performance positively. Writing in the *National Guardsman,* he boasted of how the guard had "fought and won a complete 'pocket war'" in South LA. It was a "civilian insurrection," and they were lucky to have triumphed. "As late as Sunday, 15 August, there was sincere doubt that the state's full resources would be enough." Those fighting the "Battle of Watts," already a rich source for war stories, faced harsh conditions "bivouaced in USC dormitories, the race track, public schools and armories." All in all, he was proud of his boys: "From division down it was great training under fire and under operationally charged conditions."[99]

Others were not so sanguine. James McCauley was of the opinion that "one must fear what would happen to California if a foreign foe invaded the shoreline." Others were quite concerned about the numbers of guard uniforms stolen during the deployment and where they might wind up.[100] Still others were concerned about the civil liberties implications of turning a state militia loose against civilians and the de facto martial law conditions in the curfew zone. A writer for the *Yale Law Journal* worried that "judicial abnegation in this context is especially unjustified since the involvement of Negroes as objects of these deprivations increase the likelihood that Fourteenth Amendment standards are being violated."[101]

But like the contretemps over Anderson's actions, Lieutenant General Hill of the guard came in for his share of criticism that blamed him not for the civil liberties violations but for the failure to suppress the revolt sooner. In a shrewd effort to increase his budget appropriation, Hill conceded that his force was "grossly deficient for streetfighting action"; but he disagreed with the widespread idea that his failure to divert a guard unit traveling through Long Beach to the curfew zone was somehow responsible for slowing suppression of the disturbances.[102] County Supervisor Warren Dorn felt that Hill's explanations were "misleading."[103]

Hill—a fifty-one-year-old veteran of the Asia-Pacific theater in the Second World War—conceded weaknesses, so better to advance: "We are short [of] radios; quite a bit short for tactical operations" like Watts. The guard was not armed properly, he insisted. The Third Brigade proceeding north from San Diego was armed only with ".45 caliber pistols; to a lesser degree with .45 caliber military type submachine guns, and a few rifles. . . . None of these weapons, except the rifles . . . are suitable to use in civil disorder emergencies." The submachine guns were "a very poor choice of weapons." The guard had prepared for the wrong kind of conflict, and disaster loomed if the mistake was repeated. This kind of argument was not so persuasive to LA elites as Parker's bluster. They continued to press Hill as to why the guard did not arrive sooner and whether he would back their charges against Lieutenant Governor Anderson.[104]

LA elites seemed to be more trusting of Major General Charles Adam Ott, a commanding general of the 40th Armored Division of the guard. His credentials suggested his reliability: resident of Santa Barbara; Stanford B.A., Class of 1941; and president of Ott Hardware. He was appointed by the governor in a decision "concurred in by Congress." There were 111 units and 10,800 men under his supervision, though they were "primarily weekend soldiers" and only 150 were full-time.

Like others, he tried to maintain that he was prepared for the uprising. One year earlier he had designated a rifle battalion in mostly white Glendale—550 men—for such contingencies. He was in touch with the LAPD then, and at the department's "request" he augmented its complement of "rifles, bayonets," and gas masks for tear gas. But he too insisted there were logistical problems that hampered an effective response by the guard. His troops stretched "from Bakersfield and Taft on the north to Barstow and Calexico on the south, and you couldn't expect a unit from Atascadero to be in the Los Angeles metropolitan area in less than six to eight hours, in any kind of effective strength." California was simply too large an administrative unit, overwhelming the transport capabilities of the guard. Even if they had gotten enough airplanes, there were other problems. "Yes. We flew over the riot area, but because of the continuing news reports of aircraft being shot at, I did not allow the pilot to go down below approximately 4000 feet, and we circled the area once before landing at Long Beach."[105] They had to rely on air transport aid from the Arizona National Guard and the U.S. Army.[106]

The official guard evaluation raised the specter that "rioters planned to take over the 97th Street Police Station at midnight [13 August] . . . considerable concern about what might happen should the looters turn their attention to the parking lot of the Coliseum, where thousands were attending a circus." It was like "anti-guerilla combat" replete with "kamikaze attack." This was not just hyperbole, as guardsmen were "involved in the seizure [from residents] of an Armalite AR 15 automatic rifle, of the type being used by U.S. forces against the Viet Cong, along with two boxes of ammunition." Some residents had the temerity to go straight to the guard, pretending to be guardsmen, and request ammunition.

The Guard encountered other problems, such as the dearth of portable address systems and floodlights. But that was minor compared to another fear raised by others: the possibility that the deployment of the guard could increase the chances of a successful "military take-over." This was a false fear, the report insisted, though others were not so sure.[107]

Reforming the guard so that it could better confront civil disturbances was one of the many lasting legacies of the uprisings. Parker, Pitchess, Hill, and Crittenden—in that order of exemption—generally were not blamed by LA elites so heavily as Lieutenant Governor Anderson for the failure to suppress South LA sooner, even though Anderson did not have immediate oversight of those pulling the triggers.[108] The most blameworthy should have been

Parker; even the guard's excesses could have been laid at his feet, according to Bruce Tyler, since "every Guard unit had high ranking LAPD officers attached to them. . . . Parker and his officers had decisive powers over the Guard." [109] But the right wing was too strong, and the situation was considered to be too dire to risk blaming the chief. Anderson would just have to do.

■

Mike Davis has argued that after August 1965, instead of moving away from some of its failed militaristic approaches to South LA, the LAPD took the opposite tack: its airborne effort deployed so profusely during the week of rage, notably helicopters, "became the cornerstone of policing strategy for the entire city." South LA seemed to resemble a village in Vietnam, being buzzed on a regular basis by loud, whirring helicopters. Many whites began to empty out of the curfew zone; in light of "the perceived Black threat to crucial nodes of white power . . . resegregated spatial security became the paramount concern."

All this was set in motion directly at the volition of the LAPD; yet again it was the worst of all worlds for the city because the department "subconsciously . . . never recovered from the humiliation of August 1965 when it temporarily was forced to surrender the streets to a rebellious ghetto." [110] The notorious black police informant Louis Tackwood argued similarly that Watts shocked the LAPD. "Nobody believed the niggers had it in them." The department decided, as a result, to beef up its intelligence arm in the black community, "a new squad that the LAPD put together that was to work in the streets and infiltrate militant organizations and they promised me a lot more money." After Watts, he noted happily, "domestic counter-insurgency has become a 'growth' industry." All of LA was "Watts-sized"—the bell did not just toll in South LA—as the intelligence arm for the entire city was increased. [111]

Days after the embers had cooled, the directors of the Orange County League of Cities worried that an insurrection could spread to their region. They proposed that local police be mandated to hold off the hordes "for approximately eight hours. After that local forces would be depleted or used up." At that point the only remedy would be a hurried call to the governor for the guard. [112]

The official investigative arm appointed by the governor, the McCone Commission, disappointed many with the limited scope and pallidness of its recommendations. It was considered daring for William Colby of the staff to pose the similarly racist Chicago Police Department as a model for the LAPD. In Chicago, he reported, "officers stress courtesy [toward] Negroes even when they are arrested. This enables Negroes to retain their dignity. Deputy Chief said he even tips his hats to a Negro prostitute." [113]

Paul Jacobs, writing for the Kerner Commission appointed by President Lyndon Johnson, concluded that the Police Training Academy presented a "totally inadequate range of courses in problems dealing with race relations and community relations," and this should be changed. The department was simply too militaristic; even its "efficiency reports . . . are based on a form developed" by the U.S. Marines. The LAPD needed to think of its officers more as social workers than marines. The LAPD's hostility to psychology— "under Chief Parker, not even a mental health film was allowed to be shown to the Department officers"—had to go. He also indicated why the McCone Commission was so weak in its call for reform: its staff was "primarily . . . drawn from former investigators for the FBI or for other law enforcement agencies." [114]

There was no doubt that the LA elite and the McCone Commission were well aware of the need for change in the LAPD. They collected a thick sheaf of complaints that dwarfed what they had on the sheriff's office and the CHP. [115] Yet the commission rebuffed the idea of a civilian review board; it recommended only that division commanders and others in the chain of command not investigate complaints about their "subordinate officers." [116]

The Board of Directors of the Apartment Association of the county, a constituent element of the local elite, demanded a "quick and expeditious creation of auxiliary forces" of the LAPD, to "be given all necessary equipment, such as riot guns." This request was heeded. Daryl Gates has pointed out that the development of SWAT teams and heightened consciousness about fighting guerrilla war in South LA were a partial response to Watts: "Without official authorization, several of us . . . began reading everything we could get our hands on concerning guerrilla warfare." They had discussions with the military. [117] As in a Vietnam village, large numbers were painted on the roofs of public housing in order to facilitate helicopter surveillance.

On the other side of the fence, many of the concerns of blacks—though not all—were ignored. And some concerns were deemed to have been addressed inadequately. The African-American baseball player John Roseboro was appointed to a community relations post by the LAPD, but many blacks felt this was a patronizing and cynical exploitation of their interest and success in sports.[118]

Black anger was expressed sporadically in these weeks after the uprising, and this included physical attacks on white officers in incidents reminiscent of what happened to the Fryes.[119] In some cases they were just retaliating in response to what the LAPD was doing. For a time after the uprising, the LAPD, allegedly acting on "reliable and unreliable" tips, went to "private homes, private residences . . . recovering loot" with "just willy-nilly breaking in doors, claiming property" and worse.[120]

The McCone Commission did prepare a memorandum—which it ignored—recommending strengthening the ineffectual Board of Police Commissioners. Amazingly, on 18 August 1965 when the board met as flames and smoke still wafted over the city, it virtually ignored what was taking place in the streets. Not until agenda item number eight did it get to what was going on outside, passing a unanimous resolution praising Parker and the LAPD "for the many tireless hours served, the personal courageous devotion to duty."[121]

Elbert Hudson was a member of the board and voted in favor of this resolution. This similarly light-skinned son of NAACP leader H. Claude Hudson, was, in a sense, on the board because of his connections within South LA; but in praising Parker he did not represent the black masses. The militant, though erratic, *Los Angeles Herald-Dispatch* derided him: "Have you noticed how quiet Elbert Hudson, our so-called representative on the Police Commission, has been since the Watts outbreak. I guess Charlie told him to keep quiet and keep . . . his mouth closed [and] he is."[122]

Hudson's performance showed that installing reliable, mild-mannered Negroes in high-level posts could provide an aura of legitimacy, while continuing the status quo. Jesse Brewer, a black officer who benefited from this policy, declared that "after the Watts riots I saw a positive trend . . . to ensure that affirmative action was taking place." This trend, he continued, proceeded until "about 1980" when the U.S. Supreme Court rendered the *Bakke* decision; then progress was reversed. Some of the old racist and reactionary personnel, hiring, and promotion policies were amended. The eventual election of former officer Tom Bradley to the mayor's office was partly a spin-off of the changed atmosphere brought by affirmative action.[123]

The Kerner Commission's John V. Lindsay recommended in 1967 that recruiting of Negroes by police, the guard, and so on be increased, and LA was moving on this track well before the New York mayor's words.[124] Even Mayor Yorty recommended hiring thousands more Negro officers. The Community Relations branch of the LAPD, which was a de facto intelligence unit, was augmented with Negro personnel. The city council voted $6050 to finance race relations seminars for high-ranking officers. But Bill Lane of the *Sentinel* was boiling about the fact that even at these seminars there was rampant discrimination, for whites were being trained to "be bosses of the Negroes who are schooling them."[125]

■

So, after the excessive fire launched by the LAPD, there was widespread praise for Chief Parker, some flawed affirmative action, and a few other minor reforms. The black community was moving increasingly in a nationalist direction, angry at whites generally and their perceived designated representatives, a mostly white LAPD. But this sentiment was contained in crystallized form in the theological vessel of the NOI. There was the NAACP, which was perceived as being the spokesman for the middle class. There were gangs, some evolving toward the Black Panther party. And there were the so-called cultural nationalists, who pioneered in the "Black Is Beautiful" movement but allowed themselves to be manipulated against the Panthers. The Panthers had concluded that only armed struggle could repel the LAPD.

Except for the Panthers, all of these forces had rudimentary middle-class ideas about becoming entrepreneurs or middle-level government bureaucrats, or managing illicit empires, or simply finding a way to survive U.S. imperialism mentally and culturally without challenging it. In the 1990s all—except the Panthers—continue to exist.

FOUR

Impact

8

The Old Leadership

HE RED SCARE WARPED THE DEVELOPMENT OF working-class organization in South LA. From roughly the end of World War II until 1956, there was a vibrant chapter of the left-led Civil Rights Congress, which brought together communities across racial lines to combat racist and political repression. But with its passing also went a kind of interracial militance that CORE only fitfully could replace. The vacuum was filled by the growth of cultural nationalism—which can well be considered a secular outgrowth of the NOI's popularity—and the development of gangs that branched off into the Black Panther party.

The clashing of these two trends—the cultural and the political nationalists—obscured the point that both were stained with male supremacy and corruption. The Panthers, in their insistent focus on police brutality and confronting the state, helped to catalyze police reform; the liquidation of the BPP opened the way for the proliferation of cultural nationalism with its insistent focus on subjective matters, such as naming practices. Nevertheless, the NAACP remained, as ever, the primary organization in Black LA, though its relentlessly middle-class orientation did not predispose it to play a leading role in a community that was not predominantly middle class.

■

During World War II, when Black LA was just forming, organization there even then was perceived as being overly middle class in orientation.[1] By the early 1960s the thoughtful black lawyer Loren Miller was making the same point.[2] By the time Watts blew up, even John McCone was aware that Black LA was no monolith but was riven with class distinctions. He pointed to "two separate and distinct Negro populations. One east of the Harbor Freeway which is quite 'disadvantaged' and the other west of the Harbor Freeway" which was not.[3]

A striking consensus, ranging across ideological boundaries, quickly developed: the rebellion was not only against the white elite, it was also against the black elite. The progressive assemblyman Mervyn Dymally made this point. But he was not singular in this opinion. *Newsweek* declared that the unrest "represented a failure of the largely middle-class Negro leadership to reach the alienated ghetto masses."[4] Though many in Black LA quickly proclaimed that what had taken place was a righteous rebellion, the elite black sorority Delta Sigma Theta condemned the "rioters." Its spokesperson, the prominent attorney Sadie Alexander, presented a statement at the group's twenty-eighth convention in LA in August 1965 which scorned the "small number of lawless individuals" who presumably were responsible for what had transpired.[5]

In addition to underscoring "self-hatred" and "the injustices to Negroes in the South," the black psychiatrist Dr. Alvin Poussaint zeroed in on class divisions as a reason for the uprising. In working-class Black LA, "They equate the middle class Negro, the professional, with the whites. They see them sometimes not caring for what happens to the common Negro."[6]

Saul Alinksy, a noted community organizer, added his own angle: "South Central [LA] has no legitimate leadership. . . . Neither are there any legitimate organizations in South Central Los Angeles." Alinksy saw a vacuum of leadership among blacks. "The civil rights leaders are out of touch with the masses and the gut issues. As for OEO's community action groups, Los Angles can forget them; they are for the birds." This was a harsh indictment; yet, as it related to the preeminent civil rights organization, the NAACP, it resonated. The local branch had begun just after the association was founded in 1909.[7] But the branch was perpetually wracked with infighting and conflict, which seemed to accelerate after the major black migration during the Second World War. NAACP field secretary Tarea Hall Pittman said that this large population growth fueled "an ever growing group of individuals who want their chance for recognition." There was a crisis of rapid change as the branch was unable to absorb the influx of actual members and potential recruits.

The branch faced the irony of "a serious drop in membership in a city that is constantly growing"; it shrank from 14,000 members in 1945 to 2,500 by 1950.[8] This decrease was precipitated by the disarray brought by Red Scare purges, as anyone deemed too radical was ousted. By 1965 the LA branch was not well organized and was somewhat ineffectual. Weeks before Watts went up in flames, local NAACP leader H. Claude Hudson confessed that the "LA branch [is] just drifting along." This inactivity existed in a city where the police were rampaging through the black community almost daily, employment discrimination was rife, and housing discrimination was a painful reality. In the fateful year of 1965, the branch leadership was top-heavy with preachers, lawyers, and doctors, which helped to exacerbate the organization's distance from the common concerns of Black LA.[9]

■

Indeed, like a police arson squad that sets fires, the local branch seemed more preoccupied with getting black demonstrators out of the streets than into the streets.[10] Worse, there were constant rumors about mismanagement of organizational funds—by a leadership that had gained prominence by charging the left had depleted the Scottsboro funds—this was demoralizing to those members who sought to be active.[11] This state of affairs was not inevitable; it stemmed in part from the purges during the Red Scare, which sapped considerable energy from the organization. In part, it stripped the branch of some of its sounder white members, who often were prone to be Henry Wallace supporters or those otherwise most likely to be suspected of being Reds or Red sympathizers. These purges also made the branch hesitant to become involved in activities deemed to be overly controversial. It would be difficult to defend the interests of Black LA without controversy.

In 1948 NAACP leader Roy Wilkins began to warn branch leader Norman Houston about the danger of having Reds as members. Thus began a concerted effort to oust all those who could be perceived as subversive.[12] This culminated in 1956 when NAACP officialdom objected to a projected visit to LA by the organization's founder, W. E. B. Du Bois, now under siege because of his refusal to buckle under to Cold War pressure.[13] This year was a turning point for the LA branch. In the late autumn there was a fierce election battle for leadership that sharpened tensions between left and right. The anti-Communist slate was headed by Maurice Dawkins (who reappeared in the 1990s as a prominent black conservative). The progressive slate was Red-baited, characterized as "long-reputed Stalinists." This outlook made the moderates and conservatives suspicious of one of the more militant African-Americans in the state, the journalist Almena Lomax. The left, in turn, charged that Red-baiting allegations were just a cover for more nefarious activity, such as looting a $5,000 fund raised to aid the nascent civil rights struggle in Mississippi. The left lost.[14]

This ideological pall caused some association members to distance themselves from the leading progressive black attorney of LA, if not the country, Loren Miller. From 1937 to 1948 he was a battering ram for Black LA, serving as counsel in over a hundred cases involving racially restrictive covenants in conveyances of property; the removal of racial barriers facilitated the removal of formal anti-Semitic barriers. The House Un-American Activities Committee harassed him about his ties to the National Lawyers Guild, the National Negro Congress, and Henry Wallace. This was guaranteed to make him suspect in certain NAACP circles.[15] What the NAACP apparently did not realize was that no amount of purging would satisfy some who were predestined to view the association as inherently subversive simply because of its mission. As late as 1960 Roy Wilkins was being instructed that the LA branch remained subject to "communist domination." In 1962 the NAACP reaffirmed its trailblazing 1950 resolution mandating purges of the left.[16]

A year before the rupture of 1956, the branch was in a tizzy. According to Thurgood Marshall, the "local shenanigans on the West Coast" involved "personalities and individuals." Loren Miller told Marshall that the "situation is a complex one, with rivalries and misunderstandings arising out of personality complexes, differences as to regional structures and activities and differences as to program emphasis." Tarea Hall Pittman added that the "internal conflicts" involved "old alliances; the struggle of old leadership . . . the struggle for status in the LA community of leaders in church, fraternal and social groups." There were individual as well as group rivalries.[17] What all three knew was that the branch was riven with conflicts over such issues as what faction had the deepest roots in Southern California and what faction was mostly newcomers to the area. There were color conflicts. There were conflicts over the extent to which the left—and its program, which involved sharp emphasis on confronting the right and the LAPD—would be ousted.

Even after the left was weakened severely in the aftermath of the branch elections of 1956, problems remained, and some of them illuminated why the branch had such difficulty in confronting the LAPD. By late 1957

H. Claude Hudson felt obligated to request that LAPD officers, "plain-clothesmen," attend a branch meeting where "threats of bodily harm and physical violence" loomed. He was chagrined when "white uniformed officers came instead of the colored plain-clothesmen as requested." Such reliance on the LAPD led to a new battle that erupted between the right and the center for control of the branch.[18]

It would be mistaken to characterize the LA branch as hopelessly incompetent. In 1961 it campaigned against employment policies of major establishments like the Biltmore and the Beverly Hills hotels, because they "hire Negro waiters only on an extra basis when Negro social clubs have their functions at these establishments."[19] Its middle-class orientation notwithstanding, the branch made a unanimous decision to protest such bias. Yet the telling indicator of its effectiveness was the branch's continued decline in membership. Membership had grown since the dark days of 1950; by 1961 it was 5,800.[20] But, as NAACP leader Gloster Current conceded, the association was "losing support throughout the country," and that included LA. Less than a year before the uprising, Regional Secretary Tarea Hall Pittman was complaining that the branch had "reached a new low in membership and finance during the past biennium."[21]

One confidante of Current, elected as branch secretary, sarcastically referred to her organization as "the world's most messed up branch." She told him that she was tied to "the Silk Stocking group," which was bound closely to Hudson and the local black business community, including Golden State Mutual Life Insurance. They were opposed by more conservative forces tied to the black church. While they were engaging in intrigue and mutual undermining, membership was dwindling. The 1963 branch election resembled something out of a fictional thriller. The silk-stocking faction had "diagrams and charts," to monitor voters; it "also had a sheriff and a detective as observers for us." Combating police brutality was difficult when the branch leadership relied so heavily on law enforcement to keep the membership in line.[22]

One of the reasons the branch was so bogged down in internecine conflict was because this was one of the few avenues safely open to its members. The left was still deemed to be out of bounds. Nor could they safely associate with the gathering forces of black nationalism; the branch's credibility suffered when it failed to mobilize after the April 1962 clash between the NOI and the LAPD that left one black dead and others wounded.

■

In 1961 Pittman had informed Wilkins that "this Muslim movement is spreading so fast here." She asked, "Would it be possible for you to send our branches our policy statement on these people?"[23] In 1963 when the branch decided to join with the NOI in protesting police brutality, Current howled in outrage, demanding that the association "avoid, if at all possible having Muslim speakers at your rally . . . avoid at all costs any inference of a Unity Movement or that NAACP is calling for a 'common front.' . . . This is a difficult public relations problem." Yes, it was. The NAACP was obligated to capitulate to the Red Scare; then it felt compelled to capitulate to the Black Scare. Inevitably, its base of support had to shrink accordingly.[24]

Such capitulations did not spare the branch from conflicts with powerful elites. Mayor Yorty was caustic in commenting about the branch in the wake of the April 1962 shooting.[25] Hudson was distressed about the policies of the *LA Times,* a paper which in 1963 he claimed to have read "continuously for more than forty years." Its news, he charged, was "slanted against" blacks to the point where "in politics to be endorsed by the Times would be a 'kiss of death.'" Worse, the color-conscious Hudson claimed, the paper lightened photos of blacks when their visages appeared in its pages, and in any case, most of the pictures it chose to print were of the light-skinned.[26] Any negative fallout from such practices in Black LA ineluctably would fall on the light-skinned too, and to his credit Dr. Hudson objected.

The *Times* denied the allegations, but Hudson averred later that this pressure worked; its editorials on civil rights had become "ever more favorable." "If they do not change, they will soon be as effective in their editorial policy as the New York Times." This was a concession by the traditionally right-leaning *LA Times* and could be seen rightfully by Hudson as an important development.[27]

■

The NAACP branch in LA was distracted by internal wrangling, but the insurrection did lead to some changes. Branch leadership issued critical remarks about the LAPD and Chief Parker. The flames reached close to the yards and businesses of branch leaders, and they could not remain unaffected.[28]

A flaw of the NAACP was that it tended to stress court action over mass action. The latter approach would have necessitated heavy reliance on a working-class base; the former approach, buoyed by *Brown v. Board of Education* and other decisions by the U.S. Supreme Court, necessitated heavy reliance on lawyers. However, branch ties to attorneys did prove helpful when mass arrests took place in a community that had shallow roots and had been stripped of progressive leadership. Lawyers' talents were needed all the more because the public defender's performance was seen as less than adequate.[29] But this was no unalloyed success for the NAACP, partly because of its disdain for mass action. Its failure to develop a mass membership meant that the branch did not have a broad funding base.

Only days after the uprising had been quelled, Louise Springs of the branch said that "it is impossible to continue expecting a competent legal staff to give up their private practice for indigent cases without compensation. We are now going into the trial stage of the largest case load known in the judicial history of the United States." According to the *Sentinel* the NAACP had been "swamped by appeals for legal and bail bond assistance for persons wrongfully arrested in the recent riot."[30] The stark reality of this burden helped to shake the branch leadership out of its lethargy.

This was notably true of Norman Houston, the branch leader in 1965. This forty-two-year-old native of LA had attended Jefferson High School and UCLA and thus had the requisite roots. Just as Hudson played a major role on the national board of the NAACP, Houston was the major force locally. President of the branch, his silk-stocking credentials were impeccable: he was vice-president and treasurer of Golden State Mutual Insurance Company. He had felt the sting of racism. He was drafted in 1943 and court-martialed for insubordination in a case with racial overtones; subsequently he was "assigned to a disciplinary company in [a] Northern Burma combat zone." By 1965 his well-appointed office on Western and Adams with its invaluable murals were within hailing distance of another kind of combat zone.[31]

In a "confidential report" to Gloster Current, Houston minced no words in terming the "riot . . . a spontaneous rebellion against white authority." He too saw that the rapid population growth had outstripped the association's ability to respond. In this vacuum, he argued, "black nationalism, gang organization, or complete apathy have been allowed to develop." Once the wick was lit, these groupings—gangs and nationalists—gave the uprising "some form of organization. Hate groups and radical revolutionaries were definitely present and contributed to continuation of rioting . . . organized gangs joined forces in venting their wrath . . . I have personal knowledge of this." Houston maintained that the association had to "shift from the problems of the Negro associated with the obtaining of basic constitutional rights to the problem of

big-city housing, education, etc." Practically, this meant more focus on electing officials and lobbying, but not necessarily on organizing a working-class
base for the chapter.[32]

The uprising caused Houston to become more forceful. In response to
his motion, the branch moved to censure radio station KNX because of its
"offensive editorials" about blacks. He even criticized the "so-called middle
class Negro [that] has not given sufficient support to the total problem"; this,
he said, "has caused great resentment." Houston had a fascinating opinion
about the sociopolitical context of Black LA and the city generally: "Opportu-
nistic 'leaders' both white and Negro, find it easy to operate within an area
such as Los Angeles. The newness of the population, the broad geographic
area and the absence of any seasoned leadership . . . create conditions which
are easily exploited. It has been truly said that within Southern California
anybody with a wild idea can find a following." The NAACP branch would
have been stronger, he thought, if there had been organizations and cells
grouping and mobilizing blacks spread over a "broad geographic area."[33] So
in a momentous move Houston hurried to organize a NAACP chapter of the
association in Watts that would focus—among other items—on the demand
that white merchants should use their profits to invest in the community to
create employment.[34] But this remedy had the perhaps unintended consequence of placing more pressure on these merchants, which caused some to
sell their holdings—to the kind of black middle-class professionals that dominated the association.

The NAACP leadership struggled to come to grips with August 1965.
Roy Wilkins conceded that the revolt had helped, though it did have a downside.[35] His friend the social psychologist Kenneth Clark noted bleakly that
"the wonder is there have been so few riots."[36] But their insight could not
overcome regressive patterns ignited in part by having to observe the Red and
Black scares.

In late October 1965 the branch had a reorganizing meeting at the home
of James Flournoy, an attorney. Yvonne Brathwaite, soon to be a congresswoman, was there. However, the inability to focus on the substantive ideological and political questions inevitably meant that the subjective would be
stressed. "Immediately a very bitter and decisive argument occurred." These
middle-class Negroes came close to activity they might have condemned
among blacks in Watts. Flournoy at one point "suggested his arms from up-
stairs [would be useful] to restore order." The piquancy worked; "at this point,

order was restored."[37] But not the kind of order that would facilitate growth of the ranks; by January there were further complaints about membership loss.[38]

NAACP officials were a bit contrite and wary before the McCone Commission. Houston apologized for not having the "statistics and facts to back" up some of his salient assessments. Though perceptive when writing confidentially and bold when operating within NAACP circles, here he was timorous. After he testified about the precipitous drop in membership, McCone pounced, wondering if the NAACP reflected "the opinion of the total Negro community." He scored Houston for objecting to racial designations in the press of blacks charged with crimes. Houston began to spread blame, attacking CORE and then the NAACP national office; he stated that "we are looked upon almost as the Siberia of the NAACP and that we are not at all satisfied with the level of service that we receive from the national office," which was a major faux pas. He was more restrained about Chief Parker, referring to him as "stubborn" and a "terrible diplomat."[39]

Dr. Christopher Taylor, a dentist and leading NAACP member, also testified. He assailed the War on Poverty as a "gigantic hoax on the Negro community" and urged "federally financed low-cost private housing" as an answer. With a rare prescience he endorsed quotas, arguing that without them tokenism would prevail: "It will always be one, two or three." He raised questions about the secular religion of anticommunism. "John Smith I guess was the first Communist, he said, 'If you don't work, you don't eat.'" He raised questions about the future of blacks in an age of automation and said that Sheriff Pitchess's forces were less brutal than the LAPD because he was elected and Parker—who "over the years has become a power to himself, checked by no one"—was not. Perhaps the fact that Dr. Taylor did not hold an administrative post in the NAACP allowed him to be more direct. Perhaps he was just an outspoken person. However, without a mass base, even his obvious political acumen would be insufficiently utilized.[40]

■

The inability of the NAACP to play a more effective role was one of the factors sparking the uprising. A black community that was overwhelmingly working class saw no effective channel through which grievances, like police brutality, were being met. This was in part due to the middle-class orientation of the NAACP branch. The National Urban League and the NAACP were the dominant organizations in Black LA, but they were not—or not allowed to be—militant; this meant that gangs and cultural nationalists would flourish in the wake of Watts. However, gangs and nationalists were not able to transcend the middle-class approach and, in many ways, reflected it.

The NAACP had helped to form the United Civil Rights Committee—which included the NUL and CORE—in 1963, but the orientation of the league and association dominated over that of the committee. The UCRC was helpful in electing Bradley, Gilbert Lindsay, and Billy Mills in 1963; LA was one of those anomalous cities where the ratio of black to white council members reflected the racial proportions in the city. This was one aspect of LA that caused many to view it as a paradise on earth.

The question was to what extent by 1965 there was a "trickle down" that would benefit some beyond the black middle class of attorneys seeking city business, entrepreneurs seeking contracts, and a number of public sector workers. Many blacks in the streets of Watts would have argued that they were not even tinkled by the trickle. That is one reason why scores of local activist organizations sprang up in the aftermath of August 1965, but for various reasons they did not have staying power. Susan Mary Strohm has argued persuasively that their impact was not for naught. "Despite short-run fragmentation, the militant organizations of this period may have helped to strengthen the position of established black leaders and organizations in the long run."[41]

The fate of the United Civil Rights Committee provides instructive lessons about Black LA. From its inception it targeted school desegregation as a major issue. It was multiracial, combining seventy-six groups who generated much mass action, picketing, jammed meetings, and so on. However, after the flames of Watts and the white-hot heat of Euro-American reaction ignited black nationalism, it fell apart. In 1966 in its wake there was developed a Black Congress, an organization which led to a focus away from integration and toward community control.[42] The left, with its multiracial ranks and emphasis on self-determination, could absorb both impulses; its absence meant the two were polarized.

As Susan Strohm has suggested, the NUL may have been the largest beneficiary in Black LA after August 1965. It was a respectable organization that could benefit from the fear generated by the tumult. One NUL official was keen to recognize that many blacks did not necessarily react the same way as white elites. Instead, the revolt promoted a "class feeling toward the middle class and professional Negro. The Urban League itself has been charged as being middle class."

The NUL's John Crawford outlined the links between his organization's moderation and many nationalists: "Most people say that they are burning the stores because they are trying to burn the white man out so that Negroes can get a chance to establish more businesses." The rage that in August 1965 drove many potential and actual cultural nationalists and gang members may have caused hard feelings among a stratum of blacks, but it also ultimately benefited the black middle class. With the decline of progressive trade union-ism, there was no other channel for this rage. Gangs and nationalists strength-ened the black middle class by "trying to burn the white man out." This is why gangs and nationalists also, ironically, could be deemed middle class as well. The NUL could proclaim the need for a Marshall Plan to aid Watts, but if a constituency was not mobilized to demand this, it was a wasted exercise.[43]

The Westminster Neighborhood Association was influential. It was founded in 1959–60 by the Presbyterian church. By August 1965 it was a significant indigenous community organization with a staff of seven and a budget of $100,000.[44] The leaders—Executive Director Archie Hardwick and Public Relations Director Booker Griffin—were known in South LA; they performed useful social services, such as helping residents to navigate through various public bureaucracies, from the LAPD to welfare offices. It was not coincidental that the Frye family turned to the WNA for help on 11 August 1965. Its mix of responsibilities guaranteed that it would "do well by doing good" after August 1965; by 1966 its budget had grown to $1 mil-lion and its staff to 100. Both the federal Office of Economic Opportunity and the U.S. Department of Labor ensured that funds to WNA flowed copi-ously. But this was like a velvet trap, for soon charges of corruption were flying, along with allegations of theft and stealing. Soon WNA had grown less effective.

CORE in LA was revived in the summer of 1955 by "chiefly white paci-fists." By 1961 it had thirty members.[45] During the 1960s it was on the front lines of protest about Birmingham and Selma and represented a militant al-ternative. By 1962 it had shifted its focus from solidarity with the South to the pressing problems of LA itself; it mounted a continuing picket line in Torrance over the issue of housing. But militance was just the approach that the FBI and other powerful fores did not favor, so by 1965 the chapter was in the process of disintegrating in mutual recriminations, with the Non-Violent Action Committee emerging from these ashes.[46]

This was unfortunate for South LA. CORE had the militant, multiracial approach that would have been a fresh tonic for the community. It attracted people like Don Smith, a leader on the executive board, who was born in the Virgin Islands and graduated from the University of Puerto Rico.[47] He was familiar with a multiracial reality. Another leader was Wendell Collins, first vice chairman. He had lived in LA since 1948 but like Smith did not have the deep roots that the NAACP preferred. He had attended Dillard University in Louisiana and was not unfamiliar with color contradictions.

Unlike Houston, Collins was not intimidated by the McCone Commission; at one point after being asked who organized the insurrection, Collins mused: "I think there is a certain mystic in the Negro community in which people do things almost mystically together. It happens like that [witness snaps fingers]."[48] Collins's wit was not appreciated by all on the McCone Commission. In any event, in the aftermath of 1965 CORE became a faint and distant memory.

The impending arrival on the scene of the Southern Christian Leadership Conference's Martin Luther King, Jr., was viewed cynically in certain quarters of South LA. It was not only that the growth of various forms of black nationalism had been positioned in angry opposition to King's nonviolent, multiracial approach. It was also that some had difficulty understanding why King would come to various cities and what he would be up to once he got there. The *Sentinel* quoted a "young college graduate" to stinging effect. "By the end of the week old liver lipped Martin Luther King will come in here and everybody will be talking about how he came in and soothed the savaged beasts. He'll come in here with that old mess about 'Violence whether black or white, is wrong.' Just wait he'll be here."[49]

So when the SCLC's King came to Los Angeles as the uprising ebbed, it was recognized that his arrival would not be universally acclaimed. Perhaps as a result, King was not hesitant to issue indictments. He was critical of the lack of leadership in LA. "What we find is a blind intransigence and ignorance of the tremendous social forces which are at work here," and he promised to raise this matter with President Lyndon Baines Johnson as soon as "Friday night." King was saddened by certain widely held perceptions of blacks. "There are serious doubts that the white community is in any way concerned

or willing to accommodate their needs. There is also a growing disillusionment and resentment . . . toward the Negro middle class." These feelings of
the black masses were isolating and gave birth to nationalism. "This ever
widening breach is a serious factor which leads to the feeling that they are
alone in their struggle and must resort to any method to gain attention to
their plight."[50] The rebellion was the "language of the unheard," he said elo-
quently, terming it "a sort of blind and misguided revolt against the nation
and any authority."[51]

Despite his soothing words and presence, King was not welcomed by all
to LA. Governor Brown termed his visit "untimely."[52] Watts residents were
less diplomatic. They heckled him when a meeting of 500 was held at the
Westminster Neighborhood Association headquarters on 18 August. It was
tragicomic. With his rolling cadences King began, "All over America . . . the
Negroes must join hands . . ." "And burn," added a heckler.

Another man made a fair point. "With respect to Dr. King, we need
people like Parker and Yorty down here—not Dr. King. They're the ones
responsible for what's going on here." King agreed, adding he would do "all
in my power" to get them there. He continued, "I know you will be courteous
to them." At that, the crowd roared with laugher. This was beyond the métier
that Dr. King had honed in the Deep South. This was South LA, which had
a different history, a different demographic makeup, a different reality. It was
a reality to which the traditional civil rights forces had not paid sufficient
attention.[53]

Dutifully, Dr. King sought to implement his promise to bring Yorty to
Watts. What resulted was a stormy closed-door meeting between the two.
The pugnacious mayor excoriated King for having the nerve to discuss "lawlessness, killing, looting and burning in the same context as our police department." They hotly debated King's farsighted proposal for a civilian police
review board. Yorty was unyielding, insisting that King "shouldn't have come
here."[54] King and the powerful publisher of the *Times,* Otis Chandler, did
not reveal what they discussed in their own "lengthy off the record conference"; but King's words no doubt aided the evolving shift toward the left by
this paper of record.

Toward the end of King's trip, it was becoming clear that the events of
the past week had had a dramatic impact on him. He was self-critical, ruefully
admitting that "we as Negro leaders—and I include myself—have failed to
take the civil rights movement to the masses of the people."[55] Later he ac-

knowledged that "the flames of Watts illuminated more than the western sky." Yes, it was true; his movement was heavily oriented toward the Deep South. Blacks in the North were reading and hearing constantly that a revolution in race relations was taking place, but many of them had difficulty in discerning it in their own lives. "The North, at best," he said, "stood still as the South caught up."

He was objective about what had happened. "Los Angeles could have expected riots because it is the luminous symbol of luxurious living for whites. Watts is closer to it and yet further from it than any other Negro community in the country. The looting in Watts was a form of social protest very common through the ages as a dramatic and destructive gesture of the poor toward symbols of their needs."[56]

King demonstrated keen insight in Los Angeles. Not surprisingly, and unlike the NUL and NAACP, his SCLC was more hesitant about purging the left. But at this point the black community—or at least sectors of it—was turning a deaf ear. Even so, King should have considered himself lucky. His comrade in nonviolence, the activist comedian Dick Gregory, received an even ruder reception from the "bloods" of LA. As he sought to calm the excited in August 1965, the police handed him a bullhorn so that he could "plead for peace." "Go home!" exhorted Gregory. The blunt reply was the bullet he received in his leg at the hands of a random gunman. The philosophy of nonviolence was receiving a direct challenge in Black LA.[57]

9

The New Leadership

REMARKABLE CONSENSUS HAD DEVELOPED, CROSS-
ing even class and racial divides: black leadership was too middle class and
had lost touch with the masses. This was part of the explanation for the
increased popularity of the Nation of Islam, the sect that rushed to fill the
gap. This was also a reflection of the decline of the organized left, namely, the
Civil Rights Congress. The resultant vacuum meant that grievances were not
being addressed via organized channels; like police brutality, problems generally were being ignored. Watts 1965 convinced many blacks that the way to
receive attention, particularly when much of the leadership worshipped nonviolence and appeared to be middle class, was through various physical
means.

James William Gibson has maintained that there is a "warrior" mentality
that pervades this nation's culture and connects everything from LA gangs to
mercenaries to militarism. The connective tissue defines "adult masculinity"
as the "complete opposite of the 'feminine' characteristics." [1] When the "female of the races"—as some analysts described blacks—finally is allowed to
evolve in a manner similar to its white counterpart, it engenders heightened
masculinity; for blacks, this updated masculinity was a heady brew. The rise
of the NOI and its traditional views of gender roles complicated the process.
The gangs that arose also were suffused with traditional views of masculinity,
bluster included. Some chose to define their newfound selves in "gay bash-
ing," attacking those who appeared to be white male homosexuals; this was
at once an expression of race and gender definition by the gangs. It was also

indicative of the rise of lumpen culture, which in a real sense was the reflection in a class mirror of the U.S. elite's "fly-by shootings" then taking place in Vietnam. This insistence on brute force was something the lumpen knew well; thus, the new masculinity was designed to afford them prominence. All sides had to contend with black women, who often did not recognize fully that this new burst of militance and nationalism was pregnant with a masculinity that could be misogynist.

■

As South LA rested in ruins, the *Times* revealed, "Negro leaders also find that they draw more attention when they hint or threaten a 'long, hot summer of violence.'"[2] This reflected what the sociologist Herbert Haines has told us: that the flourishing of "black radicalism," however defined, has led to more concessions being granted to African-Americans.[3]

But there was a downside to what some might term an increase in aggressive attitudes, particularly among black males, and what others might call a healthy counterreaction to oppression. Ocie Pastard of the Westminster Neighborhood Association was blunt: "I would say that before the riots this was an unhealthy community. Now it's healthy. That riot helped to drain some of that tension they had stored up in them. Before the riot they were in bad shape, but now they're ready to take part in the Great Society." So far, so good, despite the questionable optimism of his prediction for the future. But Pastard went on to claim that a negative aspect had arisen that may have been tied to the scads of researchers unleashed in South LA to ask obvious questions. "These people," he said "resents studies. They say, 'Later for the studies.'"[4]

A problem with the brute force of adult masculinity was that it was accompanied too often by an anti-intellectualism.[5] The decline of the left and its post-Enlightenment views paved the way for the increased intellectual hold of a number of regressive religious sects. This had disastrous consequence for a discrete racial minority in need of allies. Confrontation was stressed without its necessary complement, study. Black nationalism in an atmosphere of biracial polarity was one thing; but this nationalism in a region where other minorities had legitimate grievances was something else altogether. Sadly, this dilemma was not contemplated sufficiently.

This was the United States, where slave insurrections were a time-tested tactic; this was the western United States, where violence was inured in the culture. This matrix facilitated the rising influence of what were called gangs.

And similar factors also facilitated the increasing influence of sundry national-ists. The ultimate vision of each did not transcend the idea of constructing business empires; Hollywood itself exemplified how ties to mobsters could aid an industry or certain nationalities.[6] Indeed, some black performers attained a form of class mobility in Los Angeles within the entertainment industry, but this was precisely the industry where the display of an organized brute force was prevalent. If one was black and unprotected against brute force, the man-tras of cultural nationalism could help in coping with this brutal reality.

Belatedly, the *Times* caught up with this trend by talking to Mervyn Dymally, who told it: "Black nationalist groups have militant followings. No one really knows how strong they are, but we can't continue to ignore them."[7] The *Times* can be excused for its tardiness, for Watts 1965 was the catalytic event that made black nationalism known to the country at large. This was a resurgence of trends that had not been expressed so forcefully since the hal-cyon days of Marcus Garvey. But this nationalism was much more militant than that of the 1920s, much more muscular.

There were two key nationalist trends: the "cultural" nationalists exempli-fied by Maulana Ron Karenga and the "revolutionary" nationalists exempli-fied by the Panthers. The Panthers were touched by the Civil Rights Congress, and its emphasis on confronting the state, and by the gangs.[8] The influence of the gangs pushed the BPP in an ultraleft direction that reached fruition with the Weathermen and their "Days of Rage."[9] As self-proclaimed descen-dants of Malcolm X, the members of the BPP declared themselves to be "black and proud." The cultural nationalists did not tend toward confronting the state, but they did believe in black pride.[10] When the state crushed the BPP with the aid of cultural nationalists, the gangs that had been influenced by the BPP descended further into crime. Black pride was left as one of the central legacies of the 1960s to the 1990s.

The nationalism that survived the demise of the BPP stressed blacks de-veloping businesses as a strategic remedy; this was not distant from the vision of the doctors and lawyers that dominated the NAACP and NUL and much of the civil rights leadership scorned by many of these same nationalists. The irony was that all sides were actually middle-class advocates.

■

It was fortifying for many younger blacks particularly to confront the authori-ties physically and watch them flee. Dr. Harold Jones, a black psychiatrist with the county Department of Mental Health, was struck by what he was witnessing in August 1965 at his office on 1145 East Compton Boulevard. Many of these youngsters were referrals from probation officers and thus were likely to have had a recent brush with the law. Dr. Jones proclaimed that he was seeing a resonant pride among these youth, pride that they had stirred up so much consternation among those who often ignored their existence. To Dr. J. Alfred Cannon, a black neuropsychiatrist at UCLA, this pride was liberating because it suggested "the Negro isn't going to have to destroy himself in his frustration by drinking and similar behavior"; now he or she could externalize anger toward presumed foes. This change was viewed widely as a gigantic step forward.

Dr. Cannon added that the increased "Negrotude," as he called it, the pride in blackness, was having the binding effect of causing the black middle class to "re-identify with the masses."[11] The downside was that what they were uniting against was not necessarily the establishment, as represented by the movie moguls, real estate barons, Pentagon contractors, the *Times*—the elite. Yes, this affluent class was 100 percent white; but aiming at this target sometimes was transposed—in the absence of a well-defined class politic—into uniting against all whites, 100 percent of them.

The mainstream black leadership was not attuned at times to the needs of the black working class. But its more militant counterpart among gangs and nationalists could only channel black rage so that the black middle class could benefit.

The majority view was that "Negroes should band together, form businesses to provide all of their services and to boycott all white owned and operated businesses."[12] The black businessmen had already started down the first path, by definition; the boycott served to bind them with developing nationalist trends in the streets. It also served to underscore the age-old point that the class interests of black middle-class elements merge easily with the nationalists, since the former are keenly interested in having the black market all to themselves, and the nationalists were useful in fomenting this process.[13] Many of the black nationalists in the streets received a positive psychological jolt from slogans like "Black Is Beautiful" to counter racist assaults on their self-esteem; many in the black middle class were able to claim the liquor stores and other businesses once controlled by whites, as the latter fled Black LA in the face of nationalist demands for black control.

This should not all be viewed with a jaundiced eye. The black bard Langston Hughes had his character Simple say: "Looting and robbing is not the same thing. When you loot a credit store you are just taking back some of the interest they been charging you for years on them high-priced installment things they sell you on time—$10 down and $2 a week for 900 weeks, plus interest." There was a rationale for assaulting stores, and this rationale violated societal norms, which only increased the attraction in the eyes of many young blacks. The blatant exploitation of Black LA by many white-owned businesses provided the soil in which these trends developed. Without the soil, it is doubtful if the trends would have developed to the same extent; with the soil, the developing was preordained.[14]

■

The Non-Violent Action Committee was tied closely to CORE. Active before and after the rebellion, it was multiracial and collaborated with Assemblyman Dymally. Some of its leaders—Woodrow Coleman and Danny Gray, for example—remained active politically in 1992 LA. Yet, symptomatic of the strength of the prevailing discourse was the effort by one of N-VAC's leaders, Robert Lee Hall, to borrow $1,000 to open an office in South LA that offered job training along the lines of the Reverend Leon Sullivan's enterprise. This Philadelphia model was being favored by most funding authorities, notably the government and foundations, as it tended to move away from mass action to service, along the lines of the tamed National Urban League. Within months of the uprising N-VAC was able to develop a program that encompassed matters ranging from low-cost public housing to income tax exemption to conversational Spanish (with the mandate that it be "taught on a par with English at the elementary school level"). Nevertheless, this effort was swept aside by the growth of cultural nationalism and gangs.[15]

Government and foundations also played a key role in shaping the destiny of many of the groups arising out of the ashes. The Sons of Watts, for example, formerly "shot dice, smoked pot and drank cheap wine" in the area along 103d Street.[16] Watts 1965 helped to transform this group's consciousness in a nationalist direction, and Standard Oil helped to assuage its demands for control of institutions in the black community by funding a gas station controlled by SOW. Perhaps not coincidentally, SOW soon picketed and harassed a left-wing bookstore in the neighborhood. These demonstrations were covered by national television and the press, thereby ensuring that the clash would be widely known and possibly prompting those blacks who desired to see their image broadcast widely to emulate SOW.[17]

Some of the younger black men who might have drifted into N-VAC if it had survived entered the Sons of Watts. Others entered various social networks that were denoted as gangs. Why LA generally and Black LA particularly developed these networks in a more organized form than other cities—St. Louis, for example—is a useful question to explore. Some of the gangs stemmed from the need of so many migrants tossed so quickly into an alien environment to band together. Some stemmed from the desire of blacks to band together to confront racist whites who attacked them when they crossed certain city boundaries. Scholar J. Max Bond has stated that LA Negroes were even more influenced by movies—Southern California's most famous product—and glorified gangster characters played by James Cagney, Edward G. Robinson, Humphrey Bogart, and the like. Certainly Hollywood, a neighborhood not far from South LA, provided a keen example of the value of using organized brute force.[18]

Journalist Leon Bing has suggested that the gang phenomenon was sparked by Mexican-Americans, "who first walked the walk and talked the talk. It was the Mexican-American pachucho who initiated the emblematic tattoos, the signing with hands, the writing of legends on walls." The oldest street gang in LA, she has argued, dates back to the 1930s and is Chicano. Others have maintained that these gangs stemmed from the arrival of thousands of immigrants from Mexico, in a massive influx not unlike what happened to blacks, in the aftermath of the chaotic events gripping Mexico between 1910 and the end of World War I; these networks were a mechanism by which chaos and bigotry could be confronted in an alien environment. Bing has declared that black gangs came later, "in the late fifties, early sixties, with the black social clubs—young guys who got together and ran around and hung out, like the Chicano guys did in their car clubs . . . banded together for camaraderie and, to a certain extent, for protection."[19]

When the dispossessed could not be absorbed in agriculture or in primitive industry in Elizabethan England, many turned to begging or theft. This was a prelude to a new stage in the evolution of capitalism.[20] By 1965 basic industry was fleeing South LA, but blacks often were without the transport to follow. At this stage a number turned to organized crime, which was a refusal to conform to the established order. This was also a time when the organized trade union movement was in decline.[21]

Other reasons to explain why gangs arose range far from the usual black-brown arguments. For example, there was a massive influx of a dissident Russian sect, the Molokans, from the rural Transcaucasion area to East LA in the aftermath of World War I. The youthful Molokans began to rebel as they matured in LA; the sect was ridiculed for their habits, such as eating from a common dish, for the long flowing robes they wore, and for their religion itself. They had "astronomical" delinquency rates and loose networks of youth that could be easily termed gangs.[22]

Various ethnic, religious, and racial groups migrating and immigrating to the alien environment of Southern California felt the need—for various reasons—to bind together. Such wrenching moves often placed inordinate strain on traditional family structures; among male youth, gangs were an adaptation. The persistence of black gangs is a partial reflection of the inability to solve the kinds of problems that caused these networks to develop in the first place. Eric Hobsbawm has noted that "there are always groups whose social position gives them the necessary freedom of action. The most important of them is the age-group of male youth between puberty and marriage."[23] This age and gender group happened to be the prime recruiting area for gangs. Likewise, it is not unknown for gangs to take a political direction, as described by Robert Cribb in post–World War II Indonesia, or as occurred in post–August 1965 LA.[24]

Unsurprisingly, contemporary analysts were not so benign in analyzing the phenomenon of what was happening to black male youth. Robert Glasgow in the conservative *Arizona Republic* sniffed that "perhaps" the "young males" in Watts were "beyond saving." Irvin Williat, a senior citizen from Hollywood, focused on race, not age, in his analysis. He felt that the main reason for the rambunctiousness that erupted in Watts was "that the Negroes are Africans and [react] like Africans." He said the darker the Negro is, the more difficult he is to get along with. His remedy was something that would have met with approval among some of the nationalists now emerging in some gangs. "He said the government should finance a state for the Negroes in Africa and ship all there who wish to go."[25]

The relationship of various authorities to the gangs has stoked concern. For example, LA County's probation department has been charged with going beyond its normal duties to influence gangs. The department had a Group Guidance program that presumably was designed to be a benign official link with gangs. But there was a real fear that these "supervised gangs" tended to get into more trouble, while the fact of their supervision gave them more status.[26] The LAPD, on the other hand, fomented discord between gangs. These supervised gangs were pushed in a political direction away from the left.

The question of these gangs' "very big delinquency rates" was posed directly to Harold Muntz, the chief deputy probation officer of the county, who hotly denied that his staff had been involved in "assembling of youths into organized predatory gangs." In fact, he protested, "none of the gangs who were receiving service from our Group Guidance staff were significantly involved in the riots." [27]

In early 1963 the Crenshaw Coordinating Council, a locally based organization, faced sabotage of a program it had developed with local gangs. Police officers would lie in wait while the council met and afterward question, pick up, and otherwise harass gang members. Often, rather than arresting them, they would drive them away and drop them off far from their homes, sometimes in the territory of a gang that might not smile on their presence. At times the officers would go to employers and get them fired. [28] John Buggs and the county Human Relations Commission hired fifteen "community indigenous aides" to work with gangs. Though it may be not have been his intent, the direct legacy of this effort was the employment of provocateurs like Louis Tackwood and others whose activities were questionable at best. [29]

Though the gangs did not start the uprising, they were blamed for being an organized force that kept things going. John Buggs estimated that in 1965 there were 300 gangs in Black LA, mostly comprising those in their teen and early adult years, with a hard core in each of 25 members; there were others in the orbit of these hardcore members, so-called satellite groups, of about 50 each, and so-called satellites of these satellites, of 150–300 each. Another estimate presented lower figures. [30] But whatever the exact figure, it was apparent that the number and membership of gangs had grown tremendously by 1965. They were one of the few organized formations that encompassed youth.

Their presence was felt widely. Al Alevy, who operated Atlas Amusement Company, told the McCone Commission that it was "his practice when setting up a show to determine the predominant juvenile gang in the area and hire these individuals." [31] But it was not just this tangible benefit that affiliating with a gang could bring; it was also the ethos of fraternity and belonging and even caring the gangs provided when traditional family structures were under assault.

There were claims that when the uprising began on 11 August, the gangs formed a war council. [32] Certainly, if testimony of gang members can be believed, their role was not negligible during those tumultuous days. Nor was it always negative. Developing an organized force to confront the LAPD led directly to the BPP. Less than a year after the revolt, Buggs told an audience at Fisk University that the gangs had organized a "police patrol" replete with a two-way radio system in cars; they had "movie cameras and flash bulbs," befitting a region near Hollywood, to accomplish their task of monitoring the LAPD. But their cheek may have backfired because the "police are now following the police patrol." [33]

■

In 1965 Winston Slaughter was a twenty-year-old sophomore at Compton College studying sociology. He lived near 51st and Avalon and was a member of the Businessmen, a gang in that vicinity. He joined in 1960, six months after arriving from Birmingham. His grandfather was a painter and not poverty-stricken, but the tense racial atmosphere in Alabama forced his move, so that he did not arrive in LA to live with his father and stepmother in positive spirits about race relations. At that time there were 200 in the gang. "Our activities," he recalled in November 1965, "consist of car theft . . . burglary." He stated that the gang had three sections, the Babies (thirteen to fifteen years old), the Juniors (sixteen to eighteen) and the Seniors (eighteen and up). He joined after the Businessmen had tried to extort money from him.

There was no top leader per se. They met every day. They were mostly students or dropouts or graduates from Jefferson High School, and their operating area was Jefferson on the south, Washington on the north, Hooper on the east, and Vermont on the west. Car theft was a speciality in this land where an auto was seen as measuring personality, manhood, and status. "You might be walking down the street or coming from a party at night. If you was going to the west side, we wasn't old enough to drive and our parents couldn't afford cars for us, so we would see a car we would want and we would decide, 'Well, we live too far. Let's take the car and go.'" The name of this gang, the Businessmen, reflected how these youth were responding to Los Angeles. They chose a title that reflected their aspiration to be at the top of the socio-economic pyramid, and their adventures in car theft could be viewed as a reflection of the illicit business practices that traditionally formed the basis of primitive accumulation of capital. [34]

Their initiation ceremony also reflected the kind of brutality they were facing and the kind they might have to mete out in order to advance. It was a form of running the gauntlet. The prospective member would stand against a wall, and gang members would line up in front of him; he had to reach another wall twenty feet away by fighting his way through. If he succeeded, he was in; Slaughter made it and was accepted.

In addition to car theft and burglary, there was robbery, "mugging homosexuals," larceny from vending machines, and fighting with other gangs. The attacks on homosexuals reflected the homophobia of the larger society, anxiety about adult masculinity, and the forging of male bonds on an altar of antigay sentiment. Los Angeles was the capital of a developing gay and lesbian movement at the same time it was the center of a new black movement; not coincidentally, both developed in a city of constant flux, shallow roots, and a penchant for innovation.[35] There was also considerable fighting in the Businessmen between and among themselves; this was not necessarily due to enmity but a way to toughen themselves. If they were tougher, they could travel anywhere in the city they chose without fear; they could even get other gangs to run errands for them.

They were often armed with knives (by the 1990s the weapon of choice had become a gun), and fights frequently started at parties. Slaughter downplayed impressing young women as a factor in igniting fights; he maintained that the women discouraged fighting. Like many gang members, he drifted away; hence the need for constant recruitment to replenish the ranks. After the probation department began working with the gang and it became more like an ordinary club, he decided to leave it.[36]

But while he was with the Businessmen, Slaughter and his comrades were in frequent conflict with the LAPD. He too recalled being taken for long rides by officers and dropped in alien climes. Police officers often used racial epithets, along with terror tactics, such as putting a pistol to the head of a gang member in order to exact concessions. This was apparently an initiation rite of the LAPD, as such practices were more prone to be performed by rookie than older officers. This also reflected the reality that the strong right-wing presence in the LAPD of Minutemen and Birchers could merge with what could only be characterized as white gangs within the police department.

If arrested, Slaughter and his comrades would be taken to dank jail cells with cold showers and little ventilation. To Slaughter, police relations with the community in LA were much worse than in Birmingham.[37] His fury was fueled by the prevailing tense race relations nationally, symbolized by Selma. Slaughter felt that the "situation in the South had caused a climate of unrest . . . they couldn't fight 'Whitey' in the South but we sure can here." He also cited Proposition 14 as a factor in roiling attitudes. Strikingly, Slaughter rejected the idea that anti-Semitism was a factor in the revolt because most of those he knew "don't distinguish among Caucasians."[38]

Slaughter heard of the Frye incident on 12 August, the next day, at 2 P.M. He and his cohorts pulled whites out of cars, beat them, and burned their cars. Apparently they were involved in the sacking and burning of a liquor store at 51st and Avalon, in the heart of their neighborhood.[39]

Vernon James was nineteen and a graduate of Fremont High School in 1965. He was affiliated with the Slausons, a gang that grew out of Fremont High School and was composed of students or dropouts from there. Their operating area was bordered by Manchester, Slauson, Hooper, and Vermont. They were organized; they had a hand signal, the raising of the index finger and the middle finger on the right hand presenting a V and denoting Slauson Village, a local housing development. The Gladiators were a gang that operated nearby; most of them had attended Manual Arts High School, and their area of operation was bordered by Slauson, Jefferson, Avalon, and Normandie. They too had a hand signal, said to have been patterned after stories in Roman history: a closing of the four fingers and the extension of the thumb on the right hand. From Dorsey High School came the Dodge City group, and they operated in the area bounded by Jefferson, Washington, Western, and La Brea. An older gang, Watts, had been dissolved by August 1965, though their signal—three fingers of the right hand extended upward—had not disappeared.

The names of these groups were evocative. Slausons symbolized the determination of blacks to cross geographic borders; Gladiators showed they would fight. Dodge City would be the result if their determination was blunted. During the uprising many of the gangs did operate as a group, and their solidarity was forged further as they were able both to obtain consumer merchandise and to strike back at the hated LAPD. Their signals and other accoutrements were indispensable to this new solidarity. During the events of August 1965, many of the gangs chose to operate outside their normal boundaries, thus defusing a potential public relations disaster of being held responsible for the destruction of stores and other services that their neighborhoods had come to rely on.[40]

Sniping and looting of pawnshops for weapons were blamed on gangs, although it is unclear to what extent these allegations were accurate. One unnamed source, for example, said that "the uncontrolled and often unnecessary gunfire from National Guard troops and civil police resulted in false sniper reports and conceivably, could have resulted in the unnecessary wounding of civilians. The disciplined use of firearms by National Guardsmen and civil police was lacking." Yet the inflating of the role of gangs, to the extent of tarring them with the Black Scare, reached a new level on 14 August 1965 at 1:48 P.M. when reports reached the authorities about a "large truck full of male Negroes with red arm bands" riding through LA bound for vengeance and plunder.[41]

The state assembly did not feel that accounts of gang involvement in the insurrection were fanciful. Its official report expressed grave concern about "boys designated . . . as being potentially violent." There was like concern over new weapons "fired from a hand held launcher," a detailed exposition on arson and Molotov cocktails, and an expansion of the law on battery against police to include firefighters.[42]

The *Times,* on the other hand, hastened to reassure its readers that "teen age gangs had nothing to do with the outbreak of the rioting." It quoted the "former leader of [a] juvenile hoodlum band," who said that "the trouble broke out spontaneously." On the "third day of the rioting," however, "some gangs from farther north were behind some of the lootings and burnings because they wanted to show the people in Watts they couldn't be outdone."[43]

Thus, the consensus developed that the "riot" cold not be blamed on gangs, but they had substantial responsibility for carrying it forward. There was another factor that received less attention. The blazing events had the effect of not only forging solidarity among gang members but politicizing many as well. There were signs of this before August 1965. In March 1965 in Folsom prison, the NOI had been involved in a major disturbance over "segregated dining facilities" that involved some gang members.[44] This was part of a developing trend of gang members growing closer to the NOI and/ or learning more in a nationalist direction. The fact was that the NOI and gangs often recruited from the same pools, especially in prisons. This cross-fertilization could take place because both had an interest in building economic enterprises for the benefit of themselves, family members, and others.[45] Both also served as a shield, protecting members in prison from sexual assault.

Simultaneously, some gang members were moving toward the nascent LA branch of the Black Panther party and/or leaning more in a progressive, militant direction. Alprentice ("Bunchy") Carter, a founder of the local BPP, represents the confluence of these trends; he was with the Slausons, went to Soledad, became a Muslim, met BPP leader Eldridge Cleaver, and was enticed to join the Panthers.[46] But the Panthers flashed across the western sky like a meteor; their own mistakes combined with repression meant that they were virtually extinct about five years after their 1966 founding. By 1976 Woodrow Redeaux of the reorganized Watts NAACP charged that since the disorders in 1965, drugs, guns, and ammunition had been freely imported into the Los Angeles black community in a "planned program to create unrest, violence and murder." He charged that gangs as well as "political dissidents" were involved in creating this chaos; the liquidation of the BPP was an essential part of this process.[47]

By 1980 the situation had gotten worse. New gangs had developed, some of which were more violent than their predecessors, others of which had broader interests. One variety were "bottle gangs . . . informal groups of adults who spend their days—and nights—just passing bottles, passing time and passing out." They gathered at the Ace-Hi Liquor store at Imperial Highway and Wilmington, downing potent malt liquor: Olde English 800. As in 1965 there were more liquor stores per resident in South LA then in other areas of the city. The men, ranging in age from twenty to seventy, began gathering at 6 A.M. when stores opened and left at 2 A.M. the next day when they closed. More violent gangs were attracted there too because the stores cashed checks and thus had money on hand. "Nearly everyone . . . is taking pills for some kind of ailment. Pills are easy to come by, the people here say. There are certain doctors who will write prescriptions for almost anything in exchange for Medi-Cal stamps."[48]

By 1980 more politically oriented gangs, like the Slausons who formed the basis for the BPP chapter, were a fading memory. There were Crips and Bloods and Bounty Hunters and Grape Street Crips, some with members as young as nine and ten and, thus, in a position to carry the gang culture well into the future. According to one account Los Angeles County had thousands of gang members organized in around 1,000 groups by 1991. Over 700 gang-related homicides occurred in the county that year, about one-third of all its murders.[49] These warrior societies, which could replace bonds not found in families and unions, engaged in crime as a rite, a rebellion, and at times for profit. The BPP, perhaps, could have grown to channel their anger, but it did not survive.

■

Some of the gangs became nationalists, but not all the nationalists were gang members. Both drew adherents from the same source—disaffected black male youth, particularly those in prison—and held ideological affinities. The influence of the nationalists was ideological—in many ways they were a secular version of the NOI—and substantial. On the positive side they stressed self-respect, racial pride, and other practices that could mediate the harshness of living in a society where racism was pervasive. Often they changed their names to reflect African heritage and adopted various forms of West African dress. But their influence was not all positive, and they shared with the BPP and gangs a fascination with the use of force.

This was an expression of the nationalists' approach to masculinity. Like nationalist movements elsewhere, the struggle for gender equality here was constrained by group pressure to conform to hierarchical gender roles. Women seeking to assert their rights were seen as undermining the struggle. Like other nationalist movements, those in South LA often called for women to play subordinate roles. Because blacks were considered the most feminine of the races—that is, black men—and were stripped of many patriarchal privileges, black women were torn between the need to assert their equality and the desire to restore the prerogatives of masculinity denied to their men.

Some black nationalists in Los Angeles, particularly those influenced by Maulana Ron Karenga and his group, United Slaves, felt that regaining what was characterized as African culture was paramount; women were viewed as culture bearers. There was a similar trend among Chicano/a nationalists. Yet in both cases, as Leith Mullings has explained, for women "the end result may be subordination, whether the intent is to extend the 'privileges' of gender roles in the dominant society or in a real or fictive traditional culture. The material base and productive, kinship, and political relations that may have given women a real independence in traditional cultures (e.g., African, Native American) no longer exist. What is reconstructed then, is role asymmetry, which, when combined with contemporary capitalist relations, may lead to gender inequality often surpassing that of 'traditional' cultures." [50]

The perceived abuse of black women by cultural nationalists fed tensions with the Panthers and other antagonists. The position of women in these nationalist organizations was viewed widely not as an extension of traditions established by the left but, instead, a regression or repudiation. The same could be said of their fellow nationalists in the Nation of Islam. The Nation declared that it was in the nature of man to rule and woman to serve as help-mate; the cultural nationalists held a similar outlook. As one result, in many cities—and LA was no exception—five times as any men as women joined the NOI.[51]

■

Bruce Michael Tyler has been an observer and a participant in many of the events of which he has written and he has judged the nationalists harshly. He has declared that force was at the heart of the Frye incident in that a handful of blacks had swindled "several white gangsters" of $1,700 in a marijuana transaction just before 7 P.M. on 11 August 1965. The gangsters armed them-selves and returned to 120th and Avalon, where they were set upon and beaten; their weapons were taken and then used against the authorities. This act of masculinity and reprisal, according to Tyler, was the wellspring of the new nationalism.

He has suggested that John Buggs and the Human Relations Commission staff "cultivated" certain black nationalists who were manipulated against other nationalists, "and the bargain was sealed with money and jobs." All of these factions were inspired in one way or another by Malcolm X, but it was the Buggs faction that leaned more toward "cultural" nationalism and the Sons of Watts, while the other faction leaned toward the BPP. According to the cultural nationalists, "black rage was to be replaced with inward love and self-improvement through cultural identity building programs." Paradoxi-cally, elites approved of their go-it-alone approach, turning away from whites, perhaps because blacks building their own institutions would make less de-mand on public coffers.

Tyler has stated bluntly that "black nationalism was used to further isolate Watts . . . by using black cultural nationalism to turn it inward and away from outward directions." Those involved in "outward directions," like the BPP, were confronted by these cultural nationalists; "the government spon-sored . . . anti-radical persons and groups used these confrontations to gain recognition and prestige as community leaders and militants to challenge the real militants' influence within the community. This was a very sophisticated method of conflict management." Buggs and his government agency sponsored not only nationalists but gangs as well. "Their role as criminals and attackers was simply changed from outright criminals into extra-legal vigilantes . . . the County recruited the worst elements in the community to police the more law-abiding elements." This policing role was handled by the Sons of Watts.

The cultural nationalists and the SOW "'fronted' for the County . . . to act as radical black nationalists in order to contain the black ferment in the riot aftermath and to compete with 'real' radicals." It was not just the BPP that was the target. These nationalists' "tactic of denouncing in public black ministers and traditional civil rights leaders" was part and parcel of the consensus notion that these mainstream leaders had lost touch and the more "militant" nationalists who were more in touch with the masses should be listened to. It turned out, according to Tyler, that these "nationalists" were more in the hip pocket of the elites—contrary to popular opinion—than many of the traditional civil rights leaders like Dr. King.[52] But the narrow nationalist attack on King—in the name of the recently martyred Malcolm—was quite useful to elites still concerned about the reemergence of mass, interracial protest.

Tyler has raised the curious phenomenon of the substantial and mostly noncritical press attention lavished on the embodiment of cultural nationalism, Maulana Ron Karenga. Karenga, he declared "used the national media and the local press to gain prestige with radicals and gangsters. The media opened up doors to leadership roles for Karenga."[53] Though some perceived these nationalists as "anti-white," and although the press was not known to cuddle any black persons who appeared to be challenging the status quo—particularly Dr. King and the BPP—Karenga was treated quite gingerly.

Karenga was born in 1941 in Parsonburg, Maryland; his given name was Ronald McKinley Everett. He held a UCLA M.A. As the *New York Times* observed in an amazingly positive profile, Ron Ndabezitha Everett-Karenga formed the organization he led, United Slaves, or US, shortly after the uprising in order "to challenge the energies of such uprisings all over the nation." Officially he stressed the need for African-Americans to recover their African heritage.[54]

In criticizing the McCone Commission report, Karenga stated that "unless blacks create a culture of their own they will always be marginal men." (The omission of women may not have been accidental.) He cited Frantz

Fanon, who termed violence a "cleansing force." He spoke as an advocate of "black power" and a devotee of "self-determination, self-respect and self-defense," positioning himself as yet another claimant to the fallen mantle of Malcolm X.[55]

Much in this program could have been accepted by the BPP, but Karenga went further to denounce the BPP for being presumptuous enough to consort with Euro-Americans. In turn nascent and actual BPP supporters charged Karenga with recruiting gangsters with the aid of the probation department and the HRC.[56] Many of these forces confronted one another in meetings of the Self-Leadership for All Nationalities, or SLANT, which was a battle-ground for the minds of gang members and black youth generally.[57] Later some of these same forces were involved in forming the Temporary Alliance of Local Organizations, or TALO, which also included the NAACP.[58] The influence of nationalists was demonstrated when months after the uprising a proposal to create a "Freedom City," which would involve a secession of Black LA from the city of LA, received the backing not only of US but of the Communist party, Student Non-Violent Coordinating Committee, and NAACP members.[59]

The growing nationalism may have gone beyond what US intended. One result was the attacking of whites by blacks, and vice versa, for instance, a melee that erupted at the Coliseum during the Junior Olympics. Weeks after the uprising, a forty-year-old white social worker, Robert James Sutter, was "ambushed and seriously wounded" in an interracial conflict. Said the shaken Sutter, "It was just like an execution—they grabbed me and shot me."[60] This racial conflict was a price paid for the decline of the left and interracialism. But the conflict was not just interracial, as maiming violence between cultural nationalists and budding and actual Panthers also mushroomed.

Subsequently, Karenga explained that this conflict with the BPP was "essentially an ideological one and would have remained so if it had not been for the violent intervention of the police and intelligence agencies." He also criticized himself, acknowledging that "the Panthers and the left were correct when they argued against our ideological insularity"; but he was quick to add that "they were incorrect in their assessment and underestimation of the role of culture."[61] Still, in the wake of the Watts Uprising, the promising ideological trend represented by the BPP was wiped out, and US was no small factor in helping to accomplish this goal.[62]

The discourse among blacks was not just between so-called "progressive" and "cultural" nationalists. Roy Wilkins of the NAACP was a stern critic of nationalism generally, once denouncing the "hot-air hatred from American Negro cultists" that was of no help to the Africa they purported to be so concerned about. The *Economist* concluded that conflicts in Watts were part of a larger trend, the fragmenting of racial polities: "The week of the Los Angeles riots was also the week when Malaysia broke apart because brown men could not control their dark suspicions of yellow men and when black and brown resumed their efforts to slug it out in Southern Sudan."[63]

These developments made Black LA conflicts seem tame by comparison, but the point was that there were certain global developments—like the retreat of the organized left—that set the stage worldwide for internal racial cum ideological conflicts. Though Wilkins complained about their rise, the fact was that these nationalists in their call for blacks to control businesses in black communities elevated the middle class—doctors and lawyers—who were in the position to take over when some nonblack merchants began to heed the black nationalists and abandon South LA. This middle class was the foundation of the NAACP in LA.

■

The influence of gangs and nationalists reached a confluence in the initiation of the Watts Summer Festival, which began several months after the uprising. The festival was founded by Tommy Jacquette, Booker Griffin, Stan Sanders, and others in order to "honor the dead," to commemorate the uprising. It was backed by the Westminster Neighborhood Association and John Buggs of the HRC.

Progressive nationalists like Ronald Wilkins, who were leaning increasingly toward BPP ideology, were incensed when they began to perceive that the HRC had conceived of the festival as a means to stifle future rebellions. But that was not the sole basis of their concern. The festival was part of an overall initiative designed to recruit among youth—which the uprising had shown were restive—and teach them "race rhetoric," history classes, Swahili. According to Bruce Tyler, "The raising of race consciousness was now being used to pacify blacks rather than as a call to race militancy or race riots."[64]

Tyler may be viewed as overly harsh toward the growing trend of cultural nationalism. Nevertheless, to the extent that this trend inspired an inward-looking approach focused on "blackness" and an outward manifestation through dress, changed surnames, and the like, it did not necessarily represent a threat to the existing order. It definitely was not so threatening as the competing trend, which was embodied in the BPP. And most certainly, this trend was a gigantic leap backwards as far as women's rights were concerned.

Tyler has argued that there was an "interlocking directorate" that linked US, SOW, an SLANT, and that in turn these forces were influenced heavily by Buggs and the HRC, which employed many of them. There was a battle for the hearts and minds of many gang members and would-be gang members after August 1965, between cultural nationalists and those within the orbit of the BPP. That the former triumphed was due in no small part to the powerful patrons backing them. Many members of the Slausons joined the BPP, but many more would have had it not been for the HRC-bolstered trend of cultural nationalism. The Sons of Watts also helped to drain militant youth away from the BPP. Tyler's conclusion—"these leaders used militant Black rhetoric and the name of Malcolm X to cover their real motives and programs"—is not far from the mark.[65]

Tyler may be overly harsh toward Karenga. He did, after all, play a role in the formation of the Community Alert Patrols, an organization designed to monitor the police, which served as a basis for the organizing of the BPP itself, or so said the *LA Times*.[66] Still, it is understandable why Wilkins and his allies viewed the festival and the role of the cultural nationalists with suspicion. The festival was backed not only by the HRC but also by the LA Chamber of Commerce, Bekins Storage, Security Pacific, and other entities not known for their sympathy for black concerns. Antifestival forces later condemned some gender and age aspects of the festivities, namely the beauty pageant and the way youth were being "co-opted" by participating. As Wilkins saw it, gangs like the Gladiators, Businessmen, Twenties, Outlaws, and Huns, which had banded together to fight the authorities in August 1965, now were monitoring beauty pageants. As others saw it, such exercises only reinforced patriarchy. Wilkins and his comrades were infuriated that Coca Cola (which they noted had invested heavily in apartheid South Africa) and the Century-Industrial Freeway Project (which was designed to "displace over two thousand 'curfew area' Black families") were key funders of the festival and these nationalists.[67]

The summer festival was more than just a yearly event; it represented an overall approach to youth militancy that was designed to draw them away from the BPP. Once the BPP was extinguished, there was then little need for major funders to co-opt youth; they could then be allowed to devolve into gang violence. By 1979 the festival was a shadow of its former size and also gone were the militant symbols of race pride, now viewed increasingly as being somewhat passé. By 1982 the festival was being shut down temporarily due to "neighborhood gangs."[68] Shortly after that, it disappeared altogether, though a remnant of it did reemerge in the 1990s. What had disappeared with it was a kind of militance that the BPP symbolized. Fear of that trend forced the authorities to promote a countertrend, but the eradication of the BPP had the unintended consequence of not providing a framework for militant youth to express themselves and find fraternity. The proliferation of gangs filled that breach, along with a suffocatingly narrow and xenophobic nationalism.[69]

The leadership of many of the gangs, the nationalists, and the NAACP leadership all reflected different aspects of a middle-class approach that discounted confrontation with the LA elite. The decline of working-class parties and organizations created an opening for this.[70] Even the BPP, which disdained this nonconfrontational approach, was still influenced in this direction and can be said to have been—in many respects—"petty-bourgeois revolutionists."[71] Their impatience, their objectification of armed struggle—turning a tactic into a sacred principle—and the tainted tactics of gangsters they inherited had a sad impact on the New Left generally.

But ultimately, what was driving blacks toward and away from the BPP or SOW or cultural nationalism or the NAACP or gangs was a felt need to respond to the special crisis afflicting South LA. This crisis was pervasive and multifaceted; it encompassed the basic issues—employment, education, and the like. But the experience of women and youth—as the evolution of the festival demonstrated—was a prime concern for protesters and law enforcement authorities alike.

■

Black nationalism grew, in part, because of the perception that the criminal justice system was operating with racial bias. Left lawyers like Sam Rosenwein called for a political defense of the defendants, casting what happened as a revolt. Robert Kenny, former National Lawyers Guild president, wanted the issue of amnesty for the defendants raised. On the other side, in addition to bail problems, defendants were being given harsh sentences, while Chief Deputy District Attorney Harold Ackerman was being charged with using peremptory challenges to remove blacks from jury panels. By 1965 the voices of Rosenwein and Kenny were barely heard, while a white backlash propelled a black nationalism.[72]

Even the conservative district attorney Evelle Younger felt judges had gone too far in their animus against defendants. They raised bail so high, he said, that "probably the only ones that made bail were the Muslims and professional hoods." Both nationalists and gang members could depend on comrades in times of need; others were left to fend for themselves, particularly youthful defendants. Younger did not interpose this objection vigorously in court, however, and was pleased with his high conviction rate. Younger, who called "my first boss," J. Edgar Hoover, "the smartest politician in the country," felt that increased intelligence operations would be needed to forestall the growth of black militance.[73]

Sheryl M. Moinat concluded that "there is no typical riot participant."[74] Yet one glaring aspect of the rebellion was the participation of youth and their concomitant growth in militance. The civil rights movement, at various stages, had been a youth movement. Be it SNCC or those arrested in Birmingham in 1963, it did seem that youth were in the vanguard of the thrust for black advance in the 1960s. During the uprising the *LA Times* noted on 13 August that "young people were blamed for much of the trouble."

The "typical" juvenile arrested in August 1965 was a "17 year male Negro with little or no previous contact with the police"; he was "not a gang member" and was a "native of California who had lived in Los Angeles County for more than five years." According to the *Times,* he was from a "broken home . . . father was absent," and there was a "total family income . . . [of] $300 a month." He faced a "charge of looting within one mile of his home" and "usually was with companions of one sort or another." He was "in school— the ninth or tenth grade"—but not doing very well. There was a high dropout rate in this group. Over 80 percent were Protestants and attended church.

Not the least problem was the strain these arrests placed on the juvenile justice system. Said the *Times* on 26 August 1965, "Never in the history of the county's juvenile court system have so many youngsters been arrested in so short a period. . . . Those detained included 41 boys and 5 girls under 13 years of age."[75] There were 450 boys and 72 girls altogether arrested. As a result, Yvonne Brathwaite counseled that in "future emergencies" note be taken of one judge's move on 13 August when "he decided that the usual procedure for handling juveniles should be suspended." Usually a probation officer spoke with the juvenile in cases not considered severe and he or she would be sent home; emulating this judge would mean that the juvenile remained in custody pending a "predentention hearing."[76] Thus, black boys and girls would be detained even though they might be innocent of any crime.

The LA County probation department's liaison with gangs had attracted attention in the past. Similarly noteworthy was its postrebellion study that blamed girls for inciting gang wars among boys. "Girls get a thrill out of seeing a rumble," it concluded, a contention disputed by some male gang members. Some gangs also had female affiliates.[77] The report's conclusion was misleading—another more rigorous study later found the opposite—but the point was no less striking since it provided further confirmation of the popularity of Daniel Patrick Moynihan's thesis that feisty black women dominating black boys and men was a central problem of African-Americans.[78]

■

The popularity of the Moynihan thesis was a distorted response to a real issue. It was fairly apparent that black women had played a role in the streets in a way deemed inconsistent with traditional decorum. Black women tended to be arrested more than white women anyway, reflection of and a reaction against racism influenced by sexism.[79] Just as black men historically had been "feminized," black women had been "masculinized."

In August 1965 Jean Turner was eighteen and living at 9623 South San Pedro; she was born in New York City and had lived in LA for seven years. She was on parole from a girls' reformatory. Her mother was dead, and her father was "mentally unbalanced." Her religious affiliation was uncertain, but her intelligence was of a high quality. She and two girlfriends had been in Huntington Park shopping during the midst of the tumult; they stopped on their way home at Thrifty's, a local store. A boy they knew, she claimed, came up behind them with an armful of men's shoes, and at the same time a police officer approached them and arrested them all. Winifred Penelope, a twenty-two-year-old from Oakland, had been living in LA only six weeks when she endured an experience strikingly similar to Turner's. She was with her mother in a car, and they stopped to see what was going on in a store that apparently was being ransacked. She was arrested, along with her mother, for burglary.[80]

She was reluctant to complain about what happened, but that was not the case for Lovella Brumsey, twenty-seven, of 510 West 87th Street. She was angry about being "shoved" by police officers when she was arrested; "we were told that we were niggers who would be better off in Africa." Ilene Miles, fifteen, lived at 807 East 90th Street with her father, a painter, and mother, a shirt trimmer. Like Brumsey, she was irate about the violence of the LAPD. She wanted to be a secretary, but their arresting her for burglary complicated her career potential.[81]

Lucille Lacy of 11303 Success was thirty years older than Miles and had been living in LA since 1953. Like so many other women arrested, there were material reasons for her situation. "My 11 year old hasn't had a school book since [he was] 5 years old." Like many black mothers she wished to improve the life chances of her child but saw this avenue being blocked because of inferior schools. Housing was inadequate also; there were "rats in sewers as big as cats . . . when sprinklers are turned on and the sewers fill up the rats run in the house if you leave the door open." She was arrested for burglary, but she was operating in the best traditions of the nation in seeking to improve her child's life. Joyce Rodgers, twenty-nine, of 825¾ 82d Street, was born in Galveston and had been in LA only three months when she was arrested during the revolt. She claimed she was a passive bystander, "watching" rock throwing—she "didn't throw any"—at Broadway and Manchester.[82]

It was not only black women who were being driven to prison. The revolt also catalyzed a militance developing among Chicanas, particularly among those who identified with the civil rights movement. Gloria Garcia, twenty-one, of 1216½ East 62d Street, had lived in LA for her entire life. Proud of her Indian heritage, she complained bitterly about the discrimination she found in her community. "My brother-in-law is white and he threw me out because I associate with Negroes. They tried to take my children." On 14 August she was arrested for burglary. Esther Seniga, thirty-seven, was also a lifelong Angeleno and resided at 818 East 105th Street. She confessed that she knew how to make Molotov cocktails and justified looting because of "hated credit practices." She too was arrested, but her misdemeanor charge was dismissed.[83]

Nevertheless, a masculinist black tradition received a boost during the revolt, for many more men than women could claim credit for being in the vanguard of the confrontation with the despised LAPD. The only gender role models many could emulate were those that involved subordination of women; this was true of the mainstream civil rights leadership, the nationalists, the gangs—and the elite with their fascination with the Moynihan Report. It appeared that in return for some masculinist privileges, some black men wound up seeking to subordinate some black women deemed too belligerent.

■

The McCone panel decided to interview those who had been arrested. Though many of the interviewers were white and those being asked questions were not, it is striking how candid the defendants were in providing political explanations of what had transpired. Equally striking was their attraction to nationalism and their penchant for condemning the LAPD.[84] According to Nathan Cohen, these were "signs of a New Militance. . . . The militants are making strong efforts to build a sense of pride in Negro color and to build a sense of ethnicity."[85] This was true particularly of black male and female youth, whose adventurist spirit was so pervasive that it infected many adults.

James Brown was thirty-five in 1965 and had been living in LA since 1955. After dropping out of school, he "had to get a job to live" so he started working as a garbageman in Beverly Hills. What he saw in this posh area contrasted sharply with his neighborhood. He was arrested as he was driving home during the midst of the rebellion, which he insisted was unfair because he had not done anything. His interviewer agreed that he was a "very nice, very gentle, very cooperative man. I felt he truly was not a participant and was a law abiding citizen who had worked hard to gain what little he has." It did not matter; he now had been tarred with an arrest record. Perhaps understandably he had soured on the LAPD; remarkably, these developments also soured him on black leadership as well.[86]

In their haste to quell the uprising, the police swept up a number of otherwise innocent persons in their dragnet. In their haste to reestablish law and order, they often strayed beyond their normal discourtesy and incivility. It may not have been the intention, but the result was to induce antipolice sentiment and increased militance. Arthur Burke, thirty-four, was a painter living at 1561 South Spaulding. While coming from 76th and Compton, he attempted to drive past a section of 46th and Central that was blocked off because of burning. He stood there watching when a police van arrived, and he was arrested along with others who were milling about.[87]

Peer pressure was instrumental in the formation of the new nationalism. How was it that some who theretofore had gone along in order to get along with racists and/or the LAPD decided to resist? Some could be induced into taking militant actions because of the actions of a few; a psychology was de-

veloping which posited that the appropriate response to racism or police misconduct was hitting back, not passive resistance. Malcolm X was their symbol,
not Martin Luther King, Jr. Calvin Joe Jones, twenty-three, of 1313 West
66th Street, told his listener as much.[88]

However, the provocation of law enforcement and an unequal society at
times was so severe that even Mahatma Gandhi himself might have felt compelled to strike back. Willey Shorty, twenty-seven, of 510 West 87th Street,
was born in New Orleans but had been in LA since 1952. He was working
at a car wash but was making $55 per week, though "a white man starts at
$100 per week." He wanted to work at Bethlehem Steel on Slauson; he had
never heard of the War on Poverty. During the revolt he was attacked physically by a police officer who was also verbally abusive, saying, "You niggers
think you are going to take over this town like Mississippi." He heard another
officer say, "I haven't shot a nigger since yesterday." Shorty was a prime recruit
for black nationalism; like virtually all of those interviewed, he was contemp-
tuous of black leaders like Buggs, Brookins, and Hudson. "None," he felt,
"are worth anything; [they] don't care about poor people."[89]

John Harris, nineteen, of 6103 South Avalon, had a similar experience.
He encountered a police officer who told him, "If you make a move I'll blow
your head off." This was a continuation of the pre-August pattern, for the
LAPD "consistently" stopped "me as well as my friends . . . asking questions—where have you been . . . [where] are you going." His conception of
black leaders and organizations was akin to Shorty's; he had never heard of
the War on Poverty, or of Brookins and others deemed to be leaders.[90]

Robert Smith, twenty-seven, of 825 East Century Boulevard, was a lifelong resident of LA and a truck driver. He spoke of how the flux presented
by the revolt was transforming consciousness. "If I had my way I would blow
all of them up including Parker! They always mistreat us—rough us up—
even LAPD Negro officers are bad." He knew how to make Molotov cocktails
and had an attitude that indicated he might have used them.[91]

Robert James, thirty-two, of 1327 Wright Street, also knew how to make
Molotov cocktails and had endured an experience that might have led him to
use them too. After being handcuffed by the LAPD, he "was struck across
[the] shoulders near [the] neck with shotgun—officers also used vile language." As John Harris said, this was nothing new; he had been "stopped
numerous times" previously by the LAPD. John Cottrell, twenty-eight, of
601 West 80th Street, was angry too. He had been "placed under arrest with-

out anything in my possession." But then he was taken to the 77th Street precinct and photographed "with looted merchandise in foreground. They "made it appear from photo as though it was merchandise that I took." [92]

Clarence Dyas, thirty-three, of 1010 East 43d Street, was a lift-truck operator born in Louisiana. His tale of economic woe, leading inexorably to conflict with the authorities, represented the experience of many. Work was "difficult to find. Construction work was seasonal and weather often prevented construction." He had a family to support and, as it turned out, received "stolen property" during the revolt, for which he was arrested. "There were 3 police officers that came to my home and arrested me and handcuffed me in front of my 8 year old daughter, all the other kids tease her and call her father a jail bird. The police have my sewing machine and record player, the finance company wants me to pay the payments but I refuse." This would mean a negative credit rating, further worsening his economic woes. But it was the LAPD that stirred his wrath. "They talk to a man like he is a dog. Because you're in jail you're treated like a criminal and called [all] kinds of names." [93]

The economic dilemma of Clarence Dyas was that of many in South LA. Economic constraints led him and others to the snapping point, whereby they were willing to cross the line and defy the established rules of society. This was not a political decision per se, but the process of defiance was political in an objective sense and did lead to transformed political consciousness. This is why this was not just a riot but a revolt in that the end result was political, even if the subjective motivations of all of the participants were not.

Everett Williams, thirty, was typical of those who were swept up by the winds of change. He came to LA from North Carolina with his sister and her two children only to find he could not support them even though he was getting up at 4 A.M. to walk or hitchhike from their tiny apartment at 226 West 78th Street to ask for jobs in Torrance, Santa Monica, Burbank, Glendale, and Pasadena. When it seemed that law had been suspended in August 1965, it was not difficult for an Everett Williams to take to the streets and participate in an urban revolt that could lead to a confrontation with the authorities that would transform consciousness. [94] But this consciousness was transformed not in the context of an organized struggle—like a strike—but in a disorganized, fluid context; thus, the transformation could be ephemeral or even negative.

Robert James was asked why certain stores were burned. "Because they were owned by whites and especially Jews," he replied. Raymond Lee Pollard agreed. "Negroes [are] not getting fair deal from stores owned and operated by Jewish people."[95] The rise in the black community of nationalism fueled Islamic sects; combined with preexisting anti-Semitism in the United States, this often led to jaundiced views of Jewish people, which served to undercut the high moral ground theretofore occupied by the movement for black equality.

There were other causes feeding rebelliousness in South LA. Clarence Dyas observed that "people come to California believing they could do better," but "they found the same problems here as in Louisiana. Things cost twice as much in this area as in other areas."[96] It all came back to economic distress driving many blacks to cross the line of legality, which inevitably brought confrontation with law enforcement and transformed their consciousness. But civil society—organizations and associations—was unprepared for what happened, and black defendants quickly discovered that the NOI and the gangs took care of their own while others were left to fend for themselves.

Harold Bell, twenty-eight, of 1332 East 112th Street, had been arrested for burglary during the revolt. He felt that certain shops were being attacked because these merchants "had been sarcastic to Negro people." He assailed the LAPD. "Negro people [are] tired of being misused by [the LAPD]—do not respect our women folk. Talk down to them. . . . More like slavery times." Seeking to protect black women and conform to the patriarchal norm was seen as a step forward for many; this step strengthened a masculinist nationalism viewed as the best alternative.[97]

Quite a few of those arrested had learned the simple art of constructing a Molotov cocktail. Others had experience with weapons because they hailed from rural areas where hunting was common or because they had served with the armed forces in Korea. Some questioned whether snipers existed, but Patrick Lee Henry claimed to have seen them firing from "on top of [the] Figueroa Hotel" at Figueroa and Santa Barbara. Why would residents of South LA be moved to take such extreme measures? He "thought snipers were shooting because of innocent people being shot and in self-defense a number of persons began using weapons rather than to be shot without provocation."[98]

But once the guns were fired by blacks and it was seen that order could break down, the idea could grow that the existing order could be replaced altogether. This was a form of revolutionary consciousness. But the only leaders present who might have exploited that consciousness were a coterie of NAACP-style leaders, gangs, and NOI followers who were not able to build on it. The old and new leadership lacked the experience in building collectivity that characterized the left; since the missions of these groups were congruent with some of the key aims of the order they were supposedly challenging, this leadership proved insufficient.

Marco Atterbury, who also had been arrested, concurred with the opinion that law enforcement was helping to ignite black militance. While in custody, he "heard in jail that the next time it will be worse. His co-prisoners want to get back at the police." They were furious because "innocent people" were "going to jail for nothing thus losing their jobs, lose their cars and everything they have. Tremendous resentment is now being built up within the prisoners."[99]

Latinos were affected also. Martin Ayala, thirty-five, lived at 1151 South Hicks but had lived in Chavez Ravine in East LA before Mexican-Americans were ousted so that the Dodgers could build a stadium. He too knew about Molotov cocktails from his experience in the armed forces. Like his black brothers, he was resentful of the LAPD and how easily it could provide an unwanted arrest record that would lead to drastically circumscribed opportunity.[100]

The destruction of Ayala's old neighborhood threw blacks and Latinos together even more. This could spur conflict, but it also could have the opposite effect. Antonio Alfaro, thirty-one, was defined as black and lived at 229 West 51st Street. Born in Earl, Arkansas, he had lived in LA for twelve years. He had worked at a car wash but had spent considerable time in Mexico because he was "treated like a man down there." He was a nascent nationalist and "used to go to the mosque before he left LA for Mexico."[101] He too was familiar with Molotov cocktails and seemed to have possessed enough anger to throw one.

Antonio Alfaro was an example of another postrevolt trend: cross-fertilization between African-Americans and Mexican-Americans. The evolution of gangs is one example. The creation of the Brown Berets as conscious invocation of the Black Panthers was another. Similarly, the nationalism of the Nation of Aztlan was a counterpart of the Nation of Islam. In the 1990s the nationalist groupings in both communities have survived while their more leftist counterparts have disappeared.

10

The State and
Civil Society

AFRICAN-AMERICANS FOUND IT DIFFICULT TO OB-
tain mortgage loans to buy new housing or loans for home improvement.
There was no effective rent control to curb the growing share of income
soaked up by housing costs. Above all, there was a pervasive bias that locked
blacks into a ghetto and locked them out of housing opportunities. This kind
of housing bias also limited the educational opportunities available in that
neighborhood schools were predominant. The struggle around Proposition
14 on the November 1964 ballot crystallized many of these problems and
simultaneously heightened tensions to the point where an urban uprising ensued. This problematic housing-school nexus also was fueled by related factors: a pervasive poverty that circumscribed opportunity and black institutions, for example, the church, that often were not able to confront the
challenges to be faced.

This failure was pronounced during the hearings held to determine how
and why people were killed during the revolt. When justifiable homicide was
announced in these cases and police escaped prosecution, the aggrieved of
South LA witnessed not only the failure of government and justice but a failure of civil society, including associations, party cells, churches, and the like.
In part because of the nationalist fervor of the revolt, it became difficult to
attract allies in the struggle for justice. Certainly the expressions of anti-
Semitism did not help. Similarly unhelpful was the pronouncement that the
black family was the major source of instability that created the revolt.

■

There were structural reasons for the housing crisis in Los Angeles. John C. Monning, superintendent of the Department of Building and Safety at the time of the uprising, recalled that the layout of LA featured both alleys and garages. When population began to swell during World War II, "the easiest thing to do was to convert that garage that had never been designed for a dwelling unit, or the woodshed [into residential housing], or add on illegally to the garage."

Government may have worsened the problem by seeking to halt this process without constructing alternatives, thereby only curtailing overall housing stock. Beginning in 1954—in Watts particularly—thousands of sheds, shacks, and illegal additions were removed; moreover, about 25 percent of the existing residential buildings were demolished because they were dilapidated. The substandard housing—in Watts especially—was reduced from 40 percent of the dwellings in 1950 to 3 percent in 1960, but this laudable accomplishment also reduced housing opportunities where racism locked blacks out of opportunities beyond the ghetto. Community residents may have sensed this dilemma, for both before and after the uprising, housing inspectors were harassed; it got so bad in the Adams–Long Beach Boulevard area that inspection activities had to be temporarily suspended.[1]

There was a ceaseless flow of black migrants flooding into Los Angeles— and not finding housing opportunities beyond a narrow area. Since 1940 the black population of LA had increased at a rate three to four times faster than that of New York City.[2] These migrants encountered a hardened bias in the real estate industry. In the 1950s as blacks began to escape from the straitjacket of South LA and move farther north to Baldwin Hills, View Park, Windsor Hill, and Crenshaw, the pattern of bias increased.

The process of buying a home involved complex interactions between blacks and, mostly, whites in neighborhoods, banks, and offices. There may not have been the de jure discrimination that had driven the civil rights movement in the South; Loren Miller and other farsighted activists had seen to that. However, there remained a smog of de facto discrimination that seemed to be beyond the reach of sanction.

This led to the formation of a group called the Crenshaw Neighbors, designed to reverse this discrimination and "preserve integration." According to Jean Gregg, leader of this community-based organization, "brokers were discouraging Caucasian buyers." Yet, contrary to popular opinion, there was "no decline in the real value of property in Crenshaw" after blacks moved in; in fact, she told the McCone Commission, "our impression is that Negroes maintain their homes better than Caucasians." The prejudice rippled into the school system. Problems at nearby Dorsey High School were the "most frequent topic of discussion" at the meetings of the Crenshaw Neighbors. As young people accustomed to segregated existence were thrown together in schools, "serious racial problems" ensued, leading to an "unnecessary number of violent incidents . . . serious fights."[3]

Government was not an innocent bystander, passively watching the real estate industry. Though the popular columnist Drew Pearson blamed the "real estate lobby," he was caustic about the role of government in ousting families from Chavez Ravine—where a housing project had been planned—turning over that key parcel of real estate to the Dodgers for a baseball stadium, and leaving those mostly Latino families to fend for themselves. Many

6. South LA businesses burn in August 1965.

of them moved to South LA, which placed them in conflict with blacks over a dwindling number of viable housing opportunities. Housing activist Frank Wilkinson observed, "Had the Chavez Ravine and Rose Hill developments been allowed to bear their fruit, 25,000 to 30,000 persons, the majority of them children, could have been lifted from the stifling pressures of the ghetto into the good air of integrated, beautifully designed and low rental communities of good living." Thus, he concluded, "the sixties reap the follies of the fifties."[4]

African-Americans faced "the burning of crosses, acts of vandalism, threats of violence . . . neighborhood demonstrations, rumor," and worse when they sought to move from Black LA.[5] When violence accompanied integration of neighborhoods in the late 1940s and early 1950s, the vibrant, multiracial Civil Rights Congress intervened and mobilized. It had been long

7. On 15 August 1965 the National Guard's 40th armored division sets up a machine gun to confront "rioting" residents of South LA.

gone by 1965. By the mid-sixties both the rental and home purchase markets were marked by this kind of racial harassment; it had impact on all blacks, regardless of class, and thus fed nationalism. The real estate industry fueled this harassment. It was well known that certain blocks were staked out for blacks and others for nonblacks. Those so bold as to violate these informal rules faced an angry retribution.[6]

Residential desegregation was resisted fiercely by various Euro-Americans of all classes and thus fed white chauvinism. Warren Christopher, then an attorney for the McCone Commission, cracked at one point, "Someone has said . . . that integration is the period between when the first Negro family moved in and the last [white] family moves out."[7] This was a familiar trend in the United States, but once again LA had its own peculiarities. It was one of the few cities that did not suffer a severe loss of whites in the years preceding 1965; in turn this further lessened the housing available for the burgeoning black population.[8]

LA did not have the kind of rent control that graced New York City; this

8. The LAPD and the National Guard search these South LA residents in August 1965.

also meant that it did not have the fierce battles to maintain these controls, which helped to engender class conflict between landlords and tenants and class consciousness as well.[9] Unrestrained landlords in LA could not resist subdividing already small one-family dwellings and renting them to several families without maintaining the property. When faced with health department condemnation, they would simply tear down the rickety structures and sell the land. This reduced housing stock further and made the remaining residences in the ghetto more valuable; still, the record showed that at least 22.5 percent of homes in Watts, for example, were deteriorating or dilapidated.[10]

When HUD secretary Jack Kemp visited LA in 1989, he discovered that as many as 40,000 families continued to live in garages with no running water, toilets, or sometimes even windows. LA also had one of the highest rates of homelessness in the nation. African-Americans in search of housing in LA in 1965 found it difficult to get loans, FHA or otherwise. The major realty board in Southern California virtually prohibited providing opportunities for blacks to move beyond a well-contained ghetto.[11] According to California real estate commissioner Milton Gordon, "four out of five brokers interviewed will do business with Negroes only on a limited basis, if at all."

Confirming the existence of a compounded racism, he added, "Americans of Chinese, Japanese or Filipino descent apparently receive better treatment"; but they enjoyed no paradise since "less than half of the realty firms covered by this study were ready to give them equal service based on ability to pay." There were 80 blacks on a LA Realty Board of 2,080. They were not able to put a dent in the

9. On 15 August 1965 Euro-American buyers crowd a gun shop on North La Brea in LA.

powerful pattern of racial steering and outright bias, in part because of the absence of mass organizations that could address this problem.[12]

Those testifying before the McCone Commission singled out the housing question as a major cause of black discontent. Watts real estate broker Edward Warren had an office at 1204 Compton Avenue and was a a member of the black Consolidated Realty Board, organized after World War II when blacks were barred from the main board. He recalled a time during the war when "a Negro did not live any further south around Wilmington and Compton than 120th Street." He added: "Now, Lynwood, if you know—you have been down in the area—we have a Berlin wall. Poverty begins on the west side of the tracks this time."[13]

NAACP branch member Christopher Taylor was caustic in his testimony.

10. Martin Luther King, Jr., flanked by Bayard Rustin, meets with this skeptical black audience in LA in August 1965.

"I know Don Wilson, I visited him down in Torrance, and not only did he get federal money to build, he built a colored tract in Centerville and a colored tract in Dominguez, and then built a white tract, and he decided where these people would live. . . . Just think now, most of the Negroes in the Watts area live in houses [for] approximately $75 a month that are many years old, but a man could go out to West Covina somewhere and buy a house with wall to wall carpet and all of the built-ins, drapes, and [his] note will be $80 a month and no impounds." John Buggs confirmed this bias and commented that "not only are minority group persons living in sub-standard housing but that, generally speaking, they pay more for sub-standard housing than does the white population for standard housing."[14] In the "Dream Factory" that was Los Angeles, where luxurious homes were an inescapable part of the landscape, blacks were allotted only inferior homes in South LA.[15]

The prominent jurist Loren Miller, who litigated some of the leading cases against racially restrictive covenants in deeds, declared that "the great problem faced by citizens in the United States" was this issue of residential

11. A black merchant seeks to protect his shop by using a nationalist appeal.

segregation. It was, he said, "an open invitation to conflict; . . . it in fact breeds conflict." This was an area where the Golden State had pioneered when the constitution drawn up in the 1870s attempted to codify residential segregation, aimed primarily at Asian-Americans. Residential segregation, in short, was no accident or "act of God." It was the logical result of intentional acts. "The Southeast Realty Board particularly worked in season and out to confine Negroes to the traditional Watts." In 1947, he told the McCone Commission, an African-American was jailed "because he wanted to occupy his own home on East 92nd Street east of Central Avenue." In Compton, he recalled, echoing the testimony of Edward Warren, "the rallying cry . . . at that time was to keep Negroes north of 130th Street." When many whites objected to the building of homes for workers, including blacks, near Douglas Aircraft's Santa Monica plant, they were built instead in Watts, further locking African-Americans into the ghetto.[16] Racially restrictive convenants were enforced by the courts until 1948, but changing the law did not necessarily change the practice of residential segregation.

A decision by the NAACP leadership helped ensure the continuation of

12. This blockade is one of those the LAPD and National Guard set up in August 1965.

this practice: this mass organization would rely not on its base of members—which might provide opportunity for infiltration by Reds and worse—but on the wizardry of its attorneys, including their West Coast leader, Franklin Williams, and their national leader, Thurgood Marshall. This decision was certainly helpful to the careers of those who executed it; in the long run it was less helpful to the presumed beneficiaries of their largesse, for their skills could be successful only in an atmosphere transformed by mass action.

By 1965 the pattern of bias was so deeply ingrained that even black-administered institutions felt constrained to observe the status quo, according to Ben Bingham, president of Fortune Homes. He recalled going to Broadway Savings and Loan—controlled by NAACP leader H. Claude Hudson—in 1962 to get financing to build homes. He was told that the company would make no loans in Watts because there was "too much transient traffic in Watts and the loans there are not good."[17]

There was conflicting evidence as to whether Watts and South LA provided good risks for mortgage loans. Emil Seliga, the president of the Catholic Human Relations Council, felt that the market was bad in Watts, homes were

13. At this wrecked shop on Avalon near Slauson, the LAPD seeks to apprehend "suspects."

hard to sell, and foreclosures were frequent. But Yvonne Brathwaite, who did an exhaustive survey and did not rely on hearsay alone, concluded that the "rate of delinquency" there was comparable to other areas.[18]

Reasonable persons could disagree as to whether lending money in Watts was risky; what was undeniable was that it was difficult to obtain loans for housing, whatever the risk factor. B. O. Corbett of Corbett Construction was of the opinion that lending institutions simply made the decision that the area was not worthy of receiving loans, a process denoted subsequently as "redlining." When savings and loan institutions did deign to lend money in Watts and South LA generally, often they did so at exorbitant interest rates larded with special charges.[19]

■

When the NAACP, Assemblyman Byron Rumford, and other forces sought to pass legislation to curb the most draconian residential segregation excesses, their efforts were rebuffed in November 1964 when Proposition 14 was passed. This was a key factor in stoking alienation in South LA and making

14. At a September 1965 hearing, a Molotov cocktail stands between Chief William Parker of the LAPD and City Councilman Tom Bradley.

many blacks feel that there was a concerted plan to keep them locked into a
ghetto and locked out of housing opportunity.[20]

The importance of Proposition
14—and the statewide debate on racism and discrimination it engendered—
cannot be underestimated. Sensitive issues were raised—Would you want
your daughter to marry one? Would you
want one to live next door?—in the
context of a national debate on race
sparked by the civil rights movement.
When the debate rested in November
1964, the result was a signal of who had
won and lost. Proposition 14 repealed
the Rumford Fair Housing Act, a measure designed to alter entrenched pat-

15. Augustus Hawkins was congressman
from South LA in August 1965.

terns of bias in the housing market; the proposition passed by a huge two-to-
one margin. Ultimately its thrust was reversed by the courts, but the message
to Black LA had been sent clearly by then: their presence was not desired in
many neighborhoods.[21]

A NAACP official, whose opinion was shared widely by many blacks, felt
that the campaign to pass Proposition 14 was "characterized by half truths
and lies, it is based on the false contention that private property rights take
precedence over civil rights and the public welfare."[22] This scurrilous campaign only deepened the anger and alienation among blacks and fed nationalism. Yet no one could paint the campaign for Proposition 14 as a simple
black-versus-white issue, for many Euro-Americans worked tirelessly against
the measure. Celebrities like Gregory Peck, William Wyler, Burt Lancaster,
and Frank Sinatra banded together in Hollywood Stars against Proposition
14. The Japanese-American Citizens League and the Mexican-American Political Association stood with them, though—interestingly—the Mexican
Chamber of Commerce did not.[23] It was not white versus black, but diminished class consciousness made it easier to characterize Proposition 14 as such
in South LA; this broadly shared opinion fed black nationalism.

The California Real Estate Association denied vehemently that Proposition 14 was a factor in sparking the conflagration, but its opinion was not

accepted universally.[24] The direct rebuttal in the streets in August did not stifle the efforts of the industry to continue profiting from bias, however. Racial steering continued, as did more sophisticated forms of bias. For a while it seemed that scams became sharper; Van Nuys Savings and Loan apparently did not stop swindling homeowners in South LA out of their homes by the use of second mortgages and aggressive foreclosures. Again, government was not innocent, for one of the central figures in this scandal was close to "high political circles in California," and monitoring agencies were asleep.[25]

Housing stock was not the main target hit by the fires of August, but there was some damage to homes. Sadie Rubenstein was a landlord at a building in Willowbrook that was torched; six of her ten tenants were displaced. She had no plans to reinvest, and because of government policy there was "no disaster relief of any kind . . . designated for her or the other owners" so affected.[26] In the wake of August 1965, loans on real estate—which were difficult to obtain anyway—were hardly available at reasonable interest rates in Black LA. Insur-

16. In August 1965 Ronald Wilkins (*in jacket, left*) confronts the LAPD. He went on to play a leading role in the Community Alert Patrol, a precursor of the Black Panther Party.

ance—also difficult to get anyway—was made available only at excessive rates. Loans for commercial real estate were hardly available either.[27]

In the San Fernando Valley, a bastion of housing opportunity for the white working class, blacks continued to face a bar. According to the Valley Fair Housing Council, in the weeks following the uprising, sixty-three black families came to its door in search of housing, nineteen to buy, thirty-three to rent apartments, and eleven to rent houses. Of these, five succeeded in buying, sixteen in renting apartments, and one in renting a house. However, most of these families were steered to Pacoima, a section of the valley that was being designated for African-Americans.[28] This was a de facto moderate option: providing housing beyond the ghetto of South LA meant constructing another ghetto in the valley. Integration remained distant.

Meanwhile, it seemed that after the fires had been extinguished, a lingering aftereffect remained the gulf separating Watts from its northern neighbors in Crenshaw, Baldwin Hills, and other areas where some blacks were allowed to buy houses in 1965. One study suggested that blacks in Watts were more likely to approve of the rebellion, to be hostile to whites, and to oppose integration than those farther north. South LA was the epicenter of the rebellion; it was where conditions were worst. Blacks of all colors were found north of this area, but the lighter skinned and the more affluent seemed more prevalent in Baldwin Hills and thereabouts, which might help to account for this difference in attitudes toward integration. The rebellion heightened this process of differentiation. The study's conclusion that "it is probably inappropriate to talk about 'the Negro in Los Angeles' or 'the Negro community'" signaled certain distinctions that growing black nationalism could not altogether assuage.[29]

Urban renewal signified to some building new housing and to others continuing the process of tearing down substandard homes. Days after the uprising city Planning Director Calvin Hamilton was mulling the prospect of "land clearance–urban renewal" and considering even more seriously "the antagonism it would generate." With typical bureaucratic hesitancy the city council voted in November 1965 to appropriate $98,000 to study the question.[30] Months later the *Herald-Dispatch* was reporting "panic" in South LA over the prospect of urban renewal and the possibility that existing homes would be seized "via legal methods." The increasingly nationalistic black weekly scorned the role of the NAACP and Yvonne Brathwaite in this process. "There are teams of real estate investors operating . . . representing to owners that if they do not sell their homes immediately, the city will take their homes, offering little or no compensation." In the targeted area, McKinley to Hooper and 43d to 46th Street, there were many elderly blacks, but the central fear was that the urban renewal proposal was designed to blunt the black political power that was the upside of concentrating blacks into certain neighborhoods.[31]

The battle over urban renewal raged over the next few decades in South LA, and it turned out that fears of black displacement were not misplaced. Moreover, racial steering, housing segregation, and the like continued. Watts residents like Freita Shaw, who had lived there thirty years, wanted to move; her light-skinned husband had been stoned during the uprising, and the neighborhood now seemed not so comfortable. But she could not sell her house. She blamed the negative connotations now attached in certain circles to the very term *Watts* and argued passionately that Watts "definitely is not a slum. This isn't like Harlem." The black celebrity Sammy Davis, Jr., could afford to live almost anywhere in Southern California, but he was being steered away from the more affluent regions that he preferred.[32] That was the dilemma for African-Americans. Powerful forces were pushing them inexorably toward ghettoization, but this process was serving to create a steaming anger that had no outlet; it could only explode from time to time, engulfing the entire city. Residential segregation fed black nationalism and white chauvinism.

■

The neighborhood school was a concept defended fiercely in LA. A problem, however, was that housing bias often locked African-Americans into deteriorating neighborhoods, bereft of the kind of political power needed to provide decent schools. As a result, blacks often could not get the kind of education that would give them the skills needed to obtain housing—assuming bias could be overcome—and so on. Thus, inadequate education was a cofactor in spurring revolt and part of a cycle of pain.[33]

Southern California had its own peculiarities with regard to black education. The U.S. Civil Rights Commission stated that before 1947 the California education code allowed for segregation of "Indian . . . Chinese, Japanese, or Mongolian"; Latinos were included within this sweeping ambit but there was no mention of blacks.[34] This oversight should not be interpreted to suggest that there was equality in education for African-Americans. This was just another expression of the state's compounded racism.

Housing bias led to circumscribed housing choices, which led to overcrowded schools. According to Jack Crowther, superintendent of schools in the city of LA in August 1965, "Growth in the curfew area since 1955 averages 434 pupils per school; only in the West San Fernando Valley has growth and enrollment occurred more rapidly . . . [but] the average elementary school size in the curfew area is 1100 students and the average in the West San Fernando Valley is 869."[35]

Short sessions and double sessions were more prevalent in schools populated by African-Americans and Chicanos. According to Marnesba Tackett of the Education Committee of the United Civil Rights Committee, there were at the same time a "great number of empty classrooms in other sections."[36] According to Lois Massey, a former PTA president in LA, officialdom paid little or no attention to complaints about the schools before the revolt. Yet "the majority of the substitute, conditional and probationary teachers work in the minority community"; then, after their teaching skills improved, they were removed. There was overcrowding, with thirty-five to thirty-nine pupils per class, and harsh discipline, including "corporal punishment . . . to the point of sadism." That this discipline often was dispensed by white male teachers on black youth already harassed by the LAPD served to increase alienation and anger and made many suspect the traditional left argument looking to the public sector for remedy.

Meting out homework was rare, supplies were sparse, buildings were decrepit, children were called names by teachers—"monkeys or even thugs and tramps." Parents were "berated before the child" by school officials, thus undermining parental discipline and at times confirming that Negro men were the "female" of the races. Few students were counseled to go to college. The schools were a mess.[37]

Jordan High School, in the heart of the curfew zone, epitomized inequality. This school did not have chemistry classes and until 1965 was the only city high school without a chemistry laboratory. Just as dental school students practiced on the mouths of the poor before moving on to more agreeable climes, Jordan was afflicted with a similar process. This was the opinion of X. L. Smith of 724 East 116th Street, a Jordan alumnus who returned to teach there. There seemed to be an unwritten rule, he said, that if a teacher or principal can survive at Jordan, this proved his or her mettle for higher posts. In 1965 the school had fifty-one white and forty-six black teachers, but it was considered a proving ground for the former.[38]

Naturally, protest against such travesties was not absent. There was a Student Committee for Improvement in Watts, which was an outgrowth of SURE, Students United for Racial Equality. Both organizations worked on issues in and around Jordan, including fighting blight and registering community residents to vote.[39] This tradition of protest was carried to the streets in August 1965, and that spirit continued to percolate after that date; after all, those in Jordan's age cohort were disproportionately represented in the streets. They were not necessarily profligate in protests, however; though fires consumed store after store, no schools were damaged, despite the fact that troops often were bivouacked there.[40]

A rebellious spirit spread in the schools after August 1965. According to Superintendent Crowther, discipline became "more difficult within the schools . . . more of our teachers are being subjected to even bodily pressures." At that point, he went off the record.[41] John R. Doyle, Jr., a principal on the front lines, confirmed that after August 1965 students became more difficult to control.[42] There was fear that teachers would transfer en masse out of South LA.

The executive secretary of the American Federation of Teachers local, Jean Thompson, urged reforms to forestall a future uprising, such as reducing class size and teaching loads as incentives for teachers not to leave South LA.[43] Some teachers sought to incorporate the lessons of the uprising into the curriculum.[44] After the revolt South LA gained a sort of cachet that inspired some to seek ties and identification with this now highly publicized area.

Segregation was even more apparent in higher education. Despite their support through taxes, blacks were largely absent from the University of California, and those few who were enrolled at UCLA often faced an alienating and hostile atmosphere. The university's response to the August events was multifaceted. Westwood was not close to the curfew zone, but the smoke invaded the sky over the affluent neighborhood. The university arranged to continue regular salary payments to those employees called by the guard to put down the revolt.[45] On the other hand, the University Religious Conference was in the forefront of those collecting nonperishable food to take to churches and other distribution centers in South LA in the wake of the destruction of grocery stores.[46]

UCLA established tutorials and other programs in South LA staffed by its students,[47] and later the administration embarked on a conscious campaign to increase the number of minority students. The smoke over Westwood in August 1965 opened the eyes of those who had been blind to many problems in South LA. Postpuberty youth were driving the civil rights movement in Birmingham and the South, and they were a moving force in LA too. Some thought that training more blacks to be skilled workers and consumers would be useful for the economy. Education reform, as a consequence, was a priority after August 1965.[48]

■

The black nationalists' idea that "their" women should be subordinate dovetailed neatly with the elite's idea that the black family was overly matriarchal. Both saw black women as the problem. As a result, black nationalism received a boost, and black women were denigrated.

Despite the problems of housing and education confronting African-Americans, some seeking to understand what was hurting blacks saw another problem. Their target became the flaws they saw in the black family. What was happening to the black family—the weakening of the nuclear family, proliferating divorce, single-parent households—eventually would become national questions; but in 1965 it was not difficult for some to view this as simply something endemic to African-Americans. Blacks were having difficulty in securing adequate housing and education and being transported to job sites, but to some it appeared that a major reason for the plight of blacks was weakness in family structure.

Curiously, the role of black women in the family was targeted when the civil rights movement was mounting a serious challenge to racism and the feminist movement was just beginning to challenge patriarchy. Targeting black women was part of a parallel initiative—the "culture of poverty" thesis—that displaced concern from unemployment, housing, education, and transport to family structure and gender. Lost in this morass was the fact that the family is socially constructed. It is not just a biological arrangement but a product of specific conditions shaped by the socioeconomic structure. It is not a separate sphere; that is, it cannot be comprehended in isolation from factors like housing and education. But focusing intently on the presumed flaws of black women in the family was a bridge linking concerns of black and white men about the atmosphere that both were facing at home.[49]

As early as 14 August 1965, a page-one *LA Times* headline blared, "Racial Unrest Laid to Negro Family Failure." The *Wall Street Journal* followed up with a front-page article claiming, "Family Life Breakdown in Negro Slums Sows Seeds of Race Violence . . . Racing a Booming Birth Rate." This focus on the black family did not materialize mysteriously; it was largely a product of the well-known study conducted by Daniel Patrick Moynihan. When CBS-TV produced a report on the uprising, he was interviewed at length and repeated his themes about the alleged weaknesses in the black family that provided fertile soil for rage and violence.[50]

Moynihan stated that the furor which accompanied the report and hampered the immediate implementation of his recommendations was somehow to blame for the explosion in LA. One analyst asserted bluntly that "if the so-called 'Moynihan Report' . . . had been heeded, the riots perhaps could have been avoided." Soon the *LA Times* was spouting the new line, arguing that the cause of the August events was "the structure of Negro family life." Why? "To a tragic degree, the black ghetto is a matriarchal society of fatherless homes."[51]

The *Times* and others maintained this view dauntlessly, while ignoring contrary analyses. For example, in a detailed critique of the Moynihan Report in the *Nation,* William Ryan outlined its "methodological weaknesses." He scored Moynihan's "highly sophomoric treatment of illegitimacy," especially his failure to note that this phenomenon was "more underreported for whites" because such births often took place in private hospitals where "sympathetic" doctors helped to conceal them. Moynihan, said Ryan, did not engage the issue of a greater number of "shotgun marriages" among whites and their greater access to abortion services and contraception and adoption agencies. Moynihan, he said, tended to portray white families as stable, but there was substantial evidence, including spiraling divorce rates, to indicate that this was inaccurate.[52] Others questioned the accuracy of using terms like *matriarchy* to describe a black family that perhaps was matrifocal; some questioned whether the problem with single-parent families where a man was absent was not primarily the absence of a man but the lack of material resources that a father could bring to a struggling family afflicted by racism. Still others questioned Moynihan's analysis of the black family under slavery.

For those less interested in grappling with difficult questions of housing and education, the black family was an easier hook on which to hang the problems of South LA. John McCone and Warren Christopher pressed this line—with some effect—on the influential black clergyman H. H. Brookins and other black leaders, as well as on Opal Jones, director of the Neighborhood Adult Participation Project and director of the Avalon Community Center. Christopher asked her about the "matriarchal society" and its "advance effect."[53]

Families without fathers were heavily dependent on welfare, according to the conventional wisdom. In fact, the idea was prevalent that these families moved to California from elsewhere to take advantage of the more liberal benefits in the West. Experts like Professor Francis Feldman of the University of Southern California contradicted this widely circulated notion, as did social welfare officials in Sacramento, but to little avail.[54] Others suggested that there was a direct link between welfare and the rebellion: Not only did it lead to a certain enervation of the work ethic, but since welfare checks came every two weeks, by the second week in August these welfare recipients were running out of funds and decided to seize what they wanted.[55]

Thus, it was predictable that Ellis P. Murphy, director of the Bureau of Public Assistance in LA, would be questioned at length when he appeared before the McCone Commission. He informed the commissioners that the issue they were most concerned about—AFDC, or Aid to Families with Dependent Children—averaged a paltry $177 per family per month. Even for families with nine or more children, there was a maximum grant of $375 per month. So small was this sum, families could not secure housing with it. Obtaining this money was not easy for Watts families, for they had to travel to Bell or Maywood to apply, and many did not have cars to get there. Murphy lamented the fact that welfare often operated to break up families, because often it was easier for households without fathers present to obtain these funds. A criminal complaint would be filed if the "Man Assuming the Role of Spouse" was not working but living with a woman and children that were not his.

The McCone Commission was barely interested in other welfare questions such as aid to the blind, aged, or general relief, just Aid to Families with Dependent Children. McCone himself set the tone, stating: "What concerns me even more is the fact that going from 1963 to 1964 you had a two and a half per cent increase in population. You had about a 30 per cent increase in adult with children persons aided, and a 15 per cent increase in the expenditures." Murphy began to speak of "medical aid to the aged," but McCone interrupted him brusquely to drag the dialogue back to AFDC.

Murphy rebutted the easy notion that welfare recipients should find jobs. His bureau was engaging in job training, but it was plainly insufficient. "The problem that we face, though, Mr. McCone, is the fact that these people are minority group people and the job opportunities that are available for them are practically nil . . . job opportunities which we previously found and provided a pretty ripe field in for these people are rapidly disappearing, such as your routine work in manufacturing that is being automated now. . . . Even the ones we train, sometimes when we train them they can't get a job. . . . There is nothing . . . for them to do." McCone interpreted this to mean that a single mother might be better off on welfare than making $1.25 per hour, but Murphy countered that by "law and regulation" she would have to take that low-paying job, if it was available. Yet, despite Murphy's clear and forceful testimony, the idea remained extant that welfare was eroding the work ethic and was a cause of the uprising.[56]

In some sort of Gresham's law, myths served to override reality in the welfare debate. McCone, despite Murphy's testimony, continued to present the conventional notions about welfare. When Paul Ward of the California Health and Welfare Agency and consumer advocate Helen Nelson came before the commission, like Murphy they sought to provide a comprehensive view of welfare, including aid to the blind and disabled. But McCone would have none of this. "I think what concerns us more than anything else is this AFDC group . . . it seems to be almost an incentive to have illegitimate children."

With patience and care Ward sought to explain the facts to the skeptical McCone. "The typical AFDC family consists of a 31 year old mother and three children. The family is likely to be of a minority group (27 percent are Negro and 23 percent are Mexican-American). . . . When she is employed her usual occupation is some form of service work such as waitress or domestic help." Almost 75 percent of AFDC recipients were nonblack, and the children of the typical thirty-one-year-old recipient were not of the age cohort of those most involved in the August events.

Welfare was an issue in sparking the uprising but not in the way that McCone imagined. Ward conceded that "there was a strong feeling of hostility between several of the residents and the county social welfare case workers." The latter, spurred on by cost-cutting politicians, often were looking for men in the home so that benefits could be sliced or deriding recipients because of their plight. Helen Nelson lamented the difficulties that AFDC recipients had in cashing their checks, as some stores charged as much as $1.25 to cash meager checks of little more than $100. When the fires began, many of these stores—which happened to be owned mostly by nonblacks—were targeted.[57]

All the same, welfare expenditures in the state amounted to a hefty $1 billion, with 37 percent of that in LA County alone. But this included aid to the aged, blind, etc., and not just AFDC, which received most of the commission's attention. This LA County figure did not result from more benign procedures there; in fact, only 58 percent of those applying in the county were successful, compared to 89 percent in the state as a whole.[58] As one analyst explained it, for the most part welfare in the state was helping the "middle class family." Welfare, it was argued, was obtained more readily by those with verbal skills more plentiful among those who were not poor and/or black.[59] This was an overly ingenuous explanation; fewer blacks were on welfare most likely because of discrimination rather than because of a reputed dearth of verbal skills. However, welfare was not just a Negro program; nor could it be argued credibly that welfare was the cause of the rebellion, though some on the McCone Commission tried to make this point. The ascendant conservative forces were seeking to take advantage of racial stereotypes by blaming higher taxes and public spending on welfare.

The *Daily Trojan,* the student newspaper at the private University of Southern California, counseled that "the influx into California [of] the type of people who are in need of welfare" should be limited because of the propensity of this "type" to "riot."[60] Such targeting left many welfare recipients in ill humor, and their irritation often was exacted on already beleaguered social workers. The chaos created by the uprising—not least the difficulty in getting mail and checks—worsened the situation. By late August 1965 social workers in LA were described as shell-shocked, "edgy and nervous," and "almost in a state of collapse."[61] Those on AFDC were in an even worse condition, reeling from the accusation that they were a major problem in LA. Despite the battering, by 1967 their numbers in the curfew area had risen by 19 percent. There were larger forces—unemployment, housing, education, transport—beyond the black woman and the black family that created this phenomenon.[62]

■

The church played a major role in South LA. It was a critical component of the civil society that extended beyond the reach of the state. The church often was a haven of escape. It was not only a spiritual retreat but a place to commune, make friends, seek solace, and pursue more practical ends, such as getting tips on reasonably priced housing. Churches abounded in Watts. It was not unusual to find three of four crowded on a single block, crammed between the small boxlike houses and run-down shops.[63] But in many ways these crucial nodes in South LA replicated patriarchal patterns that hand-cuffed the area, for the leaders of black churches were men. Many concentrated on distracting blacks' attention away from mass protest and toward the nirvana that awaited once they left this earth. Others panicked during the uprising and cried out for martial law. Only a few sought to emulate Dr. Martin Luther King, Jr.

From the beginning of the August turmoil, clergy were deeply involved, especially Reverend Casper Glenn. On 13 August at 9 A.M., fifteen clergy met at Praises of Zion Baptist Church and decided to request the presence of the National Guard. The next day they met with Lieutenant Governor Anderson and suggested that martial law be imposed; Rev. Glenn was in the forefront. Though Glenn was an influential black minister, only 20 in his congregation of 865 hailed from Watts; its budget was $58,000, with a substantial percentage allocated to a nursery school. Glenn himself recognized that the revolt in many ways was a revolt against the church, which he admitted "represented too much a middle class philosophy" that the poor found "repugnant." Glenn conceded, "Our middle class dress has kept the poor from participating. . . . We don't have a single parishioner from the apartments just a block away on Avalon Boulevard."

On 15 August clergy sought to address a tense community at Friendship Baptist but were hooted with calls like "We've been listening to you preachers for 100 years, all you've been telling us is how to bear our burdens."[64] Part of this anger was directed against Martin Luther King, Jr. and his philosophy of nonviolent resistance, which in the eyes of many in South LA was inadequate. This hostility was transferred toward Christianity and often was accompanied by a more positive attitude toward the Nation of Islam, which was viewed as something of a militant antipode. Many black churches were passive in the face of oppression; others tried to emulate their activist counterparts in the Deep South. But in the eyes of some younger blacks, they all seemed to pale in comparison to the NOI. On Sunday, 16 August, attendance at churches was down an understandable 80 percent in South LA. This was, of course, a reflection of the chaos in the streets, but it was also a metaphor for a growing disillusion with the church.[65]

To its credit, the church responded. The following Sunday churches throughout the city resonated with parables and sermons about the searing experience that the city had just endured. Though some ministers had called for martial law, a group of Methodist pastors instead turned their focus on police brutality. Dr. Edwin T. Dahlberg, past president of the National Council of Churches, likened what happened in LA to the increasingly unpopular war in Vietnam.[66] Two chastened Episcopal clergymen declared as the fires were still raging, "As white Christian priests, we accuse the churches of [LA] of a disastrous failure to act morally or provide leadership in race leadership."[67] After the uprising, in more than three hundred Catholic parishes in Southern California, a letter from the cardinal was read at every mass explaining a new job initiative for South LA.[68]

Other clergy responded in a more traditional fashion. In December 1965 Billy Graham launched a three-day crusade in Will Rogers Park that, according to a spokesman, was intended to "hold out spiritual direction to the people of Watts in solving their difficulties." Reverend Don Boyd of the First Methodist Church recounted a recurrent theme heard in many churches, citing Isaiah and the promise of hope to the exiled Jews in Babylon. Methodist bishop Gerald Kennedy sought to raise $25,000 to underwrite an interdenominational program in South LA to improve race relations.[69]

Christian clergy responded to the crisis by launching a material and spiritual offensive. But one critic of the black church lambasted the clergy's "lucrative tie-ins with morticians" and the large "number of illegitimate children" they had fathered by women parishioners. Another critic scored the tithing that often decimated the income of domestic workers.[70] Others argued that the clergy were simply out of touch, preaching pie-in-the-sky while communities withered on the ground.

Though most of this fire was leveled at Baptist and Methodist pastors, the Catholics did not escape criticism either. The reform group Catholics United for Racial Equality complained that the church had an unwritten policy that a priest could be removed from his duties for preaching about racial matters. CURE added, "The policy of the Cardinal is to discourage . . . integration in white areas of the Diocese." Housing and education were two of the major problems faced by South LA, and the Catholic church was a major landowner and controlled many schools. However, during the bitter debate over Proposition 14, the cardinal insisted that this important issue not be discussed by priests. There was de facto segregation in Catholic schools. The cardinal pulled out of the Commission on Race and Religion of the National Conference of Christians and Jews because it was not cautious enough about avoiding controversial questions. CURE picketed the pope during his visit to New York City in October 1965.[71]

Over twenty years later a joint task force on South LA was formed by the American Jewish Committee, the LA Urban League, and the National Conference of Christians and Jews. The members issued a report saying that little had changed since 1965 and lamenting that the hopeful initiatives of that period, especially those in housing and education, had not worked.[72]

■

The rules of the game, the law that upholds order, had been suspended. The state was no longer in control. South LA was wild and chaotic, but it also had demonstrated that the existing order was not necessarily eternal or irrevocably stable. There were thousands of blacks in the streets, and many wound up in jail. By 13 August at 4 P.M., the LAPD found it "necessary to open old Main Jail due to volume of arrest activity." By 15 August the *Times* was reporting that "detention facilities were swamped by mass arrests of Negro rioters." A few days later Stanley Malone, president of the black Langston Law Club, complained that many of his clients and neighbors were being "hysterically punished and prejudged" due to "racial overtones" and "overall hysteria." Unfair jailings were being conducted because exorbitant bail was being set, such $2,000 for a misdemeanor, not the usual $1,000. Even Celes King, a chief bail bondsman for Black LA, could not meet the demand.[73]

Ben Margolis of the mostly white National Lawyers Guild echoed his black colleague. "Hysteria" was also the term he used to describe what swept through the courts. "People were being arrested at the drop of a hat. There was also something like a kind of civil war going on."[74] Though guild stalwarts like Margolis, John McTernan, William Esterman, Hugh Manes, and Frank Pestana stood out in their effort to halt this tide of hysteria, many of their friends in the American Civil Liberties Union were reproved by critics. Some of the attorneys affiliated with this more centrist group were said to be pursuing the virtues of free enterprise by asking for "fees as high as $1500."[75]

Judge Kenneth Chantry, presiding judge of the superior court in the county, did not agree with Margolis. What he was concerned about were the juveniles who, he said, were "raising hell" in jail and in the streets; "they tore up the plumbing, broke windows, etc.," after being taken into custody. The judge declared that arraignments were being held within forty-eight hours. What he did not mention was an ongoing problem in securing legal counsel for these defendants because private attorneys were charging excessive fees. Judge Ray Roberts was amazed that some private practitioners were drumming up business by spreading the rumor that the public defender's office would sell out the defendants.[76]

Hugh Taylor, a consultant to Governor Brown's staff, ventured on 20 August 1965 at 8 A.M. to the Westminster Neighborhood Association's Community Center at 10125 Beach Street. The unease he found was miasmic. "Scores of people were milling around inside [and] outside. The people's faces reflected anger, pride and despair." At 1:30 P.M. there was a meeting "teeming with people inside and out." It was a cross section of about two hundred "young people, middle aged and older people."

The forceful words of black women struck him. One spoke of how "the police called the Negro women to their car and asked for a date. She stated that if the woman refuses to have any sexual activity with the police, then they go to jail on some trumped up charge." Youth complained about being picked up by the LAPD and charged for no reason; that meant a criminal record and limited employment opportunity. Officers were often intoxicated for they were able to get free alcohol from liquor stores.

The atmosphere was heated. One speaker took sharp exception to the consensus and "had to be escorted from the floor before he finished his speech." Another engendered antiwar sentiment: "Black men are fighting all over the world. They are willing to fight and die anywhere. In Watts, we are willing to fight and die. We have a cause." An "old lady" who had been arrested declared that on her way to jail she was asked by an officer if she "would buy a ticket to the police function and that if she would, they would release her without booking her." She refused and was booked.[77]

Many blacks saw their battle against the LAPD through the prism of Vietnam's battle against the U.S. military. Both were seen as linked wars against various forms of colonialism. Often forgotten was that in Vietnam the left was directing the struggle, while in Los Angeles black nationalists buoyed by a right-wing atmosphere were rapidly ascendant. Moreover, South LA was not well organized; this was part of the weakness of civil society. A South Side Citiz[ ]ns' Defense Committee did arise and chant the provocative slogan "Let My People Go," which resonated particularly among families of the thousands that had been arrested. But this resonance was too often the exception and not the rule. Compton provides an example. Its judges refused bail altogether, and this deprivation faced little challenge.[78]

This is one reason why Professor Quentin Ogren of Loyola Law School could crow, "Compton, by the Watts standard at least, came out of the riots smelling like the proverbial rose." The Reverend Jim Patterson, who was Euro-American, could understand why. He spent the night in a jail there on 13 August. "Friday night and Saturday night, from about eleven p.m. until three or four in the morning, were the hours when things were the hottest." It was "hot, and it was crowded, and tension was high." Blacks were being jailed in droves; some had "been drinking, perhaps some with dope and so on; they were irrational, some had passed out, a lot of them were—you could almost say—vicious. . . . they just hated the policemen."[79]

Many blacks remembered what happened after the riots in Oxford, Mississippi, accompanying desegregation. Not only were all southern whites not condemned, no one was convicted of anything, "not even disturbing the peace," as Edwin O. Guthman, a special assistant to Attorney General Kennedy, recalled. In contrast, the LA County grand jury impaneled to handle the cases arising from the rebellion proclaimed that those arrested should be punished to the "fullest extent of the law." The foreman of this jury was Pete Schabarum, a future leader of the state's right-wing forces.[80] This double standard helped to convince many that antiblack racism should be confronted with black nationalism; the white right wing, which had eroded the influence of the black left, was now re-creating a black right wing.

Of course, what happened in Oxford paled in comparison to the LA events. As one analysis put it, "One in every seven persons in an area the size of San Francisco participated actively in a week-long insurrection against law and order, an insurrection which had successfully overthrown constituted legal authority about half of that time." The uprising involved about 10,000 people by one count, 34,000 by another, and about 4,000 were arrested. Another estimate put forward the figure of 80,000 participating in this carnival of the oppressed.[81] Strain was placed on the criminal justice system as a result. According to Special Counsel A. L. Wirin, "Never in the four decades of its existence has the ACLU of Southern California been confronted with so grave a challenge to civil liberties as posed by the criminal prosecutions in the aftermath of the Watts incident."[82]

During the period of 11–18 August 1965, 4,060 were arrested, including 133 for drunkenness; 556, or 14.2 percent, were juveniles; of the arrests, 3,200 were made by the LAPD, 500 by the sheriff's officers, 136 by the Compton police, 83 by the Long Beach police, and 3 by the California Highway Patrol; 2,761 were detained on felony charges, mostly for burglary, though 120 were for aggravated assault and 94 for robbery. Of the 3,170 adults arrested, 27.4 percent had no prior record; 38.4 percent had a prior record classified as minor, that is, serving ninety days or less. Of the adults arrested, 3,107 were black, 151 were white, and 68 were Chicano. Of the adults arrested, only 80 had an annual income of $500 or more, and 205 had income less than $400.[83]

Richard Simon of the LAPD prepared a "confidential" tabulation of the arrests showing that 6 Japanese-Americans and no Chinese-Americans had been arrested, and many more whites than Latinos; for example, among eighteen-year-olds, 10 white males and no white females were arrested versus 3 Latinos and no Latinas. The corresponding figure for blacks was 149 males and 23 females.[84] The question was not only why more blacks overall were arrested but why such a higher percentage of black women.

The pattern of these arrests mimicked prevalent trends. In 1964, 9,927 violent crimes were committed by blacks and 4,017 by whites, though it is possible that racism led to the detection of more of the transgressions by blacks. Still, blacks were 16 percent of the population but 60.2 percent of the suspects.[85] Even with thousands being arrested and many thousands more participating, somehow the notion was afoot, notably in the press, that those involved in the rebellion were merely "riffraff" or an "economic underclass."[86] Though not much housing stock was destroyed, the destruction of shops (some of them black owned) did disrupt the lives of many blacks; yet sympathy for the uprising reigned nonetheless, in part because of the sweeping arrests of blacks. Indeed, one analysis concluded that the rebellion predisposed more blacks toward questioning the hegemony of nonviolence as a strategy and thereby paved the way for the Black Panther party.[87]

■

There was an eerie scene in South LA after August 1965. Dead dogs and cats littered the streets, the victims of promiscuous gunfire and surging flames. Scattered about were abandoned cars riddled with bullet holes.[88] And a number of people were dead: thirty-four by the official account and hundreds according to the *Los Angeles Herald-Dispatch*.[89] This latter figure may have been inflated, but hard to question was the dual idea that the LAPD had taken its dehumanization of blacks to an ultimate degree and that in reaction black militance had grown. The fact that virtually all of these deaths at the hands of the LAPD were ruled justifiable homicide only weakened faith in the institutions of the state.[90]

City Councilman Billy Mills was sworn to uphold, indeed shape, the law, but in assailing the inquests into these deaths, even he warned that citizens might be forced to take "protective measures" against the LAPD. District Attorney Evelle Younger disagreed, but his was not a voice that was being heard in South LA.[91] Though he was a lawyer, Younger ignored the obvious flaws in the inquest process. A study commissioned by the McCone panel criticized the maneuver that barred the decedents' families from having attorneys present to intervene, declaring this decision "mechanical and formalistic." At common law "full participation" by counsel "was the rule." The study questioned the repeated incantation in the inquests that "decedent was killed while committing a felony." What should have been examined more thoroughly was the actions of those pulling the trigger.[92]

It seemed to many blacks that the inquests were further evidence that there was a de facto return to a chattel status that reduced the humanity of African-Americans. The scholar Stanley Lieberson was forced to conclude, "I wonder: Would white looters have been shot in Los Angeles?"[93] Perhaps they would have been; however, the fact that it was probably easier to shoot those who were black illustrated how racism animated the protection of private property and buoyed conservatism.

■

With Tom Bradley, Gilbert Lindsay, and Billy Mills sitting in the city council by 1965, Black LA had reached a level of representation relative to population unmatched in most other major U.S. cities. However, this may have been an example of good news masking bad news; for this representation may have been a function of compound racism in that many local elites were more frightened by the potential size and strength of Latinos than blacks and may have been more willing to make concessions to the latter as a result. So compromised, officials like Bradley and Lindsay particularly often found it difficult to lead working-class struggles. They had to express a version of middle-class leadership backed by attorneys, lobbyists, and real estate developers.

Despite this representation at the highest level of government, city services were doled out in a racially discriminatory fashion. Bureau of Sanitation bureaucrat Robert Bargman bragged that "refuse collection is rendered uniformly throughout the entire city and has been provided on that same [basis] continuously for many years."[94] But one would have a hard time convincing many in South LA of this.

The library was better. There were fourteen branches in the curfew areas.

During the unrest the branch at 4504 South Central was closed seven days and the Watts branch at 1501 East 103d for six days, but most were closed only two days. There was no injury to the staff and no damage to library property except for one small window at the Muir branch. The library system assessed the local attitude toward it realistically, noting that "there is some question as to whether the libraries were saved because the rioters simply didn't think about them or because they had a positive feeling about the libraries. There is some evidence to support either conclusion. It is true, however, that the burning did stop virtually at the front doors of two libraries."[95] Children visited libraries; it was a de facto day care center. Education was valued among blacks; it was viewed as a path to a better life. Few institutions exceeded the library in responding with renewed energy to the challenges presented by the revolt. As a result, the libraries in South LA fed a post-1965 "Watts Renaissance" in the arts and writing particularly.

Griffith Park and the Children's Zoo were closed for two days. Unlike the library, they had received "threatening phone calls." Though only minimal damage was done to their property, a number of staff members were upset by such pressure and resigned. The Department of Public Utilities, like the zoo, had trouble protecting staff and was fearful of losses; that may have inspired it to suggest all manner of reform in the aftermath of the revolt. Civil Service took a different approach; it was proud that only 21 of the 40,000 people within its jurisdiction were arrested. The housing authority boasted that out of the six projects housing 15,000 people that were in the curfew zone, "not more than one or two residents" were arrested.[96] Others felt this estimate was too low and that public-housing residents were very likely to have been in the streets; this is one reason why urban renewal or Negro removal became so popular with the city administration.

Surrounding city governments also were affected by the unrest. Both Venice and Santa Monica had "Negro areas" that were described as "Little Watts," and both suffered major problems, though on a smaller scale than their counterparts in South LA. Nearby Centinela Valley and South Bay were looking to file suit against whoever had a deep pocket as a result of the problems inflicted on them by Los Angeles.[97]

■

Blacks had been hamstrung by economic woes, then brutalized by the police when they protested. Many of their leaders and organizations were perceived as being out of touch and more interested in feathering their own nests or filling their own bellies than addressing the common interest. Black women were targeted as a problem by the Moynihan Report, and local elites; many black leaders, and some black nationalists, shared this outlook. However, black women themselves were simultaneously drawn by the militance of the nationalists but repelled by their male supremacist practices. Black youth were attracted more and more to the NOI (and its secular acolytes in Karenga's organization) and the BPP.

Bruised sentiments might not have flared if there had been a perception of justice emerging from the criminal justice system, but more blacks were beginning to think that "just us" were being criminalized in a system devoid of justice. Blacks were angry, wondering when this civil rights movement they were hearing so much about would affect their lives. Instead, it seemed that the South was simply catching up with a Los Angeles mired in stagnation.

The end result of these disparate forces was to bolster a black militance that was increasingly to become the norm among black youth. Positively, this militance was motivated by antiwar sentiment, a refusal to be used as cannon fodder in an unpopular war in Vietnam while rights at home were deprived. A problem, however, was that this black militance could be sexist, disorganized, and negatively manipulated.

Black LA had endured a painful encounter with the state and its institutions. The fact that they had representatives on the city council did not lessen the pain. Elected officials determining how public-sector funds would be dispensed could be more easily overrun by corporate lobbyists—most of whom were not black—in the absence of the black working and middle class leveraging their strength in numbers through mass-based organizations. The elected officials, clerics, and others with key roles to play in civil society were unable to confront the crisis effectively. The absence of organization and a well-developed civil society meant not only that the consciousness transformed by the revolt could be easily frittered away; it also meant that those arrested had a rougher time in navigating the criminal justice system. This was to prove true once more in 1992.

FIVE

Class versus Class

11

A Class Divided
by Race

THE *LA TIMES* CAPTURED THE POINT IN ITS
14 December 1965 editorial: "Hearts of Watts Crisis: Jobs."[1] African-
Americans had difficulty securing adequate housing and adequate education in Southern California. Contributing to this situation was a soaring rate
of black unemployment. According to some, augmenting black unemployment was the presence of a sizable Chicano population that too comprised a
sizable sector of the working class. This perception at times fueled conflicts
between these two groups. In addition, just as in 1910, there was a lingering
fear among white workers that minority workers would take their jobs.

•

Joe William Trotter has argued persuasively that there is an alternative to the
so-called ghetto synthesis in black urban history that posits hostile race contacts—the reference point is primarily black-white—as the key to understanding and interpretation. Trotter has put forward a "proletarianization
framework" that focuses on class structure and the process by which African-
Americans became urban industrial workers, or proletarians.[2]

Though the rainbow reality and compounded racism of LA is not at the
heart of Trotter's analysis, his approach has merit for understanding what led
to the insurrection. John McCone in his own blunt way helped to capture
this point. During the hearings he remarked that a major reason blacks started
coming to LA in droves in the 1940s was "they started to build ships." How
did he know this? "I brought them all in here, I know."[3] Proletarianization

was a major part of the making of Black LA. Many of these jobs emerged as a result of government contracts let to defense contractors, which meant that antidiscrimination measures were more likely to be in place than in other parts of the private sector. Certainly such jobs were more appealing than whatever positions the blacks were vacating in the South. Organizations of proletarians have been more influential and prevalent than organizations of, for example, sharecroppers; and this could mean added militance and increased concessions.

But from 1950 to 1960 blue-collar employment in LA declined. According to one study, that decline meant that by 1960 Black LA was 65.3 percent blue collar and 23.7 percent white collar (and half of the latter group were clerical). Most of the blue-collar jobs may have been more attractive than what was abandoned in the South, but they were still low-skill and "most subject to job displacement." Automation was eliminating jobs as dishwashers and eroding other positions that some blacks may have been able to obtain previously. By 1960 unemployment in Black LA officially was 12.5 percent and most likely was higher. By 1960, 44.5 percent of Watts families were at the poverty level, earning under $4,000 annually.[4]

The LA region was diverse. In Pasadena a substantial number of blacks worked as servants in the mansions of the affluent; some were able to become property owners nearby as a result. But by 1965 the black South African scholars Bernard Magubane and Anthony Ngubo, then graduate students at UCLA, were detecting parallels between this county suburb and their homeland. Men waited on corners to be recruited for labor. They were not necessarily unemployed, though it may have seemed that way to the uninitiated. Some worked irregular hours, part-time, temporary jobs; others were in construction, and many were on corners after finding no work at the union hall. This too was part of the proletarianization process and facilitated the sharing of bonhomie and grave concerns. These men on corners could just as easily be transformed in August 1965 to fathers and husbands deciding to seize goods for their families.[5]

When these black men gathered on corners, they had a lot to discuss when it came to employment discrimination. Harvey B. Schecter of the Anti-Defamation League acknowledged frankly in 1965 that among employers and recruiting firms "there is still widespread discrimination against Negroes and that many practices are employed . . . there are 'understandings' that Negroes will not be sent out to certain firms." Dwight Zook, director of personnel at North American Aviation and a Fair Employment Practices Commission member, was said to consider LA "probably the most segregated city in the U.S." He complained about the veritable absence of black bellhops in hotels, unlike a number of other cities, and the relative absence of black employees in local restaurants; even the railroads, he recalled, were more racially discriminatory than those in Texas.[6] Some of the larger employment agencies in LA orally excluded blacks from consideration for employment, apparently feeling that such discriminatory practices were necessary to stay in business.[7] Such practices were propelled by the spatial isolation of blacks. Alameda Street was a virtual Berlin Wall separating Black LA from mostly white Lynwood and Huntington Park; the Harbor Freeway bisected what was now being referred to as the ghetto. Interracial conflict was part of life on this border.[8]

Blacks were an integral part of the working class and were facing discrimination and limited opportunity. The racism fueled other distinct problems, such as distance from employment and difficulty in being transported beyond the ghetto. The Kerner Commission concluded that a "resident of Watts who wishes to go to the Sears shopping center three miles northeast of Compton must take one bus into the City of Compton and then take a bus from another company to the shopping center at a total cost of 45 [cents] and it takes one and a half hours." According to consumer advocate Helen Nelson, transport consumed 17.5 percent of family income in LA generally—in part because of the critical importance of the automobile combined with a high cost of living—and 14.7 percent elsewhere in the United States. Angelenos spent 17 percent more on autos than others in the United States; 23.4 percent more than Chicago, 29 percent more than Baltimore.[9] The Douglas Aircraft plant in Santa Monica could not be reached easily from 103d Street without a car, and even then it was a long ride; it could take almost four hours to get there by bus. Reaching the General Motors plant in Van Nuys could take longer. As industry developed in LA County—soon to be the most industrialized region in the nation—many blacks were left without work, away from higher-wage union jobs.[10]

But transportation was not the only problem. Automation meant that it was no longer enough to know how to use a towel on dishes; one had to know how to operate a machine.[11] Housing kept blacks distant from newly emerging employment opportunities; black efforts to desegregate certain neighborhoods met heavy resistance, and even public housing used negative quotas to limit their presence.[12] Deindustrialization was taking jobs away from the areas to which blacks were consigned.[13]

■

Unions were not always vigorous in fighting against racial bias. This glaring omission by class-based organizations often made blacks rely on racial appeals and formations, thus facilitating the growth of nationalism and the popularity of the NOI. The NOI's slogan, "Do for Self," made more sense when organizations of the working class did not stand tall against racial bias.

AFL-CIO unions adopted the view that they had no figures on the racial background of their membership, which meant they could better argue that they had no idea of how many blacks were in their ranks. Yet a visual inspection would have revealed the existence of a number of lily-white locals.[14] Some of the worst offenders were the building trades. In a region where freeways, universities, housing, and shopping centers were being thrown up at a breakneck pace, this was no small matter. The burning down of stores and other structures in August 1965 meant their labor would be at a premium for rebuilding. Yet the flames came dangerously close to white working-class homes in Lynwood, Huntington Park, Compton, and elsewhere. This mixed effect of the revolt may help to explain the mixed response of the unions. Immediately after the revolt AFL-CIO leaders urged a relaxation of hiring procedures in the building industry in order to hire more workers from Black LA. The building trades rejected this idea, though in all fairness they were not exclusively to blame, as contractors and developers were responsible for racial bias in hiring as well.[15]

The United Auto Workers was a more enlightened union. Its leaders, including Walter Reuther, were helpful to civil rights organizations and were keenly aware of the strategy of granting concessions to blacks in order to undermine the left, domestically and internationally; Reuther was busily fighting off the left in his own ranks. The UAW leader in the West, Paul Schrade, was shrewd. He was educated at Yale, worked at Reuther's shoulder, and came to California in 1947; by 1965 the union under his leadership had 65,000 members in the state. There was an influential black membership and, for those times, the amazingly high number of three black business agents of the union in the curfew zone alone. But the union had been weakened by internal Red Scare scrapes, and as a result some of the more militant black members and antiracist whites had been ousted from influence.[16]

Nevertheless, the UAW made distinct gestures to blacks after the revolt, offering to put up $10 million in seed money for housing in Watts and placing tens of thousands of dollars in deposits in black-owned savings and loans in the area.[17] Even before the revolt, the UAW had provided a two-story office building at 8501 South San Pedro for a dollar a year to the United Civil Rights Committee. It did seem that after the flames the union focused creatively on Black LA. Schrade proposed the novel idea that "neighborhood unions" be organized in Black LA as a means of achieving gains. He suggested that a University of California campus be placed in Watts. He questioned how the problems of Black LA could ever be addressed when there was no major program to alleviate unemployment. He was even self-critical, acknowledging that there were "very few Negroes that work in the Van Nuys plant," which was a UAW shop. Repeatedly, he instructed McCone and Christopher that it was folly to speak of training black workers if there were no real jobs for them to fill. But the two officials did not seem to hear and to Schrade's consternation continued to criticize union practices on race as if unions controlled hiring in the workplace.[18]

Unions were understandably defensive in the aftermath of the revolt. Some like the building trades were being pressured because of their abysmally low rate of black membership. Others like the UAW may have been on the side of the angels during the civil rights struggle, but they were not escaping criticism either. The unions of the booming film industry continued to maintain close ties to organized-crime figures, providing a model for South LA gangs in how force could be leveraged for economic gain. The LA County AFL-CIO manifested these tensions. It backed the Rumford Act and opposed Proposition 14; according to Max Mont of its staff, it provided the "single largest source of funds" to fight this measure.

But Mont was reluctant to criticize member unions, like the building trades, and he was strafed by McCone and Christopher as a result. He said little about the biased practice of using distorted tests to bar blacks from unions. Angrily, McCone suggested that the National Labor Relations Board should take "remedial action" to address racial bias in shops "before they recognize unions." By 1965 unions sapped of strength by anti-Communist purges and frightened by the specter of job competition were reluctant to confront racial bias on the job. When it appeared that elites like McCone and Christopher—less concerned about job competition from blacks—were more vigorous in confronting bias, many blacks were convinced that alliances with unions could not be realized and alliances with elites made more sense. Simultaneously, this strengthened the middle-class leadership in the NAACP, which would have to rely on unions in order to pursue a strategy of mass mobilization, and its mirror image among nationalists and gangs, who now could argue credibly that there was no alternative to a "go it alone, do for self" approach.

Mont defended union opposition to hiring Watts residents to rebuild LA: "They cannot bypass seniority . . . they adhere strictly to their hiring hall practices." The Laborers and Hod Carriers locals had a number of blacks and Latinos, and to the trades this seemed to be quite enough; but even those minority workers often had to provide kickbacks to get work. Earl Broady of the commission also raised the issue few wanted to confront, the "last hired, first fired" principle that harmed so many black workers and the attendant apparent conflict between affirmative action and seniority. [19]

The kind of pressure the trades were subjected to by the commission and others and the influence of more forward-looking unions like the UAW compelled the AFL-CIO in LA to be somewhat more receptive to appeals for reform and change. Its member unions called unanimously for a hospital to be built near Watts, though admittedly this massive construction job was just the kind of program that the building trades could endorse.[20] Ralph Merola, president of AFL-CIO Local 685, the city's probation officers, was contrite about his union's role in possibly helping to bring on the revolt and was open to suggestions for change.[21] But organized labor generally did not respond to the crisis with alacrity. Regressive racial thinking and the perception that black labor was a competitor out to get the jobs of white labor were powerful forces militating against serious reform.

■

The unions may have responded differently to the revolt, but others were of the firm opinion that more jobs would be an antidote preventing a repeat of August 1965. That certain elites were more advanced in their thinking on a key racial question—pushing for jobs for blacks—than some working-class organizations complicated the building of a class-based progressive movement and accelerated black nationalism. Perhaps as a partial result, there were some incremental gains for black workers in the aftermath of the uprising; more were hired as parimutuel clerks at racetracks, for example.[22]

Yet a festering sore was the sight of white contractors and workers being paid to clean up Black LA while unemployed black workers stared sullenly from the sidelines. At times they moved from staring to marching, but there was little surcease. And even when they were hired, problems remained. Joe Murdoch of Local 300 of the Laborers Union, AFL-CIO—one of the few that had a complement of black members—complained that when hired, they were "exploited at sweatshop wages."[23]

Elites were split. Some thought that jobs would douse rebellious spirits and would be a boon. Lieutenant Governor Anderson complained that there was a "chronic shortage of many kinds of professional people," such as nurses, and it made simple good sense to prepare African-Americans for such posts. However, Mayor Yorty blasted the proposal of the county Human Relations Commission to increase employment opportunity—at least 5,000 new jobs—for blacks, terming it "extremely dangerous" and "ill conceived"; instead of dousing rebellious spirits, he thought that such an offering was "building up a case for potential riot."[24]

Fortunately for Black LA and the city as a whole, the mayor did not have the final word. U.S. secretary of labor Willard Wirtz moved to create a task force in the uprising's aftermath to look into job training and employment; like others, he hoped that such programs "would prevent future riots."[25] Some "anti-poverty" jobs resulted, but the ultimate impact was short-lived. Simultaneously, unionized jobs in the proletarian sector were still escaping the grasp of many black workers. When Douglas Aircraft needed 1,500 skilled workers, the company recruited from the East Coast.[26]

Union and government maintained that their slowness in confronting black unemployment was not all their fault. City Councilman Billy Mills was informed confidentially that certain employers were saying that "they will never trust or hire another Negro as they can't be sure they aren't criminals" or potential rioters. The informant noted that contrary to the usual practice, "I never hired a Japanese gardener—I hired a Negro. I never hired a Mexican maid—I hired a Negro." But now even this person was about to move away from blacks, because he "had 5 working for me when the riots came and I have not seen them since."[27] Many seem to have viewed blacks as too wild, untrustworthy, and unreliable after the revolt. One twenty-year-old black migrant from Arkansas, who had been in LA since July 1964, complained weeks after the revolt that white bosses had become more aloof after August 1965.[28] Furthermore, in the rainbow of races that was LA, employers looking for cheap labor had alternatives beyond hiring blacks. In the next two decades, wars in Indochina and Central America helped to create more pools of cheap labor, as mainstream civil rights organizations, many nationalists, and gangs alike stood apart from antiwar protest.

The effort to put a dent in black unemployment provided mixed results. Despite the Douglas Aircraft recruitment in the East, one report detailed that Watts residents were able to garner 1,207 "permanent placements . . . largely in the aerospace industry." [29] This was partially due to the labors of Chad McClellan, a businessman who was designated by local elites to secure employment for black workers in the rebellion's aftermath. But according to McClellan and his staff, a number of blacks complained about the wages offered in certain jobs and refused the work. Others did not bother to show up after they were hired. Apparently a high percentage of the unemployed had arrest records—evidently because of police harassment—and this hampered them in securing jobs. Like Councilman Mills's confidant, those surrounding McClellan had heard the rumors about blacks not being hired because of their stained postrevolt reputations; they could read of black maids being dismissed in Beverly Hills and Bel-Air and replaced by Mexican-Americans. [30]

Many employers became hostile to blacks because of the damage inflicted on stores, the disruption of their city, and the eye-irritating smoke that wafted into their neighborhoods. Many blacks, especially the youth, were hostile to whites, and not necessarily just white elites. Just after the uprising the black city councilman Billy Mills went to speak at a curfew-zone junior high school about police work as a career, and he was almost chased out of the auditorium. The police were perceived as the intimidating local lurking presence of whites and were wildly unpopular. [31]

Black anxiety was helped along by the obviously biased inequities in the law. There were many problems, later to be lessened by the *Griggs v. Duke Power* case in the high court, of non–job-related requisites for hiring, such as a high school degree for a janitor. With inferior education being meted out in Black LA, requirements that seemed to be neutral could be devastating. There were other flaws: affirmative-action remedies for veterans, or "veterans' preference," were firmly in place; and the low level of participation of blacks in the military made this a form of built-in bias against them. Affirmative action for minorities was yet to mature. [32]

It would take years for *Griggs* to arrive and affirmative action for minorities to be firmly in place. Meanwhile, in 1970 the *Times* reported that "the Negro jobless rate in the Watts area was 2½ times the rate for Negroes on a national basis." The jobless rate for black women was rising even faster than that for black men.[33] The failure to build any class-based organization—a failure that was not totally self-inflicted—meant that whatever gains arrived could not last for long. Others argued that it was the Mexican-American population that was eroding opportunity for blacks and not elites who administered the political economy.

■

Mexican-Americans in Southern California were often ignored. At times this was due to simple "New York–centrism," or the usual U.S. pattern of seeing the world in terms presented by the nation's largest city or in black-and-white terms, akin to the early television set. There may have been other questions, such as the fact that some Chicanos were visibly and phenotypically of European descent and thus blended in easier with the region's majority; they may have enjoyed a certain race privilege that could complicate relations with other minorities. Other Chicanos were darker and thus suffered race penalties. As late as 1898 California had a higher incidence of unsolved homicides than all of the other states in the Union put together, and the Los Angeles area had a higher incidence than the rest of the state. In many instances these were Native Americans—and Mexicans, difficult to distinguish from Native Americans—being killed by lynch mobs. The scholar Ralph Guzman shared this bit of information after Warren Christopher had asked him if Mexican-Americans had an easier time—presumably than blacks—in Southern California.[34] This was a common, though not necessarily accurate, belief; certainly it seemed that what drove this opinion was whatever race privilege a small minority of Chicanos enjoyed. The widespread circulation of this opinion did influence black-brown relations negatively.

Simultaneously, there was substantial evidence of black-brown cooperation, especially in trade unions. In 1955 in El Centro, African-Americans and Mexican-Americans jointly filed a class suit in an effort to end school segregation in California. Cooperation in voter registration and political organizations was also prevalent. But the decline of the left, which toiled overtime to bring peoples together across racial lines and on a class basis, did not help black-brown relations. There had been a perceptible decline in dialogue by the time August 1965 arrived.[35]

There was cooperation culturally and socially. Raymond Paredes has written of the *vato loco,* or crazy guy, whose reckless abandon also seems prototypically U.S., Californian, and African-American: Blacks and browns were both subject to prison culture, which also forged bonds and irritations. Low-riding, dress, language, voice inflections, and, ironically, a valorization of a certain stoicism, or "cool" (which was often useful for confronting racism without falling victim to a lynching), were commonalities between black and brown male culture. The rise of lumpen culture after World War II had a similarly potent impact on brown and black alike.[36]

Ralph Guzman was that rare breed, a Chicano scholar with ties to UCLA (though his full-time post was at Long Beach State). The Ford Foundation had provided the Westwood campus a $450,000 grant to conduct a massive study of Chicanos, and Guzman was playing a key role in assembling the findings. He found the obvious: there were differences and similarities between the two communities. Chicanos were more scattered across LA, yet like blacks they did not have "a very good history with the police department" or sheriff either. Evidence of that was the Zoot Suit Riot during World War II, which too was different from and similar to Watts 1965.[37]

Another similarity was that employers often preferred to hire the lighter-skinned Chicanos and African-Americans over their darker-skinned counterparts. The problem was that often blacks took this to indicate that Chicanos were favored over African-Americans; after all, the latter were the darkest of all.[38] Yet, it would be one-sided to stress this side of the equation in isolation. There were tensions between blacks and whites, lighter- and darker-skinned blacks, Jews and gentiles, the newly arrived and those already there. Conflict was inescapable in part because a class exploitation was exacerbated by inadequate organization.[39]

Richard Griswold del Castillo has suggested that "the Chicanos living in Southern California have had a different kind of history than that of those living in other well-defined regions of the Southwest."[40] Unlike Texas, Southern California had a substantial Asian-American population that arguably deflected bigotry from Chicanos, just as these two groups' presence could deflect bigotry from blacks, as compounded racism operated. That was not the end of the uniqueness. Agriculture remained one of LA County's principal industries well into the 1930s. Many farmworkers of Mexican descent could live in the city and take the Red Line cars to work in the fields; this rural-urban experience—virtually unique in large U.S. cities—helped to create a distinct culture. Moreover, the rapid growth of LA—faster than any other metropolis—provided further distinctiveness.[41]

Whether they were called gangs or social clubs, groups often grew out of migrants banding together for mutual protection in the wake of fleeing revolution and/or chaos in Mexico; as early as 1926 Emory Bogardus was noting their presence among Mexican-Americans in Los Angeles. By the early 1940s there were an estimated forty-five to seventy such organizations in LA. As among blacks, discrimination was one reason for their existence. As late as the early 1940s, Mexicans were required to sit in a separate section of movie theaters in the San Fernando Valley; like blacks, Mexicans found on the "Anglo" side of the tracks could be harassed, beaten, or worse. But unlike blacks, Chicanos and Mexican-Americans had a distinct language that could serve to guard a distinct culture and, in a sense, bind their organizations tighter.[42]

The Zoot Suit Riot during the Second World War showed that there was no racial privilege for many Chicanos. Alfredo Guerra Gonzales has suggested that the events should be termed the "Servicemen's Riots" to name the aggressors and instigators of this attack on the Mexican-American community. It was these events that caused the intense focus on Chicano gangs, he has said. He also has challenged the idea that the presence of LA gangs can be traced to the post-1910 turmoil in Mexico and has suggested further reasons why difference and similarity are the hallmarks of black-brown relations. When they were under siege in California, Chicanos had the benefit of a Mexican government that protested directly to Washington, while U.S. blacks had no such direct intervention in 1965. In contrast, Gonzalez has argued that "before the war [i.e., World War II], the black in [California] was considered to hold a position above that of the Native American, Asian and Mexicano/Chicano."[43]

Before joining the LA City Council in 1949, Edward Roybal—the doyen of Chicano politicians—was a social worker and did community organizing. By 1965 he was representing the ninth councilmanic district. Thus, he had a close view for a lengthy period of what had happened to his community. The LAPD rousted youth in Chicano Boyle Heights, just as they did in Black LA; they would line up teenagers, make them place their hands over their heads, and then go through their pockets. Roybal had seen a Watts which during the war was "primarily composed of Mexican-American people." He had seen a city that before World War II featured signs reading "No Mexicans or Negroes allowed." Yes, Roybal agreed, it was true that the Spanish language was a guardian of Chicano culture, an advantage not enjoyed by blacks; but the latter had a number of colleges under their domain nationally and that might have been deemed a stronger guardian of culture. [44]

After World War II, Mexican-American soldiers returned to a city still infused with bigotry even though they had just fought to repel the same phenomenon in Europe and elsewhere. Complicating this difficult situation was a large influx of African-Americans who were moving into neighborhoods, competing for scarce housing, and applying for scarce jobs. The national character of the African-American organizations, combined with their advantage of having a sophisticated internationally acclaimed cadre of leaders like W. E. B. Du Bois and Paul Robeson, often caused U.S. and even LA elites to focus more attention on the needs of blacks as the Cold War got underway. At times this complicated black-brown relations.

If ever Chicanos needed mutual protection, it was after the war. Not surprisingly, it did seem that gangs proliferated at this point in Southern California. These organizations were dehumanized, referred to as "rat packs" and "wolf packs," which was just a prelude to bestial attacks by the authorities. Often these organizations turned on each other and "rumbled."[45] By the 1960s racially based gangs were present not only in black and brown communities but in Anglo neighborhoods as well, and their clashes and conflicts reverberated on the job, in the schools, in the streets.[46]

Black-brown tensions could not be separated from the context of white racism and white supremacy. At times this tendency was manifested in ways so obvious they would have been derided if in a novel. According to Eduardo Quevedo, the state president of the Mexican-American Political Association, the "metropolitan press . . . attempted to cause a conflict between" blacks and browns and whites. When a black killed Lawrence Gomez, a bottled-water delivery man, the incident was given wide publicity as the murder of a "white Caucasian." But when "Spanish surnamed persons" attacked blacks in Watts, they were not called "Caucasian" but "Mexican-American." Though race was a prime topic of discussion, the language employed was often so nebulous and euphemistic—"Caucasian"?—that it contributed to confusion and not clarity.[47]

■

As August 1965 approached, black-brown relations were not improving. On the eleventh anniversary of the *Brown v. Board of Education* decision, 17 May 1965, the county Commission on Human Relations reported that there was a "high degree of tension between the Negro and Mexican-American tenants and the LAPD had instituted heavy patrols" in the "Florence-Firestone and Ramona Gardens areas."[48]

The picture was mixed. Since 1918 Vincente R. Bonilla had lived near

Watts; his family owned a grocery store, and it was spared because of the positive relationships he had developed with neighbors who lived between 109th and 110th streets on Wilmington Avenue.[49] But on 15 August 1965 there were ten to fifteen blacks and two whites in a cell at the 77th precinct. Then a "drunken Mexican was thrust into the cell" by an officer "with a big grin on his face"; they were all told that this new prisoner had been "arrested for burning down a Negro church." The African-Americans knew enough not to respond to the provocation, and the two whites "were both convinced that the police officers were looking for an excuse to beat up the Negro inhabitants of the cell."[50] As this incident illustrated, the authorities seemed to foment black-brown conflict, which hastened nationalism in both camps and retarded the development of class-based alliances.

August 1965 was a turning point for black-brown relations in LA for many reasons. David Rieff has argued that "1965 was just about the time when the Third World, too, began to move into a kind of fast forward" in Southern California; this was partly due to the 1965 immigration law changes which caused a substantial increase in the Latino and Asian populations of the region.[51] Others felt that the spectacle of rebellious Negroes lessened their attraction as a labor force and increased that of the immigrants.

The absence of class consciousness at the workplace and the presence of race consciousness in the neighborhood may help explain Edna Guillary's outlook. Born in Louisiana and raised in Port Arthur, Texas, she moved to LA in the 1940s to find a job in the aircraft industry. She worked for Douglas Aircraft for thirty-one years. However, when she made distinctions among "whites," she excoriated the "Jews" who allegedly controlled the stores in her neighborhood and not the bosses who had hegemony over her livelihood.[52]

Anti-Jewish attitudes were part of a general antiwhite outlook held by many blacks; anti-Latino attitudes were often part of the same outlook. But one lesson emerging from this stew was causing dismay across racial lines: if the lesson was learned that expressions of black militance—however chaotic or nationalistic—brought gains, then what were Mexican-Americans—make that Chicanos—waiting for? Councilman Roybal asked plaintively, "Now, must we riot in order to get attention?" This lesson had various permutations. Jerry Rosen of the McCone Commission said that the "Mexican-American feels that the Negro is advancing at the Mexican's expense." Their answer was to "organize and start pushing like the Negro does. The consensus of the intimate discussion was Watts was a good thing for the Negro."[53]

The commission had an in-depth discussion about Mexican-Americans with Eduardo Quevedo of MAPA; Manuel Ruiz, an attorney; and Frank Paz, an engineer. The men were angry, arguing that their community had been largely overlooked. "They indicated that there was a possibility that the Mexican American community would have to riot in order to become recognized by the appropriate officials so that the poverty problems they have could be resolved." Improvements had to take place, they pleaded, since "there is a greater number of Mexican-Americans living in a state of poverty in Los Angeles County than there are Negroes."[54]

John Buggs of the Human Relations Commission echoed these assessments. Later Buggs warned publicly that "if attention is not given to the needs of the Mexican-American community, [then] we may be creating a tension situation between Negroes and Mexican-Americans in this community and particularly in the Boyle Heights–East Los Angeles area." There was fear that if Mexican-Americans "begin to feel that the only way that one gets attention is burning down a thousand buildings, we are likely to have this kind of thing happen over there."[55]

Part of this frequently stated fear was not necessarily reflected in South LA. Hugh Taylor attended a meeting at the Avalon Center, 4272 Avalon, on 24 August 1965 and found that many of the blacks there "expressed concern for the treatment of the Mexican-Americans and stated that their conditions were similar and that the attention they wanted for themselves they wanted for all of the poor, especially the Mexican-American. . . . several Mexican-Americans were present. They appeared to feel as the rest of the group felt although none spoke out." Possibly they did not speak out because they were aware that the rhetoric at the meeting might not be matched elsewhere. The dean of Chicano Studies, Rodolfo Acuña, has written that "a by-product of the Watts riots was a further shift in control of poverty funds to blacks. . . . In turn, many blacks felt that the poverty programs generally resulted from their civil rights movement. . . . White politicians encouraged tensions between the two groups by playing them against each other."[56]

Struggle over jobs and funds did exacerbate tensions, though at times this happened more at the white-collar level. The Ford Foundation was wary about providing funds to the black-oriented Opportunities Industrialization Center, for if funds went to a mostly black operation, then other funds would then have to be found for a mostly brown operation.[57] This apparent dilemma may have motivated the ill-timed headline on 10 October 1965 in the *LA Times:* "Mexican-Americans in LA Called Anti-Negro." Seventy Latino leaders denied the truth of this headline, but the damage had been done. Soon the *New York Times* took up the cry: "Negro Gains Vex Coast Mexicans . . . anti-Negro feeling is running so strong among Mexican-Americans that some residents and community leaders express fear of renewed rioting." It claimed that Mexican-Americans feared they would be fired so that African-Americans could be hired.[58]

The press was not inventing this antagonism out of whole cloth. There were tensions in antipoverty programs.[59] Leaders like Fernando Del Rio, executive committee chair of the Mexican-American Adult Leadership Conference, was complaining that federal dollars were going to blacks while Chicanos were being ignored.[60] But again, there is little question that Watts 1965 had a catalytic impact on Mexican-American militance and the emergence of the Chicano movement.[61]

The press also did not invent Ignactio Laznao, publisher of *L'Opinion,* a graduate of Notre Dame and quite wealthy. He expressed surprise as to why anyone would want to interview him since "he had little knowledge of conditions and tensions" in East LA or Watts. But he did know enough to offer the point that "he would be surprised and shocked to see any thing like the Watts riot occur in Mexican-American communities" because "the Mexican-American is much more passive than the Negro."[62] This intended compliment actually was a gauntlet tossed down to Mexican-American youth who particularly felt constrained to contradict this statement.

■

As time passed, more Mexicans came across the border to live in California, followed by Central Americans fleeing civil wars and civil conflict. Patterns gradually developed in response. One scholar found in 1968 that Mexican-American children were "almost uniformly hostile" and fearful "toward Negroes, amounting to a sub-cultural stereotype that Negroes are by nature bad and violent."[63]

By 1980 the *LA Times* was recording an "influx of Latinos into the [Watts] area"; this first "became apparent to established residents about seven years ago, and they have seen it pick up momentum over the last three years." The reporter found little enmity between "second and third generation Chicanos raised in the neighborhood" and blacks. "There is even an integrated gang, the WVG—Watts Vario Grape." Watts was changing. In La Colonia, "the area bordered generally by Alameda Street, Wilmington Avenue, 103rd

Street and Santa Ana Boulevard . . . last year nearly 40% of the homes . . . were purchased by Latinos. Just three years ago the figure was closer to 10%. Latinos now own about 17% of the homes in the neighborhood." At Martin Luther King, Jr., Hospital, built as a direct result of the Watts Revolt, "three out of every four children born are Latino. Hospital admissions records show that this year, for the first time, Spanish sur-named patients have surpassed blacks." Despite the general quiet between the races, conflict over jobs erupted as unemployment continued to persist.[64]

As time passed, black-brown relations continued the pattern of cooperation and conflict, differences and similarities. Tensions arose over government posts, as blacks were represented at a more significant rate in the city council and in the state legislature than Latinos. It was almost as if local elites found it easier to deal with a small black population and their needs—particularly given the national impetus to do so—than a large Latino population with not as much clout.[65]

By the 1990s Compton had undergone a process that a number of urban centers may pass through in the next century. Once lily-white, it had acquired a black majority and a mostly black city administration. Then the Latino population began to expand, and began to charge that the blacks were treating them like the whites once had treated the blacks.

The dearth of strong class-based organizations inevitably spawned racial militance by blacks and browns, which could bring both gains in employment—and other areas—and conflict. There was a U.S. left still vainly struggling to have influence and there was a growing ultraright whose influence was felt broadly. The hegemony of the latter guaranteed that all racial relations would have to be played out on the difficult terrain of a racist context.

12

Right, Left, and Center

THE WATTS UPRISING WAS A PIVOTAL TURNING
point in the evolution of the political left, right, and center. By 1965 the
LA left had shrunk to a shadow of its former self. The international left
was torn with tensions between Moscow and Peking, while their socialist relative in Vietnam was fighting the United States to a standstill. However, all
saw an opportunity for increased popularity of their ideas and more recruiting
of militants, especially blacks, to the organized left in the United States. The
right had suffered a setback in the U.S. presidential election of 1964, but the
domestic battle over the war helped to strengthen and revive them, as did the
uprising. Naturally, the possibility that the left might grow brought increased
attention and funding to the centrists, particularly those with ties to trade
unions like the UAW.

August 1965 had brought a new militance to South LA: one strand was
clearly nationalist, the other had aspects of anti-imperialism as expressed in
staunch opposition to the war in Vietnam. One strand led to the right toward
cultural nationalism and the NOI, away from engagement with the state;
the other led to the left toward the Black Panther party and various Marxist
formations. With the assistance of gangs and nationalists, the authorities were
able to squash the left; this hampered antiwar organizing in South LA and
gave hegemony to gangs and nationalists. The price paid was also wounded
race relations that would fester and explode again in 1992.

∎

LA provided fertile territory for the growth of the ultraright. As Christopher Rand put it, the city "has few of the Abolitionist memories that have helped move Northern consciences." LA may have been a victim of what Rand has termed the "horizontality to the U.S. migration camp," whereby northerners migrate to the San Francisco Bay area and southerners to LA, thus bolstering racist and regressive sentiment; there was enormous rightward pressure on elected officials like President Lyndon Johnson and Governor Pat Brown.[1] By 1965 Southern California generally had developed a well-deserved reputation for being a headquarters of the U.S. right. The right in this region had developed a taste for violence that reached back at least to the racist Chinatown Massacre of 24 October 1871 that cost eighteen lives.[2] The image of gun-toting blacks in 1965 Watts was perceived by some ultrarightists as a challenge that had to be met. Other militant rightists responded by deserting LA in droves for Orange County to the south, which played a role in boosting this populous region into the forefront of right-wing politics nationally.[3]

Because of the growing influence of the NOI and other Islamic groupings, there were expressions that were characterized by some as black anti-Semitism; this was an indication of rightward tugs on blacks. At the same time the Jewish community, like African-Americans, was receiving Cold War–inspired concessions that were making some more affluent. Writing in the 6 October 1965 *New York Herald Tribune,* the columnists Rowland Evans and Robert Novak stated that before August 1965 the Democratic National Committee was slated to raise funds for black voter registration by charging $1,000 per ticket for an LA luncheon with Dr. King. After the uprising the plan was "dropped." They added: "The reason: the Jewish businessmen who were counted on to attend the lunch now wouldn't pay $1000—or even $1— to hear [Dr.] King."[4]

The extent of Jewish anger can be easily overstated. One study done shortly after the uprising found that "white attitudes," presumably including Jewish attitudes (which traditionally were more liberal than those of others defined as white), "show a rather surprising degree of sympathy with the riot." Nevertheless, the fact that "over half the whites felt some fear" was indicative of a trend that could grow further. Moreover, some of the study's conclusions were just continuations of outlooks that had long hampered the growth of progressive organizations while strengthening racism: "The all-white low socio-economic community generally tended to react most antagonistically to the riot. . . . the all-white high socioeconomic status community . . . was the most sympathetic." Inevitably, integration was a working-class phenome-non—it was easier to integrate blacks in that class rather than the ruling class—and the study found that there was "higher general antagonism toward Negroes in integrated areas than in all-white areas."[5] The difficulties in inte-grating may have pushed some in the Euro-American working class to the right.

There were other factors pushing many Euro-Americans to the right. In Southern California, where many spent hours on the road with little com-pany beyond a radio, right-wing talk radio shows were becoming popular. One white man, Sam Bowman, was asked what he thought of welfare. He replied that he "heard [a] Bob Grant radio show and" it sounded "like . . . ladies [are] having so many children [but] not using money for them."[6] The *Manion Forum* was read widely by ultrarightists, binding them together na-tionally, and it was also popular in Southern California. In September 1965 it advised that "offering" blacks "pretty houses and fatter welfare checks will not curb their lawless passions." This publication was angered by the image of blacks with guns and made a number of nervous references— as did many others—to Radio Dixie and Robert Williams's broadcasts to the black com-munity from abroad, in addition to the usual citation of the NOI and the Communist party.[7]

The Southern California ultraright was growing. The regional John Birch Society and the Young Americans for Freedom seemed to be gaining mem-bers, along with other like-minded groupings.[8] According to City Council-man Billy Mills, many ultraright racists were involved in an organized effort to foment racial discord.[9] There was also a bonding of various strands on the right, as symbolized at a 8 September 1965 lecture at San Marino High School by W. Cleon Kousen, former FBI agent and alleged "authority on the Communist Party." Present were "police officers from surrounding communi-ties," who were introduced; "Chief Parker . . . had been invited but was out of the city." Many of these forces had a relationship to the Birch Society.[10] The growing hegemonic influence of these groups can be measured by the volume of incoming letters to the McCone Commission that expressed hard-line racist, anti-Communist, and conservative viewpoints.[11]

The ultraright was concerned about Red influences growing among blacks, or so they said. They feared that the war in Vietnam and the promi-nence given to Ho Chi Minh and other Communists would ignite growth in the ranks of the Communist party and benefit other self-avowed Marxist-

Leninists like Mike Laski and the Progressive Labor party. Unlike the Communist party, the forces around Laski and those in the PLP both had supported China in its ongoing conflict with the Soviet Union. These doctrinal differences kept these small forces from uniting or engaging in mutually beneficial alliances. But the increasingly influential Fred Schwarz, president of the Christian Anti-Communist Crusade, usually did not deign to distinguish them. Speaking in Long Beach on 24 August 1965, he warned that Marxists of any stripe would "use the grievances of the Negro, both legitimate and illegitimate, to destroy the constitutional governmental system of the United States." President Schwarz sought to posit connections between the CP and NOI in the usual effort to link the "black and red scare."[12]

What were some of the ideas that were being circulated and actions being perpetrated by the ultraright? After a six-day trial, Herman Lee Henry, a forty-one-year-old welder, was convicted of a felony for planning to exterminate blacks by selling them poisoned food at a 10 percent discount. He also revealed a plot to kill Dr. King and pointed the finger of accusation at the LA Citizens' Council.[13] Many retired military men were flocking to such banners; San Diego was a center for military bases, and the region stretching north to Los Angeles was becoming a beacon of attraction for conservatives. They were taking diverse names, such as the Defenders of the American Constitution. They hated Dr. King and saw him as an ally of Communists in an international Red plot to destabilize the United States.[14]

The growth of these trends was not just in Los Angeles and can be traced in the statewide press. On 10 December 1965 the *Arcata Union* reported that J. B. Smith presented a film at the local Kiwanis Club on the "riot . . . sponsored by the Committee on Truth About Civic Turmoil." He urged citizens to support and cooperate with the local police.[15] He also included standard ultraright boilerplate about race and communism, Reds manipulating blacks, and the like. The 29 December 1965 *Oroville Mercury Register* worried that one upshot of the revolt would be stricter gun-control laws that would harm the interests of their constituents, including hunters. The uprising was a rebellion against white supremacy, but it also may have been a successful recruiting message for the right wing.

■

James Conant, former president of Harvard University, expressed the concern of elites when he worried that black dissatisfaction would cause them to turn to communism: the "fate of freedom in the world hangs very much in [the] balance. Our success against the spread of communism" was at stake because the left "feeds upon discontented, frustrated, unemployed people" like those found in multitudes in South LA.[16]

This concern had fed the simultaneous repression of the left and granting of concessions to the blacks. This approach succeeded in that the ranks of the Communist party in LA in 1965 were smaller than they had been in 1948. But one right-wing study felt that this victory was just temporary because "the rise of the civil rights movement" meant that "leftists of all kinds . . . have leaped to new opportunity." Roy Wilkins was the only "true moderate" among the civil rights leadership who did not require inoculation; the rest, it was felt, were unreliable. The Student Non-Violent Coordinating Committee was reviled by ultrarightists when it decided to reject the traditional anti-Communist bars to membership.[17] Angela Davis, Franklin Alexander, and a generation of black Marxists who were to wield some influence into the 1990s emerged from SNCC in Southern California.

M. J. Heale has noted that "California was unusual in the intensity and duration of its red scare." This surge weakened the organized left to the point of evaporation, feeding a profound California conservatism that included Richard Nixon, Ronald Reagan, and a generation that pioneered in prosecuting the Cold War. Heale also has suggested that California conservatism was due more to Pentagon spending than "specific demographic or economic features." Furthermore, "the low partisan tradition of California contributed to the political power of newspapers, often controlled by right wing press barons, and of interest groups." Witness the *LA Times,* the historic voice of anti-unionism.[18]

So when Watts erupted, it was inevitable that leading figures in the black community would be charged with being Communist agents. Mervyn Dymally took to the floor of the assembly to denounce a film by the Peace Officers Research Association of California that depicted him and Congressman Augustus Hawkins as "the two leading Communists in the state and the instigators of the Watts riot."[19] This was a self-fulfilling prophecy for many conservatives who had warned that political and economic concessions to blacks would only strengthen Reds.

The cant of anticommunism meant that those who took a position akin to that of Communists, such as opposing the war in Vietnam, were Red. And this war—popular among conservatives—was increasingly unpopular in South LA. Even the quirky black weekly the *LA Herald-Dispatch* opposed the war, albeit on the idiosyncratic grounds that "the fight against Communism is not in Africa, Asia nor Latin America, it's right here in America." [20] Anticommunism was a secular church that could encompass black nationalism, but the fact that this weekly was nationalist meant that it could adopt a mildly dissenting, Baptist-like form.

The hysteria that accompanied the Watts Uprising was generated not only by the fires, the guns, and the violence but by the specter of Red advance among blacks. Civil rights leaders were seen as defenseless targets of opportunity for the Communists, here and in Vietnam. The CBS radio affiliate KNX in an editorial broadcast on 19 August 1965 was quick to note the "strange connection between civil rights leaders and the increasing propaganda against American foreign policy. There is a direct connection—and it is beginning to jell into a broad based campaign aimed at American society itself." [21] Confirming its suspicions was the fact that, like other African-Americans who remembered the popular front, leaders like Hawkins had cooperated with the left and had not forgotten the support of Jim Crow by the Dixiecrats.

Though the NOI was singled out by many, particularly the LAPD, as the instigator of the uprising, other right-wing forces still insisted on blaming the Communists, even though they had virtually run the party out of business by 1965. The *Intelligence Digest* of Gloucestershire, England, pursued this tack, as did the House Un-American Activities Committee. [22] The *Independent American* blamed Robert Williams with his radio broadcasts from Cuba and his calls for militant self-defense, and saw him as a de facto Red. [23] *Heads-Up,* published in Oroville and "dedicated to fighting Communism," felt that the revolt "represented the greatest advance ever made by the Communists to defeat us by direct insurrection." This evil plan was "born in Moscow" and "did not accidentally take place during the most critical period of the war in Vietnam." [24] The shooting at planes and helicopters, the rhetorical comparisons, the question of color all led many conservatives and ultrarightists to conclude that just as the opposition in Vietnam was led by Communists, the opposition in South LA was too.

■

Did the revolt aid the international and domestic left by forcing attention back to pressing domestic concerns and diluting the struggle against communism? Probably not, though Nathan Cohen raised this inferentially when he suggested, "In a sense we seem to be back to the unfinished business of the thirties when the entire world was in the throes of ideological conflict." The *Economist* was of like mind: "Outbreaks like this are part of the price we are going to pay for a society in which more and more people live in cities and do deadly dull work and waste their leisure."[25]

Momentarily it did seem that the revolt would spur the mobilization of the more realistically minded, particularly among elites. A change did occur at the *LA Times,* and the election of Tom Bradley as mayor showed that the impulse to tackle real issues—as opposed to demonizing as Red those who tried—was ascendant. But when the left was weakened, the glue that held diverse forces together was weakened too, as the defeat of Bradley in his effort to become governor in 1982 and 1986 suggests.

The rise of former actors and celebrities to political prominence—not only Ronald Reagan but George Murphy and others—on a platform of conservative anticommunism was more suggestive of post-1965 trends. This era marked the rise of right-wing elected officials buoyed in part by the revolt. The former song-and-dance man turned politican Senator George Murphy remarked worriedly on 18 August 1965 that "Communist groups are moving in to capitalize on the disorders."[26]

City Councilman John Gibson blamed the rebellion on "an increase in Communist activity in the last 18 months."[27] The Reds, he argued, "had a great influence."[28] Councilman Gibson felt that "the riot wasn't started by an organized group, but I think the second day it was pretty well organized." He singled out the "Los Angeles Provisional Organization Committee for a Marxist-Leninist Communist Party and Freedom," which had "distributed literature to the students at Jordan High." The councilman from the 15th district lived in industrial San Pedro; he represented Watts, though he was not African-American. Warren Christopher asked the seasoned pol if he had "noticed in recent weeks or months any emphasis by this Communist group in focusing their attention on VietNam, or protests against the war in Viet-Nam." Yes, was Gibson's immediate reply.[29]

Elites were concerned that the revolt boosted the fortunes of the domestic and international left, whatever this unrest's other vices and virtues. As early as 15 August 1965 the *LA Times* was reporting that the story was being "given big display in [the] world press." Two days later it reported that the president feared a "Red Publicity Spree" focused on the "riots." A few days later President Johnson received an angry telegram from N. N. Semenov, the vice president of the Soviet Academy of Sciences and Nobel Laureate; N. G. Basov, another Nobel Laureate; Dmitri Shastakovich; and others. They condemned police violence in LA. "How could this happen?" they asked. Linking it to the war, they declared: "The events in Los Angeles can only be associated in the mind of the people with the barbarous actions of the American soldiers in Vietnam and the Dominican Republic. . . . . The flame flaring up over the Negro ghetto recalls the burning towns and villages of Vietnam." They went on to affirm: "Mankind has the right to say at the top of its voice to you, Mr. President: Look at Los Angeles. Here you have the 'freedom' which the [U.S.] wants to impose upon other peoples through bayonets and bombs . . . here you have an endless field of work for statesmen and legislators who are hypo-critically caring for the good of '[captive] nations.'"[30]

Moscow and Peking may have been feuding about doctrinal matters and approaches to U.S. imperialism, but they were united in their view that Watts was a telling signal. The People's Republic of China termed the revolt a "veri-table revolutionary movement."[31] The New China News Agency was as assid-uous as Tass in circulating this viewpoint. Chinese premier Chou en-Lai, speaking at a 17 August Peking reception given by the Indonesian ambassa-dor—weeks before the U.S. inspired coup in Jakarata that led to over 500,000 people being slaughtered—assailed the U.S. government's response to the revolt.[32]

The fiery missive from Moscow received massive publicity worldwide; it was printed in *Pravda* and distributed in English by Tass. Washington coun-terattacked by "quietly making available to Americans abroad a four page memorandum to guide them in answering embarrassing questions about" the revolt, forwarded by the U.S. Information Agency to embassies abroad. There was grave concern that the revolt had hurt the struggle against socialism; "the uprising in Los Angeles has seriously damaged the reputation of the United States abroad for a long time to come." Even the *Torrance South Bay Daily Breeze,* prototypically Southern Californian, saw fit to seek comment from USC's Research Institute on Communist Strategy and Propaganda; the paper was concerned that the revolt was "the year's biggest [story] in Moscow and Peking."[33]

If one looks at the miniscule ranks of the LA left in 1965, it is hard to understand why U.S. elites were in such a lather. Nevertheless, some conser-vative anti-Communists accepted implicitly the leftist premise of the day that a "single spark can start a prairie fire," that the revolt might prove the cause of explosive growth in socialist forces in the United States. At the American Sociological Association meeting in LA in late August 1965, the scholars L. A. Coser and T. B. Bottomore not only said that the revolt showed the class struggle was alive, they also chided elites: "The two professors said if Karl Marx had not been so neglected in the United States, the current unrest among the Negroes and poor would not have come as such a surprise to students of politics and sociology." [34]

■

The Communist party had not neglected Karl Marx, and Watts probably did have a positive impact on its fortunes in LA for the short term. When the revolt began, the LA party leadership was hundreds of miles away in Northern California having a coastwide meeting. Led by Dorothy Healey, they left San Francisco immediately and got back home hours later. Instantly they called an emergency meeting at the home of their black leader, William Taylor. As Healey remembered, "We invited to that meeting some of the Black Communists who lived directly in Watts." She expressed no deep regret for much of the burning. To her way of thinking, much of what was burned were big stores, "including one owned by my cousin by marriage, Martin's, where there [were] credit rackets of all kinds."

Perhaps this is why concern grew over her safety after she had hurried back to her home in the heart of LA. "I was home alone. . . . I got frantic calls from everybody in the city urging me to leave, that it was just too dangerous to be here." She was cautious and careful. There were those who would love to be able to pin this revolt on the Reds, so as to avoid looking at the conditions that caused LA to be imperiled. As a woman who was auguring what might occur among women if those like her gained influence, Healey was vulnerable; at a time when the angry revolt of black women in the streets was raising concern, she was even more vulnerable.

Yet it seems that the worrying devoted to the Reds may have been pointless, for there were real questions about the perceptions of leading comrades. Healey found it hard to believe that many blacks seemed to welcome the National Guard because she knew that they feared and hated the police. "We were very surprised by this, taken aback, because our first reaction had been to oppose the calling-out of the National Guard. It was the Black comrades in Watts who kept saying, 'You just don't know what you're talking about.' . . . There was a lot of criticism of the party by our young comrades, most particularly for the fact that Black communists weren't seen in any public way in terms of helping to give leadership to this mass upsurge." [35]

The nationalism of the revolt had an impact on the party. It gave impetus to the slogan of "Nationalist in Form, Anti-imperialist in Content," which in giving legitimacy to all-black formations was a throwback to the party's view of Negroes as a nation. This idea was often derided as an inappropriate import from Moscow, but it actually just represented the fact that the party recognized earlier than most the potential explosiveness of black nationalism and sought a fruitful channel to harness it.

Healey was perceptive in lamenting the imposition of the mass curfew, which presented an ominous challenge to civil liberties and could foreshadow something else much worse. "The most terrible part of it to me was the acceptance by people of the fact that they couldn't go out." [36] This was taken quite seriously by Communists who had encoded in their memory what had happened under fascism.

The organization of the Che-Lumumba Club within the CP was an attempt to accommodate nationalism, while not balkanizing unduly by race and thereby opening the door further for advance by the ultra-right. The problem was that the kind of black nationalism the party once hailed in the 1930s had mutated under relentless pressure from a right-wing environment into something that often resembled racialism.

The Communists were able to alter their approaches and enjoy some growth. Setting "up the Che-Lumumba Club, which was an all-Black collective," was "very controversial." Some comrades wondered if this was a capitulation to the influence of the NOI and the right wing. The black Communist William Taylor did play a leading role during these times of commotion, Healey's report notwithstanding. The iron curtain obstructing left thinkers from the mass media was lifted long enough to allow Taylor to go on the radio to present party views. He hammered home relentlessly his anger at continuing racism. "No white newspaper publisher has ever been subjected to being stopped and searched in front of his own newspaper office, and then forced to await the pleasure of the police van while he calls the central office and 'does a make.'" This indignity to the *Sentinel* publisher was unconscionable, he thundered.

But what Taylor stressed—and what pushed the party inexorably in the direction of starting the Che-Lumumba Club—was the ignominy of a racial double standard which the CP linked to larger issues, like the war in Vietnam or the economy. Those blacks interviewed on television, he recalled, "expressed their feeling of utter futility about the idea of the fighting in Vietnam under the slogan of defending democracy while they were denied democracy in their own homes. They indicated their lack of confidence in the 'power structure.' Racial bias, he maintained, was profitable; for example, "many of the larger grocery chains have two grades of meat—one for the middle class white community, and one for the poor, Negro community."[37]

The West Coast Red paper, *People's World,* also linked the revolt to Vietnam, contending that the recent escalation in Asia "obstructs a serious war on poverty in Watts . . . the commitment to kill Vietnamese made it impossible to save lives in Watts."[38] Others felt that Korea was the more appropriate analogy; in 1965 more blacks had served in that war. One fan of right-wing radio host Bob Grant recalled that Watts reminded him of Korea when "school children" were "rioting to get Sigmund Rhee out." He was more perceptive than some Communists in pointing out that these Koreans were "trying to overthrow" a government, while in Watts they were just "trying to make a point. To be heard."[39] Both Communists and their right-wing opponents would have done well to heed this distinction, but often both did not, though it is understandable why the mistake was made.

The Communist youth organization, the W. E. B. Du Bois clubs—which shared an interlocking directorate with Che-Lumumba—made recommendations that could be viewed as contradictory. They demanded that white cops be removed from the 77th precinct, while arguing for higher standards for hiring officers—at least two years of college—that could have a disproportionately negative impact on black applicants.[40] Captain Thomas E. King, commander of the 77th, in turn contended that the uprising represented a rejection of the Marxists. When they passed out literature at Jordan High School, "it was heartwarming to see the students throw the material on the ground."[41]

Yet these same students reacted positively to a major case that the Communists focused on in the wake of the revolt. Philip Bentley Brooks was twenty-three, married, and the father of three children in 1965 when he was charged with murder. He was accused of slaying a deputy sheriff during the revolt, although the deputy seems to have been shot by his own partner. Brooks said the deputy aimed a gun at him, "then he hit me with the butt of it. When he hit my elbow and the top of the door, it went off." He was in jail six months without bail. His case was assisted by lawyers close to the party;

Rose Chernin, executive director of the LA Committee for Defense of the Bill of Rights—an outgrowth of the banished Civil Rights Congress—was resolute in Brooks's defense, but this was to little avail.[42]

The authorities may have spent too much time reading Communist publications that led them to inflate the Reds' influence. Herbert Aptheker, the Red historian, termed the revolt a "turning point in history, just as the Nat Turner slave uprising" was; elites, he chuckled, "are shaking in their boots and they can smell their doom."[43] Many elites were too quick to believe their own rhetoric about outside agitators and Reds stirring things up. The revolt was happening as tensions with Moscow—the presumed patron and ally of domestic Reds—were growing; naturally, this distraction obviated the necessity to consider more reflectively what real ills led to insurrections. Such an atmosphere strengthened the U.S. right, undermined some liberals, and pushed still more to the right.

Aptheker detected these ominous trends and patterns that would lead to the election of the right-wing favorite, Ronald Reagan, as governor in 1966. Radio and television sets, he observed, "blare for hour after hour—especially in the evening with messages from the extreme Right." The fanatical Billy Hargis and his "Christian Crusaders" had been gaining support steadily in the region and drew huge crowds "the week-end before the outbreak." The Communist historian was aware of the growing ties between these organized rightists and the police. "Having Parker responsible for 'law and order' in Watts is comparable to placing Himmler in charge of police in Tel Aviv."[44]

Aptheker usually represented mainstream opinion among Reds, but Ben Dobbs, who was a party leader in LA, felt that the historian had overstated the case. Indeed, many California Reds felt that the party center in New York City often was out of touch with the unique reality of the West. In contrast to Aptheker's references to Nat Turner, Dobbs was more sober, warning that this uprising was a "spontaneous upheaval" made up of "individual acts which were not preceded by political actions and demands." Because of this lack of planning or intent, "cynicism and despair" could easily result as dreams did not pan out. A remarkable sign already was that the efforts to build a movement for general amnesty for those arrested proceeded very slowly: "Since the arrests were in large measure the result of individual actions, the defense is reduced to individual defense." He was all too aware, as was Healey, that the years of the Red Scare had taken its toll: "The majority of the Negro leadership welcomed the National Guard as an antidote to Chief of Police Parker, also as a means to stabilize the situation."[45] Dobbs was closer to the scene and may have been more perceptive as a result; however, Aptheker's points could not be discarded either. Watts did lead directly to some forms of organization, such as the Black Panther party, and some organized militance that did bring some gains. Nevertheless, Dobbs's insights are helpful in judging the ultimate legacy of Watts 1965.

Early on, the FBI concluded that the party; its fraternal ally among youth, the W. E. B. Du Bois clubs; and the NOI did not engage in "organize[d] planning" of the uprising. But if this conclusion had been trumpeted widely, it might have undermined the effort to ignore pressing social problems and might have forced an effort to ascribe the uprising to these same problems.[46] It was easier to inflate Aptheker's viewpoint further and argue that a Red-black overthrow of U.S. imperialism was nigh.

The CP may not have been involved in an organized way, but the authorities were not so sure about other left forces. The barrage aimed at the party via COINTELPRO, the FBI's counterintelligence program, and the image of China as leading the colored downtrodden against white hegemony inevitably influenced many to drift to newer and theretofore lesser-known forces. One example of this trend was the rise of the LA Provisional Organizing Committee for a Marxist-Leninist Communist Party and its leader Michael Laski. As early as the electoral campaign of 1964, Councilman John Gibson had begun monitoring the M-Ls. He was concerned about the flyer they handed out at 7 P.M. on 30 October 1964 at 1634 East 103d Street. Apparently they were trying to organize car wash workers.[47]

Laski and his small band were monitored during the uprising. They were far from being instrumental in sparking disturbances,[48] yet they did become more visible and active in the early aftermath of August 1965. Inspired by China, they felt that the CP was too staid and, like their presumed patrons in Moscow, not sensitive enough to questions of color. Their fiery focus on class questions at a time when this key issue was being overlooked also may have heightened their visibility. Continuing to organize car wash workers, they also picketed the Giant grocery store at 103d and Beach, accusing it of exploiting customers and workers.[49]

In the fall of 1965, the Sons of Watts began picketing the M-Ls' bookstore at 92d Street and Compton Avenue. Despite their allegiance to China and sensitivity to color concerns, the M-Ls were mostly white, and this fact—whatever their ideology—did not go down well in the increasingly inflamed nationalist setting. The M-Ls did not help their cause by suggesting that blacks should arm themselves against the "ruling class." Some felt that the M-Ls were setting up militant blacks to be cannon fodder hurled futilely at militarily superior police forces, in the pattern subsequently made notorious by the BPP. The M-Ls were unrelenting in their criticism of the SOW, whom they called "paid police agents" and "running dogs of police." Their searing rhetoric aside, the M-Ls had noticed that uniformed police stood nearby when SOW picketers tore down the sign on the bookstore and marked the bookstore front with black spray paint. They had to be curious about the presence of Willard Murray, Mayor Yorty's "Negro aide," as all this was taking place.[50]

Things got worse for Laski and his dwindling coterie in the coming months. In February 1966 a homemade bomb, a length of pipe filled with gunpowder, was exploded at their store, now in the 1300 block of Firestone Boulevard. It had the impact of four sticks of dynamite and was heard over two miles away.[51] Then the mayor attacked them, and another leftist sect, the Progressive Labor party, and suggested that the city faced "sacking" and "urban guerilla warfare" at their hands.[52] By the time of the first anniversary of the uprising, Laski and his comrades were arrested for civil disobedience and then beaten badly at the city jail; ultimately they were stamped out of existence.[53] Some of the forces, such as the Communist party, who were facing the same severe treatment at the hands of the authorities were so alienated by the M-L rhetoric and the political disputes then raging that they did not find it useful to protest loudly.

■

While Laskie was being pulverized, others were receiving kinder treatment. Some elites tried to address pressing social problems, albeit in their own way. At times this effort was designed to fulfill other agendas, such as building up centrist organizations in order to undermine whatever residual appeal held by the left and growing BPP-oriented forces. Yet some of these attempts were motivated sincerely by a realistic assessment that domestic reform of some sort must ensue if another revolt was to be avoided.

The Watts Labor Community Action Committee was formed before the summer of 1965 as a nonprofit organization. It was organized by trade unions, principally the UAW, as a way to meld community and union concerns about South LA. Ted Watkins was the chair. He was born in Meridian,

Mississippi, and after migrating to LA, he began working with Ford and rose quickly in the UAW as a leader. The WLCAC controlled a poultry ranch and a Mobil Oil station. The powerful Southern Pacific was persuaded to provide it with a refrigerated trailer for its entrepreneurial efforts. The committee represented an alternative in ideology and approach to obstreperous leftists chanting about the "ruling class" and police brutality.[54]

Just as Laski was being pummeled, Watkins was being boosted; the former was white and the latter was black, and what was happening to them did not dovetail with popular nationalist analyses that said punishment turned exclusively on melanin content. The WLCAC established a headquarters at 10406½ Wilmington Avenue that was not being picketed by the SOW or anyone else.[55] It was the centrist alternative, backed by a labor-corporate alliance; it was designed to show that it was not necessary for blacks to align with the left, or for the United States even to have a left. It was well within the mainstream consensus represented by the NAACP. Eventually the WLCAC stretched its influence beyond the UAW to include the International Association of Machinists, the Teamsters, the International Longshore Workers, and the Industrial Union Department of the AFL-CIO.[56] It received high praise in *LA Times* editorials, and its office was a de rigueur stop for visiting officialdom like Robert Kennedy, who became a patron of the WLCAC.[57]

Watkins was able to provide some jobs for local residents with his various projects. Could more have been done if the unions and the WLCAC had not distanced themselves so completely from various left-wing and militant forces? Not only did Watkins and the unions avoid various leftists, they were not keen on nationalists either; mainstream civil rights leaders and corporations were their chief allies. This may have endeared them to liberal and conservative anti-Communists, but it did not win them a sturdy foothold in Watts. On the other hand, an alliance with leftists or nationalists might have jeopardized the meager gains they did obtain. Nevertheless, even within the narrow constraints within which they had to operate, one can question the long-term value of the WLCAC. The absence of a left and the inadequacies of the nationalists reduced the bargaining power of centrists. In 1967 the Department of Youth Authority, which also worked closely with gangs and SOW, thanked the WLCAC profusely for accepting "each of our highly delinquent, educationally retarded, economically deprived referrals." Many in South LA regarded this language as offensive and deemed it indicative of their reduced bargaining power in the wake of the left's demise.[58]

Watkins did good work. By leveraging funds adroitly from the UAW and other sources, the WLCAC controlled a considerable portion of the economy of Watts. It even planted 22,000 trees at a time when environmental consciousness was not widespread.[59] The fact was undeniable that it was part of the positive legacy of and response to the conflagration. However, what it gained was difficult to separate from the onslaught against the left. The effort by Watkins and his allies to build businesses was well within the hegemonic discourse of private enterprise and free markets and contrasted sharply with the left's insistence on castigating a ruling class and expanding the public sector. Eventually, the maneuvers by centrists and leftists were overshadowed by the growing strength of the right, which was able to prepare the path not only for seizing high electoral office in Sacramento but also for influencing officials in Los Angeles, Washington, D.C., and elsewhere in the country and the world.

13

Politics:
Local and Beyond

THE GROWTH OF THE ULTRARIGHT IN THE WAKE of and in reaction to the uprising had widespread impact. This growth was taking place as the left was being increasingly marginalized and various nationalist influences were spreading among blacks. These crosscurrents complicated the political trajectory of figures as diverse as Martin Luther King, Jr., Lyndon Johnson, and Pat Brown. Simultaneously boosted were the fortunes of Ronald Reagan, who had proved his political reliability during the 1946 Conference of Studio Unions strike. The mayor of LA, Sam Yorty, felt that he too could capitalize on the postrebellion situation, but this turned out to be not so feasible a prospect as he thought. Chief Parker also was disappointed by the turn of events.

■

The Democratic party had an uphill battle in seeking to establish a foothold in California. From the black point of view, its weakness was acceptable so long as the GOP was considered the main engine of black progress, but beginning in 1932 African-Americans tied their political aspirations to the Democrats. The party historically had been identified not only with the white working class but with rabid Dixiecrats as well. Hence, the Democratic rise provided a mixed blessing at best; black leverage against this party had been weakened, however, by the erosion of left influence in the United States. The setback for the civil rights movement—the defeat of Fannie Lou Hamer and the Mississippi Freedom Democratic party—at the 1964 Democratic convention in Atlantic City had suggested this. Yet there was no other party to turn to, because the GOP's rightward tilt was accelerating. Jan Bernstein has stated that there has been a weakened party structure in California, due in part to Progressive Era reforms, but by the 1950s after "sixty years of nearly unbroken Republican dominance," the Democrats began to surge and strengthen their structure. The influx of blacks during World War II aided this rise of the Democrats.[1]

But with Watts 1965 what commenced was the era of the so-called white backlash. As Allen J. Matusow has put it, "Legions of moderate whites who had so recently demanded justice for the meek, Christ-like demonstrators of Selma began melting away." Looking back from 1991, Thomas and Mary Edsall concluded that Watts "undermined the liberal premise behind civil rights legislation." It also undermined the Democrats while the GOP was "provided the opportunity to change the direction of the national debate by initiating a full-scale assault on liberal social policies."[2]

The opinion of Mary Landis of Long Beach was becoming typical of many. As the embers were still burning, she bluntly told the president that "white people . . . are getting real tired of the kinky haired, thick lipped blacks who are giving so much trouble . . . you and the Kennedys have given them everything they have asked for—when do you plan to stop?"[3]

Cleveland Sellers of SNCC was typical of a polar opposite view. Watts, he recalled, "motivated us to begin a search for ways in which we could mold the discontent in the urban ghettos to revolutionary advantage." The United States and more specifically Southern California were facing the two sharply contrasted tendencies of heightened black militance along with increased white chauvinism; both were unleavened generally by left and class influences. These polar opposites came face to face in LA in November 1965 when the notorious Sheriff Jim Clark of Alabama visited at the invitation of the local Citizens' Council. Even the NAACP flocked to the protest.[4]

Black militance and white blacklash were becoming totems for a changing political situation that was crippling the massive electoral mandate that the Democrats thought they had received in November 1964. Columnists Rowland Evans and Robert Novak not only claimed that usually liberal Jewish Democrats in LA had reacted negatively to perceived anti-Semitic expressions in Watts 1965; they went further to state that in Bel-Air and Beverly Hills these families were "thrown into such unreasoning panic that scores of families laid off Negro servants." This was creating enormous opportunities, they suggested, for Mayor Yorty, who "has a new popularity among whites" throughout the region. Ronald Reagan, they reported, "also rides the white backlash."[5]

This perception of a white backlash helped to create a momentum of its own and a self-fulfilling prophecy. Though certain studies showed substantial sympathy across racial lines for the grievances of South LA, this was not the message being broadcast by acolytes of the right. The governor of the state felt the heat. Brown had beaten Richard Nixon in 1962, but in 1966 he was defeated by Reagan, whose campaign, he felt, emphasized "law and order," a code for Watts 1965. Brown declared that Reagan played on and propelled the "so-called 'white backlash' to black militancy," portending a trend that "came earlier to California than to the rest of the nation."[6]

The tidal wave symbolized by Reagan was to sweep eastward from California and eventually reach all three branches of government in Washington, D.C. In the eyes of many, the Reagan administration was principally responsible for what was seen as a victorious outcome of the Cold War. A disturbing signal was sent early on when the usually reliable Senator Thomas Kuchel decried "the rule of the jungle" in Watts, a turn of phrase seen as more worthy of Chief Parker.[7] The notion that blacks had gone too far proved to be a critical factor driving the rise of contemporary conservatism. More respectable rightists were saying the same thing, if less grossly. William F. Buckley, for example, felt that the Watts community was not such a bad place to live but in August 1965 the residents there simply had "become animals."[8] The dehumanization of blacks was a necessary prelude to heightened maltreatment of them.

President Johnson quickly sensed the changing political environment engendered by the LA events. Allen Matusow may not have exaggerated when he suggested that "no white man in America was more stunned by Watts than the president himself." Johnson had invested political capital in the civil rights movement, getting behind the Civil Rights Act of 1964 and the Voting Rights Act of 1965. In part this was a response to the negative impact of lingering Jim Crow on the international position of the United States, but the fact remained that he was politically exposed. His aide Joseph Califano recalled that the president was so affected that "he refused to look at the cables from Los Angeles. . . . He refused to take calls from the generals who were requesting government planes to fly in the National Guard." He recognized instinctively that his "close identification with the cause of black Americans" would become a "political liability. By the time of the 1966 congressional elections, the trend toward racial conservatism was unmistakable."[9]

One California politico analogized the position of Democratic officials to

Lady Macbeth "trying to wash out 'that damned spot.' But the spot will not wash out."[10] The Democrats were in a quandary. A more balanced political spectrum would have provided the opportunity to scapegoat the organized left for Watts, but that would not work because an excellent job had been done of lessening their influence. The Black Scare could not be used either, for blacks were too closely identified with the Democrats. Indeed, the Voting Rights Act, which had been signed five days before the conflagration, supposedly had strengthened the Democrats' effort to retain the Solid South by adding millions of newly enfranchised black voters in that region. Watts meant in part that some white voters would respond to the GOP appeal to abandon the Democrats and their embrace of blacks for a more racially homogeneous party. The White House was aware of all this; fellow Texan and Attorney General Ramsey Clark filed away a column by David Lawrence that included these themes. But Johnson and his allies felt powerless to reverse the twist that fate had presented them.[11]

August 1965 defined a previous era and marked the initiation of a new one. The ominous concurrence of the historic legislative victory of the Voting Rights Act and one of the most destructive urban conflicts in U.S. history highlighted the fact that few of the dramatic hard-won gains of the 1960s had reached the lives of many black urban dwellers beyond the South.[12] Johnson was baffled when in a single week black registration under the new act began in the South while deadly turmoil spread through LA.[13] But he should have recognized that even though the Civil Rights Act of 1964 and the Voting Rights Act were to cover and assist some in South LA, their effectiveness depended on enforcement by courts and agencies affected by the increasingly conservative environment that arose most powerfully in California.

Johnson was on the defensive not only because of his now ill-timed embrace of civil rights. Rivals, real and putative, were sniping. Dwight Eisenhower spoke of those "disgraceful riots," and leading Republicans generally were quite hostile toward South LA. As if interparty conflict were not enough, Robert Kennedy—suspected as a contender for the 1968 Democratic presidential nomination—resisted the pull to the right and staked out a position to the left; many feared that Kennedy's appeal could further erode the president's base of support within the party. Linking the urban crisis with the war in Vietnam was to come later for Kennedy and others, but the farsighted could anticipate this linkage. Such developments could endanger LBJ's role in history and the party he led.[14]

On 19 August 1965 in the *LA Times*, Kennedy gave succor to South LA by stating, "I think there is no doubt that if Washington or Jefferson or Adams were Negroes in a northern city today they would be in the forefront of the effort to change the conditions under which Negroes live in our society." Kennedy agreed that "we have a long way to go before law means the same thing to Negroes as it does to us." The former attorney general acknowledged that "the laws do not protect them from paying too much money for inferior goods, from having their furniture illegally repossessed. The law does not protect them from having to keep lights turned on the feet of children at night, to keep them from being gnawed by rats."

Pressed from the right by the GOP and from the left by Kennedy, LBJ was paralyzed intellectually and politically. Joseph Califano, then his top aide, has recalled that when he tried to reach the president on Friday, 13 August, and again on Saturday, "he didn't return my calls—the only time in the years I worked for Lyndon Johnson that this occurred." As a result, Califano provided White House approval for shipping supplies to the National Guard in Southern California without even talking to LBJ. On 14 August 1965, another aide, Jack Valenti, noted for the president, "at 6:20 P.M. Texas time, Secretary McNamara talked to Joe Califano and strongly recommended that the President send C-13s or comparable aircraft to transport California National Guardsmen."[15]

Califano has stated that LBJ was "depressed." During this Second Reconstruction, LBJ was worried that as in the post-Civil War period, "Negroes will end up pissing in the aisles of the Senate," "making fools of themselves" by their boisterous behavior. But all of the president's perceptions were not so distorted; he wanted the conservative John McCone to head the investigation, not only to provide ideological cover but also to disprove the idea that Communists were behind the rebellion. In 1965 to be "soft on communism" was political suicide, so that Johnson knew how carefully this matter had to be handled. And, said Califano, the rebellion "had put the stamp of urgency on LBJ's desire to mount a concerted assault on slum conditions."[16]

The president was told that events in Watts were all too similar to some recent U.S. foreign adventures. "It is not a bit different than what we saw happening in the Elizabethville area of the Congo" was one conclusion.[17] Many thought that a strain of the primitive sparking such outbursts was common to both Africans and African-Americans. Hitting closer to home, the Washington humorist Art Buchwald compared Watts to the recent U.S. incursion in Santo Domingo and mused that "Pres. Emmanuel El Finco . . . of Enchilada" sent troops to LA to "protect the lives and property of Enchiladas who have been caught there in the recent riots."[18] If the liberal Buchwald could display such racial insensitivity and ridicule the basis for the president's recent "victory" in the Caribbean, then the problem haunting the White House was larger than most thought. Dr. F. L. King of Texarkana was blunt with LBJ. He knew many "long time supporters" of the president, and most felt that "had the arsonist, looters, etc. in the riots . . . been shot on the spot— all of them—by the National Guards, there would have been no repetition . . . for fifty years." He assured Johnson that "I am not a racist."[19]

When LBJ aide Leroy Collins arrived in LA on 18 August 1965, he found the "air was more filled with tension than smog. Everyone was criticising and blaming everyone else." It was chaos. "Even reporters at the airport were abrasive in their questioning." Leaders were wrangling. He wanted to call a press conference with the mayor and governor, but they got "along like the gingham and calico cat." LBJ's coordinator of antipoverty money, the Kennedy in-law Sargent Shriver, "continued to swap transcontinental insults" with Yorty.[20]

Other administration officials were having similar difficulties. Lloyd Hand, yet another aide to LBJ, later to run for office in 1966, informed Ramsey Clark weeks after the uprising about some "Negro friends who are students" at Yale and other "Eastern Law schools" who "have [come] home to see their parents terrorized by the new power in the Negro community. The snipers are still at large . . . and they are acting under direction" and are "regarded as patriots." He felt that many Negroes wanted to ignite conflict in LA so as to divert the attention and energy of the White House from Vietnam. "They work at odd jobs by day . . . no one reports them for fear of reprisal." He told the attorney general: "I trust that our national security forces know of this or are on top of it. Can it be reported or is it too dangerous for public consumption? The implications are bizarre but they are there."[21] Hand was half-right; the scene was certainly bizarre but not in the way he imagined. His idea of a black community held hostage reflected an awareness of the increased and at times chaotic black militance (and a reason for frightened calls for martial law). The reach of the militants was overstated, however. His inattention to the corresponding growth in ultraright sentiment only heightened the antiblack atmosphere.

This was the conflict faced by Johnson, and the response was fitful. On

21 August 1965 at a White House conference on equal employment opportunity, high-ranking officials compared people in South LA streets to the KKK. Later the administration was more sober, warning that "the clock is ticking, time is moving" toward LA-style "uprisings in other major cities." But indicative of LBJ's dilemma was the fact that House GOP leader Gerald Ford quickly retaliated, suggesting that the president was inviting "race violence."[22]

Ramsey Clark was the son of Johnson's Texas comrade former U.S. Supreme Court justice Tom Clark; the father's conservatism, his judicial outlook, and his diligence as Truman's attorney general in hounding the left were presumed to have been inherited by the son, an inaccurate presumption as it turned out. Indeed, some were surprised by his appointment at the Justice Department, for he was already exhibiting the kind of independent spirit that eventually would take him further to the left. When told of the flames engulfing LA, he was incredulous. "That can't be. There must be a great distortion in the communication of the facts, and that just can't be."[23] On arrival in Los Angeles he was blunt, warning that if "California cannot resolve difficulties such as this, I don't know what state can."[24]

He scrambled to help to mobilize troops as far away as Spokane and Colorado and sought to patch up the ripped social fabric of the city. Clark spent about ten days in LA and helped in rushing $29 million in federal aid there, worried all the while about the "great concern that what we would do might appear to reward rioters." Obviously, this dilemma hampered and "lent a certain ambiguity to our mission." Clark was also worried about the "reverberations from a cataclysm like Watts" that "are felt all through the country, and you can sense tensions rising and psychological warfare sets in so that people all around are making threats and fear is a major factor."[25]

Clark was subjected to righward tugs also. On 26 August 1965 Benjamin Mandel, research director of the Senate Internal Security Subcommittee, sent him instructive texts like *Communist Anti-American Riots, Mob Violence as an Instrument of Red Diplomacy,* and a *Guide to Communist Tactics among the Unemployed;* he also sent the "very valuable" book *The Mob* by a "French author, Le Bon." The president's men, Collins, Hand, and Clark, were pulled in different directions, but the momentum in the nation still listed inexorably toward the right.[26]

Roger Wilkins was the nephew of Roy Wilkins of the NAACP and was thought to have inherited his uncle's moderation; in 1965 he was serving at the Justice Department. He was with Clark quite a bit during those days and remembered that "Watts hit Washington like a thunderstorm," washing away illusions about what it would take to dissolve centuries of encrusted racism. He intimated that the uprising might have been sparked by the city's laggard approach to participating in administration antipoverty initiatives. Like Collins he was amazed by the Shakespearean infighting among local officialdom: "Every politician had a knife out, and every politician was protecting his own back. We seemed to have endless meetings to no particular purpose." Many Democrats in California were like LBJ, paralyzed intellectually and politically, so they compensated for this deficiency by turning the undermining of fellow officials into a sport. Wilkins's sour reflections may have been colored by a grave experience. He was harassed by the LAPD during his mission in 1965, a "brush with death that filled me with fear." The White House also had difficult experiences with Mayor Yorty, who set the tone for the LAPD and conservatives in the city. He already had insisted that LBJ provide his local rival, James Roosevelt, a post at the United Nations; "Yorty's price for signing the community-action agreement was for the President to get Roosevelt out of his hair." Then Watts exploded, and the fallout worsened relations.

McCone became irritated when he found that Clark, Wilkins, and others were assigned to provide a full report of what happened in Watts and why. The ex-CIA man "had thrown a fit when he heard" about this, feeling "it would pre-empt the work of his commission. He would quit if we were published." Needing the conservative ideological cover, LBJ acquiesced to McCone's demand.[27] The report by the Johnson team was filed in September to little fanfare, months before the McCone report. The task force had arrived in LA on 26 August and left by 3 September and thus did not explore extensively. The report was signed by Andrew Brimmer, then an assistant secretary of commerce, and Jack T. Conway, the deputy director of the War on Poverty.

The team's report focused on riot control and existing federal programs. Like the U.S.-backed policy in Guatemala in the 1980s, this could well be characterized as a "beans and rifles" or a *frijoles y fusiles* approach. It noted that the Civil Rights Act of 1964 and the Voting Rights Act of 1965 had not yet had much relevance to Watts, but it criticized the perception that the civil rights movement has not been "particularly germane." The authors pondered nervously the growing popularity of the increasingly atavistic phrase "white power structure," which had been invoked repeatedly by some in the streets.[28]

Even before the report was filed, the administration did more than just dispatch troops. As early as 25 August 1965, Secretary of Agriculture Orville Freeman was working to deliver 231,000 pounds of food to the curfew zone. Freeman also told LBJ about all manner of education and jobs programs.[29] On 2 September forty-nine projects were approved, amounting to $8.5 million, but the desire to avoid the perception of rewarding insurrection made White House efforts decidedly ambiguous.[30]

The signals sent from the White House became even more confusing in 1966. Wilkins, rapidly becoming the firefighter of choice for urban areas, was said by LBJ press aide Bill Moyers to have "prevented another and more serious riot in Watts . . . by intervening in a case in which a Negro was fired on [at] the picket line. . . . It was getting close to exploding when Wilkins stepped in."[31] Wilkins was putting out fires, but Lloyd Hand was starting them. Eyebrows were raised when he went from analyzing the scene in August 1965 to running against the scapegoated and besieged Lieutenant Governor Anderson, denouncing him as "indecisive." Hand's challenge strengthened the right-wing forces seeking to sabotage his party and his former boss in the White House.[32]

Yet it was LBJ who paid a price higher than Anderson in the wake of August 1965. He had been identified closely with blacks, and they now were being associated with noisy and difficult activity. Years later the historian Joe B. Frantz asked LBJ's aide Lee White if "the President had any intuition that this was a start of a phase." White answered simply, "Yes, I think so."[33]

■

Some racists argued that not only LBJ but Governor Brown too was stuck to the tar baby of black militance. Brown acknowledged later that "people always felt I was too friendly with the blacks anyway." Voters, he felt, were reacting sharply to black advances; before voting against him, they had decided to "put a guy in there that'll put these colored guys in their place." The GOP was bound to benefit from this trend toward racial conservatism, the longing for the good old days of Jim Crow when blacks knew their place. Ronald Reagan, Brown recalled ruefully, "very cleverly handled that thing." Neither Brown nor LBJ nor many other leading Democrats for the next few decades could figure out a way to explain all of the reasons—including the Cold War competition for hearts and minds globally—why overturning Jim Crow was necessary.

It was the bad luck of Governor Brown to be abroad on 11 August 1965, which allowed some to criticize him for being out of touch or asleep on the job. He had been invited to Greece by the Order of AHEPA, a fraternal grouping. He left immediately and was met in New York City by Califano; Brown recalled later that the aide "offered all the assistance in the world . . . they flew me back in a Presidential jet."[34] Lee White, another LBJ aide who met with the governor in New York City, had more negative memories of the encounter and Brown himself: "If you took a line and drew it underneath, you might have a little trouble finding where the substance was and where the fluff was." Watts was not just Brown's fault, he thought; "but at least we were doing more than anybody else at the moment."[35] Lieutenant Governor Anderson and some of the governor's top aides were attacked for tardy responses to the conflagration. The governor noted subsequently that "the severity of the incident was beyond the scope of anything anticipated by me or my advisers."[36]

By the time he got to LA, things had become even more chaotic, and on 15 August his attempt to tour the curfew zone was "curtailed by sniper fire." Brown, said the *LA Times,* "returned to a holocaust of rubble and ruins not unlike the aftermath in London when the Nazis struck, or Berlin after Allied armies finished their demolition." This World War II rhetoric set the tone for more military metaphors: "The negroes of Los Angeles stabbed him in the back politically. . . . In doing so they strengthened the right wing. . . . They also strengthened the right wing and segregationists all over the United States."[37]

Brown acknowledged that the rebellion did him no good politically.[38] Senator George Murphy agreed, saying that Brown "came out badly." Fellow Republican George Christopher, gubernatorial aspirant and former mayor of San Francisco, ridiculed Brown: he "fiddled while Los Angeles was burning." Like many others, Christopher linked the revolt to the Berkeley student rebellion of 1964 as an example of what liberal policies produced.[39] A further problem faced by the embattled governor was his prickly relationship with the city's mayor and police chief.[40] Moreover, Brown's ties with his attorney general, Thomas Lynch, were not the best either. During the hectic moments of August 1965 when proper coordination was at a premium, the existence of these bad feelings complicated everything.

■

On hearing of the disturbances, Lynch immediately set up a statewide network of intelligence to determine if the situation threatened to provoke outbreaks elsewhere. There was "near panic" in the state, he recalled. "In one community early Saturday afternoon many working mothers suddenly left their jobs and hurried home, gathering up their children from baby-sitters and playgrounds to take refuge in their homes. Rumors of an impending riot prompted their action. In another town, rumors spread that householders could protect themselves against an impending riot by displaying red. Anything red was grabbed up and displayed in windows and on mail boxes." This grasping for the usually reviled red was symptomatic of the hysteria gripping all too many in the state.

There was fear that groups like the NOI would take advantage of the turmoil for their own ends. "There was one [incident] in Santa Barbara which we know was definitely a Black Muslim operation, which was quieted down by the police and nothing came of it but it was a potential dangerous thing," Lynch said. "There was another incident in Berkeley . . . beatniks, there were both white and colored people here, only a few were trying to inspire them to carry on a Watts type operation . . . there was an incident in San Diego, there was potential trouble in San Bernadino, and the one in San Diego . . . there were rumors before Labor Day that there would be more riots here in Los Angeles."

But as staggering as this reaction was, it was dwarfed by the call for martial law, in which a number of black leaders joined. This call—by blacks in particular—was an indication not only of a failure to consider the implications of this extreme measure but also a reflection of how they would respond in other contexts. A call for martial law showed that black leaders in LA would not be unreliable in a pinch. Even Lynch was taken aback by their enthusiasm for martial law since it "completely removes and transfers over to the military all functions of government, including the operation of our system of justice . . . every factor of government then comes under the military." It could mean abolition of jury trials, rule by the military, a constitutional coup d'état. This is what Southern California came dangerously close to in 1965, and some black officials endorsed it. No wonder the Communists, who often used blacks as their lodestar, were confused.[41]

If this measure had been taken, it would have exacerbated the chaos that already obtained, for politicians and law enforcement agents were already using Watts as a tool to score points against rivals. Both the LAPD and the county sheriff's office had their own intelligence units, and both guarded their information jealously; compounding this was the existence of forty-eight independent law enforcement agencies in the county.[42] One of the reasons that

South LA spun out of control was turf battles grounded in jealousy. Separation of powers could be a check against overconcentration of power, but it could also make a coordinated response difficult in the midst of a crisis. Politicians like Glenn Anderson were taking fire from rivals like Robert Finch, a GOP aspirant for lieutenant governor. Others were busily undermining officials in competing branches of government. It was not a pretty picture.[43]

Also seeking to manipulate the situation was Speaker of the Assembly Jesse Unruh. He did not get along with the governor, though they belonged to the same party, and his own political ambitions drove him into alliances with unlikely allies, like the mayor. Unruh even sought to take advantage of the postrebellion food shortage in South LA. "It seems to me it would have have been wonderful if the 'hated' cops who had been 'brutalizing' the Negroes could have been the ones to dispense this food—thereby benefacting after having 'oppressed.'"[44]

Though Mayor Sam Yorty was expected to ride the white backlash to higher office, it did not happen. Many felt that his intransigence had led directly to the insurrection and that this pattern would only be repeated if he became governor. Sargent Shriver echoed Vice President Hubert H. Humphrey when he singled out LA as being "the only major city" without a "well-rounded community action program because of the failure of local officials to establish a broad-based community action board representing all segments of the community."[45] As late as mid-October 1965, two-thirds of the $29 million in antipoverty funds targeted for LA were "bogged down."[46] Yet the contretemps over antipoverty funds did not represent a total loss for the mayor, for others felt that the promise of a "war on poverty" itself had fueled unrealistic expectations "far beyond any possibility of fulfillment" and, consequently, had hastened an eruption.[47] The mayor's stand against the War on Poverty may help explain why much of his mail in the immediate aftermath of August 1965 was favorable.[48] His supporters feared that this poverty money would buoy programs beneficial to a black community that mostly voted liberal, not conservative.

But Yorty's dreams of riding the antirevolt wave came crashing to earth, in no small part because the *LA Times* opposed him. As one study of the powerful newspaper put it, "Soon after the Watts riots, antagonisms between Yorty and the *Times* reemerged for the first time since 1961. The *Times* disliked Yorty's cultivation of his small town image and was angered by his Watts tactics. This paper was increasingly committed to a modern, liberal approach to the problems of the inner cities, and had modified its own previous position on many questions, such as open housing."[49] The nation was drifting rightward, but not the *Times*. The paper criticized Yorty for allowing "practical communications between city authorities and the Negro community" to break down.[50] Other local elites were upset with his intemperate remarks, such as suggesting that nuclear weapons be used in Vietnam, and his absentee style of management, which included a trip out of town as his city was going up in flames.[51]

Close watchers of the mayor were sanguine about his political prospects, however. After all, wasn't Yorty the embodiment of the surging white backlash? As one study put it, "The major beneficiary of the Watts riots, in a political sense, was the Little Giant of City Hall. Yorty's staunch law and order position was exactly what many voters wanted to see . . . [he] had emerged from the ashes of Watts with a new image—an enforcer of laws and anything but a coddler of criminals."[52] But Yorty was making too many enemies. Not only was there the *Times*, but on the national level, the White House was no fan of his either. LBJ aide Lee White confessed candidly, "I really don't have a very [high] regard for him."[53] The McCone panel could not fathom why he would fly out of town in the middle of an insurrection.[54] And black and liberal voters felt betrayed by Yorty because he had been elected in 1961 on the promise that he would oust Chief Parker and now he had become a clone of the LAPD leader.[55]

Still, it was understandable why Yorty continued to have delusions about rising to higher office. His identification with Chief Parker was winning rave reviews in certain circles. J. Allen Carmien, president of New Plastics Corporation of Sycamore, California, warned Yorty that "I will make it my business to watch carefully what our public officials say in regard to the attack on Chief Parker and will act energetically and accordingly at election time."[56] Even the otherwise liberal Chester Bowles had praise for the chief. And Yorty could not ignore the slavish praise for Parker coming from the state assembly.[57]

Yorty had to interpret two separate trends pointing in opposite directions. Black leaders were pledging to halt his political career in its tracks if he sought to run for governor, as expected.[58] And whatever praise he received from the *Times*, which had virtual hegemony in the market, came when he stepped out of character and acted like a liberal, as when he helped to get the black baseball star John Roseboro appointed to a public relations job with the LAPD.[59]

Yet, as Yorty surveyed the county, it was easy to see that a new generation of politicians was rising to power based on opposition to what Watts represented. In the San Fernando Valley, for example, there was Bobbie Fiedler, soon to be elected to Congress. Born and educated in Santa Monica, she had moved—as did many others—in 1966. She was Jewish but had attracted a base of support among Eastern European émigrés, some of whom had backgrounds steeped in anti-Semitism, when she launched a campaign against "forced busing," which her newfound allies saw as a form of communism. She was a "small business-person" and a beneficiary of feminism as well. She had thought it would be more credible to have a man leading the charge against busing, but the changing times helped to convince her otherwise; when she ran for the school board, her male opponent had difficulty in conducting a campaign against a woman. Soon she was in the House of Representatives, and it was easy to see why the mayor, when viewing figures like Fiedler, could assume that his political trajectory was upward too.[60] Such was not the case. He was defeated by Brown in the Democratic primary race for governor in 1966. And but for a Black-Red Scare at the last minute, Yorty would have been defeated by Bradley in 1969 for mayor.

■

A number of South LA's leaders were black and performed poorly, as did a number who happened to be white. John Gibson was in the latter category. Born in Geneseo, Kansas, on 11 August 1902, he failed to graduate from college and like many migrants wandered into the real estate business. He was also president of the city council in 1953–57.[61] John Ferraro, president of the Board of Police Commissioners, a native of LA and a former All-American football player at USC, was as cautious and conservative as Gibson when the times demanded boldness.[62]

Leadership at the county level was little better. To be fair, as noted by Supervisor Ernest Debs, "this county took the first leadership in human relations in all of these United States, the first one to have a Commission [on Human Relations]," though his colleague Warren Dorn may have gone a bit too far when he said that LA was "the outstanding area as far as civil rights in the entire world." [63] Although the city was a sizable part of it, the county also included large areas as conservative as the San Fernando Valley.

But this vaunted county agency focused on human relations was not able to meet the challenges at hand, and this cast doubt on the capabilities of those supervisors who were supposed to be providing the oversight. Meeting on

16 August 1965 as smoke billowed outside of its building, the first item on the commission's agenda was a problem concerning a boys' baseball team. When the commissioners finally got around to discussing the insurrection going on all about them, one decided that the proper course of action was to issue a resolution condemning the "criminal element." John Buggs sought to bring them back to earth by scoring the black leadership of which he was a part and ruminating on why youth joined gangs—it was to provide a source of identity, he thought—but the meeting adjourned soon thereafter.[64]

Kenneth Hahn, a representative of South LA on the board of supervisors, was another inadequate leader. Born at Slauson and Flower, educated at Pepperdine and USC, he was quite familiar with the region. He was elected to the city council in 1947 and later to the assembly before being elected to the powerful county board in 1952. Some of his constituents stoned him on 11 August 1965; "my collar was full of blood." The next morning he suggested the disastrous Athens Park meeting intended to calm the black youth. The presence of this Anglo at this tumultuous gathering, representing an increasingly nationalistic community, served to inflame passion even more.

Perhaps to provide cover for himself, Hahn sought to downplay the events of August, pointing out that there were only "four deaths . . . in Watts . . . in the so-called Watts riot." He argued that property damage losses would be much less than initially claimed and contended that attorneys for damaged businesses "might ask more than they receive." But Hahn's experience on 11–12 August 1965 belied his cautious assessment. He was present at Imperial and San Pedro at 12:25 A.M. on 12 August when stoning accelerated. "People stumbled from the cars with a look of bewilderment. . . . Some were bleeding. Some were women. There were Negroes and white." Minutes later, as he was being chauffeured by a police officer, "suddenly, again with no warning, several rioters ran into the streets. Sergeant Rankin, who was driving, yelled, 'I'm hit! I'm blacking out!'" Hahn jumped from the back seat and steered the car while Rankin kept his foot on the gas; they were able to drive to safety. This experience did not shake any new ideas into his head, however. Like leaders of various races and class backgrounds, he saw gender as a major problem, arguing that the "man should be head of the house" and this is what was needed among blacks. In saying this, Hahn was responding to a sentiment that was rising in the increasingly nationalistic black community.[65]

Hahn was not a progressive leader, but neither were some of his black counterparts. During the height of the revolt, Brown's director of finance,

Hale Champion, met with a number of black leaders. "All present agreed that maximum force should be employed to bring the riots to an end, and they also agreed to provide as much information and intelligence on the activities of the rioters as was possible. . . . Some of the information received later indicated that there was some planned activity, if only a limited coordination between small bands or gangs." [66] Other black leaders were urging that martial law be imposed. These measures could mean the death of some of their neighbors, perhaps their friends.

Celes King was a black Republican, an NAACP vice president, and a local leader of CORE. He was instrumental in helping Yorty get elected in 1961. During the revolt he sent his wife and children fifty miles away from the city to Val Verde. He acknowledged that black leadership was out of touch with those in the streets: "It was a new situation for all of us." To his credit, his bail bond business was quite useful in making sure that a number of blacks did not waste away in jail. He knew that "people were being picked up almost at random, mothers and children were being picked up, working people coming home from work." King "dropped all of the normal standards—collateral, payment in advance . . . payment at all. . . . We knew we were gambling the entire business. . . . They were acceptable losses . . . no agency had as much experience in getting out large numbers of people like our agency had."

King's response showed a certain compassion. But, of course, as the situation evolved, persons like himself were beneficiaries of the turmoil. "We had opportunity . . . to take over most of the businesses that were in the black community. . . . Basically the white merchants wanted to flee the district, take their capital . . . it was very, very easy to take a small amount of capital and go in and to buy out those businesses. This was the golden opportunity." There was also "black flight"; some moved to Fontana and Pomona and many more to Leimert Park, Crenshaw, and other areas of the city. But some black leaders and/or their allies who stayed, many of whom had sought to bring the iron fist of repression down even harder on their community, wound up benefiting directly from the rebellion.[67] And their rise was aided by the nationalists' insistent demand for black control of the black community, a point that was viewed widely as democratic but, as time passed, could not by itself lead to an improvement in the standard of living of the black masses. However, it could reward handsomely those few with the capital to buy out a fleeing white merchant.

Black leaders could be stampeded into calls for martial law and use of maximum force because they were frightened. The Reverend Thomas Kilgore, a prominent black cleric, has recalled a meeting on Central Avenue during those days when those assembled were debating whether "to march on Beverly Hills and maybe set some fires out there."[68]

When Yvonne Brathwaite served on the McCone panel, she noticed "the lack of communication that many leaders had with the masses of people." Seeking to correct this, she ran successfully for the assembly, moved on to Congress, became a regent of the University of California, and then a member of the county board of supervisors.[69]

But it was City Councilman Thomas Bradley who was the largest beneficiary. He barely lost to Mayor Yorty in 1969 in the race for city hall and then was elected in 1973; in 1982 he barely missed becoming governor. Bradley had served as a police officer before going to law school and getting elected to the council. Before August 1965 he had been pushing measures leading to job creation but was blocked repeatedly by his colleagues. He also "made the prediction . . . that this growing hostility and friction between the police department and a large segment of the black community could result in a major confrontation." After the revolt he came under attack by Yorty because he questioned the behavior of the LAPD.[70]

Like Kenneth Hahn, Bradley revealed his inadequacies when analyzing the black family. On 15 August on KCBS-TV he suggested that children be taken away from their parents in Watts as a means to motivate them to improve their lives.[71] Bradley too had his weaknesses when it came to being in touch with the black masses, though he had the excuse that he did not represent a majority black district. Yet Bradley was quick to rebuke City Councilman Holland's idea that "welfare as it is presently constituted tends to discourage family responsibility and tends to perpetuate itself" and urged that he use the term *civil disturbance,* not *riot.*[72] Bradley's ability to navigate through conflicting currents helps to explain his post-August electoral success. Mike Davis has argued that "a multiracial coalition, based on Jewish (10 percent of electorate) and black voters under the dispensation of Downtown boosters led by Otis Chandler's 'liberalized' *Los Angeles Times*" propelled Bradley into city hall.[73] Juggling these often conflicting constituencies was a skill that few mastered as well as Tom Bradley.

To the left of Bradley on the council and more in touch with the black working class was Billy Mills. He lived in South LA—at 92d and Beach, then 113th and Belhaven—and went to Compton College. "Incidentally I went to school there at a time in Compton when there were no Negroes in Compton except those who played ball." He then lived at 52d and Broadway, married in 1953, and moved to Adams and Arlington. He went to UCLA, where he had to leave home at 5 A.M. to get to Westwood "without even the benefit of a token or car fare. I was able to get there by devices which I refuse to reveal under the 5th." His experience in South LA convinced him that many blacks came to the state "with preconceived ideas of what [California] was like . . . how shocked we were when we alighted from the bus and the train and we found that our first house was in a ghetto to end all ghettoes."

He was all too familiar with the tactics of the LAPD; in 1957–60 he was a probation officer, working with gangs. He was well aware that "a very common entreaty for instruction to a Negro motorist is 'Nigger, get out of [that] car.'" It was this maltreatment, he maintained, that fed the insurrection. "In the past, circumstances have forced a suppression of this anger. But each time the fire has been banked and the coals fanned hotter and hotter. . . . The burning in South Central Los Angeles was but the cinder spawned from a much bigger fire." While others were prating about a white backlash, Mills felt that "this period is best described as the period of black backlash, which is a direct result of hopelessness."

But Mills did not downplay the white reaction. After August 1965 "we probably could have gotten 10 or 12 votes for a Human Relations Commission. Today [28 September 1965] I would say we might able to get nine. Two weeks from now we will probably be able barely to get seven . . . a division . . . exists between the Negro Councilman and the white Councilman. And some times it even turns out where you have got the Negro Councilman on one side and the Jewish Councilmen on the same side and all the other Councilmen on the other side."

Mills was not invited to the Athens Park meeting, and his militance may help explain why. Warren Christopher was concerned about his statement that "those of us who are not handicapped by the sophistication of education, employment, property and self-control are going to strike back physically until there can be seen with our own eyes, in our own community, that some changes are effected and that injustices are corrected." This seemed a tad militant for Christopher, even though Mills was simply trying to keep pace with his constituents.

Even such overheated rhetoric could not keep Mills from being deemed "conservative . . . in my district." This was partly because he favored the deployment of the guard and partly because all elected leadership was questioned in the wake of August. Yet this lowered opinion of him did not cause his hate mail from the ultraright to cease; after August it tripled. This was the dilemma of black leadership. Their constituents pushed them one way, and the opponents of their constituents—who happened to be more powerful and conservative—pushed them in the opposite direction.[74]

Assemblyman Mervyn Dymally did not have the light skin of NAACP leader H. Claude Hudson, but he did have the wavy hair that was associated with this color (Bradley appeared to add pomade to achieve his level of the de rigueur straightened hair preferred by the local black celebrities like Sammy Davis, Jr., and Nat "King" Cole). Dymally represented South LA in Sacramento. He was elected in 1962 and ever since had gained a reputation as a tribune of his people. But just as Mills was not invited to Athens Park, when Glenn Anderson met "so-called Negro leaders," Dymally was not invited; nor was he invited to a meeting with Governor Brown during the revolt.

Dymally was not at the Athens Park meeting because he was out of town, but he did not take this passively. "I met Lieutenant Glenn Anderson and I bawled him out about it, and I bawled the Governor out about it." It seemed that one tactic being pursued toward black leaders was to reach out only to those who might tend to agree with draconian remedies. Like Mills, he too wanted the LAPD curbed and regretted that it had not happened. "I lived in New York in Harlem, Chicago['s] South Side and believe it or not I have never been as harassed as I was in Los Angeles. . . . I just have this deadly fear of the Los Angeles police." At one point an officer threatened to shoot him when the assemblyman protested the arrest of an innocent man.

But even Dymally's militance was exceeded by that of some of his constituents. On 13 August 1965 as flames leaped around him, Dymally allegedly was asked by a newsman for Channel 5 if he was with those who were rebelling. His answer was yes. Then someone handed him a Molotov cocktail and said, "If you are with them, here is the bottle, throw it." This story may have been apocryphal, but it indicated the dilemma of the black elected official, like Dymally, whose militance was being defined by some by how one cast missiles, not votes.

Dymally admitted that he was "probably the only public official in this city, county, or state who can communicate with John Shabazz," the NOI leader. More than most, he was in touch with the indigenous leadership, such as the "little neighborhood clubs, Athens Park community clubs or the Little

Democratic clubs." But there were still those who charged him with being out of touch with his constituents.[75]

Congressman Augustus Hawkins, who represented South LA in the House, might have had a reason for being out of touch; he lived in Washington, D.C., for much of the year. But there was another reason why he kept a low profile during the rebellion, besides the fact that "after the telephone lines were severed," it became difficult for him to stay in touch. As he admitted later, "I did walk some of the streets, although, because of my complexion, I had to be somewhat careful." Like NAACP leader Hudson, Hawkins's light skin had become a target for abuse in an increasingly nationalistic and color-conscious South LA.

"The feeling of hostility" was not only directed against those who were melanin deficient but also against those "who had left the area and who were living in the so-called better areas of the city." Hawkins found this "alarming," but it was a reflection of the fact that class and color divisions were sharpening in Black LA. Black nationalism became the way these differences could be bridged, but like any nationalism, this kind too could splinter into its component parts.

Yet Hawkins was sufficiently perspicacious to place the rebellion in a larger context, pointing out that "not only Watts, USA but two-thirds of the peoples of the world . . . live in similar conditions or worse." For this reason, what happened was not just a "riot" but a "combination of social disorders."[76] Bradley, Mills, Dymally, and Hawkins were all in LA and, thus, received conflicting pressures from all sides in reaction to the revolt. Speaking from New York, Adam Clayton Powell may have faced less pressure; in noting the "volcano of discontent and hatred" released in Watts, he also denounced the "white power structure" and the use of "selected 'Uncle Toms' and 'Uncle Tom' organizations." Powell, ever sensitive to shifts in public opinion, was responding to the fact that Watts had accelerated a process that deepened ideological rifts among blacks. To Powell the legislator, the Civil Rights Act of 1964 and the Voting Rights Act of 1965 both were "absolutely of no value or meaning to Negroes in the North." If the man who played a key role in the passage of what had been called the Magna Carta for African-Americans could now deride this measure, then one can only imagine what alienation and militance was brewing in South LA.[77]

Martin Luther King, Jr., by this time, faced more constraints than Powell. Watts presented a challenge to his philosophy of nonviolence and passive resistance. It complicated his relationship with the White House, already fraying because of his antiwar viewpoints. Watts inspired him to go to Chicago where he and his aides held nonviolence workshops for the gangs. His colleague James Bevel even showed them a film about the revolt, contending that thirty blacks had died there and only five whites and that "the same cops were still in power." He contrasted those results with the campaign against Sheriff Jim Clark in Selma to prove that nonviolence worked. But, indicating the increasingly complicated situation, Mayor Richard Daley then accused Bevel of provoking violence![78]

When Watts erupted, King was at the world convention of the Disciples of Christ in San Juan, Puerto Rico. He rushed to LA to confer with leaders and walk the streets. His widow has recalled that "Martin almost felt that on that night the response had been so strong that a new movement might have been founded, so ready were the people to follow him." Nevertheless, others hooted the cleric and pounced on him verbally. According to his aide Bayard Rustin, in LA they "told the young Negroes they must put an end to rioting." In response the youth screamed, "'Go back where you come from. We are winning.' One of them lit a match, held it up and said, 'This is our manifesto and it's winning.'" Rustin saw no victory at all, but his doubts fell on deaf ears.[79]

Despite King's distaste for burning and ransacking shops, some blamed him for what had happened. KNX radio sought to tie him to a "left" and "revolutionary program" and to link his views on Vietnam to what had transpired in Watts.[80] Conservative pundit James J. Kilpatrick agreed that King was responsible for the revolt. The columnist's gender-conscious remedy was "to treat the Negro like a white man. God knows his race had done little enough to deserve a fate so difficult and demanding."[81] Still, this advice could not obscure the point that the revolt had inspired a heightened conservative assault on King.

LBJ was worried that he had tied his political fortunes to a people now engaged in insurrection and a leader who was blamed for their actions. White House aide Lee White confided to his boss that King "views Los Angeles as basically an economic conflict between the haves and the have-nots, definitely not a racial dispute."[82] This interpretation was not altogether inaccurate and only sharpened the dilemma for the president, for it meant more spending to resolve this problem at a time when the war he was committed to prosecuting was soaking up more and more dollars.

Ralph Bunche was both distant—he was residing in New York, still toiling for the United Nations—and close, for he had been raised in LA. Many of his close relatives lived in the curfew zone, and this may help to explain his vitriolic response. To the color-conscious and light-skinned international civil servant, it was all "deplorable" and "senseless . . . insane, wicked and suicidal." This was no "insurrection," he added for good measure. But Bunche undermined his position by refusing to condemn the authorities, even the LAPD. His recommendation—"there is but one remedy . . . begin the dispersal of every black ghetto in this land"—would win no plaudits from backers of Proposition 14 or newly nationalistic blacks who planned to leverage the concentration of blacks for political gain.[83] Negroes like Bunche had been promoted and had done well in the process so that Washington could better fight the Cold War by claiming a nonracist record; he was a direct beneficiary of his people's struggle. It is understandable that he suggested only that his fellow blacks continue to try to disappear into white America.

Jackie Robinson, who had been raised in Pasadena before attaining stardom by integrating professional baseball, felt that the "massive police power invoked to quell the lawlessness . . . was necessary," though unlike Bunche, he expressed sympathy for the motives of the dispossessed.[84] Roy Wilkins was

> not prepared for the sheer scale of the violence . . . I don't know which was worse—the grief I felt or the anger . . . those were frightening days. The country was on the edge of a very destructive time, with eruptions of violence on one side and a real threat of repression on the other. . . . I still remember how shocked President Johnson was by what had happened. I don't think he wanted to believe the first reports. He seemed to take the riot as a personal affront, a rejection of all he had done for black Americans. . . . Those first weeks after Watts were a miserable time for the civil rights movement. . . . In one direction we had to keep the South from making a Jim Crow comeback in Congress; in the other, we had to do something about the ghettos in the cities. No one was really prepared with a strategy or workable program. We seemed more and more often to fall out among ourselves.[85]

■

Democrats from the president on down felt that Watts had harmed their fortunes irreparably. Black Democrats faced the special question of having to satisfy angry constituents while fending off hate mail from outraged white conservatives. Against this backdrop the pivotal elections of 1966 loomed. Black Democratic operative Louis Martin felt that the party's prospects were gloomy, not only because of Watts but also because of the internecine conflict gripping the top leadership. Like Leroy Collins, he knew there was a "fierce rivalry for power between the camps of Jesse Unruh and Governor Brown. This rivalry is probably more intense among the lieutenants than between the principals." As a result, there was a "chaotic state of Democratic Party affairs" in California.[86]

Pat Brown was boosted when with the help of the black vote he defeated Sam Yorty in the 1966 Democratic primary. Brown may have been helped by a record number of black candidates leading to a huge black turnout. There was a black challenger in the primary, the popular and prominent publisher Carleton Goodlett, who received a small percentage of the vote but whose presence on the ballot hampered Yorty's effort to tie Brown to the black vote.[87] Contrary to the popular wisdom of coming decades, Goodlett's presence did not lead to the election of the most conservative white man.

However, Brown did go down to a ringing defeat at the hands of Ronald Reagan in the general election in November 1966, and a major issue was Watts.[88] Reagan tried to co-opt the newly fashionable language of black nationalism by lauding "Negro self-help" while adding his main theme that "too many of the government programs—what they're really trying to get you to do is to exchange one kind of paternalism for another." [89] This was a continuation of his effort to attract black and moderate voters, begun when he started his campaign. But according to the pundit Murray Kempton, when Watts erupted, the Birchers denounced Reagan as a moderate, and he began to sing a different tune.[90] Like many politicians, Reagan often shifted campaign themes depending on whom he was addressing. Yet recurrent throughout was his appeal to the "white backlash" against black militance. His opponent suffered substantial losses of support among the white working class, especially union members and among lower-income and educational groups that had been Brown's chief source of strength in 1958 and to a degree in 1962.[91] White voters of Bell, Downey, and Norwalk voted for Brown in 1958 and rejected Goldwater in 1964; but "they could look across Alameda Street and see the flames rising from the Negro ghetto" and voted against Brown in 1966. He received only 24,612 out of 70,635 votes there.[92]

The response to Watts on the national level was contradictory as befit a situation governed by conflicting tendencies of black militance and white backlash. James Button has pointed out that antipoverty funds were pumped into Watts and other urban areas. Simultaneously, "the seeds of a national domestic intelligence apparatus were planted by 1965–1966 due mainly to the large scale Watts outburst, and this incipient surveillance network foreshadowed much of the federal response that developed more fully later in the decade."[93] This was the contradictory beans and rifles policy later to be popularized in Central America, a result of the contradictory currents of white backlash and black militance.

Likewise, black leaders were buffeted by conflicting tendencies—notably those relating to ideology and class—that could not be avoided. Weaknesses on gender questions and acceptance of the Moynihan thesis were virtually uniform among all male leaders: black, white, nationalist, and conservative (Marxists, of course, were excepted, but there were far fewer of them by 1965).

■

If African-American leaders wished to survive politically in the long term, they could not match their fellow white leaders' response to the developing concern about law and order—calls for martial law by some blacks notwithstanding—because their constituencies were represented significantly in the ranks of those who had been arrested. Blacks were beginning to feel that the backlash generating calls for law and order was just another way to impugn their community.

Those few days in August 1965 had involved the emission of decades—if not centuries—of pent-up rage that led to a transformed black consciousness. Catalyzing this process was a traumatic confrontation with the state: the LAPD and the criminal justice system. By 1965 civil society in South LA had regressed. Churches, a prime source of community, did not—and perhaps could not—act as an effective shield against racism. Organizations that depended heavily on legal acumen, such as the NAACP, were unable to meet the challenge. Unions were on the defensive.

This had impact on black men and women. Black women were being told that they were too matriarchal and should be more subordinate in the family. But on the streets they were being kicked and punched like any man. Politically and ideologically they could look to either middle-class civil rights leadership that was deficient on gender issues or nationalists of various stripes who were little better and often worse. Youth were faced with a similar dilemma; they perceived the civil rights leadership as insufficiently militant, and the dreams of nationalists and gangs at that time were incapable of realization.

All those arrested, women, men and youth alike, found it difficult to secure adequate representation. The leftist Lawyers Guild, which would logically be expected to step forward, had been weakened by the Red Scare. The black Langston Law Club was small and, in any case, was composed heavily of private practitioners who were obliged to charge fees. The growth of conservatism in the region meant that the state, in the form of the public defender's office, did not have the funding or the staff to handle such a mass of arrests. The rest of the bar too had been buffeted by ubiquitous market forces; they had to charge defendants. Conservatives disputed the Marxist idea of "bourgeois democracy"—or that the exercise of certain rights was dependent on the size of one's pocketbook—but even they may have noticed this trend in South LA in August 1965.

Though he was not an elected official, John Buggs was viewed as a black leader by dint of his post with the Human Relations Commission of the county. In that capacity he was expected to be a liaison between the county and blacks; the uprising meant that he was being pressured from both ends. Buggs was a native of Brunswick, Georgia; he graduated from high school in 1933 and attended Dillard University in New Orleans, where he graduated in 1939. He went on to earn an M.A. in sociology at Fisk University and had worked with the NAACP before moving to LA in 1951. He worked as a newspaper editor and a caseworker before becoming a deputy probation officer, a position that provided him with insight and knowledge of gangs. In 1954 he went to work for the HRC, where he was serving as executive director in 1965. He was one of the few blacks heading such a government agency.[94]

From the beginning local elites looked to Buggs to provide analysis and explain why such upheaval had been visited on their city. He was also expected to do the impossible, which was to halt the turbulence. On 13 August 1965 the *LA Times* reported that Buggs "got a disappointingly small show of hands when he asked how many in the audience would work to prevent violence."

Like Bradley, Dymally, and other black leaders, Buggs could not afford to be wholly censorious of his fellow blacks. He told the *Times* candidly that "if legal approaches fail, if passive resistance fails, there is only the vengeancy of Malcolm X and the fire of James Baldwin left—and it will come here." Buggs's response—provide concessions on civil rights issues as specified by civil rights leaders or reap the whirlwind—was a familiar entreaty of the times. This response did not condemn or praise those in the streets, though this fact did not keep Buggs from being criticized by many blacks who felt their leadership was still too cozy with those responsible for their plight.[95]

Buggs was not able to demand, for example, improvements in labor laws that would facilitate the rise of militant and leftist union leaders who could demand economic justice. Hence, when he came to testify before the McCone panel on 28 September 1965, he arrived sullied by the reprimands of some blacks, particularly those who had been ensnared by the law during the rebellion. Perhaps as a result, Buggs concentrated his fire on law enforcement. He admonished the LAPD's 77th Street Division for its hostility to the surrounding black community.[96]

The inadequacies of the police, especially those who happened to be white, were a prime reason explaining why things spun out of control on 12 August; their presence is what induced a "shower of bricks." It was not just the local authorities, it was also Chief Parker and his "patronizing" and "authoritarian personality," his belief that "Negroes are inferior," and his "frigid relations" with Sheriff Peter Pitchess.[97]

Buggs's black critics were heartened by his candor in assailing the LAPD. Like other black leaders, he went much further than his white counterparts in reproach. Also unlike his white counterparts, he was affected by black nationalism, a facet that was reflected when he proposed on 12 August that white officers be replaced by black. This proposal was something of a turn-about for a civil rights leader who had promoted integration as not only a tactic but a principle. Buggs's proposal was both a response to an emergency and a result of increased black nationalism in the community at large that he could not ignore.[98] It was also, in part, an affirmative-action legal measure.

Buggs was sensitive to his position as a buffer between the government and the blacks and took pains to ensure that the latter would know he was not wedded irrevocably to the interests of the former. In mid-October 1965 he told the *Times* forcefully that "we have two alternatives. . . . One is to solve the troubles . . . and the other is to line up several hundred thousand Negroes and shoot them down."[99] By posing the alternatives so starkly, Buggs was serving notice that law and order advocates would not find solace with him and was turning up the pressure for more civil rights concessions. Though his comments on race were in tune with his community, his comments on class were self-serving. He pleaded that those of the "upper class," like the Chandler family of the *LA Times,* take actions like inviting black leaders "home for dinner parties" and publicize such social interactions. Presumably he thought this would go beyond ingratiating Buggs with elites to spread a residue of goodwill among blacks at large. However, McCone panel member Asa Call reminded him of the problem that "there may be efforts made to have others come in" to these lofty circles "who will be of much less acceptable quality." [100]

This colloquy illustrated how racism, by imposing a ceiling on black advance, drove black middle strata back to the arms of the black masses. It also showed how middle-strata black leaders could pursue their own interests at times when many viewed them as defending the interests of the black masses. Black leadership in LA often was taken by the idea that some blacks were acceptable and some were not. The former tended to look and dress and live like the leaders; the problem was that the bulk of Black LA did not fit this description. Civil rights concessions were limited inherently, because Buggs's agenda could not go far beyond the idea of economic justice and dinner party invitations for individuals like himself.

There may have been white elite resistance to including Buggs in dinner parties involving the "upper class," but many of these same elites could agree on his analyses and remedies involving gender. There was a racial gap and a class gap between Buggs and the U.S. elites, but there was agreement on gender. Like Kenneth Hahn and many others, Buggs agreed with the "Moynihan diagnosis of Negro society," which had become the widely accepted wisdom. More intriguing was his addendum that when he lived in the South, he never went shopping with his wife because there might be "incidents" only "alone could [she] handle," tensions "might arise" that his presence as a male would exacerbate. [101] Black men could be rendered mute, and the only substitute was a residue of paternalistic privilege "benefiting" black women, yet another factor to be widely ignored in coming decades. Some agreed that this policy had to go, but what was to replace it?

Almost in passing, Buggs had touched on a key question of gender. Buggs's comment illustrated that there was common ground on which local elites, black leaders, and black nationalists could stand. The role of black women in the family needed reconfiguring; in partial return for reining in black women, certain leaders would be included on dinner lists of elites. This admitted caricature of the accomplishments of a number of black leaders nevertheless has a degree of accuracy. The absence of class- and mass-based organizations left many black leaders at the mercy of elites in Washington, Sacramento, and downtown LA. This pattern was to endure through another periodic expression of blunted outrage in the spring of 1992.

14

Business

THE REVOLT NOT ONLY TRANSFORMED THE CON-sciousness of African-Americans. It had a similar impact on all sectors of business. Although in the popular imagination what was involved was the destruction by blacks of their own neighborhoods, in fact business, including elite business sectors owned by those who lived far from South LA, also was affected significantly by the events of August 1965. Such a broad impact helps to explain the concern and response from elites, including philanthropies allied with the Ford and Rockefeller fortunes.

Businesses, including the outposts of major chains like Giant's supermarkets, were targeted by those setting fires during the revolt. It was suspected that this was not accidental. A city council report argued that there "were definite patterns established which would lead to the conclusion that those involved knew what, when, who and where their attacks would be aimed—in short, some form of organization." [1]

The revolt represented not so much a sharp departure but a continuation of trends that had been in place for some time. South LA contained 12 percent of the city's population but reported 37 percent of all fires set by juveniles and 33 percent of the false alarms. [2] It appeared that for some years black anger had been expressed through the liberal use of fire. Sam Yorty was not engaging in his usual hyperbole when he testified that "there were indications of a pattern, a very clever way of setting the fires one place, and then another, and running our fire department around, and decoying our police department with false calls." The problem for businesses in South LA was that such creative tactics often were aimed—successfully—at them.[3]

It seemed that the cooling of the flames of August 1965 did not cool at all the ardor of those interested in torching businesses. On 2 September 1965 the *LA Sentinel* reported a spate of fires in Watts: "Police said they had received reports of a roving group of youths carrying cans of gas which led firemen to believe all the fires were intentionally set." On 3 September the *Times* reported that arsonists set fire to a liquor store at 7658 South Central Avenue, "causing an estimated $4000 damage." On 9 September the *Sentinel* reported yet another incident of suspected arson, and fires continued to bedevil South LA for some weeks to come. On 26 September the *Times* reported that a "fire believed set by arsonists swept through a large shoe store" in the curfew zone.

There was legitimate concern that profiteering businessmen were burning down their businesses for insurance money. This cannot be ruled out altogether, though it does not diminish the fact that the frequent fires were making the business sector nervous. Nor does it negate the point that the fire department in LA was being strained to the breaking point; further, firefighters—regardless of who was setting the fires—had to contend with "a considerable increase in verbal abuse of firemen" in South LA. After 1965 it became common to toss rocks at LA's finest; since "arson cases [were] occurring with double the frequency" of the pre-August pattern, the situation was viewed with grim seriousness.[4]

Why would residents of South LA set fire to businesses that were their main source of food, clothing, and wherewithal generally? One reason was a sense that these very businesses were exploiting them mercilessly. Even McCone believed that prices were higher in South LA. Harvey Claybrook, a consumer activist, agreed. A familiar tactic was to mark up items for sale so that the down payment was all markup. He singled out Martin's, located at 16661 103d Street but owned by a resident of Huntington Park. It was burned down.[5]

Daniel Panger of the California Department of Industrial Relations was caustic in his assessment of certain business practices. "Like a plague of locusts, door-to-door salesmen, collectors, customer peddlers and others that are generally classified as the 'suede shoe boys' prey" on South LA residents. They "pressure the residents to sign conditional sales contracts," with the "greatest kind of exploitation [exercised] by owners of furniture [and] jewelry stores." This problem of the "sharp businessman" and "the loan shark" could not be overestimated, he continued.[6]

The McCone panel was advised that "chickens which are in such a state that they cannot be sold as whole or cut-up fowl, and pork which is not saleable in its raw state, are utilized in the barbecue shop of Ralph's Market at Figueroa Avenue and Vernon Avenue."[7] After the revolt a flood of revelations emerged presenting a picture of a black community that was being fleeced. Now chagrined, one white businessman expressed guilt about selling $0.87 rings for $10 to blacks "by displaying a sign reading 'Jack Johnson paid $10,000 for a ring like this.'" His apology came a bit late, for many of these jewelry stores had been reduced to ashes and rubble.[8]

It would be one-sided to portray every business in the curfew zone as owned by bloodsucking parasites. Meyer Stein owned a store at Vernon and Central and denied that he had engaged in such sharp practices: "Our prices had to be and were lower in price than those of the downtown stores." In fact, in the "forty years I've been there I've known only one store which sold merchandise that was completely misrepresented." His contention that the Communists were "behind . . . black nationalist groups" might have impeached his credibility among many; however, he was correct in saying that all stores in the area were not grossly unfair.[9]

For example, the ABC market at 50th and Main was not touched; one reason, according to Assemblyman Dymally, was the owner's policy (and he happened to be Jewish) of hiring local residents, providing scholarships, and pursuing other policies of benevolence.[10] On the other hand, a store like Gold's—which also had a positive reputation—was burned to the ground.[11] A number of used car agencies and automobile dealerships were not affected at all.[12] Such inconsistencies led some to conclude that the revolt was not altogether planned. This was not a centrally directed revolt; there was an incentive for businessmen to burn down their businesses and an opportunity for aggrieved individuals to torch specific businesses even if the business had enjoyed an overall positive reputation in South LA.

Giant's markets were a fixture in South LA and sustained heavy damage. Not only was Giant's a convenient target to loot for food and other basic necessities; this chain was suspected widely of engaging in highly questionable practices. Carl Margolis, the proprietor of the Giant store at 1756 East 103d Street, remained unrepentant even after his store suffered severe damage. A McCone panel staff member paraphrased his words at an angry meeting of community residents in October 1965: "We do not have prime or choice meats, we carry commercial meats. We don't think the people in this area can afford to purchase prime or choice meats . . . the conditions you are complaining about are those you have created yourselves. . . . You women [came] into our market and used the phone booth for a latrine." [13]

During the revolt Giant's was under siege. In a subtle reinforcement of the Moynihan thesis, "only women shoppers were allowed to enter" their stores during this period. Clerks at cash registers brandished guns. Food and milk were delivered under arms. [14] After the revolt Giant's became an ongoing target for protesters. Though Margolis had complained about his customers, protesters were complaining about the filthy conditions in his store, his "charging to cash welfare checks," his "overcharging," and his "spoiled and discolored meat." [15] On 4 November 1965 about four hundred students from Markham Junior High School, Jordan High School, and "some of the grammar schools in the area, marched down 103rd Street and gathered in and around" the store. They then entered it and threatened to ransack the place and burn it to the ground. As they began shattering the windows, the store's proprietor decided to make a hasty departure. [16]

This organized demonstration was a manifestation of a heightened consciousness and militance among black youth that was not limited to LA. On 26 September 1965 the *Times* reported that "150 Negro youths loot San Bernadino store." The store was owned by Bruce Van Horn, who happened to be white, and it had been attacked by black youth in August as well. At this juncture several voices were raised in opposition to the significant number of liquor stores that marked the landscape of South LA. Some felt that alcohol fueled the angry acts of the residents, while others just viewed these stores as eyesores that contained health hazards. Assembly minority leader Robert T. Nonagan called for a reduction of their number in the curfew zone. [17] But this did not occur; in fact, Congressman Cecil King, chair of the state's congressional delegation, requested that the Small Business Administration give "special consideration . . . with respect to the easing of regulations governing loans to any enterprise where 50% of the revenues come from the sale of alcoholic beverages." [18]

In 1967 Walter Raine conducted a study of "the ghetto merchant." "White graduate students from UCLA" interviewed seventy-nine merchants, including forty who were Jewish, fourteen non-Jewish whites, ten blacks, ten Asian-Americans, three Mexican-Americans, and two "others." The conclusion of this study was frank: "The situation for [the] businessman in the Los Angeles ghetto is not unlike the one faced by Chinese merchants in Malaysia or Indian merchants in Africa. In all three situations, the merchant is a member of an elite, better-educated group and resentments between merchants and customers abound."[19]

Some businesses sought to take advantage of this bad situation. One merchant took out a full-page advertisement in the 29 August 1965 *Times,* blaring: "It took armed guards to bring you this sale! Because of the recent riot in South Los Angeles, Merchandiser International was forced to move their entire inventory from their South Broadway location with the help of armed guards to their main warehouse and showroom." Other merchants were not so creative and chose to shut down rather than continue in business; this increased the social isolation and hypersegregation of South LA and boosted black nationalism.

■

Those who thought the impact of the revolt was limited strictly to South LA should have consulted the insurance industry. These companies were being asked to compensate the businesses and individuals whose interests had been damaged or destroyed. They did so unwillingly and, in a number of cases, not at all. It was becoming increasingly clear that despite racial segregation, the problems of Black LA could not be contained simply in one region; thus, attention to these problems of necessity became a regional and national question.

African-Americans felt aggrieved by the insurance industry. Again, the LAPD was a cofactor in that its perceived targeting of black motorists for traffic infractions caused their insurance premiums to rise.[20] Other blacks complained about redlining, or refusing to provide insurance to designated areas in South LA. On the other hand, many who were ransacking stores did so confident in the belief that the insurance industry would have to pick up the tab and suffer the losses.[21]

When the Kerner Commission investigated the civil disturbances of the 1960s, it was told by former New Jersey governor Richard Hughes that the insurance industry was feeling the full impact of urban unrest.[22] This industry had its tentacles in other industries through its investments, and thus, when the insurance industry was affected, the entire economy was touched. Harold Ullman, an LA businessman who owned "store properties" in the curfew zone, was worried about the impact of the revolt on his insurance and property values. But he insisted this was not just a problem for the curfew zone alone, for if property values fell, tax revenues would fall too, and "the entire county will have to pay much higher taxes to compensate for [the] loss."[23] Further, this could have negative impact on major institutions like the University of Southern California, one of the largest property owners in the vicinity of the curfew zone. Indeed, an eroding tax base, accelerated by the passage of the tax-cutting Proposition 13 in the 1970s, led to government layoffs and reduction of services that helped to make the civil unrest of 1992 virtually inevitable.

South LA businessmen were not the only ones nervously watching the insurance industry and wondering how they would respond to the crisis. Johnson administration officials were reluctant to declare LA a disaster area. Eugene Foley of the Small Business Administration was "afraid if we make an early declaration [then] the insurance companies might seize this as an opportunity not to pay off their policies."[24]

Perhaps in response, county damage estimates fluctuated wildly from $50 million to ten times as much. As the *Times* noted, "None of the estimates includes the incalculable losses in wages and business revenues." Foley proved prescient, however, for days after the uprising the Central Empire Insurance Company of Santa Ana canceled insurance policies on fifteen liquor stores, while others balked at paying what businesses deemed to be adequate value.[25] For example, Felix and June Bell received only "partial payment" of their $12,000 loss at their store at 1456 East Florence, where 90 percent of the contents was taken.[26]

The insurance industry was not alone in its penny-pinching practices. County counsel Harold Kennedy ruled that LA County should not be liable for eighty-three damage claims totaling over $9 million for alleged transgressions and oversights by firefighters and other public safety personnel accused of inadequately arresting fires and preventing damage or not doing so at all.[27] Local governments were penurious in part because of the losses they themselves had suffered. Mayor Yorty's preliminary estimate was that the city's costs had exceeded $2 million, including $1.6 million in extra police costs, as a result of the unrest.[28] The city and county both tried to escape liability, and their insurers were expected to pick up the tab.

One early decision the insurance industry had to make was whether a "riot or an insurrection" had taken place. Despite its conservative political orientation, the industry felt forced to conclude that it was the latter. This decision was reached not necessarily because the industry thought consciousness had been transformed as a result of the August 1965 events; it was more because most policies had a clause exempting coverage in the event of an insurrection. Conveniently, Lieutenant General Roderic Hill of the guard agreed, saying that what was happening was an "armed insurrection in which a significant number of the population of Los Angeles was participating."[29]

In addition to avoiding payments by virtue of this clause, insurance companies began dropping some clients and increasing the rates of others.[30] Like the tactic of fire employed by South LA residents, the companies had started this practice before August 1965 and continued afterwards. Michael Steiner, president of the Southern California Liquor Dealers Association, told the *Herald Examiner* on 2 September 1965, "I've also heard that as long as six months ago some insurance companies started canceling compensation insurance in southeast Los Angeles." Other reports indicated that some of those lucky enough to get insurance were paying five times the pre-August rate.[31] One insurance company increased an annual premium from $380 to $5,000.[32]

Naturally this caused an uproar, quickly followed by proposals that the insurance industry viewed with horror. Richard Roddis of the state insurance department pondered whether the industry should be viewed as an industry or "as a social plan to guarantee reimbursement to every individual for every loss on every occasion."[33] He decided on the former but even hearing the latter suggested distressed insurance moguls. Soon various bills were introduced in Congress, but the thrust was not to nationalize the industry, as Social Democrats and the left would argue in Western Europe and Canada, but to socialize the losses of the industry in areas like South LA by having the government set up special insurance programs targeting these areas. Yet the insurance companies remained concerned that stiffer regulations might be imposed, such as those that "generally require that companies operating [in] different parts of a state shall make the same types of insurance available in different parts."[34]

As time passed, businesses in South LA continued to have problems obtaining insurance. Companies refused to write policies covering theft, vandalism, or malicious mischief in the area. But again, this kind of penalty was viewed through a racial and geographic prism. Even the *Times* and Kenneth Hahn recognized this as early as 1961 when the huge Bel-Air fire took place.

At that time insurance losses were spread statewide, so that Watts paid for it too; an orgy of policy cancelations and rate hikes did not occur.[35] But when the same recourse did not obtain in 1965, the message was not lost on black nationalists.[36] This discrimination by the insurance industry hindered economic growth in South LA and ensured that the region would continue to wither, which equally ensured the coming of another social explosion.

Banks also were not left unaffected by the revolt. Gene Meyers was a businessman who could attest to this. He controlled Patten Escrow at 8211 South Broadway and Sands Restaurant in the same vicinity. He had been in the area for twenty-two years. His business dropped 75 percent after the rebellion, and his insurance rates went up fourfold though there was no damage to his buildings. He commented that banks, especially savings and loan associations, had a gold mine in his neighborhood because the foreclosure rate was no higher than elsewhere but they could charge higher interest and loan charges. But with the revolt, many of these banks seized the chance to flee; one executive told Meyers that they had wanted to leave for some time and now they had a reason. The problem was for businessmen like Meyers—he had a quarter of a million dollars invested in the area—whose investments could suffer if banks allowed South LA to decline further.[37]

Congressman Augustus Hawkins found it "notorious that east of certain streets, and usually it is the Harbor Freeway, that loans are not available from financial institutions."[38] Yvonne Brathwaite agreed. "Most brokers felt that the savings and loan institutions had abandoned the area completely, except for the Negro savings and loans and Lytton Savings and Loan." But like Meyers, she could not understand any financial reason for this. Her sources "did not believe that this is a risk area or that there are any more foreclosures in the area than in other areas."[39] Perhaps racism was involved. If so, even the Negro-owned institutions hailed by Brathwaite may not have been immune. In 1962 Ben Bingham of Fortune Homes went to Broadway Savings and Loan, controlled by NAACP leader H. Claude Hudson, and to Safety S&L, also black owned, for financing of home construction in South LA. "At both institutions the loan officers told them that the institutions would make no loans in the Watts area because there was 'too much transient traffic in Watts and the loans there are not good.'" If racism is deemed to be institutional, then it is comprehensible why even black-owned entities bowed to the prevailing racial norms. As it happened, Bingham was able to get financing, however, and by August 1965 had six projects under construction; "there was not a single bit of damage, even to a window, in any of the six homes under construction in the riot area."[40]

The inability to obtain loans to improve or construct buildings contributed mightily to the deterioration of South LA. But the banks were not the only culprit responsible. On 9 December 1965 the *Long Beach Independent* reported that "large corporations in [LA] are wary of an area near Watts and Willowbrook. After the riots, at least some gas stations in Compton had difficulty getting deliveries." The city administration was also responsible. By December not a single building permit had been issued for construction purposes for 155 buildings damaged beyond repair.[41] Again, more than a glimmer of black militance emerged from this situation. J. C. Monning of the city's Department of Building and Safety argued strenuously that permits were slow to emerge in part because of the "abuse inflicted by many of the residents in the area and a certain amount of personal danger to the inspectors."[42]

A number of business executives saw considerable investments going up in smoke in August 1965. The *Times,* itself a large asset for the Chandler family and considered a major economic force in the region, evoked this viewpoint on 15 August 1965 when it editorialized, "Now, as on Wednesday night, the first grim order of business is to put down what amounts to civil insurrection, using every method available." "Every method available" was perilously close to the black admonition "by any means necessary"; this amounted to a black irresistible force confronting a capital immovable object with the inevitable flying sparks.

It was obvious that chains like Giant's had suffered losses, but there were others. A number of television and radio stations had equipment stolen or vehicles fired on.[43] Pacific Telephone also was hurt; there were added labor costs, losses from coin phones, customers deprived of service. However, propelling the idea that what was involved was more than just a wild free-for-all was the company's notion that "some of our employees sensed that the rioters were conscious of a 'need for communications' and at times took care to avoid damaging telephone installations."[44]

Another monopoly, Southern California Gas, also was affected. Fire destroyed meters and regulators, and offices suffered related damage.[45] The privately owned bus line that traversed South LA shut down for the first time in forty years.[46] A number of gas stations in the area were damaged.[47] A major target were those companies holding "credit and 'easy payment' files," such as

furniture stores.[48] Though some blacks could be accused of not being sufficiently conscious of their role as members of the working class, others could
not be accused of ignoring those on the other side of the class barricades
perceived as oppressive.

Business executives were quick to respond in diverse ways to the challenge
of August 1965. They consulted with the fire department, and this agency
decided to plan for "future disturbances of this nature, and perhaps of an even
greater magnitude."[49] But all sides recognized that the defensive preparations
might not be sufficient and other measures were needed. They told Governor
Brown that he should seek to aid business by setting up depots for "looted
goods and weapons." This would not only be a boon to merchants; "participation by these minors in returning these items will act as a stimulus for moral
and legal rehabilitation and restoration of personal dignity. The return of
weapons would lessen the possibility of future outbreaks of violence and
crime involving area gangs."[50]

■

Business recognized that it would take more than defensive measures and psychological operations to deter future rebellions. A number of elite business
interests banded together to determine what should be done. The local
Chamber of Commerce established a Committee on Rehabilitation that included representatives from Southern Pacific, Marsh & McLennan, Bank of
America, Union Oil, Crocker Bank, and Southern California Edison; cooper-
ating were Northrop, Uniroyal, and TWA. Interestingly, the most lukewarm
response came from Universal, the film studio.[51]

H. C. ("Chad") McClellan was chosen to head this effort. Chairman of
Old Colony Paint and Chemical Division, he had served previously as assistant secretary of commerce. In 1965 he was sixty-eight years old and had
lived in Southern California since 1912. He was on the board of the National
Association of Manufacturers and had traveled widely in many different nations, frequently on business for the U.S. government. For example, in 1959
he had set up the U.S. exhibit at an important trade fair in Moscow where
over seven hundred firms were participating.[52] Hence, he was well aware of
the international effect of a state of insurrection in the nation's third largest
city.[53]

The role of social reformer was something new for this businessman who
had served faithfully in the Eisenhower administration. He was not distin-

guished during his business career for hiring minorities; "some years ago" his company had no black salesman on the payroll. "I tried it," McClellan explained, "but it didn't work." What led him to reverse field was simple economic reality. "Our foremost economic counselors" in "their analysis of the economic indexes" told him that "we are probably confronted in 1966 with a labor shortage."[54] Black labor was a languishing resource that could fill the employment gap and then use wages to buy goods in order to keep the economy functioning.

But this pact was to be worked out on McClellan's terms. "We told the Negro committee that we would not participate in marches, boycotts, picketing or the like. . . . If the Negroes insisted on militant action, I, for one, would depart the program and devote my time to my orchids." Though black militance had helped to bring business interests to consider reform, McClellan was not going to bow to it. He recognized that if he did, it would only bring on more militance as blacks came to see that passivity did not bring concessions. As a consequence, McClellan's plans faced a rocky road, for at the moment even centrist blacks at least had to appear militant from time to time. This left the elderly business leader shaken and "convinced . . . that the depth and suspicion among [Negroes] is far greater than most people realize."[55]

Like other local elites, McClellan was concerned that providing concessions to blacks would provide an unfortunate lesson for Latinos, who would come to believe that militance was the sure route for obtaining gains. This was a central topic of concern when he appeared before the McCone panel. Commissioner Asa Call also was concerned and mentioned in passing that recent legislative efforts to prevent Mexicans coming across the border to work in the fields could lead to blacks taking their place.[56] But this was not to occur; the major thrust of McClellan's campaign was to secure employment for blacks in service and industrial fields.

By November 1966 McClellan was reporting that 201 companies had hired 17,903 new employees; if this figure was accurate, it is unlikely that they all came from the curfew zone.[57] In fact, a minor furor erupted when it appeared that local companies were importing labor from outside the region while unemployment rates in South LA continued to spiral upward. The Watts Manufacturing Company was "the only major business started in Watts since the 1965 riots," according to the 27 August 1967 *Times.* It provided 438 jobs turning out tents under a $2.5 million contract with the Pentagon.

An industrial park was inaugurated in Watts in 1969. But there was "fully leased" a fifty-two acre park of a similar nature in nearby Lynwood whose "tenants, except for Lockheed, make no special commitment to hire from the surrounding [Watts] community." By 1972 recruitment of tenants for the Watts park was difficult. "Simply put, white businessmen find South Central Los Angeles . . . just plain frightening. . . . Some employers frankly admit that they do not hire many local blacks."[58] The Sons of Watts were rewarded with a grant from Standard Oil and opened gas stations in the area but were crushed by the 1973 oil crisis.[59] In 1977 there was 20 percent unemployment in South LA, twice the city average. It seemed that little had changed since 1965.

■

Philanthropy, especially the Ford Foundation, responded with alacrity to the crisis in Southern California. A major question is whether this influence was altogether benign or even positive. Ford particularly poured money into entities with which it was ideologically compatible, and as a result these entities were able to play a leading role in South LA. Moreover, the foundations were instrumental in influencing the funding priorities of government in the region.

Before providing funds, the Ford Foundation analyzed the problems in South LA. It was concerned that black mistrust of major institutions could lead to increased violence.[60] It was similarly concerned that black leadership, notably from the clergy, was weak and a contributing factor to instability. Overall, it was worried that the enormous population growth in the region was producing undue strain and instability.[61]

Ford executives were stunned by the devastation they found when they inspected South LA in September 1965. They found it curious that Safeway stores were hit severely while Standard Oil service stations were hardly harmed; Bank of America similarly was barely touched though its record of hiring blacks left much to be desired. They expressed anger at black political leaders like Mervyn Dymally, phonetically spelling his name as "Dimoly" and thus revealing their unfamiliarity with him.[62] On the social level they worried about black-Latino clashes over funds and wondered at the fact that it was middle-class Negroes who seemed to be attracted to the Swahili classes and cultural nationalism of Ron Karenga.[63] The social scientists they hired to do the analysis apparently did not recognize that this emerging nationalism proved to be particularly attractive to middle-class Negroes in frequent contact with whites and in search of a psychological shield to deflect the widespread idea that to be of African descent was to be inferior.

Ford's major thrust was support for the Watts Labor Community Action Committee, the Westminster Neighborhood Association, and the Opportunities Industrialization Corporation, based in Philadelphia and headed by the Reverend Leon Sullivan. The OIC, which specialized in job training, was seen as an appropriate model for LA.[64] Quickly it obtained funding from Raytheon, Bank of America, United California Bank, Hughes Electronics, Douglas Aircraft, and Southern California Edison.[65] However, Ford's backing was the key to OIC's improved fortunes in South LA. The foundation in turn wielded significant influence on the internal operations of OIC, including veto power over the appointment of executives.[66]

Though Ford had pointed criticisms about black leadership, especially that it was out of touch with the masses, the charge quickly arose that instead of solving this problem the foundation was inflating it by supporting the OIC. The OIC was charged with creating a middle-class movement and only hiring staff from the hills, not the flatlands. It was noted ironically that anger was not only being directed at the whites the OIC had on its staff but at the middle-class blacks that were being hired as well.[67] That was not the only problem. The Urban League was smarting because the OIC seemed to be invading its turf.[68] Others were irked that the OIC seemed to be engaged in inappropriate hiring not only in race and class but in region as well; many of its top executives were from Philadelphia.[69]

Despite these criticisms Ford funded the OIC handsomely; in part this was done at the behest of both John McCone and the federal Office of Economic Opportunity.[70] Under the leadership of the Reverend Edward V. Hill, the OIC used its $450,000 grant from Ford to lease a building on East 103d Street and another at 62d and Central to establish job-training facilities. The plan was to train 1,400 day and evening students every six months, targeting those in the eighteen to thirty age bracket. However, the general approach was a throwback to the ideas of Booker T. Washington. According to Rev. Hill, its mission was not only teaching a worker added skills but also counseling about "a change in hair-do . . . taking a bath, not being mad at the world." But even after these tasks were accomplished, the OIC graduate still had to enter an economy where black unemployment was 20 percent and OIC's disdain for confronting local elites was not designed to increase the overall job base.[71]

This distaste for confrontation guaranteed funding for the OIC and criticism of those who would not take the OIC's path.[72] However, this support did not guarantee the viability of the OIC. Within a few years of the revolt, it was closed. It left a decidedly poor record in fulfilling its stated goal of employment training. The OIC was beset with problems throughout. It faced growing anger from the surrounding community; its buildings were subjected to arson, and some of its executives had to carry weapons. Moreover, businesses often could not use those who were trained by the OIC, and—the Moynihan thesis notwithstanding—it seemed to have an easier time placing black women workers.[73] This last point was even more curious in that many local executives accepted wholly the idea that the black family was disintegrating and that this was a function of undermining the role of the African-American man.[74] Perhaps the fact that sexism meant women must work for less overrode executives' fondness for the Moynihan thesis.

Philanthropy also was quite generous toward Ted Watkins and the Watts Labor Community Action Committee. But the Rockefeller Foundation was their main patron, along with the federal government's Department of Labor, Department of Health, Education, and Welfare, and Department of Commerce.[75] Watkins maintained ties to the Rockefeller family and other national elites, like Thomas Watson of IBM.[76] However, even these powerful connections did not allow the WLCAC to make more of a dent in South LA's pressing problem of unemployment than the OIC had, partly because there was a basic gulf between the needs of business for cheap labor and the needs of South LA residents for high-wage jobs. The chairman of Southern Pacific proposed a redevelopment plan for Watts that involved massive Negro removal, while many residents of that area understandably opposed displacement. Neither the OIC nor the WCLAC could square this circle.[77]

Nor could they erode underlying biased attitudes. Wesley Brazier of the Urban League acknowledged that the attitude of employers he encountered often were not "as rigid against the Japanese[-Americans] as it is against the Negro. I have had personnel managers to say, 'I will take all the Japanese girls you can send me.'" Not only that, but employers wanted "nothing to do with the government's money" that could be used for worker training. Only a bruising confrontation could shake these calcified biases, but the favoring of organizations like the OIC and the WCLAC was designed precisely to forestall such an approach.[78]

■

Business's approach to South LA was not uniform. As Brazier noted, there was an inured prejudice that was hard to dislodge. Ben Perry, a South Central LA businessman, accused the party of big business, the Republicans, of writing off blacks and considering them all "rioters." He ruefully pointed out the double standard: "We don't see you people going in sack cloth and ashes because of your John Dillingers and Cosa Nostras." On the other hand, the local GOP reached out to black businessmen like Lee Jackson, whose furniture and appliance store was burned and looted. Its aid helped him to reopen for business within days of the revolt's conclusion; the GOP was "stirred to action by Jackson's determination to help himself rather than wait for possible government aid." A number of other black businessmen were motivated similarly to invest in South LA in the aftermath of the rebellion.[79]

Nevertheless, as time passed, it did seem that the kinds of economic conditions that produced the revolt in August 1965 got worse. Business did not ride to the rescue with investment and jobs. On 21 August 1980 the *Times* reported on 103d Street, the fabled Charcoal Alley of 1965. "Many fire ravaged businesses, hardware and appliance stores for example, were never rebuilt. Shop Rite and White Front—two major chains—went out of business. Neighborhood movie theaters, such [as] the once popular Southside Theater on South Vermont Avenue near Imperial Highway, were shut down and converted to churches. Today there are no large, wide selection supermarkets within Watts proper. . . . And since Sears, Roebuck & Co. closed its Compton store in 1978, Montgomery Ward in Lynwood has been the only department store within several miles of Watts' 29,000 residents."

At that point in South Central LA, 5 percent of business owners were of Asian extraction, 7 percent were Latino, and 9 percent were black. Of the eighty-five banks that had branch offices in LA County, only a few did business in South Central; only twelve of the county's eighty savings and loans were to be found in that area. According to the *Times,* malls in Carson, Hawthorne, and Fox Hills helped "kill black shopping areas at Manchester and Vermont Avenues and Vermont and Slauson avenues, and brought some hard times upon the Crenshaw area and Inglewood." Though business, the private sector, was viewed in the United States as the savior of humankind, it seemed that in South LA business was part of the problem.

15

Representing Rebellion

T HE WATTS UPRISING BECAME A CAUSE CÉLÈBRE
in part because of massive press coverage. In turn, the uprising had an
impact on mass media, including television, films, newspaper, and radio,
and on the arts and social sciences; in fact, there was a similar impact on
intellectual life generally, with some envisioning a Watts Renaissance akin to
the Harlem Renaissance of the 1920s. Philanthropy had a material impact in
shaping the direction that the arts took in post-August 1965 South LA.
Though at times it did not appear that way, South LA was indeed part of Los
Angeles; flames there can be seen from elsewhere; smoke from there can even
drift into executive suites in Culver City, Burbank, and Westwood and homes
in Bel-Air and Brentwood.

■

Television was a major factor in the economy of Southern California, as a
number of programs broadcast nationally were filmed there. Television also
was given credit for both propelling and exacerbating the revolt. Loren Miller,
the prominent black jurist, told the McCone panel that TV helped to spread
the flames of revolt because South LA residents by simply turning on their
sets could ascertain where police and firefighters were not and proceed accordingly.[1] Newspaper columnist Hal Humphrey wondered if TV coverage
"heightened the hysteria with inflammatory commentary and unconfirmed
reports." Creativity in coverage was a hallmark in the region; still, he was

concerned that one channel "scored some of their riot film with 'chase' music."[2]

Almena Lomax, a black columnist, felt that one reason the incident involving the Fryes exploded was television. Flames of resentment were "first fanned by hopeful speculation on the part of bored television newsmen that maybe the quiet of Los Angeles' hot summer was perhaps to be broken by a riot similar to last summer's Harlem."[3] Similarly, LBJ aide Bill Moyers was told that "many of the misguided hoodlums are having a field day as they see their images on the television screens, knowing that they have the attention of a world-wide audience."[4] Though some viewed television as aiding the insurrection, those participating in the streets often directed their anger at television personnel. Perhaps they were responding to the "inflammatory" commentary, viewed as racist by some, or it may have been a simple reaction to the fact that most of the personnel were white. In any case, the industry was staggered by the ferocity and vehemence of the attacks. Its cars were pelted with rocks, its newsmen were beaten, the lenses of its cameras were shattered.[5] According to the *Times* of 13 August 1965, Ray Fahrenkopf of ABC-TV was missing for two hours on 12 August before he turned up at a hospital. He had been stripped, badly beaten, and robbed after his automobile was overturned and burned. It is probable that even more reporters would have been beaten but for the intervention of the Human Relations Commission and its operatives.[6]

Those assaulting television personnel may have been spurred to action by an incendiary program hosted by Joe Pyne broadcast on a local station. On 14 August 1965 on his regularly scheduled program, Pyne was interviewing a black man who displayed a pistol. On camera Pyne then drew his own gun to show that he was ready for the worst. "I bought one of these. You ought to do the same thing," was his untimely advice to his massive audience.[7] Off-stage it was discovered that the black's gun was a toy, but by that time the effect of having such tension-filled interracial images broadcast throughout the region had been felt disastrously.[8] The fake pistol versus the real pistol was an all too appropriate metaphor for LA in August 1965.

Channel 5 in LA was criticized by Richard Kline, aide to Governor Brown, for "broadcasting every single rumor of every single incident . . . people who lived in that area would become panicked . . . television compounded" the panic.[9] A correspondent to the McCone panel recounted that on "Thursday evening the presence of several television and radio marked cars and the lights necessary for night-time . . . did attract crowds." Others argued that the cameras inspired the crowds to engage in demonstrative actions that otherwise might not have occurred.[10]

Joe Pyne was censured for inciting whites. Louis Lomax was scored for inciting blacks. City Councilman John Holland was told that Lomax's TV show "appears on Channel 11 tv at 10:30 pm on Saturdays. During the weeks prior to the riot, and during the riot period, the comments by Lomax and the format of his program were definitely inflammatory." Particularly upsetting was Lomax's "repeated use of expressions such as 'long hot summer,' 'burn Charley.'"[11]

Blacks were not so upset by Lomax's program as by others that were run. "Joe," identified by the *Times* as a "rioter," was incensed that TV "kept showing 'Uncle Tom' movies about Africa" during the rebellion.[12] Other blacks were upset by TV editorials, such as those broadcast repeatedly in August 1965 by KABC-TV enthusiastically praising Chief Parker.[13] Still others were irked by stations like KTLA, which bragged about how its "telecopter was utilized by law enforcement agencies as a source of information and communication." The "telecopter" was a helicopter that transmitted TV images, and protesters in the streets were not happy when the station turned this advanced technology over to Chief Parker.[14]

Subsequently, many civil libertarians were upset when TV footage was used to apprehend those accused of crimes during the revolt. The police used a CBS broadcast to obtain a voiceprint of Edward Lee King, eighteen, of 1221 East 28th Street; with his face shrouded, he had confessed on camera to engaging in firebombings. The voiceprint was used to track him down and arrest him, a precedent found disturbing by some.[15] This CBS broadcast was part of a flood of documentaries examining the roots and aftermath of the revolt, albeit with mixed results.[16]

Television was not just passively transmitting images but was a material force affecting behavior on all sides. Concern was so great that the McCone panel commissioned a legal opinion on the "Constitutionality of Exclusion of Press from Riot or Disaster Areas."[17] This was nothing new to McCone, who confessed that "I have had a great deal of experience with this sort of thing in the Defense Department, AEC and CIA."[18] Perhaps that is why the legal opinion provided was that despite the First Amendment, such an exclusion would not be unconstitutional. Another option suggested to the McCone panel was voluntary restraint on the part of the press; the press would withhold "voluntarily . . . news of racial flare-ups until the danger of increasing tension has passed." Obviously, said this correspondent, "helter-skelter coverage without feeling for the total community interest, cannot be tolerated in the future."[19]

Ben Holman, one of the few top black officials in the Justice Department, agreed with the idea of voluntary restraint and urged it on LA authorities.[20] He advocated the model in Chicago; there in 1959 the press had adopted a policy to "not publicize any potentially explosive racial situation without first clearing it with the police. . . . only television networks have caused [difficulty] in this regard but networks are becoming more cooperative."[21]

Newspapers came in for their share of criticism too, and reforms were proposed. Unlike television, critics could compare newspaper coverage of the so-called Zoot Suit or Servicemen's Riot of 1943 with the events of 1965. According to one analyst, in 1943 "temperate journalistic practices were abandoned as newspapers rivaled one another for sales."[22] Since then the press had sobered, but the events of August 1965 showed that there had been no radical transformation.

Newsweek concluded that "before the riots . . . the ad-fat *Los Angeles Times* . . . had done no regular racial reporting in Los Angeles. The Hearst owned afternoon *Herald-Examiner* is even less attuned to the Negro's plight."[23] Neither paper had reporters well versed in South LA or black reporters who might be less subject to physical attack while covering the revolt. As one study put it, "Ordinarily when there was trouble in the ghetto, the *Times* desk men downplayed it, according to one *Times* staffer, 'as a bunch of black jigaboos down there making trouble.' When the first reports came into the *Times* skeleton crew on the evening of August 11, the desk treated it as a routine matter."[24] Editor Nick Williams later admitted that the paper did not anticipate what was to come. "We knew things were tough in Watts—very acutely, because our circulators were having one hell of a time there. It was very hard to keep men on the job, black or white. It was the poorest section of Los Angeles, with the exception of Skid Row, but we didn't foresee an explosion. Hell, we didn't even have a single black reporter on the staff."[25]

Caught flat-footed, the *Times* responded fitfully. In a 13 August 1965 editorial, it acknowledged that "what happened the other night may well have been symptomatic of more serious underlying conditions, which should and are being treated." Yet, despite the facts, it stated that "the police are doing their job, and doing it well." As time passed during that fateful week, its words became tougher. "Terrorism is spreading . . . the sternest possible steps must be taken to quell the madness before mob violence becomes mass murder."[26]

Perhaps in response, *Times* reporters were assaulted in the curfew zone. Phil Fradkin of its staff was struck in the shoulder by a huge rock and had to be rushed to the hospital. Several photographers obtained flak jackets. The *Times* felt compelled to dispatch one of its few black employees, Robert Richardson—who was not a reporter—to cover what was happening. Of course, the *Times* reporters were not the only ones assaulted. Nevertheless, the revolt probably had a larger impact on the *Times* than any other organ of the press. As one study noted, "Watts changed the terms of the local community identity. It changed the terms of *Times* urban coverage. The full flavor of the 1960s . . . hit the *Times* like a blast from a furnace. A 'before and after' consciousness developed at the paper; Watts marked the point of departure."[27] The *Times* was located downtown, not in Malibu; it was harder from its vantage point to ignore the flames and smoke of a nearby neighborhood.

■

One frequent radio listener told the *Times* that "conversation radio" was responsible for the insurrection; "these 'conversation' programs continued unchecked and repeatedly unidentified callers made incredibly damaging statements on the air at the height of the trouble. . . . One station went so far as to proudly air two and one-half hours of totally irresponsible and completely unpredictable telephone questions."[28] What was to be known as talk radio came of age in 1965.

Like television, radio had been transformed from being a passive transmitter of information to a material force shaping actions. As such, radio also came under attack. The tower of KNX-AM was sabotaged, and it was off the air for twenty-four hours; since it was a major news source for the region, this blocked the free flow of information and may have been a factor in creating more confusion.[29]

KMPC-AM was proud of its reportage. During the turbulence it provided "eight in-depth reports given every hour" and "made special arrangements with the Angels broadcasters to break in during the five games which were broadcast during this period. Frequent reports on the civil disorder were given during the ball games. The facilities of the 18 station Angels baseball network . . . were used to disseminate live news reports to outlying areas." Its coverage was adequate, but that did not prevent its helicopters from being fired on "numerous times" by "snipers." Hence, some of its reporters chose to carry weapons.[30]

All radio reporting was not reviled. The local noncommercial Pacifica station was hailed for the range and diversity of its coverage. Black radio too played a central role in this regard; however, radio as a whole—like television and newspapers—paid the price not only for having an insufficient number of black reporters but also for ignoring South LA.[31]

During the midst of the rebellion, irate citizens flooded the LAPD with calls demanding that Montague, a local disk jockey on black radio, be stopped from using the word *burn,* or more precisely, his repeated phrase "Burn, baby, burn." This term was a reference to music and musicians and to a style of life, not necessarily a call to arson. It was his wont to come on the air screaming this phrase or "Get yourself together now and burn" or "Burn with Montague." Police officers visited him and demanded that he say something else because Montague's words were frightening some, while inspiring others.[32]

The "magnificent" Nathaniel Montague had just arrived in 1965 from New York City where he had known Malcolm X; his experience in the field of radio helped him to secure employment with KGFJ-AM, the local black station. Like many disk jockeys, he was looking for a way to distinguish himself from his competitors. Someone would call and say, "My name's Thomas Rush! I go to John Muir Junior High and I want to say, 'Burn, baby, burn!'" Montague would respond, "Burn, baby!" By the third day of the revolt, he reluctantly agreed to drop his provocative phrase. He did not intend for it to have political content, he recalled later. Subsequently he recalled the popular song of 1975, "Disco Inferno," which used the same phrase.[33]

This was all true but disingenuous. The use of *burn* may not have been intended as an incendiary cry, but its frequent invocation by disk jockeys and others was a reflection of the strength of this term and its resonance in black folk culture. In LA fire was a constant menace, arson was becoming ever more popular, and many of the blacks came from a region where fire and arson were favored tactics during slave rebellions; the popularity of the phrase "Burn, baby, burn!" was difficult to separate from this context.

It was understandable, in a sense, why the LAPD would take time away from crushing the rebellion to visit a disk jockey, for the black press was the lifeline for South LA. Paul Udell of the local CBS television affiliate agreed with this approach; he castigated the coverage of the black press as inflammatory. Montague's station, KGFJ, operated from Melrose and Normandie; it played rhythm and blues and had high ratings among blacks, a daily audience of about forty thousand. Though deemed a black station, it was not black owned; the general manager was not black, nor were seven of its eight engineers. However, six of its eight disk jockeys were African-American. For whatever reason, the station was accused of being slower than KMPC, KNX, and other mainstream stations in covering the revolt. It collaborated with the LAPD, lending its microphones to the police for broadcasts urging residents to leave the streets. Yet, unlike KMPC, its units, which were "clearly marked," "were the only radio or television mobile units not stoned or wrecked."[34]

The *LA Sentinel* was a black newspaper that was begun in 1932 to compete with the progressive *California Eagle;* it was more moderate than its competitor, which fell victim to the Red Scare and stiff competition. But the third Black LA paper, the *Herald-Dispatch,* was hard to categorize ideologically. Founded in 1952, it was attracting so much attention by 1965 that its office at 1431 West Jefferson was being bombed periodically. One analyst has concluded that this paper "probably did help set the stage for the revolt" and added that the selective burning and looting of pawnshops, department stores, and furniture stores "is probably reflected by the *Herald-Dispatch*'s many comments against Jews."[35]

Certainly the *Herald-Dispatch* was erratic and contradictory. It was militant, covering African affairs, connecting Goldwater's rise to the concomitant ascendancy of the ultraright, and the like.[36] But the paper was a stern critic of interracial dating and marriage: "The white woman is the last weapon of defense the white race has. They are using her to conquer without guns."[37] This was becoming a popular nationalist line, but what did it mean for the legions of lighter-skinned blacks in the region who were either products of such interracial unions or had a white under the woodpile somewhere in their family background? Should they despise the "white blood" in their veins? Wouldn't this paper's approach lead inevitably to the move in the 1990s by some light-skinned blacks to be counted as "biracial"—not black—in the U.S. Census, thereby heralding the disintegration of the 1960s definition of what it means to be black?

Strikingly, despite its militance, the paper also sang the praises of black conservatives.[38] And despite its criticism of Goldwater, it praised Yorty and defended the John Birch Society against charges of anti-Semitism.[39] Yet a few days earlier it attacked the Birchers for being akin to the hated Communists.[40] This paper was an authentic voice of right-wing nationalism; it was Black LA's unique response to the growing conservatism in the region and nation.

It attacked black leaders as diverse as Martin Luther King, Jr. and Ron Karenga.[41] Naturally, Sammy Davis, Jr., the popular black entertainer, was attacked—"the little black Jew"—for dating white women and for allegedly being close to the Communists.[42] Later it expressed concern about the "Jewish Federation" becoming the "boss" of the "Negro community."[43] It hailed the "bloody revolt against the meanest form of oppression—cheating, over-charging, wage attachment." Thrifty's drugstores, it said, were a symbol of "discrimination" and "oppression" and merited assault.[44] It was around this time that the paper's offices were bombed; but instead of blaming the ultra-right, the probable culprit, it pointed to a "Communist conspiracy," a charge that reassured certain elites and guaranteed their continued existence.[45] Though its readership was not so wide as the *Sentinel*'s, its often bizarre journalism was a material factor in the production of ideological confusion in Black LA.

The *Herald-Dispatch* was quite close to the Nation of Islam and often circulated its tracts. This paper is best viewed as an example of a militant and conservative black nationalism that was most visible in South LA but not unique to that region. This nationalism was useful to some, insofar as it hampered the organizing of unions in the workplace and hindered calls to distribute public-sector booty more equitably; but it could combine with lumpen organization, and this could present problems, from time to time, beyond South LA.

■

One outgrowth of the revolt was a move toward inclusion of blacks on the staffs of major press organs. Another outgrowth was a flowering of intellectual and artistic production in South LA. This was seen at the Watts Tower, the imposing symbol of the area constructed by Simon Rodia, where an arts center was developed on a fourteen-acre complex that included instruction in arts and crafts, music and dance, and children's theater.[46]

The raw materials were already present for a resurgence of the music scene in South LA. The city itself was an entertainment capital, in any case, and attracted migrants who wished to express themselves artistically. This was the case for music. As Mark Newman has pointed out, LA played a "strong role" in the evolution of "rhythm and blues music."[47] The origins of the migrants to Black LA cannot be ignored either, for Texas and New Orleans particularly had long been known as bastions of creativity in music.[48] John Eric Priestley, who was born in 1943 and lived at 1105 105th Street, recalled the ubiquitous presence of pounding drums in the area.[49] These factors may help to explain why LA produced some of the premier jazz artists of the era, including Dexter Gordon, Eric Dolphy, Charles Mingus, Ornette Coleman, and Horace Tapscott.[50]

After the revolt there was a growth in places where music could be played and, as a partial result, a renaissance in music. There was the Watts Happening café and Studio Watts. It was apparent that the old idea of music soothing the savage breast impelled many who were promoting the development of music in the area.[51] This trend was to continue through the 1990s. The critic Armond White commented in 1991, "Compton has overtaken Harlem as the characteristic *place* of African-America's class and potential" in music; he was referring to rap, but the overriding point was that the revolt spurred a continuing renaissance in music.[52] This was also an aspect of the fact that South LA had replaced Harlem as the incubator of epochal trends for Black America. But even here there was something special about South LA, for the kind of rap that emerged from this area—"gansta' rap"—reflected the dominance of lumpen culture, a phenomenon deeply rooted in Los Angeles.

The Watts Happening café was a seedbed not just for music but for creative writing as well. The café opened in October 1965; it spawned the Watts Writers Workshop, and from there came leading black figures in drama like Yaphet Kotto, Marla Gibbs, Roger Moseley, and Ted Lange and writers like Louise Merriwether. The Watts Prophets, a precursor of rappers, also emerged from there.[53] Watts Happening was like an indoor Hyde Park; it was a community theater, a jazz venue, a painting and sculpture studio, a writers' workshop, a filmmaking class, and an all-around neighborhood hangout.[54] It was located at 103d Street between Wilmington and the tracks and was funded by the Southern California Council of Churches and the federal government's Department of Housing and Urban Development.

Watts Happening was not an isolated entity; there was also the Douglas House, which was instituted by the Westminster Neighborhood Association in August 1965 and played a similar role in artistic production. There were also programs in the arts for children, teenagers, and adults at the Watts Tower Art Center.[55] The most prominent sources of funding for such activities were the local entertainment industry and the Rockefeller Foundation. Budd Schulberg, scion of a well-known Hollywood family and a well-respected screenplay writer and novelist in his own right, was the sparkplug driving this process. He was able to attract other personalities like Sam

Goldwyn, Sidney Poitier, Gregory Peck, Shirley MacLaine, Jack Lemmon, Groucho Marx, Janet Leigh, John Steinbeck, Irving Stone, Irving Shaw, Norman Mailer, Elia Kazan, Richard Burton, and many others.[56] Schulberg's was an insistent voice, criticizing the McCone panel, urging those of his class to get involved in Watts, and sharing his skills and contacts with blacks in South LA.[57]

Schulberg was moved by what had befallen his city. "I had not seen such devastation since, as a member of an OSS team in World War II, I had driven into German cities."[58] Inspired, he invited seventy-five leaders of the entertainment industry to his home to discuss what should be done. Embarrassed, Schulberg admitted that "as a writer, in the tradition of Jack London and Frank Norris, I should be informed about what was going on. But I wasn't."[59] Schulberg had been a man of the left, close to the Communist party, and remained a liberal-minded person.

From the Writers Workshop, backed by Schulberg, came a number of programs that were produced by the major television networks. Its program "The Angry Voices of Watts" was broadcast on NBC on the first anniversary of the revolt and "according to NBC . . . received more attention, provoking more phone calls and mail" since the "telecast of the Johnson election."[60] NBC also was a donor to the Writers Workshop, which suggests that investment and not charity was involved. Columbia Records contracted to release an LP of writings from the workshop narrated by Sidney Poitier, entitled "From the Ashes." The government's Department of Health, Education, and Welfare contracted with Douglas House to "write pamphlets for them, explaining their social programs in terms people in ghetto communities can understand."[61]

But the promise of these efforts was not to be realized. Watts Happening and the Writers Workshop began to split apart.[62] A number of black writers, including Quincy Troupe, broke away from the Writers Workshop, charging Schulberg with "literary sharecropping" and "subtle censorship rendering their poetry sterile."[63] One Rockefeller Foundation memorandum lamented that the "on rush of do-gooders after the 1965 revolt has largely petered out. The white matrons have returned to Brentwood." Others felt that there was too much patronizing by whites. For example, the same memorandum commented, "The art seems to be a medium through which people, who are held down and completely frustrated, find the possibility to express themselves with a form of intelligence that may have nothing to do with the intelligence required in mathematics, literature or other standard disciplines."[64] As usual, a patronizing white person had managed not only to insult black people but Sean O'Casey, Pablo Neruda, and millions of nonblacks.

This condescension was on the record; other varieties, such as looking at blacks as creative "primitives," were not on the record, but the disintegration of the Writers Workshop and related efforts was a reflection of how white chauvinism could clash with black militance and derail the most laudable of efforts. It also may help to explain why the subsequent inclusion of some black themes in movies was so grudging and stereotyped.

The Writers Workshop was the most visible but not the only effort that arose from the ashes of Watts. August 1965 marked the acceleration of increased affirmative action in the film and television industry. Much of this was related to the fact that the flames of the revolt could be seen from the executive suites in Burbank, Culver City, and other industry headquarters.[65]

A critic's evaluation of the black comic Bill Cosby days after the rebellion suggests how the revolt affected blacks in the industry: "The tall, laconic performer projects a style free of the underlying bitterness, chip-on-the-shoulder racial intensity common in many Negro stars."[66] There was a felt need to project milder and calmer black images to counteract the image of black militance, and Cosby was able to translate this style into hundreds of millions of dollars. This development had important repercussions for related industries like advertising, which sought to be more inclusive as a result.[67]

Sports were another important part of the entertainment industry that was not left unaffected by the events of August 1965. The Coliseum, where the Rams played football, was across the street from the University of Southern California and in the heart of the curfew zone. Their game with the Dallas Cowboys was scheduled during the height of the turbulence and had to be postponed "in the interest of public safety." Most of their fans were white, and the real question was whether they would have come there for the game. It was played a few days later "under a heavy concentration of National Guardsmen and police"; only 31,579 attended in a stadium that seated over 90,000.[68] Eventually, like many of their white neighbors, the Rams fled to Orange County. The racetracks, which were heavily dependent on fan attendance, also suffered a significant decline in attendance during this period.[69] Ringling Brothers and Barnum and Bailey Circus had to cancel six shows and had to endure heavy losses.[70]

Live sports and entertainment suffered grievously during the entire week of turmoil and felt repercussions thereafter.[71] Still, the LA Dodgers, perhaps guilty about their material role in fomenting the uprising by using up land for their stadium, continued to reflect the legacy bequeathed by their predecessor, the Brooklyn Dodgers, that made Jackie Robinson of Pasadena the first black man to play in the major leagues in decades. They continued to hire black athletes like John Roseboro, Tommy Davis, Willie Davis, Maury Wills, Jim Gilliam, Don Newcombe, and Tommy Hawkins; unlike some clubs, they even hired black athletes as coaches and executives. Sports continued to be a major venue for male bonding and—along with Hollywood's later cinematic fascination with male bonding across racial lines—stood as one of the few examples nationally where black men were allowed to excel. Unfortunately, the primary field where blacks were allowed to excel—entertainment—happened to be influenced deeply by organized crime; this provided an incentive and model for the rise of black gangsters.

■

Many of the homes in South LA were extraordinarily small, and this increased the value of open space in parks as a place to commune, enjoy sports, and play music. Many activities were sponsored there by the churches, high schools, Kiwanis, and Boy Scouts. There were nine parks in the curfew zone, and some had to be closed during the revolt. Though the LAPD chose not to withdraw white personnel from the curfew zone, the Department of Parks and Recreation did so.[72] It may have been coincidental that the parks suffered "very little actual damage . . . primarily the damage was limited to the carrying off of trash cans, bleachers, picnic tables and picnic benches to use as street barricades."[73]

The University of Southern California was not only a repository of open space in the curfew zone, it was also a major employer in that area. There was fear that the revolt, which came right to its doorstep, would frighten away its present and future student body—not to mention its faculty—which had been traditionally drawn from white neighborhoods. Thus, the school's administration was extremely cooperative with the authorities in their effort to quell the unrest. The National Guard was bivouacked on campus and freely utilized dormitories and food services there. A major communications center for law enforcement during the revolt was housed on campus. The school had to close for a few days, not least because there was fear for the safety of students and employees and members of the university community had difficulty getting to and from the campus.[74]

USC emulated the Dodgers and continued to have no small amount of success in the coming years by offering athletic scholarships to black athletes like Anthony Davis, Marcus Allen, Charles White, Ronnie Lott, and O. J. Simpson. This opened the door for the Trojans to accept superior Chicano athletes like Anthony Muñoz and Samoan-Americans like Junior Seau. When they battered erstwhile lily-white teams like the Crimson Tide of the University of Alabama, it inspired their athletic department to bend to the national will and admit black athletes. This opened doors further for the admission of black women students, for these authorities often did not want the resident heroes and big men on campus—black athletes—to consort with white coeds. When television began to rely more heavily on sports events for images and revenue, the entire nation received a lesson in the virtues of interracial relationships among athletes and male bonding.

There were a number of museums across from USC at Exposition Park, but they suffered no physical damage; however, attendance decreased afterwards because many were afraid to visit an area that was increasingly being viewed as some sort of "heart of darkness."[75] Television, radio, newspapers, the arts, universities, libraries, and museums all were affected by the revolt. Some of these institutions saw the light and moved to correct perceived injustices that were seen as igniting the flames. Others were more laggard in their approach. But none could remain indifferent. The Watts Uprising marked a turning point in the evolution of Southern California and helping to drive this point home to all was the McCone Commission.

■

The McCone Commission could not have done its job as well as it did without the tireless labor of social scientists and academics, particularly at UCLA and USC. Academics flourished, particularly those specializing in alleged "ghetto pathologies" that could purport to explain what was wrong with these black people; still, they provided some insights.

A number of social science surveys of the curfew zone were generated. One involved a random probability sample of 585 "Negro respondents residing in the 182 census tracks which made up the riot curfew area . . . interviewed by indigenous Negro interviewers." This survey revealed that it was a "myth that an overwhelming majority of the Negro community disapproves [of the rebellion] . . . at least 34% and perhaps as high as 50% express a sympathetic understanding." The idea that blacks saw the rebellion as a "haphazard, meaningless event" was equally wrong, for "62% saw it as a Negro protest, 56% thought it had a purpose and 38% described the riot in revolutionary rhetoric"; 56 percent thought the rebellion was intended to be a blunt message delivered to the "power structure," a term increasingly accepted by those influenced by the BPP. Still, 71 percent expressed dismay about the "burning, destruction and killing." Attitudes of militance were most likely to be found among the youth.[76]

Nathan Cohen conducted 2,700 interviews of two hours each in the immediate post–August 1965 period. He found that "traces of racial nationalism intrude at several points." He concluded that 30 percent were "militant," 35 percent were "uninvolved," and 35 percent were "conservative." Strikingly, "merchants doing a heavy credit business were more likely to attribute support for the riot to racists, Muslims and Communists." While it was estimated that upwards of 30,000 participated in the events of August 1965—"looting," breaking the curfew, milling in the street, and providing succor—it was estimated that another 70,000 were "close spectators." Whatever the exact number, what had happened clearly was no small event pulled off by "riffraff."[77]

The social scientists David Sears and John McConahay also tried to refute the Moynihan thesis blaming family breakdown for the revolt and to disprove the idea that recent southern migrants were more likely to be arrested. Writing in 1973, they did not accept the idea that a white backlash had set in, finding that "white Southern Californians are if anything more racially liberal than other white northerners." But they posited that this may have been because of a "profound degree of black invisibility" and the "racial isolation" afflicting blacks; since whites did not come in contact with blacks that often, it was easier for them to maintain liberal attitudes. But this isolation also helped to create in LA a group of "New Urban Blacks" with a "more positive racial identity relative to older southern migrants. . . . The riot clearly speeded up this process of historical change."[78]

The social scientists were premature. Certainly the popularity of Governor Brown's children as elected officials suggested that liberalism and even black militance could survive the conservative onslaught. But their setbacks and, particularly, the defeat of Tom Bradley in his race for governor in 1982 suggested that the idea of a white backlash or racist reaction was not far-fetched—even against as mild and, as often said, nonthreatening a person as LA's first black mayor. The specter of marauding blacks who could inspire or combine with students and even unions was too ghastly to contemplate for some.

■

This was part of the dilemma. Those—whether at the *Times* or in Westwood—who were representing rebellion to a larger audience may have possessed certain liberal sentiments; but as the political spectrum began to shift to the right, their lack of contact with black people as a partial result of still enforced policies of segregation and the evolving attitudes toward whites among blacks themselves, along with a growing conservatism nationally, negated much of the positive impact that was represented by liberals. By the 1990s it seemed that liberal intentions toward blacks were the rankest form of "political correctness"; it was considered by many as paternalism personified while the twin triumphs of conservatism and nationalism preached "Do for self" and don't rely on the government, except for a few thousand kinds of things ranging from Pentagon contracts to maintaining the freeways.

Certainly it could not be said that all blacks were doing badly. As the doors opened further in sports, black athletes from UCLA like Lew Alcindor (soon to be known as Kareem Abdul-Jabbar) and Jamaal Keith Wilkes were able to translate their basketball skills into real wealth in fields as diverse as real estate, acting, and producing; their altered names reflected the Islamic and African influences brought by nationalism and cultural nationalism. Their reality and the reality of many other blacks who seemed to have overcome the economic barriers of racism suggested to some that blacks who complained about racism might be slackers, unable to compete and grousing all the time about it. As the years passed between 1965 and 1992, such ideas reflected real popularity—and real resentment.

SIX

Meanings

16

After the Fire

TENSION CONTINUED TO ESCALATE IN THE IMMEDI-
ate aftermath of the revolt. It reached a crescendo in the spring of 1966
when South LA almost exploded again. The panel appointed by Governor Brown busily investigated what happened in August and why; but when
it released its eagerly awaited report in December 1965, it was greeted with
derision and criticism from diverse circles. Although elites were concerned
that improving conditions in South LA might leave the impression that there
was a value to insurrection, inevitably concessions flowed to this area. As a
result, part of the meaning of the 1960s that was perceived widely was that
black militance could bring gains.

■

After the turmoil subsided South LA resembled Baghdad in the aftermath of
the Gulf War. Shattered glass was everywhere; crumbled brick and mortar
littered the sidewalk and spilled grotesquely into the alleys. Steel beams stood
twisted and bent like so many hairpins and pretzels. The incidence of flat tires
on equipment assigned to cleanup was astronomical. Putrefied animal and
vegetable materials created a nauseating smell, and there were so many flies
the area had to be sprayed before crews could be sent in. Cleaning up this
mess involved "extraordinary expenditures." [1]

Fortunately for the residents of South LA, few single-family residences
were lost. Some residents made a concerted effort to return stolen merchandise.[2] Nevertheless, many outside South LA were not viewing the past week's

events benignly. Some were demanding that those who participated in the revolt be subjected to forced labor to clean up their neighborhood. "Put them under the surveillance of the National Guard . . . don't pay them for this work. . . . Why can't the able bodied men and women be sent up to Fresno and Salinas to harvest the crops . . . lighten the burden of their keep on us hard-working, tax-paying white people."[3] This desire for vengeance also helped to explain the record number of guns sold "nearly all to whites . . . in a five day period after" the rebellion.[4]

After spending almost fifty hours in Watts in the immediate aftermath of the revolt, William Becker informed Governor Brown he had found "an almost universal bitterness toward the 'establishment,' both white and Negro." He was told repeatedly that "'this is not a war against the whites' . . . but a 'war against the police'" or the "well-to-do." At the same time his interlocutors felt "the stature of the Muslims has increased as a result of the riots." The conflict in Southeast Asia was ever present, for he was told, "How can the US send so much money overseas and not have enough to put Watts on its feet."[5]

The revolt was not squashed altogether on 18 August 1965. A spate of arson erupted soon thereafter.[6] What terrified some was that the anger seemed to be spilling out of South LA. On 23 August three "colored marauders invaded . . . Diamond Jim Brady's swank establishment [on Wilshire Boulevard] and at gunpoint made some 35 guests and a dozen employees lie face down on the floor while they robbed them. One employee had managed to get [to the] phone and when the two backed out, they were mowed down by arriving police. Two died instantly." After that, "just across from the Ambassador, . . . a guest from the Gaylord entered his car, only to be bopped over the head by a bottle, wielded by one of two Negroes, who had hidden in the back seat and who relieved the LA visitor of all his valuables. Numerous similar incidents were reported in Hollywood, Pasadena and even Beverly Hills. Actually guest cancellations to better hotels have been reported because of the fear that further troubles may develop."[7] In September scores of blacks stood by as five blacks attacked two white police officers who had tried to arrest them on a minor traffic charge.[8]

LA was becoming a city of fear. It was apparent that containing anger in South LA might prove to be difficult. Heightening the tension was the fact that the LAPD had not become kinder and gentler after August. Judge Earl Broady was told that in South LA "tensions are increasing. . . . [Officers] are continuing to stop motorists and they are continuing to cause men with their families to remove themselves from automobiles and stretch their bodies face downward across the hoods of their cars and be searched by the police in the presence of their wives and children."[9]

The revolt unleashed a torrent of boycotts and protests. One official said that he was frightened by the "sense of power" the revolt had given blacks. For their part, many in the LAPD were upset by this turn of events and the fact that what had happened was being called a revolt, not a riot. On all sides there was a recognition of a heightened prestige for the Nation of Islam and, inevitably, for its beliefs.[10] This perception was an outgrowth of an increased solidarity. Those in Watts, who felt that they lived in a backwater, now could feel they were on the cutting edge of Black America. As one resident put it, "Since the riot we feel more together. We look at each other and say hello 'brother' to other Negroes who we don't even know." This statement reflects the contradictory nature of the postrevolt dispensation. The increased solidarity was welcome, but the failure to include "sisters" may not have been accidental and, in fact, signaled the acceleration of a black nationalism laced with a spiraling masculinity that was to continue through the 1990s.

Other trends that were evident before August 1965 deepened afterwards. One black saw a robbery of a store and was questioned by the police. He spotted the suspect in the mug book but would not say so. He did not want to turn a brother over to the "fuzz."[11]

■

It was in this context of sharpened black militance and stiffening white resistance that Governor Brown appointed John McCone to head a panel to investigate what had happened in August 1965 and why. McCone was appointed because his impeccable conservative credentials would provide a much-desired credibility for the liberal governor and his party colleague in the White House who were fearful that they both would be tarred with the brush of being soft on blacks. McCone, a former CIA director, had the added advantage of being familiar with Watts. He had known "Watts for a long time; 45 years. I played ball down there when I was a kid in intermediate school and a Watts team used to come up and play us."[12] McCone agreed to chair the investigation "for only one reason and that is because you persuaded me that it was the thing to do."[13]

McCone's colleagues on the panel were not so well known nationally. There were two blacks among the eight commissioners, Judge Earl Broady and the Reverend James Jones.[14] The staff was sizable, including a general counsel, an executive director, ten investigators, and twenty-six consultants. There were sixty-four meetings over about a three-month period. Most of the meetings were closed. Tens of thousands of dollars were spent with a good deal of the money coming from the Ford Foundation.[15]

Some of the hearings had a bit of contention, and McCone often was at the heart of it. When representatives from the ACLU came to testify, tensions rose. McCone brusquely told the witnesses: "We don't want opinions. We don't want extreme statements. We don't want emotional statements. We want facts." Police brutality, he argued hotly, was a "device . . . [of] our adversaries, those who would like to destroy the freedom that this country stands for."[16] Rev. Jones, on the other hand, had been a persistent critic of the LAPD and was not inclined to agree with McCone on this and other issues.[17]

McCone's attitude did not inspire confidence in South LA, but if the investigation was to be thorough, then its residents would have to be convinced that the panel would be evenhanded. This was an obstacle the panel was not able to surmount. The new spirit in South LA—not to mention simple pragmatism—meant that its residents wanted hearings in their neighborhood, not in areas where McCone might feel more comfortable.[18] The presence of Rev. Jones was supposed to reassure skeptical blacks, but it did not. When he traveled to Watts to encourage participation, some he encountered "said they'd never heard of Mr. Jones." Some felt that the panel would produce a whitewash and did not want to be party to it. Congruent with the gathering black nationalism, some would not cooperate with the "white man's" body. Some of a more conspiratorial outlook were mistrustful of how their information would be used.[19]

This skepticism was not just endemic among the black masses. The normally staid and moderate Norman Houston of the NAACP rapped the commission. He hinted why he had appeared so timid in his own appearance before them, when he complained that the panel "has let itself become a sounding board for those protecting their own positions and respectability but this has not succeded in exploring in depth, the problems involved. They have failed to assure the community that they can or will protect the necessary witnesses."[20] Houston was expressing the widespread sentiment that any frank testimony about the depredations of the LAPD would lead to swift and sure retaliation. This may have inspired Governor Brown's staff to arrange to make payments to those witnesses with significant tidbits of evidence.[21]

Overcoming the reticence of South LA was a problem throughout, but it did not altogether handcuff the McCone panel. It established field offices in South LA and hired bright young black staffers like Samuel Williams and Yvonne Brathwaite; and they were able to accumulate as much significant qualitative information as had ever been produced on a single black community in the 1960s.[22]

Still, some were doubtful about the McCone panel. Not only was there fear of the LAPD, but there were also more hidden, though still potent, issues like clashes between the leadership of the police and the FBI. This may explain the extraordinary security precautions that were used for ultrasensitive communications: the "services of a paper disintegrating company to reduce to powder all note paper scribbled on."[23] David Butterfield of the staff felt that the telephone lines at one field office were being monitored. "Each time he receives a telephone call, or places a call, he hears a clicking tone."[24] When McCone decided to travel to the White House to confer with LBJ, he wanted his visit to be "off the record." When he did get to Washington, his suite at the Shoreham was burglarized anyway.[25]

■

The commission's report— *Violence in the City: An End or a Beginning?*—was released in December 1965; it did not do justice to the massive amount of data and material collected. In pedestrian and sparse terms it recounted what happened and detailed where and how it happened. It made recommendations concerning the pressing issues—the LAPD, jobs, schools, etc.—but the points raised seemed either overly cautious or obvious. One controversial aspect was the panel's idea that riffraff were involved in the revolt, which many felt unduly downplayed the breadth of what had happened, while others felt it had stumbled accidentally on the critical role of gangs and the lumpen. To be fair, the panel did recommend more spending on preschool programs, class-size reduction, elimination of double sessions in schools, and the like.[26]

The commission tried to straddle the conflict between and among various constituencies and wound up pleasing no one, not even those from whom praise was expected. The CBS radio affiliate provided a tepid editorial endorsement and a pointed criticism. "Some say the report is trite . . . in part, that's true. . . . KNX believes the Commission was in error [in] saying the Watts riot was not a racial affair. . . . KNX also challenges the Commission criticism of news media."[27]

Governor Brown was not targeted for criticism by those he had appointed, although Glenn Anderson, his second in command, was. On radio the governor stated portentously: "Some day a scholar will read this report, in a generation or more. He [will] say one of two things. He will say it was delivered in time and Los Angeles did something about it, or he will say we were warned and we didn't pay attention." Brown tried to ensure that the first option prevailed when he announced that he would "ask approval of a program to train 5000 people for skilled jobs" in LA. But even if this program had proceeded, it is doubtful it would have put a dent in the region's black unemployment rate.[28]

The *LA Times* was quick to endorse the report and call for immediate action. But years later, after the conflagration that beset the city in 1992, the paper had second thoughts, calling the report "not a magnificent document or a tremendous sociological study."[29] Its later view was the immediate view of many blacks. Rev. Jones disagreed "violently" with the report's idea that welfare was luring the poor to California.[30] This pastor at Westminster Presbyterian Church on West Jefferson Boulevard received criticism for his candor about the panel; the *Herald-Examiner* reported that "sources close to the commission declared" he had "hindered its work."[31]

Looking back, Warren Christopher too was critical of what he had labored to produce. Testifying before the Kerner Commission, he was at pains to say the deficiency did not result from lack of trying. The panel, he said, tried to establish an "educational . . . rather than a courtroom atmosphere." It sent investigators on an "overt and covert basis in the riot area." The panel even wrote the report itself, as opposed to the staff. But with all that, Christopher conceded, "we did well on some areas and poorly on other areas. I think we did poorly in the housing area and we did not adequately consider by any means the family problems, birth control problems, which I think ought to be inquired into." Moreover, he was disappointed with the panel's effort to reach South LA itself, and vice versa. When he was appointed twenty-five years later to head a local panel to investigate the LAPD, the *LA Weekly* noted that Christopher "was really trying to atone for what went wrong in 1965 . . . he vowed to us that this would not be another McCone Commission."[32] A major problem with the report, beyond Christopher's reservations, was that the panel had a fixed set of biases—for example, on welfare and the black family—no established format, no enforcement power, a budget perceived as inadequate, and a deadline that gave it no time to resolve conflicting testimony.[33]

Though the *LA Times* supported the report initially, other press organs distant from the scene and with no immediate stake in the city were not so generous. *Newsweek* praised the panel for conducting the "deepest investigation of a race riot ever attempted" but termed the report "a flawed accounting, a skimpy 101 pages in length, nomadic in organization." The news magazine was amazed that the LAPD "got a virtually clean bill from McCone & Co." and added that "even some of the commission's own expert consultants were disappointed with the distillation of their studies." It warned that "the investigation could become a substitute instead of a catalyst for visible, meaningful action." [34]

Governor Brown appointed an attorney, Alexander Pope, to coordinate the follow-up to the report. McCone had urged earlier that the commission not be disbanded immediately after the report was filed, and his wish was honored. But despite these precautions, Bill Boyarsky of the *LA Times* observed twenty-five years later that "the lack of follow-up" was "the greatest failure" of the McCone panel. After a "follow-up report six months later, the McCone commissioners dropped out . . . with nobody nagging, then Mayor Sam Yorty, the City Council and the Police Commission resisted any change." [35]

As early as 1967 Warren Christopher agreed with this critique. He was far from being "satisfied with the progress made in implementing the recommendations of the commission." There were exceptions, of course. "By 1966 every elementary school in the disadvantaged area had a Class A library. The Commission's recommendation was fully implemented. . . . With minor modifications the Commission's recommendation for establishment of an Inspector-General reporting directly to the Chief of Police and outside the chain of command has been established." The prominent black lawyer Clifford Alexander was not glowing in his evaluation, however. In mid-1966 he told LBJ aide Marvin Watson that "the basic condition of the Negro in that part of Los Angeles . . . is fundamentally unchanged since the riots." [36]

Dissatisfaction with the report was widespread. The U.S. Commission on Civil Rights was "sorely disappointed . . . it prescribes aspirin where surgery is required"; it was "elementary, superficial, unoriginal and unimaginable." The USCCR found the panel's inattention to Proposition 14 shocking and scorned its attack on Glenn Anderson, who "has a long record of devotion and service to the cause of civil rights." The commission could not understand the report's failure "to come to grips at all with the incendiary issue . . . of police misbehavior . . . [or] racial discrimination." But since the USCCR had as members such figures as Loren Miller and Mervyn Dymally, its carping was discounted by some.[37]

Partisan or not, the substance of the USCCR's complaint about the shallowness of the report had merit. Even before the final report was issued, San Francisco attorney George Brunn was disappointed that the McCone panel did not pay more attention to the repetitive complaints from South LA about high interest rates, poor merchandise, unfriendly treatment, wage garnishments, and collection agency abuses.[38] His concern was justified, for these fundamental issues were not highlighted; a dearth in class consciousness could mean ignoring of class-related issues.

Black leaders were some of the more stringent critics of the report. One exception was Roy Wilkins of the NAACP, who said he was encouraged by the report despite its weaknesses. But black leaders who were closer to the scene in LA and who were feeling the heat from their constituents were much more unkind. Billy Mills found the report "pitiful." Wesley Brazier of the Urban League—who termed what had transpired a "revolt"—felt that the report did not go far enough. He thought that a top priority should have been a "large scale increase in government subsidies to firms hiring unskilled Negroes" and a "massive public works program."[39] The Reverend H. H. Brookins was highly critical. In fact, one of the few leaders of blacks who was not critical of the report was County Supervisor Kenneth Hahn, who happened to be white.[40]

Allies of Black LA were similarly critical. The local AFL-CIO found the report "inadequate and unimaginative." The American Civil Liberties Union focused its criticism on the report's recommendation that an inspector general be appointed for the LAPD, chiding the commission for not recommending more independence for this figure.[41] Pacifica Radio wondered why the report covered the same territory as a 1963 report done by the county Human Relations Commission. Latino leader Louis García was also reproachful.[42]

Critics from academia were numerous. Frances Lomas Feldman was an academic consultant on social welfare for the panel. What concerned her were its "difficulties" in examining the "evidence objectively and not through the haze of preconceived notions." She was referring to the fact that the growth in the welfare population was slower than population growth as a whole, which undermined the report's contention that welfare was a lure increasing the state's population. Though many commissioners kept returning to this idea of the lure of welfare when questioning witnesses, "none, when asked for details, could provide them."[43]

David Olson captured the sentiments of many analysts of the McCone report when he observed, "The myth that disorders are pathological manifestations of anomic behavior by a few riffraff must be rejected insofar as blacks view contemporary civil violence as meaningful protest activity."[44] He could have added that in the absence of working-class organizations to negotiate demands in an ordered and peaceful manner, lumpen organizations fueled by nationalism could ascend in South LA. Robert Fogelson of Columbia University contended that 80,000 out of a black population of 650,000 in the county were involved in the revolt, not the McCone figure of 10,000.[45] This larger figure is probably closer to the truth; that so many could cross the bounds of order was riveting.

A two-day seminar at USC held on the first anniversary of the report dismissed it as too cautious, written by people too frightened to confront the magnitude of the trauma the city had endured.[46] Yet the McCone panel was not without support. Conservative ideologue William F. Buckley generally endorsed it. Oddly, his words were echoed, in a sense, by Robert Kennedy, already viewed by many as positioning himself to challenge LBJ for the White House. Kennedy urged cities across the nation to set up bodies similar to the McCone Commission in order to spotlight urban problems before "they flamed into similar 'catastrophes.' "[47]

The response from South LA reflected that of its leaders, like Billy Mills and Rev. Brookins. However, it seemed that Kennedy had the gift of prophecy when South LA almost erupted again in the spring of 1966. He was not alone in sensing future problems. In September 1965 McCone himself expressed concern about potential outbreaks and added, "We must move very rapidly."[48] This concern led McCone to avoid making ambitious recommendations because doing so could "risk the danger of encouraging riots . . . if all of these things do not materialize."[49] As it turned out, the weak recommendations did not forestall future eruptions but may have incited them.

Tensions flared on 15 March 1966 when a black threw a rock through the windshield of the car of a white teacher leaving Jordan High School. In a confused manner this led to a black-Latino confrontation. The resultant fracas attracted police who proceeded to line up shoulder to shoulder at 104th Street and Wilmington with drawn guns and loudspeakers. Hundreds of patrol cars prowled the darkened streets through the neighborhood stopping everyone on foot and all in cars. Hundreds were stopped, searched, and advised to go home immediately.[50]

It could have been worse, or at least that was the initial impression. At first the incipient outbreak seemed to have been quelled without a shot being fired by the police; one black was killed, apparently by a sniper. However, a coroner's jury was told that the police fired numerous shots and that one of these probably hit the deceased. William Clay Lane, a reporter for the *Sentinel,* estimated that forty shots had been fired. Officers charged that "two or three Negro men wearing yellow sweatshirts bearing pictures of the late black nationalist Malcolm X agitated the crowd and tried to direct it against police."[51]

The response was predictable. McCone blamed hotheaded blacks. Norman Houston of the NAACP blasted McCone and "white leadership" generally. In a letter to Governor Brown, McCone was more restrained, indicating that "statements coming to me from various sources (mostly anonymous) indicate that the frustration and the rage remain widespread."[52]

Despite the intense introspection and investigation generated by the McCone report, it seemed that nothing had changed for the better. In early May 1966 in South LA, a handcuffed suspect was forcibly taken from four deputy sheriffs by a crowd of two hundred blacks. In mid-May, police shot and killed Leonard Deadwyler, a black man, and the officer involved was cleared in the inquest.[53] Similar incidents continued throughout the month and into the summer. The National Association of Evangelicals was able to raise considerable sums by contending that Reds and black nationalists were trying to launch another uprising. Some of the funds raised were to go to the Evangelicals broadcasts on Sundays on the black-oriented 50,000-watt KDAY-AM.[54]

■

The flames engulfing LA helped many to see the light. The recognition was growing that unless something was done, the prospect for further disruption was on the horizon; it was this concern that the Evangelicals were able to capitalize on. However, they were not the only ones. Though some were arguing persuasively that a white backlash meant that it would be foolhardy to appear to reward insurrection, others were arguing with similar passion that there was no alternative. The latter could point to studies showing "large numbers of whites were in some degree sympathetic to the rebellion."[55] Those positing the former view could point to equally cogent arguments that this sympathy was not sustainable given the growing strength of conservatism.[56]

What happened was predictable: the granting of some concessions, but not enough to alleviate the pressing problems of South LA. Naturally this was disappointing to many in the curfew zone. Robert Richardson, an African-American who was drafted on the spot by the *Times* to report on the revolt, recalled later, "The thinking was if we burn down some of these old, decaying stores, maybe whitey would come back and rebuild, and we'd have gleaming glass and steel, like in the suburbs."[57] This dream did not become reality. The vaulted civil rights movement that was sweeping the nation had more impact in the Deep South than in an urban area like LA. Paul Bullock was not totally wrong when he said that "civil rights measures at both federal and state levels" were "almost completely irrelevant" to the Far West.[58]

It cannot be said that liberal elites were unaware of what was needed. However, the correlation of political forces shifted to the advantage of the right wing, limiting what could be done. Days after the revolt one high-level state appointee told Governor Brown that there should be a "significant expansion of our highly successful but severely limited affirmative action program." Even the conservative McCone conceded a year after his report was filed that "if one segment of society cannot [advance] then the dynamics of our economy will be adversely affected."[59] Somehow McCone's logic was to be submerged in the subsequent debate. It was left to the general in the War on Poverty, Sargent Shriver, to articulate the liberal consensus that the "investment of $1.5 million in Harlem social projects and nothing in Los Angeles' Watts section made the difference between a quiet summer in Harlem and a riot in Watts."[60] "Investing" in South LA was seen as a way to forestall increased costs in prison construction and related social ills in the long term. Somehow this view too was submerged in the debate.

Right after the McCone report was filed, Governor Brown moved to request $15 million from the legislature to train 5,000 in South LA for skilled jobs.[61] By April 1966 Chad McClellan was claiming that 4,671 in the curfew zone had obtained employment since 1 September and that he was in touch with 267 employers; but even if this figure was accurate, it was a small portion of what was necessary.[62]

Still, it would be a distortion to claim that there were no advances on the employment front in the aftermath of the rebellion. Sam Anderson, who taught at Jordan High School for nineteen years, recalled that there were no black telephone line workers or gas meter readers and few black school administrators before August 1965 and quite a few afterwards.[63] Ronald Powell, then a reporter for the *Santa Barbara News Press,* later contended that the revolt had a similar impact on hiring patterns in the press.[64]

This effect was not just limited to LA, either. Oakland's Stanley Robertson in January 1966 maintained that "before Watts Negroes were still finding it tough to get into certain jobs but now, every place you go, you can expect to find a black face. . . . A year ago this progress would have been unheard of."[65] It did seem that powerful economic forces had taken more of an interest in South LA. After the rebellion the Life Insurance Association provided $1 billion for "housing and job opportunities" in a number of cities; cities in California received "more benefits under the . . . program than any of the other 41 states assisted."[66] In February 1966 the Southwest Branch of the LA Realty Board voted 50-13 to change its bylaws to allow the admission of black realtors. This was the direct result of a "secret" U.S. Justice Department investigation based on the premise that racial discrimination is a violation of federal antitrust laws in that it restrains trade.[67] Others sought to take advantage of the changing environment by suggesting that what was in their interest was equally in the interest of blacks.[68] The owners of KTYM-FM sought an AM station so as to provide "an immediate, valuable voice" for the "Negro colony."[69]

Soon a tour of South LA was mandatory for visiting dignitaries like Rodman Rockefeller and Robert Kennedy.[70] But with all the announcements and visits, the fact remained that insurance remained difficult to obtain for businesses on 103d Street and other neighborhoods in the curfew zone, banks continued to redline, and forces were still in motion that would propel a deindustrialization of the region, thus removing factory jobs that could have supported many a black family. Two years after the revolt, the once ebullient Chad McClellan was conceding that "there have been very few gains" in South LA.[71]

The private sector was reluctant to invest in South LA, and there was not sufficient pressure to compel it to do so. The public sector was more responsive, but it was subject to the shifting vicissitudes of politics. However, one still existing result of the rebellion was a large hospital constructed in the middle of the curfew zone. The carnage of August 1965 placed quite a strain on medical facilities in the region. One hospital official recalled later the distinct "hazard of being fired on while giving medical attention." Even the authorities would have benefited if there had been more hospitals available to treat injured police officers and firefighters.[72] At least this might have allowed the county to avoid the often exorbitant charges levied by private hospitals.[73]

After the revolt USC sought to develop "revolutionary neighborhood family health centers."[74] President Norman Topping of USC, recognizing that he was heading an institution surrounded by insurrectionists, confessed that "as a consequence of the Watts riot, USC opened an important and badly needed health facility in the area." Billy Mills was pushing the city and the county to move in a similar direction.[75] Inspired, the *Times* on 21 December 1965 editorialized in favor of a "large, modern hospital" for South LA. A proposition was placed on the ballot to build such a facility, though the *Times* recognized "whether we want to admit it or not, there are among us some who look at Proposition A as a sop to the Negroes, as a reward or a pacifier."[76] This attitude reflected opposition to the initiative, and Martin Luther King Hospital was not built until 1972. It was "a direct result of the fire and pain that swept the community."[77]

Perhaps the largest beneficiary of the revolt was the social science community. Funds poured into the pockets of social scientists who could provide—or pretend to provide—a clue as to why South LA had erupted and what was on the minds of those who revolted.[78] Similarly, there was a push to build an institution of higher education in South LA. A branch of the California State University system, originally slated for affluent Palos Verdes, instead was built at Dominguez Hills; this was an attempt to "bring the state college system into closer communication with the Negro community in south Los Angeles."[79]

This initiative was part of a larger thrust by the state and federal government to respond to the agony emanating from South LA. In October 1965 the U.S. Census sent three hundred interviewers to fan out through the curfew zone in order to "determine the changing needs of the region." Even Mayor Yorty jumped on the bandwagon for a while, showing up at 96th and Central in mid-October to dedicate a community center that would provide child-care clinics, legal aid, and youth employment services. Jesse Blye of Watts reflected the opinion of many of those assembled when he said, "They should have done this 20 years ago and they might have avoided that riot."[80]

Since youth were disproportionately involved in the revolt, many of the programs were aimed at them. The government was not unresponsive to the new spirit of militance; in fact, it tried to channel that spirit in a direction it found congenial. This was where the cultural nationalists were useful, for their growing ideological hegemony and their stress on African names and dress were not frowned upon. Many of them wound up being hired by the government and were paid to spread their ideas.[81]

In May 1966 Calvin Hamilton, director of planning for the city, outlined an ambitious program for South LA involving "highway improvements . . . a county hospital, civic center, senior citizens building, health building, library, police station, fire station . . . enlargement of junior high and elementary schools . . . child care center and a youth recreation center."[82] Local bond measures and antipoverty funds led to the realization of a number of these plans.[83]

The depth of the concern about the volatility in South LA was revealed when real estate mogul John Factor announced plans to build a $1 million youth center in Watts. This announcement took place at a World Jewish Congress banquet in Beverly Hills, though conventional wisdom was that the Jewish community had been alienated by expressions of anti-Semitism during the revolt.[84]

There were other concessions. Transportation in South LA was improved; for example, through bus service along Avalon Boulevard between Vernon and Florence was initiated.[85] Arts programs were improved. A film festival was started at a school at 104th and Compton, and in July 1966 Janet Leigh, Dick Van Dyke, and Pernell Roberts ventured out of Hollywood to attend.[86] The summer festival started in Watts attracted the masses and celebrities alike. The Inner City Cultural Center was begun and would make major contributions to black theater over the years.[87] But with all that, as the 1990s unwound many in South LA were arguing stoutly that things were worse than during the 1960s.

■

This folk wisdom was confirmed by the *Times* on 10 September 1988. "Despite a high rate of poverty in black ghetto areas before 1960, rates of joblessness, out-of-wedlock births . . . serious crime, drug addiction and gang violence did not begin to rise rapidly until after the mid-1960s and did not begin to reach catastrophic proportions until the mid-1970s." Trends barely glimpsed in the 1960s—particularly deindustrialization, an influx of drugs and guns with a resultant impact on crime rates, increasing incarceration—exploded in the 1980s.

In 1966 Paul Jacobs lamented that "there are three systems of justice in

Los Angeles . . . one for the rich, one for the poor and one for the police." This remained no less true as time passed.[88] By 1969 the U.S. Civil Rights Commission was reporting sadly that "four and one half years" after the filing of the McCone report, "few changes have been made in . . . the handling of civilian complaints alleging misconduct by law enforcement personnel"; with sorrow it concluded that this was "still an unresolved issue."[89]

What had happened was that the ultraright had continued to grow after Ronald Reagan was elected governor in 1966, while black militance was overwhelmed, most conspicuously with the smashing of the Black Panther party and its focus on police brutality. Cultural nationalists and the NOI were not up to the task of confronting the authorities. Police misconduct, as a result, flourished in LA.

The decline of the BPP was a reflection of a spreading political alienation. This was evident as early as 1966 when less than 1 percent of an estimated four hundred thousand eligible people participated in antipoverty elections.[90] This could be deemed a conscious boycott of a program initiated by a discredited president, but political participation in other spheres declined as well. Thus, when the proposal was made in 1968 to extend freeways in a way that would displace thousands of residents in South LA, community organization was insufficient to halt this effort. Indeed, the process of urban renewal, which often was packaged as a benevolent reform, devastated South LA in the wake of August 1965.[91]

On the fifteenth anniversary of the uprising, the police were referring to South LA as "Dodge City" and speaking of themselves as "sort of modern day Marshal Dillons." This was all too familiar. So was the existence of unemployment, which was "more than twice the rate of the city of Los Angeles." Such relics of the 1960s like the Sons of Watts and Watts Happening café were gone.[92]

All was not bleak. By 1985 there were the hospital and better bus service; there was a shopping center. This center covered four hundred thousand square feet and was patterned after one opened in 1981 at Vermont and Slauson. Named after Dr. King, it was expected to take in $45 million in sales in its first year, or $350 per square foot, "more than three times the average earnings of first-year shopping centers." Since August 1965 more than five thousand housing units had been built.

But GM, Firestone, and Goodyear all had moved. A steel mill at 109th and Central was now a Catholic high school. Ted Watkins, a veteran of the region, bewailed the fact that "our economic base is worse now than it was at the time of the riots."[93] Even the service industry was lagging in South LA; it was only in November 1991 that the first sit-down restaurant was opened in Watts since August 1965.[94]

■

On 1 October 1965 Marquette and Ronald Frye were sentenced; the former got a 180-day suspended sentence and three years' probation; his brother got a 120-day suspended term, was fined $250, and received three years' probation. In early December after a two-week trial, their mother, Rena Frye, was convicted of obstructing an officer in the performance of his duty. She was sentenced to pay $250 in monthly installments or serve twenty-five days in jail. Said Judge George Dell, "I have a reason for this. . . . On the first day of every month when you have to pay $10 you will be reminded of this case." She chose to be reminded.[95]

Marquette Frye was back in the news in May 1966 when he received ninety days for battery in a bar at 11646 South Main.[96] He continued to have run-ins with the LAPD, and many said the officers had a vendetta against him. Subsequently he was sprayed with Mace by an officer and suffered severe burns around his eyes; his skin was bleached, and it took several months for his melanin to return. On 31 August 1980 the *Times* reported that his day "begins with television, blurs into drinking beer with the guys, and ends with television." He was a living symbol of the failed promise of the uprising. A few years later he had transcended the symbolic annihilation of the removal of his melanin: he was dead.

Meanwhile, in August 1967 the McCone panel ended operations and submitted a report to the Kerner Commission. The *New York Times* of 24 August 1967 quoted John McCone as saying that "tensions are still high" in South LA.

EPILOGUE

The 1990s

O N 3 MARCH 1991 BLACK MOTORIST RODNEY KING was stopped by LAPD and CHP officers after a high-speed car chase. After forcing King to stop and demanding that he leave his car, the officers fiercely beat the hulking African-American. Unfortunately for the officers involved, the beating was captured on videotape by George Holliday, who was trying out his new camera in a nearby apartment. When this tape was broadcast on television locally and then nationally, yet another cause célèbre erupted.[1]

The officers were tried criminally for their acts; a defense motion, however, forced removal of the trial from the city of Los Angeles to Simi Valley, a mostly white suburb with a significant concentration of LAPD officers. As a result, a jury with no blacks was selected. When the officers were acquitted in April 1992, the city again exploded in a "revolt" that was both similar to and different from its predecessor in 1965. Again, a fierce beating was captured on tape. The victim, a white truck driver named Reginald Denny, happened to be driving through South LA. A group of black men pounced on him and flailed away, as a helicopter with a camera broadcast the ugly scene live to a stunned audience. Latinos, those of Asian extraction, and others who did not resemble African-Americans were also assaulted. Apparently, light-skinned blacks were not targeted this time. Black nationalism had taken hold, chasms between darker- and lighter-skinned blacks that had seemed to widen in August 1965 apparently had been bridged, but at what price?

Many more were arrested in 1992—16,291—and a larger number were injured, 2,383. In 1992 at least 52 were killed, and estimates for property damage ranged as high as $1 billion. This time it took approximately 20,000

LAPD, CHP, National Guard, and seven related military forces to subdue those who were "looting" and burning. Unlike 1965, this time a plurality, 36.9 percent, of those arrested were Latino (475 of whom were "illegal aliens" and were deported), and only 29.9 percent were black; a higher percentage of whites also were arrested this time. The fire this time swept well beyond South LA into Hollywood, the West Side, the San Fernando Valley, and the edge of Beverly Hills.[2]

Like 1965, there were rumors about organization and participation by gangs. There were allegations about excessive use of force by the authorities. And there was the sense that what was now the second largest city in the United States had descended once more into a chaotic and riotous anarchy. Even those things that had changed bore a resemblance to the past. Unlike 1965 when it seemed that conflict between Jewish shopkeepers and black customers was a driving force, now it appeared that Korean and Korean-American merchants were being blamed. The shooting of a young black girl, LaTasha Harlins, in an altercation with a Korean-American shopkeeper—which too was captured on videotape—had inflamed passions between the two groups.

But again, the local industry, Hollywood, was not necessarily a passive bystander in this process. As a columnist in the local *Korea Times* pointed out, a number of films released before and after the unrest—*Menace II Society, Quick Change, Falling Down, Do the Right Thing,* and *Crossing Delancey*—all featured Korean-American or Asian-American shopkeepers in various stages of conflict with other races. This seemed to be the only role that Hollywood could envision for a minority whose growing presence in LA had caused a section of the city to be known as Koreatown—joining Little Tokyo and Chinatown. Worse, Korean-Americans were the butt of offensive jokes in a film, *Boomerang,* featuring Hollywood's biggest black star, Eddie Murphy, and were a constant source of repulsive humor in the television show "Martin," starring another popular black comedian, Martin Lawrence.[3]

The passage of civil rights laws and the momentum of the civil rights movement had sparked a liberalization of immigration laws that had been viewed as racially discriminatory. Since this liberalization in 1965, Los Angeles had been the recipient of waves of immigrants fleeing wars in Central America and political repression and economic dislocation in Korea and other parts of Asia.[4] Just as blacks had bought stores from Jewish merchants fleeing the tumult of 1965, in the period leading up to 1992 black merchants had begun selling stores to Korean immigrants.

The black-Korean tension was flaring against the backdrop of the Cold War's end and the heightened focus on Tokyo as Moscow's replacement as the international enemy of choice. This process reignited anti-Asian sentiments always lurking beneath the surface in California. The crude anti-Nippon sentiment often ignored distinctions among Asians, sweeping within its ambit immigrants from Korea, a nation that had suffered under the brutal lash of Japanese colonialism.[5] Nationalism and chauvinism both had well-deserved reputations for spurring anti-intellectualism, and this was just one more example. Moreover, many of the Korean immigrants resembled their Cuban counterparts in that they were fleeing the specter of socialism or its actual existence and often arrived on these shores with attitudes congenial to the right-wing consensus on blacks and related matters. Some of the anti-Asian sentiment was stirred by general hysteria about the growth of the economy in Japan, Korea, and other parts of Asia and its possible effect on the United States, which had endured great sacrifice in order to "triumph" in the Cold War and emerge as the "sole remaining superpower." Some doubted if the heralded coming of the Pacific Century would include California. Others concluded that the dissolution of socialism in the Soviet Union should mean the destruction of the "socialist-inspired" public sector of the U.S. economy that had employed so many blacks.

Though receiving less publicity, there were other ethnic and racial conflicts tearing at the fabric of LA that gave 1992 a different flavor from 1965. Latino immigrants in the Pico Union section of LA, close by Koreatown, had conflicts with Korean-American merchants. Latinos also had streamed into South LA, and there tensions developed with their new black neighbors.[6] Though the area was represented politically by African-Americans like Maxine Waters, Rita Walters, Mark-Ridley Thomas, and Walter Tucker, South LA was rapidly becoming a predominantly Latino enclave as Los Angeles reverted to its historic origins.

The city and state were facing unique challenges. Like New Mexico and Hawaii, California was becoming a "minority majority" state where Native Americans, Latinos, African-Americans, and Asian-Americans comprised the majority of the population. But unlike its western neighbors, California had a sizable black population in a nation where their enslavement had been a central issue and where discrimination against the darkest of citizens remained prevalent. A compounded racism—featuring black-Latino, Latino-Korean, black-Korean, Anglo-Latino, and other forms of bias stretching far beyond the biracial polarity that marked the rest of the nation—was the hallmark of California and its largest city. Many African-Americans felt that the pernicious bias they faced was often lost in the welter of concern about Latinos and Asian-Americans. Many of the latter felt they were the ones being ignored, while many working-class Euro-Americans felt it was they who were being cast aside as they slowly and inexorably dwindled into minority status.

Amid all of this diversity, there still was a dearth of trade union activity and working-class organization that could cross and merge sensitive racial and ethnic boundaries. As a frontline state during the Cold War, the United States had to enforce the Red Scare more pervasively than Japan, Germany, or France; in those nations to be a "democratic socialist" was not considered a sign of immaturity, opprobrium, or imbecility. In the United States to be deemed a liberal was often grounds for marginalization. Ultimately, this difficulty in forging a diverse commonweal harmed race relations.

■

But what had inspired the awesome conflagration of 1992 was not a black-Korean or Latino-Korean conflict but an incident strikingly similar to what had transpired in 1965. Once again, the LAPD's treatment of blacks had deepened old wounds. Once again, Warren Christopher stepped forward, this time to investigate the LAPD. In a sense, this commission was necessary because the McCone Commission had not been sufficiently audacious in rooting racism out of the LAPD.

The Christopher Commission made a number of recommendations, most notably its call for "community policing." If implemented, this model would do away with Chief Parker's old idea of treating South LA as a community that needed to be subdued. Instead, community policing would focus on crime prevention, with officers becoming quasi-social workers, working closely with residents and merchants in solving problems rather than just arresting criminals.[7] The local elite finally was determining that it might be better if the LAPD emulated social workers rather than Marines.

The core of the project is the establishment of a network of police advisory boards, panels that the department hoped eventually would draw hundreds of volunteers and form the focal point of police-community relations. However, two years after the 1992 civil unrest, a study found that many of the commission's recommendations—considered rather mild by some critics—had not been implemented; most notably, the community policing model remained on the drafting board.[8] Likewise, the plan to retest officers psychologically during the course of their careers was not in place. If implemented, community policing and such testing could go a long way to ensure that those officers most prone to brutalizing blacks and others would be removed.

Another change greeted warmly in South LA was the replacement of the combative Daryl Gates as police chief with Willie Williams, formerly of Philadelphia, who happened to be African-American. Yet resistance to reform continued unabated in the ranks of the LAPD, as evidenced by the fact that in July 1994 the city council bent to pressure from officers and refused to place civilians on police disciplinary boards.[9]

The LAPD—the constant that linked 1965 with 1992—was mired in difficulties that perhaps could not be resolved by measures as meaningful as hiring a new chief, providing new tests, or changing the model of policing. A study released by the American Civil Liberties Union in March 1994 concluded that 83.1 percent of LAPD officers lived beyond the city limits. A total of 293 officers resided in Simi Valley, while fewer than 200 lived in the area covered by the department's Central Bureau. The ACLU made a number of recommendations to rectify the situation, including low- and no-interest mortgage loans to lure officers back to the city. It did not call for residency requirements because a 1974 amendment to California's constitution appeared to bar them. Instead, it pointedly wondered how true community policing could be implemented when so many officers lived beyond the community they policed.[10] The ACLU also suggested that this failure to reside in the city contributed to the LAPD's image as an "army of occupation in the urban communities" and added that the lengthy distance between officers' homes and workplaces may have "played a role in compromising responses to major emergency incidents."[11]

The LAPD's penchant for brutality was not only of moment for racial minorities; male officers also had developed a reputation for strong sexual harassment of female officers, many of whom were white.[12] Indeed, studies had shown that adding more women to the force was an antidote to brutality.[13] The atmosphere for law enforcement in Los Angeles was not the best. In 1988 an investigation revealed that deputies in the county sheriff's office were stealing millions of dollars from drug dealers; during the same period a number of LAPD officers were found to be running a prostitution service, dealing automatic weapons, and committing insurance fraud, armed robbery, and murder for hire.[14]

In such an atmosphere, police brutality against racial minorities seemed like a minor peccadillo; similarly, tolerance of internal racism and sexism made it difficult to police any transgressions of the LAPD. Likewise, there was a link between the depredations of the LAPD's Red Squad of the 1930s, designed to bash labor and the left, and the civil unrest of 1965 and 1992. It was difficult to focus police lawlessness exclusively on unpopular political and racial minorities without this cancer spreading to other parts of the body politic.

The unrest of 1965 and 1992 was linked in other ways. The failure of the LAPD to stop the disturbances engendered mass insecurity throughout the region. Stores were abandoned to be looted and burned; some families felt abandoned. Both times, as the columnist Lars-Erik Nelson pointed out in *New York Newsday* on 8 May 1994, there was a rush to buy weapons and a heightened atomizing of society as the feeling spread that the controls of government and the authorities had broken down. Not surprisingly, the weakening of government was a lifelong dream of the right wing, which then benefited as faith in controls plummeted and a survivalist atomizing spread.

In 1965 and 1992 there was a revival of nineteenth-century vigilantism. Professor James Lasley of Arizona State University, a former adviser to the LAPD's Office of Operations and Personnel, observed in the 13 May 1994 *LA Times* that there were an estimated sixty-five vigilante groupings in LA with membership ranging from twenty five to five hundred. "These groups outnumber the LAPD and Sheriff's Department by 5 to 1. Some wear uniforms, drive patrol cars and even carry weapons." There are patrols by such forces in Koreatown and by members of the Jewish Orthodox community in the Beverly-Fairfax district. Almost all of these forces arose after the unrest of 1992, in a process similar to what happened in the immediate aftermath of 1965. With such role models, it was little wonder that gangs would increase their numbers in South LA.

■

Even if the LAPD had been transformed profoundly in the aftermath of the 1965 revolt, the 1992 civil unrest still might have happened because of the deteriorating economic environment facing so many in the city. The deindustrialization that had been glimpsed in 1965 was accelerated by the end of the Cold War. Southern California had been a major recipient of Pentagon contracts, and in fact, its economy had been pumped up by the steroids of defense spending.[15] The fall of the Berlin Wall in 1989 helped to change all that.

As of 1992, the largest employer in the LA metropolitan area was government—the county, the federal government, the city, and the school system.[16] Yet the prevalence of conservatism had forced cutbacks in government spending that hit racial minorities hardest. The entertainment industry, that other pillar of the region's economy, had not changed appreciably its historic policies of slighting blacks in employment.[17]

The microeconomy of South LA was bleak, with even the victories only underscoring the depth of the problem. Between 1965 and 1990 the number of supermarkets in South LA dropped from fifty-five to thirty; the area has 25 percent fewer supermarkets per capita than other areas of the county. When the Alpha Beta supermarket chain pledged in April 1994 to build a store on Adams and Vermont on a plot of land that had been vacant for nine years, this decision captured headlines.[18] When the Denny's restaurant chain, under fire because of charges of racism, pledged that same year to open shop in the Watts-Willowbrook area, it was noted that this would be "the first full-service restaurant to open in the area since the Watts riots of 1965."[19] The cinema in Baldwin Hills, opened in 1949 in the then predominantly white Crenshaw district, was closed in the spring of 1994, after it had become "the only black owned movie house in L.A."[20] The Baldwin Hills/Crenshaw Plaza, a major shopping and retail center, was facing difficulty in staying open for business despite substantial governmental aid.[21]

On the second anniversary of the civil unrest of 1992, one study found half of the 607 properties severely damaged or destroyed then had not been rebuilt. The pace of rebuilding proceeded at a more rapid pace north of the Santa Monica Freeway, where 63 percent of the properties had been rebuilt or were under construction; south of the freeway—where racial minorities were more prevalent—only 44 percent had been rebuilt.[22]

This time, instead of government taking the lead in reconstruction, an entity backed by the private sector—Rebuild LA—was in the vanguard. This development was part and parcel of the conservatism—given a major boost after 1965—that posited that government was the problem and the private sector should take its place. But as the *LA Times* concluded, "The mixed success of rebuilding efforts raises serious questions about the private sector as a panacea, particularly at a time when cities and counties are increasingly turning toward privatization as a solution to budget woes."[23]

Black LA was a chief victim of deindustrialization and its companion, the decline of unions. Since 1965 no militant substitute for the Nation of Islam had arisen; militant multiracialism had declined with the disappearance of the Civil Rights Congress. Narrow nationalism continued to maintain a foothold, particularly among black youth. The NOI and gangs continued to recruit from the same vast pool: the growing number of black inmates populating California's prisons, the residue of deindustrialization.[24] At times it seemed that there had been a confluence of the gangs and nationalists, as NOI spokesmen like Khalid Abdul Muhammad were fixtures at "gang summits" called to try to halt the internecine violence that coursed between and among gangs. Muhammad sought to update the NOI's theology, downplaying the concept of blacks as Asiatic and stressing the precept of mainstream black nationalism, that is, that blacks were African.[25]

There was also evidence of another confluence, that of the NOI with the middle class, as NOI members demonstrated considerable influence on a number of budding black business establishments in Los Angeles by conducting themselves in a manner not dissimilar from organized crime figures that arose in 1930s Chicago.[26] The NOI also wielded influence on rappers of various persuasions, many of whom dreamed of constructing business empires in the presumed manner of other racial and ethnic groups.[27]

Evidence of the NOI's influence among black youth arose when a furor was stirred at Howard University—the nation's largest predominantly black university—by a mass rally featuring anti-Jewish expressions that was held in early 1994. The chief organizer was Malik Zulu Shabazz, a second-year law student from Los Angeles.[28] Los Angeles remained a center of NOI influence; weekly figures showed that its newspaper, the *Final Call*, usually sold more copies there than in New York City where the black population was more substantial and had deeper roots.[29]

By 1992 the Black Panther party was a distant memory. It did manage to achieve headlines in 1994 when Larry Joseph Stiner, a cultural nationalist involved in the murder of two Panthers at UCLA in 1969, surrendered to the FBI after escaping twenty years earlier from San Quentin.[30] This historical postscript was a reminder that nationalism attained hegemony over the left in Black LA through means fair and foul.

The NAACP was in the process of changing leadership nationally in 1992. Chosen to replace the Republican minister Benjamin Hooks was Benjamin Chavis, who had developed ties to the left when he was a "political prisoner" in North Carolina in the 1970s as a member of the "Wilmington Ten." However, his efforts to reach out to those influenced by the NOI, as well as controversial figures like the Marxist scholar-activist Angela Davis who had worked tirelessly to free him, sparked outrage; his alleged mishandling of a sexual discrimination case led to his dismissal during the summer of 1994.[31]

Tom Bradley, who was catapulted into higher office as a direct result of the 1965 revolt, served as mayor of Los Angeles from 1973 to 1993. However, his political career exemplified the contradictory nature of the compounded racism of Southern California. On the one hand, he was able to serve two decades as mayor while New York City did not elect its first black mayor until 1989. Bradley also was nominated by the state Democratic party as its gubernatorial nominee in 1982 and 1986. New York's Democrats have yet to nominate an African-American for this highest statewide office. On the other hand, Bradley was defeated both times by a conservative Republican in what was viewed widely as an expression of white backlash.[32]

Speaking of New York Democrats, Daniel Patrick Moynihan had advanced to new heights; by 1994 he was the senior U.S. senator from that state. Yet it seemed that this lofty perch had not improved his view of women; in the midst of his reelection race, he extended the import of his famed report, charging that the phenomenon of unwed motherhood was leading to "speciation," or the creation of a new species.[33] NOI leaders making intemperate remarks were hounded, while those making inflammatory remarks that appeared to target blacks and others not deemed to be powerful barely created a ripple; such double standards only served to increase the nationalist appeal of the NOI.

The Watts Revolt of 1965 led to certain concessions being made to African-Americans; but as the 1990s unfolded, the black middle class—a major recipient of those concessions—remained dissatisfied, even enraged.[34] One could only imagine the feelings of the black working class, which had borne the brunt of conservative-inspired reductions in government spending. Still, all was not bleak, and the 1965 revolt was not without consequence for the 1990s. Since 1965 a number of popular and affluent black entertainers had joined Bill Cosby in this privileged category. Sports, particularly basketball, had been one of the areas that opened their doors to black participation.

Rudy Washington grew up in Los Angeles playing ball and eventually coached at Verbum Dei and Locke high schools, Compton College, and USC. But in August 1965 Washington was a teenager living not far from

115th Street and Avalon. "I could sit on my porch and listen to the windows breaking. At the time, there was a place around the corner from me on 120th called Shop-Rite. The drug store was there and I . . . could sit on my front porch and [watch] people running up and down my street with couches and televisions. . . . As a child, I saw the whole thing transpire. I watched the police come, the National Guard. I watched the looting. I watched the killings. That was at 14 years old."

Today, Washington is a basketball coach at Drake University and is working closely with the Congressional Black Caucus in its efforts to end bias in the National Collegiate Athletic Association and to divert some of the billions generated by athletes toward their education; many of these basketball players are black. In January 1994 the Black Coaches Association, which Washington heads, threatened to shut down college basketball unless the NCAA negotiated in good faith. At this juncture the NCAA became more forthcoming, and more serious negotiations resumed.

This struggle continues, and Rudy Washington speaks openly about being marked and inspired by what he witnessed in South LA in August 1965.[35] This too is the legacy—and meaning—of the 1960s.

NOTES

Introduction

1. David O. Sears and John B. McConahay, *The Politics of Violence: The New Urban Blacks and the Watts Riot* (Boston, 1973), p. 13.

2. *LA Times,* 11, 14 Aug. 1965.

3. LA Fire Department, "Riot Area," statistical summary, structure and content damage, from 12 Aug. 1965 at 9 P.M. to 16 Aug. at 8 A.M., issued 20 Aug. 1965 by Raymond Hill, McCone Transcript. After 103d Street, in second place for property destruction was Central Avenue from Santa Barbara Avenue to 49th Street with 15 buildings housing 37 separate occupancies suffering 100 percent loss and an additional 5 buildings housing 7 occupancies partially destroyed. In third place was Broadway from Santa Barbara Avenue to 49th Street with 20 buildings housing 23 occupancies totally destroyed.

4. *Hollywood Reporter,* 12 Feb. 1947; David Caute, *The Great Fear: The Anti-Communist Purge under Truman and Eisenhower* (New York, 1978), p. 487; see also Dorothy Healey, *California Red: A Life in the Communist Party* (Urbana, Ill., 1993). The stakes in Southern California were large; there was a booming aerospace industry buoyed by Cold War spending and there was Hollywood, which made millions in profits and massaged consciousness. This is one reason why the Red Scare here was so fierce; those who were battle-tested here had shown mettle and were on the fast track to bigger and better things. See Stephen Vaughn, *Ronald Reagan in Hollywood: Movies and Politics* (New York, 1994); Oliver Carlson, *Red Star over Hollywood* (New York, 1947); Lester Cole, *Hollywood Red: The Autobiography of Lester Cole* (Palo Alto, Calif., 1981); Larry Ceplair and Steven Englund, *The Inquisition in Hollywood: Politics in the Film Community, 1930–1960* (Garden City, N.Y., 1980). The ferocious class wars, particularly during the strikes and lockouts of 1945 and 1946, led to moguls and the state collaborating with organized crime figures to crush the left. This unfolded in "Hollywood," (e.g., Culver City and Burbank), not distant from South LA where other gangs were forming. William Knoedelseder, *Stiffed: A True Story of MCA, the Music Business, and the Mafia* (New York, 1993); Dan Moldea, *Dark Victory: Ronald Reagan, MCA, and the Mob* (New York, 1986); Justine Picardie and Dorothy Wade, *Music Man: Ahmet Ertegun, Atlantic Records, and the Triumph of Rock n' Roll* (New York, 1990). See also my forthcoming book, *Class Struggle in Hollywood: Mobsters, Moguls, Stars, Politicians, Trade Unionists, and Reds, 1946.* In the postwar era the idea grew that gangsters, even "gang-bangers," were part of a culture of resistance, particularly among African-Americans. There is a scintilla of accuracy imbedded in this notion but often ignored is the salient point that gangsters of whatever race or ethnicity in the United States have been highly accommodating to larger cultural norms and to the requisites of social production. Ultimately, their defiance is limited to symbolic suggestion and often remains on the level of appearance. Indeed, the experiences of nonblack gangsters suggest that their goals are congruent with and help to sustain the goals of capitalism itself. The heralding of the alleged resistance represented by gangsters obscures their true role in social reproduction, subverts actual resistance, and helps to suppress true alternatives. See Alisse Waterston, *Street Addicts in the Political Economy* (Philadelphia, 1994).

5. U.S. Congress, House, Committee on Un-American Activities, *Communist Activities among Professional Groups in the Los Angeles Area*, pt. 1, testimony of Max Silver, 82d Cong., 2d sess., 21 Jan. 1952, 2444.

6. "How a Negro Came to Marxism," c. 1960, box 1, folder 1, Pettis Perry Papers; see also Al Richmond, *A Long View from the Left: Memoirs of an American Revolutionary* (Boston, 1973); James Goodman, *Stories of Scottsboro: The Rape Case That Shocked 1930's America and Revived the Struggle for Equality* (New York, 1994).

7. Jay Rand, "Hitlerites in Hollywood," *New Masses* 16, no. 4 (23 July 1935): 29–30; see also Greg Mitchell, *The Campaign of the Century: Upton Sinclair's Race for Governor of California and the Birth of Media Politics* (New York, 1992).

8. Gerald Horne, *Black Liberation/Red Scare: Ben Davis and the Communist Party* (Newark, Del., 1994).

9. Charlotta Bass to John Howard Lawson, 18 July 1946, box 12, folder 3, John Howard Lawson Papers.

10. "Marge and Roger" to Emil Freed, 26 Sept. 1949, Emil Freed Papers; see also Charlotta Bass, *Forty Years: Memoirs from the Pages of a Newspaper* (Los Angeles, 1960).

11. Charlotta Bass to Arna Bontemps, 30, 7, 9 Aug. 1961, box 2, Arna Bontemps Papers; Kirkland C. Jones, *Renaissance Man from Louisiana: A Biography of Arna Wendell Bontemps* (Westport, Conn., 1992).

12. Minutes of the Provisional Committee of the Civil Rights Congress, Los Angeles, 11 July 1946, reel 45, box 77, P16, Civil Rights Congress Papers; Sponsors of CRC, Oct. 1946, reel 45, box 77, P11, ibid. For further information on CRC and for documentation of what follows, see Gerald Horne, *Communist Front? The Civil Rights Congress, 1946–56* (London, 1988).

13. Horne, *Communist Front?* pp. 333, 324. Robert Wesley Wells was an example of a person from the black workingclass who collaborated with the left when it had more strength. His mother died when he was quite young, and he migrated from Fort Worth to Denver then to Los Angeles, where he lived with an aunt who had three children of her own and no husband; they all resided in a tiny two-room flat near a swamp. In 1921, when he was twelve, he was sent to reform school for two years for stealing a car. By 1928 he was imprisoned in San Quentin, and by 1931 he was residing in Folsom prison where he faced racism, beatings, and solitary confinement. Despite these hardships Wells became an articulate writer and spokesman for prisoners' rights. Eventually, Wells was freed because of a national and international campaign; unfortunately, this took place well after the Civil Rights Congress—which had led the fight for his freedom—had gone out of business in 1956. With no political anchor, Wells did not realize the promise foreshadowed by his earlier writings and leadership in prison; likewise, with the demise of the CRC, the Nation of Islam stepped into the breach as the major defender of the rights of black prisoners.

14. Ibid., p. 59.

15. *California Eagle*, 7 Nov. 1946; *LA Sentinel*, 19 Sept. 1946.

16. Conference program, 12 March 1947, box 40, folder 4, Dalton Trumbo Papers; see also Bruce Cook, *Dalton Trumbo* (New York, 1977); John Carver Edwards, *Berlin Calling: American Broadcasters in Service to the Third Reich* (New York, 1991).

17. *LA Sentinel*, 31 Oct. 1946; Ingrid Scobie, *Center Stage: Helen Gahagan Douglas, a Life* (New York, 1991).

18. Horne, *Communist Front?* pp. 66–67; U.S. Congress, House, Committee on Un-American Activities, *Communist Political Subversion, Los Angeles*, 84th Cong., 2d sess., 5 Dec. 1956, 6620–6859; idem, *Investigation of Communist Activities in the Los Angeles Area*, pt. 7, Los Angeles, 84th Cong., 2d sess., 16 April 1956, 3657–4071; idem, *Investigation of Communist Activities in the Los Angeles Area*, p. 1, Los Angeles, 84th Congress, 1st sess., 27–28 June 1955, 1437–1905; idem, *Subversive Influences in Riots, Looting, and Burning*, pt. 3A, Los Angeles, 90th Cong., 2d sess., 28 June 1968, 1815–59; idem, *The Southern California District of the Communist Party: Structure, Objectives, Leadership*, pt. 1, Los Angeles, 85th Cong.,

2d sess., 24–27 April 1962, 53–221. This attack on the left apparently took its toll on some whites who had been involved with the Communist party. By 1958 Pettis Perry, the black party leader, was complaining "we hear that in L.A. . . . that when Negro people move into an area, that white Left and Communists, immediately flee to other areas, that are still lily white. . . . Is it not clear, that such action, undermines the confidence of the Negro Communist and non-Communist of the sincerity of white comrades?" Report, c. 1958, box 2, folder 11, Pettis Perry Papers. Just as Robert Wells drifted away from a weakened left after leaving prison, the bludgeoning of the left not only hindered interracial unity but also eroded the racial sensitivities of some white leftists.

19. Press release, 13 June 1950, reel 9037, Federated Press Papers. The sharp battles around education energized right-wing Republicans in the state also. See Max Rafferty, *Max Rafferty on Education* (New York, 1968); Max Rafferty, *Suffer, Little Children* (New York, 1962); Max Rafferty, *What They Are Doing to Your Children* (New York, 1964). Besides class and race, age and youth particularly were major issues in the state and South LA.

20. *Hollywood Reporter,* 13 June 1952.

21. Study, 26 April 1952, box 40, folder 5, John Howard Lawson Papers.

22. *New York Times,* 28 July 1963, 14 March 1969.

23. Karl Marx, *The Eighteenth Brumaire of Louis Bonaparte* (New York, 1968), p. 75. Here the lumpen is described as "vagabonds, discharged soldiers, discharged jailbirds, escaped galley slaves, swindlers, mountebanks, lazzaroni, pickpockets, tricksters, gamblers, maquereaus [procurers], brothel keepers, porters, literati, organ-grinders, knife grinders, tinkers, beggars." Three points should be made here: this lumpen should not be confused with the unemployed, nor should it be confused with the proletariat itself; indeed, this is a class that tends to prey on the proletariat and working class generally. See also Jurgen Kuczynki, *The Rise of the Working Class* (New York, 1975); Friedrich Engels, *The Condition of the Working Class in England* (Stanford, Calif., 1968). For the impact of lumpen culture on the Panthers and the black struggle combined with an analysis and definition of this class that I largely share, see Henry Winston, *Strategy for a Black Agenda: A Critique of New Theories of Liberation in the United States and Africa* (New York, 1973). A key reason for the NOI's increased popularity among men in prison was that joining their ranks there helped to ensure that one would not be sexually assaulted. In turn, this underlined the NOI's role as guardian of black masculinity.

24. Cynthia Enloe, *Bananas, Beaches, and Bases: Making Feminist Sense of International Politics* (Berkeley, Calif., 1990). Similarly, racism and class exploitation are linked. Victor Perlo, *The Economics of Racism: Roots of Black Inequality* (New York, 1975); Gary Becker, *The Economics of Discrimination* (Chicago, 1971); Mel Leiman, *The Political Economy of Racism: A History* (Boulder, Colo., 1993).

25. Gerald Horne, "Race Matters: The Trajectory of Anti-Racism," *Science and Society* 57, no. 4, (1993–94): 441–45; Virginia Dominguez, *White by Definition: Social Classification in Creole Louisiana* (New Brunswick, N.J., 1986). For a case study of how compounded racism plays out in literature, see Mary Horne Young, *Mules and Dragons: Popular Culture Images in the Selected Writings of African-American and Chinese-American Women Writers* (Westport, Conn., 1993).

26. Joao Jose Reis, *Slave Rebellion in Brazil: The Muslim Uprisings of 1835 in Bahia* (Baltimore, 1993); Yvonne Y. Haddad, ed., *The Muslims of America* (New York, 1991); E. U. Essien-Udom, *Black Nationalism: A Search for Identity in America* (Chicago, 1962).

27. Gerald Horne, *Black and Red: W. E. B. Du Bois and the Afro-American Response to the Cold War, 1944–1963* (Albany, 1986), pp. 60, 45.

28. Eric Williams, *Capitalism and Slavery* (Chapel Hill, N.C., 1944); Seymour Drescher, *Econocide: British Slavery in the Era of Abolition* (Pittsburgh, 1977); Seymour Drescher, *Capitalism and Antislavery: British Mobilization in Comparative Perspective* (New York, 1987); Thomas C. Holt, *The Problem of Freedom: Race, Labor, and Politics in Jamaica and Britain, 1832–1938* (Baltimore, 1992).

29. Ernest Allen, "When Japan Was 'Champion of the Darker Races': Satokata Takahashi and the

Flowering of Black Messianic Nationalism," *Black Scholar: Journal of Black Studies and Research* 24, no. 1 (1994): 23–46; cf. Evelyn Iritani, *An Ocean between Us: The Changing Relationship of Japan and the United States* (New York, 1994). Tokyo also launched balloons with bombs that detonated on the west coast of the United States.

30. Hugh Pearson, *The Shadow of the Panther: Huey Newton and the Price of Black Power in America* (Reading, Mass., 1994), pp. 108, 101–4: The Community Alert Patrol in South LA, organized after the revolt to monitor the LAPD, was the embryo from which grew the BPP.

31. Gerald Horne, "Civil Rights/Cold War," *Guild Practitioner* 48, no. 4 (1991): 109–15; Gerald Horne, "Hell in the City of Angels, 1965–1992," ibid., 49, no. 3 (1992): 65–72.

32. Juan Gomez Quiñones, *Chicano Politics: Reality and Promise, 1940–1990* (Albuquerque, 1990); Juan Gomez Quiñones, *Development of the Mexican Working Class North of the Rio Bravo: Work and Culture among Laborers and Artisans, 1600–1900* (Los Angeles, 1982); Juan Gomez Quiñones, *Mexican Nationalist Formation: Political Discourse, Policy, and Dissidence* (Encino, Calif., 1992); Juan Gomez Quiñones, *Roots of Chicano Politics, 1600–1940* (Albuquerque, 1994); Tomás Almaguer, *Racial Fault Lines: The Historical Origins of White Supremacy in California* (Berkeley and Los Angeles, 1994).

33. Gerald Horne, "Hands across the Water: Afro-American Lawyers and the Decolonization of Southern Africa," *Guild Practitioner* 45, no. 3 (1988): 110–28; see also Fatima Meer, *Higher than Hope: A Biography of Nelson Mandela* (London, 1990); Joe Slovo et al., *Southern Africa: The New Politics of Revolution* (Harmondsworth, Eng., 1976); Joe Slovo, *Has Socialism Failed?* (Chicago, 1990).

34. Janet G. Vaillant, *Black, French, and African: A Life of Leopold Senghor* (Cambridge, Mass., 1990), p. 187.

35. Ibid., pp. 286–87; Horne, *Black and Red*, p. 260.

36. Ian Tyrell, *Woman's World, Woman's Empire* (Chapel Hill, N.C., 1991).

37. Sudarshan Kapur, *Raising Up a Prophet: The African-American Encounter with Gandhi* (Boston, 1992).

38. Peter Benson, *"Black Orpheus," "Transition," and Modern Cultural Awakening in Africa* (Berkeley, Calif., 1986); G. Wesley Johnson, *The Emergence of Black Politics in Senegal* (Stanford, Calif., 1971); Mort Rosenblum, *Mission to Civilize: The French Way* (San Diego, 1986); Jacque Louis Hymans, *Leopold Sedar Senghor: An Intellectual Biography* (Edinburgh, 1971); Mercer Cook, "Some Literary Contacts: African, West Indian, and Afro-American," in *The Black Writer*, ed. Lloyd W. Brown (Los Angeles, 1973) pp. 119–40; Nathan Huggins, *The Harlem Renaissance* (New York, 1971); J. Ayo Langley, *Pan Africanism and Nationalism in West Africa, 1900–1945: A Study in Ideology and Social Classes* (Oxford, 1973); A. James Arnold, *Modernism and Negritude: The Poetry and Poetics of Aimé Césaire* (Cambridge, Mass., 1981); Irving Leonard Markovitz, *Leopold Sedar Senghor and the Politics of Negritude* (New York, 1969). That France and the United States often had conflicts about policy toward Africa and other matters during the Cold War period makes the influence of Senghor and Negritude on African-Americans even more intriguing. This influence can be seen in the development of United Slaves, the main cultural nationalist grouping in LA and the progenitor of the December holiday of Kwanzaa; it can also be seen more widely on campuses, viz., certain forms of "Afro-centricity," in the recrudescence of mysticism and stress on the subjective. Maulana Karenga, *The African American Holiday of Kwanzaa: A Celebration of Family, Community and Culture* (Los Angeles, 1988); Maulana Karenga, *Kawaida Theory: An Introductory Outline* (Inglewood, Calif., 1980); Clyde Halisi and James Mtume, *The Quotable Karenga* (Los Angeles, 1967); Molefi Asante, *The Afrocentric Idea* (Philadelphia, 1987); Molefi Asante, *Afrocentricity* (Trenton, 1988). It is striking that two of the major avatars of black nationalism, Karenga and Asante, had roots in LA.

39. Mark Juergensmeyer, *The New Cold War? Religious Nationalism Confronts the Secular State* (Berkeley, Calif., 1993); Gerald Horne, "Myth and the Making of 'Malcolm X,'" *American Historical Review* 98 (April 1993): 440–50; Martin Walker, *The Cold War: A History* (New York, 1994); *LA Times*, 8 Feb. 1993.

40. Toni Morrison, *Playing in the Dark: Whiteness and the Literary Imagination* (Cambridge, Mass.,

1992); See also James Baldwin, *The Price of the Ticket: Collected Nonfiction, 1948–1965* (New York, 1985); James Baldwin, *The Fire Next Time* (New York, 1963). Perforce when considering the future of Africans and African-Americans one must consider, e.g., Japan, China, the European Union and their at times conflicting relations with the United States. See generally, Gerald Horne, *Race for the Planet: The U.S. and the New World Order* (Thousand Oaks, Calif., 1994). For ruminations on contemporary LA and California, see Peter Theroux, *Translating LA: A Tour of the Rainbow City* (New York, 1994); Bill Barich, *Big Dreams: Into the Heart of California* (New York, 1994).

1. Toward Understanding

1. Kenneth Kusmer, "Black Urban History in the U.S.: Retrospect and Prospect," *Trends in History* 3 (Fall 1982): 71–92, p. 84; Kenneth Kusmer, "Urban Black History at the Crossroads," *Journal of Urban History* 13 (Aug. 1987): 460–70; see also Paul Groves and Edward Muller, "The Evolution of Black Residential Concentrations in Late 19th Century Cities," *Journal of Historical Geography* 1 (April 1975): 169–91; Reynolds Farley, "The Urbanization of Negroes in the United States," *Journal of Social History* 1 (Spring 1968): 241–58; Roger W. Lotchin, "The City and the Sword in Metropolitan California, 1919–1941," *Urbanism Past and Present* 7 (Summer–Fall 1982): 1–16; Neil Shumsky and Timothy Crimmins, eds., *Urban America: A Historical Bibliography* (Santa Barbara, Calif., 1983); see also Lawrence E. Guillow, "Rancheria, Barrio, and Chinatown: The Origins of Race Relations in Los Angeles, 1781–1900" (Ph.D. diss., Arizona State Univ., 1992).

2. W. W. Robinson, "Myth-Making in the Los Angeles Area," *Southern California Quarterly* 45, no. 1 (1963): 83–94; Beasley, *Negro Trailblazers of California,* p. 18; see also Douglas Henry Daniels, *Pioneer Urbanites: A Social and Cultural History of Black San Francisco* (Philadelphia, 1980); Albert S. Broussard, *Black San Francisco: The Struggle for Racial Equality in the West, 1900–1954* (Lawrence, Kans., 1993).

3. Lawrence B. DeGraaf, "The City of Black Angels: Emergence of the Los Angeles Ghetto, 1890–1930," *Pacific Historical Review* 39 (Aug. 1970): 323–52, p. 327.

4. Joseph Franklin, *All through the Night: The History of Spokane Black Americans, 1860–1940* (Fairfield, Wash., 1989), p. 111. See also p. 13 quoting Robert O'Brien: "In both Oregon and Washington, Negroes were treated essentially as individuals during the period from the Civil War to World War I. . . . Negroes and those of Negro ancestry were elected to positions of Mayors or as representatives in the state legislature." However, as black populations grew in the West, Jim Crow grew also. See Joan Reese, "Two Enemies to Fight: Blacks Battle for Equality in Two World Wars," *Colorado Heritage* 1 (1990): 2–17, p. 3: In Denver, before the 1960s there "was no eating in downtown restaurants . . . or staying in downtown hotels. Schools were for all purposes segregated because of housing restrictions that didn't even begin to break down until the late 1950s. The 'crow's nest' was endured in theaters downtown—when it was full you were turned away even if half the seats downtown were empty. These were just the more obvious restrictions."

5. Roger Daniels and Harry H. L. Kitano, *American Racism: Exploration of the Nature of Prejudice* (Englewood Cliffs, N.J., 1970).

6. Gordon DeMarco, *A Short History of Los Angeles* (San Francisco, 1988), pp. 31, 32, 35; see also Michael Feldberg, "Urbanization as a Cause of Violence: Philadelphia as a Test Case," in *The Peoples of Philadelphia: A History of Ethnic Groups and Lower-Class Life, 1790–1940,* ed. Allen F. Davis and Mark H. Haller (Philadelphia, 1973), pp. 53–69; Richard Hofstadter, "Reflections on Violence in the United States," in *Violence in America: A Documentary History,* ed. Richard Hofstadter and Michael Wallace (New York, 1970), pp. 3–43; Arthur F. Raper, *The Tragedy of Lynching* (Chapel Hill, N.C., 1933); David R. Roediger, *The Wages of Whiteness: Race and the Making of the American Working Class* (New York, 1991); John Warner, *Reaping the Bloody Harvest: Race Riots in the United States during the Age of Jackson, 1824–1849* (New York, 1986). Though most violence in California during the nineteenth century may have been aimed at nonblacks, African-Americans were not able to escape lynchings and brutality in the West either.

7. Barry Crouch, "A Spirit of Lawlessness: White Violence, Texas Blacks, 1865–1868," *Journal of Social History* 18 (Winter 1984): 217–32; Randolph B. Campbell, *An Empire for Slavery: The Peculiar Institution in Texas, 1821–1865* (Baton Rouge, La., 1989), p. 224; Joe Gray Taylor, *Negro Slavery in Louisiana* (Baton Rouge, La., 1963), p. 212; see also Lorraine Adams and Dan Malone, "Abuse of Authority," *Southern Exposure* 20, no. 4 (1992): 41–44, p. 41: "Texas police have been investigated and prosecuted more frequently for beatings, torture, coerced confessions, rapes and needless deaths than police in any other state."

8. William Ivy Hair, *Bourbonism and Agrarian Protest: Louisiana Politics, 1877–1910* (Baton Rouge, La., 1969); William Ivy Hair, *Carnival of Fury: Robert Charles and the New Orleans Race Riot of 1905* (Baton Rouge, La., 1963), p. 212; Wonda Fonténot, *Secret Doctors: Ethnomedicine of African Americans* (Westport, Conn., 1994). Blacks in Louisiana developed a distinct culture based in part on their Bambara origins and their relations with local Choctaw, Cherokees, and Creeks.

9. James J. Parsons, "The Uniqueness of California," *American Quarterly* 7 (Spring 1955): 45–50; see also Carey McWilliams, *California: The Great Exception* (New York, 1949); Carey McWilliams, *Southern California Country: An Island on the Land* (New York, 1946).

10. Jack Forbes, *Afro-Americans in the Far West: A Handbook for Educators* (Washington, D.C., 1967), p. 12; Ramon Eduardo Ruiz, *Triumphs and Tragedy: A History of the Mexican People* (New York, 1992). A strong theme emerging from the latter work is the color consciousness in Mexico. See also Frank Dikotter, *The Discourse of Race in Modern China* (London, 1992).

11. *LA Herald Examiner,* 15 Jan. 1891.

12. *LA Sentinel,* 3 Sept. 1992.

13. *LA Times,* 2 March 1994.

14. DeGraaf, "The City of Black Angels," p. 334; Lawrence DeGraaf, "Negro Migration to Los Angeles, 1930–1950" (Ph.D. diss., UCLA, 1962), p. 21. There was also an attempt to segregate blacks in privately owned and unregulated buses. See DeMarco, *A Short History of Los Angeles,* p. 101.

15. Christopher Cocolthchos, "The Invisible Government and the Viable Community: The Ku Klux Klan in Orange County, California, during the 1920s" (Ph.D. diss., UCLA, 1979). The author concludes that the KKK was focused mostly on the Japanese, though his relatively benign view of the Klan tends to make questionable his overall thesis.

16. Emory Joel Tolbert, "The Universal Negro Improvement Association in Los Angeles: A Study of Western Garveyism" (Ph.D. diss., UCLA, 1975); see also Tony Martin, *Race First: The Ideological and Organizational Struggles of Marcus Garvey and the Universal Negro Improvement Association* (Westport, Conn., 1976).

17. Scott L. Bottles, *Los Angeles and the Automobile: The Making of the Modern City* (Berkeley, Calif., 1987), p. 208.

18. Lonnie G. Bunch III, "A Past Not Necessarily Prologue: The Afro-American in Los Angeles since 1900," in *20th Century Los Angeles: Power, Promotion, and Social Conflict,* ed. Norman Klein and Martin Schiesl (Claremont, Calif., 1990), pp. 101–30, 115.

19. Loren Miller, "Relationship of Racial Residential Segregation to Los Angeles Riots," 7 Oct. 1965, box 12, 26F, McCone Papers; *LA Times,* 10 Oct. 1965.

20. Douglas S. Massey and Nancy A. Denton, *American Apartheid: Segregation and the Making of the Underclass* (Cambridge, Mass., 1993); see also Ken Auletta, *The Underclass* (New York, 1982); William Julius Wilson, ed., *The Ghetto Underclass: Social Science Perspectives* (Newbury Park, Calif., 1989); Michael Katz, ed., *The "Underclass" Debate: Views from History* (Princeton, N.J., 1993).

21. Arna Bontemps, *God Sends Sunday* (New York, 1931), pp. 118–19; Sonora McKeller, "Watts: Little Rome," in *From the Ashes: Voices of Watts,* ed. Budd Schulberg (New York, 1967), pp. 213–18, 213.

22. Franklyn Rabow, "Watts: A History of Deprivation," July 1965, LACHRC Papers; Patricia Rae Adler, "Watts: From Suburb to Black Ghetto" (Ph.D. diss., Univ. of Southern California, 1976), p. 139.

The close friend of Langston Hughes presents a graphic picture of Watts during this early period: "This section before the blacks came, had evidently been a walnut grove. A few of the groves were still standing. Beneath them crude shacks had been built and vines—morning-glory, gourd and honeysuckle—had promptly covered them, giving the whole neighborhood an aspect of savage wildness. . . . The streets of Mudtown [Watts] were three or four dusty wagon paths. In the moist grass along the edges cows were staked. Broken carts and useless wagons littered the front yards of the people, carts on the spokes of the wheels and wagons from the beds of which small dark mules were eating straw. Ducks were sleeping in the weeds, and there was on the air a suggestion of pigs and slime holes. Tiny hoot-owls were sitting bravely on fence posts while bats wavered overhead like shadows. . . . The small group in Mudtown was exceptional. Here, removed from the influences of white folks, they did not acquire the inhibitions of their city brothers. Mudtown was like a tiny section of the deep south literally transplanted." Bontemps, *God Sends Sunday*, pp. 118–19.

23. DeGraaf, "Negro Migration to Los Angeles," pp. 78–88.

24. Martin Wachs, *Auto, Transit, and the Sprawl of L.A.* (Los Angeles, 1983), pp. 4, 6, 7. See also *Fifteenth U.S. Census, 1930*, vol. 3, pt. 2, p. 279; pt. 1, pp. 609, 1131, 248, 1338; *Sixteenth U.S. Census, 1940*, vol. 2, pt. 5, pp. 137, 177; pt. 2, p. 639; pt. 3, p. 889; pt. 1, p. 629; pt. 4, p. 448; *LA Times*, 26 Nov. 1967.

25. Fred W. Viehe, "Black Gold Suburbs: The Influence of the Extractive Industry on the Suburbanization of Los Angeles, 1890–1930," *Journal of Urban History* 8 (Nov. 1981): 3–26; Greg Hise, "Home Building and Industrial Decentralization in Los Angeles: The Roots of the Postwar Urban Region," *Journal of Urban History* 19 (Feb. 1993): 95–125.

26. Arnold Rampersad, *The Life of Langston Hughes* 1 (New York, 1986): 236; see also Faith Berry, *Langston Hughes, before and beyond Harlem* (Westport, Conn., 1983).

27. J. Max Bond, "The Negro in Los Angeles" (Ph.D. diss., Univ. of Southern California, 1936), p. 98; James McFarline Ervin, "The Participation of the Negro in the Community Life of Los Angeles" (M.A. thesis, Univ. of Southern California, 1931).

28. James Gregory, *American Exodus: The Dust Bowl Migration and Okie Culture in California* (New York, 1989), pp. 164–69, p. 168; see also Reed Massengill, *Portrait of a Racist: The Man Who Killed Medgar Evers* (New York, 1994). The convicted murderer of Evers, a NAACP leader, was Byron De La Beckwith; a section of his family moved from Mississippi and the South to Colusa, a region in California known as the "Little South" because of historic ties to the Confederacy.

29. John Arthur Maynard, *Venice West: The Beat Generation in Southern California* (New Brunswick, N.J., 1991), p. 11; see also Bruce Henstell, *Sunshine and Wealth: Los Angeles in the Twenties and Thirties* (San Francisco, 1984): "The legend . . . is that Los Angeles is a hastily thrown together smear of pink and blue stucco doll houses, inhabited by long-haired men and short-haired women, clairvoyants, herb doctors, swamis, chiropractors, nature lovers, depraved motion-picture actors, psychopathic murderers, painless dentists, bonds salesmen, gunmen, winos, radio announcers"; John Caughey, *California* (Englewood Cliffs, N.J., 1953).

30. Jill Marie Watts, " 'Shout the Victory': The History of Father Divine and the Peace Mission Movement, 1879–1942" (Ph.D. diss., UCLA, 1989), pp. 313, 324, 357, 423: Divine's movement made its "greatest impact in Los Angeles"; moreover, "while in most Peace Mission outposts, black and white disciples continued to worship separately, by 1934 the Los Angeles membership had surmounted racial lines and class barriers." In LA "late night orgies" and "homosexuality" were common. Jill Watts, *God, Harlem USA: The Father Divine Story* (Berkeley, Calif., 1992).

31. Jerry Cohen and William S. Murphy, *Burn, Baby, Burn!: The Los Angeles Race Riot, August 1965* (New York, 1966), p. 19.

32. Liabna K. Baebner, "Raymond Chandler's City of Lies," in *Los Angeles in Fiction,* ed. David Fine (Albuquerque, N.M., 1984), pp. 109–31, p. 124; see also S. U. Peters, "The Los Angeles Anti-Myth," in

Itinerary Seven: Essays on California Writers (Bowling Green, Ohio, 1978), pp. 21–34. Peters pointed to LA not as the site of the "American Dream" but its disastrous finish. The recurring symbol sketched is LA as a symbol of chaos and collapse, a charnel house for dreams, a world gone wrong, a Nathaniel West nightmare. For an even darker view of LA by an author who captures the city in fiction as well as Chester Himes, Nathaniel West, or Raymond Chandler, see Octavia Butler, *Parable of the Sower* (New York, 1993).

33. Lizette LeFalle-Collins, ed., *Home and Yard: Black Folk Expressions of Los Angeles* (Los Angeles, 1988), pp. 6–7.

34. Chester Himes, *Lonely Crusade* (New York, 1986), p. 17.

35. Robert Fogelson, *The Fragmented Metropolis: Los Angeles, 1850–1930* (Cambridge, Mass., 1967); Alonzo N. Smith, "Blacks and the Los Angeles Municipal Transit System," *Urbanism Past and Present* 6 (Winter–Spring 1981): 25–31; P. L. Clay, "The Process of Black Suburbanization," *Urban Affairs Quarterly* 14 (June 1979): 405–24; Kathryn P. Nelson, "Recent Suburbanization of Blacks: How Much, Who, and Where," *Journal of American Planning Association* 46 (July 1980): 287–300; David Gebhard and Hariette Von Breton, *L.A. in the Thirties, 1931–1941* (Salt Lake City, 1975).

36. DeGraaf, "Negro Migration to Los Angeles," 186; Smith, "Blacks and the Los Angeles Municipal Transit System," p. 28. See also Don Carleton, *Red Scare!: Right-Wing Hysteria, Fifties Fanaticism, and Their Legacy in Texas* (Austin, Tex., 1985).

37. Gerald D. Nash, *The American West Transformed: The Impact of the Second World War* (Bloomington, Ind., 1985), p. vii; Adler, "Watts," p. 262; Harlan Dale Unrau, "The Double V Movement in Los Angeles during the Second World War: A Study in Negro Protest" (M.A. thesis, California State Univ.–Fullerton, 1971), p. 118; Mark S. Foster, "Giant of the West: Henry J. Kaiser and Regional Industrialization, 1930–1950," *Business History Review* 59 (Spring 1985): 1–23; see also Kevin Allen Leonard, "The Impact of World War II on Race Relations in Los Angeles" (Ph.D. diss., Univ. of California–Davis, 1992).

38. John Modell, *The Economics and Politics of Racial Accommodation: The Japanese of Los Angeles, 1900–1942* (Urbana, Ill., 1977), p. 181; see also Bill Ong Hing, *Making and Remaking Asian America through Immigration Policy, 1850–1990* (Stanford, Calif., 1993).

39. Maya Angelou, "I Know Why the Caged Bird Sings," in *West of the West: Imagining California*, ed. Leonard Michaels et al. (San Francisco, 1989), pp. 221–24, p. 222: "The Yakamoto Sea Food Market quietly became Sammy's Shoe Shine Parlor and Smoke Shop. Yashigira's Hardware metamorphosed into La Salon de Beaute owned by Miss Clorinda Jackson. The Japanese shops which sold products to Nisei customers were taken over by enterprising Negro businessmen. . . . where the odors of tempura, raw fish and cha had dominated, the aroma of chitlings, greens and hamhocks now prevailed. The Asian population dwindled before my eyes . . . The Japanese area became San Francisco's Harlem in a matter of months." A similar process unfolded in the Pacific Northwest. See Quintard Taylor, Jr., "A History of Blacks in the Pacific Northwest, 1788–1970" (Ph.D. diss., Univ. of Minnesota, 1977), p. 225: "Blacks in Seattle and Portland moved into residential areas formerly occupied by Japanese citizens when the latter were placed in inland detention centers. In Seattle Afro-Americans also took over many of the small Japanese businesses." See also Quintard Taylor, *The Forging of a Black Community: Seattle's Central District through the Civil Rights Era* (Seattle, 1994).

40. Arna Bontemps and Jack Conroy, *They Seek a City* (Garden City, N.Y., 1945), p. 205.

41. Alonzo Nelson Smith, "Black Employment in the Los Angeles Area, 1938–1948" (Ph.D. diss., UCLA, 1978), p. 142. See also Gwendolyn Midlo Hall, *Africans in Colonial Louisiana: The Development of Afro-Creole Culture in the 18th Century* (Baton Rouge, La., 1992), pp. 323, 343. Tensions existed there between darker and lighter blacks; slave resistance in New Orleans in the eighteenth century often involved arson. See also Arnold Hirsch and Joseph Logsdon, eds., *Creole New Orleans: Race and Americanization* (Baton Rouge, La., 1992).

42. Walter Mosley, *A Red Death* (New York, 1991), pp. 15, 197.

43. Dorothy Dandridge and Earl Conrad, *Everything and Nothing: The Dorothy Dandridge Tragedy* (New York, 1970), pp. 79, 154.

44. Smith, "Black Employment in the Los Angeles Area," p. 17; Unrau, "The Double V Movement in Los Angeles during the Second World War," p. 140; E. Frederick Anderson, *The Development of Leadership and Organization Building in the Black Community of Los Angeles from 1900 through World War II* (Saratoga, Fla., 1980).

45. Nash, *The American West Transformed,* pp. 93, 94.

46. Interview with Buddy Collette, 11 Oct. 1990, Southern California Library.

47. Woody Strode and Sam Young, *Goal Dust: An Autobiography* (Lanham, Md., 1990), pp. 4, 7, 11, 50, 65, 125.

48. Taylor, "A History of Blacks in the Pacific Northwest."

49. Chester B. Himes, *If He Hollers Let Him Go* (Garden City, N.Y., 1945), p. 49.

50. Kenneth T. Jackson, "Race, Ethnicity, and Real Estate Appraisal: The Home Owners Loan Corporation and the Federal Housing Administration," *Journal of Urban History* 6 (Aug. 1980): 419–52; Kenneth T. Jackson, *Crabgrass Frontier: The Suburbanization of the United States* (New York, 1985); Sally Jane Sandoval, "Ghetto Growing Pains: The Impact of Negro Migration in the City of Los Angeles, 1940–1960" (M.A. thesis, California State Univ.–Fullerton, 1973). See also Francine F. Rabinowitz and William J. Siembieda, *Minorities in Suburbs: The Los Angeles Experience* (Lexington, Mass., 1977); Dorothy Slade Williams, "Ecology of Negro Communities in Los Angeles County: 1940–1959" (Ph.D. diss., Univ. of Southern California, 1961).

51. Rabow, "Watts," LACHRC Papers.

52. Lloyd H. Fisher, *The Problem of Violence: Observations on Race Conflict in Los Angeles* (Chicago, 1947), p. 11.

53. Harold Draper, "Jim Crow in Los Angeles," Workers Party file, 1946, Tamiment Institute.

54. Fisher, *The Problem of Violence.*

55. Smith, "Black Employment in the Los Angeles Area," pp. 317, 318, 340, 359.

56. Adler, "Watts," pp. 279, 293, 294; see also Mary Ellen Bell Ray, *The City of Watts, California: 1907 to 1926* (Los Angeles, 1985); R. L. Williams, "The Negro Migration to Los Angeles, 1900–1946," *Negro History Bulletin* 19 (1956): 112–13; Keith Collins, *Black Los Angeles: The Maturing of the Ghetto, 1940–1950* (Saratoga, Calif., 1980).

57. John Caughey et al., eds., *Los Angeles: Biography of a City* (Berkeley, Calif., 1977), p. 426.

58. Editorial, "Need for New Leadership," 17 Aug. 1965, broadcast 8:15 A.M., 6:25 P.M., 8:55 P.M., KNX-AM radio, no. 250, 107, box 21, McCone Papers; editorial, 17 Aug. 1965, KNX-AM radio, box 61, folder 5, John Holland Papers.

59. *New York Daily News,* 8 Dec. 1965; M. B. Jackson, c. Aug. 1965, KMPC-AM radio, box 61, folder 1, John Holland Papers; "Policy Statement of the National Lawyers Guild on the Watts Revolt," c. Aug. 1965, box 14, 102, McCone Papers; Sears and Conahay, *The Politics of Violence,* 9.

60. *LA Times,* 22 Aug. 1965.

61. Memo from Kevin O'Connell re interview with Curt Moody, 27 Sept. 1965, box 14, 31N, McCone Papers; *LA Times,* 22 Aug. 1965. Added the *Times,* "A ghetto with palm trees, flowers and some open space is as difficult for persons acquainted with eastern city slums to conceive as it is for them to envision it sprawled over 50 square miles."

62. *LA Times,* 15 Sept. 1965.

63. *Economist,* 21 Aug. 1965: "Many of the Los Angeles rioters are brothers under the skin to the baffled young men from London and its suburbs who spend their holidays stomping along the front at Brighton and Margate or breaking up bars in Calais and Ostend."

64. *Agenda* 2, no. 1 (1966), Record Group 7, box 10, James Corman Papers.

65. Robert Blauner, "Internal Colonialism and Ghetto Revolt," in *Conflict and Competition: Studies in the Recent Black Protest Movement,* ed. John Bracey et al. (Belmont, Calif., 1971), pp. 210–26, p. 214.

66. Della Rossa, *Why Watts Exploded: How the Ghetto Fought Back* (Los Angeles, 1966).

67. *LA Times,* 22, 19 Aug. 1965.

68. *LA Daily Journal,* 28 March 1966.

69. Donald J. McCrone and Richard J. Hardy, "Civil Rights Policies and the Achievement of Racial Economic Equality, 1948–1975," *American Journal of Political Science* 22 (Feb. 1978): 1–17, p. 1.

70. J. J. Morrow, "American Negroes: A Wasted Resource," *Harvard Business Review* 35 (Jan.–Feb. 1957): 65–74; *Newsweek,* 3 Sept. 1962; Jeffrey B. Nugent and Michael E. DePrano, "Productivity Costs to Society of Discrimination Including Educational Differences," vol. 17, McCone Transcript.

71. *LA Free Press,* 10 Feb. 1967.

72. W. J. Wethersby, *James Baldwin: Artist on Fire* (New York, 1989), p. 246; Fred L. Standley and Louis Pratt, *Conversations with James Baldwin* (Jackson, Miss., 1989); James Baldwin, *The Devil Finds Work* (London, 1976).

73. *New York Times Magazine,* 12 June 1966.

74. Vernon Allen, "Toward Understanding Riots: Some Perspectives," *Journal of Social Issues* 26, no. 1 (1970): 1–18.

75. President's Commission on Law Enforcement and the Administration of Justice, "Riots and Crime," in Simon Dinitz, et al., eds., *Deviance: Studies in the Process of Stigmatization and Societal Reaction* (New York, 1969), pp. 117–26, p. 120.

76. Joseph Boskin and Victor Pilson, "The Los Angeles Riot of 1965: A Medical Profile of an Urban Crisis," *Pacific Historical Review* 39 (Aug. 1970): 353–65; Kent Lloyd, "An End or a Beginning? Urban Race Riots vs. Effective Anti-Discrimination Agencies," 25 March 1966, box 61, folder 3, John Holland Papers; Robert M. Fogelson, "Violence and Grievances: Reflections on the 1960s Riots," *Journal of Social Issues* 26, no. 1 (1970): 141–63; Margaret J. G. Adudu et al., "Black Ghetto Violence: A Case Study Inquiry into the Spatial Pattern of Four Los Angeles Riot Event Types," *Social Problems* 19, no. 3 (1972): 408–26; Anthony Oberschall, "The Los Angeles Riot of August 1965," ibid., 15 (Spring 1968): 322–41; Lynne B. Iglitz, "Violence and American Democracy," *Journal of Social Issues* 26, no. 1 (1970): 165–86; David O. Sears and John McConahay, "Racial Socialization, Comparison Levels, and the Watts Riot," ibid., pp. 121–40.

77. Dr. Vernon Mark to Lyndon Baines Johnson, 8 Aug. 1967, reel 14, 0104, Kerner Commission Papers; see also Jack Harrison Pollack, "Psychiatrists Seek Secrets of the Riots," *Today's Health* 45 (Nov. 1967): 27–30; Nathan Cohen, ed., *The Los Angeles Riots: A Socio-Psychological Study* (New York, 1970); Philip Mercanto, ed., *The Kerner Report Revisited: Final Report and Background Papers* (Urbana, Ill., 1970).

78. *LA Herald Examiner,* 26 Aug. 1965, box 32, folder 9, Mervyn Dymally Papers.

79. *LA Times,* 15 Sept. 1965.

80. Interview with Archie Hardwick, 27 Oct., 23 Nov. 1965, vol. 15, McCone Transcript. Gov. Brown was also reputed to have said after the uprising, "Why, this is the worst disaster since my election." *New York Times Magazine,* 21 Aug. 1994.

81. *Fortune,* Nov. 1965; Paul Bullock, *Fighting Poverty: The View from Watts* (Los Angeles, 1967), p. 1; see also *LA Sentinel,* 19 Aug. 1965: Father Samuel Morrison, "a young white Episcopal priest and vice president of Los Angeles CORE known as 'Father Sam' said: 'This is the best thing that could happen. We've been asking, pleading for better housing, better facilities and by burning these buildings down we can show Mayor Yorty and his friends that they just can't sit on that anti-poverty money and not let us have it"; *LA Times,* 2 Sept. 1965: University of Southern California professor C. T. Hadwen noted that the "rioters were exhilirated and happy . . . for once they were released from their customary role of patient, long suffering victims of white indifference." The activist and entertainer Dick Gregory, who was wounded as he tried to calm the situation in LA, nonetheless retained his irreverence: "Course, I look at Watts as Urban Renewal without graft. . . . They're having an uprising against tyranny—against oppression. . . . There's no such thing as having a cancer in your foot, and then come by my house for dinner and tell me you haven't brought that germ with you." *Dick Gregory: An Interview* (Berkeley, Calif., 27 Sept. 1966), Niebyl-Proctor Library.

82. Chester Himes, *The Quality of Hurt: The Early Years, the Autobiography of Chester Himes* (New York, 1990), p. 73; *LA Sentinel*, 2 Sept. 1965; James Conant, "Social Dynamite in Our Large Cities," LACHRC Papers; James Conant, *My Several Lives: Memoirs of a Social Inventor* (New York, 1979); James Hershberg, *James B. Conant: Harvard to Hiroshima and the Making of the Nuclear Age* (New York, 1993).

83. Charles E. Fager, *Selma, 1965* (New York, 1974); David Garrow, *Protest at Selma: Martin Luther King, Jr., and the Voting Rights Act of 1965* (New Haven, 1978).

84. H. Edward Ransford, "Isolation, Powerlessness, and Violence: A Study of Attitudes and Participation in the Watts Riot," *American Journal of Sociology* 73 (March 1968): 581–91, p. 590.

85. *New York Times*, 17 Aug. 1965; *LA Weekly*, 24 Feb.–2 March 1989.

86. *LA Times*, 13 Oct. 1965.

87. Ibid., 13 Dec. 1965.

88. Albert Grundlingh, *Fighting Their Own War: South African Blacks and the First World War* (Johannesburg, South Africa, 1987), p. 1.

89. Bruce Michael Tyler, "Black Radicalism in Southern California, 1950–1982" (Ph.D. diss., UCLA, 1983), p. 1.

90. Iver Bernstein, *The New York City Draft Riots: Their Significance for American Society and Politics in the Age of the Civil War* (New York, 1990); Paul Gilje, *The Road to Mobocracy: Popular Disorder in New York City, 1763–1834* (Chapel Hill, N.C., 1987); see also Roger B. Manning, *Village Revolts: Social Protest and Popular Disturbances in England, 1509–1640* (New York, 1988).

91. John Dittmer, *Black Georgia in the Progressive Era, 1900–1920* (Urbana, 1977), pp. 123–30; Peter Whelan, *Captain Swing* (London, 1979); George Rudé, *The Face of the Crowd: Studies in Revolution, Ideology, and Popular Protest* (Atlantic Highlands, N.J., 1988).

92. Holt, *The Problem of Freedom*, p. 419.

93. Dileep Padgaonkar, ed., *When Bombay Burned* (New Delhi, 1994). Bombay is also the headquarters of India's booming film industry, which, like its counterpart in the United States, has attracted organized crime.

94. Donald Crummey, ed., *Banditry, Rebellion, and Social Protest in Africa* (Portsmouth, Eng., 1986); Baruch Hifson, *Year of Fire, Year of Ash. The Soweto Revolt: Roots of Revolution* (London, 1979).

2. Rising Up

1. Howard Jewel to Attorney General Stanley Mosk, 25 May 1964, box 60, folder 5, John Holland Papers: "I think it is truly a situation where a stitch in time would save nine. I only wish I could tell you where to start sewing—but you know [Police Chief William] Parker better than I do." See also testimony of Governor Edmund Brown, vol. 4, 53, McCone Commission Transcript.

2. E. R. Haines to McCone Commission, 14 Oct. 1965, 23a, box 12, McCone Papers. See also *Hearings before the United States Commission on Civil Rights*, in Los Angeles, Calif., 25–26 Jan. 1960 (Washington, D.C., 1960).

3. Hugh Manes, "A Report on Law Enforcement and the Negro Citizen in Los Angeles," c. 1962, LACHRC Papers–Bilbrew; *LA Sentinel*, 17 Aug. 1961.

4. Speech by H. H. Brookins, 18 Sept. 1965, Southern California Library; J. Gregory Payne and Scott C. Ratzan, *Tom Bradley, The Impossible Dream: A Biography* (Santa Monica, Calif., 1986), pp. 67, 70.

5. Harry M. Scobie, "Negro Politics in Los Angeles: The Quest for Power," Los Angeles, UCLA Institute of Government and Public Affairs, 1 June 1967; see also Beeman C. Patterson, "The Politics of Recognition: Negro Politics in Los Angeles, 1960–1963" (Ph.D. diss., UCLA, 1967).

6. Notecards, 11 Aug. 1965, box 4, McCone Papers.

7. "The Warning That Was Ignored," 23 Dec. 1965, BB4769, Pacifica Radio Archives.

8. Clipping, 12 Nov. 1964, box 20, ser. 3, Bustop Papers.

9. Harry M. Scobie, "Negro Politics in Los Angeles: The Quest for Power," in Cohen, *The LA Riots,* pp. 638–75.

10. *LA Sentinel,* 28 Jan., 4 Feb., 4 March 1965; *LA Times,* 3, 9 March 1965.

11. Minutes, 18 Jan. 1965, meeting of LA County on Human Relations Commission, LACHRC Papers. Vada Somerville, a close friend of W. E. B. Du Bois, served on this body.

12. Mike Davis, "Chinatown Revisited? The 'Internationalization' of Downtown Los Angeles," in *Sex, Death, and God in LA,* ed. David Reid (New York, 1992), pp. 19–53, p. 24.

13. Minutes, 15 March 1965, LACHRC Papers. Interestingly, the intial version of the minutes stated that the progressive Pacifica Foundation station, KPFK, should be asked to broadcast the segments, but— perhaps in a capitulation to Red Scare pressures—this was changed in the 19 April 1965 minutes to KGFJ.

14. *LA Free Press,* 19 March 1965; *LA Times,* 20 March 1965.

15. *LA Free Press,* 4 June, 9 July 1965.

16. *LA Herald-Dispatch,* 12 Aug. 1965.

17. Minutes, 28 April 1965, Los Angeles Board of Police Commissioners.

18. Elizabeth Poe, "Nobody Was Listening," in Caughey, *Los Angeles,* pp. 426–31.

19. *LA Times,* 31 May 1992.

20. Report by William Colby, 11 Nov. 1965, box 18, 16, McCone Papers.

21. "The Los Angeles Negro: Hidden Community—A Special Report," *Frontier,* June 1955, p. 6, cited in Adler, "Watts," p. 295.

22. Richard M. Elman, *Ill-at-Ease in Compton* (New York, 1967).

23. John Gibson, "Watts Area Improvements since 1951," LA City Council Report, Sept. 1965, box 62, folder 3, John Holland Papers. In 1960 the census showed 34,000 in Watts; the slow growth by 1965 was partially a reflection of harsh and unattractive conditions.

24. Eldridge Cleaver, *Soul on Ice* (New York, 1968), pp. 26–27.

25. Interview with Stanley Sanders, 2 Oct. 1990, Southern California Library.

26. Testimony of Herbert Atkinson, 4 Nov. 1965, 10:30 A.M., 11100 South Central Avenue, McCone Transcript.

27. Thomas Hines, "Housing, Baseball, and Creeping Socialism: The Battle of Chavez Ravine, Los Angeles, 1949–1959," *Journal of Urban History* 8 (Feb. 1982): 123–43, p. 141.

28. Samuel Yette, *The Choice: The Issue of Black Survival in America* (New York, 1971), p. 68: "The mayor's argument was that an all-white, five member group called the Youth Opportunity Board was sufficiently large to receive and disperse the funds." The Office of Economic Opportunity objected.

29. Memo from Ben Farber, Sept. [1965] Chron. file, box 14, McCone Papers.

30. "Hard Core Unemployment and Poverty in Los Angeles," prepared by the staff of the Institute of Industrial Relations at UCLA under a contract with the Area Redevelopment Administration of the U.S. Department of Commerce, 14 Dec. 1964, Bilbrew Library.

31. Thomas Sheridan to McCone Commission, 23 Nov. 1965, box 15, 16–30 Nov. Chron. file, McCone Papers.

32. Ashleigh Ellwood Brilliant, "Social Effects of the Automobile in Southern California during the Nineteen-Twenties" (Ph.D. diss., Univ. of Southern California, 1964), p. 248. Brilliant argued that "smog" was noted first in the region in 1943, citing the *LA Times,* 26 May 1943.

33. Memo to Chief Counsel, 30 Sept. 1965, box 4, McCone Papers.

34. *LA Times,* 13, 14 Aug. 1965. Nat Turner's antislavery revolt in Virginia took place in August 1831; Gabriel Prosser's revolt in Virginia took place in August 1800. John Hope Franklin, *From Slavery to Freedom: A History of Negro Americans* (New York, 1974), pp. 161–62; Herbert Aptheker, *American Negro Slave Revolts* (New York, 1943).

35. *LA Times,* 22 Aug. 1965; Lillard, *Eden in Jeopardy,* p. 238.

36. *LA Times,* 22 Aug. 1965.

37. William Colby, memorandum on "Weather," 22 Nov. 1965, box 4, McCone Papers.

38. *LA Times*, 22, 13 Aug. 1965.

39. "Booking and Property Record," 12 Aug. 1965, box 4, McCone Papers; report of Evelle Younger, LA County District Attorney, vol. 1, box 20, ibid.; see also Cohen and Murphy, *Burn, Baby, Burn!* p. 43.

40. *LA Times*, 3 Sept. 1965.

41. Thomas Sheridan to McCone Commission, 1 Nov. 1965, box 4, 2-a, McCone Papers; chronology, vol. 2, McCone Transcript.

42. *LA Times*, 13 Aug. 1965.

43. Ibid.; see also "The Fires of August," 10 Aug. 1990, 7:30 P.M., KABC-TV, LA. Bob Lewis, who was twenty-nine years old in 1965 and had served as a patrol officer for seven years, confirms the bulk of Minikus's account.

44. *LA Times*, 28 Oct. 1965.

45. Interview of Ralph Reese by Logan Lane, 22 Nov. 1965, 16–30 Nov. Chron. file, box 15, McCone Papers.

46. *LA Times*, 13 Aug. 1965.

47. Thomas Sheridan, memorandum, 1 Nov. 1965, Nov. Chron. file, box 15, McCone Papers; see also report of Evelle Younger, LA County District Attorney, 4 vol., box 20, ibid.

48. *LA Times*, 30 Aug. 1965.

49. Interview with Frank J. Beeson, Jr., 2 Nov. 1965, box 4, 4b, McCone Papers. One of the little recognized but significant factors complicating police and community relations in South LA was the distorting impact on the LAPD of being obligated to interact frequently with black "criminals." Because their experience with other kinds of blacks was limited due to hypersegregation, many white LAPD officers could believe that most blacks were, indeed, criminals.

50. Daryl Gates, with Diane K. Shah, *Chief: My Life in the LAPD* (New York, 1992).

51. Emergency Control Center Journal, box 4, McCone Papers. This account may not be necessarily accurate because most likely it was sent from the scene by a harried officer.

52. Notecards, 15 Sept. 1965, ibid.

53. *LA Times*, 12 Aug. 1965.

54. *Berkeley Post*, 22 Aug. 1965, box 32, folder 7, Mervyn Dymally Papers.

55. Testimony of Benjamin Perry, 4 Nov. 1965, 9:25 A.M., 11100 South Central Avenue, vol. 12, McCone Transcript. Perry's testimony, three months after the incident in question, may have been colored by subsequent emphases in certain accounts.

56. Interview with Leon Smith, 9 Nov. 1965, vol. 16, McCone Transcript; interview with Herbert Carter, 10 Nov. 1965, box 5c, McCone Papers.

57. John Buggs, "A Chronological Report of the Los Angeles Riot and the Staff Involvement of the Los Angeles County Commission on Human Relations," c. 1965, LACHRC Papers.

58. Oral history, Sam Yorty, 27 Sept. 1985, UCLA Oral History.

59. Notecards, 16 Sept. 1965, box 4, McCone Papers.

60. Testimony, 2:43, McCone Transcript.

61. Notecards, 16 Sept. 1965, box 4, McCone Papers.

62. Interview with Leon Smith, 9 Nov. 1965; *LA Times*, 13 Aug. 1965.

63. Emergency Control Center Journal, box 4, McCone Papers.

64. Interview of the Reverend Casper I. Glenn by David Butterfield, 5 Nov. 1965, box 5b, ibid. The interview was done on 28 Oct. 1965 and transcribed by 5 Nov. Glenn was born in Winnsboro, S.C., went to Coulter Memorial Academy, and graduated from Lincoln University and Temple University; his psychiatric training was at Temple Medical College. From 1946 to 1952 he was in Baltimore, then New Orleans in 1956–64.

65. Testimony of John Buggs, 5:34, 36, McCone Transcript. The subsequent revelation that black

leaders like Buggs would intentionally spread inaccurate rumors did not improve their relations with younger, more militant blacks.

66. Testimony, 2:43, 71, ibid.

67. Testimony of John Buggs, 5:46, ibid.

68. Interview of Rev. Glenn, McCone Papers.

69. Ibid.

70. Notecards, 28 Sept. 1965, box 4, ibid.; testimony of Opal Jones, 6 Oct. 1965, 10:16, 73, McCone Transcript: "My understanding as to what took place as was reported to me in feedback, was that Mr. Buggs was treated with disrespect as a person who, it was felt, had nothing at all to do with the work of the police department in giving any such recommendation as he was giving." Ms. Jones was director of the Neighborhood Adult Participation Project and director of the Avalon Community Center, which was funded by the United Way, the Disciples of Christ, and Christian churches generally in the region. She had served since 1958.

71. Interview of John Buggs, box 5-b, McCone Papers.

72. Ibid.

73. Interview of H. Claude Hudson, 1 Nov. 1965, vol. 15, McCone Transcript.

74. Interview of Herbert Carter by Benjamin Farber, 10 Nov. 1965, box 5c, McCone Papers.

75. Interview of Herbert Carter, Ibid.

76. Malcolm Richards and William C. Gilkey to Thomas Sheridan, 27 Oct. 1965, box 4, 3-a, ibid.

77. Report by William C. Gilkey, 4 Oct. 1965, box 5b, ibid.; memo of interview with Everette Hodge by William C. Gilkey, box 4, 3-c, ibid.

3. Death in the Afternoon, Evening, and Morning

1. *LA Times*, 15, 22 Aug. 1965.

2. *LA Sentinel*, 2 Sept. 1965.

3. John Buggs, "Report from Los Angeles," *Journal of Intergroup Relations* 5 (Autumn 1966): 27–40, 29, 31, 36; testimony of John Buggs, 5:32, McCone Transcript.

4. *Report of the National Advisory Commission on Civil Disorders* (New York, 1968), pp. 38, 498.

5. Emergency Control Center Journal, Notecards 3, 13 Aug. 1965, 3:30 P.M., box 4, McCone Papers; Michael Meyerson, "After the Massacre," *Crossroads* 1 (Sept. 1991): 18–22, p. 20.

6. *LA Times*, 16 Aug. 1965.

7. Folder, "Watts Rebellion," Aug. 1965, undated clipping, Southern California Library.

8. Testimony of Warren Dorn, 19 Oct. 1965, vol. 6, McCone Transcript.

9. Notecards 3, 13 Aug. 1965, box 4, McCone Papers.

10. *LA Times*, 15 Sept. 1965.

11. Notecards 3, 13 Aug. 1965, box 4, McCone Papers.

12. "The Fire This Time," produced and edited by Trevor Thomas for the Center for the Study of Democratic Institutions, Santa Barbara, no. 309, Pacifica Radio Archives.

13. Emergency Control Center Journal, Notecards 4, 14 Aug. 1965, 3:58 P.M., box 4, McCone Papers.

14. *LA Times*, 15 Aug. 1965. The employment of this reporter suggests how the tactic of attacking journalists because of their race did lead directly to the press hiring more blacks.

15. Testimony, 2:229, McCone Transcript.

16. Lt. Gen. Roderic Hill to Thomas Sheridan, 9 Nov. 1965, box 19, 105, McCone Papers.

17. Cohen and Murphy, *Burn, Baby, Burn!* p. 159.

18. *Berkeley Post*, 22 Aug. 1965. The use of "family disputes" as a leading indicator may suggest that the revolt allowed long-suffering black men in particular to focus their anger on the authorities rather than their loved ones.

19. Interview of Leon Smith, 9 Nov. 1965, vol. 16, McCone Transcript.

20. Report of interview with Ulysses Prince, 10 Nov. 1965, ibid.

21. *LA Herald Examiner,* 13 Aug. 1965.

22. Interview with Hugh Manes, 27 Oct. 1965, box 21, 106, v. 2, McCone Papers.

23. Notecards 2, 12:17 A.M., 13 Aug. 1965, box 4, ibid.

24. Testimony of William H. Parker, 16 Sept. 1965, 2 P.M., McCone Transcript.

25. California National Guard, "Military Support for Law Enforcement during Civil Disturbances: A Report Concerning the California National Guard's Part in Suppressing the Los Angeles Riot," undated (c. August 1965), p. 9, UCLA Law Library.

26. Testimony of Lt. Gov. Glenn M. Anderson, 22 Sept. 1965, 10 A.M., room 1070, New State Building, 107 S. Broadway, Los Angeles, vol. 3, McCone Transcript.

27. Deposition of Richard Kline, 19 Oct. 1965, vol. 9, ibid.

28. Interview with H. Claude Hudson, 1 Nov. 1965, vol. 15, ibid.

29. Notecards 2, 13 Aug. 1965, 10 A.M., box 4, McCone Papers.

30. Notecards 3, 13 Aug. 1965, 5:26 P.M., ibid.

31. Office of Chief Medical Examiner, City of Los Angeles, Medical Report no. 19911, 13 Oct. 1965, 9:30 A.M., ACLA.

32. Memorandum by Benjamin S. Farber, interview of Ulysses S. Prince, 10 Nov. 1965, box 5c, McCone Papers.

33. Office of Chief Medical Examiner, City of Los Angeles, Medical Report no. 19903, tape no 1-146A, ACLA.

34. Ibid., Medical Report no. 19905.

35. "In the Matter of the Inquisition upon the Body of George Adams, Jr.," Old Hall of Records, room 501, City of Los Angeles, ACLA.

36. Office of Chief Medical Examiner, City of Los Angeles. Medical Report no. 19906, ACLA.

37. Ibid., Medical Report no. 19915.

38. *LA Times,* 14 Aug. 1965.

39. Edward Stewart, *The Great Los Angeles Fire* (New York, 1980), p. 7; see also Margaret Leslie Davis, *Rivers in the Desert: William Mulholland and the Invention of Los Angeles* (New York, 1993).

40. Raymond Ford, Jr., *Santa Barbara Wildfires* (Santa Barbara, Calif., 1991).

41. Stewart, *Great Los Angeles Fire,* p. 109; see also Stephen J. Pyne, *Burning Bush: A Fire History of Australia* (New York, 1991); Margaret Hindle Hazen and Robert M. Hazen, *Keepers of the Flame: The Role of Fire in American Culture, 1775–1925* (Princeton, N.J., 1992); cf. M. Catherine Miller, *Flooding the Courtrooms: Law and Water in the Far West* (Lincoln, Nebr., 1993).

42. Marc Reisner and Sarah Bates, *Overtapped Oasis: Reform or Revolution for Western Water* (Washington, D.C., 1990); see also Donald Worster, *Rivers of Empire: Water, Aridity, and the Growth of the American West* (New York, 1985).

43. "Anonymous" interview with W. J. Patterson, 18 Nov. 1965, box 11, 21e, McCone Papers.

44. Memorandum of Yvonne Brathwaite, 8 Nov. 1965, ibid.

45. *LA Times,* 13 Sept. 1991.

46. Report of Carl W. Wullschlager, 14 Sept. 1965, box 6, 10b, McCone Papers.

47. Memorandum to Chief Counsel, "Rioters Arrested for Arson or Attempted Arson," 19 Nov. 1965, box 7, 12a (25), ibid.

48. Report of Interview with Father Samuels, 24 Oct. 1965, vol. 16, McCone Transcript; Col. Rex Applegate, *Riot Control: Materiel and Techniques* (Boulder, Colo., 1981).

49. Cohen and Murphy, *Burn, Baby, Burn!* pp. 162, 163.

50. Memorandum, 30 Sept. 1965, R1478, 6500377, FFA.

51. Hilton F. Jarrett, "Fire Data from the Watts Riot: Results of Preliminary Analysis and Evaluation,"

Work Unit no. 2611C, EOC Operations Study, 10 May 1966, System Development Corporation, 2500 Colorado Avenue, Santa Monica, Calif. 90406.

52. *LA Times*, 24 Aug. 1965; Paul Ditzel, "Firemen Tackle Multiple Incendiary Fires," *Fire Engineering* 1 (1966): 47–48.

53. Testimony of William Parker, 16 Sept. 1965, pp. 43, 44, McCone Transcript.

54. Interview with Hayward Erwing, 1965, box 6, 12a(18), McCone Papers.

55. Interview with Vernon B. Brooks, 1965, and interview with Thurman Moore, 1965, box 6, 12a(10), ibid.

4. Fire/Guns

1. *LA Times,* 15 Aug. 1965.

2. Ibid., 16, 17 Aug. 1965.

3. Ibid., 18 Aug. 1965; *Life,* 27 Aug. 1965.

4. *LA Times,* 25 Aug. 1965; see also ibid., 19 Aug. 1965.

5. KABC-TV editorial, 13–15 Sept. 1965, box 22, 108, no. 5465, McCone Papers; *Closer Up* 21, no. 18 (27 Aug. 1965), reel 28, no. C35, Right Wing Collections, Univ. of Iowa.

6. *LA Herald Examiner,* 21 Sept. 1965.

7. Kevin Flynn and Gary Earhardt, *The Silent Brotherhood: Inside America's Racist Underground* (New York, 1989), p. 359.

8. *LA Times,* 15 Aug. 1965.

9. Ibid., 14 Aug. 1965.

10. Ibid.

11. Deposition of John W. Billett, 19 Oct. 1965, vol. 3, McCone Transcript; John W. Billett to John A. Mitchell, 19 Oct. 1965, box 5, 6a, McCone Papers.

12. Testimony of Lt. Gen. Roderic L. Hill, 21 Sept. 1965, 10 A.M., vol. 13, McCone Transcript.

13. Notecards 4, 14 Aug. 1965, 12:30 P.M., box 4, McCone Papers.

14. *Report of the National Advisory Commission on Civil Disorders,* p. 498.

15. Notecards 4, 14 Aug. 1965, box 4, McCone Papers.

16. *LA Times,* 29 Nov. 1991; see also "Amended Rule No. 1," by Gov. Edmund Brown, 15 Aug. 1965, box 5, 7a, ibid. During the curfew no one was to be outside between 8 P.M. and sunrise, "starting at the intersection of Washington Boulevard and Alameda Street, then proceeding westerly to Flower Street, then [from] Flower Street to Adams Blvd., then westerly on Adams Blvd. to Crenshaw Boulevard, then southerly on Crenshaw Boulevard to Florence Avenue, then easterly on Florence Avenue to Van Ness Avenue, southerly to Van Ness Avenue to Rosecrans Avenue, then easterly on Rosecrans Avenue to Alameda, northerly on Alameda Street to the starting point, all named streets included."

17. Notecards 4, 14 Aug. 1965, box 4, ibid.

18. *LA Times,* 15 Aug. 1965.

19. Verdict of coroner's jury, "Inquisition upon the Body of Montague Whitmore," 21 Sept. 1965, ACLA.

20. "Inquest Held on the Body of Warren Earl Tilson," 14 Oct. 1965, ibid.

21. "In the Matter of the Inquisition upon the Body" of Albert Flores, Jr., 21 Sept. 1965, ibid.

22. Office of Chief Medical Examiner, LA, 19 Oct. 1965, ibid.

23. City of Los Angeles, Hospital Department, Coroner's Case no. 19924, Medical Report no. 19924, 20 Oct. 1965, 9:30 A.M.; and "In the Matter of the Inquisition upon the Body of Carlton Elliot," 20 Oct. 1965, ibid.

24. "In the Matter of the Inquisition upon the Body of Andrew Houston, Jr.," 22 Oct. 1965, ibid.

25. *Violence in the City: An End or a Beginning?* (Sacramento, Calif., 1965), p. 174.

26. Office of Chief Medical Examiner, LA, Coroner, Case Report no. 19928, crypt no. 30A, ACLA.

27. Ibid., Case Report no. 19926.

28. "Verdict of Coroner's Jury," 15 Sept. 1965, and Office of Chief Medical Examiner, LA County, Case Report no. 19935, ibid.

29. *LA Times,* 28 Aug. 1991.

30. *LA Free Press,* 1 Oct., 25 Dec., 17 Sept. 1964.

31. Cohen and Murphy, *Burn, Baby, Burn!* p. 73.

32. *San Francisco Chronicle,* 15 Aug. 1965.

33. Interview with Daniel Horowitz, 2 Nov. 1991.

34. Paul Bullock, ed., *Watts: The Aftermath, an Inside View of the Ghetto by the People of Watts* (New York, 1969), p. 45.

35. Memorandum from Adrian Dove, Consultant, California Department of Industrial Relations, 17 Aug. 1965, vol. 15, McCone Transcript.

36. *LA Times,* 16 Aug., 10 Oct. 1965.

37. Memorandum, 16 Aug. 1965, 11 A.M., box 33, Ramsey Clark Papers.

38. Office of Chief Medical Examiner, LA Case Report no. 19968, ACLA.

39. Ibid., Coroner's Case Report no. 19959.

40. Mercedes Madrid, Claimant, to City of LA, undated, c. 1965, no. 67-60.23.1, ibid.

41. Office of Chief Medical Examiner, LA Coroner's Case no. 19965, ibid.

42. Ibid., Coroner's Case no. 20028, tape no. 3-35B.

43. Ibid., Coroner's Case no. 19962.

44. Ibid., Coroner's Case no. 19967.

45. Ibid., Coroner's Case no. 19969.

5. "The Hearing Children of Deaf Parents"

1. Interview with Jerry Gaines, c. 1965, box 6, 12a, McCone Papers.

2. Adrian Dove to Clyde Graham, 17 Aug. 1965, box 60, folder 4, John Holland Papers.

3. Paul O'Rourke to Gov. Brown, 19 Aug. 1965, ibid.

4. Interview with Alice Harris, 11 Aug. 1990, Southern California Library. Harris observed that those burning had "turbans" and "spoke with an accent."

5. Malcolm Richards and William Gilkey, 3 Nov. 1965, interview with Lelia Hodge, 2667 South Vermont, Nov. Chron. file, box 15, McCone Papers.

6. *LA Free Press,* 20 Aug. 1965: Robert Freeman of CORE was told by some revolt participants that "although they were not a part of the non-violent civil rights movement, they had waited and hoped that the voices of protest from these people would be heeded. But, since the non-violent people had been slapped in the face, they would do it their way."

7. "The Fire This Time," 28 Oct. 1965, B1353, Pacifica Radio Archives. This idea that the events of August 1965 were in large part an expression of unhappiness with black leadership struck the black assemblyman from South LA, Mervyn Dymally, who as a result called the uprising a "class revolt," not just a race issue. *LA Herald Examiner,* 24 Aug. 1965, box 33, folder 4, Mervyn Dymally Papers.

8. *LA Free Press,* 18 June 1965.

9. Christopher Rand, *Los Angeles: The Ultimate City* (New York, 1967), p. 126.

10. Nathan Caplan, "The New Ghetto Man: A Review of Recent Empirical Studies," *Journal of Social Issues* 25, no. 1 (1970): 59–73, p. 71.

11. Notecards 3, 13 Aug. 1965, 5:30 P.M., box 4, McCone Papers.

12. Rhett Jones, "Patterns of Race Hate in the Americas before 1800," *Trotter Institute Review* 5 (Summer 1991): 4–12; see also Robert Park, *The Collected Papers of Robert Ezra Park* (New York, 1974).

13. Sidney Verba and Norman H. Nie, *Participation in America: Political Democracy and Social Equality* (New York, 1972), p. 151.

14. Interview with Yvonne Gerioux, conducted by Alice Campbell, 3 Nov. 1965, box 12, 25a, McCone Papers.

15. H. Edward Ransford, "Skin Color, Life Chances, and Anti-White Attitudes," *Social Problems* 18, no. 2 (1970): 164–79, p. 164.

16. *LA Sentinel,* 19 Aug. 1965, 16–22 Aug. 1990.

17. *LA Times,* 13 Aug. 1965; see also *Sacramento Bee,* 22 Aug. 1965.

18. *LA Times,* 14 Aug. 1965.

19. Ibid.

20. Ibid.

21. "The Wall," 10 Sept. 1965, BC0326, Pacifica Radio Archives.

22. Emergency Control Center Journal, LAPD, 15 Aug. 1965, 7:30 P.M., box 4, McCone Papers.

23. Testimony of Lt. Gov. Glenn Anderson, McCone Transcript, p. 18.

24. Adrian Dove to Clive Graham, 17 Aug. 1965, box 11, 21f, McCone Papers.

25. *LA Times,* 13 Aug. 1965.

26. Charles Silberman, "Beware the Day They Change Their Minds," *Fortune,* Nov. 1965, box 8, 18a, McCone Papers.

27. Interview with H. Claude Hudson, 1 Nov. 1965, box 10, 20k, ibid.

28. Interview with Zara Buggs Taylor, 21 Sept. 1990.

29. Testimony of John Buggs, McCone Transcript, p. 27.

30. Interview, Frieta Shaw Johnson, c. Aug. 1990, Southern California Library.

31. *LA Times,* 28 Sept. 1989.

32. Gayle T. Tate, "Black Nationalism: An Angle of Vision," *Western Journal of Black Studies* 12, no. 1 (1988): 40–64; Edith Folb, *Black Vernacular Vocabulary: A Study of Intra/Inter-cultural Concerns and Usage* (Los Angeles, 1973); Robert M. Kahn, "The Political Ideologies of Martin Delany," *Journal of Black Studies* 14 (June 1984): 415–40; Editor, "The Racial Disturbance in Los Angeles," *Frontier* 13, no. 8 (1962): 3–4: "Dire predictions have been made of future racial disturbances in Los Angeles"; see also Michael Edson Robinson, *Cultural Nationalism in Colonial Korea, 1920–1925* (Seattle, 1988); William L. Van Deburg, *New Day in Babylon: The Black Power Movement and American Culture, 1965–1975* (Chicago, 1992); John T. McCartney, *Black Power Ideologies: An Essay in African-American Political Thought* (Philadelphia, 1992).

33. Testimony of Antone Peter Jasich and Raymond Hill, 19 Oct. 1965, vol. 8, McCone Transcript; see also testimony of George Brunton, 21 Oct. 1965, vol. 4, ibid.: He reminded the commission that because it was "too dry, too windy. . . . we [could] have lost all of the southern part of Los Angeles."

34. K. E. Klinger, "Riot Fires Report—Watts Area," 11–18 Aug. 1965, ibid.

35. Jasich-Hill testimony, McCone Transcript; see also *LA Times,* 2 Sept. 1965: Deputy Fire Chief Hill averred: "There were so many fires that we had to knock one fire down and move on to the next one. We didn't have time to completely extinguish the fires . . . some of those rocks [thrown] were the size of my hat."

36. George Warheit and E. L. Quarantelli, *An Analysis of the Los Angeles Fire Department Operations during Watts,* for Office of Civil Defense, Office of the Secretary of the Army, Disaster Research Center Monograph Series, no. 7, Contract OCD-PS-64-46, Work Unit 2651-A (Washington, D.C., 1969). This detailed report was distributed widely among the armed services—e.g., chief of naval research, "Weapons Systems Evaluation Group" at the Pentagon, "US Army Combat Development Command," etc.—and to such research agencies as the Hudson Institute, Stanford Research Institute, Institute for Defense Analysis, and the Civil Defense Research Project at Oak Ridge.

37. *LA Times,* 17 Aug. 1965.

38. Ibid., 15 Aug. 1965; Frank R. Palmieri, President, Department of Water and Power, to Irvin Walden, 20 May 1966, box 60, folder 6, John Holland Papers.

39. Jasich-Hill testimony, McCone Transcript, p. 33; see also Los Angeles Fire Department, "The South-Central Los Angeles Riot Fires," c. 1965, box 61, folder 3, John Holland Papers.

40. *LA Times,* 19 Aug. 1965.

41. *LA Herald Examiner,* 1 Sept. 1965, box 33, folder 7, Mervyn Dymally Papers.

42. Marnesba Tackett, 26 April 1984, UCLA Oral History.

43. Milton A. Senn to Jerry Rosen, 19 Nov. 1965, box 5, 9-a (7–21), McCone Papers.

44. Interview with Jesse Robinson, 20 Oct. 1965, vol. 16, McCone Transcript; interview with Jesse Robinson, 20 Oct. 1965, box 14, Oct. Chron. file, 153, McCone Papers; see also Max Vorspan and Lloyd Garther, *History of the Jews of Los Angeles* (San Marino, Calif., 1970).

45. Interview with Richard Marshal, 8 Nov. 1965, box 11, 21e, McCone Papers. Marshal is identified as "Mr. Smith," a forty-three-year-old mechanic, in the interview with Mr. Smith, 8 Nov. 1965, vol. 16, McCone Transcript.

46. Memorandum from Sam Williams re interview with Hyman Hanes, 3 Nov. 1965, box 15, Nov. Chron. file, McCone Papers.

47. Report by Logan Lane, c. Nov. 1965, box 5, 9-a (7–21), ibid.

48. Report by William Colby of interview with Richard Walker, 15 Nov. 1965, ibid.

49. Report by William Colby, 3 Dec. 1965, ibid.

50. *LA Times,* 15 Aug. 1965; Emergency Control Center Journal, 15 Aug. 1965, 1:05 P.M., box 4, McCone Papers; "LAPD Photos of Damaged Buildings," Aug. 1965, box 6, 9-a, ibid. In these hundreds of photos are images of young black men and women sprawled on sidewalk with televisions surrounding them, images of police officers with rifles trained on suspects, etc. There are photos of buildings with "BURN" written on them and others with such signs as "Negro owned operated, We shall overcome."

51. *LA Sentinel,* 19 Aug. 1965.

52. *LA Herald-Dispatch,* 26 Aug. 1965.

53. Interview with Alfred Stalford, Chair, Housing and Community Development Commission of California, by Yvonne Brathwaite, 23 Nov. 1965, box 15, 16–30 Nov. Chron. file, McCone Papers.

54. Walter J. Raine, "The Ghetto Merchant Survey," in Cohen, *The LA Riots,* pp. 602–37, p. 610.

55. Notecards 5, box 4, McCone Papers; see also report by William Colby, 27 Oct. 1965, box 5, 9-a (2–7), ibid.

56. Tyler, "Black Radicalism in Southern California," p. 42; *Chico Enterprise,* 8 Dec. 1965.

57. Office of Chief Medical Examiner, LA Coroner's Case no. 19970, ACLA. The deceased's attorney, Hugh Manes, sought to intervene in the hearing, but his request was denied.

58. Ibid., Coroner's Case no. 19976.

59. Ibid., Coroner's Case no 19971.

60. *Violence in the City* 2:174.

61. Office of Chief Medical Examiner, LA Coroner's Case no. 19990, ACLA.

62. Ibid., Coroner's Case no. 19998.

63. Ibid., Coroner's Case no. 20001.

6. Black Scare

1. *LA Times,* 28 Aug. 1965; see also David Boesel and Peter H. Rossi, eds., *Cities under Siege: An Anatomy of the Ghetto Riots, 1964–1968* (New York, 1971).

2. Don Will Fong to John Holland, 20 Aug. 1965, box 61, folder 5, John Holland Papers.

3. *Long Beach Independent,* 7 Dec. 1965.

4. Ibid., 6 Dec. 1965.

5. *Paramount-Hollydale Herald American,* 9 Dec. 1965.

6. *LA Times,* 16, 19 Aug. 1965; notecards 4, 15 Aug. 1965, 1:20 A.M., box 4, McCone Papers.

7. *LA Times,* 30, 21, 17 Aug. 1965.

8. Sidney Fine, *Violence in the Model City: The Cavanagh Administration, Race Relations, and the Detroit Riot of 1967* (Ann Arbor, 1989), p. 172; Bruce Porter and Marvin Dunn, *The Miami Riot of 1980: Crossing the Bounds* (Lexington, Mass., 1984); *New York Times*, 23 July 1967.

9. *LA Times*, 22, 16 Aug. 1965.

10. Memorandum from Logan Lane, 22 Oct. 1965, box 21, 106, McCone Papers.

11. *New York Times*, 18 Aug. 1965. Watts was a question of U.S. foreign policy because the sight of blacks being gunned down in the streets weakened Washington's stance atop the moral high ground in its ongoing confrontation with Moscow.

12. Office of the Chief Medical Examiner, LA Coroner's Case no. 20006, tape no. 3-35B, ACLA.

13. *LA Times*, 18 Aug. 1965.

14. Donald Craig Parson, "Urban Politics during the Cold War: Public Housing, Urban Renewal, and Suburbanization in Los Angeles" (Ph.D. diss., UCLA, 1985), pp. 131, 133, 148, 154; Peter Levy, *The New Left and Labor in the 1960s* (Urbana, Ill., 1994); see also David Farber, ed., *The Sixties: From Memory to History* (Chapel Hill, N.C., 1994); Bret Neal Eynon, "Community, Democracy and the Reconstruction of Political Life: The Civil Rights Influence on New Left Political Culture in Ann Arbor, Michigan, 1958–1966" (Ph.D. diss., New York Univ., 1993).

15. Bruce Perry, *Malcolm: The Life of a Man Who Changed Black America* (New York, 1991), p. 167; C. Eric Lincoln, *The Black Muslims in America* (Boston, 1961); Clifton E. Marsh, *From Black Muslims to Muslims: The Transition from Separatism to Islam, 1930–1980* (Metuchen, N.J., 1984).

16. *Muhammad Speaks*, 6 Aug., 29 Jan 1965; *LA Times*, 13 Aug. 1965, 29 April 1962.

17. Perry, *Malcolm*, pp. 191–92. That those who allegedly died were not of the class responsible for the actions of the LAPD was lost amid the proclaimed "end of ideology." It was enough that the dead were white, and their ultimate sacrifice would balance the death of Stokes, a black man.

18. *Muhammad Speaks*, 12 Feb. 1965. Featured here is a picture of "nine innocent Muslims, victims of police brutality and terror tactics in Los Angeles." Dispatched by the NOI to investigate was "Supreme Captain Raymond Sharieff" of Fruit of Islam, the paramilitary arm of the NOI, and the son-in-law of Elijah Muhammad.

19. Report to Board of Police Commissioners, Minutes of 16 June 1965. The police were apparently oblivious to the First Amendment implications of their surveillance and proposals.

20. *LA Herald Examiner*, 16 Sept. 1965; *LA Times*, 9 Sept., 17 Aug. 1965; report, 15 Aug. 1965, McCone Transcript, p. 210.

21. Monna Utter to John McCone, 20 Aug. 1965, box 4, McCone Papers; Gary Allen, "The Plan to Burn Los Angeles" (John Birch Society), undated box 33, folder 5, Mervyn Dymally Papers.

22. Memorandum from Kevin O'Connell, 20 Sept. 1965, and report, "Did 'Black Muslims' Instigate the Los Angeles Riots," c. 1965, box 17, 104, McCone Papers.

23. Memorandum, 16 Aug. 1965, box 33, Ramsey Clark Papers.

24. Testimony of John Buggs, vol. 5, McCone Transcript.

25. Interview with Archie Hardwick, 27 Oct., 23 Nov. 1965, box 8, 16, McCone Papers; see also Hakim A. Jamal, *From the Dead Level: Malcolm X and Me* (New York, 1973).

26. *LA Times*, 19 Aug. 1965.

27. Ibid., 17 Oct. 1971.

28. Ibid., 19 Aug. 1965.

29. Ibid.

30. "Special Report," by Councilman Billy G. Mills, 1965, box 61, folder 2, John Holland Papers.

31. *LA Times*, 19 Sept. 1965; statement of Frank Miller, 1965, reel 12, 1022, Kerner Commission Papers.

32. *LA Times*, 21 Sept. 1965, 8 Feb. 1966, 23 Nov. 1965.

33. "Report of Investigation," 16 Sept. 1965, McCone Papers.

34. *Muhammad Speaks,* 3 Sept., 27 Aug. 1965.

35. *LA Sentinel,* 16 Sept. 1965.

36. *LA Times,* 16 Aug. 1965; *Muhammad Speaks,* 27 Aug. 1965.

37. *Muhammad Speaks,* 27 Aug. 1965. Said Powell, "An oppressed people can only internalize their anger and fury so long. . . . Los Angeles . . . [is] only the visible [spark] of the volcano of discontent and hatred which lies quietly beneath the surface now in black communities all over America."

38. *Muhammad Speaks,* 20 Aug. 1965.

39. *LA Free Press,* 3 Sept. 1965: Said Shabazz about snipers during the revolt: "A man firing pot shots is not a sniper. . . . Of course there weren't any snipers." *LA Times,* 24 Sept. 1965: Shabazz was forced to cancel a talk in Woodland Hills due to threats of bombings, etc. Notecards 5, box 4, 18 Aug. 1965, 6:40 P.M., Emergency Control Center Journal, McCone Papers: This reflects evidence of surveillance of Shabazz by the authorities: "John Shabazz and Edward Sherold, Chief Muslim Guard, just arrived at International Airport from Chicago."

40. Asa Call to Thomas R. Sheridan, 27 Sept. 1965, box 21, 106, v.4, McCone Papers.

41. Minutes of commission meeting, 13 Sept. 1965, box 21, 106, McCone Papers.

42. Memorandum from Hugh Taylor, 1 Sept. 1965, vol. 16, McCone Transcript.

43. *Sacramento Bee,* 22 Nov. 1965, box 32, folder 17, Mervyn Dymally Papers.

44. *LA Sentinel,* 3 Feb. 1966.

45. *LA Times,* 24 June 1966.

46. *Jet,* 16 Sept. 1965.

47. *LA Times,* 6 Sept. 1965.

48. James O'Toole, *Watts and Woodstock: Identity and Culture in the U.S. and South Africa* (New York, 1973), p. 126; Tom Tomlinson, "Ideological Foundations for Negro Action: Militant and Non-Militant Views," in Cohen, *The LA Riots,* pp. 326–79.

49. "Confidential" memorandum from "Office of the Commissioner," 3 Sept. 1965, "Area Training and Riot Control," 8 Sept. 1965, box 18, 105, McCone Papers.

50. "A Black Dissent from Watts," 1965, reel 9, 0125, Kerner Commission Papers.

51. Interview with Richard Simon, 15 Oct. 1965, box 13, 31I, McCone Papers.

52. "Report on the Negro Riot in Los Angeles," by American Eugenics Party, c. 1965, box 61, folder 5, John Holland Papers. The import of the rise of black nationalism was reflected in the bizarre case of the former NOI minister Yahweh Ben Yahweh. From his headquarters in South Florida, during the 1980s he presided over a multimillion-dollar religious empire that was based in part on extortion, firebombing, and murder. Despite his fiery antiwhite rhetoric, he was embraced by the Miami establishment. Why? One writer has argued that his robed and turbaned followers, who came to number in the thousands, represented "the ghetto moneyed Miami hungered for: a docile, disciplined, unquestioning supply of labor whose leaders loved capitalism." See Sydney P. Freedberg, *Brother Love: Murder, Money, and a Messiah* (New York, 1994), p. 180.

7. Iron Fist

1. *LA Weekly,* 19–25 July 1991; *Santa Barbara News-Press,* 22 July 1991. Cannon described a "police state" as a "state characterized by repressive, arbitrary authoritarian rule."

2. Payne and Ratzan, *Tom Bradley,* pp. 34–35; Martin J. Schiesl, "Behind the Badge: The Police and Social Discontent in Los Angeles since 1950," in Klein and Schiesl, *20th Century Los Angeles,* pp. 153–94, p. 153. Robert Vernon, *LA Justice: Lessons from the Firestorm* (Colorado Springs, Colo., 1993).

3. Testimony of Augustus Hawkins, 20 Sept. 1965, vol. 8, McCone Transcript.

4. *LA Sentinel,* 16–22 Aug. 1990.

5. Mike Rothmiller and Ivan Goldman, *LA Secret Police: Inside the LAPD Elite Spy Network* (New York, 1992), pp. 29–46.

6. Tyler, "Black Radicalism in Southern California," p. 183.

7. *LA Times*, 11 Oct. 1965; George M. O'Connor, "The Negro and the Police in Los Angeles" (M.A. thesis, Univ. of Southern California, 1955); Joseph G. Woods, "The Progressives and the Police: Urban Reform and the Professionalization of the Los Angeles Police" (Ph.D. diss., UCLA, 1973); Ed Cray, "The Police and Civil Rights," *Frontier* 13, no. 7 (1962): 5–11; *California Eagle*, 16 April 1964; *LA Times*, 10 May 1962.

8. McKeller, "Watts: Little Rome," pp. 213–18, p. 215; see also, "Conversation with Mr. Harold Ackerman, Chief Deputy District Attorney," 2 Nov. 1965, Nov. Chron. file, box 15, McCone Papers. This memorandum concerns the rape, allegedly by the LAPD, of an arrested woman who then died; "she was apparently pregnant and had intercourse with someone else between the incident and her appearance before the Grand Jury."

9. *National Law Journal*, 25 March 1991; see also John DeSantis, *The New Untouchables: How America Sanctions Police Violence* (Chicago, 1994).

10. Bullock, *Watts*, 141.

11. Testimony of Walter Colwell, 12 Oct. 1965, vol. 5, McCone Transcript.

12. Spencer Crump, *Black Riot in Los Angeles: The Story of the Watts Tragedy* (Los Angeles, 1966), p. 27; deposition of William H. Parker, 24 Nov. 1965, vol. 11, McCone Transcript; see also, Dean Jennings, "Portrait of a Police Chief," *Saturday Evening Post* 232 (7 May 1960): 87, 89; James Gazell, "William Parker, Police Professionalization, and the Public: An Assessment," *Journal of Police Science and Administration* 4 (March 1976): 31–32.

13. *LA Mirror*, 26 Jan. 1960; *Time*, 27 Aug. 1965; *LA Times*, 11 May 1962; "Police Chief William H. Parker Speaks," undated, prepared by Community Relations Conference of Southern California, box 60, folder 4, John Holland Papers.

14. Testimony of William H. Parker, 16 Sept. 1965, 2 P.M., vol. 11, McCone Transcript.

15. *LA Times*, 12, 7 Oct. 1965.

16. Deposition of Winslow Christian, 18 Oct. 1965, 9:30 A.M., 5:59, McCone Transcript: "There was a general feeling on the part of people who were observing and participating in these events from the point of view of the state that Chief Parker was resistant to communication on the part of the Negro leadership . . . indeed resistant to communication on the part of our people at times. We did not find with him the easy and helpful exchange that one would expect in dealings with another jurisdiction that is trying to handle a common problem. . . . Well, I remember hearing regret expressed at his statement to the effect that 'They are underneath and we are on top at this point' which did not seem to us a statesman like thing to say."

17. Testimony of John Ferraro, 13 Oct. 1965, vol. 6, ibid.; testimony of William H. Parker, 17 Sept. 1965, 2 P.M., 11:93, ibid.

18. Michael Hannon, "Behind the Watts Revolt," *New Politics* 4, no. 3 (1965): 36–40, p. 39; Crump, *Black Riot in Los Angeles*, p. 26.

19. *LA Times*, 12 Sept. 1965.

20. *Village Voice*, 16 April 1991.

21. R. E. Driscoll to Jim Corman, undated, group 7, box 10, James Corman Papers.

22. LAPD Community Relations–Public Information Division, Oct. 1965, box 18, 105, McCone Papers.

23. Tom Bradley to Sam Williams, 15 Sept. 1965, box 14, 101, v. 2, ibid.

24. William Becker to Warren Christopher, 13 Oct. 1965, box 14, 102, McCone Papers; interview of Capt. Thomas King by James White, Nov. Chron. file, box 15, ibid. Concluded the interviewer: "He tends to categorize people and causes and to make generalizations without adequate supporting data. This is unfortunate in men with his responsibilities." See also testimony of James Fisk, 10 Oct. 1965, and deposition of Jack L. Eberhardt, 18 Oct. 1965, vol. 6, McCone Transcript.

25. *LA Times*, 19 Aug. 1965.

26. Meeting with James Williams, 23 Sept. 1965, Sept. Chron. file, box 14, McCone Papers.

27. Interview with Willie F. Brown, 4 Oct. 1965, vol. 15, McCone Transcript. See also interview with Herbert Atkinson, 31 Oct. 1965, ibid.

28. *LA Sentinel,* 2 Sept. 1965.

29. Interview with Thomas G. Neusom, 10 Nov. 1965, vol. 16, McCone Transcript.

30. ACLU Report, reel 13, Kerner Commission Papers.

31. *LA Sentinel,* 19 Aug. 1965; Ben Fraber to Thomas Sheridan, 29 Sept. 1965, box 4, 3-c, McCone Papers.

32. *LA Times,* 13 Aug. 1965.

33. "Police Malpractice and the Watts Riot," report by the ACLU of Southern California, reel 12, 0999, Kerner Commission Papers.

34. Photographs, box 23, McCone Papers.

35. *LA Times,* 15 Aug. 1965.

36. ACLU Report.

37. Interview with DeKovan Richard Bowie, undated, box 6, 12a (14), McCone Papers. The desire to return to Africa could be heightened given such comments.

38. ACLU Report.

39. Ibid. The competing explanation—which stressed that blacks were brutalized at the behest of an elite so they would be stigmatized, work for less, and not object—had been nullified by the Red Scare.

40. *LA Times,* 22 Nov. 1965.

41. Memorandum from Logan Lane, 2 Nov. 1965, box 13, 31K, McCone Papers.

42. ACLU Report.

43. *LA Sentinel,* 2 Sept. 1965; Thomas Sheridan to John Ferraro, 22 Nov. 1965, box 15, 16–30 Nov. Chron. file, McCone Papers; W. Fitzhugh Brundage, *Lynching in the New South: Georgia and Virginia, 1880–1930* (Urbana, Ill., 1993).

44. "Report from Los Angeles," 1965, BB1557, Pacifica Radio Archives. A key aspect of NOI theology was the idea that African-Americans were Asiatic; this reflected the long-standing ties between the NOI and Tokyo that appeared again when Elijah Muhammad was accused of being of Japanese ancestry; see also Louis Farrakhan, *Back Where We Belong: Selected Speeches* (Philadelphia, 1989); Louis Farrakhan, *Seven Speeches* (New York, 1974).

45. Testimony of Tom Bradley, 30 Sept. 1965, 11:55 A.M., vol. 3, McCone Transcript.

46. Gary Marx, "Civil Disorder and the Agents of Social Control," *Journal of Social Issues* 26, no. 1 (1970): 19–57, pp. 21, 35.

47. LAPD, "Seven Days in August," *Police Chief* 34, no. 4 (1967): 26–32, p. 26; memorandum from H. C. Sullivan, 18 May 1966, box 60, folder 6, John Holland Papers.

48. Sullivan memorandum.

49. Notecards 3, 13 Aug. 1965, 4:30 P.M., box 4, McCone Papers.

50. Testimony of Roger Murdock, 12 Oct. 1965, vol. 10, McCone Transcript; see also *LA Times,* 13 Oct. 1965: Murdock was criticized by the McCone Commission for allegedly stating that blacks should be sent into South LA to quell the uprising because they are seen less easily. See also Marx, "Civil Disorder and the Agents of Social Control," p. 39: "The directors of the LA Human Relations Commission had worked out a plan to send in 400 black plainsclothes officers and several hundred anti-poverty workers to make inconspicuous arrests and spread positive rumors ('the riot is over'). . . . Young gang leaders promised to use their influence to stop the riot and were led to believe that these conditions would be met."

51. Testimony of Thomas Reddin, 14 Oct. 1965, vol. 12, McCone Transcript; cf. also James G. Fisk, Inspector, LAPD, to John Holland, 23 Nov. 1964, box 61, folder 1, John Holland Papers; press release, undated, c. 1966, box 62, folder 4, ibid.: This concerns the interim report, issued after twenty-six hearings, of the Police, Fire, and Civil Defense Committee of the LA City Council.

52. Testimony of Richard Simon, 13 Oct. 1965, vol. 13, McCone Transcript, pp. 8, 36.

53. Memorandum from Daryl Gates, 27 Oct. 1967, reel 10, 0736, Kerner Commission Papers.

54. Notecards, 2 Nov. 1965, box 4, McCone Papers.

55. Judge J. B. Lawrence to Warren Christopher, 1965, box 14, 101, vol. 3, ibid.

56. Cohen and Murphy, *Burn, Baby, Burn!* p. 94.

57. *LA Times*, 16, 18 Aug. 1965; "On Duty Injured as a Result of the Riot," 1965, box 4, McCone Papers.

58. Interview with Sgt. Vivian Strange, 1965, box 13, 31I, McCone Papers.

59. Cohen and Murphy, *Burn, Baby, Burn!* p. 195.

60. J. A. Mitchell to Warren Christopher, 22 Nov. 1965, box 15, McCone Papers.

61. Testimony of William Parker, 16 Sept. 1965, 4 P.M., vol. 11, McCone Transcript.

62. *LA Sentinel*, 2 Sept. 1965; *LA Times*, 11 Dec. 1965.

63. *LA Times*, 14 Dec., 16 Sept. 1965.

64. Ibid., 17 Oct. 1965.

65. Testimony of Mrs. Ozie Gonzaque, 4 Nov. 1965, 2:15 P.M., vol. 7, McCone Transcript.

66. Minutes, Executive Committee, 15 March 1965, LACHRC Papers.

67. Testimony of John Gibson, vol. 7, McCone Transcript.

68. "Region I: Disaster Law Enforcement Instructional Guide [for] Crowd and Riot Control," Coordinator, Peter Pitchess, Jan. 1963; "Region I: Disaster Law Enforcement Operations Plan Supplement No. 3: Manpower and Resources," Coordinator, Peter Pitchess, April 1963; and "Region I Disaster Law Enforcement Planning Guide Disaster Operations," Coordinator Peter Pitchess, June 1963, box 4, McCone Papers. The roles of the highway patrol and local police, like that of Downey, were detailed; see also Jack J. Roth, *The Cult of Violence: Sorel and the Sorelians* (Berkeley, Calif., 1980).

69. Notecards, 20 Sept. 1965, ibid.

70. Testimony of James F. Downey, 26 Oct. 1965, vol. 6, McCone Transcript.

71. Testimony of Willie F. Brown, 4 Nov. 1965, 11:40 A.M., vol. 4, ibid.; Himes, *Lonely Crusade*, p. 32.

72. Testimony of Peter Pitchess, 20 Sept. 1965, 12: 6, 10, 25, McCone Transcript; *LA Herald-Examiner*, 5 Nov. 1965.

73. Testimony of Chief William H. Parker, 17 Sept. 1965, 2 P.M., 11:118, McCone Transcript.

74. Testimony of William K. Ingram, 22 Sept. 1965, 2 P.M., 8:87, 111, ibid.

75. Memorandum from Sam Williams, 22 Sept. 1965, box 14, Sept. Chron. file, McCone Papers.

76. *LA Sentinel*, 19 Aug. 1965.

77. Transcript, "Meet the Press," 29 Aug. 1965, box 33, Ramsey Clark Papers; James White to Thomas Sheridan, 15 Sept. 1965, box 4, 2-a, McCone Papers.

78. Testimony of Bradford M. Crittenden, 17 Sept. 1965, 10 A.M., 5:67, McCone Transcript; Bradford M. Crittendon to Thomas Sheridan, 15 Oct. 1965, box 4, 2-a, McCone Papers.

79. Lt. Gen. Roderic Hill to Arthur Alarcon, 27 Sept. 1963, box 19, 105, McCone Papers; testimony of Roger Murdock, 10:47, 50, McCone Transcript.

80. "Emergency Plan for the State Military Forces," Cal-EP-62, 20 Nov. 1962, Military Department, State of California, box 5, 6c, McCone Papers.

81. Gen. Roderic Hill to Arthur Alarcon, 30 July 1963, box 5, 6a, ibid.

82. Testimony of William H. Parker, 17 Sept. 1965, 2 P.M., 9:98, McCone Transcript.

83. Testimony of Lt. Gov. Glenn Anderson, 22 Sept. 1965, 10 A.M., 3:4, 22, 24, 137, 58, ibid.

84. Memorandum of Kevin O'Connell, 12 Oct. 1965, box 4, McCone Papers.

85. Anderson testimony, pp. 67, 62.

86. Glenn Anderson, "100 Hours," 21 Aug. 1965, box 60, folder 5, John Holland Papers; *LA Times*, 14 Dec. 1994: Anderson, a World War II infantry sergeant, was also a real estate developer in Hawthorne before his election.

87. Deposition of Richard Kline, 19 Oct. 1965, 9:15,34, McCone Transcript.

88. Memorandum by John McCone, 23 Sept. 1965, box 14, McCone Papers.

89. *San Francisco Chronicle,* 14 Aug. 1965, box 32, folder 7, Mervyn Dymally Papers; *Long Beach Independent,* 17 Dec. 1965.

90. Richard G. Lillard, *Eden in Jeopardy; Man's Prodigal Meddling with His Environment: The Southern California Experience* (Westport, Conn, 1966), pp. 40, 97.

91. "National Guard Troops Commitment to Los Angeles Riot Area," box 4, McCone Papers; see also Robert W. Coakley, *The Role of Federal Military Forces in Domestic Disorders, 1789–1878* (Washington, D.C., 1988).

92. *LA Times,* 22 Aug. 1965.

93. Ibid., 26 May 1990.

94. Ibid., 19 Aug. 1965.

95. Report from Adrian Dove, 17 Aug. 1965, box 60, folder 4, John Holland Papers.

96. Memorandum from Adrian Dove, 17 Aug. 1965, vol. 15, McCone Transcript.

97. *LA Times,* 26 May 1990.

98. *LA Sentinel,* 19 Aug. 1965; *LA Times,* 18 Aug. 1965, box 33, folder 6, Mervyn Dymally Papers.

99. Julian Hartt, "Riot Duty: The California National Guard at Watts," *National Guardsman* 19 (Oct. 1965): 8–13.

100. *Long Beach Telegram,* 22 Dec. 1965; William Becker to Lt. Gen. Roderic Hill, 8 Sept. 1965, box 14, 101, vol. 2, McCone Papers.

101. Note, "Riot Control and the 4th Amendment," *Yale Law Journal* 81, no. 3 (1968): 625–37.

102. *LA Times,* 17 Dec. 1965; see also *LA Herald-Examiner,* 17 Dec. 1965.

103. Memorandum of John McCone, 23 Sept. 1965, Sept. Chron. file, box 14, McCone Papers.

104. Deposition of Roderic Hill, Adjutant General, 23 Nov. 1965, vol. 8, McCone Transcript.

105. Testimony of Charles Adam Ott, 18 Oct. 1965, vol. 1, ibid.; see also J. A. Mitchell memorandum of conversation with Lt. Gen. Hill, 5 Oct. 1965, box 5, McCone Papers.

106. Winston Wilson, Major General, National Guard, to Chief of Staff, U.S. Army, 19 Aug. 1965, box 19, 105, McCone Papers; see also Roderic Hill to Thomas Sheridan, 23 Nov. 1965, vol. 8, McCone Transcript.

107. California National Guard, "Military Support of Law Enforcement during Civil Disturbances," undated (c. Aug. 1965), UCLA Law Library.

108. *LA Times,* 23 Oct. 1965: Lt. Gen. Hill was decorated for actions during the uprising.

109. Tyler, "Black Radicalism in Southern California," p. 193.

110. Mike Davis, *City of Quartz: Excavating the Future in Los Angeles* (New York, 1990).

111. Louis Tackwood et al., *The Glass House Tapes* (New York, 1973), pp. 30, 222.

112. *LA Times,* 10 Sept. 1965.

113. Memorandum from William Colby, 22 Nov. 1965, box 15, 16–30 Nov. Chron. file, McCone Papers.

114. Paul Jacobs memorandum, reel 9, 0115, Kerner Commission Papers; see also David H. Bayley, *Police for the Future* (New York, 1994).

115. "Complaints to Commission, re: LAPDD," undated, box 13, 31a, McCone Papers.

116. *Violence in the City,* p. 32.

117. Resolution, Board of Directors of the Apartment Association of LA County, 6 Oct. 1965, box 61, John Holland Papers; Gates, *Chief.*

118. *LA Sentinel,* 28 Oct. 1965; *LA Times,* 21 Oct. 1965.

119. *LA Sentinel,* 23 Sept. 1965.

120. Testimony of Billy Mills, 10:66, McCone Transcript.

121. Memorandum of Harold Horowitz, 1 Nov. 1965, Nov. Chron. file, box 15, McCone Papers; Minutes, Board of Police Commissioners, 18 Aug. 1965, ACLA.

122. *LA Herald-Dispatch,* 18 Sept. 1965.

123. *LA Sentinel,* 1 Aug. 1991.

124. John V. Lindsay and Otto Kerner to Lyndon Baines Johnson, 10 Aug. 1967, reel 15, 0370, Kerner Commission Papers.

125. *LA Times,* 21 Oct., 17 Nov. 1965; *L.A. Sentinel,* 27 Jan. 1966.

8. The Old Leadership

1. Unrau, "The Double V Movement in Los Angeles during the Second World War."

2. *California Sun-Reporter,* 25 Aug. 1962.

3. Memorandum from John McCone, 6 Oct. 1965, box 14, Oct. Chron. file, McCone Papers.

4. *LA Times,* 26 Aug. 1965; *Newsweek,* 30 Aug. 1965.

5. *LA Times,* 18 Aug. 1965.

6. Ibid., 14 Aug. 1965.

7. Report by Kevin O'Connell of interview with Saul Alinsky, 30 Nov. 1965, box 8, 18-c, McCone Papers; Gloria Harrison, "The National Association for the Advancement of Colored People in California" (M.A. thesis, Stanford Univ., 1949). For an account of the life and career of a leading member of LA's black middle class, who happened to be related to NAACP patriarch H. Claude Hudson, see Karen Hudson, *Paul R. Williams, Architect: A Legacy of Style* (New York, 1993); see also Louis E. Lomax, *The Negro Revolt* (New York, 1963).

8. Tarea Hall Pittman to Gloster Current, 30 Dec. 1958, box 15, NAACP Papers–West.

9. H. Claude Hudson to Gloster Current, 23 July 1965, Frederick Spann to Norman Houston, 30 March 1965, NAACP Papers.

10. Tarea Hall to Roy Wilkins, 30 July 1964, box A155, NAACP Papers–West.

11. Leonard Carter to Lucille Black, 3 Aug. 1965, NAACP Papers; see also *LA Sentinel,* 29 July 1965.

12. Roy Wilkins to Norman Houston, 29 Dec. 1948, box 15, NAACP Papers–West.

13. Herbert Wright to Bennet Johnson, 10 April 1956, ibid.

14. Lester Bailey to Roy Wilkins, et al., 21 Nov. 1956, Estelle Van Meter to NAACP, 5 June 1956, NAACP Papers.

15. Biography of Loren Miller, box 19, 105, McCone Papers.

16. Del Coffey to Roy Wilkins, 22 April 1960, NAACP Papers; "Resolution No. 73," NAACP 53d Annual Convention Resolution, July–Aug. 1962, Atlanta, NAACP–West Papers.

17. Thurgood Marshall to Franklin Williams, 3 March 1955, Loren Miller to Thurgood Marshall, 1 March 1955, Tarea Pittman to Franklin Williams, 12 March 1955, box 15, NAACP Papers–West.

18. Zella Taylor to Roy Wilkins, 26 Dec. 1957, NAACP Papers; see also affidavit re 1958 LA Branch Election-Protest, 18 Dec. 1958, box 15, NAACP Papers–West.

19. Press release, LA Branch, 24 Aug. 1961, NAACP Papers. In a bit of mythmaking that illustrated the complexity of a compounded racism, novelist Bebe Moore Campbell spoke recently of a time "in the 40's and 50's . . . [in] the downtown hotels . . . everybody serving your table is going to be an older black man. Well, now they are Latino." *New York Times Magazine,* 25 Dec. 1994.

20. Roy Wilkins to H. Claude Hudson, 5 Oct. 1961, ibid.

21. Gloster Current to Ed Warren, 5 Feb. 1962, ibid.; Tarea Hall Pittman to Gloster Current, 4 Sept. 1964, NAACP Papers–West.

22. "Gwennie" to Gloster Current, 11 Jan. 1963, NAACP Papers.

23. Tarea Hall Pittman to Roy Wilkins, 24 Jan. 1961, ibid.

24. Editorial comment, Robert Sutton, VP-KNX-LA, broadcast 9 May 1962, and Gloster Current to Branches, 26 March 1963, ibid.

25. *LA Herald Examiner,* 1 Aug. 1962.

26. H. Claude Hudson to *LA Times,* 18 April 1963, NAACP Papers.

27. H. Claude Hudson to Roy Wilkins, 24 May 1963, ibid.

28. Legal Redress Committee, LA NAACP, 1965 Annual Report, ibid.

29. Minutes, NAACP Board, 11 Oct. 1965, ibid.

30. Louise Springs to Leonard Carter, 7 Sept. 1965, ibid.; *LA Sentinel,* 2 Sept. 1965; press release, 8 Oct. 1965, box 8, 18-a, NAACP Papers–West.

31. Biography of Norman Houston, box 19, 105, McCone Papers.

32. Norman Houston to Gloster Current, 8 Sept. 1965, box 19, 105, ibid.; see also Norman Houston to Gloster Current, 8 Sept. 1965, NAACP Papers.

33. Minutes, NAACP Board, 13 Sept. 1965, and Norman Houston to Roy Wilkins, 13 Oct. 1965, NAACP Papers.

34. *LA Times,* 4 Oct. 1965.

35. Ibid., 27 Oct. 1965.

36. *New York Times,* 5 Sept. 1965.

37. Leonard Carter to Gloster Current, 27 Oct. 1965, NAACP Papers.

38. *LA Sentinel,* 27 Jan. 1966.

39. Testimony of Norman Houston, 12 Oct. 1965, 8:9, 12, 13, 18, 19, McCone Transcript.

40. Testimony of Christopher L. Taylor, 25 Sept. 1965, 13:17, 28, 21, 42, ibid.

41. Susan Mary Strohm, "Black Community Organization and the Role of the Black Press in Resource Mobilization in Los Angeles from 1940 to 1980" (Ph.D. diss., Univ. of Minnesota, 1989), pp. 88, 90, 119, 122, 150.

42. Joyce Marie DeLoach Brooks, "A Case Study: The Role of Black Groups in Achieving Educational Equity for Black Children in the Los Angeles Unified School District" (Ph.D. diss., UCLA, 1979), pp. ix, 43.

43. John W. Crawford to Wesley R. Brazier, 9 Oct. 1965, box 8, 16, McCone Papers; see also biography of Wesley Brazier, executive director of NUL, c. 1965, box 17, 105, ibid.; *LA Times,* 15 Oct. 1965: Here Brazier called for a Marshall Plan for Watts.

44. Mitchell Gordon and Robert Goldman, "The Unsettled Settlement House: An Evaluation of the Neighborhood Association," Aug. 1969, 002321, FFA.

45. August Meier and Elliott Rudwick, *CORE: A Study in the Civil Rights Movement, 1942–1968* (New York, 1973), pp. 74, 150, 358.

46. William Russell Ellis, Jr., *Operation Bootstrap: A Case Study in Ideology and the Institutionalization of Protest* (Ph.D. diss., UCLA, 1969), pp. 3, 72.

47. Interview with Don Smith, 3 Nov. 1965, vol. 16, McCone Transcript; see also report by William Gilkey of interview with Don Smith, 3 Nov. 1965, box 8, 18-a, McCone Papers.

48. Testimony of Wendell Collins, 4 Nov. 1965, vol. 5, McCone Transcript.

49. *LA Sentinel,* 19 Aug. 1965.

50. *LA Times,* 21 Aug. 1965; see also Sydarshan Kapur, "Gandhi and the Afro-American Community, 1919–1955: A Study of the Image and Influence of the Gandhian Movement in the Black Communities of America before the Coming of Martin Luther King, Jr." (Ph.D. diss., Univ. of Denver, 1989).

51. *Nation,* 3 March 1991; *LA Times,* 18 Aug. 1965.

52. *LA Times,* 18 Aug. 1965.

53. Ibid., 19 Aug. 1965.

54. Ibid., 20 Aug. 1965.

55. Ibid., 19 Aug. 1965.

56. Martin Luther King, Jr., "Beyond the Los Angeles Riots," *Saturday Review,* reel 12, 0930, Kerner Commission Papers.

57. *LA Times,* 22 Aug. 1965. By 1994 the NAACP in LA was still mired in stagnation. A columnist in the *Los Angeles Sentinel* of 15 Dec. 1994 noted that in the previous five years "the branch membership dropped from 8,000 to back under 2,000. The branch's annual meeting had less than fifty people in atten-

dance. . . . About 280 people (mostly from one group) voted in this last election, down from 1,600 five years ago."

9. The New Leadership

1. James William Gibson, *Warrior Dreams: Paramilitary Culture in Post-Vietnam America* (New York, 1994), p. 304. By the 1990s many of these gangs were mired in murderous internecine conflict. There were numerous slayings, "drive-by shootings," and worse. Unlike the gangs that had been so helpful in crushing left-wing unionism at film studios in Culver City and Burbank, these gangs were not allowed to expand into other territories, because of racism and hypersegregation. See also E. Anthony Rotundo, *American Manhood: Transformations in Masculinity from the Revolution to the Modern Era* (New York, 1993); Richard Slotkin, *Regeneration through Violence: The Mythology of the American Frontier, 1660–1860* (Middletown, Conn., 1973); Klaus Theweleit, *Male Bodies: Psychoanalyzing the White Terror,* vol. 2 of *Male Fantasies,* trans. Erica Carter and Chris Turner (Minneapolis, 1977). Unfortunately, intimate past relations between black and white men could be infected with violence; this was part of being deemed the "female of the races." *State v. Maner,* 2 Hill 453, Dec. 1834: "The defendant and Phail [a slave], who . . . were on terms of intimacy, got into a quarrel and a fight ensued, after which the defendant shot him"; "the defendant was indicted for an assault . . . with an intent to murder . . . verdict of guilty," in Helen Honor Catterall, ed., *Judicial Cases concerning American Slavery and the Negro* (Washington, D.C., 1926–37), p. 355. It is well recognized that rape of black women by white men during and after slavery has roiled race relations; the extent to which rape and sexual assault of black men by white men occurred is unclear. Recent allegations in New York City concerning the rape of black men by a nonblack police officer illuminates how the issue of rape has shaped black masculinity. See *Village Voice,* 3 Jan. 1995, 27 Dec. 1994. See also George Chauncey, *Gay New York: Gender, Urban Culture, and the Making of the Gay Male World, 1890–1940* (New York, 1994).

2. *LA Times,* 22 Aug. 1965; see also ibid., 14 Aug. 1965: "Area Appears Devoid of Community Leadership." See also Carlton Goodlett to Leon Washington, 6 July 1963, Franklin Williams to Carlton Goodlett, 25 Aug. 1965, reel 1, Carlton Goodlett Papers: These letters concern an effort to hold a California Leadership Conference to fill the presumed leadership void; *L.A. Sentinel,* 22 July 1965.

3. Herbert Haines, *Black Radicalism and the Civil Rights Mainstream, 1954–1970* (Knoxville, Tenn., 1988).

4. *LA Times,* 17 Oct. 1965.

5. Richard Hofstadter, *Anti-Intellectualism in American Life* (New York, 1963).

6. Dwight C. Smith, *The Mafia Mystique* (New York, 1975); Robert Kelly, ed., *Organized Crime: A Global Perspective* (Totowa, N.J., 1986); Perry Bruce Kaufman, "The Best City of Them All: A History of Las Vegas, 1930–1960" (Ph.D. diss., Univ. of California–Santa Barbara, 1974); Jonathan Kwitny, *Vicious Circles: The Mafia in the Marketplace* (New York, 1979); Dennis Eisenberger et al., *Meyer Lansky: Mogul of the Mob* (New York, 1979); Peter Reuter, *Disorganized Crime* (Cambridge, Mass., 1985); Robert Lacey, *Little Man: Meyer Lansky and the Gangster Life* (Boston, 1991); Knoedelseder, *Stiffed;* see also, forthcoming, Horne, *Class Struggle in Hollywood.*

7. *LA Times,* 22 Aug. 1965.

8. Pearson, *The Shadow of a Panther;* Rufus Schatzberg, *Black Organized Crime in Harlem, 1920–1930* (New York, 1993); Elaine Brown, *A Taste of Power: A Black Woman's Story* (New York, 1992); Huey Newton, *Revolutionary Suicide* (New York, 1974); Bobby Seale, *A Lonely Rage: The Autobiography of Bobby Seale* (New York, 1978); David Hilliard, *This Side of Glory: The Autobiography of David Hilliard and the Story of the Black Panther Party* (Boston, 1993).

9. Todd Gitlin, *The Sixties: Years of Hope, Days of Rage* (New York, 1987); Kirkpatrick Sale, *SDS: Ten Years toward a Revolution* (New York, 1973).

10. Van Deburg, *New Day in Babylon.*

11. *LA Times,* 17 Oct. 1965.

12. Memorandum from K. V. Hansen, 24 Nov. 1965, Nov. Chron. file, box 15, McCone Papers.

13. Winston, *Strategy for a Black Agenda.*

14. *New York Post,* 20 Aug. 1965.

15. *LA Free Press,* 3 Sept. 1965; *LA Times,* 1 Oct. 1965; flyer N-VAC, "Boycott, Baby, Boycott!" Southern California Library.

16. *LA Times,* 2 Sept. 1966.

17. Douglas G. Glasgow, *The Black Underclass: Poverty, Unemployment, and Entrapment of Ghetto Youth* (San Francisco, 1980), pp. 112, 138, 145.

18. Bond, "The Negro in Los Angeles," p. 139. See also Carlos Clarens, *Crime Movies: An Illustrated History* (New York, 1980).

19. Leon Bing, *Do or Die* (New York, 1991), pp. xiv, 148; Kody Scott, *Monster: The Autobiography of an L.A. Gang Member Sanyika Shakur, a.k.a. Monster Kody Scott* (New York, 1993); Martin Sanchez Jankowski, *City Bound: Urban Life and Political Attitudes among Chicano Youth* (Albuquerque, 1986); Martin Sanchez Jankowski, *Islands in the Street: Gangs and American Urban Society* (Berkeley, Calif., 1991).

20. Maureen Cain and Alan Hunt, *Marx and Engels on Law* (New York, 1979); David Greenberg, ed., *Crime and Capitalism: Readings in Marxist Criminology* (Philadelphia, 1993); David Cantor and Kenneth Land, "Unemployment and Crime Rates in Post–World War II United States: A Theoretical and Empirical Analysis," *American Sociology Review* 50 (Spring 1985): 317–32.

21. Arnold J. Heidenheimer, Hugh Heclo, and Carolyn Teich Adams, *Comparative Public Policy: The Politics of Social Choice in Europe and America* (New York, 1983); Gosta Esping-Anderson, *Politics against Markets: The Social Democratic Road to Power* (Princeton, N.J., 1985).

22. Pauline Young, *Pilgrims of Russian-Town* (New York, 1967).

23. Eric J. Hobsbawm, *Bandits* (New York, 1985), p. 31; Tony Platt, "'Street Crime': A View from the Left," *Crime and Social Justice* 9, no. 1 (1978): 26–34.

24. Robert Cribb, *Gangsters and Revolutionaries: The Jakarta People's Militia and the Indonesian Revolution, 1945–1949* (Sydney, Aus., 1990); Louis Perez, *Lords of the Mountain: Social Banditry and Peasant Protest in Cuba, 1878–1918* (Pittsburgh, 1989); Rosalie Schwartz, *Lawless Liberators: Political Banditry and Cuban Independence* (Durham, N.C., 1989).

25. *Arizona Republic,* 9 Sept. 1965; interview with Irvin Williat, c. 1965, box 14, 32g, McCone Papers.

26. Malcolm W. Klein, "Juvenile Gangs, Police, and Detached Workers: Controversies about Intervention," *Social Service Review* 39, no. 2 (1965): 183–90, p. 189.

27. Presentation of Harold Muntz, box 19, 105, 5 Oct. 1965, McCone Papers.

28. Report of interview with Selma Lesser, 20 Sept. 1965, vol. 16, McCone Transcript.

29. Address delivered by John Buggs, 29 June 1966, LACHRC Papers.

30. Interview with John Buggs, 28 Sept. 1965, vol. 15, McCone Transcript; "Arresting the Development of Delinquent Gangs with the Employment of Indigenous College Students," by Special Service for Groups, Inc., c. 1965, box 12, 25a, McCone Papers.

31. Memorandum of call from Al Alevy, 14 Oct. 1965, box 12, 23b, McCone Papers.

32. *Economist,* 21 Aug. 1965.

33. Address delivered by John Buggs, 29 June 1966, LACHRC Papers.

34. Testimony of Winston Slaughter, 4 Nov. 1965, vol. 13, McCone Transcript; interview, 28 Oct. 1965, vol. 16, ibid.

35. Stuart Timmons, *The Trouble with Harry Hay: Founder of the Modern Gay Movement* (Boston, 1990). In 1995, the NOI raised a cry about a black youth accused of murdering two white gay men after they allegedly sought to rape him. *Final Call,* 11 Jan. 1995.

36. Slaughter testimony.

37. Memorandum from Ben Farber on interview with Winston Slaughter, 1 Nov. 1965, box 15, Nov. Chron. file, McCone Papers.

38. Slaughter testimony.

39. Ibid.

40. Interview with Vernon James, 19 Nov. 1965, box 13, 30, McCone Papers; interview, c. 1965, vol., 16, ibid.

41. Anonymous memorandum, undated, reel 11, 0510, Kerner Commission Papers; Notecards, 14 Aug. 1965, 1:48 P.M., box 4, McCone Papers.

42. "Riot and the Criminal Law," Report and Recommendations by Assemblyman Pearce Young, Chair, Assembly Interim Committee on Criminal Procedure, Jan. 1966, LACHRC Papers.

43. *LA Times,* 5 Nov. 1965.

44. Tackwood, *The Glass House Tapes,* p. 108.

45. Gilbert Geis, "Juvenile Gangs," June 1965, for President's Committee on Juvenile Delinquency and Youth Crime, box 12, 25a, McCone Papers.

46. *Black Panther,* 17 Oct. 1970.

47. *LA Sentinel,* 29 Jan. 1976.

48. *LA Times,* 15 Aug. 1980.

49. Ibid., 28 Aug. 1980, 17 May 1992.

50. Leith Mullings, "Images, Ideology, and Women of Color," in *Women of Color in U.S. Society,* ed. Maxine Baca Zinn and Bonnie Thornton Dill (Philadelphia, 1993), pp. 265–89, p. 282.

51. Maulana Karenga, *The Roots of the U.S./Panther Conflict: The Perverse and Deadly Games People Play* (San Diego, 1976); Kenneth O'Reilly, *"Racial Matters": The FBI's Secret File on Black America* (New York, 1989); Seale, *A Lonely Rage; Muhammad Speaks,* 28 Oct. 1966; Elijah Muhammad, *Message to the Blackman in America* (Philadelphia, 1965), p. 127.

52. Tyler, "Black Radicalism in Southern California," pp. 225, 231, 240, 283, 293, 295, 300, 357.

53. Ibid., p. 283.

54. *LA Free Press,* 2 Sept. 1966; *New York Times,* 2 Sept. 1968; Robert Weisbrot, *Freedom Bound: A History of America's Civil Rights Movement* (New York, 1990), p. 228.

55. Ron Everett-Karenga et al., "A Black Power View of the McCone Commission Report: A Cultural Approach," reel 9, 0132, Kerner Commission Papers.

56. Tyler, "Black Radicalism in Southern California," pp. 364, 381; deposition of Ron Karenga, 22 Feb. 1968, 7 A.M., reel 14, 0763, Kerner Commission Papers.

57. *LA Times,* 17 Oct. 1965; *Muhammad Speaks,* 28 May 1965.

58. Newsletter, FCL California Report, 15, no. 6 (1966): 1–4, folder: "Watts 1960s," Southern California Library.

59. *LA Free Press,* 8 July 1966.

60. *LA Times,* 1, 25 Sept. 1966; Elman, *Ill-at-Ease in Compton,* p. 68; T. George Harris, "Is the Race Problem Insoluble," folder: "Watts 1960s," Southern California Library.

61. Karenga, *The Roots of the U.S./Panther Conflict. The Economist,* 17 Dec. 1994, noted that Karenga was founder of the African-American holiday Kwanzaa, marked every December after Christmas. Hallmark, a card company, and other corporations have profited handsomely from this holiday. According to the conservative weekly, "Clearly, corporate America sees potential in Mr. Karenga's creation."

62. Robert L. Allen, *Black Awakening in Capitalist America: An Analytic History* (Garden City, N.Y., 1970), pp. 82, 139, 188.

63. Statement of Roy Wilkins, 5 Aug. 1959, NAACP Papers–West; *Economist,* 21 Aug. 1965.

64. Bruce Tyler, "The Watts Riot and the Watts Summer Festival," *Journey of Kentucky Studies* 5 (Sept. 1988): 76–95, p. 83.

65. Ibid.

66. *LA Times,* 11 June 1966.

67. "The Pamphlet about the Watts Summer Festival," c. 1972, file: "Black Leadership," box 14, Urban Policy Research Institute Papers; *LA Sentinel,* 27 June 1991; interview, Stanley Sanders, 2 Oct. 1990, Southern California Library.

68. *LA Times,* 20 Aug. 1979, 15 Aug. 1985, 21, 23 Aug. 1966.

69. Robert S. Browne and Robert Vernon, eds., *Should the U.S. be Partitioned into Two Separate and Independent Nations—One a Homeland for White Americans and the Other a Homeland for Black Americans* (New York, 1968), Niebyl-Proctor Library.

70. André Gunder Frank, *Lumpen Bourgeoisie/Lumpen Development: Dependence, Class, and Politics in Latin America* (New York, 1972); William Z. Foster, *The Negro People in American History* (New York, 1973); James E. Jackson, *Revolutionary Tracings* (New York, 1974).

71. Boris Leibson, *Petty-Bourgeois Revolutionism* (Moscow, 1970).

72. Kevin O'Connell to McCone Commission, 25 Oct. 1965, box 7, 12b, McCone Papers; see also Hugh Manes, "A Report on Law Enforcement and the Negro Citizen in Los Angeles," 1963, box 13, 31e, ibid.

73. Testimony of Evelle J. Younger, 28 Oct. 1965, vol. 14, ibid., report of Evelle Younger to the McCone Commission, 28 Oct. 1965, box 61, folder 2, John Holland Papers; see also Leo Branton et al., "Watts Riots: Guild Amicus Brief," *Guild Practitioner* 24, no. 3 (1965): 57–66.

74. Sheryl M. Moinat et al., "Black Ghetto Residents as Rioters," *Journal of Social Issues* 28, no. 4, (1972): 45–62; *Watts Riot Arrests: Los Angeles, August 1965, a Statistical Accounting of 30 June 1966,* prepared by the Bureau of Criminal Statistics (Sacramento, Calif., 1966), box 49, folder 13, Urban Policy Research Institute Papers; Allen Barton, *Communities in Disaster: A Sociological Analysis of Collective Stress Situations* (Garden City, N.Y., 1969).

75. *LA Times,* 23 Nov. 1965; "Riot Participation Study . . . Juvenile Offenders," prepared by Los Angeles County Probation Department, Nov. 1965, LACHRC Papers.

76. Yvonne Brathwaite to Chief Counsel, 29 Sept. 1965, box 7, 12b, McCone Papers.

77. *LA Herald Examiner,* 24 Jan. 1966; testimony of Harold R. Muntz, 5 Oct. 1965, McCone Transcript.

78. Lee H. Bowker et al., "Female Participation in Delinquent Gang Activities," *Adolescence* 59, no. 15 (1980): 509–19. This study was based on data collected in Jan.–March 1964.

79. Barbara Ann Filo, "Reclaiming Those Poor Unfortunates: The Movement to Establish the First Federal Prison for Women" (Ph.D. diss., Boston Univ., 1982), p. 17; Jane Chapman Roberts, *Economic Realities and the Female Offender* (Lexington, Mass., 1980); Lee Bowker, ed., *Women, Crime, and the Criminal Justice System* (Lexington, Mass., 1978); Laura Crites, ed., *The Female Offender* (Lexington, Mass., 1976); Cora R. Mann, *Female Crime and Delinquency* (Tuscaloosa, 1984); Charles Owens and Jimmy Bell, *Blacks and Criminal Justice* (Lexington, Mass., 1977); Barbara R. Price and Natalie Sokoloff, *The Criminal Justice System and Women* (New York, 1982).

80. "Interview of Persons Arrested," 1965, box 6, 12 (9) and 12a (8), McCone Papers.

81. Ibid., 12a (3) and 12a (7).

82. Ibid., 12a (3) and 12a (8). See also, ibid., 12a (9): Lula Reese, thirty-four, lived at 500 East 35th Street, was born in Montgomery, Ala., and had resided for eight years in LA; she had left school due to pregnancy. On 14 Aug. she was arrested for burglary. Thelma Blanton, forty-four, lived at 1006½ East 75th Street, was born in Oklahoma, and had resided in LA since 1943; she dropped out of school to marry her husband and wound up working as a janitor. She was arrested 14 Aug. for burglary.

83. Ibid., 12a (9) and 12a (3).

84. *LA Times,* 3 Oct. 1965; see also Albert E. Hale to Logan Lane, undated, box 5, 9a (1), McCone Papers.

85. Nathan Cohen, "Los Angeles Riot Study—Summary and Implications for Policy," 1 June 1967, funded by OEO, reel 21, LBJ Papers.

86. "Interview of Persons Arrested," 1965, box 6, 12a (8), McCone Papers.

87. Ibid., 12a (3).

88. Ibid., 12a (2).

89. Ibid., 12a (7).

90. Ibid.

91. Ibid., 12a (3).

92. Ibid., 12a (2).

93. Ibid., 12a (3).

94. *LA Times,* 13 Oct. 1965.

95. "Interview of Persons Arrested," 1965, box 6, 12a (2), McCone Papers.

96. Ibid., 12a (3).

97. Ibid.

98. Ibid., 12a (7).

99. Ibid., 12a (10).

100. Ibid., 12a (3).

101. Ibid., 12a (8). By the 1990s in LA the hegemony of gangs was reflected in the preferred dress of youth—e.g., baggy pants sagging to the knees, without a belt (this style was appropriated from local jails where a belt was a potential weapon)—and music, "gangsta rap." Marion "Suge" Knight, one of the leading rap music entrepreneurs in his capacity as chief executive of Death Row Records in LA and manager of Snoop Doggy Dogg and Dr. Dre—leading "gangsta rappers" from that city—was charged in 1994 with criminal conspiracy and firearms violations in connection with an investigation of a major cocaine distribution operation: *Village Voice,* 3 May 1994. Previously Knight had been convicted of weapons violations. In 1994 Death Row Records had revenues of $75 million, while Knight was billed as "the [Steven] Spielberg of hip-hop." *New York Times,* 2 Jan. 1995.

10. The State and Civil Society

1. Testimony of John C. Monning, 26 Oct. 1965, 10:9, McCone Transcript; John C. Monning to McCone Commission, 25 Oct. 1965, box 60, folder 6, John Holland Papers.

2. Elizabeth Poe, "Watts," *Frontier* 16, no. 11 (1965): 5–7, p. 5.

3. Statement of Jean Gregg, 21 Oct. 1965, box 18, 105, McCone Papers.

4. Drew Pearson, newspaper column, 3 Sept. 1965, box 22, 108, McCone Papers; Frank Wilkinson, "And Now the Bill Comes Due," *Frontier* 16, no. 12 (1965): 10–12, p. 12.

5. "Minority Housing in Metropolitan Los Angeles: A Summary Report," prepared by the Health and Welfare Department, LA Urban League, July 1959, LACHRC Papers–Bilbrew.

6. Testimony of Milton G. Gordon, 20 Oct. 1965, 7:17, McCone Transcript.

7. Testimony of Loren Miller, 17 Oct. 1965, 10:20, ibid.

8. Nelson, "Recent Suburbanization of Blacks."

9. Neil Lebowitz, "'Above Party, Class, or Creed': Rent Control in the United States," *Journal of Urban History* 7 (Aug. 1981): 439–70; see also Arthur James Krim, "Imagery in Search of a City: The Geosophy of Los Angeles, 1921–1971" (Ph.D. diss., Clark Univ., 1980); B. Marchand, *The Emergence of Los Angeles: Population and Housing in the City of Dreams, 1940–1970* (London, 1986); John Beach and John Chase, "The Stucco Box," in Charles W. Moore et al., eds., *Home Sweet Home: American Domestic Vernacular Architecture* (New York, 1983), 118–29; Mark Rose, *Interstate: Express Highway Politics, 1941–1959* (Lawrence, Kans., 1979); Paolo Ceccarelli, "'Ex Uno Plures': A Walk through Marxist Urban Studies," in Lloyd Rodwin et al., eds. *Cities of the Mind: Images, Themes of the City in the Social Sciences* (New York, 1984), pp. 313–35; Ronald Bayor, "Roads to Racial Segregation: Atlanta in the 20th Century," *Journal of Urban History* 15, no. 1 (1988–89): 3–21; Richard Bernard and Bradley Rice, eds., *Sunbelt Cities: Politics and Growth since World War II* (Austin, Tex., 1983); William G. Robbins, *Colony and Empire: The Capitalist Transformation of the American West* (Lawrence, Kans., 1994); Arnold R. Hirsch and Ray-

mond A. Mohl, *Urban Policy In Twentieth Century America* (New Brunswick, N.J., 1993); Williams, "Ecology of Negro Communities in Los Angeles County." Part of the story of LA in the 1960s is how this metropolis was coming to supplant New York as a dominant metropolitan power. Just as New York complemented London in an era of Atlanticism, LA complemented Tokyo as capital moved steadily west. Martin Shefter, ed., *Capital of the American Century: The National and International Influence of New York City* (New York, 1993); Mark Joseph Williams, "From 'Remote' Possibilities to Entertaining 'Difference': A Regional Study of the Rise of the Television Industry in Los Angeles, 1930–1952" (Ph.D. diss., Univ. of Southern California, 1992).

10. *LA Times,* 15 Oct. 1965; see also National Urban League analysis, appendix to Wesley Brazier testimony, c. 1965, vol. 4, McCone Transcript.

11. *LA Times,* 31 May 1989; interview with B. O. Corbett, 4 Oct. 1965, vol. 15, McCone Transcript; Robert Sollen, "And They Wonder Why," *Frontier* 16, no. 11 (1965): 1, 14, 24.

12. Statement of Milton G. Gordon, 20 Oct. 1965, box 18, 105, McCone Papers.

13. Testimony of Edward Warren, 25 Sept. 1965, 14:13, McCone Transcript.

14. Testimony of Christopher L. Taylor, 25 Sept. 1965, 13:48, and testimony of John Buggs, 5:10, ibid.

15. See Hudson, *Paul R. Williams, Architect.*

16. Testimony of Loren Miller, 7 Oct. 1965, 10:4, 5, 7, McCone Transcript; *LA Times,* 8 Oct. 1965.

17. Report of interview with Ben Bingham, 11 Nov. 1965, vol. 16, McCone Transcript.

18. Report of interview with Emil Seliga, 1 Nov. 1965, ibid.; memorandum from Yvonne Brathwaite, 20 Nov. 1965, box 12, 26, McCone Papers.

19. Statement by B. O. Corbett, c. 1965, and report by Ken Hansen, 22 Sept. 1965, box 12, 26e, McCone Papers; see also John Buenker et al., *Urban History: A Guide to Information Sources* (Detroit, 1981).

20. Lawrence Paul Crouchett, "Byron Rumford: Symbol for an Era," *California History* 66 (March 1987): 13–23, 70–71; *LA Times,* 24 Nov. 1965.

21. Lawrence P. Crouchett, *William Byron Rumford: The Life and Public Service of a California Legislator* (El Cerrito, Calif., 1984), p. 68.

22. Jack Woods to Mildred Bond, 24 Nov. 1964, A47, NAACP Papers.

23. Flyers, c. 1964, box 5, ser. 2, Max Mont Papers; see also Gov. Edmund Brown to Roy Wilkins, 15 June 1964, A47, NAACP Papers; flyers, c. 1964, reel 106, R-63, Right Wing Collections, Univ. of Iowa; Stephen Berger, "The Social Consequences of Residential Segregation of the Urban American Negro," Metropolitan Applied Research Center, paper no. 2 (New York, March 1970).

24. *LA Times,* 2 Dec. 1965.

25. Memorandum from Logan Lane, 10 Nov. 1965, box 12, 26e, McCone Papers.

26. Report by William Colby, 3 Dec. 1965, box 5, 9a, ibid.

27. Testimony of Milton Gordon, 7:12, McCone Transcript.

28. *LA Times,* 17 Oct., 12 Dec. 1965.

29. Edward Ransford and Melvin Seeman, "Attitudes and Other Characteristics of Negroes in Watts, South Central, and Crenshaw Areas of Los Angeles," vol. 18, McCone Transcript.

30. *LA Times,* 22 Aug., 23 Nov. 1965.

31. *LA Herald-Dispatch,* 10 Feb. 1966.

32. Testimony of Freita Shaw, 4 Nov. 1965, vol. 9, McCone Transcript; Sammy Davis, Jr., et al., *Yes I Can* (New York, 1965), p. 191.

33. Marilyn Green Douroux, "The Black Education Commission: Its Genesis, Structure, and Function within the Los Angeles Unified School District, 1970–1979" (Ph.D. diss., UCLA, 1980); Clifford Linden Davis, Jr., "Black Student Movements and Their Influence in Ten High Schools in the Los Angeles Unified School District" (Ph.D. diss., UCLA, 1971); Nathaniel Hickerson, "Comparisons between Negro

and Non-Negro Students in Participation in the Formal and Informal Activities of a California High School" (Ed.D, Univ. of California–Berkeley, 1963).

34. *A Generation Deprived: LA School Desegregation,* Report of the U.S. Commission on Civil Rights (Washington, D.C., 1977).

35. Testimony of Jack Crowther, 3 Nov. 1965, 6:22, McCone Transcript; biography of Jack Crowther, undated, box 18, 105, McCone Papers. Crowther was born in 1909 in Salt Lake City and received an honorary doctorate in 1964 from Pepperdine University. He taught in the high schools of LA for a number of years and was appointed superintendent in 1962.

36. Interview with Marnesba Tackett, 3 Nov. 1965, box 15, Nov. Chron. file, McCone Papers.

37. Memorandum from Lois Massey, 20 Oct. 1965, vol. 16, McCone Transcript.

38. Memorandum from Yvonne Brathwaite, 18 Oct. 1965, box 14, Oct. Chron. file, McCone Papers; interview with X. L. Smith, 22 Oct. 1965, box 12, 22g, ibid.

39. Testimony of Linda Bryant, 25 Sept. 1965, 4:3, McCone Transcript.

40. Testimony of Jack Crowther, p. 35.

41. Ibid., p. 39.

42. Memorandum from Yvonne Brathwaite, McCone Papers.

43. *LA Sentinel,* 2 Sept. 1965.

44. *Scholastic Teacher* 47, no 4 (7 Oct. 1965): 1.

45. Memorandum from H. R. Wellman, Office of the Vice President, 31 Aug. 1965, box 2, ser. 401, Franklin Murphy Papers.

46. Flyer, 18 Aug. 1965, box 6, UCLA Student Activism Collection.

47. Memorandum from Academic Senate Special Committee for the Advancement of Education for Secondary School Students, 2 Feb. 1966, ibid.

48. Robert A. Rutland to Charles Young, 25 June 1968, box 124, ser. 401, Franklin Murphy Papers.

49. Mullings, "Images, Ideology, and Women of Color," p. 274; Cheryl Gilkes, "From Slavery to Social Welfare: Racism and the Control of Black Women," in *Class, Race, and Sex: The Dynamics of Control,* ed. Amy Swerdlow and Hanna Lessinger (Boston, 1983), pp. 288–300; Amirah Inglis, *The White Women's Protection Ordinance* (New York, 1975); Patricia Morton, *Disfigured Images: The Historical Assault on Afro-American Women* (New York, 1991); Janet Simms-Wood, "The Black Female: Mammy, Jemima, Sapphire, and Other Images," in *Images of Blacks in American Culture: A Reference Guide to Information Sources,* ed. Jesse Carney Smith (Westport, Conn., 1988), pp. 235–54; Linda Grant, *Sexing the Millenium: Women and the Sexual Revolution* (New York, 1994).

50. *Wall Street Journal,* 16 Aug. 1965; *LA Times,* 7 Dec. 1965; Daniel Patrick Moynihan, "The Negro Family: The Case for National Action," in *The Moynihan Report and the Politics of Controversy,* ed. Lee Rainwater and W. L. Yancey (Cambridge, Mass., 1965), pp. 39–124.

51. *Richmond Independent,* 7 Dec. 1965; *LA Times,* 19 Dec. 1965.

52. *Nation,* 25 Nov. 1965; see also Jill Quadagno, *The Color of Welfare: How Racism Undermined the War on Poverty* (New York, 1994).

53. Testimony of H. H. Brookins, 29 Sept. 1965, 4:60, McCone Transcript; testimony of Opal Jones, 6 Oct. 1965, 9:30, ibid.

54. *Long Beach Independent,* 9 Dec. 1965.

55. *LA Free Press,* 20 Aug. 1965.

56. Testimony of Ellis P. Murphy, 20 Oct. 1965, 11:16, 22, 23, 27, 30, 39, 41, 42, 43, McCone Transcript.

57. Testimony of Paul Ward and Helen Nelson, 17 Nov. 1965, 13:52, 14, 27, ibid.

58. Ibid., p. 28.

59. Memorandum from Alice Campbell, 22 Nov. 1965, box 15, 16–30 Nov. Chron. file, McCone Papers.

60. *Daily Trojan,* 20 Aug., 14 Sept. 1965.

61. Report by Patricia Dear, Director, Bureau of Public Health Social Work, LA County Health Department, 26 Aug. 1965, vol. 15, McCone Transcript; testimony of Hugo Fisher, 17 Nov. 1965, vol. 6, ibid.; Douglas Glasgow, "Patterns in Welfare: Bureaucracy to Neighborhood Services," *Journal of Black Studies* 2 (Dec. 1971): 171–88; Jerome Cohen, "A Descriptive Study of the Availability of Social Services in the South Central Area of Los Angeles," Institute of Government and Public Affairs, UCLA (Los Angeles, 1 June 1967).

62. *LA Times,* 5 Feb. 1967.

63. Gregory Holmes Singleton, "Religion in the City of the Angels: American Protestant Culture and Urbanization, Los Angeles, 1850–1930" (Ph.D. diss., UCLA, 1976); Roger Lee Ragan, "Attitudes of White Methodist Church Members in Selected Los Angeles Metropolitan Area Churches toward Residential Segregation of the Negro" (Th.D., Southern California School of Theology, 1963); *LA Times,* 19 Aug. 1980.

64. Interview with Casper Glenn, McCone Papers; see also James F. Findlay, Jr., *Church People in the Struggle: The National Council of Churches and the Black Freedom Movement, 1950–1970* (New York, 1993).

65. *LA Times,* 16 Aug. 1965; photographs, box 23, McCone Papers.

66. *LA Times,* 23, 19, 22 Aug. 1965.

67. Ibid., 19 Aug. 1965.

68. Undated news clipping, c. 1965, box 49, folder 13, Urban Policy Research Institute Papers.

69. Statement of H. H. Brookins, c. 1965, box 17, 105, McCone Papers; *LA Times,* 4, 13 Dec., 21 Nov. 1965.

70. Report by Marlen Neumann, 24 Nov. 1965, box 8, 16, McCone Papers; interview with "Mr. Smith," 24 Nov. 1965, vol. 16, McCone Transcript; Roger Finke and Rodney Stark, *The Churching of America, 1776–1990: Winners and Losers in Our Religious Economy* (New Brunswick, N.J., 1992).

71. Memorandum from William Colby, interview with Leon Aubry, 28 Nov. 1965, box 15, 16–30 Nov. Chron. file, McCone Papers.

72. *LA Times,* 23 June 1986.

73. Notecards, 3, 13 Aug. 1965, box 4, McCone Papers; *LA Times,* 19 Aug. 1965.

74. Oral history, Ben Margolis, 17 May 1985, UCLA Oral History.

75. Benjamin S. Farber to McCone Commission, 27 Oct. 1965, box 7, 12b, McCone Papers.

76. Kevin O'Connell to Chief Counsel, 29 Oct. 1965, ibid.

77. Hugh Taylor to William Becker, 1 Sept. 1965, box 60, folder, 4, John Holland Papers.

78. Petition from South Side Citizens Defense Committee to Gov. Brown, undated, box 14, 101, v. 3, McCone Papers; *LA Times,* 19 Aug. 1965.

79. "Why No Fire That Time? The Compton Council on Human Relations," KPFK, 30 May, 7 June 1966, Pacifica Archives.

80. *LA Times,* 22 Aug., 12 Dec. 1965.

81. David O. Sears and John B. McConahay, "Riot Participation," in Cohen, *The LA Riots,* pp. 258–71, p. 279; Robert M. Fogelson, "White on Black: A Critique of the McCone Commission Report on the Los Angeles Riots," in *Mass Violence in America: The Los Angeles Riots,* ed. Fogelson, pp. 113–43, p. 120.

82. J. R. Hicks, "Watts," *ACLU Open Forum* 67, no. 5 (1990): 1.

83. *Watts Riot Arrests,* box 49, folder 13, Urban Policy Research Institute Papers.

84. Richard Simon to Thomas Sheridan, 25 Oct. 1965, box 4, McCone Papers.

85. "Special Arrest Analysis by Selected Population Categories 1964," LAPD, ibid.

86. *New York Times,* 30 June 1967; article, c. 1967, box 10, Record Group 7, James Corman Papers.

87. T. M. Tomlinson and David O. Sears, "Negro Attitudes toward the Riots," in Cohen, *The LA Riots,* pp. 288–325, pp. 288, 318. See also Richard Majors and Janet Mancini Billson, *Cool Pose: The*

Dilemmas of Black Manhood in America (New York, 1992). The case of Emmett Till, the black youth lynched in Red Scare Mississippi because of alleged indiscretions involving a white woman, illustrated for many the value of being "cool" or unprovoked by racism, deflecting subordination. What was cool began to evolve during the changed 1960s and what happened to black men had implication for manhood in the United States generally. Coolly facing down police officers was a specialty of the BPP; for a black working class that at times seemed defenseless in the face of LAPD brutality, the "effective coolness" of the BPP—or that of their Fruit of Islam counterparts—seemed to be a welcome evolution.

88. "The Curfew Zone," 22 Feb. 1991, KPFK, Southern California Library; photographs, 17 Aug. 1965, box 23, McCone Papers.

89. *LA Herald-Dispatch,* 11 Sept. 1965; Edmund Lester to William Becker, undated, box 13, 31e, McCone Papers: the writer commented on an 18 Aug. 1965 *LA Herald Examiner* article reporting the death of Katie Lester at the hands of the LAPD, which was "not directly connected" to the revolt. This suggests that the official total of thirty-four may be underestimated.

90. Thomas T. Noguchi with Joseph DiMona, *Coroner* (Boston, 1984). This book confirms the hoary bromide that if one is seeking ultimate power in government, the coroner's office may be a better bet than City Hall.

91. *LA Times,* 22 Oct. 1965; Evelle Younger, "Report to the Governor's Commission on the Los Angeles Riots," 28 Oct. 1965, McCone Transcript.

92. James N. Adler, "Coroner's Inquests and the Los Angeles Riots," 12 Nov. 1965, box 5, 8a, McCone Papers; the same document can also be found in vol. 17, McCone Transcript.

93. *LA Times,* 1 Sept. 1965.

94. Testimony of Robert D. Bargman, 19 Oct. 1965, vol. 16, McCone Transcript.

95. Harold Hamill, Chief Librarian, to John Holland, 18 May 1966, box 60, folder 6, John Holland Papers.

96. William Frederickson, Jr., General Manager, Recreation and Parks, to City Council, 20 May 1965, memo from Robert Russell, Chief Engineer and General Manager, Department of Public Utilities, 19 May 1966, Muriel Moore, General Manager, Civil Service, LA, to City Council, 12 May 1966, box 60, folder 6, John Holland Papers; R. F. Johnson to Irwin Walder, 18 May 1966, box 66, folder 6, ibid.; summary of CRA activities, c. May 1966, box 6, folder 6, ibid.; see also *LA Times,* 17 Jan. 1966.

97. *LA Times,* 9 Sept. 1965; see also Ernest Gellner, *Conditions of Liberty: Civil Society and Its Rivals* (New York, 1994).

11. A Class Divided by Race

1. *LA Times,* 14 Dec. 1965.

2. Joe William Trotter, Jr., *Black Milwaukee: The Making of an Industrial Proletariat, 1915–1945* (Urbana, Ill., 1985).

3. Testimony of Richard Simon, 13 Oct. 1965, 13:22, McCone Transcript.

4. William James Williams, "Attacking Poverty in the Watts Area: Small Business Development under the Economic Opportunity Act of 1964" (Ph.D. diss., Univ. of Southern California, 1966); California Department of Employment, LA Metropolitan Area, Research and Statistics Section, "Measurement of Job Vacancies, LA–Long Beach Metropolitan Area, December 1964, April 1965" (Los Angeles, 1965); "Hard-Core Unemployment and Poverty in Los Angeles," prepared by Institute of Industrial Relations, UCLA, Dec. 1964.

5. *LA Times,* 17 Oct. 1965.

6. Harvey B. Schecter to Ben Farber, 16 Nov. 1965, box 10, 21, McCone Papers; interview with Dwight Zook, 20 Oct. 1965, box 10, 21a, ibid.

7. Memorandum from Jerry Rosen, 15 Nov. 1965, Nov. Chron. file, box 15, ibid.

8. Bullock, *Watts,* p. 18.

9. Memorandum, c. 1967, 0709, Kerner Commission Papers; statement by Helen Nelson, c. 1965, box 60, folder 4, John Holland Papers; Bradford Snell, "Roger Rabbit and the Politics of Transportation in Los Angeles," *Urban Affairs Quarterly* 27, no. 1 (1991): 51–86.

10. Samuel Hayakawa, "Reflections on a Visit to Watts," c. 1965, box 32, folder 8, Mervyn Dymally Papers; see also David Brodsly, *LA Freeway: An Appreciation* (Berkeley, Calif., 1981); Rose, *Interstate;* E. Gordon Erickson, "The Superhighway and City Planning: Some Ecological Considerations with Reference to Los Angeles," *Social Forces* 28 (May 1950): 429–34; Bruce Stave, "The Spatial Dimensions of Social Control," in *Modern Industrial Cities: History, Politics, and Survival,* ed. Bruce Stave (Beverly Hills, Calif., 1981), pp. 79–128.

11. Interview with Wade McClain, State Service Center in Watts, 24 Nov. 1965, box 15, 16–30 Nov. Chron. file, McCone Papers.

12. Collins, *Black Los Angeles,* p. 26.

13. Testimony of Opal Jones, 6 Oct. 1965, vol. 9, McCone Transcript.

14. Interview with William J. Bassett and Max Mont, LA County AFL-CIO, 24 Nov. 1965, vol. 15, ibid.

15. *LA Times,* 28 Aug., 10 Sept. 1965; *LA Sentinel,* 16 Sept. 1965.

16. Memorandum from J. A. Mitchell, 23 Sept. 1965, box 21, 106, McCone Papers. The UAW was in a dilemma when the McCone Commission requested data on the racial and ethnic composition of its membership; though it may have recognized the necessity of knowing these numbers, it resisted compliance because the authorities did not seem to evince any interest in the racial and ethnic makeup of boards of directors of corporations. See *LA Sentinel,* 16 Dec. 1965. See also Roger Keeran, *The Communist Party and the Auto Workers Union* (Bloomington, Ind., 1980); Stephen Amberg, *The Union Inspiration in American Politics: The Autoworkers and the Making of a Liberal Industrial Order* (Philadelphia, 1994).

17. *LA Herald Examiner,* 13 Sept. 1965; *LA Times,* 30 Nov. 1965.

18. Testimony of Paul Schrade, 26 Oct. 1965, vol. 12, McCone Transcript.

19. Testimony of Max Mont, 13 Oct. 1965, 10:22, 31, 32, 36, ibid.

20. *LA Citizen,* 21 Jan. 1966.

21. *LA Sentinel,* 2 Sept. 1965; *LA Times,* 2 Sept., 24 Aug. 1965; memorandum from K. V. Hansen, 1 Nov. 1965, box 15, Nov. Chron. file, McCone Papers.

22. *Golden State Newsletter* 1, no. 7 (1966), box 22, 108, McCone Papers.

23. *LA Times,* 30 Nov. 1965; *LA Herald Examiner,* 11, 22 Sept. 1965; testimony of Eugene Purnell, 4 Nov. 1965, vol. 12, McCone Transcript.

24. Testimony of Glenn Anderson, 22 Sept. 1965, vol. 3, McCone Transcript; *LA Times,* 4, 13 Nov. 1965.

25. Fine, *Violence in the Model City,* p. 85.

26. Memorandum from Ben Farber, 28 Oct. 1965, box 21, 106, McCone Papers.

27. "A Sad American" to Councilman Billy Mills, 29 Sept. 1965, box 19, 105, ibid.

28. *LA Times,* 10 Oct. 1965.

29. Ibid., 20 Nov. 1965.

30. Ibid., 17 Oct. 1965, 29 Dec. 1966.

31. Testimony of Billy Mills, 28 Sept. 1965, vol. 10, McCone Transcript.

32. Testimony of Muriel M. Morse, 20 Oct. 1965, 10:17, 38, 46, 47, ibid.

33. *LA Times,* 7 Aug. 1970.

34. Testimony of Ralph Guzman, 27 Oct. 1965, vol. 7, McCone Transcript.

35. Ralph Guzman, "The Mexican-American Community," Oct. 1965, box 18, 105, McCone Papers.

36. Raymond Paredes, "Los Angeles from the Barrio: Oscar Zeta Acosta's 'The Revolt of the Cockroach People,'" in Fine, *Los Angeles in Fiction,* pp. 209–22.

37. Testimony of Ralph Guzman, 27 Oct. 1965, 7: 11, 18, 26, 41, McCone Transcript; "Negroes and Mexican Americans in South and East Los Angeles: Changes between 1960 and 1965 in Population, Employment, Income, Family Status, an Analysis of a Special U.S. Census Survey of November 1965," State of California, Department of Industrial Relations, Division of Fair Employment Practices, July 1966, LACHRC Papers–Bilbrew; Mauricio Mazon, *The Zoot Suit Riots: The Psychology of Symbolic Annihilation* (Austin, Tex. 1984). These events lasted from 3–13 June 1943, longer than the seven days of Watts 1965, but no one was killed, and no one sustained massive injuries. Property damage was slight; convictions were few and highly discretionary.

38. Paul Bullock, "Combating Discrimination in Employment," Institute of Industrial Relations, UCLA (Los Angeles, 1961), Southern California Library.

39. Interview with Yvonne Gerioux, 3 Nov. 1965, vol. 15, McCone Transcript.

40. Richard Griswold del Castillo, "Southern California and Chicano History: Regional Origins and National Critique," *Aztlan: A Journal of Chicano Studies* 19, no. 1 (1988–90): 109–24.

41. George Joseph Sanchez, "Becoming Mexican American: Ethnicity and Acculturation in Chicano Los Angeles, 1900–1943" (Ph.D. diss., Stanford Univ., 1989), pp. 90–91, 97; George Sanchez, *Becoming Mexican American: Ethnicity, Culture, and Identity in Chicano Los Angeles, 1900–1945* (New York, 1993).

42. Joan Moore, *Homeboys: Gangs, Drugs, and Prison in the Barrios of Los Angeles* (Philadelphia, 1978), pp. 42, 70, 169.

43. Alfredo Guerra Gonzalez, "Mexicano/Chicano Gangs in Los Angeles: A Socio-historical Case Study" (D.S.W., Univ. of California–Berkeley, 1981), pp. xii, 14, 49, 58, 143–44.

44. Testimony of Edward R. Roybal, 28 Oct. 1965, 12: 19, 26, 33, 36, McCone Transcript.

45. *People's World,* 18 May 1950; memorandum, 19 July 1950, 100–2572, San Diego, FBI.

46. "Statement of Events Leading Up to Arrest of Thirty-Seven Mexican American Youths," 24 Sept. 1962, Southern California Library.

47. Minutes, meeting of LACHRC, 21 May 1966, LACHRC Papers.

48. Ibid., 17 May 1965.

49. Interview, Vincente R. Bonilla, 13 Sept. 1990, Southern California Library.

50. Memorandum from Benjamin Farber, 18 Oct. 1965, box 14, Oct. Chron. file, McCone Papers.

51. David Rieff, *Los Angeles: Capital of the Third World* (New York, 1991), pp. 179–80.

52. Interview, Edna Guillary, 8 Oct. 1990, Southern California Library.

53. Testimony of Edward R. Roybal, 28 Oct. 1965, 12:25, McCone Transcript; memorandum from Jerry Rosen, 11 Oct. 1965, box 14, Oct. Chron. file, McCone Papers.

54. Report of interview, 27 Oct. 1965, vol. 16, McCone Transcript.

55. John Buggs to Andrew Brimmer, 7 Oct. 1965, box 75, Ramsey Clark Papers; testimony of John Buggs, McCone Transcript, p. 29.

56. Hugh Taylor, Department of Industrial Relations, to William Becker, Assistant to the Governor for Human Rights, 1 Sept. 1965, box 60, folder 5, John Holland Papers; Rodolfo F. Acuña, *A Community under Siege: A Chronicle of Chicanos East of the Los Angeles River* (Los Angeles, 1984), p. 132.

57. Malcolm Moos to W. McNeil Lowry, 22 Dec. 1965, R1478, 650037, FFA.

58. *LA Times,* 10, 11 Oct. 1965; *New York Times,* 17 Oct. 1965.

59. *LA Times,* 16 Sept. 1966.

60. *LA Herald Examiner,* 7 Oct. 1965.

61. *LA Times,* 8 May 1966.

62. Report of interview, by Kevin O'Connell, box 12, 26f, McCone Papers.

63. Ralph Dunlap et al., "Young Children and the Watts Revolt," *Community Mental Health Journal* 4, no. 3 (1968): 201–10.

64. *LA Times,* 24 Aug. 1980.

65. Rufus Browning et al., "Black and Hispanics in California City Politics," *Public Affairs Report* 20,

no. 3 (1979): 1–9; Ralph H. Turner, "Responses to Uncertainty and Risk: Mexican-American, Black, and Anglo Beliefs about the Manageability of the Future," *Social Science Quarterly* 65 (June 1984): 665–79: Turner found that blacks were more fatalistic about earthquake preparedness and survival than Anglos; Mexican-Americans were "significantly less so"; Susan Welch et al., "Dismissal, Conviction, and Incarceration of Hispanic Defendants: A Comparison with Anglos and Blacks," *Social Science Quarterly* 65 (June 1984): 257–64; Biliana C. S. Ambrecht, *Politicizing the Poor: The Legacy of the War on Poverty in a Mexican-American Community* (New York, 1976).

12. Right, Left, and Center

1. Rand, *Los Angeles*, p. 129.

2. Howard H. Earle, *Police Community Relations: Crisis in Our Time* (Springfield, Ill., 1967).

3. *LA Times*, 22 June 1992.

4. "B'Nai B'rith Messenger," 17 Sept. 1965, box 21, 107, McCone Papers; Kenneth Lamott, *Anti-California: Report from Our First Para-Fascist State* (Boston, 1971).

5. Richard T. Morris and Vincent Jeffries, "The White Reaction Study," in Cohen, *The LA Riots*, pp. 480–601, pp. 485, 497, 508.

6. Interview with Sam Bowman, c. 1965, box 6, 12a (18), McCone Papers.

7. *Manion Forum*, Sept. 1965, reel 174, M69, Right Wing Collections, Univ. of Iowa; see also, Leo Ribuffo, *The Old Christian Right: The Protestant Far Right from the Great Depression to the Cold War* (Philadelphia, 1983); Leo Ribuffo, *Right, Center, Left: Essays in American History* (New Brunswick, N.J., 1992).

8. *Evolve* 6, no. 1 (1965), reel 44, E8, Right Wing Collections, Univ. of Iowa; see also "Activities of Private Organizations" and Alexander Miller, "Crisis without Violence: The Story of a Hot Summer," Anti-Defamation League of B'nai B'rith, foreword by Leroy Collins, introduction by Burke Marshall, New York City, undated, box 5-a, McCone Papers.

9. *LA Herald Examiner*, 29 Sept. 1965.

10. Memorandum from R. V. Hansen, 22 Sept. 1965, box 14, 32g, McCone Papers.

11. Correspondence, 1965, box 14, 101, ibid.

12. Fred Schwarz to Dear Friends, 24 Aug. 1965, reel 20, C14, Right Wing Collections, Univ. of Iowa.

13. *Los Angeles Sentinel*, 30 June 1966.

14. Ibid., 23 June 1966; G. L. Southwell to John McCone, 9 Sept. 1965, box 14, 32a, McCone Papers.

15. *Arcata Union*, 10 Dec. 1965; *Anaheim Bulletin*, 20 Dec. 1965; *Oroville Mercury-Register*, 29 Dec. 1965.

16. James Conant, "Social Dynamite in Our Large Cities," undated, LACHRC Papers.

17. Lee Edwards and Terry Catchpole, eds., *Behind the Civil Rights Mask* (Washington, D.C., 1965); Terry Cannon, "The Movement," SNCC-California, Aug. 1966 (in possession of author).

18. M. J. Heale, "Red Scare Politics: California's Campaign against Un-American Activities, 1940–1970," *Journal of American Studies* 20 (April 1986): 5–32, pp. 6, 7, 32.

19. *San Francisco Chronicle*, 7 April 1966.

20. *LA Herald-Dispatch*, 16 Sept. 1965.

21. Editorial, KNX Radio, broadcast 19 Aug. 1965, 8:15 A.M., 8:55 P.M., box 61, folder 5, John Holland Papers.

22. *Intelligence Digest*, Sept. 1965, box 14, Sept. Chron. file, McCone Papers; "Subversive Influences in Riots, Looting, and Burning," pt. 3 (Los Angeles–Watts), *Hearings before the House Un-American Activities Committee*, 90th Cong., 1st sess., 28–30 Nov. 1967 (Washington, D.C., 1968).

23. Karl Prussion, *Communist Influence in the Los Angeles Riots* (New Orleans, 1965), box 60, folder 5, John Holland Papers. This was mailed to Gov. Brown on 10 Dec. 1965.

24. "Heads-Up," Aug. 1965, reel 60, H-5, Right Wing Collections, Univ. of Iowa.

25. Nathan Cohen, "1965 to 1970: Crisis and Responsibility," in Cohen, *The LA Riots*, pp. 706–28, p. 723: *Economist*, 21 Aug. 1965.

26. *LA Times*, 18 Aug. 1965.

27. Ibid., 30 Sept. 1965.

28. Testimony of John Gibson, 29 Sept. 1965, vol. 7, McCone Transcript.

29. Ibid., p. 17.

30. *LA Times*, 15, 17 Aug. 1965; telegram from Soviets to President Johnson, 20 Aug. 1965, HU2/ST5, box 25, LBJ Papers.

31. *LA Times*, 16 Aug. 1965.

32. *Peking Review* 8, no. 34 (20 Aug. 1965): 4.

33. *LA Times*, 21 Aug., 4 Sept. 1965; *Torrance South Bay Daily Breeze*, 14 Dec. 1965.

34. *LA Times*, 31 Aug. 1965. Scholars in the United States have been allowed to take more liberal positions, particularly when compared to other professions, the domestic scientific nomenklatura, and others; this trend reaches back to C. Wright Mills—but not Herbert Aptheker—and suggests why Coser and Bottomore could sound so adventurous. See, e.g., Herbert Aptheker, *The World of C. Wright Mills* (New York, 1960); Howard Press, *C. Wright Mills* (Boston, 1978).

35. Dorothy Healey, 19 April 1973, UCLA Oral History, pp. 809, 811, 813, 816.

36. Ibid., p. 816.

37. William Taylor, "Watts Upsurge: A Communist Appraisal," "Radio Talk," 25 Aug. 1965, brochure, folder: "Watts 1960s," Southern California Library.

38. *People's World*, 18 Dec. 1965.

39. Interview with Sam Bowman, box 6, 12a (18), McCone Papers.

40. W. E. B. Du Bois Clubs of LA, "The Fire This Time," Nov. 1965, box 60, folder 4, John Holland Papers.

41. *LA Times*, 21 Oct. 1965.

42. Pamphlet, *Charged with Murder*, Southern California Library; press release, Committee for the Defense of Philip Bentley Brooks, 18 Feb. 1965, folder: "Watts 1960s," Southern California Library.

43. Herbert Aptheker, "The Watts Ghetto Uprising," *Political Affairs* 44 (Oct. 1965): 16–29.

44. Herbert Aptheker, "The Watts Ghetto," ibid., 45 (Nov. 1965): 28–44, pp. 29, 34.

45. Ben Dobbs, "The Meaning of Watts," ibid., pp. 21–27.

46. FBI Report, "Racial Riot" (LA), 17 Aug. 1965, HU2/ST5, box 25, LBJ Papers.

47. "Communist and Trotskyist Activity within the Greater Los Angeles Chapter of the Fair Play for Cuba Committee," Report and Testimony of Albert J. Lewis and Steve Roberts, 26–27 April 1962, House of Representatives, Committee on Un-American Activities, 87th Cong., 2d sess.; flyer, John Gibson file, box 18, 105, McCone Papers.

48. *LA Herald Examiner*, 18 Aug. 1965.

49. Report of A. V. Branche, 2 Nov. 1965, Nov. Chron. file, box 15, McCone Papers.

50. *LA Times*, 26 Oct. 1966.

51. Ibid., 3 Feb. 1966.

52. Ibid., 29 June 1966.

53. Pamphlet, folder: "Watts," Southern California Library; brochure, SLCAC, undated, folder: "Watts 1960s," ibid.

54. Pamphlet, folder: "Watts," ibid.; brochure, WLCAC, undated, folder: "Watts 1960s," ibid.

55. *LA Herald-Dispatch*, 12 Aug. 1965.

56. Release, 7 April 1967, folder: "Watts 1960s," Southern California Library.

57. *LA Times,* 12 June 1967; *Star-Review,* 18 May 1967, folder: "Watts 1960s," Southern California Library.

58. Victor Mack to WCLAC, 12 June 1967, reel 18, 0174, Kerner Commission Papers; *LA Times,* 17 Oct., 17 Nov. 1971.

59. *LA Herald Examiner,* 11 Aug. 1978

13. Politics: Local and Beyond

1. Jan G. Bernstein, "Realignment and Political Party-Building in California, 1952–1963" (Ph.D. diss., Cornell Univ., 1986), p. 1.

2. Allen J. Matusow, *The Unraveling of America: A History of Liberalism in the 1960s* (New York, 1984), p. 196; Thomas Byrne Edsall and Mary D. Edsall, *Chain Reaction: The Impact of Race, Rights, and Taxes on American Politics* (New York, 1991), p. 49; J. Anthony Lukas, *Common Ground: A Turbulent Decade in the Lives of Three American Families* (New York, 1985).

3. Mary Landis to Pres. Johnson, 21 Aug. 1965, box 177, LBJ Papers. See also the similarly acerbic responses to the revolt in the Papers of Governor Brown located at the University of California–Berkeley.

4. Cleveland Sellers, *The River of No Return: The Autobiography of a Black Militant and the Life and Death of SNCC* (New York, 1973); *Pasadena Star News,* 9 Nov. 1965.

5. *New York Herald Tribune,* 6 Oct. 1965; *White Sentinel* (Fort Lauderdale), Sept.–Oct. 1965, reel 151, W27, Right-Wing Collections, Univ. of Iowa.

6. Edmund G. Brown, *Reagan and Reality: The Two Californias* (New York, 1970).

7. *Sacramento Bee,* 14 Aug. 1965.

8. *LA Times,* 20 Aug. 1965.

9. Matusow, *The Unraveling of America,* pp. 196, 214.

10. Press release, 7 Sept. 1965, box 23, Thomas Rees Papers.

11. Article by David Lawrence, box 32, Ramsey Clark Papers.

12. Nick Kotz and Mary Lynn Kotz, *A Passion for Equality: George Wiley and the Movement* (New York, 1977), p. 155.

13. *LA Times,* 21 Aug. 1965.

14. *Pasadena Star-News,* 2 Sept. 1965.

15. Joseph A. Califano, Jr., *The Triumph and Tragedy of Lyndon Johnson* (New York, 1991), p. 59; Jack Valenti to LBJ, 14 Aug. 1965, HU2/ST5, box 25, LBJ Papers.

16. Califano, *Triumph and Tragedy,* p. 126.

17. N. C. Ribble to Arthur Perry, 16 Aug. 1965, box 29, HU2/ST5, LBJ Papers.

18. *Portland Oregonian,* 29 Aug. 1965.

19. Dr. F. L. King to LBJ, 12 Nov. 1965, box 30, HU2/ST5, LBJ Papers.

20. Leroy Collins to LBJ, undated, c. Aug. 1965, box 25, ibid.; oral history, Leroy Collins, acc. 81–54, 24 Dec. 1980, LBJ Library.

21. Lloyd Hand and attached typed note to Ramsey Clark, 21 Sept. 1965, box 32, Ramsey Clark Papers.

22. *LA Times,* 21, 27 Aug. 1965.

23. Oral history, Ramsey Clark, 21 March 1969, LBJ Library.

24. *LA Times,* 27 Aug. 1965.

25. Clark oral history.

26. Benjamin Mandel to Ramsey Clark, 26 Aug. 1965, box 32, Ramsey Clark Papers.

27. Roger Wilkins, *A Man's Life: An Autobiography* (New York, 1982), pp. 162, 163, 165, 166, 167, 169, 173.

28. "Report of the President's Task Force on the LA Riots, 8/11/65," 17 Sept. 1965, box 10, LBJ Papers.

29. Orville Freeman to LBJ, 25 Aug. 1965, box 25, HU2/ST5, ibid.

30. Ramsey Clark to Gus Hawkins, 13 Oct. 1965, box 75, Ramsey Clark Papers.

31. Bill Moyers to LBJ, 16 March 1966, box 25, HU2/ST5, LBJ Papers.

32. *LA Times*, 26 April 1966.

33. Oral history, Lee White, 16 July 1979, LBJ Library.

34. Oral history, Edmund G. Brown, 11 March 1975, ibid.

35. Lee White oral history.

36. *LA Times*, 29 Aug. 180.

37. Ibid., 16, 20 Aug. 1965.

38. Oral history, Edmund G. Brown, LBJ Library.

39. *LA Times*, 28, 19 Aug. 1965.

40. Testimony of Edmund Brown, 16 Sept. 1965, 4:25, McCone Transcript.

41. Testimony of Thomas Lynch, 27 Oct. 1965, vol. 9, ibid.

42. Testimony of Evelle Younger, 28 Oct. 1965, vol. 14, ibid.

43. *Palo Alto Times*, 9 Dec. 1965. Interestingly, Mervyn Dymally, who eventually became lieutenant governor himself, defended Anderson strenuously. *Sacramento Bee*, 8 Dec. 1965.

44. Jesse Unruh to Jack Valenti, 18 Aug. 1965, HU2/ST5, box 30, LBJ Papers.

45. *LA Times*, 29 Oct., 19 Aug. 1965.

46. Ibid., 18 Oct. 1965.

47. Report, 27 Oct. 1965, box 8, 17, McCone Papers; see also, Richard Rioux, "The Los Angeles County Manpower Maze: A Study of the Impact of Federal Manpower Programs on the Politics and Government of Los Angeles County, 1960–1975" (Ph.D. diss., Univ. of Southern California, 1978); testimony of Mrs. Anabelle Williams, 4 Nov. 1965, vol. 14, McCone Transcript.

48. *LA Times*, 21 Aug. 1965: Yorty received 3,751 favorable and 68 unfavorable letters; ibid., 24 Oct. 1965: Yorty claimed that he had received more than 60,000 letters and telegrams since mid-August asking him to run for governor.

49. Robert Gottlieb and Irene Wolt, *Thinking Big: The Story of the* Los Angeles Times, *Its Publishers, and Their Influence on Southern California* (New York, 1977), p. 405.

50. *LA Times*, 29 Aug. 1965.

51. *People's World*, 18 Dec. 1965.

52. John C. Bollens and Grant B. Geyer, *Yorty: Politics of a Constant Candidate* (Pacific Palisades, Calif., 1973), p. 154; see also Ed Ainsworth, *Maverick Mayor: A Biography of Sam Yorty of Los Angeles* (Garden City, N.Y., 1966): Yorty's obstinance, his right-wing philosophy, and bureaucratic concern about where antipoverty money from Washington would go and who would supervise its dispensation led to his turning his back on this major LBJ initiative; see also Marc Pilisuk and Phyllis Pilisuk, eds., *How We Lost the War on Poverty* (New Brunswick, N.J., 1973); Jonathan James Bean, "Beyond the Broker State: A History of the Federal Government's Policies toward Small Business, 1936–1961" (Ph.D. diss., Ohio State Univ., 1994).

53. Lee White, oral history, 16 July 1979, LBJ Library.

54. "Yorty's Flight," undated, box 5-b, McCone Papers.

55. Raphael Sonenshein, "Biracial Coalition Politics in Los Angeles," *PS* 15 (Summer 1986): 582–91, p. 584.

56. J. Allen Carmien to Mayor Yorty, 20 Aug. 1965, box 61, folder 4, John Holland Papers. Other letters expressing similar sentiments came from Joseph Zahradka, president of the Wilshire Chamber of Commerce, 17 Aug. 1965; the Northeast Realty Board, 25 Aug. 1965; Jack Reinhold, president of Reinhold Plastics, 25 Aug. 1965; Warren Clendening, president of the Santa Monica Junior Chamber of Commerce; and J. P. Hughes, president of Hughes Market, 25 Aug. 1965 (this last letter carried scores of signatures).

57. Chester Bowles to Sam Yorty, 21 Jan. 1965, Minutes of Board of Police Commissioners, 27 Jan. 1965, ACLA; *LA Times,* 17 Oct. 1965.

58. *LA Times,* 19 Oct. 1965.

59. Ibid., 22 Oct. 1965.

60. Bobbie Fiedler, oral history, 17 Nov. 1988, California State University–Northridge.

61. Biography of John Gibson, box 18, 105, McCone Papers; *LA Times,* 31 Aug. 1980.

62. Biography of John Ferraro, box 18, 105, McCone Papers.

63. "Before the County Board of Supervisors for the County of Los Angeles," In the Matter of the Riot Situation in the Watts Area of the City of Los Angeles, Hearing of 14 Sept. 1965, ACLA.

64. Minutes of meeting, 16 Aug. 1965, LA County Commission on Human Relations, LACHRC Papers.

65. Testimony of Kenneth Hahn, 30 Sept. 1965, vol. 7, McCone Transcript.

66. Testimony of Hale Champion, 18 Oct. 1965, vol. 5, ibid.

67. Celes King, oral history, 14 July 1985, UCLA Oral History.

68. Rev. Thomas Kilgore, oral history, 3 Feb. 1987, ibid.

69. Yvonne Brathwaite, oral history, 26 April 1982, ibid.

70. James Lee Robinson, Jr., "Tom Bradley: Los Angeles' First Black Mayor" (Ph.D. diss., UCLA, 1976), p. 98; Tom Bradley, oral history, 25 Aug. 1978, UCLA Oral History; Payne and Ratzan, *Tom Bradley,* p. 73.

71. *LA Times,* 16 Aug. 1965.

72. Tom Bradley to John Holland, 25 April 1966, box 60, folder 6, John Holland Papers.

73. Davis, "Chinatown Revisited?: The 'Internationalization' of Downtown Los Angeles"; Raphael J. Sonenshein, "Bradley's People: Functions of the Candidate Organization" (Ph.D. diss., Yale Univ., 1984); I. R. McPhail, "The Vote for Mayor of Los Angeles in 1969," *Annals of the Association of American Geographers* 61, no. 4 (1971): 744–58; John M. Allswang, "Tom Bradley of Los Angeles," *Southern California Quarterly* 74, no. 1 (1992): 55–105.

74. Testimony of Billy Mills, 28 Sept. 1965, 10:6, 9, 10, 14, 52, 61, 37, 44, 29, 30, 34, McCone Transcript.

75. Testimony of Mervyn Dymally, 13 Oct. 1965, 6:15, 66, 73, ibid.

76. Testimony of Augustus Hawkins, 20 Sept. 1965, 8:52, 63, 78, ibid.

77. Press release, Adam Clayton Powell, 17 Aug. 1965, box 10, James Corman Papers.

78. Stephen B. Oates, *Let the Trumpet Sound: The Life of Martin Luther King, Jr.* (New York, 1982), pp. 392, 410; James R. Ralph, *Northern Protest: Martin Luther King, Jr., Chicago, and the Civil Rights Movement* (Cambridge, Mass., 1993).

79. Coretta Scott King, *My Life with Martin Luther King, Jr.* (New York, 1969), p. 271; Bayard Rustin, *Down the Line* (Chicago, 1971).

80. Editorial, KNX, 20 Aug. 1965, box 61, folder 5, John Holland Papers.

81. "The White Sentinel," Feb.–March 1966, reel 151, no. W27, Right Wing Collections, Univ. of Iowa.

82. Lee White to Lyndon Johnson, 20 Aug. 1965, Files of Lee White, box 6, LBJ Papers.

83. Statement by Ralph Bunche, 17 Aug. 1965, and Ralph Bunche to "Doug," 17 Aug. 1965, box 127, Ralph Bunche Papers; Brian Urquhart, *Ralph Bunche: An American Life* (New York, 1993).

84. *Pittsburgh Courier,* 28 Aug. 1965.

85. Roy Wilkins, *Standing Fast: The Autobiography of Roy Wilkins* (New York, 1982), pp. 312, 313.

86. Louis Martin to John Bailey, 23 Aug. 1965, HU2/ST5, box 25, LBJ Papers; see also *LA Herald Examiner,* 26 Aug. 1965; clipping, 16 Oct. 1965, box 9, folder 32, Mervyn Dymally Papers; *LA Times,* 20 Aug. 1965.

87. *LA Sentinel,* 9 June, 5 May 1966; see also Hanes Walton, "The Recent Literature of Black Poli-

tics," *PS* 18 (Fall 1985): 769–80; Harlan Hahn and Timothy Almy, "Ethnic Politics and Racial Issues: Voting in LA," *Western Political Quarterly* 24, no. 4 (1971): 719–30; Totton Anderson and Eugene Lee, "The 1966 Election in California," ibid., 20, no. 2 (1967): 535–54; Melvin Steinfeld, "California Black Legislators: Leadership Roles," *Black Politician* 3, no. 1 (1971): 81–84; Wilhelmina Perry, "Black Political Leadership Styles: The Black Elected Officials of California" (Ph.D. diss., United States International Univ., 1975).

88. Lou Cannon, *Ronnie and Jesse: A Political Odyssey* (Garden City, N.Y., 1969), pp. 83–84.

89. *LA Times*, 1 Feb. 1966.

90. *Spectator*, 20 Aug. 1965, box 14, 32a, McCone Papers.

91. Anderson and Lee, "The 1966 Election in California," pp. 543, 547.

92. Frederick B. Tuttle, "The California Democrats, 1953–1966" (Ph.D. diss., UCLA, 1975), p. 281.

93. James Button, *Black Violence: Political Impact of the 1960s Riots* (Princeton, N.J., 1978), pp. 153, 158, 121, 31.

94. Biographical sketch of John A. Buggs, undated, LACHRC Papers–Bilbrew; résumé, John Buggs, box 17, 105, McCone Papers.

95. *LA Times*, 22 Aug. 1965.

96. Testimony of John Buggs, 28 Sept. 1965, 5:17, McCone Transcript.

97. Interview with John Buggs, box 5b, McCone Papers.

98. *LA Times*, 3 Feb. 1966.

99. *LA Times*, 17 Oct. 1965.

100. Buggs interview; Buggs testimony, p. 67.

101. Buggs interview.

14. Business

1. LA City Council, Police, Fire, and Civil Defense Committee, "Report on Los Angeles Riot," City Council files 125, 342–43.

2. Testimony of Raymond Hill and A. P. Jasich, McCone Transcript.

3. Testimony of Sam Yorty, 21 Sept. 1965, vol. 14, ibid.

4. *LA Times*, 20 Oct. 1965. Rev. Samuels of the Westminster Neighborhood Association argued that fires were not necessarily being set by arsonists but rather were ignited by broken electrical connections. Report of interview with Rev. Samuels, 24 Oct. 1965, vol. 16, McCone Transcript.

5. Testimony of Harvey Claybrook, 4 Nov. 1965, vol. 5, McCone Transcript.

6. Report by Daniel Panger, 17 Aug. 1965, box 11, 21f, McCone Papers.

7. Memorandum from Logan Lane, 22 Nov. 1965, box 12, 27c, ibid.

8. *LA Times*, 17 Oct. 1965.

9. Statement by Meyer Blue Stein, c. 1965, box 5, 9-a, McCone Papers.

10. Testimony of Mervyn Dymally, 6:77, McCone Transcript.

11. Interview with Seymour Phillips, 2 Nov. 1990, Southern California Library.

12. Testimony of Harvey Claybrook, McCone Transcript.

13. Memorandum from Loring D. Emile, 2 Nov. 1965, box 12, 27c, McCone Papers.

14. *LA Times*, 17 Aug. 1965.

15. *LA Sentinel*, 4 Nov. 1965.

16. Report by Loring D. Emile, 5 Nov. 1965, box 5, 9-a, McCone Papers.

17. *LA Sentinel*, 9 Sept. 1965.

18. Cecil King to Ross Davis, 20 Sept. 1965, box 29, HU2/ST5, LBJ Papers.

19. Walter J. Raine, "Los Angeles Riot Study: The Ghetto Merchant Survey," Institute for Government Affairs, UCLA, 1 June 1967; see also, Howard Aldrich, "The Effect of Civil Disorders on Small Business in the Inner City," *Journal of Social Issues* 26, no. 1 (1970): 187–206.

20. Interview with Linda Cerletta, 5 Nov. 1965, box 21, vol. 106, v. 2, McCone Papers.

21. Interview with Mrs. Earsie Burton, box 11, 21b, ibid.

22. Richard Hughes to Editor of *Washington Evening Star,* 4 Oct. 1967, reel 14, 0893, Kerner Commission Papers; Mercanto, *The Kerner Report Revisited.* Through various maneuvers the insurance industry was able to escape substantial liability in 1965. The ultimate victim was South LA, which was starved of capital as a punitive result.

23. Harold Ullman to Kenneth Hahn, 22 March 1966, box 61, folder 3, John Holland Papers.

24. Eugene Foley to Marvin Watson, 18 Aug. 1965, box 25, HU2/ST5, LBJ Papers.

25. *LA Times,* 21 Aug., 2, 24 Sept. 1965.

26. Ibid., 11 Sept. 1965; see also *LA Herald Examiner,* 5 Sept. 1965.

27. Memorandum of Harold Kennedy to Board of Supervisors, 9 Dec. 1965, 67/60.23, ACLA; *LA Times,* 15 Dec. 1965.

28. *LA Times,* 26 Aug. 1965.

29. Ibid., 17 Aug. 1965.

30. Ibid., 16 Aug. 1965.

31. Comment, "Riot Insurance," *Yale Law Journal* 77, no. 3 (1968): 541–58; *Time,* 25 Aug. 1967.

32. *LA Herald Examiner,* 7 Oct. 1965.

33. Richard Roddis, report on "Special Insurance Problems," 21 March 1966, box 61, folder 3, John Holland Papers; see also Note, "Compensation for Victims of Urban Riots," *Columbia Law Review* 68, no. 1 (1968): 57–84.

34. Henry B. Taliaferro, Jr., to David Ginsburg et al., 21 Aug. 1967, reel 17, 0237, Kerner Commission Papers.

35. *LA Times,* 13 Jan. 1966.

36. Ibid., 18 July 1967; motion by Kenneth Hahn, 15 March 1966, 67/60.26, ACLA.

37. Interview with Gene Meyers, 9 Nov. 1965, vol. 16, McCone Papers.

38. Testimony of Augustus Hawkins, 20 Sept. 1965, vol. 8, McCone Transcript.

39. Interview with James Woods (president of Woods Construction Co.), conducted by Yvonne Brathwaite, 8 Nov. 1965, box 12, 26e, McCone Papers.

40. Interview of Ben L. Bingham, 11 Nov. 1965, ibid.

41. *LA Times,* 6 Dec. 1965.

42. J. C. Monning to LA City Council, 24 May 1966, box 60, folder 6, John Holland Papers.

43. John Wagner to Irwin Walder, 6 June 1966, ibid.

44. G. L. Hough to Irwin Walder, 23 May 1966, ibid.

45. R. A. Gormsen to Irwin Walder, 10 May 1966, box 66, folder 6, ibid.

46. Report by William Colby, 8 Dec. 1965, box 10, 20e, McCone Papers.

47. Felix Chappellet, Vice President and General Manager, Western Oil and Gas Association, to Sheriff Peter Pitchess, 19 Aug. 1965, 60.15, ACLA.

48. H. H. Brookins speech, 17 Sept. 1965, box 60, folder 4, John Holland Papers.

49. Raymond Hill to Irwin Walder, 20 May 1966, box 60, folder 6, ibid.

50. Paul O'Rourke to Gov. Edmund Brown, 19 Aug. 1965, ibid.

51. H. C. McClellan, "Interim Report, President's Committee on Rehabilitation," LA Chamber of Commerce, 28 Sept. 1965, vol. 9, McCone Transcript.

52. Biography of H. C. McClellan, box 19, 105, McCone Papers.

53. *LA Times,* 2 July 1967.

54. Testimony of H. C. McClellan and Murray Lewis, 1 Nov. 1965, 9:11, McCone Transcript.

55. *LA Times,* 2 July 1967.

56. Testimony of H. C. McClellan, McCone Transcript, pp. 37, 53; See also *LA Times,* 20 Nov. 1965.

57. *LA Times,* 2 July 1967. See also KABC-TV editorial, 17–18 Nov. 1966, R1486, 66–171, FFA. The editorial praised Aerojet General for putting a plant in Watts creating two hundred new jobs.

58. *LA Times,* 7 Dec. 1980.

59. Ibid., 15 Oct. 1981.

60. McNeil Lowry to Judge Charles Wyzanski, 25 March 1966, R1486, 66–171, FFA.

61. Report on OIC-LA by Systems Development Corporation, 14 Dec. 1966, ibid.

62. Malcolm Moos to McNeil Lowry, 14 Sept. 1965, R1478, 650377, ibid.

63. Confidential memorandum from Arnold Nemore, 4 Jan. 1967, R1486, 66–171, ibid.

64. Memorandum from Kevin O'Connell, 17 Nov. 1965, box 15, 16–30 Nov. Chron. file, McCone Papers.

65. OIC Progress Report, 1 May 1966–28 July 1966, R1486, 66–171, FFA.

66. Chris Edley to Rev. Rakestraw, 12 Sept. 1966, ibid.

67. OIC Board Minutes, 15 Aug. 1966, ibid.

68. Chris Edley to Rev. Thomas Kilgore, 13 June 1966, ibid.

69. Circular, c. 1966, ibid.

70. Chris Edley to file, 30 Nov. 1966, ibid; see also form, 29 March 1966, R1486, 66–170, ibid.; *LA Times,* 31 March 1966.

71. *LA Times,* 30 March 1966.

72. *Chicago Sun-Times,* 29 May 1966.

73. Mitchell Gordon to Robert Goldmann, Nov. 1969, 002084, FFA.

74. Carl to Marvin Feldman, 19 Jan. 1966, R1486, 66171, ibid.

75. Mitchell Gordon to Robert Goldmann, Aug. 1969, 00215, ibid.

76. *LA Times,* 11 Dec. 1965; memorandum, 12 June 1968, box 105, Rockefeller Archives; see also confidential memorandum from Arnold Nemore, 4 Jan. 1967, R1486, 66–171, FFA.

77. S. D. Bechtel to Paul Ylvisaker, 9 Aug. 1966, R1486, 66–171, FFA.

78. Testimony of Wesley Brazier, 14 Oct. 1965, 14:10, 27, McCone Transcript.

79. *LA Times,* 27 Sept., 31 Aug., 15 Sept. 1965; see also Martin O. Ijere, *An Overview of Black Entrepreneurship in Los Angeles* (Los Angeles, 1971).

15. Representing Rebellion

1. Testimony of Loren Miller, 7 Oct. 1965, vol. 10, McCone Transcript.

2. *LA Times,* 17 Aug. 1965.

3. *Berkeley Post,* 22 Aug. 1965.

4. Max Lockwood to Bill Moyers, 20 Aug. 1965, box 29, HU2/ST5, LBJ Papers.

5. *LA Times,* 17 Aug. 1965; Robert Howard, General Manager, KNBC-TV, to LA City Clerk, 18 May 1966, box 60, folder 5, John Holland Papers; Peter Bart of the *New York Times* carried a gun while reporting from the curfew zone: *LA Weekly* 16–22 Dec. 1994.

6. John Buggs to Irwin Walder, 25 May 1966, box 60, folder 6, John Holland Papers.

7. Deposition of Richard Kline, 19 Oct. 1965, vol. 9, McCone Transcript.

8. Crump, *Black Riot in Los Angeles,* 103; letters, 1965, box 14, 101, vol. 3, McCone Papers; *Long Beach Independent,* 18 Dec. 1965.

9. Kline deposition.

10. C. J. Bride, Jr., to McCone Commission, 15 Nov. 1965, box 4, 3-b, McCone Papers.

11. George Dunlop to John Holland, undated, box 61, folder 1, John Holland Papers; letters, 1965, box 4, McCone Papers.

12. *LA Times,* 22 Aug. 1965.

13. Editorial, Aug. 1965, box 21, 107, no. 65–28, McCone Papers.

14. A. M. Mortensen, Vice President and General Manager, KTLA, to Ben Waple, FCC, 10 Sept. 1965, box 60, folder 6, John Holland Papers.

15. *LA Times,* 2 June 1966.

16. "Watts: Riot or Revolt?" broadcast 7 Dec. 1965 by CBS-TV, and "The Cities: Dilemma in Black

and White," broadcast 25 June 1968 by CBS-TV, Museum of Television and Radio; "The Racial Issue in San Diego . . . A Report of a Television Program and the Reaction to It from the San Diego Community," box 6, 11a, McCone Papers.

17. Legal memorandum from Henry Steinman, 1965, vol. 16, McCone Transcript.

18. John McCone to Thomas Sheridan, 17 Nov. 1965, box 15, 16–30 Nov. Chron. file, McCone Papers.

19. C. J. Bride to John McCone, 15 Nov. 1965, box 4, 3-b, ibid.

20. Memorandum from Ben Holman, Assistant Director for Media Relations, U.S. Justice Department, Community Relations Service, to Chief Counsel Thomas Sheridan, 28 Oct. 1965, box 7, 13b, ibid.

21. William Colby to McCone Commission, 23 Nov. 1965, ibid.

22. Solomon James Jones, *The Government Riots of Los Angeles, June 1943* (Los Angeles, 1969), p. 29.

23. *Newsweek,* 30 Aug. 1965.

24. Gottlieb and Wolt, *Thinking Big,* p. 377.

25. Marshall Berger, *The Life and Times of Los Angeles: A Newspaper, a Family, and a City* (New York, 1984), p. 134.

26. *LA Times,* 14 Aug. 1965.

27. Gottlieb and Wolt, *Thinking Big,* 380.

28. *LA Times,* 30 Aug. 1965.

29. Editorial, KNX-AM, 17–20 Sept. 1965, broadcast thirteen times, box 21, 107, no. 255, McCone Papers.

30. "Fact Sheet," "KMPC Coverage of LA Riot," press release, Aug. 1965, box 61, folder 1, John Holland Papers.

31. *LA Free Press,* 8 Oct. 1965; A. J. Williams, President, Trans-America Broadcasting Corporation, to LeRoy Collins, 11 Sept. 1965, box 30, HU2/ST5, LBJ Papers; Edmonde A. Haddad, "A Code for Riot Reporting," reel 6, 0750, Kerner Commission Papers.

32. *LA Times,* 19 Aug. 1965.

33. Ibid., 12 Aug. 1985.

34. Frederic C. Coonradt, "The Negro News Media and the Los Angeles Riots" (School of Journalism, Univ. of Southern California, 1965); see also, Valerie Stephanie Saddler, "A Content Analysis of *Ebony*'s and *Life*'s 1955–1965 Reporting on Black Civil Rights Movement Issues" (Ph.D. diss., Ohio Univ., 1984); Lee Finkle, *Forum for Protest: The Black Press during World War II* (Cranbury, N.J., 1975).

35. Coonradt, "The Negro News Media and the Los Angeles Riots."

36. *LA Herald-Dispatch,* 25 July 1964.

37. Ibid., 6 May 1965.

38. Ibid., 12, 29 Aug., 18 Sept. 1965.

39. Ibid., 11, 25 Nov. 1965.

40. Ibid., 4 Nov. 1965.

41. Ibid., 6 May 1965, 21 July 1966.

42. Ibid., 13 May 1965.

43. Ibid., 11 Nov. 1965.

44. Ibid., 19 Aug. 1965.

45. Ibid., 26 Aug. 1965.

46. *LA Times,* 7 Feb. 1966; see also David Smith, "The Black Arts Movement and Its Critics," *American Literary History* 3, no. 1 (1991): 93–110; Sam Bluefarb, *Set in LA: Scenes of the City in Fiction* (Los Angeles, 1986); interview with Wendell Collins, 11 Oct. 1965, box 18-a, McCone Papers; California Afro-American Museum Foundation, "1960s: A Cultural Awakening Re-Evaluated, 1965–1975" (Los Angeles, 1989).

47. Mark Newman, *Entrepreneurs of Profit and Pride: From Black Appeal to Radio Soul* (New York,

1988), p. 86; see also Johnny Otis, *Upside Your Head! Rhythm and Blues on Central Avenue* (Hanover, N.H., 1993).

48. Alan Govenar, *The Early Years of Rhythm and Blues: Focus on Houston* (Houston, Tex., 1990), pp. 5, 17.

49. Interview, John Eric Priestley, 21 Dec. 1990, Southern California Library.

50. Robert Gordon, *Jazz West Coast: The Los Angeles Jazz Scene of the 1950s* (New York, 1986); David W. Stowe, "Jazz in the West: Cultural Frontiers and Region during the Swing Era," *Western Historical Quarterly* 23 (Feb. 1992): 53–74; Patricia Carr Bowie, "The Cultural History of Los Angeles, 1850–1967: From Rural Backwash to World Center" (Ph.D. diss., Univ. of Southern California, 1980); Ted Goia, *West Coast Jazz: Modern Jazz in California, 1945–1960* (New York, 1993); Charles Mingus, *Beneath the Underdog* (New York, 1971). Looking back from 1994, pianist-composer Horace Tapscott recalled that one of his band's "legendary performances took place in the back of a flatbed truck" during the height of the revolt in August 1965; "we had been playing like that before the rebellion began . . . and the music continued while the media was claiming that nothing but destruction was going on, [but] the people in Watts, were dancing to the Arkestra and music of 'The Dark Tree'": *San Francisco Bay Guardian*, 3 Aug. 1994. Jazz musicians, most of whom were black, also had to confront organized crime. See Ronald L. Morris, *Jazz and the Underworld, 1880–1940* (Bowling Green, Ohio, 1980).

51. *LA Times*, 7 Feb. 1966.

52. *City Sun*, 7–13 Aug. 1991.

53. Interview, Father Amde Tsion (also known as Anthony Hamilton), 1 Oct. 1990, Southern California Library; Jones, *Renaissance Man from Louisiana*.

54. Brochure, folder: "Watts 1960s," Southern California Library; see also *LA Times*, 12 Aug. 1970; LeFalle-Collins, *Home and Yard*.

55. Circular, 4 Oct. 1967, folder 4010, box 469, Rockefeller Archives.

56. Budd Schulberg to Gerald Freund, 25 Sept. 1968, folder 4011, box 470, and "A Brief History of Douglas House," 20 Oct. 1967, 200R, folder 4010, box 469, ibid.; see also memorandum from Ben Farber, 26 Oct. 1965, box 14, Oct. Chron. file, McCone Papers.

57. *LA Times*, 15, 22 May 1966.

58. Schulberg, *From the Ashes*, p. 3.

59. *Bakersfield Californian*, 8 Dec. 1965.

60. "Accomplishments of Douglas House," Oct. 1967, folder 4010, box 469, Rockefeller Archives; *New York Times*, 20 Feb. 1967.

61. Progress report from Douglas House, Watts Writers Workshop, 1 April–31 July 1968, folder 4011, box 470, Rockefeller Archives.

62. Memorandum on Watts Happening Coffee House and Watts Writers Workshop, 30 April 1968, ibid.

63. Woodie King, Jr., to Norman Lloyd, 9 Dec. 1968, ibid.; see also *Hollywood Reporter*, 30 Oct. 1968; *Variety*, 1 Nov. 1968.

64. Memorandum on $25,000 grant to Watts Writers Workshop, 13 March 1968, and related memorandum, 4 Oct. 1967, folder 4010, box 469, Rockefeller Archives.

65. Leonard Archer, *Black Images in the American Theater: NAACP Protest Campaigns—Stage, Screen, Radio, and Television* (Brooklyn, N.Y., 1973); Philip Davies and Brian Neve, *Cinema, Politics, and Society in America* (New York, 1981); Nancy Signorelli, *Role Portrayal and Stereotyping on Television: An Annotated Bibliography of Studies Relating to Women, Minorities, Aging, Sexual Behavior, Health, and Handicaps* (Westport, Conn., 1985); Donald Bogle, *Blacks in American Films and Television: An Encyclopedia* (New York, 1988); Sammy Davis, Jr., and Jane and Burt Boyar, *Why Me? The Sammy Davis, Jr. Story* (New York, 1989); Sammy Davis, Jr., *Hollywood in a Suitcase* (New York, 1980).

66. *LA Times*, 27 Sept. 1965.

67. Ibid., 9 Sept. 1965.

68. Ibid., 15, 18 Aug. 1965.

69. Ibid., 17 Aug. 1965.

70. Ibid., 18 Aug. 1965.

71. Neil J. Sullivan, *The Dodgers Move West* (New York, 1987), p. 172; see also interview, Robert Oliver, 18 Sept. 1990, Southern California Library: Oliver lived next door to Willie Crawford of the Dodgers; the outfielder had trouble leaving his neighborhood in South LA to get to the game because of police lines. Like their counterparts in cinema, black athletes also had to confront the influence of organized crime in sports. See Dan Moldea, *Interference: How Organized Crime Influences Professional Football* (New York, 1989).

72. E. R. Haines to McCone Commission, 14 Oct. 1965, box 12, 23a, McCone Papers.

73. William Frederickson to Robert L. Goe, 21 Oct. 1965, vol. 16, McCone Transcript; see also Sandra Freitag, *Collective Action and Community: Public Arenas and the Emergence of Communalism in North India* (Berkeley, Calif., 1989).

74. *Daily Trojan* (USC), 20 Aug. 1965; Norman Topping with Gordon Cohn, *Recollections* (Los Angeles, 1990), p. 267.

75. Report by William Colby, 1965, box 5-b, McCone Papers; Charles M. Weisenberger to Evelyn Geller, 28 Sept. 1965, box 12, 22e, ibid.

76. T. M. Tomlinson, "The Development of a Riot Ideology among Urban Negroes," In *Racial Violence in the United States*, ed. Allen D. Grimshaw (Chicago, 1969), pp. 226–35, p. 227.

77. Nathan Cohen, "The LA Riots Study," in Cohen, *The LA Riots*, pp. 1–40, p. 1, 4, 15, 20.

78. Sears and McConahay, *Politics of Violence*, pp. 13, 29, 127, 136, 188; see also *LA Times*, 13 Aug. 1967: A study at UCLA said that the rebellion "got much support;" 15 percent of adults "took part" and another 35 to 40 percent were "active spectators." In Detroit it was estimated that there was an 11 percent participation rate: Fine, *Violence in the Model City*, p. 343.

16. After the Fire

1. *LA Sentinel*, 19 Aug. 1965; Ben R. Paris, Director, Bureau of Street Management, to Louis Dodge Gilliam, Department of Public Works, 19 May 1966, A. J. Fink, Safety and Disaster Services, to Irwin Walder, 20 May 1966, box 60, folder 6, John Holland Papers.

2. *LA Times*, 20 Aug. 1965.

3. *Santa Monica Evening Outlook*, 21 Aug. 1965.

4. *LA Herald Examiner*, 24 Aug. 1965.

5. William Becker to Gov. Brown, 30 Aug. 1965, box 60, folder 4, John Holland Papers.

6. *LA Times*, 3 Sept. 1965.

7. *Pacific Coast Record*, Oct. 1965, box 21, 107, McCone Papers; *LA Herald Examiner*, 24 Aug. 1965.

8. *LA Times*, 22 Sept. 1965.

9. Report of interview by Earl Broady of Peter Guidry, 18 Oct. 1965, box 4, 3-a, McCone Papers.

10. Clipping, 14 Nov. 1965, box 32, folder 7, Mervyn Dymally Papers.

11. Memorandum from J. Rosen, 22 Nov. 1965, box 15, 16–30 Nov. Chron. file, McCone Papers.

12. Testimony of H. H. Brookins, vol. 4, McCone Transcript, p. 100.

13. John McCone to LBJ, 7 Dec. 1965, HU2/ST5, box 25, LBJ Papers.

14. *New York Times*, 31 Oct. 1965; see also Anthony Platt, ed., *The Politics of Riot Commissions, 1917–1970: A Collection of Official Reports and Critical Essays* (New York, 1971).

15. *LA Times*, 7 Dec. 1965; testimony of Warren Christopher, c. 1967, reel 1, no. D225, Kerner Commission Papers; memorandum from John Joannes, 20 Nov. 1965, box 15, 16–30 Nov. Chron. file, McCone Papers; Secretary of Ford Foundation to Gov. Brown, 5 Oct. 1965, R1478, 6500377, FFA.

16. Testimony of George Slaff et al., 12 Oct. 1965, vol. 13, McCone Papers.

17. "Secrecy vs. the Public Interest," KNX-AM radio, 24 Sept. 1965, box 61, folder 1, John Holland Papers.

18. Virna M. Coarson to Gov. Brown, 23 Aug. 1965, box 60, folder 4, ibid.

19. *LA Times,* 17 Oct. 1965; see also ibid., 17 Sept. 1965.

20. Circular, attached to letter from Norman Houston to McCone Commission, 14 Oct. 1965, box 19, p. 105, McCone Papers.

21. Winslow Christian to Alan Cranston, 4 Oct. 1965, box 14, 101, v. 3, ibid.

22. *LA Times,* 15 Oct. 1965.

23. John and Laree Caughey, *School Segregation on Our Doorstep: The Los Angeles Story* (Los Angeles, 1966), p. 35.

24. Memorandum from Samuel Williams, 22 Sept. 1965, box 14, Sept. Chron. file, McCone Papers; see also memorandum from John Joannes, 20 Nov. 1965, box 15, Nov. Chron. file, ibid.; interview, David Butterfield, 20 June 1990, Santa Barbara.

25. John McCone to Joseph Califano, 1 Oct. 1965, HU2/ST5, box 25, LBJ Papers; *Time,* 24 Dec. 1965.

26. "Fiscal Summary McCone Commission Recommendations . . . Los Angeles City Schools," box 11, 22, McCone Papers.

27. Editorial, KNX-AM, 15 Dec. 1965, broadcast 6:25 P.M. and 8:55 P.M., box 60, folder 4, John Holland Papers.

28. Message recorded by Gov. Brown, 10 Dec. 1965, KNXT radio, box 60, folder 5, ibid.

29. *LA Times,* 7–10 Dec. 1965, 13 May 1992.

30. Ibid., 7 Dec. 1965.

31. *LA Herald-Examiner,* 13 Dec. 1965.

32. Testimony of Warren Christopher, c. 1967, reel 1, no. D225, Kerner Commission Papers; *LA Weekly,* 19–25 July 1991.

33. Comments by Thomas Sheridan, c. 1967, reel 9, 0121, Kerner Commission Papers.

34. *Newsweek,* 13, 20 Dec. 1965.

35. *LA Times,* 21 Dec., 2 Nov. 1965; 10 July 1991.

36. Warren Christopher to David Ginsburg, 9 Oct. 1967, reel 16, 0317, Kerner Commission Papers; Clifford Alexander to Marvin Watson, 5 July 1966, HU2/ST5, box 25, LBJ Papers.

37. "Report on the McCone Commission Report: 'Not with a Bang but a Whimper'" by the Southern California Advisory Commission to the U.S. Commission on Civil Rights, Dec. 1965, box 75, Ramsey Clark Papers; *LA Times,* 14 Dec. 1965.

38. *LA Times,* 9 Nov. 1965.

39. Ibid., 20, 8, 15 Dec. 1965.

40. Ibid., 8 Dec. 1965.

41. Ibid., 7, 18 Dec. 1965.

42. "Up from the Ashes," 11 April 1966, BB5317, Pacifica Archives; Louis Garciá to John McCone, 29 Dec. 1965, box 33, folder 2, Mervyn Dymally Papers.

43. Frances Lomas Feldman, critique of McCone report, reel 9, 0103, Kerner Commission Papers.

44. David J. Olson, "Black Violence as Political Protest," in *Black Politics: The Inevitability of Conflict,* ed. Edward Greenberg et al. (New York, 1971), pp. 273–89, p. 283.

45. *LA Times,* 11 Sept. 1967.

46. Kendall O. Price, "A Critique of the Governor's Commission on the Los Angeles Riot," A Pilot Project in University-Urban Intergroup Relations in LA, 1967, reel 9, 0063, Kerner Commission Papers; see also *LA Times,* 16 Dec. 1966; critique by Paul Bullock of McCone report, c. 1966, reel 9, 0097, Kerner Commission Papers.

47. *LA Times,* 22 Dec. 1965; *New York Times,* 17 Dec. 1965.

48. *LA Times,* 26 Sept. 1965.

49. John McCone to Warren Christopher, 21 Sept. 1965, box 14, Sept. Chron. file, McCone Papers. In addition to playing a leading role with the Central Intelligence Agency and the Atomic Energy Commission, McCone was also a principal at Bechtel's, the huge transnational engineering corporation based in California which has built significant developments in the United States and abroad; two leading members of the Reagan administration, Caspar Weinberger and George Schulz, also were executives at Bechtel's. See Laton McCartney, *Friends in High Places: The Bechtel Story, the Most Secret Corporation and How It Engineered the World* (New York, 1988). In addition to being a partner in a major LA law firm, Christopher later played a pivotal role as deputy secretary of state in the Jimmy Carter administration in the negotiations concerning U.S. hostages in Iran. Paul H. Kreisberg, ed., *American Hostages in Iran: The Conduct of a Crisis* (New Haven, 1985).

50. *LA Times,* 16 March 1966; *LA Herald Examiner,* 16 March 1966.

51. *LA Times,* 13 April 1966.

52. NAACP press release, 17 March 1966, box 33, folder 1, Mervyn Dymally Papers; John McCone to Gov. Brown, 31 March 1966, box 9, folder 32, ibid.

53. *LA Times,* 9, 17 May 1966; *LA Herald Examiner,* 17 May 1966.

54. Press release from National Association of Evangelicals, 28 June 1966, box 32, folder 8, Mervyn Dymally Papers.

55. Richard T. Morris and Vincent Jeffries, "Violence Next Door," *Social Forces* 46, no. 3 (1968): 352–58, p. 353; see also Vincent Jeffries and H. Edward Ransford, "Interracial Social Contact and Middle-Class White Reactions to the Watts Riot," *Social Problems* 16, no. 3 (1969): 312–24.

56. Jonathan Martin Kolkey, "The New Radical Right, 1960–1968" (Ph.D. diss., UCLA, 1979), p. 408; see also Daniel Bell, *The Radical Right* (Garden City, N.Y., 1964); Benjamin Epstein and Arnold Foster, *The Radical Right: Report on the John Birch Society and Its Allies* (New York, 1967); Howard Glennerster and James Midley, *The Radical Right and the Welfare State: An International Assessment* (Savage, Md., 1991).

57. *People,* 13 Aug. 1990.

58. Paul Bullock memorandum, c. 1967, reel 4, 0536, Kerner Commission Papers.

59. Clive Graham to Gov. Brown, 18 Sept. 1965, box 11, 21f, McCone Papers; address by John McCone, accepting Public Service Award of Advertising Council, Plaza Hotel, New York City, 14 Dec. 1966, reel 9, 0194, Kerner Commission Papers.

60. *New York Herald Tribune,* 11 Oct. 1965.

61. *Sacramento Bee,* 13 Dec. 1965.

62. *LA Times,* 9, 13 April 1966: McClellan's figures are disputed here.

63. Interview, Sam Anderson, 4 Oct. 1990, Southern California Library.

64. Interview, Ronald Powell, 1 Oct. 1990, Santa Barbara.

65. *LA Sentinel,* 6 Jan. 1966; see also Paul Bullock to John Buggs, 3 Jan. 1966, LACHRC Papers: Bullock attached his "Final Report on Employment and Training" done for the McCone panel.

66. Frederick E. Case, *Black Capitalism: Problems in Development, a Case Study of Los Angeles* (New York, 1972), p. 5; Allen, *Black Awakening in Capitalist America.*

67. *LA Times,* 3, 23 Feb. 1966.

68. Reports of Actions Taken to Implement the Recommendations in the Commission's Report, Staff Report 2, 18 Aug. 1966, reel 6, Kerner Commission Papers; *LA Times,* 20 Aug. 1967.

69. A. J. Williams, President, Trans-American Broadcasting, to Gov. Leroy Collins, Sept. 1965, box 10, 20i, McCone Papers.

70. *LA Times,* 11 Dec. 1965.

71. Ibid., 8 Oct. 1967.

72. Kearney Sauer to LA City Council, 16 May 1966, box 60, folder 6, John Holland Papers.

73. Mrs. Frances Wolfe, Bon Air Hospital, 250 West 120th Street, to LA General Hospital, 13 Oct. 1965, 67/60.24, ACLA.

74. *LA Times,* 11 Jan. 1966.

75. Topping, *Recollections,* p. 267; motion by Billy Mills, 7 Dec. 1965, box 61, folder 4, John Holland Papers.

76. *LA Times,* 31 May 1966.

77. Ibid., 20 Dec. 1965, 17 Aug. 1980; see also Dr. Milton L. Roemer, "Health Services in the Los Angeles Riot Area," 1965, vol. 18, McCone Transcript.

78. Louis Masotti and Don R. Bowen, eds., *Riots and Rebellion: Civil Violence in the Urban Community* (Beverly Hills, Calif., 1968) (almost all of the articles in this collection were funded by government grants); McCone Commission to Thomas Sheridan, 1965, box 7, 12b, McCone Papers; Development Research Associates, "An Analysis of Surveys, Plans, and Studies Undertaken in South Central Los Angeles, California," prepared for Economic Development Administration, U.S. Department of Commerce, Project No. 07-6-09275, 1970: "Before the Watts riots, study and planning activity was virtually nonexistent. . . . In the months immediately following the disturbances, large quantities of money and attention flowed into the area. . . . Watts student projects were in vogue both at UCLA and USC in the months immediately following the riots"; Willard Hertz to Rev. E. W. Rakestraw, 21 Dec. 1966, R1486, 66-171, FFA; Dale Marshall, *The Politics of Participation in Poverty: A Case Study of the Board of the Economic and Youth Opportunities Agency of Greater Los Angeles* (Berkeley, Calif., 1971).

79. *LA Times,* 21 Oct., 23 Sept. 1965, 1 July 1966.

80. Ibid., 2, 16 Oct. 1965.

81. Ibid., 19 Oct. 1965, 21 Feb. 1966.

82. Calvin Hamilton to City Council, 20 May 1966, box 6, folder 6, John Holland Papers.

83. John Johnson to Hyman Bookbinder, 4 Aug. 1967, reel 14, 0027, Kerner Commission Papers; see also San Francisco Federal Executive Board, "'Watts': Information Exchange Project: A Report on Federal Activities in the Watts Community," Jan. 1966, LACHRC Papers.

84. *LA Times,* 16 Sept. 1966.

85. Ibid., 3 Feb. 1966.

86. *LA Free Press,* 22 July 1966.

87. *LA Times,* 3 March 1991; see also resolution introduced by John Gibson, 22 Nov. 1966, no. 129596, sup. 2, ACLA; "Watts Bureau Round-up," 28 July 1970, BB4771, Pacifica Archives; *LA Times,* 19, 8 Dec. 1965.

88. *Beverly Hill Tribune-Advertiser,* 22 Dec. 1966.

89. "Report of the California State Advisory Committee to the U.S. Commission on Civil Rights" and "Police Community Relations in East Los Angeles, California," 1969, LACHRC Papers.

90. *LA Times,* 3 March 1966.

91. "Watts: Ten Years after the Flames," 11 Aug. 1975, BC2420, Pacifica Archives.

92. *LA Times,* 27, 10 Aug. 1980; see also ibid., 13 Aug. 1980.

93. Ibid., 11 Aug. 1985; see also Weisbrot, *Freedom Bound,* p. 310.

94. *LA Times,* 8 Nov. 1991.

95. Ibid., 2 Oct., 3 Dec. 1965.

96. Ibid., 19 May 1966.

Epilogue

1. Raphael J. Sonenshein, *Politics in Black and White: Race and Power in Los Angeles* (Princeton, N.J., 1993); Robert Gooding-Williams, *Reading Rodney King, Reading Urban Uprising* (New York, 1993); Tom Owens with Rod Browning, *Lying Eyes: The Truth behind the Corruption and Brutality of the LAPD and the Beating of Rodney King* (New York, 1994); Joe Domanick, *To Protect and To Serve: The LAPD's Century of War in the City of Dreams* (New York, 1994); Mark Baldassare, ed., *The Los Angeles Riots: Lessons for the Urban Future* (Boulder, Colo., 1994).

2. *Wall Street Journal,* 4 May 1992; *USA Today,* 5, 6 May 1992; *LA Times,* 8 May 1992.

3. *Korea Times,* 30 June 1993.

4. Edward T. Chang, "New Urban Crisis: Korean-Black Conflicts in Los Angeles" (Ph.D. diss., Univ. of California–Berkeley, 1990); Ella Stewart, "Ethnic Cultural Diversity: An Ethnographic Study of Cultural Differences and Communication Style between Korean Merchants and Employees and Black Patrons in South Los Angeles" (M.A. thesis, California State Univ.–Los Angeles, 1989); Eui-Young Yu et al., eds., *Koreans in Los Angeles* (Los Angeles, 1982). On immigration generally and the impact of the 1965 changes, see Virginia Yans-McLaughlin, ed., *Immigration Reconsidered: History, Sociology, and Politics* (New York, 1990); Thomas Muller, *Immigrants and the American City* (New York, 1993).

5. Gerald Horne, *Studies in Black: Progressive Views of the African-American Experience* (Thousand Oaks, Calif., 1992); Horne, *Race for the Planet;* Gerald Horne, "Re-educating the U.S. Working Class on Race and Class," in Joseph Wilson et al., eds., *The Re-Education of the American Working Class* (Westport, Conn., 1990), pp. 171–82; Gerald Horne, "Racism and the New World Order," in Stephanie Baker, ed., *New Walls in Europe: Nationalism and Racism—Civic Solutions* (Prague, 1992), pp. 31–35; see also Paul Ong, Edna Bonacich, and Lucie Cheng, *The New Asian Immigration in Los Angeles and Global Restructuring* (Philadelphia, 1994); Liah Greenfield, *Nationalism: Five Roads to Modernity* (Cambridge, Mass., 1992); Michael Ignatieff, *Blood and Belonging: Journeys into the New Nationalism* (New York, 1994); William Pfaff, *Barbarian Sentiments: How the American Century Ends* (New York, 1989); William Pfaff, *The Wrath of Nations: Civilization and the Furies of Nationalism* (New York, 1993); Walker Connor, *Ethnonationalism: The Quest for Understanding* (Princeton, N.J., 1994).

6. Armando Navarro, "The South Central Los Angeles Eruption: A Latino Perspective," *Amerasia Journal* 19, no. 2 (1993): 69–85; *LA Times,* 8, 9 July 1992; Manuel Pastor, *Latinos and the Los Angeles Uprising: The Economic Context* (Claremont, Calif., 1993); *LA Weekly,* 1–7 April 1994.

7. *LA Times,* 17 April 1994.

8. Ibid., 5 April 1994. For example, the Mollen Commission, which investigated similar problems afflicting the New York City Police Department, recommended, among other things, using polygraphs when questioning officers during corruption investigations, halting the "dumping" of officers with problems in poor neighborhoods, stripping pensions from officers convicted of crimes, giving stiffer penalties to officers who violate departmental regulations, punishing officers who fail to report corruption, disqualifying applicants with a history of domestic violence, and many other recommendations that the LAPD could well consider. *New York Newsday,* 21 April 1994.

9. *LA Times,* 28 July 1994.

10. Ibid., 29 March 1994.

11. Ibid., 6 April 1994.

12. Ibid., 19 May 1994.

13. Gerald Horne, *Reversing Discrimination: The Case for Affirmative Action* (New York, 1992); Nijole V. Benokraitis and Joe Feagin, *Affirmative Action and Equal Opportunity: Action, Inaction, Reaction* (Boulder, Colo., 1978); Nijole V. Benokraitis and Joe R. Feagin, *Modern Sexism: Blatant, Subtle, and Covert Discrimination* (Englewood Cliffs, N.J., 1986); Gertrude Ezorsky, *Racism and Justice: The Case for Affirmative Action* (Ithaca, N.Y., 1991); for a contrasting view, see Frederick Lynch, *Invisible Victims: White Males and the Crisis of Affirmative Action* (Westport, Conn., 1989).

14. *LA Times,* 2 Dec. 1993; Jan Golab, *The Dark Side of the Force: A True Story of Corruption and Murder in the LAPD* (New York, 1993); see also Independent Commission on the Los Angeles Police Department, *Report of the Independent Commission on the Los Angeles Police Department* (Los Angeles, 1991); Independent Commission on the Los Angeles Police Department, *Status Report on the Independent Commission on the Los Angeles Police Department* (Los Angeles, 1992).

15. Roger Lotchin, *Fortress California, 1910–1961: From Warfare to Welfare* (New York, 1992); Seymour Melman, *The Defense Economy: Conversion of Industries and Occupations to Civilian Needs* (New York,

1970); Seymour Melman, *Our Depleted Society* (New York, 1965); Seymour Melman, *Pentagon Capitalism: The Political Economy of War* (New York, 1970).

16. *LA Sentinel,* 16 Sept. 1993.

17. Marc Eliot, *Walt Disney: Hollywood's Dark Prince* (New York, 1993).

18. *LA Times,* 22 April 1994.

19. *New York Times,* 25 March 1994.

20. *LA Weekly,* 15–21 April 1994.

21. *LA Sentinel,* 31 March 1994.

22. *LA Times,* 22 April 1994.

23. Ibid., 29 April 1994.

24. Gerald Horne, "Race Backwards: Genes, Violence, Race, and Genocide," *Covert Action Quarterly* 1, no. 43 (1992–93): 29–35; Horne, "Myth and the Making of 'Malcolm X'"; Allan Chase, *The Legacy of Malthus: The Social Costs of the New Scientific Racism* (New York, 1977).

25. *New York Amsterdam News,* 16 April 1994; *Forward,* 27 May 1994. Note that the decline of the left and the rise of gangs and nationalism is not unique to Black LA. This trend can also be detected in Eastern Europe. See Claire Sterling, *Thieves' World: The Threat of the New Global Network of Organized Crime* (New York, 1994).

26. *LA Times Magazine,* 26 June 1994; see also *Village Voice,* 19 April 1994: "Each Saturday at Muhammad's mosques 7 and 7C in Harlem and Flatbush, members of the sect's security arm, the Fruit of Islam, conduct a kind of religious boot camp, called 'Manhood-Brotherhood Training Sessions,' for community members who want to 'clean themselves up.' All the borough jails have chapters of the Nation." The keynote speaker at this event, NOI leader Conrad Muhammad, "invoked the United States government as the 'biggest gang in the world' and went on to remind his audience that where 'white people have Boy Scouts and youth groups and ball teams,' blacks have only the 'Crips and Bloods.'" See also Karl Evanzz, *The Judas Factor: The Plot to Kill Malcolm X* (New York, 1992). Playthell Benjamin, columnist and critic, in the *New York Daily News* of 29 July 1994, raised questions about the frequent use of violence by the NOI, not against the alleged hated white foe but other blacks. He made reference to Louis Farrakhan's incendiary 4 Dec. 1964 editorial in *Muhammad Speaks* calling for severe punishment for Malcolm X and a pastoral letter in 1994 signed by five black Christian clerics in Boston that underscored the "1973 attack on black women and children of the Hanafi Muslim sect in Washington, D.C. mansion of basketball great Kareem Abdul Jabbar." The NOI did not evolve in a vacuum; in the areas where its members lived were not only violent police officers but similarly violent gangs trading in illegal drugs. The latter was another example of the growth of lumpen, as opposed to working-class, organization. The impact of the lumpen, particularly on popular music and literature, is demonstrable in the influential and misogynist work of Robert Beck. See Robert Beck, *Long White Con: Trick Baby's Newest Score!* (Los Angeles, 1977); Robert Beck, *Trick Baby, the Biography of a Con Man* (Los Angeles, 1967). NOI leader Khalid Abdul Muhammad spent his youth "between his native Houston and Los Angeles, where he still maintains close family and personal connections." He attended Dillard University in Louisiana. He once headed the mosque in LA and has appeared on rap music recordings with Ice-Cube, Public Enemy, and X-Clano. See Sylvester Monroe, "Khalid Abdul Muhammad," *Emerge* 5, no. 11 (Sept. 1994): 42–46. Indeed, the pervasive influence of Black LA on black politics and culture suggests that there is not only a "Black Atlantic" but also a "Black Pacific." See Paul Gilroy, *The Black Atlantic: Modernity and Double Consciousness* (Cambridge, 1993).

27. Brian Cross, *It's Not about a Salary: Rap, Race, and Resistance in Los Angeles* (New York, 1994); Tricia Rose, *Black Noise: Rap Music and Black Culture in Contemporary America* (Hanover, N.H., 1994); Ice-T, *The Ice Opinion: Who Gives a Fuck?* (New York, 1994): the nihilism and misogyny that is apparent in the work of a number of rappers can be detected in the words of this LA-based performer. The influence of "Iceberg Slim" is evident in the names and practices of a number of rappers who have emulated the misogyny of this notorious pimp. Such influence is indicative of how lumpen culture has eroded working-

class culture generally and among blacks; this makes the popularity of "gangsta' rap" outside of the community of blacks easier to explain: it is popular not for racial reasons but for class—lumpen—reasons. Iceberg Slim, *Pimp: The Story of My Life* (Los Angeles, 1969); Christina Milner and Richard Milner, *Black Players: The Secret World of Black Pimps* (Boston, 1973); Susan Hall and Bob Adelman, *Gentleman of Leisure: A Year in the Life of a Pimp* (New York, 1972). Compton, the headquarters for a number of "gangsta' rappers," symbolized the dilemmas of blacks in the region. By 1994 it was the oldest black majority–governed city west of the Mississippi. But the black government had inherited depleted coffers; like the French colonialists who had been forced out of Guinea during the Cold War, white Compton had left the cupboard bare, halting the building of schools and parks and not seeking to raise public capital for new infrastructural improvement. The passage of Proposition 13 in the 1970s which reduced the ability of state and local government in the state to address pressing problems exacerbated the problem. Merchants and businesses fled to nearby Torrance, Long Beach, and elsewhere, which forced the city administration to try hiking taxes on homeowners; as banks continued to redline, the result was the fleeing of a number of working-class blacks and their replacement by those much poorer—who often were Latino. Like other politicians in the nation, those in Compton often saw fit to line their pockets with tax dollars when they were not being bribed by entrepreneurs in return for tax giveaways. This set the stage for angry conflict between a mostly black city administration and a growing Latino population that charged discrimination and mismanagement. In this deteriorating environment, black and Latino gangs flourished. In some parts of the county there was a merger between black and Latino gangs, and fortunately in the aftermath of the "gang truce" clashes between the two groups were not frequent. *LA Times,* 21 Aug. 1994; *Nation,* 19 Sept. 1994; *LA Weekly,* 19–25 Aug. 1994. This relative dearth of murderous interethnic conflict was even more astounding when one considers that 81 percent of all small-caliber, inexpensive handguns in the nation were produced in this region and, inevitably—despite exports—pistols were not that hard to find in Compton and other parts of the county where hope was barely alive. *LA Times,* 23 Sept. 1994.

28. *Washington Post,* 6 April 1994. Stanley Crouch, a contributing editor at the *New Republic* and an influential and conservative critic, also hails from Black LA.

29. *Final Call,* 13, 20, 27 April 1994.

30. *Santa Barbara News-Press,* 5 Feb. 1994.

31. *New York Times,* 19 Jan., 29 July 1994; *Forward,* 15 July 1994; Ben Chavis, *Psalms from Prison* (New York, 1983); see also Michael Dawson, *Behind the Mule: Race and Class in African-American Politics* (Princeton, N.J., 1994).

32. Payne and Ratzan, *Tom Bradley.*

33. *Village Voice,* 26 July 1994; *New York Times Magazine,* 7 Aug. 1994; *New York Amsterdam News,* 23 July 1994; see also, Douglas E. Schoen, *Pat: A Biography of Daniel Patrick Moynihan* (New York, 1979). Sadly, regressive attitudes were not unique to Moynihan. In the November 1994 election a majority of blacks in South LA evidently voted for Proposition 187, a statewide initiative designed to deprive "illegal immigrants" of health care, education, and other services. This measure was backed avidly by the GOP incumbent governor, Pete Wilson, who also was able to garner a substantial black vote. See *Los Angeles Sentinel,* 22 Dec. 1994; *LA Weekly,* 16–22 Dec. 1994.

34. Ellis Cose, *The Rage of a Privileged Class* (New York, 1994); Joe R. Feagin, *Discrimination American Style: Institutional Racism and Sexism* (Malabar, Fl., 1986); Joe R. Feagin, *Living with Racism: The Black Middle Class Experience* (Boston, 1994).

35. *LA Times,* 17 March 1994; Nelson George, *Elevating the Game: Black Men and Basketball* (New York, 1992). I ran for the U.S. Senate from California in 1992, amassing 305,000 votes while running on a platform that evoked memories of the Civil Rights Congress, the Conference of Studio Unions, Pettis Perry, Charlotta Bass, Frank Barnes, and Loren Miller. This too is part of the legacy—and meaning—of the 1960s and 1990s.

A Note on Sources

THE PRIMARY SOURCE FOR THIS STUDY IS THE
Papers of the Governor's Commission on the Los Angeles Riots; this panel
was chaired by John McCone (cited in the notes as McCone Papers).
These papers are located at the library of the University of California–
Berkeley. Also at the library are the Papers of the West Coast Branches of the
NAACP (NAACP Papers–West) and the papers of Governor Brown.

The Niebyl-Proctor Library in Berkeley is an independent institution that
contains numerous rare pamphlets and books, not only on the left—its speciality—but also on various strands of nationalism.

The McCone panel also held hearings; that transcript can be found at the
law library of the University of California–Los Angeles (McCone Transcript).
Also at UCLA are the Ralph Bunche Papers, the Franklin Murphy Papers,
and the UCLA Student Activism collection. UCLA is also the depository for
a useful collection of oral histories of such figures as Dorothy Healey, Tom
Bradley, Sam Yorty, and many others.

The papers of Thomas Rees and Yvonne Brathwaite are located at the
University of Southern California.

Other than the Los Angeles Police Department, city and county agencies
were generally helpful. The Office of the Chief Medical Examiner provided
me with records on those killed during the revolt from the archives of the city
and county of Los Angeles (ACLA). The city's Board of Police Commissioners
and city council provided me with access to some of their records. The Los
Angeles County Commission on Human Relations opened its files to me
(LACHRC Papers). There is also a collection of LACHRC records at the
Bilbrew Public Library in South Los Angeles (LACHRC Papers–Bilbrew),
along with other materials relevant to this study. The archives of Pacifica
Radio are located in North Hollywood and must be consulted by anyone
conducting research on post–World War II history.

California State University–Los Angeles has the voluminous papers of
Mervyn Dymally and John Holland; both collections are invaluable for gaining an understanding of LA. California State University–Northridge holds
the papers of former congressman James Corman and AFL-CIO official Max

Mont, along with a valuable collection of oral histories, including that of former congresswoman Bobbie Fiedler; the library there also contains the Bustop Papers, an important collection of an organization that adamantly opposed busing for the purposes of school desegregation. The Schomburg Center of the New York Public Library contains the papers of Pettis Perry and the Civil Rights Congress. The Tamiment Institute collection at the library of New York University is invaluable in doing research on any aspect of the history of radicalism; there are numerous rare pamphlets and books there. The Museum of Television and Radio in New York City is a necessary stop for any doing research on recent U.S. history. The Ford Foundation Archives (FFA) in Manhattan and the Rockefeller Archives in Pocantico Hills, N.Y., are both rich sources for the study of virtually any aspect of recent history. The library at Columbia University holds the Federated Press Papers. The papers of Arna Bontemps are at Syracuse University.

The central depository for papers of the NAACP is the Library of Congress in Washington, D.C. This major civil rights organization has not yet received a thorough and comprehensive study.

The papers of the noted black publisher and activist Carleton Goodlett are at the University of Wisconsin–Madison, as are the papers of Dalton Trumbo. The papers of John Howard Lawson are located at Southern Illinois University in Carbondale. The Right Wing Collections of the University of Iowa in Iowa City are a significant—indeed, profound—assemblage of materials on a political phenomenon that has shaped the destiny of the planet.

The papers of Lyndon Baines Johnson (LBJ Papers) and members of his cabinet and staff, e.g., Ramsey Clark, are located at the University of Texas–Austin. There are also a number of worthwhile oral histories in the Johnson collection.

I have saved the most important part of this bibliographic note for last, for the following is intended not as a pro forma acknowledgment but also as an appreciation: The Southern California Library for Social Studies and Research (Southern California Library) is located in the former curfew zone in Los Angeles and, as my notes indicate, contains numerous files on the history of this community. In August 1990, after I had been residing in this zone conducting informal interviews, we collaborated in organizing a conference marking the twenty-fifth anniversary of the revolt, and simultaneously, we conducted a number of important oral histories featuring community residents that now form a permanent part of their collections.

The library of the University of California–Santa Barbara not only was useful in procuring a number of dissertations and books via interlibrary loan but also obtained important reels of primary material, e.g, the papers of the Kerner Commission.

Ula Taylor, Cynthia Hamilton, and Sarah Cooper, all longtime residents of LA, were particularly helpful in guiding me to persons to interview and sources of all types.

Likewise, the library of the University of Virginia—during the year I spent as a fellow at the Carter G. Woodson Institute for African and Afro-American Studies working on this study—was extremely helpful in procuring microfilm versions of the *Los Angeles Times, Los Angeles Sentinel, Los Angeles Herald-Dispatch, Los Angeles Herald Examiner,* and other newspapers that were used to construct this book.

To them and to the countless others in Los Angeles and elsewhere who assisted securing sources for this study, I give profuse thanks.

INDEX

Buchwald, Art, 283–84
Buckley, William F., 281, 347
Buena Park area, 120
Buggs, John, 65, 105, 192, 193, 202, 293,
    380 n.70
  at Athens Park meeting, 62
  background, 303
  criticism of police by, 304
  on housing problems, 220
  in manipulation of black nationalist move-
      ment, 199–200, 203
  on Mexican-American community, 260
  on Nation of Islam, 125
  at outbreak of uprising, 58, 59, 60
  political position of, 147, 303–4
  recommendations of, 47, 60, 304–5
Bullock, Paul, 40, 349
Bunche, Ralph, 300
Burke, Arthur, 208
Burks, James, 62, 99
Burroughs, Miller, 89
Bush, George, 49
Businessmen street gang, 193–95
Business practices, 308–11
  after uprising, 316–18, 321
  banking industry, 314–15
  insurance industry, 311–14, 350
  investment in Watts after uprising, 350–51,
      353–54
  in 1990s LA, 361
Butterfield, David, 343
Button, James, 302

Cabral, Amilcar, 22
Caldwell, Orville, 32
Califano, Joseph, 281, 283, 288
California Eagle, 6, 7, 328
California Highway Patrol, 54–55, 56, 57, 68,
    156
Call, Asa, 130, 152, 305, 317
Cannon, J. Alfred, 188
Cannon, Lou, 134
Carmien, J. Allen, 291
Carson, Clay, 101
Carter, Alprentice, 197
Carter, Dick, 53
Carter, Herbert, 58–59, 63, 153
Caston, William Vernon, 89
Cauley, Leon, 88

Causes of uprising
  black anger, 39–40
  black characteristics as, 39
  black residents' interpretation of, 334–35
  Chief Parker on, 137–38
  class conflict within black community, 172
  communists in, 268, 275
  economic and employment factors, 37–39, 47
  gangster reprisal theory, 199
  as insurrection, 36–37, 312–13
  LAPD practices in, 140–41
  Martin Luther King, Jr. on, 184
  NAACP on, 177–79
  police response as, 159–60
  political agitators in, 52–53
  political elites on, 159–60, 163–64
  sociocultural tradition, 41, 42
Caute, David, 5
Chaisson, Claude, 86
Champion, Hale, 294
Chandler, George, 89
Chandler, Otis, 183, 295
Chandler, Raymond, 30
Chantry, Kenneth, 237
Chavis, Benjamin, 362–63
Che-Lumumba Group, 272–73
Chernin, Rose, 274
Chou En-Lai, 270
Christian, Winslow, 138
Christian Anti-Communist Crusade, 266
Christian Defense League, 80
Christopher, George, 288
Christopher, Warren, 149, 151, 217, 231, 255,
    269, 296
  career, 417 n.49
  criticism of McCone Commission by, 344,
      345
  in Rodney King investigation, 358–59
Churches and religious organizations, 234–37,
    302
Civil Rights Act of 1964, 281, 282, 286, 298
Civil Rights Congress, 7–9, 11, 171, 187, 216–17
Civil rights movement
  anticommunist attacks on, 267, 268
  in Los Angeles, 46–49
  Watts Uprising in context of, 38–39, 40, 52
  See also specific organizations of
Clark, Jim, 280
Clark, Kenneth, 178

Other titles of interest

**THE SUMMER THAT
DIDN'T END**
**The Story of the Mississippi Civil
Rights Project of 1964**
Len Holt
New preface by Julian Bond
351 pp.
80469-7 $14.95

THE TROUBLE THEY SEEN
**The Story of Reconstruction in the
Words of African Americans**
Edited by Dorothy Sterling
512 pp., 152 illus.
80548-0 $15.95

THE UNKNOWN SOLDIERS
**African-American Troops in
World War I**
Arthur E. Barbeau and
Florette Henri
New introd. by Bernard C. Nalty
320 pp., 20 photos
80694-0 $14.95

WE SHALL OVERCOME
**Martin Luther King, Jr., and
the Black Freedom Struggle**
Edited by Peter J. Albert and
Ronald Hoffman
304 pp., 6 illus.
80511-1 $14.95

THE ENEMY WITHIN
**The McClellan Committee's
Crusade against Jimmy Hoffa and
Corrupt Labor Unions**
Robert F. Kennedy
New introduction by
Edwin Guthman
363 pp., 24 photos
80590-1 $14.95

KENNEDY IN VIETNAM
American Vietnam Policy 1960–63
William J. Rust
272 pp., 19 photos
80284-8 $10.95

TET!
**The Turning Point
in the Vietnam War**
Don Oberdorfer
400 pp., 42 photos
80210-4 $11.95

JACK RUBY
Garry Wills and Ovid Demaris
276 pp.
80564-2 $13.95

BLACK TALK
Ben Sidran
228 pp., 16 photos
80184-1 $10.95

Available at your bookstore

OR ORDER DIRECTLY FROM

DA CAPO PRESS

1-800-321-0050